HOLOCAUST

HOLOCAUST

Critical Concepts in Historical Studies

Edited by David Cesarani

Editorial Assistant: Sarah Kavanaugh

Volume II

From the Persecution of the Jews to Mass Murder

Routledge
Taylor & Francis Group

LONDON AND NEW YORK

First published 2004
by Routledge
11 New Fetter Lane, London EC4P 4EE

Simultaneously published in the USA and Canada
by Routledge
29 West 35th Street, New York, NY 10001

Routledge is an imprint of the Taylor & Francis Group

Typeset in Times by Wearset Ltd, Boldon, Tyne and Wear
Printed and bound in Great Britain by MPG Books Ltd.,
Bodmin, Cornwall.

British Library Cataloguing in Publication Data
A catalogue record for this book is available from the British Library

Library of Congress Cataloging in Publication Data
A catalog record has been requested for this book.

ISBN 0-415-27509-1 (Set)
ISBN 0-415-27511-3 (Volume II)

Publisher's Note
References within each chapter are as they appear in the original
complete work.

CONTENTS

CONTENTS

ACKNOWLEDGEMENTS
Volume II

Author's acknowledgements

I wish to thank my former Ph.D student Dr Sarah Kavanaugh for her unflagging assistance, my colleagues Professor Mark Roseman and Dr Neil Gregor for their helpful comments on an early draft of the introductory material, and the Arts and Humanities Research Board for its support. These volumes represent part of the output of the research project on 'The Holocaust and its Legacy' carried out under the auspices of the AHRB Parkes Centre for the Study of Jewish/non-Jewish Relations, University of Southampton.

The publishers would like to thank the following for permission to reprint their material:

Yad Vashem for permission to reprint Frank Bajohr, 'The beneficiaries of "Aryanization": Hamburg as a case study', *Yad Vashem Studies*, 26 (1998), 173–202.

Hans Safrian, 'Expediting expropriation and expulsion: the impact of the "Vienna Model" on anti-Jewish policies in Nazi Germany, 1938', *Holocaust and Genocide Studies*, 14:3 (2000), 390–414. Published by Oxford University Press in association with the United States Holocaust Memorial Museum. Reprinted by permission of Oxford University Press.

Berghahn Books for permission to reprint Konrad Kwiet, 'Forced labour of German Jews in Nazi Germany', *Leo Baeck Institute Yearbook*, 36 (1991), 389–410.

Yad Vashem for permission to reprint Wolf Gruner, 'Poverty and persecution: the Reichsvereinigung, the Jewish population, and anti-Jewish policy in the Nazi state, 1939–1945', *Yad Vashem Studies*, 27 (1999), 23–61.

Berghahn Books for permission to reprint Sybille Steinbacher, 'In the shadow of Auschwitz. The murder of the Jews of East Upper Silesia', in Ulrich Herbert (ed.), *National Socialist Extermination Policies. Contemporary Perspectives and Controversies,* New York/Oxford: Berghahn, 2000, pp. 276–305.

Simon Wiesenthal Center, Los Angeles, for permission to reprint Götz Aly and Susanne Heim, 'The economics of the Final Solution: a case study from the General Government', *Simon Wiesenthal Center Annual*, 5 (1988), 3–48.

Yad Vashem for permission to reprint Bogdan Musial, 'The origins of "Operation Reinhard": the decision-making process for the mass murder of the Jews in the *Generalgouvernement*', *Yad Vashem Studies*, 28 (2000), 113–53.

Christopher Browning, 'Jewish workers in Poland. Self-maintenance, exploitation, destruction', in Christopher Browning, *Nazi Policy, Jewish Workers, German Killers*, Cambridge: Cambridge University Press, 2000, pp. 58–88. Copyright © C. Browning 2000, reproduced with permission of Cambridge University Press and the author.

Berghahn Books for permission to reprint Walter Manoschek, 'The extermination of the Jews in Serbia', in Ulrich Herbert (ed.), *National Socialist Extermination Policies. Contemporary Perspectives and Controversies*, New York/Oxford: Berghahn, 2000, pp. 163–85.

Berghahn Books for permission to reprint Christoph Dieckmann, 'The war and the killing of the Lithuanian Jews', in Ulrich Herbert (ed.), *National Socialist Extermination Policies. Contemporary Perspectives and Controversies*, New York/Oxford: Berghahn, 2000, pp. 240–75.

Berghahn Books for permission to reprint Christian Gerlach, 'German economic interests, occupation policy, and the murder of the Jews in Belorussia, 1941/43', in Ulrich Herbert (ed.), *National Socialist Extermination Policies. Contemporary Perspectives and Controversies*, New York/Oxford: Berghahn, 2000, pp. 83–103.

The Royal Historical Society for permission to reprint Ian Kershaw, 'Improvised genocide? The emergence of the "Final Solution" in the "Warthegau"', *Transactions of the Royal Historical Society, 6th Series*, vol. 2, (1992), 51–78.

Christopher Browning, 'From "ethnic cleansing" to genocide to the "Final Solution": the evolution of Nazi Jewish policy, 1939–1941', in Christopher Browning, *Nazi Policy, Jewish Workers, German Killers*, Cambridge: Cambridge University Press, 2000, pp. 1–25. Copyright © C. Browning 2000, reproduced with permission of Cambridge University Press and the author.

Disclaimer

INTRODUCTION TO VOLUME II

Volume II covers the economic and physical destruction of the German Jews and the impact of Nazi rule on the Jews of Poland 1939–41. The basic information about the despoliation of German and Austrian Jewry has been available since Raul Hilberg's magisterial study, *The Destruction of the European Jews* (1961).[1] However, the campaign for restitution and redress in the 1990s and the scrutiny of German banks exposed how little was known in detail. As several inquiries revealed the extent to which banks, companies and individuals were involved in the seizure of assets belonging to Jews and the liquidation or take-over of Jewish-owned businesses, questions arose about the origins of the policy. Was such a ramified process centrally controlled or was it the result of local initiatives? If so many Germans were implicated in this gigantic robbery, were they driven by ideology or greed? When legal inquiries and a change of archival attitudes made access to key documents easier it became possible to answer some of these questions.[2]

Frank Bajohr is one of the new wave of German historians to delve into the newly opened records. His findings challenge both the Marxist analysis of fascism that reduces policy to profit-seeking and the view of Götz Aly and Suzanne Heim that the economic measures against the Jews can be seen as rational and utilitarian. Using Hamburg as a case study Bajohr shows that a determination to strip the Jews of their wealth was always a part of Nazi emigration policy and grew out of the desire to break the alleged economic power of the Jews. Yet the stated motive was often just a fig leaf to cover envy and corruption. Party bosses and municipal officials grew fat on the money and property extorted from Jews as a condition of their departure. The most acquisitive sections of the population were party activists and small businessmen. A majority of big enterprises initially held aloof from the bonanza because it offended their belief in the sanctity of property and for fear of offending foreign trading partners. However, when the 'aryanisation' of Jewish concerns accelerated in 1938 they could no longer risk standing aside. At that point numerous firms plunged into the murky dealings that surrounded the brutal transfer of wealth from

1

persecuted Jews to Germans. A new class of criminal grew around this trade. Many thousands of 'innocent' Germans participated in the auctions at which confiscated property, including the contents of sequestered apartments, were sold off. Those bombed out of their homes during the war were compensated with clothing and furniture that once belonged to Jewish families deported from the Reich and from countries such as the Netherlands. In this sense, 'ordinary Germans' were the direct beneficiaries of expropriation and genocide.[3]

The violent, sweeping enforcement of 'aryanisation' policy in Vienna after the *Anschluss* has typically been seen as a radicalisation of already existing practices in the Reich. Götz Aly and Suzanne Heim argued, furthermore, that it was an experiment in economic rationalisation that was intended to serve as a model for use elsewhere.[4] However, Hans Safrian challenges these interpretations in his study of 'aryanisation' in Vienna. He shows that the lunge for Jewish assets and property preceded the establishment and functioning of the Nazi institutions in Austria. It was, in fact, a spontaneous and unruly outburst of greed and hatred. The incoming Nazis struggled to impose order on the despoliation and to ensure that they got their cut. Once they had established their authority they looked for ways to legalise the expropriations and came up with laws that would later be employed in Germany proper. In this sense, the events in Vienna fed the process of radicalisation in Germany. Safrian also explains that the depredations inflicted on the Viennese Jews filled the Nazi administration with anxiety that the mass of impoverished Jews would be unable to afford emigration or find anywhere willing to take them. To solve this dilemma they came up with a system of funding enforced emigration out of relief money coming from Jews abroad and from 'taxing' wealthy Jews. This system was set up and administered by the rising SIPO–SD officer Adolf Eichmann and it worked so well that it was imported into the Reich.[5]

German Jews were not only exploited for their cash, assets or property. From 1938 onwards the regime exploited their labour, too. In his research on another neglected aspect of the persecution, Konrad Kwiet draws our gaze to the plight of over 20,000 German Jews who were compelled to work on road-building projects and in the armaments industry. The regime inaugurated this compulsory labour in the wake of the November 1938 pogrom. As more and more Jews were made unemployed, the SIPO–SD apparatus, which now controlled the affairs of Jews in the Reich through its domination of the so-called Central Emigration Office, conscripted them for forced labour. When the shortage of skilled labour became increasingly acute during the war a premium was placed on this reserve labour force: pragmatism rubbed up against ideology. Eventually Hitler personally consented to demands for the remaining German Jews to be deported. Kwiet notes that the Führer's intervention to resolve tension between those who wanted to exploit Jewish labour and those who wanted to exterminate the Jews immediately is a further demonstration of his centrality to the annihilation process.[6]

The Jewish community adapted as best it could to the policy of social isolation and deliberate pauperisation. In 1995 the publication of Victor Klemperer's diaries of the 1930s and the 1940s created a sensation by enabling readers vicariously to experience the narrowing world of German Jews and the humiliations to which they were exposed. The personality of Klemperer also revealed the doggedness with which Jews hung on and the resistance of the spirit.[7] Wolf Gruner details the efforts which the *Reichsvereinigung*, the Nazi-controlled central Jewish community organisation, made to support the unemployed, indigent, sick and aged Jews who formed a growing majority of the German Jewish population from 1939 onwards and who, like Klemperer, were denied the benefits of state welfare. The *Reichsvereinigung* was intended by the Nazis to provide services for a segregated population and to promote emigration, but it was used by German Jews to ameliorate Nazi policy. By mid-1941 some 53,000 German Jews were performing compulsory labour and it seemed as if the community had reached some kind of stability. It was not to last: by the end of the year the *Reichsvereinigung* was forced to pay the costs of deporting Jews 'to the East'.[8]

Each town and city with a Jewish population has its own sad story but few are as paradoxical as that of Auschwitz, as Oswięcim became when the region of East Upper Silesia was annexed to the Reich from Poland in September 1939. The Jews of East Upper Silesia were quickly subjected to forced labour and became a significant part of the labour force in this heavily industrial zone. Albrecht Schmelt, an SS official, set up a network of camps and started supplying Jews, at a price, to local industrial enterprises. In a bizarre turn of events the SS acquired a vested interest in these 'work Jews' and defended them against the civilian authority that wanted to make the region 'free of Jews'. Sybille Steinbacher's study of this overlooked corner of the Third Reich yet again exposes the conflict between ideology and pragmatism. She also challenges the view of Götz Aly that Germanisation policies and ethnic cleansing inevitably doomed the Jews. In East Upper Silesia the Jews remained in place while it was the Poles who were deported to make way for 'ethnic Germans'. Conditions of work were so good, relatively speaking, that Polish Jews smuggled themselves into the district. While Jews from across Europe were being murdered in the gas chambers at Auschwitz, over 20,000 Jews were being preserved as a valued labour force a few miles away. Work proved to be a temporary reprieve, but this local study disrupts the picture of a monolithic policy emanating from the centre and enforced locally by SS automatons.[9]

During the 1990s a string of similar local studies using new sources from Polish and Russian archives added to the impression that middle-ranking officials, regional authorities and police commanders had far more latitude than was previously thought to be the case. Götz Aly and Suzanne Heim played a searchlight on the economic, demographic and social planners who advised the Nazi leaders. They unearthed documents that suggested there was a logical and rational vision for developing the conquered east, involving the 'removal' of 'surplus' Jewish and Polish populations.[10] This thesis aroused intense controversy. Critics pointed out that many of the plans cited by Aly and Heim never left the drawing board and, if they found implementation, were frequently a mere rationalisation for racist policies and greed. Even if the language of modernisation had some purchase in Poland, it had no relevance in modern industrial countries where Jews suffered a similar fate.[11]

The contingency of mass murder is made evident by the meandering path to genocide in the General Government, the area of German-occupied Poland which was not annexed to the Reich and which was the home to over a million Jews. Bogdan Musial maintains that the genocide in the General Government resulted from a series of failed efforts to remove the Jews by means of expulsion or deportation. Musial focuses on Odilo Globocnik, the SS police chief in Lublin, and his ambitions to create settlements for Germans on land cleared of Jews and Poles. Globocnik was thwarted in 1939, but hoped for a second chance following the German invasion of Russia. When the prospects of deporting the Polish Jews into Russia faded and the regional authorities were faced with food shortages as well as a perceived threat to security, they turned to mass murder to get rid of the Jews. In October 1941 Globocnik initiated the construction of the Belzec death camp, which became the prototype for other camps in Poland although its small capacity suggests that as first envisaged it had a limited function. On the strength of this evidence Musial argues that the Nazi leadership had to take further steps to arrive at the decision to annihilate all the Jews in Poland, let alone in all of Europe.[12]

Even then the genocide was not carried out consistently. Christopher Browning explains that there was constant friction between elements of the regime in occupied Poland over the relative merits of preserving substantial numbers of Jews for economic uses. The Schmelt organisation described by Sybille Steinbacher was a template for the economic exploitation of Jews in the Polish cities and ghettos, although there were great variations, such as the differences between the centralised system in Lodz and the private enterprise fostered in Warsaw. On the other hand, Himmler was never reconciled to the survival of the Jewish population in any numbers and insisted on one barbarous cull after another, whittling the population down to those who could work and compressing them into ever smaller units. Browning argues, contra the thesis of Aly and Heim, that the utilisation of Jewish labour was always subordinate to the racial–ideological goals of the National Socialist government in Berlin.[13]

During the late 1970s and 1980s, much energy was devoted to identifying the moment at which Hitler and his immediate entourage made the decision to exterminate the Jews of Europe.[14] Historians had always regarded the commencement of mass killings in the course of the invasion of the Soviet Union from June 1941 onwards as a pivotal moment, a quantum leap in Nazi policy and indicative of an order by Hitler to proceed with genocide. But argument raged over whether the murderous spree of the *Einsatzgruppen*, the mobile killing units tasked with the murder of commissars, communists and Jews amongst other functions, had been ordered before the invasion or if it had escalated with infusions of manpower and fresh orders. And what was the precise connection between the mass killings in Russia and developments in Poland, let alone the rest of Europe, given the time lag and apparent inconsistencies separating mass murder in Russia from the initiation of death camps in Poland?[15]

The chapters in Part 3, many by the 'new wave' of German historians, cut a swathe through this debate by showing that mass murder frequently developed out of local initiatives. They may have been loosely incited by the leadership in Berlin and received its sanction, but they were never explicitly ordered. Moreover, in many cases the slaughter of Jews grew out of pre-existing policies and attitudes that were only broadly aligned with the racial–biological National Socialist *Weltanschauung*. They were not a simple, straightforward outcome of anti-Jewish policy and were paralleled by measures against other groups, such as Soviet prisoners of war and Gypsies who could not be seen as the targets of an 'eternal anti-semitism'.

Walter Manoschek demonstrates that the brutal repression of the Jews in Yugoslavia began as soon as the German army had conquered the country in April 1941. The army, not the SS or the security apparatus, acting on its own initiative was responsible for the mass internment of Jewish men, the registration and marking of Jews, the expropriation of Jewish property and forced labour. When partisan activity flared up in mid-1941, the army decided in reprisal to shoot interned Jews and Communists. Indeed, in their eyes, there was no difference between the two. The mass executions were intensified when a ruthless new commander arrived in Serbia in October 1941 to curb the uprising. Meanwhile, the representatives of the German Foreign Office demanded that Jews be removed from Serbia. When this was not permitted, the civil authorities grew restive about the 'burden' of maintaining Jewish women and children as well as the surviving men who were held in camps. Dr Harald Turner, head of the civil administration, requested the despatch of gas vans to deal with this unwanted human residue. By May 1942, Serbia was 'free of Jews' as the result of a process that had begun locally and developed autonomously from Berlin. The army, the Foreign Office and the civil administration were the driving forces, rather than Himmler's and Heydrich's SS men.[16]

The mass shooting of Jews in Lithuania, White Russia and south eastern Poland, detailed by Christoph Dieckmann and Christian Gerlach indicate a similar pattern after the opening of 'Operation Barbarossa'. The German army intended to 'live off the land' during the invasion and made no allowance for feeding the local population or prisoners of war. In fact, rudimentary planning for the occupation of Russia decreed that millions of Russians in urban centres would be left to starve while the Germans transported all available foodstuffs back to the Reich to make up for shortfalls in the German harvest. This merciless policy was underpinned by racist assumptions about the Germans' right to *Lebensraum* versus the sub-human status of so-called Slavs. The pre-invasion decision to write-off Russian industrial centres (which the Germans could not supply with raw materials) doomed the Jewish population that was concentrated in these locations. But they were seen as fair game anyway. Hitler regarded the USSR as the seat of Jewish power because he automatically conflated Jews with Bolsheviks. Consequently, he mandated the SS to execute all male Jews in the Communist Party and state apparatus. But the identification of Jews with Bolsheviks permeated the military, too. Harsh action against the Jews was seen by senior army figures as necessary for security against the 'Bolshevik enemy' as well as a corollary of the tight supply situation. Military and logistical considerations thereby enmeshed lethally with National Socialist doctrine.[17] The question of who ordered the *Einsatzgruppen* to do what and when, a question which had once dominated the historiography on this phase of Nazi policy, paled by comparison with these insights into the origins of genocide in Russia.[18]

Evidence that the SS was not the only element involved in the killing further undermined the significance of the earlier historiographical strife. Dieckmann found that, in Lithuania, the initial killing was carried out on an ad hoc basis by mixed groups of border police, troops, air force ground crew and personnel from the civil administration. They acted locally without reference to Berlin. In Galicia the mass murder was organised with chilling efficiency by one SS man, Hans Krüger. He arrived in July 1941 with 25 SIPO–SD men but recruited local auxiliaries and drew on the civil administration for help. By the following spring, Krüger and his scratch force had accounted for 70,000 Jews shot locally and 12,000 more deported to death camps.[19]

The impression of 'improvised' genocide with a regional horizon is strengthened by Ian Kershaw's study of the Warthegau, the slice of western Poland annexed to Germany in September 1939. Arthur Greiser, the Nazi gauleiter of the new district, had no wish to retain the 350,000 Jews who came with the territory and Hitler gave a rhetorical indication that he wanted them ejected, too. As a temporary measure Heydrich ordered the Jews to be concentrated in major towns and cities prior to their removal to a 'reservation', but where and how? Early efforts to deport the Jews to the further reaches of the General Government were frustrated by a combination of factors. Reception facilities did not exist and there was insufficient transport. The ruler of the Government General, Hans Frank, objected to the influx of displaced Jews and Poles which added to the economic problems of his domain. Himmler and his organisations had their hands full resettling tens of thousands of ethnic Germans brought 'home to the Reich' from Eastern Europe. As Browning shows, in the winter of 1939–40, Nazi policy in Poland was stymied. Meanwhile, the Jews who were stripped of their rights and livelihoods and confined to poor, overcrowded quarters of towns and cities, fell victim to starvation and disease. For a time the conquest of France in May–June 1940 offered the Nazi leadership the hope of deporting Europe's Jews to Madagascar. But this proved unworkable, too. Greiser and Frank responded to the impasse by allowing Jews to work for the Germans so that they could pay for food and medicines imported into the ghettos. But the long-term goal remained removal. For a time it appeared that the invasion of Russia would deliver a solution, but this was not to be either. When Hitler demanded that Greiser take German Jews deported from the Reich the only way it seemed possible to accommodate them was by using the techniques of the 'euthanasia campaign' to kill off Jews already in the ghetto who were deemed 'useless' because they could not work. Hence an improvised death camp using the kind of gas vans developed for the 'euthanasia campaign' was set up at Chelmno, near Lodz. In December 1941 deportations from Lodz to Chelmno began. But Kershaw argues that this was not a sign that the 'Final Solution' had begun, as most historians once assumed. Instead, he maintains that the Chelmno operation was a local initiative that stemmed from local frustrations.[20]

Notes

1 Raul Hilberg, *The Destruction of the European Jews* (revised edition, New York, 1985, first published 1961), pp. 81–154. See also Barkai, *From Boycott to Annihilation*.
2 See the comment by Frank Bajohr, *'Aryanization' in Hamburg. The Economic Exclusion of the Jews and the Confiscation of their Property in Nazi Germany* (Oxford, 2002), pp. 1–10.
3 Frank Bajohr, 'The beneficiaries of "Aryanization": Hamburg as a case study', *Holocaust: Critical Concepts in Historical Studies* (*HCC*), 2:1, pp. 13–33. For other examples of research based on new documents, see Albert Fischer, 'The Minister of Economics and the expulsion of the Jews from the German economy', in David Bankier (ed.) *Probing the Depths of German*, pp. 213–25 and Simone Ladwig-Winters, 'The attack on the Berlin department stores (*Wärenhauser*) after 1933', ibid., pp. 246–67.
4 Götz Aly and Susanne Heim, 'The Holocaust and population policy: remarks on the decision on the "Final Solution"', *YVS*, 24 (1994), 45–71.
5 Hans Safrian, 'Expediting expropriation and expulsion: the impact of the

"Vienna Model" on anti-Jewish policies in Nazi Germany, 1938', *HCC*, 2:1, pp. 34–58. Cf. Götz Aly and Suzanne Heim, *Architects of Genocide*, trans. A.G. Blunden (London, 2002), pp. 16–23.

6 Konrad Kwiet, 'Forced labour of German Jews in Nazi Germany', *HCC*, 2:1, pp. 59–81.

7 *I Shall Bear Witness: The Diaries of Victor Klemperer 1933–1941*, trans. and ed. Martin Chalmers (London, 1998, first published in German in 1995) and *To The Bitter End: The Diaries of Victor Klemperer 1942–1945*, trans and ed. Martin Chalmers (London, 1999, first published in German in 1995).

8 Wolf Gruner, 'Poverty and persecution: the Reichsvereinigung, the Jewish population, and anti-Jewish Policy in the Nazi state, 1939–1945', *HCC*, 2:1, pp. 82–109.

9 Sybille Steinbacher, 'In the shadow of Auschwitz. The murder of the Jews of East Upper Silesia', *HCC*, 2:1, pp. 110–36.

10 Götz Aly and Susanne Heim, 'The economics of the Final Solution: a case study from the General Government', *HCC*, 2:2, pp. 139–80.

11 Dan Diner, 'Rationalization and method: critique of a new approach in understanding the "Final Solution"', *YVS*, 26 (1994), pp. 71–108; David Bankier, 'On modernization and the rationality of extermination', *YVS*, 26 (1994), pp. 109–30; Ulrich Herbert, 'Racism and rational calculation: the role of "utilitarian" strategies of legitimation in the National Socialist "*Weltanschauung*", *YVS*, 26 (1994), pp. 131–46; Martin Housden, 'Population, economics and genocide: Aly and Heim versus all-comers in the interpretation of the Holocaust', *HJ*, 38:2 (1995), 479–86. See also the articles in 2:3.

12 Bogdan Musial, 'The origins of "Operation Reinhard": the decision-making process for the mass murder of the Jews in the General Government', *HCC*, 2:2, pp. 181–210. Cf. Thomas Sandkühler, 'Anti-Jewish policy and the murder of the Jews in the district of Galicia', *HCC*, 3:3, pp. 320–41.

13 Christopher Browning, 'Jewish workers in Poland. Self-maintenance, exploitation, destruction', *HCC*, 2:2, pp. 211–37. See also, Ulrich Herbert, 'Labour and extermination: economic interest and the primacy of *Weltanschauung* in National Socialism', *PP*, 13 (1993), 144–95.

14 For example, Martin Broszat, 'Hitler and the genesis of the "Final Solution": an assessment of David Irving's theses', *YVS*, 13 (1979), pp. 72–125; Christopher Browning, 'A reply to Martin Broszat regarding the origins of the Final Solution', *SWCA*, 1 (1984), pp. 113–32; Hans Mommsen, 'The realization of the unthinkable: the Final Solution of the Jewish Question in the Third Reich', in Gerhard Hirschfeld (ed.) *The Policies of Genocide: Jews and Soviet Prisoners of War in Nazi Germany* (London, 1986), pp. 93–144.

15 Alfred Streim, 'The tasks of the SS *Einsatzgruppen*', *SWCA*, 4 (1987), pp. 309–28; 'Exchange between Helmut Krausnik and Alfred Streim', *SWCA*, 6 (1989), 311–29; Yehoshua Büchler, '*Kommandostab Reichsführer-SS*: Himmler's personal murder brigades in 1941', *HGS*, 1:1 (1986), 11–26; Yaacov Lozowick, '*Rollbahn Mord*: the early activities of *Einsatzgruppe C*', *HGS*, 2:2 (1987), 221–41; Ronald Headland, 'The *Einsatzgruppen*: the question of their early operations', *HGS*, 4:4 (1989), pp. 401–12 and the discussion in Christopher Browning, 'Beyond "Intentionalism" and "Functionalism": the decision for the Final Solution reconsidered', ibid., *The Path to Genocide* (New York, 1992), pp. 86–120.

16 Walter Manoschek, 'The extermination of the Jews in Serbia', *HCC*, 2:3, pp. 241–61.

17 Christian Gerlach, 'German economic interests, occupation policy, and the

murder of the Jews in Belorussia, 1941/43', *HCC*, 2:3, pp. 295–321; Christoph
Dieckmann, 'The war and the killing of the Lithuanian Jews', *HCC*, 2:3, pp.
262–94. See also, Michael McQueen, 'Nazi policy toward the Jews in the *Reich-
skommisariat Ostland*, June–December 1941', in Zvi Gitelman (ed.) *Bitter
Legacy: Confronting the Holocaust in the USSR* (Bloomington, Ind., 1997), pp.
91–103. But see also Hans-Heinrich Wilhelm, ' "Inventing" the Holocaust for
Latvia: new research', in Gitelman (ed.) *Bitter Legacy*, pp. 102–22.
18 See note 15. On the crimes of the Wehrmacht in general, see Hannes Heer and
Klaus Naumann (eds) *War of Extermination. The German Military in World
War Two 1941–44* (New York/Oxford 2000) and in addition, Daniel Uziel,
'Wehrmacht propaganda troops and the Jews', *YVS*, 29 (2001), pp. 27–63.
19 Dieckmann, 'The war and the killing of the Lithuanian Jews'; Dieter Pohl,
'Hans Kruger and the murder of the Jews in the region of Stanislawow
(Galicia)', *YVS*, 26 (1998) 239–64.
20 Ian Kershaw, 'Improvised genocide? The emergence of the "Final Solution" in
the "Warthegau" ', *HCC*, 2:3, pp. 322–50; Christopher Browning, 'From
"ethnic cleansing" to genocide to the "Final Solution": the evolution of Nazi
Jewish policy, 1939–41', *HCC*, 2:3, pp. 351–72.

Part 1

THE DESPOLIATION AND
DESTRUCTION OF GERMAN
AND AUSTRIAN JEWRY

15

THE BENEFICIARIES OF "ARYANIZATION"

Hamburg as a case study

Frank Bajohr

Source: *Yad Vashem Studies*, 26 (1998), 173–202. Translated by William Templer.

Although the "Aryanization" of Jewish assets under National-Socialist rule was one of the most prodigious property transfers in modern times, historians have exhibited only limited interest in this important aspect of the Nazi persecution of Jews in Germany. The groundbreaking studies by Helmut Genschel[1] and Avraham Barkai[2] are significant surveys of the destruction of German Jewry's economic basis under Nazism, and these works have been subsequently supplemented by a number of other articles[3] and regional studies.[4] Nonetheless, our knowledge about key facets of this topic remains inadequate. One of the remaining intriguing questions pertains to the persons who profited from this expropriation process, which began its insidious course in 1933, and was then systematized in a raft of pseudo-legal forms in 1937–38. Who were the beneficiaries?

For the most part, historians have interpreted the so-called Aryanization of Jewish assets as a National-Socialist measure motivated by ideology rather than economic interests, as an important stage in Nazi Jewish policy, leading on to deportation and the mass murder.[5] In public declarations the Nazis themselves never tried to conceal that, in their eyes, the "Jewish Question" was "racial and *völkisch*, not an economic question."[6] Nonetheless, some scholars have tried to reduce Aryanization to an economic-utilitarian, functional core, denying its ideological underpinnings. Thus, for example, Marxist-Leninist historiography repeatedly underscored "the culpability of German finance capital for the persecution and murder of the Jews."[7]

In their study *Vordenker der Vernichtung*, Götz Aly and Susanne Heim, using Vienna as an example, conceptualized Aryanization as part of an

13

economic modernization strategy seeking to resolve structural deficiencies in transposed economic sectors; they argue that it became a kind of paradigm for Nazi policies of occupation and annihilation in Eastern Europe.[8]

This analysis steers clear of such functionalist reductions of Nazi Jewish policy. Nonetheless, the economic dimensions of *Judenpolitik* need to be examined from a differentiated perspective. Utilitarian motives did not play a central role in the ideological justifications advanced for the National-Socialist policy of Aryanization. Yet such motives did give impetus to the institutions and persons involved, guiding their actions. Above all, they shaped the concrete forms Aryanization took on, and the ambience in which it was carried out.

Focusing on a regional investigation of Hamburg, I wish to explore the beneficiaries of Aryanization as well as its economic and material spillover effects. We will first examine the respective benefits for the German Reich, the Nazi party and its functionaries, those who acquired Jewish property and the effect on the economy. Then I would like to probe the contours of a veritable sub-branch of commerce, a "utilization business" that sprang up around the Aryanizations. This trafficking in Jewish property, almost totally neglected to date by scholarship, had fluid boundaries with a criminal milieu that unscrupulously exploited the parlous predicament in which many Jews found themselves. I conclude by looking at the role of the German population, by no means merely an uninvolved bystander, and the form and scope of its participation.

Aryanization as expropriation

To pilfer and expropriate from the Jews and thus destroy their economic basis for survival was an essential component of National-Socialist Jewish policy. The pressure on Jews in Germany to emigrate mounted with every further turn of the economic screw. With an onslaught of economic restrictions, the National Socialists moved ever closer to their declared ideological aim of rendering the Reich *judenrein*. This immediate nexus between expropriation policies and forced emigration became especially evident during the course of Aryanizations in Vienna in the spring of 1938.

After being stripped of their belongings, Jews were subsequently forced to emigrate. This procedure was supervised by the Central Office for Jewish Emigration (Zentralstelle für jüdische Auswanderung) under the control of the SD (Sicherheitsdienst) of the SS.[9] Ultimately, this model was extended to encompass the entire Greater Reich, with the establishment of the Reich Central Office for Jewish Emigration (Reichszentrale für die jüdische Auswanderung) in January 1939.

However, the National Socialists also had an immediate financial rationale in pursuing a policy of forced Aryanization. After 1933, the Nazi state had embarked on a step-by-step program to create a machinery of repression in financial policy: this made it possible not only to compel Jews to sell off their businesses and property immediately, but also to divert a lion's share of the proceeds from such sales into the coffers of the Reich.

Preoccupied with the policies of the Economics Ministry and the 1937–38 "change in course" after Schacht stepped down as economics minister, historians to date have failed to appreciate the true importance of this repressive apparatus in the financial policy for Aryanization. Its most important elements included the development and expansion of currency-control agencies within the Regional Tax Administrations (Oberfinanzdirektionem) to monitor foreign exchange and audit other transactions and the creation in Berlin of the Investigation Agency for Foreign Currency Violations (Devisenfahndungsamt) in the summer of 1936.[10] Under the direction of Reinhard Heydrich, this central office assured the SS direct influence on regional investigative offices for foreign currency and customs violations. Foreign-currency laws were made ever more stringent, reaching a new high point on December 1, 1936, with the new legislation termed Revision of the Law on Exchange Control.[11] This affected German Jews most adversely. A newly introduced paragraph (§ 37a) empowered foreign-currency officials to strip owners of all rights of disposal over their assets if there were any suspicion that such capital was being illegally exported abroad. Although the scope of this law extended to all "non-foreigners" (Inländer), in actual fact, the practical effect was antisemitic. The Regional Tax Administration in Hamburg made immediate use of the new opportunities, initiating measures that triggered a wave of Aryanizations in Hamburg, especially of large Jewish concerns.[12]

At the same time, a thickening web of taxes and obligatory levies led, in actual fact, from 1938 on, to the total forced confiscation of Jewish assets.[13] The most important components in this policy of special compulsory taxes and levies were the Reich Flight Tax, the ever-spiraling fees gouged for capital transfer transactions, the Jewish property tax (Judenvermögensabgabe), fees for emigrants and the "de-Jewification gains tax," the so-called Entjudungsgewinnsteuer:

- The Reich Flight Tax or Reichsfluchtsteuer, introduced by the Brüning government in 1931 as part of reparations policy, was made increasingly more stringent after 1933, and developed, for all practical purposes, into an anti-Jewish punitive tax. In the last fiscal year of Weimar (1932–33), revenues from the Reich Flight Tax amounted to some 0.9 million Reichsmarks. By fiscal 1938–39, under the Nazis, they had soared to RM 342 million.
- In January 1934, the "commission" in capital transfer, i.e., the fees deducted from emigrants' blocked accounts by the German Gold Discount Bank (Dego) in connection with currency exchange, was approximately 20 percent of the total amount transferred. By June

1935, it had jumped to 68 percent; in October 1936, it zoomed to 81 percent, and, in June 1938, to a staggering 90 percent of the total. From September 1939, the fee was uniformly 96 percent.[14] Since Aryanization of Jewish property was usually followed by the emigration of the former owner, the National Socialists were able to drain off a substantial portion of all Jewish assets solely by utilizing this Dego commission.

- On November 12, 1938, in the wake of the *Kristallnacht* pogrom of November 9–10, the Decree on an Atonement Tax of Jews with German Citizenship (*Verordnung über die Sühneleistung der Juden deutscher Staatsangehörigkeit*) was promulgated, levying a sum of one billion Reichsmarks on German Jewry. Collected in five payments slapped with an additional 5 percent surcharge, it brought a total of RM 1.126 billion into the coffers of the Reich.

- In December 1938, the Hamburg Gestapo introduced an additional compounder: the "emigration tax" for Jewish emigrants, calculated at 20 percent of the Reich Flight Tax.[15] This *Auswanderungsabgabe* did not become common practice throughout the Reich until March 1939. In Hamburg, revenues from this tax were directed almost exclusively to the Jewish community, which had lost its most important funding source due to the emigration of its wealthiest members.

- The Decree on the Use of Jewish Assets promulgated on December 3, 1938, made it possible for the authorizing agencies to levy a tax to be paid to the Reich in connection with Aryanizations.[16] According to a directive of the Economics Ministry dated February 8, 1939, the amount payable was 70 percent of the difference between the officially assessed value and the actual purchase price. On June 10, 1940, Hermann Göring, in his capacity as Plenipotentiary for the Four-Year Plan, issued a Decree on the Audit of De-Jewification Business Transactions.[17] It specified a compensatory tax, effective from January 30, 1933, for all Aryanization sales in which the purchaser had gained an "improper financial advantage." This decree could have been applied retroactively to virtually all Aryanizations, since an attractive windfall for the purchaser at the Jewish seller's expense was a veritable distinguishing mark of such sales. However, in Hamburg, for example, this late decree was rarely actually applied and brought in a total sum of only about 50 million Reichsmarks. As in other parts of the Reich, the political leaders in Hamburg had already devised far more efficient means for skimming off profits.[18]

Two examples from Hamburg can serve to illustrate how the compounded practical effect of these taxes and compulsory contributions was to divest the Jewish owner of all assets. In July 1938, Albert Aronson was still one of Hamburg's wealthiest entrepreneurs.[19] He was the sole proprietor of the chocolate factory Reese & Wichmann GmbH, the cigarette import firm Havana-Import-Compagnie and the owner of thirty-six properties, some in prime locations. His total worth was estimated to be more than four million Reichsmarks. When Aronson emigrated to London six weeks later, all he had managed to salvage and transfer abroad was 1.7 percent of his assets. In order to obtain funds for emigration, he had arranged a credit of RM 800,000 from his bank, M.M. Warburg & Co. Of this, only 66,000 Reichsmarks (= £5,413, at a rate of RM 12.19 to the pound sterling) could be transferred, while RM 734,000 (= £60,213) was paid as a commission to the German Gold Discount Bank. To cover this loan, Aronson had been obliged to sell off most of the real estate he owned at throwaway prices, while his two companies were forcibly Aryanized. The proceeds from the sale of the firms, RM 800,000, which did not reflect the companies' actual value, were transferred to a special security account. Yet Aronson could not freely control these funds, since the Regional Tax Administration in Hamburg had issued a security order against him on July 12, 1938. Aronson was required to pay a Reich flight tax of 613,713 Reichsmarks, RM 245,510 in Jewish property taxes, and the sum of RM 100,000 to a secret slush fund of the Hamburg *Gauleiter* (district party leader) in order to have his passport released. The remaining assets and properties were confiscated for the German Reich under the 11th Decree in the Reich Citizenship Law of November 25, 1941: thus, 98.3 percent of all his wealth had been expropriated.

Our second example is the Hamburg private bank M.M. Warburg & Co., one of the ten largest and most respected private banks in the Reich.[20] Under the general pressure of Aryanization, the bank was changed in 1938 from a family firm to a limited company. The Hamburg merchants Dr. Rudolf Brinckmann and Paul Wirtz assumed management. The Warburg family was fully compensated in this "amicable Aryanization"[21] with 11.6 million Reichsmarks for the balance of net assets, but the actual proceeds from the sale were reduced to RM 6.4 million, because the value of the affiliate Warburg & Co. in Amsterdam was calculated into and deducted from the purchase price. Of these 6.4 million, 3 million marks remained as a "silent deposit" in the firm; very soon this money, too, had to be paid out in one form or another. In the subsequent period, proceeds from the sale were completely eaten up by taxes and levies. Thus, the Warburgs paid RM 850,000 in flight tax, an authorization fee of one million Reichsmarks for the Aryanization, RM 1,221,000 in Jewish property taxes, and an emigration fee of 450,000 Reichsmarks. For permission to continue operating Warburg & Co. in Amsterdam as a family firm, they had to exchange an additional RM 1.2 million in Dutch guilders into Reichsmarks to a blocked account. This saddled them with a further loss of 1,080,000 Reichsmarks as a result of a commission of 90 percent paid to the Gold Discount Bank.

On the surface these transactions seemed to constitute fair, indeed "amicable," Aryanization. Yet upon closer scrutiny their true nature emerged; they were an out-and-out swindle. Even the moderate forms assumed by this property transfer did nothing to change that fact, since the fair compensation received by the Jewish owner was gobbled up by the voracious web of National-Socialist fees and levies.[22] In fact, one might argue, the fairer and more "amicably" the Aryanization was implemented and the greater the sale proceeds for the Jewish proprietor, the larger was the ultimate gain for the Nazi state. In most instances, the latter turned out to be the main beneficiary of the Aryanizations.

Corruption of party officials

One of the special features of the National-Socialist system of rule, especially at the regional level, was a policy of cliques and clienteles that systematically rewarded Nazi functionaries for their "idealistic" efforts. Corruption and nepotism were important NSDAP techniques of domination. These were used in particular by the *Gauleiters* in order to assure the political loyalty of party members.[23] Since the public coffers could not be plundered without limit for the benefit of the party and the NSDAP national treasurer pursued a restrictive policy of economy vis-à-vis regional party organizations, many *Gauleiters* made use of the Aryanizations as a much-welcome local source of lucre. They regarded Jewish property as a personal reservoir they could dispose of in order to satisfy the needs of the party and its functionaries. Helmut Genschel alluded to this link between Aryanization and corruption in connection with the NSDAP district of Franconia, where the district leadership pocketed 25 percent of the transacted purchase price.[24] Yet he characterized this as "untypical," since he believed they were due largely to the vicious antisemitism of the Franconian *Gauleiter* Julius Streicher.

In reality, these events in Franconia were only the tip of a nationwide iceberg, since virtually all other NSDAP districts practiced similar methods. Thus, the Gau leadership in Thuringia siphoned off 10 percent of the purchase price in Aryanizations in order to fund an old-age pension scheme for "veterans of the movement."[25] In the party district Saar-Palatinate, Jewish owners were even forced to funnel 40 percent of the sale proceeds into a special account of the district leadership.[26] In Hamburg, *Gauleiter* Karl Kaufmann had created a personal slush fund outside of the municipal budget in the form of the Hamburg Foundation of 1937 (*Hamburger Stiftung von 1937*). With this he financed NSDAP formations, personal protégés, and the "indemnification of deserving veteran Party comrades." In addition, Kaufmann used foundation funds as financial backing for front men to buy up all the shares of a Jewish factory, Chemische Fabrik Siegfried Kroch AG, Wandsbek.[27]

The capital in the Hamburg Foundation of 1937 came in part from

"Aryanization contributions," which usually had to be paid by the Jewish owners, but sometimes also by the buyers. While the Nazis put the screws on the Jewish proprietors when commercial enterprises were Aryanized, extorting sums of up to RM 100,000 by threat and intimidation,[28] the "Aryan" purchasers were required to kick back a fee in cases of Aryanized real estate; frequently, such new owners had picked up Jewish properties below their appraised value.[29]

Jewish prime real estate held a special fascination for the Hamburg NSDAP and its leading functionaries. Thus, the *Gauleiter* and Reich Governor Kaufmann was ensconced in the former villa of a wealthy Jewish family, the so-called Budge Palace, where he had set up his offices.[30] His deputy Ahrens and many other party functionaries in Hamburg had procured Jewish residential buildings at preferential prices as part of the Aryanization of real estate.[31] Various offices of the Hamburg NSDAP also grabbed up Jewish real estate with no compunction. Thus, the Academy for District Leadership Cadre (Gauführerschule) of the Hamburg NSDAP established itself on property in Barsbüttel that had belonged to a large Jewish shareholder in the Deutsch-Amerikanische Petroleum-Gesellschaft who had emigrated. Although the market value of the realty was in excess of RM 450,000, the NSDAP district treasurer had deposited only 60,000 Reichsmarks in a closed account. In cynical candor, he characterized this sale price as being "so ludicrously low that at best, it can only be regarded as some kind of symbolic payment."[32]

The SS was able to acquire a villa on the Aussenalster lake in 1942, to be used as a "guest house," at an even more attractive price. After the Jewish owner had died from a heart attack during interrogation, the Gestapo forced the estate custodian to sell the property. The formal purchaser was not the SS, but the Hamburger Elektrizitätswerke AG (HEW) under its general manager Otte, who was a prominent SS member; he later transferred the property to the SS cost-free.[33]

The NSDAP was given further lucrative opportunities after the compulsory authorization for Aryanizations was introduced in 1938. The office of *Gauleiter* Kaufmann had been designated the chief authorization agency for Hamburg as a result of the decrees on Registration of Jewish Wealth (*Verordnung zur Anmeldung des Vermögens der Juden*) of April 26, 1938, and the Use of Jewish Assets (*Verordnung zum Einsatz jüdischen Vermögens*) of December 3, 1938. Kaufmann exploited this position rigorously for the benefit of NSDAP functionaries. Thus, he sometimes denied authorization for submitted sale contracts, making sure that the Jewish firms were handed over to heads of local party groups (*Ortsgruppenleiter*) or party district chiefs (*Kreisleiter*)—persons who had never been involved in business, let alone managed a company.[34]

Other high-ranking officials central to setting Nazi Jewish policy in Hamburg also felt no compunction in capitalizing on their influence in order to line their private pockets. Thus, the *Judenreferent* ("expert on Jewish affairs") in the Hamburg Gestapo, Claus Göttsche, transferred over RM 237,000 for his personal use from a Gestapo account in which the proceeds from Jewish property sold at auction had been deposited.[35] Willibald Schallert, head of the section of Labor Deployment for "Jews and Gypsies" in the Hamburg Labor Office, systematically enriched himself by exploiting the Jews under his control. He extorted their assets, molested women sexually, and denounced persons he disliked to the Gestapo, which then arranged their deportation to Auschwitz.[36] The actual circumstances so prevalent in the practice of National-Socialist Jewish policy refuted the official, pseudo-moral rationale for Aryanization as set forth in the Nazi propaganda. The public was told that Aryanization was being carried out in strict accordance with the principles of "efficiency and decency."[37]

Astonishingly, the Nazi state seldom took any steps against the damage done to its financial interests as a result of corruption. It is pointless to speculate whether the National-Socialist state acquiesced in the personal enrichment of Nazi functionaries as a lucrative concession to the "movement." Even structurally, National Socialism had no effective control mechanisms to combat corruption. Three aspects in particular impeded the development of any functional controls: (1) the dictatorial elimination of any critical public sphere; (2) the atavistic "*Führer* principle" that was geared to unconditional loyalty rather than the control of power and favored the formation of mafia-like cliques; and, above all, (3) the total deprivation of the rights of the victims, who were helpless and at the mercy of the arbitrary will of the National Socialists.

The behavior of the acquirers

Discrimination and persecution created the basic armature for Aryanization from which those who acquired Jewish property and wealth ultimately profited. Thus, for example, in determining the sale price, it was forbidden to include the intangible value of a firm, a composite based on its reputation, market position, clientele, and earning prospects in an assessment of the value of a firm. In the Nazi view, Jewish companies did not enjoy such public "good will." Furthermore, there were specific instructions to underestimate the value of the stocks, inventory, and net book amount in assessments conducted by estimators from the chambers of industry and commerce. Many stocktaking procedures, which customarily had taken several days in the annual firm inventory, lasted only a few hours; more often they were perfunctorily completed in a couple of minutes.[38] Even easily marketable items were valued far below the wholesale trade price. In general, the estimators based their assessment on the bankruptcy value, which was only half the trade price.[39] In one case, an arbiter of the Hamburg Chamber of Commerce even offered the prospective purchaser the option of buying the firm for some 10–15 percent of its inventory value, telling him outright that he should "not be so stupid and cash in on the situation."[40]

These conditions were common particularly for Aryanizations in 1937–38, which were subject to a compulsory authorization. But there had been a tendency in that direction even earlier, in Aryanization sales prior to 1937. From December 1938 on, the Jewish owners, many of whom had been interned in concentration camps following *Kristallnacht*, were stripped of all property rights and appointed trustees were authorized to sell the firms at cut-rate prices without even the agreement of the owner.

Despite the discriminatory conditions in effect for Jewish proprietors, not all Aryanizations turned out to be a profitable deal for the purchaser. This was especially the case with Jewish export firms, which accounted for almost one-third of all Jewish-owned enterprises in Hamburg. As a rule these were boycotted by their previous Jewish business partners abroad after being taken over by an "Aryan." With the outbreak of the war in 1939, virtually all commercial ties were broken off. Many firms had to shut down; others tried to keep themselves afloat through barter arrangements. Moreover, the Allied bombing raids on Hamburg in 1943, as part of Operation Gomorrah, took their toll, demolishing more than half of all commercial firms in the city. After 1945, many an Aryan owner who had acquired Jewish property was confronted with claims for restitution and reimbursement for a firm that had actually yielded no profit.[41]

Those who acquired Jewish property represented a broad cross-section of the German entrepreneurs and were by no means a homogeneous group. The spectrum ranged from ruthless exploiters who plundered Jewish owners to sympathetic businesspersons who were willing to pay a fair price for acquisition. Actually, there were three main categories:[42]

– The first category consisted of active and unscrupulous profiteers, and comprised some 40 percent of the total. They undertook personal initiatives of their own toward the Jewish owners over and beyond the discriminatory framework of Aryanization in order to depress the sale price even further, taking ruthless advantage of the predicament of the owners to stuff their own pockets. They extorted the owners by threatening to denounce them to the Gestapo or to bring the Gestapo in on the transaction; they arranged to have the owner's passport confiscated,[43] refused to keep contractual obligations,[44] and pressured the owners by bringing to bear their good connections with the party.[45] Sometimes they came to the first encounter sporting their Nazi uniform and forbade the Jewish owners to enter the premises of their firm in the future.[46]

It is not surprising that NSDAP functionaries were heavily represented in this group. Yet some may find it astounding that the most unscrupulous antagonists of the Jewish proprietors often came from the ranks of their own employees. Propelled by avarice, they made common cause with the institutions of the Nazi state behind the back of the Jewish owner in order to arrange an attractive takeover deal at the expense of their former employer.[47] "Now we want a chance to run the place," an employee told his Jewish boss after he had schemed behind his back to have his lease for the firm cancelled and had then finessed a new lease for himself.[48]

- The second group, also about 40 percent of the total, can best be characterized by the term "sleeping partner." They garnered their personal gain within the Aryanization framework, such as by underestimation of inventory and stocks; yet they did not call any further attention to themselves, and tried to transact the property transfer in an outwardly proper manner. In this way, they maintained the illusion of a "standard" property deal; after 1945, they were often bewildered when confronted with formal claims for restitution raised by the former Jewish owners.[49]

- The remaining 20 percent of the purchasers, and thus the smallest of the three categories, consisted of well-meaning and sympathetic businesspersons who tried to give Jewish owners an equitable price for their property. Many in this category counted Jews among their friends. Often, they had decided to get involved only after being specifically requested to do so by their Jewish friends. Upon closer examination of these contracts, it is clear that buyer and seller had concluded a secret pact against the authorities. An attempt was frequently made to mask the value of the firm (which was not permitted to be paid) by means of other artificially inflated budgetary items,[50] or clandestinely to pay the price to the Jewish owner.[51] Such transactions were well-intentioned, but due to the rigid Nazi policies regarding special taxes and fees, they rarely fulfilled their objective of providing Jewish proprietors with a reasonable price for their property.

Only a small number of buyers went a perilous step further and resorted to measures deemed illegal under National–Socialist law. For example, they left the Jewish owner with the firm's accounts receivable abroad, outstanding funds which had been concealed in the contract.[52] One purchaser even personally smuggled Swiss watches and gold chains to Amsterdam and arranged for funds covering the true value of the firm to be taken abroad in a suitcase in order to reimburse the full fair price to the Jewish owner.[53] Such actions were not only quite risky for the buyer, but also point up how Aryanization transposed basic moral principles: persons who wanted to uphold the traditional principles of business ethics and did not aim to capitalize on the innocent plight of others—i.e., who wished to preserve their basic "decency"—had to act criminally and violate existing laws. This moral dilemma of well-meaning buyers also discloses the under-lying amorality of Aryanization itself.

If we examine the purchasers of Jewish property as a group, it is notable that, at least in Hamburg, there are comparatively few people from the established economy.[54] A large proportion of the buyers were social climbers, careerists and young businesspersons who wanted to get a start by availing themselves of the boon of Aryanization; on the other hand, there were also a good many bootlicking profiteers and subalterns who were seeking some source of livelihood in the political wake of Nazi rule. The Hamburg banker Max Warburg characterized this latter cat-egory as "vile flunkies."[55]

This relative reserve on the part of the established sector of the economy toward Aryanization evident down to 1938 certainly did not spring primarily from compassion or moral scruples. It was rooted in other considerations, openly addressed by the Hamburg *Gauleiter* Kaufmann in a speech before the Hamburg Chamber of Commerce:

> Aryanization has been a bit disconcerting for some Hamburg Aryans. I've heard rumors that certain older gentlemen here in town have been giving serious thought to just when this kind of Aryanization might befall them as well. Now that's something you can only think, talk about and expect if you're totally ignorant about the racial problem or not completely confident about your own race. Remarks like that are so childish—please excuse the expression—so childish that they're quite worrisome. So when you hear someone voice such apprehensions, I'd like you to dispel those foolish misconceptions. Be vigorously clear in refuting these notions; if necessary, you can refer to me. Everyone who works hard is going to remain economically just the same as before, no change.[56]

Aryanization was greeted with a certain skepticism in some sectors of the Hamburg business establishment, especially due to concerns about the protection of private rights. By expropriating a person's life's earnings, the Nazi state was seriously intruding into the realm of private property, and this clashed with middle-class notions of security. Some thus interpreted Aryanization as the harbinger of a "brown Bolshevism" in the offing.

Starting in 1938, however, a new attitude about Aryanization began to crystallize among a majority in the Hamburg business world. By this time, the effects of the global Depression had finally been overcome. The mono-structural Hamburg economy had been especially hard hit by that crisis: since it was oriented mainly to foreign trade, the Hamburg economy had suffered significantly longer from the slump than other regions in the Reich. Now it no longer seemed necessary to take any special economic considerations regarding Jewish firms. Moreover, with Schacht's demise as economics minister in 1937, an additional brake on Aryanization had been removed, and that policy now was radicalized, visibly and inexorably. Moreover, as a result of its foreign-policy "successes" chalked up in 1938, the regime had consolidated itself in a way that convinced many it would remain in power for a long time to come.

Above all, that changed perspective on Aryanization was evident in the activities of the Hamburg Chamber of Commerce; up to 1938, it had inclined to be more neutral and restrictive vis-à-vis Aryanization. It now undertook initiatives of its own to benefit purchasers of Jewish property. It suggested to the Economics Ministry to subject sale contracts concluded before 1938 retroactively to the same discriminatory conditions in force for contracts authorized after 1938.[57] This step was designed to make it possible for purchasers of Jewish properties to worm their way out of agreed-to obligations toward their Jewish contractual partner—by removing the stated value of the firm, for example, which contracts from 1938 on no longer allowed to be paid, or by reducing pensions and lump-sum compensations.

From the end of 1938, professional organizations and trade associations in Hamburg were given a say in the forced liquidation of Jewish firms. In early December 1938 in Hamburg alone, more than 200 Jewish retail stores were closed down in just a few days.[58] The main advantage for the commercial sector lay in having Jewish businesses liquidated rather than transferred to "Aryan" hands, since in this handy way they were able to rid themselves of unwanted competition.

In the whirl of National-Socialist expansionist policy from 1938–39 on, the Aryanizations acquired a supplementary new money-making dimension for sections of the Hamburg economy. Thus, on the occasion of the annexation of Austria in March 1938, *Gauleiter* Kaufmann had already arranged behind the scenes for firms in Hamburg to participate in the Aryanization of Jewish intermediary trade in Vienna.[59] Later on, Hamburg companies were involved in the Aryanization of Jewish enterprises in the Netherlands[60] and southeastern Europe.[61] They were particularly active though in the *Generalgouvernement* in occupied Poland, where the former director of the Hamburg Senate, Walter Emmerich, served as economics minister. Emmerich felt especially obligated to helping commercial firms in Hamburg, and appointed a total of forty companies as "district wholesalers" for the *Generalgouvernement*. In this function, such enterprises could take over and absorb Jewish firms and their stocks.[62] The fact that representatives of the forty companies recited the poem "Ali Baba and the Forty Thieves," which they had composed as a token of gratitude for his birthday, indicates how deeply implicated certain elements of the Hamburg economy had become in the predatory policies of the regime. The active involvement by Hamburg entrepreneurs in the European "macro-area" under Nazi domination also points up the international dimensions of Aryanization: it was by no means limited solely to Germany, but had spread to encompass all of Europe on the heels of the National-Socialist war of aggression.

Other profiteers on the "Aryanization market"

Starting in the mid-1930s, an informal "Aryanization market" had sprung up in Hamburg and across Germany. This market was the scene of a bustling and multifarious "trade" trafficking in the sale and utilization of Jewish property. A large number of realtors and lawyers watched the potential market, keeping an eye out for suitable properties; they brokered the contacts between owners and buyers and drew up the corresponding contracts. Large commissions made Aryanization a lucrative business.

In Hamburg, the Nazi lawyer Arthur Kramm, who enjoyed the special trust of the NSDAP district leadership, had assured himself a monopoly position in connection with sales of large Jewish concerns.[63] Other realtors and attorneys specialized in various branches of the Aryanization trade. Thus, for example, all Jewish pharmacies in Hamburg were Aryanized by the realtor Ernst Zobel acting as a broker. Just how much money could be pocketed in such deals is illustrated by the sale of the Jewish-owned fashion shop G. W. Unger, centrally located on the exclusive Jungfernstieg along the Binnenalster lake, which changed hands for the sum of RM 200,000. The lawyer Dr. Dröge, head of the Hanseatic Chamber of Attorneys, demanded a fee of 30,000 Reichsmarks to draw up the sales contract. He justified this large amount by the revealing argument "that in the final analysis, the contract had only come about thanks to his good connections."[64] The fact that Dröge was simultaneously president of the association "Pro Honore," an organization active in combating "the evil of corruption," serves to point up another facet in the moral rot and muddle afflicting business ethics under Nazism.

Along with realtors and attorneys, German bankers also romped on the fields of the Aryanization market. The Deutsche Bank and Dresdner Bank in particular watched the market carefully, financed numerous sales of Jewish firms and picked up shares in Aryanized companies.[65] The Hamburg bank M. M. Warburg & Co. also combed the marketplace intensively for potential buyers, though it did so at the specific request of the Jewish owners, and followed the maxim of obtaining the highest possible terms of sale.[66]

There were moneymaking deals to be made not only in the sale of Jewish property but also in the administration of Jewish assets by trusteeship, usually ordered by the Regional Tax Administrations in line with § 37a of the revised law on foreign exchange. In Hamburg, trustees and liquidators for Jewish firms were exclusively party members.[67] One company that made a name for itself here was the Hanseatische Vermögensverwaltung und Treuhand-Gesellschaft mbH (Hanseatic Company for Asset Administration and Trusteeship Ltd., abbreviated "Treuhansa"), headed by the Nazi Hans Sixt Freiherr von Jena.[68] The trustees not only paid themselves princely salaries from the sale and liquidation of Jewish firms, but also sometimes acquired the administered enterprises themselves, or artfully arranged a personal part share during sale negotiations.[69]

On the initiative of *Gauleiter* Kaufmann, the Hamburgische Grundstücksverwaltungs-Gesellschaft von 1938 mbH (Hamburg Real Estate Administration of 1938 Ltd., abbreviated "GVG") was set up to administer Jewish real estate. Kaufmann provided the basic capital for the company from funds of the Hamburg Foundation of 1937. In order to conceal this connection, the Treuhansa appeared outwardly as the nominal partner.[70] This corrupted meshwork finally became complete when the GVG raked in "Aryanization contributions" connected with the sale of Jewish properties and deposited these in a special account of the Hamburg Foundation of 1937.

The GVG, which was notorious among Jewish property owners, initially appropriated real estate administered by Jewish realtors, but soon took over a substantial segment of all Jewish-owned real estate in Hamburg. To the detriment of the Jewish owners, the GVG sold the properties far below their market value. However, in order to avoid seriously depressing property prices in Hamburg, it offered only a limited number of Jewish properties for sale.[71]

The trade sector dealing with Jewish property had fluid boundaries with a milieu of criminal elements that ruthlessly exploited the predicament many Jews found themselves in to feather their own nests. This milieu ranged from underworld criminals who extorted "protection money" in a mafia-like manner from Jewish firms[72] all the way to shyster lawyers who proffered their services to beleaguered Jews and then absconded after pocketing large advances.[73] Others pretended to have close connections with leading Hamburg Nazis, lured Jews in difficulty with grandiose promises and cozened huge amounts of money without offering anything in return.[74]

After the number of Jews under pressure to emigrate jumped dramatically in 1938, an illegal trafficking arose in entry visas, a trade in which numerous persons lined their pockets. Thus, there was a slew of so-called "emigration agents" who arranged to procure a visa after the payment of sizable bribes.[75] In the Hamburg consulates of Central and South American countries, almost all the consuls and their staff were implicated in these despicable dealings to arrange life-saving visas. An entry visa to Argentina required a bribe of RM 5,000 per person, while a visa for Haiti went for the sum of 1,000 Reichsmarks. The Jewish Religious Association in Hamburg had no choice but to grin and bear it, participating in the payoff game in order to make it possible for at least a few indigent Jews to emigrate.[76]

The Uruguayan Consul General Rivas, the deputy doyen of the diplomatic corps in Hamburg, developed a special criminal élan in this regard. Knowing the high market value his visa commanded, he "purchased shares" cost-free in exclusive Jewish enterprises.[77] In close cooperation with his consular staff, largely Jewish, he not only extorted corresponding bribes, but also demanded numerous "fees" and foreign exchange as a deposit, which he then transferred abroad illegally. In 1939, the Hamburg district court indicted five Jewish employees of the Uruguay Consulate General for misappropriation of funds and foreign–currency violations.[78] The court termed the Consul General's behavior "incredible" and accused the defendants of having "lined their pockets in the most frivolous manner" and "drained dry" the Jewish emigrants. It was "outrageous," the court noted, that it had to admonish the Jewish defendants about "pouncing on persons in a serious predicament to plunder them of everything."[79] Such moral recriminations coming from a district court under Nazism do not lack a certain cynical hypocrisy, seeing that the plundering of helpless persons was an integral component, disguised in pseudo-legal trappings, of the everyday practice of the National-Socialist state.

The German population as material beneficiaries of the Holocaust

In February 1941, Aryanization in Hamburg reached new heights with the systematic auctioning off of Jewish property: now the entire population was drawn into the circle of beneficiaries. At the behest of the *Gauleiter*, the Gestapo in February 1941 had confiscated the chattels of Jewish emigrants that had not been shipped due to the outbreak of the war in September 1939.[80] This involved between 3,000 and 4,000 containers being held in storage up until then in the Hamburg transshipment port. These containers contained the effects of Jewish emigrants from all parts of Germany, since most had embarked via the traditional emigration port of Hamburg. Beginning in February 1941, on orders from the Hamburg Gestapo, these belongings were auctioned off to the population. The proceeds were deposited in a Gestapo account with the Deutsche Bank and reached the sum of RM 7.2 million by early 1943.[81] Both the auctioneers[82] and forwarding agents[83] bore the main burden of organizing this form of Aryanization. During the war years, these auctions became a profitable business for them.

The authorities involved stated in the public press that the auctions were intended "to make the goods available to the broadest possible segment of the population at reasonable prices."[84] Special treatment was given to those who had lost their possessions in bombing raids, young married couples and Germans who had returned from abroad and were being looked after by the Foreign Organization (*Auslandsorganisation*, AO) of the NSDAP.[85] In addition, numerous agencies of the government and party helped themselves to the so-called Jewish goods (*Judengut*).[86] The social services administration put together a corresponding reserve of furniture and household goods; the chief regional tax administrator (*Oberfinanzpräsident*) and the SD section head in Hamburg supplemented their equipment by acquiring office furniture; a commission from the Hamburg Art Museum (Kunsthalie) acquired paintings, and the Hamburg public library system augmented its holdings by appropriating many volumes from Jewish private libraries.[87]

From February 1941 until the end of the war in the spring of 1945, hardly a day went by in Hamburg without a public auction of Jewish property. For one, a sufficient supply of goods was guaranteed by the "Assets Utilization Agency" (*Vermögensver-wertungsstelle*) of the chief regional tax administrator, which channeled the furniture of deported Hamburg Jews to the auctioneers beginning in the autumn of 1941. Another source was the large amounts of Jewish chattels sent to Hamburg after being pilfered throughout Western Europe, part of Operation M.[88] What had initially been launched in Western Europe in 1940–41 as the organized plunder of art and cultural objects by the *Reichsleiter* Rosenberg Operational Staff was amplified in the course of deportations to Auschwitz to encompass all Jewish possessions in France, Belgium, the Netherlands and Luxembourg. Hamburg profited in a special way from the Operation M shipments of loot. In 1942 alone, the complete furnishings of several thousand apartments belonging to deported Dutch Jews were shipped by sea to Hamburg.[89] In addition, the German Reichsbahn transported a total of 2,699 freight cars full of Jewish possessions to Hamburg through 1944. The circle of customers for such despoiled items ranged from the simple Hamburg housewife to the department stores in the Emsland, which regularly inquired with the auctioneers about new shipments.[90]

In her autobiographical sketches, a former Hamburg librarian described her feelings about the distribution and auctioning off of Jewish property:

I can still feel today the way I thought back then. I wondered: "What will happen to us some day because of all these things we've done?" When it came to supplies of basic necessities, we didn't have any problem yet. The goods that had been pilfered, or paid for with worthless paper money, were still rolling in from all over the Europe we'd attacked and plundered. The shops were still accepting our food ration cards, clothing cards, tickets for buying shoes. The men who came home on leave were still bringing meat, wine, cloth goods and tobacco back from the occupied

28

areas. The ships with confiscated Jewish possessions from Holland were still anchored in the harbor ... I was also ordered to go down to the port and pick up some rugs, furniture, jewelry and furs for myself. It was the stolen belongings of Dutch Jews who'd already been deported to the gas chambers. I didn't want to have anything to do with it. But even if I rejected all that, I had to watch my step with those primitive people who were so rapacious in grabbing up this loot, especially when it came to the women. I had to be careful not to say out loud what I was really thinking. I could only try, with great caution, to influence a few of the women, the ones who were not so euphoric, those whose husbands I knew were staunch Social Democrats—by telling them where these ship-ments full of the choicest household goods actually came from. And by repeating the old proverb: "Stolen goods never thrive." And they paid attention, they complied.[91]

By systematically distributing and auctioning off Jewish possessions, the Nazi regime turned broad segments of the German population into accom-plices of its policies of plunder and expansion, transforming them into material beneficiaries of the Holocaust. This aspect of the pillage has received little attention to date in research on Aryanization. What began insidiously after 1933 with the sale of individual properties burgeoned into one of the most mammoth property transfers in modern times. In 1938–39, it finally shifted to a policy of plundering in the form of exorbitant taxes, culminating in a massive despoilment participated in by large sections of the German populace. Even if it was the National-Socialist state that extracted the greatest financial benefit from Aryanization, no other measure of Nazi Jewish policy ultimately involved so many actors, and above all, so many profiteers.

Notes

1 Helmut Genschel, *Die Verdrängung der Juden aus der Wirtschaft im Dritten Reich* (Göttingen: Musterschmidt, 1966) (Genschel, *Verdrängung*).
2 Avraham Barkai, *From Boycott to Annihilation: the Economic Struggle of German Jews, 1933–1943* (Hanover, NH: University Press of New England, 1989); German original, *Vom Boykott zur Entjudung* (Frankfurt am Main: Fischer Taschenbuch, 1987).
3 See, among others, Peter Hayes, "Big Business and 'Aryanization' in Germany 1933–1939," in *Jahrbuch für Antisemitismusforschung*, Wolfgang Benz, ed., 3 (Frankfurt am Main/New York: Campus, 1994), pp. 254–281; Dirk van Laak, "Die Mitwirkenden bei der 'Arisierung.' Dargestellt am Beispiel der rheinisch-westfälischen Industrieregion 1933–1940," in *Die Deutschen und die Judenverfol-gung im Dritten Reich*, Ursula Büttner, ed. (Hamburg: Christians, 1992), pp. 231–257; Avraham Barkai, "Die deutschen Unternchmer und die Judenpolitik im 'Dritten Reich,'" *Geschichte und Gesellschaft*, 15 (1989), pp. 227–247.

4 See, among others, Barbara Händler-Lachmann and Thomas Werther, *Vergessene Geschäfte—verlorene Geschichte. Jüdisches Wirtschaftsleben in Marburg und seine Vernichtung im Nationalsozialismus* (Marburg: Hitzeroth, 1992); Regina Bruss, *Die Bremer Juden unter dem Nationalsozialismus* (Bremen: Selbstverlag des Staatsarchivs der Freien Hansestadt Bremen, 1983); Hans Witek, " 'Arisierungen' in Wien," in *NS-Herrschaft in Österreich 1938–1945*, Emmerich Talos et al., eds. (Vienna: Verlag für Gesellschatftskritik, 1988), pp. 199–217.

5 See, for example, Raul Hilberg, *The Destruction of the European Jews*, revised edition (New York: Holmes and Meier, 1985), who interprets the economic expropriation of the Jews as a stage on the road to annihilation.

6 Cited in "Die Ausschaltung der Juden," *Die Deutsche Volkswirtschaft. Nationalsozialistischer Wirtschaftsdienst*, No. 33 (1938), p. 1197.

7 Kurt Pätzold, *Faschismus, Rassenwahn, Judenverfolgung, Eine Studie zur politischen Strategie und Taktik des faschistischen deutschen Imperialismus (1933–1935)* ([East] Berlin: Deutscher Verlag der Wissenschaften, 1975), p. 25.

8 Götz Aly and Susanne Heim, *Vordenker der Vernichtung. Auschwitz und die deutschen Pläne für eine neue europäische Ordnung* (Hamburg: Hoffmann und Campe, 1991) (Aly and Heim, *Vordenker*), pp. 33–43.

9 See Hans Safrian, *Die Eichmann-Männer* (Vienna: Europaverlag, 1993) (Safrian, *Eichmann-Männer*), pp. 23–67.

10 Bundesarchiv koblenz (BAK), R 58, 23a, pp. 144, 163–164.

11 "Gesetz zur Änderung des Gesetzes über die Devisenbewirtschaftung," *Reichsgesetzblatt (RGBL)*, 1936, pt. 1, pp. 1000–01.

12 Staatsarchiv Hamburg (StAHH), "Oberfinanzpräsident," 9 UA 3 (security orders against Jews as preventive measures against the flight of capital). On "Aryanizations" as the result of security orders, see, among others: Archiv des Wiedergutmachungsamtes beim Landgericht Hamburg (hereafter, AWAH), Z 21664 (Fa. Jacoby, Zucker-Export), Z 2869–1 (Metallwerk Peute), Z 2660 (Arnold Bernstein Schiffahrtsgesellschaft m.b.H.), Z 995–1 (Fa. Julius Lachmann, Im- und Export), Z-193–1 (Fa. Dammtor-Lombard, Weiss & Sander).

13 On tax discrimination against Jews and the following figures, see Günther Felix, "Scheinlegalität und Rechtsbeugung—Finanzverwaltung, Steuergerichtsbarkeit und Judenverfolgung im 'Dritten Reich,'" *Steuer & Studium*, 5 (1995), pp. 197–204; Dorothee Mußgnug, *Die Reichsfluchtsteuer 1931–1953* (Berlin: Duncker & Humblot, 1993); Martin Tarrab-Maslaton, *Rechtliche Strukturen der Diskriminierung der Juden im Dritten Reich* (Berlin: Duncker & Humblot, 1993).

14 A table of such fees for the years 1934–1939 can be found in StAHH, "Oberfinanzpräsident," 47 UA 14.

15 Leo Lippmann, *"... dass ich wie ein guter Deutscher empfinde und handele." Zur Geschichte der Deutsch-Israelitischen Gemeinde in Hamburg in der Zeit vom Herbst 1935 bis zum Ende 1942* (Hamburg: Dölling & Galitz, 1944), pp. 71–72.

16 "Verordnung über den Einsatz jüdischen Vermögens," *RGBL* 1938, pt. 1, pp. 1709–1712, esp. 1709, art. V, § 15, sec. 1.

17 "Verordnung über die Nachprüfung von Entjudungsgeschäften," *RGBL* 1940, pt. 1, pp. 891–892.

18 On such compulsory contributions and Hamburg regional levies, see below.

19 On the Aronson case and the following data, see AWAH, Z 2-Leitakte, pp. 1–5, communication from Arthur Reimann, December 12, 1945.

20 On the following figures and the Aryanization of M. M. Warburg & Co. see BAK, Z 45 F, OMGUS-FINAD, 2/181/2, communication from Eric Warburg

to the OMGUS Finance Division, January 23, 1946; Christopher Kopper, "Nationalsozialistische Bankenpolitik am Beispiel des Bankhauses M. M. Warburg & Co. in Hamburg," master's thesis, Bochum University, 1988, pp. 125–126.

21 So characterized in Genschel, *Verdrängung*, pp. 237–240.

22 This is especially true for the period after 1938, when there were no longer any alternative possibilities for transfer, such as the *Altreu* procedure or funds transfer to Palestine within the framework of the *Ha'avarah* Transfer Agreement. For a description of the *Ha'avarah* and *Altreu* schemes, see Barkai, *From Boycott to Annihilation*, pp. 51–53, 103–104.

23 Presented, using the example of Hamburg, in Frank Bajohr, "Gauleitor in Hamburg. Zur Person und Tätigkeit Karl Kaufmanns," *Vierteljahrshefte für Zeitgeschichte*, no. 2, (1995), pp. 267–295, especially pp. 277–280.

24 Genschel, *Verdrängung*, pp. 240–248.

25 For so-called *Alte Kämpfer*, BAK, NS 1/554, "Gauschatzmeister Thüringen an Reichsschatzmeister Schwarz," July 22, 1938.

26 BAK, NS 1/554, "Beauftragter des Reichsschatzmeisters für den Gau Saarpfalz an das Reichsrevisionsamt," November 18, 1938.

27 AWAH, Z 993, pp. 14–16.

28 StAHH, "Hamburger Stiftung von 1937," no. 24, "Bericht des Hamburger Oberfinanzpräsidenten an den Hamburger Bürgermeister," February 8, 1946; on individual cases see, among others, AWAH, Z 2 (Aronson), Z 2073 (Luria & Co. Succ.).

29 StAHH, "Hamburger Stiftung von 1937," no. 24, pp. 41–42, memo, February 12, 1947.

30 See Günter Könke, "Das Budge-Palais. Entziehung jüdischer Vermögen und Rückerstattung in Hamburg," in *Die Juden in Hamburg 1590 bis 1990* Arno Herzig, ed. (Hamburg: Dölling & Galitz, 1991), pp. 657–668.

31 StAHH, "Familie Ahrens," 5, p. 108.

32 BAK, NS 1/2375–2, memo, February 16, 1937.

33 AWAH, Z 1719–2, pp. 20–22, communication from Dr. Carl Stumme, July 18, 1951.

34 See, for example, StAHH, "Deputation für Handel, Schiffahrt und Gewerbe 11," 111 D 5 (Aryanization of Fa. Herz & Co.); ibid., "Senatskanzlei-Präsidialabteilung," 1939 S 11/28 (Aryanization of Campell & Co.).

35 StAHH, "Oberfinanzpräsident," 47 UA 13, communication, "Norddeutsche Bank an den Oberfinanzpräsidenten," June 26, 1950.

36 See Ministry of Justice Hamburg, "Staatsanwaltschaftliches Ermittlungsverfahren gegen Willibald Schallert beim Landgericht Hamburg wegen Verbrechen gegen die Menschlichkeit," 14 Js 278/48.

37 "*Leistung und Anständigkeit*"; see "Arisierung—eine Gesinnungsfrage," *Völkischer Beobachter*, September 11, 1938.

38 Note, for example, the instance of the Adolf Lipper jewelry store, where the assessment of the value of thousands of watches and gold jewelry was completed in two hours; or the case of the specialty clothing shop Ostindienhaus Heinrich Colm, that changed owners in the span of ten minutes. See AWAH, Z 963–4, p. 2 (Fa. Adolf Lipper); Z 28–1 (Ostindienhaus Heinrich Colm).

39 Ibid., Z 28741, p. 30, testimony by the auditor Gustav von Bargen, February 18, 1969.

40 Cited ibid., Z 1175–1, p. 9 (Fa. Fiedler's Strumpfläden).

41 On such cases, which were not so uncommon, see ibid., Z 5500–2 (Fa. Schönthal & Co.), Z 5432–7 (Fa. Bernhard Stern), Z 9343 (Fa. Dr. Emil Marx Nachf.).

42 This classification is based on some 300 Aryanizations of firms in Hamburg.

43 AWAH, Z 3103 (Chemische Fabrik Rothschild & Leers).

44 Ibid., Z 574–7 (Fa. Robert Ganz), Z 1256 (Fa. Gebr. Nathan).

45 Ibid., Z 9879/2894 (Textilgeschäft Martin Josephs), Z 2889 (Fa. H. W. Almind Nachf.).

46 Ibid., Z 2588 (Fa. H. J. Luft).

47 Ibid., Z 2522–1 (Fa. Maaβ & Riege), Z 1159–1 (Schuhwarengeschäft Speier), Z 995 (Fa. Julius Lachmann).

48 Ibid., Z 1159–1, p. 40a, communication from Dr. Samson, February 28, 1951.

49 The legislation on restitution was frequently denounced as "immoral and illegal)," and many former purchasers now claimed they were the actual victims of the political circumstances. See, for example, ibid., Z 3350–1 (Fa. Inselmann & Co.), "Brief Julius Mehldau an das Landgericht Hamburg," February 17, 1953.

50 Ibid., Z 1124 (Spedition S. Dreyer Sen. Nachf. GmbH), Z 13410 (Fa. Julius Engländer & Hinsel).

51 Ibid., Z 13984 (Fa. H. van Pels & Wolff).

52 Ibid., Z 14281/14292 (Fa. Wilheim Haller).

53 Ibid., Z 15172–1 (Fa. Julius Hamberg).

54 By contrast, Barkai emphasizes that the economic establishment was also unscrupulous in exploiting Aryanization for its own advantage; Hayes has a more differentiated argument on this, especially from the temporal point of view. See Barkai, "Unternchmer," especially p. 237; Hayes, "Big Business."

55 Cited in Archives, M. M. Warburg & Co., Hamburg, "Autobiographische Aufzeichnungen Max Warburgs," New York, 1944, chap. 2; "Die Arisierungen 1936–1938."

56 Speech by Kaufmann to the Hamburg Chamber of Commerce, January 1939, Archives, Forschungsstelle für die Geschichte des Nationalsozìalismus in Hamburg (Archiv Fst.), fasc. 12 ("Personalakte Kaufmann").

57 See communication by the attorney of the Chamber of Commerce Haage to Dr. Eller in Berlin, May 11, 1939, ibid., fasc. 227–11.

58 "Alle jüdischen Einzelhandelsgeschäfte Hamburgs werden geschlossen," *Hamburger Tageblatt*, December 2, 1938.

59 See speech by Kaufmann to the "Hamburger Nationalklub von 1919," May 6, 1938, Bundesarchiv Potsdam (BAP), "Reichssicherheitshauptamt," St 3/510, p. 11.

60 Archiv Fst., fasc. 227–11, memo by Rudolf Blohm, January 5, 1943, "betr. Hamburger Firmen in den Niederlanden."

61 BAP, "Deutsche Reichsbank," no. 6612, pp. 396–398.

62 See Aly and Heim, *Vordenker*, pp. 232–237.

63 See AWAH, Z 131 (Fa. Rudolf Reich), Z 28–1 (Ostindienhaus Heinrich Colm), Z 995–1 (Fa. Julius Lachmann), Z 995–2 (Fa. von Georg & Co.).

64 Berlin Document Center, personal file Karl Kaufmann — PK, communication (no date) "betr. Arisierung G. W. Unger."

65 See O.M.G.U.S., *Ermittlungen gegen die Deutsche Bank* (Nördlingen: Greno, 1985), pp. 165–175; Harold James, "Die Deutsche Bank und die Diktatur 1933–1945," in *Die Deutsche Bank 1870–1995*, Lothar Gall et al., eds. (Munich: C.H. Beck, 1995), pp. 315–408, especially pp. 344ff.; O.M.G.U.S., *Ermittlungen gegen die Dresdner Bank* (Nördlingen: Greno, 1986), pp. 76–84.

66 See the files on various companies in Archives, M. M. Warburg & Co., collection "Nicht durch das Sekretariat," among others, on the firms Rappolt & Söhne, Juster & Co. (not separately listed).

67 See the list of trustees in StAHH, "Bürgerschaft 11," C II d 1, vol. 2.
68 Among others, the Treuhansa was appointed as trustee for the firms Gebrüder Hirschfeld, Heinrich Abeles & Co., Adolf Salberg, Ostindienhaus Heinrich Colm and J. Lobbenberg.
69 See the case of the wholesale firm Goldschmidt & Mindus, where the trustee von Jena participated as a limited partner with a personal deposit of RM 50,000, AWAH, Z 1489–1, pp. 2–3.
70 On the GVG, see StAHH, "Hamburger Stiftung von 1937," no. 24, pp. 4–6, 41–42.
71 Thus, up to October 1939, the GVG had sold only 280 properties; see StAHH, "Oberfinanzpräsident," 9 UA 3, memo from Currency Office, October 24, 1939.
72 "Justiz Behörde Hamburg, Urteil des Amtsgerichtes Hamburg, Abt. 121, gegen Max Arthur Schlappkohl," March 7, 1939, 7 Js 181/39.
73 Ibid., "Urteil des Landgerichtes Hamburg gegen Dr. Alois Schlosser, July 18, 1941, 6 Js 1336/38; on analogous acts in Vienna, see Safrian, *Eichmann-Männer*, pp. 35–36.
74 Ibid., "Urteil des Landgerichtes Hamburg gegen Anna Korowitschka," August 21, 1940, 11 Js 121/40.
75 See StAHH, "Auswanderungsamt I," sec. II, A II 13, vol. III 1938, communication, "Auswanderungsamt Hamburg an die Reichsstelle für Auswanderung," October 21, 1938.
76 Ibid., interrogation of Dr. Max Plaut, October 3, 1938.
77 Interview with Hans Hirschfeld, August 9, 1990, p. 8 (Interviewer: Beate Meyer), Archiv Fst./Werkstatt der Erinnerung.
78 See "Urteil des Amtsgerichtes Hamburg," dept. 131, August 3, 1939, 11 Js 209/39.
79 Ibid., "Urteilstext," pp. 25–26.
80 AWAH, binder "Entziehung von Vermögenswerten durch Globalmassnahmen," "Richtlinien der Hamburger Gestapo für die Versteigerung des jüdischen Umzugsgutes," January 20, 1941.
81 StAHH, "Oberfinanzpräsident," 47 UA 17 (alphabetical list of the proceeds from auction transferred in the period 1941–1943).
82 Ibid., UA 30 (list of 22 auctioneers who took part in the auctioning of Jewish chattels).
83 Ibid., 47 UA 2 (list of the 21 shipping agencies involved in the shipping of Jewish household goods).
84 "Jüdisches Umzugsgut unter dem Hammer," *Hamburger Fremdenblatt*, March 29, 1941.
85 See the correspondence of the auctioneer Carl F. Schlüter, 1941–1943, AWAH (not separately listed).
86 On the following, see StAHH, "Oberfinanzpräsident," 23 (utilization of the property of deported Jews and Jewish emigrants).
87 StAHH, "Hamburger Öffentliche Bücherhallen," 14, memos, June 11, August 3, September 4 and September 7, 1942.
88 See "Gesamtleistungsbericht der Dienststelle Westen des Reichsministeriums für die besetzten Ostgebiete," August 8, 1944, AWAH, document collection on "M-Aktion," pp. 170–175.
89 StAHH, "Senatskanzlei-Präsidialabteilung," 1942 S II 538, memo, "Beigeordneter Martini an Reichsstatthalter Kaufmann," October 16, 1942.
90 See communications from Manufaktur- und Modenhaus Carl Möddel in Lingen/Emsland to auctioneer Carl F. Schlüter, AWAH, correspondence Schlüter, 1941–1943 (not separately listed).
91 Gertrud Seydelmann, "Lebenserinnerungen" (Hamburg: 1994), manuscript, p. 83.

16

EXPEDITING EXPROPRIATION AND EXPULSION

The impact of the "Vienna Model" on anti-Jewish policies in Nazi Germany, 1938

Hans Safrian

Source: *Holocaust and Genocide Studies*, 14:3 (2000), 390–414.

Historians of the Nazi period agree that the year 1938 marked a watershed in Nazi antisemitic policy.[1] This is especially true as it concerned the exclusion of Jews from the economy ("Aryanization")[2] and the transition from a strategy of emigration to one of expulsion. But there is no consensus about the causes of the intensification of these policies. A variety of factors contributed, of course, but I will explore two such, heretofore underrated and, I believe, decisive ones. These were the initiatives of Austrian antisemites and the concomitant new procedures introduced by functionaries in the *Ostmark* (Austria after the *Anschluss*, or incorporation) in response to these actions. An additional impetus for examining this topic is a tendency in historiography to ignore or underestimate the existence of indigenous antisemitic policies in the Ostmark,[3] suggesting either that Austria was a proving ground for more extreme anti-Jewish policy,[4] or that antisemitic measures carried out over six years in Germany had to be telescoped into a brief period in the Ostmark. In coining the phrase "Vienna Model," recent publications addressing this issue have stimulated discussion.[5] The authors of these publications, however, fail to grasp both the significance of the antisemitic mass movement that manifested itself in the spring of 1938 in Austria and its impact on the formulation of antisemitic policies in the Reich. The necessity of examining in tandem those procedures emanating from the Ostmark with those measures pursued by Nazi government agencies in Berlin will be demonstrated by exploring, as one example, the genesis of the decree concerning the registration of Jewish property. According to hitherto unevaluated documents, this decree was devised not in Berlin, but in Vienna.

"Aryanizations" before 1938

From 1933 to 1938, National Socialist policies aimed at the disintegration and marginalization of German Jewry. Legislation such as the "Law for the Restoration of the Professional Service" of April 1933 banned Jews from certain designated professions. Party formations of the NSDAP staged anti-Jewish boycott actions, particularly in April 1933 and in the summer of 1935.

In this period so-called "voluntary Aryanizations" were the norm.[6] Laws for the forced exclusion of Jews from German economic life ("compulsory Aryanization") were not issued before November 1938. Corresponding initiatives, like those in connection with decrees attached to the Nuremberg racial laws, had been rejected by the responsible ministries, and especially by Economics Minister and Reichsbank president Hjalmar Schacht.[7] Until the end of 1937, the drive to dislodge Jews from the economy (*Entjudung der Wirtschaft*) originated not with governmental agencies in Berlin but predominantly at regional and local party levels. Boycott actions and discrimination in government contracts, coupled often with the imputation of infringements of tax and currency regulations, forced Jewish owners of primarily small- and medium-sized enterprises to sell or relinquish their businesses. The tempo and scope of these "Aryanizations" varied from region to region.[8] The majority of big businesses in Germany were, according to Peter Hayes, not very interested in "Aryanizations."[9] Of the great banking concerns, it was above all the Dresdner Bank, that, beginning in 1936, facilitated "Aryan purchasers" through consultation and credits, profiting handsomely from commissions and brokerage fees, and that carried out "Aryanizations" in its own right.[10] As a rule, Jewish entrepreneurs received a certain, generally inadequate, compensation[11] for their enterprises during this phase. In isolated instances, however, expropriation without indemnification took place, as for example in the case of the Simson Weapons Factory (*Waffenfabrik* Simson) in Suhl (Thuringia), which Thuringian Gauleiter Fritz Sauckel transformed into the Wilhelm Gustloff Foundation (*Wilhelm-Gustloff-Stiftung*).[12]

Hermann Göring's appointment as Plenipotentiary for the Four-Year Plan in 1936, together with the assumption of important economic and financial agendas by officials of the Four-Year Plan and Schacht's dismissal as Economics Minister in the autumn of 1937, altered this situation by degrees.[13] The pressure on Jewish-owned enterprises grew stronger, particularly with Göring ordering reduced allocations of raw materials and foreign currencies and with a June 1938 decree providing a legally binding definition of a "Jewish firm."[14] Nevertheless a frictionless functioning of anti-Jewish legislation in the economic sphere was still not guaranteed.[15] Neither Hitler's demand in the autumn of 1936 for a law making German Jews liable for so-called "Jewish crimes" abroad[16] nor the introduction of a special punitive tax for Jews was realized.[17] Even Göring opposed the special tax in December 1937, citing potential consequences for the already severely depleted foreign currencies reserve needed to import raw materials for the rearmament program.[18]

When in June 1938 Reich Interior Minister Wilhelm Frick submitted a draft of a law for the compulsory elimination of Jews from the economy,[19] the Finance Ministry and the Reichsbank president objected. In his letter of July 7, 1938, Schacht expressed his reservations: besides the anticipated negative impact the proposed measure would have upon the capital market and German credit transactions, such a law would raise fundamental questions concerning the right of property ownership. Schacht pronounced it dangerous "in dealing with the economic aspect of the 'Jewish Question' to further pursue a path that the rest of the world will denounce as arbitrary flouting of the fundament of law and as outright confiscation of property."[20]

In terms of the legislative process, the situation in the summer of 1938 could be viewed as a stalemate. Although individual decrees chipped away at Jewish-owned businesses, a comprehensive law concerning compulsory expropriation did not yet exist.

"Open season"

At the time of the Anschluss in March 1938, more than 200,000 persons in Austria were Jews according to the Nuremberg Racial Laws.[21] They constituted approximately forty percent of all Jews living in the "Greater German Reich" at that time. Austrian Jews were concentrated in Vienna, which hosted in absolute and relative numbers the largest Jewish community in "Greater Germany."

Directly upon the heels of the Anschluss, expression of antisemitic sentiment—previously limited for the most part to oral and written articulation[22]—took a violent turn. On the evening before German troops crossed the Austrian border, anti-Jewish riots erupted. Without "orders from above," native antisemites—whether Party members or not—struck out against anyone whom they thought to be Jewish. This was the onset of a sort of "open season" during March and April of 1938, in which theft, plundering, extortion, and public humiliation rituals—such as forcing Jews to scrub sidewalks—took place on a massive scale. Jewish-owned stores were ransacked in broad daylight, cars "confiscated," and money, jewels, savings books, and valuables "taken into safekeeping" during household searches.[23]

Official organs of the police and Nazi Party contributed to this climate of open terror. The Gestapo, the SS, and its Security Service (*Sicherheitsdienst*, or SD)[24], joined Party members in hunting down alleged political opponents. Hundreds of prominent or wealthy Jewish men were arrested and their properties confiscated. One of the first actions of Adolf Eichmann[25] in Vienna was to search the administrative offices of the *Israelitischen Kultusgemeinde*, on March 18, 1938; Eichmann seized all documents and valuables and took all leading personnel, among them the managing director Dr. Josef Löwenherz, into custody. Receipts of campaign donations raised for chancellor Kurt Schuschnigg's planned plebiscite, found on the premises, were utilized in order to impose upon the Kultusgemeinde a "contribution" of half a million Reichsmark. This was the first time in "Greater Germany" that a Jewish body was forced to pay a collective levy. After the reorganization of the Kultusgemeinde under his direct supervision in May 1938, Eichmann monitored payment of the fine.[26]

In the Ostmark the line between official and unofficial terror blurred in the weeks following the Anschluss. Anyone wearing a swastika armband could take Jews into custody, sometimes settling old scores in the process. As a witness later reported, every person who at one time or another had made an enemy had to reckon with the possibility of arrest. It sufficed that an Aryan—no matter how humble or ill-reputed—appeared before the SA, SS, or other Party organization to denounce a Jewish person for some alleged infraction. Extortionists demanded payment in cash or goods: those who refused to pay were threatened with denunciation to Nazi authorities.[27]

The perspective of the victims was best summed up by a foreign observer. In April 1938, Leo Lauterbach, a secretary of the Zionist Executive in London,[28] traveled with Sir Wyndham Deedes, a leading member of the Council for German Jewry, to Vienna and Berlin to discuss relief operations on behalf of Austrian Jews with the authorities and members of the Jewish communities in those cities. Lauterbach's keen insight into the situation of Jews in the Ostmark led him to somber conclusions. He found that the catastrophe that had descended upon Austrian Jewry and the profound changes that within a few weeks' time had so drastically altered their economic, social, and legal circumstances were not the outcome of publicly-announced laws, but rather the result of spontaneous actions emanating from a variety of different sources: from the Nazi Party, the Gestapo, uniformed SS and SA, and even private citizens. He described in detail "Aryanizations," searches of private homes, accompanied by theft and extortion, mass arrests and deportations to concentration camps, sadistic violence, and demeaning forced labor. Lauterbach was especially struck by the impact of public humiliation upon Jewish victims. The behavior of the jeering onlookers was a "terrible shock" for Austria's Jews—an experience that robbed the victims of any feeling of personal security and that dashed their belief in the humanity of their neighbors: "It revealed to them that they lived not only in a fool's paradise, but also in a veritable hell [*wahre Hölle*]. No one who till then had known the average Viennese would have believed that he could sink to such a level."[29] In his opinion the situation in Vienna in April of 1938 appeared to be characterized on both the Jewish and Nazi sides by confusion, insecurity, and constantly fluctuating circumstances.

A clear policy concerning the Jewish problem in Austria has been neither publicly announced nor communicated in the few discussions we had with authorities. One cannot escape the impression, however, that this policy will be palpably different from that which is pursued in Germany, and that their goal may be the complete destruction of Austrian Jewry. According to all indications, it aims at excluding them from economic life, stripping them of all financial resources in order to force them either to starve or to leave the country penniless, at the expense of the international Jewish relief organizations and with the help of such lands which may be willing to accept them.[30]

Lauterbach's assessment was a relatively accurate prediction of the policies of the next months.

Those persons attempting to flee the terror in the Ostmark had to surrender nearly all their belongings. Legal emigration was made very difficult: new papers and dozens of certificates had to be acquired. In order to secure the indispensable documents and paperwork, one had to queue for hours, even days, before the offices of police and tax officials, and individuals standing in line in the streets were often harassed by Nazi thugs. It also became necessary to grease a number of palms in order to reduce the amount of red tape and bureaucratic chicanery. Against payment of improbable sums, attorneys well connected with Gestapo and police officials procured passports for their desperate clients. As those possibilities still existing in Germany to transfer money or property abroad had not been extended to the Ostmark, victims attempting to flee had no legal means of taking the remainder of their possessions with them. Measures like the flight tax (*Reichsfluchtsteuer*), however, did find their way to Austria. Charles Kapralik, in 1938 an official of the Kultusgemeinde responsible for its foreign currencies branch (*Devisenabteilung*) in Vienna, wrote: "The situation [in the Ostmark] was fundamentally different from that in the *Altreich* up to the summer of 1938. There [i.e., in Germany] freedom and life were not put in constant danger; there also existed various official transfer possibilities, particularly the 'Haavara' to Palestine. Furniture, household items, valuable pictures, and objects d'art could be taken across the German border without much difficulty. From the standpoint of Austrian Jews, the circumstances under which emigration from Germany was still possible were considered extremely favorable."[31] Seen in the Austrian context, the term expulsion seems more apt than that of "emigration."

38

New decrees, new institutions

In Vienna the looting of shops and households as well as various extortion attempts were committed in part by local Nazi "small fry." They knew their turf; they knew where and from whom there was something to steal. Not only were these excesses perpetrated without orders: the new authorities in the Ostmark had difficulty putting a stop to them. On March 14, two days after the Anschluss, the quasi-official *Wiener Zeitung* stated that confiscations or arrests by party or SA members were strictly forbidden without the express approval of the Gauleiter.[32] In a March 17 letter to future "Reich Commissar for the Reunification" Josef Bürckel, Reinhard Heydrich threatened Gestapo action against party comrades who "in the last days have participated in large-scale excesses in a completely undisciplined manner."[33] The antisemitic rioters and plunderers paid no heed.

Ministries in Berlin were not amused by the manner in which "Aryanizations" took place in Vienna. On March 21, Dr. Wilhelm Stuckart from the Ministry of the Interior cabled the authorities in Vienna that he had learned of "wild Aryanizations" in the Ostmark. On behalf of the minister of economics, he requested that authorities "intervene against these unauthorized proceedings and see to it that these sorts of Aryanization measures cease."[34]

The groundswell of enthusiasm for personal enrichment could not be easily suppressed. In the Ostmark, antisemitism became for tens of thousands an instrument for quick personal gain at the expense of a marginalized minority. The most striking expression of this mentality were the so-called "wild commissars" (*"wilde Kommissare"*).[35] These self-appointed commissars, an Austrian peculiarity, settled themselves into Jewish-run stores and businesses, ostensibly to control and prevent the "machinations" of the Jewish owners. In reality, most of the wild commissars, numbering more than 20,000, simply took money from the tills or seized goods for themselves and their associates.

The wide-scale looting in March and April 1938, coupled with the activities of the commissars, forced the Jewish owners of 7,000—mostly small-scale—businesses to close their doors due to lack of inventory. This first wave of "liquidations," as the closures came to be known, preceded, and set the tone for, official "Aryanization" measures in Austria. *Reichskommissar* Bürckel grumbled that "the shining history of National Socialism and the uprising in Austria has been tarnished to a certain extent by the plunder and larceny of the first few weeks." The Austrian party members, he complained, "had notions that did not correspond with our conception of property, personal integrity in financial matters, etc."[36]

Parallel and in tandem with the outright theft and plunder, the "race" for the takeover of Jewish enterprises began. As the bargaining power of Jewish owners was not very strong, so-called buyers purchased firms from

39

Jewish owners for much less than their genuine value. In April of 1938, for example, Vienna's largest brewery, *Ottakringer Brauerei*, was "sold" for a miniscule sum to an "Aryan" purchaser.[37] (The "Aryan" family remains in possession of the brewery to this day.)

To curb the worst excesses of the commissars, to introduce a measure of order into the race for Jewish property, and—not incidentally—to ensure that the state and its agencies would secure their share of the loot, Nazi authorities in the Ostmark were spurred to shape innovative decrees and forge new institutions. Arthur Seyss-Inquart's Anschluss government, and especially its trade minister, Dr. Hans Fischböck,[38] had a hand in crafting the new decrees concerning the disposal of Jewish property and the activities of the wild commissars. The commissars had already established themselves outside the existing legal framework; and the new rulers in Austria did not dare oust them, for they feared such a step would trigger heavy rioting among the local population (*"ohne weiteres zu schweren Ausschreitungen geführt"*).[39] Thus they opted to legitimize the wild commissars retroactively. In late March a *Staatskommissar* for the private economy, Walter Rafelsberger,[40] was installed to license the commissars. One of Rafelsberger's first actions, however, was not to rein in the larcenists, but to confiscate major enterprises of Jewish owners, placing, for example, the banking houses S. M. von Rothschild and Gutmann Bros. under the commissarial administration of the state-owned Austrian Credit-Institute for Public Enterprises and Works.[41]

On April 14, 1938, the "Law Concerning the Appointment of Commissarial Administrators and Supervisory Personnel"[42] was decreed, valid only for the Ostmark, which entitled commissars to handle all legal transactions regarding enterprises of Jewish owners. Another law drafted to address the Austrian situation initially encountered some delay, but when promulgated, went into force for the entire Reich: the decree concerning registration of Jewish property.

Although historians view the significance of this decree as one of central importance to the expropriation of the Jews,[43] almost nothing is known about the genesis of the decree and the April 11 conference at which it was initiated.[44] The protocol for this meeting makes it clear that the law originated not in Berlin, but in Vienna.

On April 11, 1938, a "discussion regarding currency exchange issues rising from the reunification with Austria under the chairmanship of Herr Minister President General Field Marshal Göring"[45] was convened in Berlin. The conference, held one day after the plebiscite concerning the Anschluss, was attended by Reich Minister of Economics Walter Funk; high-ranking officials from the Reichsbank and the ministries of finance and the interior; by Reich Plenipotentiary Wilhelm Keppler, and the Austrian Nazi trade minister, Fischböck. Topic five of the meeting's agenda was the policy of "Aryanization" in Austria.[46] The protocol states that after a thoroughgoing discussion of the proposal for an Austrian law requiring registration of Jewish property, Göring "made up his mind to apply it immediately to the whole Reich"[47] ("... *entschließt sich der Herr Ministerpräsident, diese Aktion gleich im gesamten Reichsgebiet durchzuführen*"). The decree was to be promulgated jointly by the Reich ministers of economics and the interior. When it was issued on April 26, 1938, it contained the ominous Paragraph 7: "The Plenipotentiary for the Four-Year Plan can undertake measures in order to guarantee utilization of the registered property in the interest of the German economy."[48] The deadline for Jews to complete the necessary registration forms was set for July 31, 1938, and for German and Austrian Jews living abroad October 31, 1938.[49]

In the Ostmark the legalization of the wild commissars had certainly created the opportunity for forced Aryanizations, but state supervision and control of all expropriation proceedings had still not been fully secured: hence the functionaries created a centralizing apparatus. In mid-May 1938, the Property Transfer Office (*Vermögensverkehrsstelle*), an institution that had no predecessors in Germany, was founded in Vienna under the jurisdiction of Minister Fischböck. Walter Rafelsberger headed the office, which was tasked with the execution and supervision of Aryanizations and the evaluation and partial replacement of the commissars.[50] It was the assignment of the Transfer Office to collect the property registrations of Jewish Austrians to approve all contracts for Aryanizations, and to assess the sales prices.[51]

But still another problem plagued the authorities in the Ostmark: the illegal nature of confiscations executed in the first months after the Anschluss. The confiscation, in the spring of 1938, of property belonging to Austrian Jews and other so-called enemies of the state and the people had yielded enormous booty. Analyzing an inventory drawn up by the SS in August 1938 that cites the confiscation of palaces, villas, hotels, factories, and 1,700 automobiles, we can conclude that property valued at a total of more than one hundred million Reichsmark was seized from Jewish owners.[52] From the perspective of the authorities there was only one slight problem: the confiscations had no legal basis. In early May of 1938, the leader of the SD Main Sector Danube (*SD-Oberabschnitt Donau*), learned jurist Dr. Stahlecker, debated the legality of the confiscations.[53] Under the pretext of maintaining law and order, the Gestapo had carried out property seizures without legal authority. A retroactive legal settlement would be difficult, however, since the Gestapo had not been the only ones to confiscate Jewish property. In a memo Stahlecker wrote. "In the meantime, the Party, its formations, and affiliated organizations have attempted in a manner surpassing every standard to appropriate the property of Jews and of enemies of the state. It is estimated that these parties have confiscated three times as many assets as were seized by the Gestapo."[54] Retroactive legalization would have to apply to all seizures. Of the party actions, only

41

a small percentage could be legally justified. Stahlecker continued. "All other confiscations have either to be legalized unlawfully [*per nefas legalisiert*] or nullified. In both cases it should be noted that the value of the confiscated items has declined appreciably in the meantime. This is not only true for automobiles, but also for real estate, from which a large portion of the inventory has been stolen."[55]

The absence of legal bases for the confiscations had to be addressed at higher levels. The Beich governor (*Reichsslatthalter*) in Austria. Arthur Seyss-Inquart, therefore demanded a decree concerning the "Confiscation of Property of Enemies of the People and the State in Austria." a decree that was finally promulgated on November 18, 1938.[56]

As a general principle, in the Ostmark transactions that had been designated "voluntary Aryanizations" were the exception, "compulsory Aryanizations" the rule. Whereas German Reich ministers debated the pros and cons of expropriation in the summer of 1938, functionaries in the Ostmark—through confiscation, through legalization of the commissars, and finally through the creation of a central agency for the supervision and execution of Aryanizations—had, by the late spring of 1938, already denied Austrian Jews any influence over the disposal of their property. Within two months' time, a system had been constructed that allowed for compulsory Aryanizations only (thus reversing the universally accepted stereotype of German thoroughness and efficiency and Austrian slovenliness).

In the Ostmark the main question was not whether to engage in compulsory Aryanizations, but rather how to divvy up the loot. As there were many fewer enterprises to Aryanize than applicants eager to take them over, a struggle ensued among individual Nazis for property rights. In letters to the Transfer Office, *Parteigenossen* (Party members), who hoped to partake of the plunder, stressed their own contributions to the movement and portrayed their competitors as shady and avaricious figures.[57] Members of the Nazi "old guard" ("*Alte Kämpfer*") demanded Aryanized property as "*Wiedergutmachung*"—as "compensation" for their earlier sacrifices to the cause. As an example, the widow of Otto Planetta, the executed murderer of Austrian chancellor Engelbert Dollfuss, requested an Aryanized fun house (*Geisterbahn*) concession in the Prater amusement park as a reward for her loss. When her comrades deemed this inappropriate, she was instead made proprietor of a cinema that had belonged to Jewish owners.

The highest echelons of government were aware of the shady transactions in the Ostmark. In a conference at his Reich Aviation Ministry (*Reichsluftfahrtsministerium*) in October 1938, at which primarily economic and financial matters were discussed, Göring stressed the pressing need for measures aimed at expropriating Jews, but sharply criticized those practices currently being applied in Austria: "The wild bustle of commissars as it has developed in Austria must be prevented under all cir-cumstances. These wild actions have to cease, and the settling of the Jewish problem should not be regarded as a system of providing for incompetent party members."[58] Hans Fischböck, who had, in the mean-time, become minister of economics and finance in the Nazi Ostmark government, revealed that there were still 3,500 active commissars. The Nazi Party in the Ostmark, he concluded, held the opinion that Aryaniza-tions had "to be connected with the recompensation of the old party members."[59] Göring took a strong stand against these "compensations." Most of the Aryanizers and commissars, however, were so firmly entrenched in the local Nazi Party that there was little to be done.

The strategy developed by the Nazis in the Ostmark in the summer of 1938 already encompassed a total solution to the "Jewish question." In an internal position paper Bürckel spelled out the issue: "One may never forget, if one wants to Aryanize and take from the Jews their livelihood, then one must solve the Jewish Question in a total manner. To regard him as a state-paid pensioner—this is impossible. So one must create the pre-conditions necessary for him to go abroad."[60] Bürckel therefore suggested the construction of occupational training and labor camps for 30,000 Jews—a proposal that was never realized.

Instead another institution was developed to foster the expulsion of Austrian Jewry. In August 1938, the *Zentralstelle für jüdische Auswan-derung* (Central Office for Jewish Emigration) was founded by authorities in the Ostmark and placed under the leadership of Adolf Eichmann. The nominal director of the office was Eichmann's superior, Dr. Stahlecker. In line with the strategies of the SD,[61] Eichmann had tried to accelerate the expulsion of Jews from Austria in the spring of 1938. But, independent of his efforts, tens of thousands had made desperate attempts to flee the country as soon as possible. When the Kultusgemeinde reopened its offices in May 1938, 45,000 applications for emigration (*Auswanderungs-formulare*) were submitted within a few days' time. Kultusgemeinde offi-cials recommended the centralization of all agencies concerned with "emigration." Eichmann transmitted this proposal, slightly modified, to Bürckel, who ordered the creation of the Zentralstelle für jüdische Auswanderung. The substance of the procedure was not altered: the total depletion of the emigrants' resources was still the pre-condition for getting a valid passport—but the bureaucratic process was speeded up. From now on, only Eichmann's underlings were entitled to harass Jewish emigrants.[62]

The financing of emigration proceeded not from the conversion of victim's Reichsmark accounts to foreign currencies, emanating from the Reichsbank, but, as Lauterbach had feared, at the expense of the international Jewish relief organizations. Beginning in July 1938, the Joint Distribution Commit-tee and the Council for German Jewry donated $100,000 monthly to the Kul-tusgemeinde. The foreign currency account was monitored by the foreign exchange office (*Devisenstelle*) of the Reich's finance ministry and by Eichmann, but the foreign currencies branch of the Kultusgemeinde carried out the distribution of funds.[63] Jews were allowed to utilize Reichsmark from their blocked accounts for the necessary expenses of emigration. The foreign currencies branch of the Kultusgemeinde sold the currencies to well-to-do persons for so-called capitalist certificates (proof of possession of 1,000 British pounds to immigrate into Palestine) purchased at two—and later at three and four times the official exchange rate; to poorer emigrants they sold them at or below the official rate for landing monies (*Vorzeigegelder*) and travel expenses.[64] In this way a certain redistribution of the costs of emigration was effected. The Kultusgemeinde utilized the proceeds stemming from these transactions to cover the rising expenses of social welfare and relief for the poor—Austrian Jews were not entitled to receive any *Sozialhilfe* (state aid)—as well as the funding of schools, retraining programs, hospitals, and homes for the elderly. Seen from the perspective of the Nazi authorities, this arrangement was convenient, for the foreign exchange that defrayed the cost of emigration came not from the critically low levels of foreign currency reserve in the Reichsbank, but from relief agencies abroad.

By May 1939 (the time of the census), more than half of Austrian Jewry had fled from the Ostmark abroad. Besides what they could carry in their luggage, they were allowed to take with them only the small amounts of foreign currency required by their respective countries of immigration. Eichmann and his superiors claimed credit for this system and successfully extolled these procedures as a prototype.

Example as rule—Ostmark inputs to decision-making

During the November pogrom (*Kristallnacht*) in Vienna, the Austrian Nazis committed the same crimes as their comrades in the Altreich, albeit on a broader scale. SS commandos set synagogues ablaze;[65] more than 6,500 Jewish men were arrested,[66] tortured in makeshift prisons, and subsequently sent to concentration camps. "It may sound absurd," one victim who experienced a makeshift prison in Vienna wrote in a postwar-report, but "after the numerous inhuman and incalculable excesses, Dachau was almost a relief" ("*war Dachau fast eine Erholung*").[67] At least twenty-seven Jewish men were killed in Vienna—nearly one-third of all Reichs-kristallnacht murder victims.[68] The most striking deviation in the Ostmark, however, was the extensive scale of plunder of Jewish homes and businesses. Local Nazis looted nearly all still-existing Jewish shops, regardless of whether they were administered by commissars or figured in the process of Aryanization. Bürckel dubbed the November pogrom in Vienna "the Day and Night of the Long Fingers," an obvious reference to the massive spoliation. A second wave of property liquidations followed the pogrom.

Bürckel and other leading functionaries had once again to cover up the deeds of their local party comrades: "5,000 Jewish businesses are closed in Vienna as a result of the excesses. That in itself is not a bad thing. Nevertheless, the planned transition that I had envisioned would have been better. Insofar as the businesses are now closed, their re-openings can take place only as long as their inventory is still available—that is, if it has not been plundered outright. ... For the liquidation ... and the utilization of the secured goods I require a legal basis."[69] Once again there was a need to shore up the existing legal framework, for ex-post-facto regulations.

At a November 12 meeting in the Reich Aviation Ministry, Göring voiced his intention to settle the economic aspect of the "Jewish problem" in the wake of Reichskristallnacht—by which he meant to fill the coffers of the Reich with stolen Jewish assets. Göring was disturbed by the destruction of what he dubbed German resources: "I would have preferred that you had killed 200 Jews and not destroyed such valuables" (*"Mir wäre es lieber gewesen, ihr hättet 200 Juden erschlagen und hättet nicht solche Werte vernichtet"*).[70]

Some of the steps already taken in the Ostmark were presented as recommendations for Reich-wide regulations. After the issue of insurance payments had been deliberated and decided, the discussion turned to the question of whether looted Jewish stores should be reopened or not. Göring had not yet made up his mind. The minister of economy and finance of the Nazi Ostmark government, Hans Fischböck, announced that he already had a plan. According to his scheme, only 3,000–3,500 out of a total of the 17,000 stores ostensibly still in existence should be Aryanized; all others should be closed. (Fischböck's strategy was a smokescreen. As shown above, a considerable number of shops in Vienna had to be closed not according to plan, but as a result of the lootings and lack of inventory.) In order to do this legally, in September 1938 the functionaries had drafted a law to empower them to withdraw licenses from artisans. If this law were to be issued, the authorities in the Ostmark would be able to close 10,000 stores as a matter of course. Göring promised, "I shall have this decree issued today."[71] Fischböck asserted that all Jewish-owned businesses could be liquidated in Vienna before the end of the year. Göring was thrilled: "I have to say that this proposal is grand. This way, the whole affair would be wound up in Vienna, one of the Jewish capitals, so to speak, by Christmas or by the end of the year."[72] Reich Economics Minister Walther Funk, held the opinion that the same thing could be done "over here [i.e., in Germany]."[73]

The question of whether Jewish owners should receive money for their Aryanized properties was raised. Göring did not support the idea because he feared Jews could use the funds to buy jewels and smuggle them abroad. Minister Fischböck explained how the procedure already practiced in the Ostmark ruled out this possibility: "We do that the following way. The Aryanizing is authorized only under the condition that the price for the purchase is to be paid in installments lasting over a long period of time, in case the buyer is unable to pay; or, in case payment is made, that the amount be placed in a frozen bank account."[74] This time it was Göring who said "We could do the same thing over here."

Later Fischböck brought up the issue of apartment buildings, bonds, and shares in the possession of Jews. Fischböck proposed confiscating real estate properties and financial papers; Jewish owners should be "compensated" with claims on the debit ledger of the Reich. Economics Minister Funk was stunned and asked, "Why should Jews not be allowed to keep bonds?" Göring and Fischböck argued that by expropriating bonds, the Reich would be able to control this portion of Jewish wealth. Funk had misgivings, because, "the Reich will become possessor of half a billion shares." Fischböck explained that this was precisely the point—this would be a business based on profits for the Reich. The last resistance was offered by Reich Finance Minister Schwerin von Krosigk, who dubbed Fischböck's approach "an entirely new idea to expropriate the Jews in this manner as well," although the intention had been to retain their nominal status as share owners. Fischböck brushed von Krosigk's doubts aside, maintaining that all their efforts would remain unsuccessful "as long as the Jews shall be in the possession of values, which they may realize quickly and employ for any other undertaking." Once again Göring whole-heartedly agreed: "I think Fischböck's proposal is very good. We should give it the form of a draft now."[75]

The practice of shaping suggestions originating in Vienna into regulations for the entire German Reich—initiated by Göring in connection with the registration of property in April 1938—now reached its apogee. Fischböck's interventions at the November conference were grounded in an already existing system of compulsory Aryanizations in the Ostmark. While in Germany, up to this point, Aryanizations had taken place in the private economy, in Austria regional state agencies had interfered heavily in the process, gained partial control of its direction, and profited from their own participation. Fischböck and other functionaries had set precedents in dealing with the "Jewish question." With these credentials he was able to lecture Reich ministers Funk and von Krosigk and to propose procedures that delighted Göring. The numerous objections raised by various Reich ministries, objections that had prevailed before the summer of 1938, were now pushed aside.

In a similar vein, Reinhard Heydrich suggested that the Central Office for Jewish Emigration in Vienna serve as a model for a parallel institution in the Reich. He boasted that, thanks to the Central Office in Vienna, 50,000 Austrian Jews had emigrated, whereas only 19,000 Jews had fled the Reich in the same period of time. "Through the Jewish Kultusgemeinde, we extracted a certain amount of money from rich Jews who wanted to emigrate. By paying this amount ... they made it possible for a number of poor Jews to leave. The problem was not to make the rich Jew leave, but to get rid of the Jewish mob."[76] Göring was obviously not aware of the fact that the foreign currency came from Jewish relief organizations abroad and that Jewish emigrants from Austria were not allowed to transfer money and asked: "But children, did you ever think this through? ... Has it ever occurred to you that this procedure may cost us so much foreign currency that in the end we won't be able to hold out?"[77] Heydrich was able to answer this objection by indicating that Austrian Jews were allowed to take with them only small amounts of foreign currency. This argument proved convincing. Göring agreed, and the way was open for Heydrich to set up "a similar procedure for the Reich," which would be the new Reichszentrale für jüdische Auswanderung. With Göring's announcement that he would impose a collective one billion RM *Sühneabgabe* ("atonement tax") upon all Jews in "Greater Germany," the meeting was adjourned. The topics discussed during the conference at the Reich Aviation Ministry were promulgated as decrees and spelled out the end of "voluntary Aryanization." With these regulations of November and December 1938, many measures that already had been practiced for months in the Ostmark became binding for the entire Reich. For example, the Decree for the Utilization of Jewish Property of December 3, 1938 (*Verordnung über den Einsatz des jüdischen Vermögens*) dictated that all still existing Jewish-owned enterprises be Aryanized or liquidated.[78]

Göring strove to adopt still another strategy practiced in the Ostmark: the preservation of Germany's limited foreign currency reserve vis-à-vis Jewish emigration. Obviously he had learned from the proceedings in Austria that relief organizations abroad could be urged to give money to support emigration from the Reich. In a December 6 Aviation Ministry discussion with the Gauleiter, provincial president (*Oberpräsident*), and Reich governor concerning the "Jewish Question,"[79] Göring informed his audience that Hitler had entrusted him to oversee and regulate all aspects of anti-Jewish policies.[80] Hitler, he asserted, had given top priority to a rapid and effective expulsion of Jews. Addressing the thorny problem of emigration. Göring had developed a strategy. Emigrating Jews should not obtain any foreign currencies from German institutions. Rather, Jewish organizations abroad and sympathetic governments should raise a large loan in foreign currencies.[81] The distribution of this foreign exchange should be administered by German officials so that "for one rich Jew, four poor Jews"[82] could emigrate—a distinct reference to methods practiced in Vienna. As collateral for the loan. Göring wanted to put up all Jewish-owned assets. In order to secure repayment of the loan, foreign Jewish organizations should effect a termination of the anti-German boycott and induce large-scale trade concerns to guarantee purchase of designated goods from Germany. "The Führer had given this plan his specific endorsement"

47

(*"Dieser Plan hat dem Führer außerordentlich zugesagt"*).[83] The scheme, intended mainly to solve German export and foreign currency reserve problems, was proposed by Hjalmar Schacht—evidently in accordance with Göring and Hitler—in the course of negotiations with George Rublee from the Inter-Governmental Committee on Political Refugees.[84]

The establishment of the Reichszentrale für jüdische Auswanderung and the January 1939 appointment of Heydrich as its head was a major breakthrough for Heydrich, his SD and the Gestapo—organizations later integrated in the Reich Main Security Office (*Reichssicherheitshauptamt* or *RSHA*): increasingly Heydrich's RSHA would become the principal institution dealing with the "Jewish Question."

The chain of command that was forged during the November conference and implemented in January 1939 did not alter in the following years.[85] Setting up the Reichszentrale. Göring concluded that order with the following sentence: "Before fundamental measures are taken my consent must be sought."[86] Heydrich complied with these instructions. Three years later, when he no longer organized the emigration of Jews, but their genocide, Heydrich deferred to Göring's authority in major decisions. In his preliminary remarks at the Wannsee Conference on January 20, 1942, Heydrich announced his appointment as the functionary responsible for the preparation of the "final solution of the Jewish question" in Europe.[87] Göring's wish to be sent a draft concerning the organizational and technical matters pertaining to a "final solution of the Jewish question" provided the impetus for the conference, since this endeavor would require the advance coordination of all authorities concerned.

Conclusions

The exclusion of Jews from the Austrian economy and their subsequent expulsion from the country were not the result of premeditated plans nor did they develop from preconceived laws. Rather, they grew out of a series of "official" confiscations and "unofficial" lootings. The new governors of the Ostmark, driven partly by the groundswell of greed, partly by their desire to fill the coffers of state agencies, were induced to invent new pseudo-legal procedures and unprecedented institutions. The expropriation of Jewish assets not only proceeded more rapidly in the Ostmark than in the Altreich, it reached its objectives more quickly.[88] Material and ideological motives for anti-Jewish policies did not contradict, but fueled each other. As Bürckel noted in the summer of 1938, the expropriation of Jews entailed a massive pauperization, which made it in his eyes necessary to envision a "total solution"—meaning, at that time, expulsion. The pressure to dispatch Jews from Vienna continued after 1938: emigration was complemented by organized deportations from Vienna beginning in October 1939—earlier than from any city in Germany.[89] In late 1940 Bürckel's successor as governor of the Ostmark, Baldur von Schirach, obtained from Hitler a written order to deport 60,000 Austrian Jews—in order, ostensibly, to alleviate housing shortages in Vienna.[90] Thus it is not coincidental that expulsions advanced at a more accelerated pace,[91] and that deportations from Vienna were completed earlier than those from the Altreich, with the last mass deportation from the Ostmark to Minsk/Maly Trostinets taking place in October 1942.[92]

Götz Aly and Susanne Heim's emphasis on a rational strategy for a planned economy in the development of the "Vienna Model" diverges from my own findings.[93] The "Vienna Model" did not spring out of the heads of technocrats like the goddess Athena from the head of Zeus. To be sure, plans did exist, but mainly on paper; they were rarely guidelines for realization. Rather, these plans were utilized as a cover for policies that had to reconcile the outcome of the massive spoliation on the part of Austrian Nazis and ordinary civilians. How futile planning proved to be in certain fields of the economy in the Ostmark can be seen from the example of Jewish-owned firms engaged in export. Originally the plan was to Aryanize these enterprises very cautiously in order not to endanger this access to foreign exchange. After the November pogrom Bürckel had to confess in a letter to Göring that the lootings of November 9 and 10 signified "a deadly blow for the various efforts to salvage and promote Ostmark exports."[94]

When Saul Friedländer maintains in reference to the ruination of Jewish economic life that "what happened in Austria after the *Anschluss* was simply the better organized part of a general policy adopted throughout the Reich,"[95] he is confusing cause and effect. He thereby diminishes the Austrian input into Nazi decision-making. The expropriations were not better organized in the Ostmark because of a general policy. On the contrary, there was much more spontaneous plunder, bickering, and infighting over the booty, much more pressure "from below." It was not the plans of bureaucrats or orders from Berlin, but the actions of tens of thousands of Austrian antisemites, combined with the eagerness of Ostmark policemen and party officials to hunt down Jews and rob them of their belongings, that made Austrian Jews surrender their properties, "sell" or relinquish their enterprises and flee more or less penniless from this "veritable hell." The new masters in the Ostmark had more leeway to take steps without restrictions and even illegally. In many instances, measures already in practice were *legalized ex post facto*, as seen in the cases of the wild commissars, the confiscations, and the wholesale plunder during the November pogrom. The lessons that were gleaned from the Ostmark were transplanted throughout the entire Reich, where they became general policy. The Ostmark example contributed to the acceleration of anti-Jewish policies in Germany in the form of laws and institutions crafted after the models in the Ostmark. Certain agencies—Heydrich's

SD, Göring's Office for the Four-Year Plan—utilized these innovative measures in the formulation and advancement of their own strategies.

Functionaries such as Eichmann or like Fischböck, who was not even a member of the Nazi party until 1940, did not act on specific orders. In 1938 Austria they rode the wave of an endemic antisemitism. They adapted their actions to a given situation and used a creative approach to shape a course corresponding with their organizational or state interests. In doing so, they developed unprecedented procedures and strategies, propelling anti-Jewish policies one step further. From this perspective they are striking examples of the role functionaries played in the system of destruction as Raul Hilberg analyzed it: "The process could not have been brought to its conclusion if everyone would have had to wait for instructions. Nothing was so crucial as the requirement that the bureaucrat had to understand opportunities and 'necessities,' that he should act in accordance with perceived imperatives. . . . Ideas and initiatives were developed by experts in its ranks. They were submitted as proposals to supervisors and returned as authorizations to their originators. . . . Within the entire system, internal directives were, if anything, few and sparse. The fact is that the initiators, formulators, and expediters, who at critical junctures moved the bureaucratic machine from one point to the next, came from within that apparatus."[96]

For Austrian perpetrators 1938 did not mark an end to their persecution of Jews, but rather the beginning of their career, which soon expanded beyond Austria and the Altreich to encompass the breadth of Nazi-occupied Europe. Whether as deportation specialists in Vienna, Berlin, Prague, Paris, Nice, Salonica. Athens, and Budapest, as masterminds in the expropriation of Jews in the Netherlands,[97] or as mass murderers in the "Reinhard" killing centers of the Lublin district, they were part and parcel of the Nazi genocides.

The research for this article dates back to the late 1980s, when I was preparing *Und keiner war dabei* in collaboration with Hans Witek. The current piece is based upon a scholarly paper I delivered at the 1998 "Lessons and Legacies" Conference, organized by the Holocaust Educational Foundation in Boca Raton, Florida. This published version was completed in the summer of 1999. This article contains no information uncovered in my research for the Austrian *Historikerkommission*, nor has it any connection with my work for that commission which began in March 2000.

Notes

1 See Saul Friedländer, *Nazi Germany and the Jews*, vol. 1, *The Years of Persecution* (New York: HarperCollins, 1997), p. 180: "Within the second phase [i.e., 1936–1939)], 1938 was the fateful turning point." See also Martin Broszat,

"Roundtable discussion at the 1984 'Stuttgart Conference'" in Eberhard Jäckel and Jürgen Rohwer, eds., *Der Mord an den Juden im Zweiten Weltkrieg: Entschlußbildung und Verwirklichung* (Frankfurt: Fischer Taschenbuch Verlag, 1987), p. 181; Konrad Kwiet, "Gehen oder Bleiben? Die deutschen Juden am Wendepunkt" in Walter H. Pehle, ed., *Der Judenpogrom 1938: Von der "Reichskristallnacht" zum Völkermord* (Frankfurt: Fischer Taschenbuch Verlag, 1988), pp. 132ff.

2 The best overall analysis of the topic remains Helmut Genschel, *Die Verdrängung der Juden aus der Wirtschaft im Dritten Reich* (Göttingen: Musterschmidt-Verlag, 1966). An examination of the expropriations in the broader context of the destruction process is provided by Raul Hilberg. *The Destruction of the European Jews* (Chicago: Quadrangle Books, 1967).

3 See, e.g., Avraham Barkai, *Vom Boykott zur "Entjudung": Der wirtschaftliche Existenz-kampf der Juden im Dritten Reich 1933–1943* (Frankfurt: Fischer, 1988), English translation: *From Boycott to Annihilation* (Hanover, NH: Published for Brandeis University Press by University Press of New England, 1989). An exception to the rule is Konrad Kwiet, " 'Material Incentives': The Lust for 'Jewish' Property" in John Milfull, ed., *The Attractions of Fascism* (New York: Berg, 1990), pp. 238 ff., where the "Aryanizations" of apartments and houses in Germany and Austria are considered.

4 See Karl A. Schleunes, *The Twisted Road to Auschwitz: Nazi Policy Toward German Jews* (Urbana; Chicago: University of Illinois, 1990), p. 229: "Austria was made the laboratory in which new ideas concerning the Jewish problem were tested."

5 Susanne Heim and Götz Aly, "Die Ökonomie der Endlösung: Menschenvernichtung und wirtschaftliche Neuordnung," *Beiträge zur nationalsozialistischen Gesundheits- und Sozialpolitik*, 5 (1987); Götz Aly and Susanne Heim, *Vordenker der Vernichtung: Ausclucitz und die deutschen Pläne für eine neue europäische Ordnung* (Frankfurt: Fischer, 1991). Without further corroboration Aly and Heim's thesis is reiterated in Peter Longerich, *Politik der Vernichtung: Eine Gesamtdarstellung der nationalsozialistischen Judenverfolgung* (Munich: Piper, 1998), pp. 163f.

6 See Hilberg, *The Destruction of the European Jews*, p. 60: "The Aryanizations were divided into two phases: 1) the so-called voluntary Aryanizations ... which were transfers in pursuance of 'voluntary' agreements between Jewish sellers and German buyers and 2) the 'compulsory Aryanization' after November 1938, which were transfers in pursuance of state orders compelling the Jewish owners to sell their property. The word 'voluntary' belongs in quotation marks because no sale of Jewish property under the Nazi regime was voluntary in the sense of a freely negotiated contract in a free society. The Jews were under pressure to sell."

7 See Helmut Genschel, *Die Verdrängung der Juden*, pp. 105ff.

8 For a comparative analysis of Hamburg and Munich in this period, see Frank Bajohr, *"Arisierungen" in Hamburg: Die Verdrängung der jüdischen Unternehmer, 1933–1945* (Hamburg: Christians, 1997), pp. 121ff. Bajohr asserts that while Munich pushed ahead in local efforts at "Aryanization," Hamburg lagged behind, a fact that corresponded chiefly to differing economic and constitutional conditions in these cities.

9 See Peter Hayes, "Big Business and 'Aryanization' in Germany, 1933–1939," *Jahrbuch für Antisemitismusforschung* 3 (1994), pp. 254ff.

10 Thus, on the "Aryanization" of the Berlin branch of the private banking house Bros. Arnhold & S. Bleichröder by Dresdner Bank, compare Christopher

Kopper, *Zwischen Marktwirtschaft und Dirigismus: Bankenpolitik im "Dritten Reich"* (Bonn: Bouvier, 1995), pp. 256f. and 278ff.

11 Peter Hayes, in "Big Business," describes cases in which large-scale enterprises paid relatively adequate compensation to Jewish owners in the early phase of "Aryanization" policy.

12 See Genschel, *Die Verdrängung der Juden*, pp. 99ff.

13 For discussion of the conflict among Schacht, Hitler, and Göring concerning the scope of deficit spending for rearmament and autarkic policies, which led to Schacht's resignation as minister, see Kopper, *Zwischen Marktwirtschaft*, pp. 209ff.

14 See Joseph Walk, ed., *Das Sonderrecht für die Juden im NS-Staat: Eine Sammlung der gesetzlichen Maßnahmen und Richtlinien—Inhalt und Bedeutung* (Heidelberg: C. F. Müller Verlag, 1996), pp. 210, 229: January 4, 1938, "Jüdische Gewerbebetriebe"; June 14, 1938, "3. Verordnung zum Reichsbürgergesetz."

15 See Uwe Dietrich Adam, *Judenpolitik im Dritten Reich* (Düsseldorf: Droste Verlag, 1972), pp. 172 ff.

16 Generally understood to mean the killing of Wilhelm Gustloff, Nazi Party representative in Switzerland, by the Jewish student David Frankfurter.

17 See Genschel, *Die Verdrängung der Juden*, pp. 141 ff. and Adam. *Judenpolitik im Dritten Reich*, pp. 160ff.

18 See Saul Friedländer, *Nazi Germany and the Jews*, p. 236.

19 See Hilberg, *The Destruction of the European Jews*, pp. 82f. and Adam, *Judenpolitik im Dritten Reich*, p. 181. Another draft in a similar vein from the same period, probably from Dr. Krüger in the Economics Ministry, was never promulgated, see *"Zweite Anordnung auf Grund der Verordnung über die Anmeldung des Vermögens von Juden"* in National Archives (NARA), Collection of Foreign Records Seized (RG 242), T 84, r. 13. fr. 10266ff.

20 Memorandum of Hjalmar Schacht to Frick, Funk, Göring, Hess, Himmler, v. Krosigk, Lammers, Ribbentrop, 7.7.1938, quoted by Kopper, *Zwischen Marktwirtschaft*, p. 276. The reply of Minister of Finance v. Krosigk to Frick's proposal is quoted in Hilberg, *The Destruction of the European Jews*, p. 83.

21 According to the census of March 1934, there were 191,481 denominationally Jewish persons living in Austria, of whom 176,034 were living in Vienna: see *Statistisches Handbuch für den Bundesstaat Österreich*, (Wien: Staatsdruckerei, 1935), p. 8. The exact number of persons living in Austria 1938 who belonged to other denominations but were designated as Jews according to the Nuremberg racial law is unknown and can only be gauged from the census of May 1939. A rough estimate suggests a ratio of 100 denominational Jews to 15 nondenominational Jews.

22 The roots of Austrian antisemitism reaching back to the nineteenth century are analyzed in Peter Pulzer, *The Rise of Political Anti-Semitism in Germany and Austria* (Cambridge, MA: Harvard University Press, 1988). Pulzer dubbed Vienna the "cradle of modern political Antisemitism": P. G. J. Pulzer, "The Development of Political Antisemitism in Austria" in Josef Fraenkel, ed., *The Jews of Austria: Essays on their Life, History, and Destruction* (London: Vallentine Mitchell, 1967), p. 429. For a concise description of interwar antisemitism in Austria, see Karl Stuhlpfarrer, "Antisemitismus, Rassenpolitik und Judenverfolgung in Österreich nach dem Ersten Weltkrieg" in Anna Drabek, et al., *Das österreichische Judentum: Voraussetz-ungen und Geschichte* (Vienna: Munich: Jugend und Volk, 1974), pp. 141ff. Bruce F. Pauley provides an overview in his *From Prejudice to Persecution: A History of Austrian Antisemitism* (Chapel Hill: University of North Carolina Press, 1991).

23 See Hans Safrian and Hans Witek. *Und keiner war dabei: Dokumente des alltäglichen Antisemitismus in Wien 1938*, with a foreword by Erika Weinzierl (Vienna: Picus, 1988), pp. 22ff.

24 For the development of the anti-Jewish policies in Heydrich's Security Service, see Michael Wildt, ed., *Die Judenpolitik des SD 1935 bis 1938: Eine Dokumentation* (Munich: Oldenbourg, 1995).

25 It should be noted that at this time Eichmann was not a Gestapo official, but a member of the SS Security Service (SD). In Germany the SD had had no executive power: in Vienna Eichmann arrogated these powers, see Hans Safrian. *Die Eichmann-Männer* (Vienna: Europaverlag, 1993), pp. 24ff. In this respect Evan Burr Bukey is wrong when he writes that the Gestapo dissolved the Jewish Community Council in Vienna: see his *Hitler's Austria: Popular Sentiment in the Nazi Era* (Chapel Hill: University of North Carolina Press, 2000), p. 134.

26 See Safrian, *Die Eichmann-Männer*, pp. 36f.

27 See Dr. Ludwig Wechsler. "Von Wien aus nach Dachan und Buchenwald." Yad Vashem Archives, 0–1/208.

28 Dr. Leo Lauterbach served as acting secretary for a department of the Zionist Executive in London.

29 Quoted in Herbert Rosenkranz, *Verfolgung und Selbstbehauptung: Die Juden in Österreich, 1938–1945* (Vienna: Munich: Herold, 1978), p. 43.

30 Ibid., p. 49.

31 Charles J. Kapralik, "Erinnerungen eines Beamten der Wiener Israelitischen Kultusgemeinde 1938/39," *Leo Baeck Institute Bulletin* 58 (1981), p. 58. Kapralik's conclusion is substantiated by a memo of the Reich Ministry of Trade and Commerce (*Reichswirtschaftsministerium*): "Übersicht über die unit dem Judenproblem zusammenhängenden Fragen für die Besprechung mit den Leitern der Devisenstellen am Dienstag, dem 22. November 1938," United States Holocaust Memorial Museum, Archives, RG 14.002 M 6, documents Devisenstelle Leipzig. According to this document 170,000 Jewish men, women, and children left Germany and transferred values of 340,000,000 RM abroad, an average of 2,000 RM per capita.

32 See Gerhard Botz, *Wien, vom "Anschluß" zum Krieg: Nationalsozialistische Machtübernahme und politisch-soziale Umgestaltung am Beispiel der Stadt Wien 1938/39* (Vienna; Munich: Jugend und Volk, 1978), p. 96.

33 Memorandum of Chief of Security Police to *Sonderbeauftragten* of the party in Austria, 3.17.1938. Archiv der Republik (AdR). Bestand Reichskommissar für die Wiedervereinigung Österreichs mit dem Deutschen Reich (Rk), 103/2010.

34 Quoted in Safrian and Witek, *Und keiner war dabei*, p. 99.

35 See Hans Witek, " 'Arisierungen' in Wien: Aspekte nationalsozialistischer Enteignungspolitik 1938–1940" in Emmerich Talos et al., eds., *Nationalsozialistische Herrschaft in Österreich 1938–1945* (Vienna: Verlag für Gesellschaftskritik, 1988).

36 Report of Bürckel to Göring, November 19, 1938. Safrian and Witek, *Und keiner war dabei*, p. 186.

37 See application for retroactive approval of "Aryanization" in Safrian and Witek, *Und keiner war dabei*, pp. 119f.

38 Hans Fischböck was born in 1895 in Lower Austria (*Niederösterreich*) and in the 1920s and '30s made a career in banking and insurance companies. When he became minister of the Austrian Nazi government on the evening of March 11, 1938, he was neither a member of the NSDAP nor SS, but had had close contact with Arthur Seyss-Inquart and Wilhelm Keppler, Hitler's liaison to and

supervisor of Austrian Nazis since summer 1937. Fischböck joined the SS in June 1940, the Nazi Party around the same time.

39 Letter of Bürckel to Göring, April 29, 1938, quoted in Botz, *Wien, com "Anschluß" zum Krieg*, p. 331.

40 Walter Rafelsberger was born in 1899 in Vienna. He studied chemistry at the Technical University and joined the Austrian Nazi Party in 1933. In Styria he soon became a leading functionary of the illegal party and was arrested by the Austrian authorities in 1935. After he was amnestied in 1936 he fled to Germany, to return to the Ostmark in March of 1938. In the same month he joined the SS and was quickly promoted: in July of 1938 his rank was SS-*Standartenführer* (colonel).

41 The Aryanization of private banks was an exception to the pattern of expropriation in the Ostmark. Because it was from beginning to end state-controlled, wild commissars played no role at all: see Hans Witek, " 'Arisierung' in Wien," pp. 209ff. and Kopper, *Zwischen Marktwirtschaft*, pp. 308ff.

42 "Gesetz über die Bestellung von konunissarischen Verwaltern und kommissarischen Überwachungspersonen," *Gesetzblatt für das Land Österreich*, 80–1938.

43 See for example Hilberg, *The Destruction of the European Jews*, pp. 65, 82, 91.

44 In Adam, *Judenpolitik im Dritten Reich*, p. 177, who analyzed most closely the development of anti-Jewish legislation, one learns only that the registration law must have arisen in connection with the "Decree Against Aiding the Concealment Of Businesses Owned by Jews" (*Verordnung gegen die Unterstützung der Tarnung jüdischer Gewerbebetriebe*) of April 22, 1938. The only mention that I have found in regard to the April conference—although without reference to documentation—is in the rarely cited article of A. J. van der Leeuw, "Der Griff des Reiches nach dem Judenvermögen," *Studies over Nederland in oorlogstijd*, deel 1, Rijksinstituut voor Oorlogsdocumentatie. Onder redactie van A. H. Paape ('s-Gravenhage: Nijhoff, 1972), p. 213.

45 Protocol of the discussion, April 11, 1938 (Besprechung über die durch die Rückgliederung Österreichs entstehenden Devisenfragen unter dem Vorsitz des Herrn Ministerpräsidenten Generalfeldmarschall Göring am 11. April 1938), comp. by ministerial director Dr. Gramsch (Office of the Four-Year Plan). Dokumentationsarchiv des österreichischen Widerstands (DÖW), Doc. 5108.

46 Ibid. The first issue discussed at this meeting was the seizure of Austria's gold and foreign currency reserves and their further utilization. Göring was eager to divert the 250 million RM in gold to the coffers of the Four-Year Plan Office, wishing to use them in part to stockpile raw materials for armaments production.

47 Protocol of the discussion, April 11, 1938, comp. by ministerial director Dr. Gramsch (Office of the Four-Year Plan), Dokumentationsarchiv des österreichischen Widerstands (DÖW), Doc. 5108.

48 See Joseph Walk, *Das Sonderrecht für die Juden*, p. 223. Evan Burr Bukey, *Hitler's Austria*, p. 135, is incorrect when he asserts "Reich commissioner Bürckel issued the Decree on the Declaration of Jewish Assets."

49 See Walk, *Das Sonderrecht für die Juden*, p. 230.

50 See Safrian and Witek, *Und keiner war dabei*, pp. 96ff.

51 Utilizing the property registration forms collected and evaluated by the Vienna Property Transfer Office, Helen B. Junz, in her "Report on the Wealth Position of the Jewish Population in Nazi-Occupied Countries, Germany and Austria." (Appendix S of the *Report on Dormant Accounts of Victims of Nazi*

Persecution in Swiss Banks (Volcker Commission Report) (Bern, 1999))
attempts to calculate the scope of assets owned by Austrian Jews before the Nazi
takeover. The results of the study are flawed as Junz bases her analysis on the
assumption that "data from the 1938 census provide a reasonable guide to the
minimum level of the wealth of the Jewish population in Austria. As the declarations were made within weeks of the Anschluss," Junz continues, "the Jewish-
owned wealth had not been eroded anywhere near the extent that it had in
Germany. Nor had the majority of the Jewish population given up hope that
they would be able to preserve a reasonable part of their assets through compliance." (p. A-141.) By the time registration forms were due, at the end of July
and October, respectively—months, rather than weeks, after the Anschluss—
Austrian Jews had already been robbed of their possessions through confiscations, "commissar actions," and "Aryan takeovers" to a much larger degree than
had their German counterparts. In late spring and early summer of 1938, a
majority of victims had made up their minds to go abroad: between March 1938
and May 1939 more than 100,000 Austrian Jews left the country. The protracted
procedures required to obtain visas and necessary documentation often meant
that months elapsed between the decision to emigrate and actual departure.
When filing their declaration forms in June and July 1938, most Austrian Jews
had few illusions about compliance: their only chance lay in scraping together
funds to pay the "flight tax" (*Reichsfluchtsteuer*) and additional fees, and to
salvage a fragment of their possessions by any means available,—including
under-reporting and hiding valuables with friends or acquaintances—so that they
might transfer them abroad. The reliability of property registration data lodged
at the Property Transfer Office is called further into question by possible lacunae
in the figures themselves: it remains uncertain, and unlikely, that the 7,000 stores
and shops ransacked and closed in March and April of 1938 and further "confiscated" assets, like those of the Louis Rothschild family, were included in the
evaluation. Taken together these caveats suggest that the data computed by the
Property Transfer Office are not a very reliable source and correspond to only a
fraction of the original holdings of Austrian Jews.

52 Nuremberg Document 3446-PS in United States. Office of Chief of Counsel for
    the Prosecution of Axis Criminality, *Nazi Conspiracy and Aggression*, vol. VI
    (Washington: U.S.G.P.O., 1946), pp. 153f. As the document relates a total of
    162 cases of confiscation, and values in Reichsmark are mentioned in only two-
    thirds of these cases (93,000,000 RM), one has to add half of the known sum to
    gauge the total value for all confiscations. In the list of valued confiscations,
    approximately one-third are from non-Jewish owners. Significantly, the list
    hints at even bigger lacunae in the accounts. The document mentions art
    objects sequestered from the Rothschilds and other well-to-do families, but
    does not present figures for these families' other confiscated properties,
    making it very likely that they were a part of the cases not valued. As the value
    of the Rothschild's family assets in Austria was much higher than that of other
    victims, the overall sum of confiscated properties would be considerably
    higher. For the pillaging of artworks owned by Jewish families, see Jonathan
    Petropoulos, *Art as Politics in the Third Reich* (Chapel Hill: University of
    North Carolina Press, 1996).
53 Memo of the *SD-Führers des SD-Oberabschnitt Donau*, Dr. Stahlecker, May 7,
    1938. Dokumentationsarchiv des österreichischen Widerstands, Doc. E 18 036.
54 Ibid.
55 Ibid.
56 Nuremberg Documents 3446-PS, 3447-PS, 3448-PS, 3449-PS, 3450-PS, *Nazi*

Conspiracy and Aggression, vol. VI, pp. 153–58. When promulgated, the law included the sentence: "Confiscations that were ordered by the Gestapo before this decree took effect are considered confiscations in the sense of this decree."

57 Cf. Safrian and Witek. *Und keiner war dabei*, p. 112.

58 Nuremberg Document 1301 PS, *Nazi Conspiracy and Aggression*, vol. III, p. 904.

59 Ibid.

60 Notation "Judenfrage in Österreich" no date (summer 1938), Archiv der Republik. Rk 144/2160.

61 According to a November 1937 memo of Herbert Hagen. SD-Hauptamt II-112, the goal was a centralization of all aspects of the "Jewish question" including financial and transfer matters, such as Paltreu and Haavara, under the rule of the SD and the Gestapo, See Hans Safrian, *Die Eichmann-Männer*, p. 28.

62 See Hans Safrian. *Die Eichmann-Männer*, pp. 44ff.

63 The scheme was set up in a June 17 meeting in Vienna among *Reichsbankrat* Dr. Wolf; Dr. Siegert from the Reich's Economics Ministry; *Reichsbankoberinspektor* Raffegerst from the foreign currencies branch Vienna, and Eichmann; see memo II 112 (*SS-Untersturmführer* Hagen), June 24, 1938, concerning financing emigration from Austria, with 3 enclosures, Bundesarchiv R 58/984, fol. 32ff.

64 See Kapralik, "Erinnerungen eines Beamten," pp. 63ff, and the report of Dr. Leo Landau, until 1939 board member of Kultusgemeinde, Yad Vashem, 0–1/244, pp. 12f.

65 See, for example, report of 89th SS-*Standarte*, where it was proudly reported that the destruction of synagogues had been accomplished in a thorough manner ("*ganze Arbeit geleistet*"), in Safrian and Witek, *Und keincr war dabei*, pp. 164f.

66 According to a Gestapo report, 6,547 Jewish men were arrested in Vienna. NARA, Collection of Foreign Records Seized (RG 242), T 84, r. 13, fr. 39814.

67 Report, quoted in Safrian and Witek, *Und keiner war dabei*, p. 182.

68 According to the findings of the Nazi Party Supreme Court, ninety-one victims were killed during the pogrom. Nuremberg Document 3063 PS, *Nazi Conspiracy and Aggression*, vol. V, p. 875. A different interpretation is given in Bruce F. Pauley, *From Prejudice to Persecution*, p. 288, where the author correlates the number of victims in November to the number of Jews in Vienna and declares them "proportionate to Vienna's share of the Third Reich's Jewish population." He would be right if these persons had been victims of random car accidents (something one could correlate proportionally) or if the murderers had had orders to kill a certain ratio. Neither was the case. The number of victims had to do with the zeal and latitude of the perpetrators.

69 Report Bürckel to Göring, November 19, 1938, Safrian and Witek, *Und keiner war dabei*, p. 187.

70 Nuremberg Document 1816-PS. Stenographic Reports of the Meeting on the Jewish Question, November 12, 1938. *Nazi Conspiracy and Aggression*, vol. IV, p. 439. The German text of 1816-PS is published in *Der Prozeß gegen die Hauptkriegsverbrecher vor dem Internationalen Militärgerichtshof, Nürnberg 1948*, vol. XXVII, p. 518.

71 Nuremberg Document 1816-PS, *Nazi Conspiracy and Aggression*, vol. IV, p. 444.

72 Ibid., p. 445.

73 Ibid.

74 Ibid., p. 447.

75 Ibid., pp. 448f.
76 Ibid., p. 451.
77 Ibid.
78 For the impact of this decree, see H. G. Adler, *Der verwaltete Mensch: Studien zur Deportation der Juden aus Deutschland* (Tübingen: Mohr, 1974), pp. 494f.
79 The protocol of Göring's speech at this meeting (*Besprechung mit den Gauleitern, Oberpräsidenten und Reichsstatthaltern über die Judenfrage am 6. December 1938, vormittags 11 Uhr im großen Sitzungssaal des Reichsluftfahrtsministeriums*) was located in Osobyi Arkhiv, Moscow 1458 (Reichswirtschaftsministerium)/3/2216, Bl, 1–33 by Susanne Heim and Götz Aly and published in "Staatliche Ordnung and 'organische Lösung': Die Rede Hermann Görings 'über die Judenfrage' vom 6, Dezember 1938." *Jahrbuch für Antisemitismusforschung* 2 (1993), pp. 382ff.
80 The protocol states that Göring had assumed responsibility for the "Jewish question" because of its close nexus with German economic issues. Hitler had given him his special consent. Göring had waived public announcement of the fact that he had been named coordinator primarily because Hitler had not wished to compromise Göring's position at home and abroad. Göring emphasized that all decrees concerning the "Jewish question" would be subject to his approval and would then be processed by the responsible offices, ministries, and party agencies, Ibid., p. 383.
81 The idea of a transfer bank and international loans to facilitate the emigration of Jews from Germany can be traced back to proposals developed by Hamburg banker Max Warburg in 1935–1936 and discussed inter alia with Hjalmar Schacht. Warburg's intentions had been to save as many German Jews as possible and to transfer their belongings from Germany abroad. See Ron Chernow. *Die Warburgs: Odyssee einer Familie* (Berlin: Goldman Verlag, 1996), pp. 526 ff.
82 Protocol of Göring's speech. December 6, 1938, p. 385.
83 Ibid., p. 386.
84 Some historians incorrectly assume that Schacht's proposals were based not on those procedures introduced by Wolf and Eichmann and practiced in Vienna for over half a year, but on a plan "apparently conceived by Hans Fischböck ... who suggested it to Göring and Schacht." See, e.g., Yehuda Baner. *Jews for Sale? Nazi-Jewish Negotiations 1933–1945* (New Haven: Yale University Press, 1994), p. 33 and Longerich, *Politik der Vernichtung*, p. 222.
85 See, for example, Karl A. Schleunes. *The Twisted Road to Auschwitz*, p. 254.
86 Plenipotentiary for the Four-Year Plan. Founding of the *Reichszentrale*, January 24, 1939, BA, R 58/276, p. 195.
87 See Minutes of the "Wannsee Conference." Nuremberg document NG 2586, quoted in Robert M. W. Kempner, *Eichmann und Komplizen* (Zurich: Europa Verlag, 1961), p. 133.
88 See Safrian and Witek, *Und keiner war dabei*, pp. 97f.
89 Concerning the deportations to Nisko on the San, see Hans Safrian. *Die Eichmann-Männer*, pp. 68ff.
90 See Hans Safrian. *Die Eichmann-Männer*, pp. 96ff.
91 See Gertrude Schmeider, *Exile and Destruction: The Fate of Austrian Jews, 1938–1945* (Westport, CT: Praeger, 1995).
92 See Florian Freund and Hans Safrian. *Expulsion and Extermination: The Fate of the Austrian Jews 1938–1945: Project "Registration by Name, Austrian Victims of the Holocaust"* (Vienna: Austrian Resistance Archive, 1997), pp. 22ff.

93 Götz Aly and Susanne Heim, *Vordenker der Vernichtung*, pp. 33ff.
94 Letter of Bürckel to Göring, December 12, 1938, AdR, Rk 167/2205.
95 Saul Friedländer, *Nazi Germany and the Jews*, p. 247.
96 Raul Hilberg. "The Bureaucracy of Annihilation," in François Furet, ed., *Unanswered Questions: Nazi Germany and the Genocide of the Jews* (New York: Schocken Books. 1989). pp. 127ff.
97 For a discussion of the "Vienna Model" as it applied to Aryanization policy in the Netherlands and for Hans Fischböck's role there see Jos Scheren, "Aryanization, Market Vendors, and Peddlers in Amsterdam," in this issue of *Holocaust and Genocide Studies*.

17

FORCED LABOUR OF GERMAN JEWS IN NAZI GERMANY

Konrad Kwiet

Source: *Leo Baeck Institute Yearbook*, 36 (1991), 389–410.

In autumn 1941, when genocide in the East was already under way and the mass deportation of German Jews was introduced, a remarkable event took place in the control centres of the Nazi system. In his capacity as *Reichskommissar* for the *Ostland*, Hinrich Lohse suspended a series of "wild" executions in the Latvian port of Libau. Lohse took this step not because he was opposed to a radical "solution of the Jewish Question", but because he had taken exception to the manner of its implementation. This interference by the highest civilian authority aroused indignation in SS headquarters, in Riga and Berlin alike. The *Reichssicherheitshauptamt* (*Reich* Security Central Office, or RSHA) made a complaint and requested further information via the *Reichsministerium für die besetzten Ostgebiete* (Ministry for the Occupied Territories in the East).[1] In a short letter of 15th November 1941, Lohse justified his ban. Furthermore, unaware of the killing directive which had been issued to the SS *Einsatzgruppen* some weeks before, he asked for further information as to whether "all Jews in the East are to be liquidated?" Lohse added: "Is this to occur without regard for age and sex and economic interests (e.g. that of the *Wehrmacht* in skilled workers in armaments factories)? Of course the cleansing of the East of Jews is an urgent task, but its solution must be reconciled with the needs of the war economy."[2] At the end of December the answer arrived. The *Reichskommissar* was instructed to contact the appropriate Higher SS and Police Leader in future. As far as the Jews were concerned, he was informed by Berlin: "In the Jewish Question, meanwhile, the matter should be settled by verbal discussions. Economic concerns are not to be taken into consideration in the settlement of this problem."[3]

This issue has been the subject of much debate among researchers, always against a background of controversy. Then as now, at the heart of the question are problems of theory and interpretation, the classification and historicisation of Nazism in general and Nazi persecution of the Jews in particular.[4] The international *Historikerstreit* (now apparently on the wane) revealed the great difficulty encountered by some historians in dealing with the German murder of the Jews. One typical feature is that much of the running has been made by noted "outsiders" such as Ernst Nolte and Arno Mayer, rather than by the experts. These historians have formulated judgements and concepts which frequently disregard historical reality and end in speculation and apologia. The approaches of Susanne Heim and Götz Aly have also met with fierce opposition. Both are concerned to attribute a "rationality" to Nazi policies of annihilation and to work out the concept of an "economy of the Final Solution". Basically, their theory holds that it was not racial hatred which led to genocide but that it was prepared and implemented by a group of the "planning intelligentsia" – consisting of "economists, agricultural scientists, population experts, labour force specialists, regional planners and statisticians".[5] Such thinking has been rejected as untenable by Ulrich Herbert,[6] Christopher Browning,[7] and Dan Diner.[8]

The present contribution addresses a theme which is touched on in all these debates but not made a central feature, since attention has been focused primarily on Nazi rule in the East.

Unlike the situation in the occupied territories, the Jews in Germany were drawn back into the production process as forced labourers. By the beginning of 1939 at the latest, the destruction of their economic existence had left behind an army of impoverished and jobless Jews, which threatened to become a burden on the German *Reich*. In taking steps to remove this burden from society, the Nazis could count on the agreement of wide circles of the population and the vigorous support of the economic and military elites. The granting of priority to material interests recommended the use of forced labour as a means of re-incorporating the Jews into economic life, at least until the "Final Solution" was agreed upon and the gaps in the workforce could be filled by the forced recruitment of workers from other sources. Until then the Jews could cling to the hope that their continued existence was guaranteed by their labour. The Nazis exploited this belief by disguising the road to the extermination camps with the familiar euphemisms of "evacuation" and "resettlement".

Jewish forced labour in Germany has been very little researched until now. It is included in some descriptions of the history of the German Jews.[9] Some description and documentation can also be found in regional studies, in the history of individual firms, in personal accounts and in literature on the concentration camps. Important as trail-blazers are the works of Ulrich Herbert,[10] who argues that, with the decision of autumn 1941 to use Soviet prisoners-of-war as forced labourers more intensively than before, the Nazi regime was free to push on with a programme of genocide based on racial ideology because the exploitation of the Jewish workforce was no longer essential. Military representatives of the war economy were involved in this change of direction. Their strategies for the "solution of the Jewish Question" will be revealed in this essay.

Initially, responsibility for the central military management of the war economy lay with the *Wehrwirtschaft- und Rüstungsamt* under General Thomas in the *Oberkommando der Wehrmacht*.[11] In the large military areas the *Rüstungsinspektionen* (armaments inspectorates) were created, while *Rüstungskommandos* (*RüKdos*) emerged in the government districts. After the outbreak and spread of the Second World War, this apparatus was extended to the occupied territories. Everywhere, and from the beginning, the military experts regarded the exploitation of Jewish labour as extremely important. They were present at every scene where the programme of the "Final Solution" was implemented. Some military representatives were dismayed by the murder actions; on occasion they offered criticism or made protests, sometimes in strong language. In so doing they always referred to "economic interests" or the "requirements of the war economy", and submitted statistics and calculations to show the "losses" and "disadvantages" resulting from the "withdrawals of Jews". A clash with the SS was inevitable. The conflict was particularly intense where there was a large potential force of Jewish workers which the military were unwilling to lose. It would seem that the conflicts were triggered less by the rival concepts of "work" and "extermination" than by a tactical question – how to determine the time when extermination should take place. In all the battles over interests and authority, there was constant evidence of one basic attitude: like the military as a whole, the military representatives of the war economy were not attempting to put a stop to the murder programme, but only to delay the "withdrawal" of Jewish forced labour until the vital "replacement question" was settled.

Measures to exploit the Jewish labour force in Germany were undertaken after the November Pogrom of 1938. The method chosen was the pseudo-legitimate route of official decree.[12] As in the other areas of repression and persecution, the complex and dynamic Nazi system of rule created a multiplicity of "offices" responsible for the introduction, organisation, supervision and liquidation of Jewish forced labour. These institutions represented the "power blocks" of State, Party and SS, of the *Wehrmacht* and the economy – at central, regional and local level. Among the participants in the discussions and decisions were the key authorities and subordinate authorities of the Plenipotentiary for the Four Year Plan, the Plenipotentiary for *Reich* Administration, the Plenipotentiary for the Labour Supply, the *Reichsarbeitsministerium*, the *Reichsfinanzministerium*, the *Reichswirtschaftsministerium* or the *Reichsministerium für Bewaffnung und Munition*, the Office of the *Führer*'s Deputy and the Party Chancellery, as well as the war economic offices of the *Wehrmacht* and the representatives of industry and trade. The SS and police apparatus asserted its claim to leadership in the issue. It also press-ganged the representatives of the remaining Jewish community. Thus the *Reichsvereinigung der Juden in Deutschland* and *Kultusgemeinden* were forced to pass on orders and provide administrative assistance. As in the other "registration actions", they were compelled to collaborate with the introduction and organisation of Jewish forced labour.

The prelude was a decree of 20th December 1938, in which the President of the *Reichsanstalt für Arbeitsvermittlung and Arbeitslosenversicherung* ordered the labour exchanges to assign all unemployed Jews who were fit to work to jobs, and "with the utmost speed". This approach was linked with a desire to divert non-Jews "to priority, politically important projects". However, a further directive was dispatched to the local authorities and firms concerned. These were to have regard to racial doctrine and take care to set the Jews to work in "self-contained" units, "separated from the main body" of workers.[13] It was obvious that only carefully chosen hard and difficult work was to be done by the Jews. Building sites, road and motorway work, rubbish disposal, public toilets and sewage plants, quarries and gravel pits, coal merchants and rag and bone works were regarded as suitable. Some fanatical Nazis were less than enthusiastic, particularly when work was assigned which threatened to undermine the dogma of "strict separation" of Germans and Jews. There was much annoyance when Jews appeared on farms, in bakeries and in other foodstuff factories. However, these reproaches died away after the outbreak of the Second World War, when the issue was seen as one of forcing Jews to work for the German war effort. There were a number of reasons for this change.

Workers, especially skilled workers, were already in short supply in 1939.[14] As more men were called up to the *Wehrmacht*, the number of unfilled vacancies rose dramatically. One result was "anarchy" in the labour market, against which the Nazis waged a vain battle. From a very early stage, German military experts in the war economy recognised that, as the war dragged on, the major problem lay less in the supply of raw materials than in the "deployment of the human labour force". The alternatives were: "Either supply new forces or curb orders".[15] Following Hitler's order for intensified efforts in armament production, they worked with the other authorities responsible for the workforce in an attempt to keep the shortage of workers within bounds. Priorities were established, based on the needs of the armament programmes. In concrete terms, this meant that firms concerned with civilian or less urgent military manufacturing were constantly examined and "combed through" so that the workers "set free" could be distributed to firms on the priority list. This redistribution of existing workers was called the "inter-firm adjustment". In addition, there were rationalisations, closures of firms, retraining schemes, introduction of the 60-hour week, increased temporary exemptions from front-line service, and the deployment of *Wirtschaftsurlauber* (soldiers seconded to "urgent" work in the factories during periods of leave). These efforts met with little success. In October 1940 the military experts in Berlin claimed that 29,400 workers were needed in the metal industry alone, with the shortage of skilled workers estimated at 15,700.[16] It became even more important to recruit new workers. The reservoir of women workers and *"Fremdarbeiter"* (foreign workers), of prisoners-of-war and Jews, was tapped to exhaustion. Public and private businesses now rushed to demand Jewish workers. Thus in October 1940 the *Oberkommando des Heeres* asked the *Reichsarbeitsministerium* for 1,800 Jews for work in the railway administration at Oppeln, Breslau and Lublin. The Lower Saxony labour exchange offered between 1,000 and 2,000 Jews to the *Hermann-Göring-Werke* in Watcnstedt-Salzgitter. At the beginning of 1941 the *Siemens-Halske-Werke* in Berlin demanded 400 workers for an "urgent manufacturing programme in communications" on behalf of General Fell-giebel; here Jewish women were put to work as forced labourers.[17]

At this stage, a total of some 30,000 Jews had already been conscripted as forced labourers, approximately 20% of the remaining Jewish community of Germany. It was not long before the decision was taken to conscript all Jews between the ages of 15 and 65 years who were fit to work. On 4th March 1941 the *Reichsarbeitministerium* ordered the introduction of general forced labour.[18] The *Rüslungsinspektion* calculated an increase of 73,000 Jews, 42,000 of whom were men and 31,000 women. For *Wehrkreis* Kassel some 5,000 workers were planned. *Rüstungsinspektion IX* noted: "It remains to be seen what the effect of the action will be in regard to the overall labour market in the area, since the accommodation and deployment of the Jews still cause especially great difficulties."[19]

Meanwhile, it had become known that Jewish workers were not only to be kept "separate from the main body of workers", but were "if possible" to be housed in self-contained camps. Only a few authorities followed this suggestion; there were barrack camps in Essen and Salzgitter, Dresden and Munich. Though the intention in early 1939 was to quarter all German Jews – in case of war – in special camps, classified as "Arbeitsdienstlager", this was not done, partly because the limited building capacity was required for other mass accommodation. In many areas, barracks were hastily erected to accept the ever-increasing number of foreign workers and prisoners-of-war, all of whom required "self-contained" accommodation. In Berlin, where Jewish forced labourers were concentrated, firms limited themselves to setting up *"Judenabteilungen"*, *"Judengruppen"*, or *"Judenschichten"* (Jewish detachments, groups or shifts). In October 1941 the *Rüstungsinspektion* registered 21,000 Jews employed in firms involved with the war economy, including approximately 11,000 in the metal indus-try. About half of them were women.[20] The *Reichsvereinigung* also gave a figure of 21,000 at the end of 1941, when some 33,450 *Sternträger* (wearers of the Yellow Star) were left behind after the first wave of deportations. Approximately 2,000 still had a job in the Jewish administrative apparatus. The rest were divided among groups who were protected from forced labour: children, the seriously ill, the seriously disabled, and Jewish partners in so-called "privileged mixed marriages".[21] At the beginning of 1943 – when Jewish forced labour in Germany was approaching its end – the SS statistician Dr Richard Korherr gave his notorious "interim balance" in his report on "The Final Solution of the European Jewish Question". Here he noted that there were still 21,659 Jews engaged in "work of importance for the war effort" in the German *Reich*.[22]

Jewish forced labour required the clarification of legal issues relating to work and pay. There were long discussions between the various departments and offices in order to develop the new *"Sonderrecht"*. This was finished when the planned deportations got under way. The *Verordnung über die Beschäftigung der Juden* (decree on the employment of Jews) came into force at the beginning of October 1941.[23]

Defined as *"Artfremde"* (ethnic aliens), Jewish workers were refused acceptance into the "works community" and therefore denied all the rights to which other members could lay claim. Jewish forced labourers received no family and child allowances, no maternity and marriage allowances, no extra payments on Sundays and holidays, no money at Christmas, no death benefits, no bonuses or loyalty payments. They received no paid holidays and no wages in the event of sickness. They were denied protection against unlawful dismissal, were not covered by safety regulations, and were not entitled to unemployment benefit or old age pension schemes. The underlying principle was that "Jewish employees have a claim to remuneration only for work actually done". Firms were provided with a charter giving them the right to virtually unlimited exploitation of their Jewish workers. For a maximum of work they had to pay a minimum in wages.[24] In the forced labour ghettos and concentration camps, it became standard practice to transfer this pay to the special accounts of the exploiters.

As a rule Jewish forced labourers were placed on the lowest wage scale. Thanks to the *Finanzamt*, taxes were deducted from their earnings at the highest rate. The *Finanzamt* also supervised the "blocked accounts" containing the remaining proceeds from the forced sale of Jewish businesses, property and other possessions, and from which only a monthly "free allowance" of up to RM 250 could be taken. At the end of 1940 a special tax was imposed on the Jews; this removed 15% from their wages and declared it to be a "social compensation payment". Other "aliens" – Polish forced labourers and gipsies – also had to pay this tribute. The average hourly pay of German workers in 1939 was just RM 0.90. Jewish forced labourers, on average, received less than half that. One young cemetery worker and gravedigger in Fürstenwald earned RM 0.16.[25] A $15\frac{1}{2}$ year old unskilled worker in a Berlin factory making uniforms received hourly pay of RM 0.30 for her day and night shifts; when she reached the age of 16 the pay rose to RM 0.34.[26] The *Siemens-Schuckert-Werke* paid its women assemblers RM 0.50 per hour.[27] One forced labourer who had been trained as a lathe operator in the *Deutsche Waffen- und Munitionsfabrik* in Berlin-Borsigwalde received RM 0.90.[28] As time passed, firms and authorities grew anxious to save wages. Municipal administrations thus preferred to employ Jewish "work columns" to sweep the streets and, in winter, to shovel the snow. The *Reichsvereinigung* was then obliged to pay welfare support. One Munich building firm took on 450 Jewish workers in spring 1941 to establish a self-contained "Jewish settlement" in the Milbersthofen area – without pay, but with the task of doing their work "in the interests of the Israelite religious community and its members".[29] Anyone evading "voluntary" deployment was threatened with transfer to the nearby Dachau concentration camp.

For many forced labourers, the pay was not sufficient to cover their cost of living. Rents had to be paid, for small, often squalid rooms where they had been forcibly quartered shortly before. As part of the *"Entjudung"* of the German residential areas, local authorities, estate agents and house-owners had pushed through the physical separation of Germans and Jews and thereby taken an essential step on the road to the envisaged "Final Solution of the Jewish Question". The seizure of desirable Jewish homes also offered a way of easing the strain on the housing market. After the outbreak and extension of the war, the general housing shortage reached catastrophic proportions. And the greater the need, the louder became the appeals from wide circles of the population for the "gathering together" and – if that did not suffice – the expulsion of the Jews. Such sentiments found their expression in the establishment of "Jewish houses" and barracks, and in the organisation of "evacuation" to the East. During this short waiting period of uncertainty and fear, of isolation and loneliness, Jewish forced labourers continued to seek extra sources of income. On top of their forced labour, some found illegal work in small firms in the major cities, especially Berlin, where concern with regulations and paper-work was rather less exact. Profound weariness and exhaustion were the consequences.

Hunger became an important factor in the suffering of Jewish forced labourers. Step by step, the authorities reduced their nourishment by continually cutting down their share of rationed foods. Jews had to go without meat and fish, eggs and fruit, chocolate and cakes, coffee and tea, wine and alcohol. The *Ernährungsämter* withdrew the special supplements for pregnant women and breast-feeding mothers, children and old people, the sick and disabled. What remained was a vestige of basic foodstuffs, relief packages which were still arriving from abroad and were deducted from the rations, the foodstuffs obtained by mutual aid or on the "black market". The *Ernährungsämter* also thought it appropriate to cancel the special rations for forced labourers. The following is taken from a report from the Berlin *Rüstungsinspektion III* in August 1941 on the "nutrition of Jewish workers":[30]

> "The *Haupternährungsamt* Berlin reports that Jewish workers may no longer receive extra cards for long, heavy and very heavy labour. Non-Aryans also may not receive the same food as the Aryan workers in a munitions firm. For the care of the Aryan workforce, the *Haupternährungsamt* of the city of Berlin supplies the works canteens of the munitions factories with supplementary foodstuffs such as rice, noodles, bacon, margarine etc. in order to make the meals tastier and more nourishing. But there is no objection if hot meals are prepared for the Jewish workers in a special kitchen solely on the basis of their food ration cards. Special cooking facilities can also be made available to non-Aryans for their own preparation. However, it is not permissible for Jews to eat in the same canteens or mess halls as the Aryans."

To hunger was added the strain of travelling to and from work. It often took forced labourers hours to reach their place of work or their homes. After the November Pogrom of 1938, motor vehicles and drivers' licences had been confiscated; bicycles were requisitioned in 1942. Jewish forced labourers could only use buses or trams, underground trains or municipal railways if they had a special pass. This privilege was granted if the distance from home to work was more than 7 km. or over an hour's walk. *Sternträger* were allowed to sit on public transport only when all the Germans had found a seat. Enforced detours were frequent, since a *Judenbann* meant that Jews could not travel through designated roads, squares or parks.

Once at work, the Jewish forced labourers had to obey the company's "Jewish regulations". Instructions on "security" issued by the Berlin electricity works in 1941 contained the following "disciplinary regulations for the surveillance of Jews":[31]

> "1. Jews must be collected by the gate-keeper before starting their work, be brought by security to their changing-room and handed over to the foreman of their work crew.
> 2. The Jews may only move about the works property under supervision. They may never stay within the works alone. Work will be undertaken by them in self-contained crews which must be under the leadership of an Aryan member of the company.
> 3. After the end of work, the Jews are to be taken by security in the same way, as a self-contained group to the exit to works property."

It was not easy for German Jews to get used to their new places of work under such conditions. Their social origins and professional training had prepared them for a world very different from the one into which they were now thrust. Vivid evidence of this is provided by the personal accounts of Jewish forced labourers.[32]

One furrier – expelled from his business – was forced to report to the Jewish labour exchange in Berlin at the end of 1939.

> "Together with a senior teacher, a factory owner and a painter, I was sent to the Lehrter station ... to clean the toilets of the incoming trains. We were set to work with only a cloth and scouring sand. I asked humbly for a scrubbing brush. At that Herr B. became furious and yelled: 'You Jews are quite used to wallowing in filth so get to the sh ..! Anyone here who rebels will make a real discovery. Do you know where I can send you?'"[33]

In 1940, a lawyer, whose practice in Gleiwitz had been confiscated, was sent to a sewage farm "where 30 Jews in all had to work... Work lasted from 7.00 until 17.00 with a short break at lunchtime, under civilian supervision and *Gestapo* control. Over the years I lost 30 pounds doing this work. I had to cultivate the humus and shovel it onto wagons, up to 150 cwt. on many days."[34] Better prepared for arduous labour was the owner of a lamp factory who had been very active in sport, including judo, in his spare time. He was dispatched to a Berlin building firm: "We had to do heavy roadwork, such as breaking up stones, carting stones and sand, and fetching the stones for the pavers. The work did not break me so much, but there were some workers among us who literally collapsed under it. When the first bombs fell, we had to tear down the badly damaged houses, which caused us many accidents."[35]

As a rule the forced labourers had to work a ten-hour day. One graduate of the by then closed Berlin *Lehranstalt für die Wissenschaft des Judentums* was employed examining and cleaning greasy shells in the *Deustsche Waffen- und Munitionsfabrik* in Berlin-Borsigwalde.[36] A woman from an upper-middle-class family which had converted to Christianity was forced to peel 6 cwt. of potatoes every day in a tiny, windowless room in the *Zeiss-Ikon-Görtz* factory in Berlin-Zehlendorf.[37] Approximately 200 workers formed the *Judenabteilung* which did piece-work manufacturing fuses and timers for U-boats in the *Dresden Göhle Werke* of *Zeiss-Ikon*. One woman forced labourer, classed as a *Mischling*, recalled: "This work required great concentration, manual dexterity and good eyesight. My eyes suffered very much from the effects of this precision work, as we worked continuously each day in artificial light using magnifying glasses and tweezers."[38] The *IG-Farben Konzern* was especially known and feared for the harsh treatment it meted out. One Jewish woman was sent to a Berlin factory specialising in silk for parachutes:[39]

"For ten hours we had to ensure that the thread on the rotating spindles did not get tangled or snap, and that the spindles did not run empty. The room was hot, the work hard and tiring. The noise made any conversation with one's colleagues impossible. During the break in the breakfast room there was only one theme: how can we get out of here? Women who had been there some time told of the harassment to which they had been subjected. Some succeeded in obtaining their release. Gynaecological illness was one reason which was accepted, we heard; this made it impossible to stand at the machine for hours on end."

Women suffered more than men from these demands and privations. In addition to the factory shifts, they also had to face their housework and the need for long and exhausting trips for food. Many women had to look after a family, and many were still caring for parents and grandparents. Mothers sent their children to kindergartens run by the Jewish community during their working hours. On occasion, they came back after work to find only empty rooms; during their absence a *Kindertransport* had been sent to the East.

Among many young Jewish people, a feeling of hopelessness set in. Banned from schools and other centres of education, they had been degraded to the level of unskilled workers without any prospect of working their way up as apprentices or journeymen. However, some young people attempted to break out of the cycle of demoralisation and isolation. In the *Hachscharah* – agricultural estates described by the Nazis as "living communities for Jewish forced labourers" in 1941 and liquidated in 1943 – Jewish and Zionist ideals survived and found expression in the will to emigrate and the longing for a new life in *Eretz Israel*.[40] Groups were also formed in munitions factories. In many cases, social barriers first had to be overcome before new friendships could be made. This problem was most severe for young people who had grown up in an upper-middle-class environment. In the factories and firms, many of them made their first-ever contacts with their companions in suffering from working-class Jewish families. There were some who found the strength and courage to embark on political resistance. For instance, the two *Judenabteilungen* in the electric motor works of Siemens contained many of the young forced labourers who formed the Herbert Baum group, an organisation with a proud place in the history of Jewish resistance and German anti-fascism.[41]

The personal accounts also reflect the experiences of the forced labourers with their supervisors. It is possible to suggest a typology of attitude and treatment which covers the various forms and levels encountered. Firstly, there were the supervisors who made no bones about their anti-Jewish feelings and who took every opportunity to torment and degrade their slave labourers and even to hand them over to the *Gestapo*. The forced labourers knew that even the slightest infringement of the "Jewish regulations" could be interpreted as sabotage and result in draconian punishment. Employees were instructed to notify their superiors of any incidents that occurred. Some were more than happy to do so. They observed every move the forced labourers made, eavesdropped on conversations, and inspected bread brought in during short breaks to see whether forbidden foods were being eaten. Alongside complaints and denunciation came verbal attacks, ranging from minor incidents to wholesale and furious attacks. Everywhere the Jewish workers faced loud commands, dressings down, bullying demands for work. These modes of speech were even adopted by people who were not fully committed either to Nazism or to antisemitism.

However, Jewish forced labourers sometimes came into contact with fellow-workers who tried to alleviate their hard conditions or to make up the deficiencies in their rations. These people had the courage to greet and encourage *Sternträger*, to help them get easier work, or to show them other, smaller kindnesses. Secretly, they might hand over sandwiches, fruit, slices of meat, tobacco, sweets or tablets. Such gestures of sympathy, compassion and help occurred frequently, and those who made them were dubbed "decent Germans" by the survivors. From their ranks was drawn the small band of Germans who went one vital step further – and began to try and save Jews. The survivors have also left accounts of such conduct; they show that forced labour offered an opportunity for the re-establishment of social contacts. After their social exclusion and banishment to a "ghetto without walls", Jewish forced labourers became acquainted with Germans who were ready to resist and, knowing that they were risking their own lives, to keep Jews out of the clutches of the *Gestapo*. Visits by the *Gestapo* were notified in advance and Jews forced to "go underground". Some Germans offered hiding places and helped to safeguard the lives of the illegal existence of the Jews underground.

From a distance, Jewish forced labourers also became aware of the existence of foreign slave labourers and prisoners of war. Some pitied these "utterly ragged figures"[42] and noted how they "searched through the canteen waste buckets after the meal break".[43] On occasion individual Jews would break out of the separate *Judenabteilung* to make contact with the "foreign workers' camp". On these journeys the Jews would take the remains of their own starvation rations for distribution among the Poles or Russians. But contact with these foreign workers also made the Jews more aware of the threat to themselves. As the army of foreign workers grew larger, some Jewish forced labourers became afraid that they would be replaced by Poles and Russians at work.

Hitler and Himmler were always determined that the use of Jewish workers – in Germany as in the occupied territories – was only a transitional solution. From autumn 1941 at the latest they made it clear that the "exemptions" from deportation or liquidation in the East were "temporary" and could be "retracted at any time". The civilian and military authorities took note of the directives and adapted to the losses involved. When the first *"Rüstungsjuden"* ("armament" Jews) were "withdrawn" in October 1941, the military representatives of the war economy complained that they had not been given an opportunity to state their views. In every report there were references to the losses in production and demands for "immediate replacements". The *Kriegstagebuch* of *Rüstungsbereich* Frankfurt a. Main contains the following entry for 20th October 1941:[44]

> "Several armaments firms, including *Voltohm Seil- und Kabelwerke AG ... Radio Braun* report that in a sudden transportation of *Jews* from Frankfurt/M to the *Generalgouvernement* on Sunday 19th October 1941, without the prior agreement of the *RüKdos*, a number of their Jewish workers had been withdrawn, the consequence of which was to damage the *Wehrmacht* manufacture involved since replacement workers could not be supplied immediately."

In Berlin the first "withdrawal" endangered the "manufacture of insulation for billets in the East".[45] At once, contact was established with the labour exchanges and the *Gestapo* in an effort to come to an arrangement. The interests of the *Rüstungsinspektion* involved "preventing the withdrawal of Jewish workers ... from armaments and special firms as far as is absolutely possible". There was sympathy for this appeal within the Berlin labour exchange. Its "Jewish expert", Eschhaus, let it be known that Jewish workers would not be withdrawn for the present. Even the deportation office of the *Gestapo* was ready to co-operate. On 28th October 1941, the *Kriegstagebuch* of *Rüstungskommando III* noted:[46]

> "It was decided in discussion that state police headquarters does not want to ignore the needs of the armament economy in any way and will examine doubtful cases in an accommodating manner. Basically the *RüKd* must get in touch with the technical specialist *Kommissar* Stübs, and *Regierungsrat* Dr. Kunz is personally available for important questions. The *Kommando* is instructed ... to send the lists of its Jewish workers with an appropriate covering letter, in which the indispensable workers are indicated with a red cross ... Basically it is to be noted that evacuations which have already taken place cannot be called off."

What was to be co-ordinated at local level had already been laid down within the central leadership. On 25th October 1941 the *Wirtschaft-Rüstungsamt* in the *Oberkommando der Wehrmacht* dispatched a memorandum to the *Rüstunginspektionen* containing the RSHA "guidelines" for the implementation of deportations. Account was taken of the needs of the war economy. Jewish forced labourers were among those whose deportation was "temporarily" postponed. Exemption would be granted only if proof was provided that "resettlement" would endanger the "carrying out of urgent armament orders on schedule".[47] *Rüstungskommandos* and firms set to work to compile the lists of names and to send them to the *Gestapo* and labour exchanges. In Frankfurt a. Main a list of 360 names was compiled with a request to delay transportation until "replacement workers" were available.[48] Such lists and reasons were provided everywhere. But the *Gestapo* promise to examine these requests "benevolently" was not always fulfilled. "Withdrawals" of Jewish forced labourers were recorded constantly. At the end of November 1941 the Berlin labour exchange would no longer accept responsibility for preventing the deportation of Jews working in the metal industry. "A non-withdrawal of Jewish armaments workers", explained the director of the labour exchange, "would only be possible if the *Gestapo Sippenlisten* (genealogical lists) were at its disposal at the correct time and if the *Gestapo* was to guarantee that only non-Aryans examined by itself [i.e. the labour exchange] are sent to the transport."[49] The labour exchange faced considerable difficulties, not only in supplying "replacements" in view of the acute labour shortage, but also in selecting the Jewish forced labourers to be deported. The "*Sippenlisten*" were long in coming. The head of the labour exchange felt it essential "as before ... to let employees from his office participate in the measures in the synagogues, in order to obtain reliable documents on the non-Aryans affected by the evacuation".[50] However, the *Rüstungskommandos* confided that the agreements made would be kept and that the "indispensable armaments Jews" would be the last Jewish group to be deported. There was full information on the scale and timetable of the deportations. On 15th November 1941, *Rüstungsinspektion III* wrote a report:[51]

"The transporting of about 75,000 Jews away from Berlin, of whom around 20,000 are employed in important jobs – about 10,000 in the metal sector alone – also affects the question of the supply of replacement workers. A replacement in the shape of German workers through the labour exchanges is out of the question. By 4th December 1941 a further 15,000 Jews, and then from February 1942 the remainder, are to be evacuated. The Jews working in the armaments industry are, if possible, to be removed from the firms at the end of the evacuation measures."

Another report summarised experiences in the period from October 1940 to December 1941:[52]

71

"The Jews who had previously worked individually in firms were collected into self-contained groups, sections in a firm, or Jewish shifts. Here they worked separate from the Aryan workforce. They were supervised only by Aryan masters or foremen. At various levels the results were very good, e.g. in the chemical and textile economy and especially in the electrical industry, where Jewish women proved to be highly skilled winders etc. ... In October 1941 there suddenly began – without the *Rüstungsinspektion* having a chance of stating its own position beforehand – a resettlement of Jews to the East. Jews engaged in urgent production were not to be evacuated for the time being. On the other hand, as the deportation was, for various reasons, to be carried out on the basis of kin, important workers were nevertheless caught up in the process in increasing numbers and lost to the armaments firms. Because of a lack of replacement skilled workers and a shortage of transport capacity, the planned further resettlement of Jews was halted at the beginning of 1942."

When the *Reichsbahn* trains were available once more and the extermination camps and gas wagons were ready for operation, the wave of deportations began anew.

Once again the military representatives of the war economy were confronted with the "Jewish Question" and the old debates revived. These arguments now took place against the background of a distinct power shift. To an increasing extent, the *Wirtschaft-Rüstungsamt* under General Thomas had lost influence: it was clear that Albert Speer as *Reichsminister für Bewaffnung und Munition* was building an empire and assuming control over the *Rüstungskommandos*. In fact, one vital decision had already been taken in occupied Poland. This illuminates the strategy which was developed by the leading military and war economy authorities for the solution of the "replacement problem". In September 1942 the *Oberkommando der Wehrmacht* was quite prepared to relinquish control of armament firms in the *Generalgouvernement* to the *Reichsministerium für Bewaffnung und Munition*. Field Marshal Keitel freely admitted that Speer was now solely responsible for debating "with the SS about of the removal of Jewish workers".[53] He expressly forbade all military offices to continue "placing themselves protectively ... in front of the Jews".[54] Indeed such protection no longer appeared necessary – Keitel announced the deployment of Polish workers.

When the "replacement" issue was due to be settled in the *Generalgouvernement Wehrkreiskommandant* General Freiherr von Gienanth made his own position clear. On 18th September 1942 he sent a memorandum to the *Oberkommando der Wehrmacht*. It included the following comments:[55]

"If work of vital importance for the war effort is not to suffer, the Jews can only be released after the training of the replacements step by step. This task can only be undertaken locally, but must be centrally directed by *one* office [emphasis in original] in cooperation with the Higher SS and Police Leader.

It is requested that the decree be implemented in this form. The guideline should be to exclude the Jews as quickly as possible without damaging work of vital significance for the war effort."

In the *Oberkommando der Wehrmacht* this request fell on deaf ears, and General von Gienanth was put on the retired list. On 10th October 1942 his successor was informed "that the Jews employed by the *Wehrmacht* in auxiliary military services and in the armaments industry are to be replaced immediately by Aryan workers".[56] The instruction gained the approval of *Reichsführer SS* Himmler, who had advanced his claims to leadership after reading the Gienanth memorandum[57] and, on 9th October 1942, had submitted a stage-by-stage plan proposing the liquidation of Jewish forced labourers.[58] The penultimate step involved "amalgamating" them in a number of "*KL-Großbetrieben*", large concentration-camp firms in the East of the *Generalgouvernement*.[59] The ultimate aim was stated in the final sentence: "However, here too, corresponding to the wish of the *Führer*, the Jews are to disappear one day." The military were also made aware of the programme of the "Final Solution". The *Oberkommando der Wehrmacht* passed on the Himmler order and simply added that "after this it [is] the task of the military offices responsible for the firms to fix the implementation of the above guidelines with the appropriate SS and Police Chief".[60]

In the *Altreich* too, the decision to remove all Jews from the armaments factories had been taken. On 22nd September 1942 Adolf Hitler gave the order to Sauckel, who was responsible for labour supply.[61] Goebbels noted triumphantly in his diary:[62]

"The *Führer* once again expresses his firm determination to get the Jews out of Berlin at all costs. Even the comments of our economic experts and industrialists, to the effect that they cannot do without so-called Jewish precision work, do not impress him. Suddenly the Jews are being praised absolutely everywhere as workers of the highest quality. This argument is repeatedly used against us in order to plead leniency for them. But they are not as indispensable as our intellectuals make them out to be. It will not be too difficult, in view of the fact that in Berlin alone we have 240,000 foreign workers, to replace the remaining 40,000 Jews – of whom only 17,000 are active in the production process – with foreign workers as well. As things stand the Jewish precision worker is becoming a constant argument of intellectual philo-semitic propaganda. Here we see again that we Germans are only too easily inclined to be too just, and to judge questions of polit-ical necessity with emotion but not with cool intellect."

Some weeks passed before the *"Entjudung"* of the armaments factories was achieved. On 20th October 1942 the deportation experts of the Berlin *Gestapo* again offered the assurance that the *"Rüstungsjuden"* would be the last group to be deported;[63] on 13th November 1942 they announced that "within the next six months the Jews would be completely removed [and replaced] by Poles".[64] Firms were exhorted to offer the "utmost col-laboration" and reminded of their duty to provide accommodation for the "replacement workers". Within the firms there was widespread regret at the withdrawal of the Jews. In October 1942 the Berlin *Rüstungskom-mando* reported:[65]

"The Jews have been described by all the works managers as excel-lent workers, on the same level as skilled workers. The evacuation of the Jews is settled. The replacement is to be provided by Poles, whose training requires many weeks. The works managers fear that they will have to set on two Poles for each Jew in order to achieve the same results. The order that the armaments firms are to be spared until last in the evacuation of the Jews has not always been put into practice. As the Jews are evacuated by family, there have been repeated instances where Jews employed in armaments firms have also been removed prematurely. This has caused a certain unrest in the *Judenabteilungen*. The works managers gener-ally regret that the original proposal to retain the Jews as workers, and to this end to quarter them and to transfer them to camps exactly like foreign workers, has not been implemented."

Some individual works managers tried to obtain further exemptions from the labour exchange or the *Gestapo*. An end was put to such intervention in January 1943. Special circulars were sent by the *Rüstungskommandos*[66] to inform the firms that all applications or visits would be "futile". Peti-tions could be submitted to the *Rüstungskommandos* only if they included detailed figures on the expected fall in production. These instructions also stipulated that the labour exchange must be informed of the disappear-ance of Jewish workers and applications for replacements directed to them. Finally, the firms also had a duty to inform the *Gestapo* immediately of every "Jew being released from manufacturing or becoming dispensable in any way whatsoever".

At the end of February 1943 the *Gestapo* was finally in a position to strike the decisive blow against the *"Rüstungsjuden"*. On 27th February the so-called "factory actions" began. Approximately 7,000 Jews were seized in arrests and raids on firms, on the streets, and on homes. The manhunt lasted for several days. In Berlin, it triggered a unique protest demonstration after Jews who were living in "privileged mixed marriages" were among those seized during the mass arrests. "Aryan" wives arrived at the assembly point in the Rosenstrasse and began to chorus demands for the release of their husbands, supported by passersby who took the side of the demonstrators. Shocked by this wholly spontaneous and large-scale resistance, the *Gestapo* gave way and began to release the Jewish husbands step by step. The successful result of the public protests inevitably led to speculation that similar actions might have changed the course of Nazi policy towards the Jews. *Reichsminister* Goebbels was highly dissatisfied with the course of the "factory action". His diary contains the following entry for 2nd March 1943:[67]

"We are now removing the Jews from Berlin at last. They were gathered together suddenly last Saturday and will now be shifted to the East in the shortest time possible. Unfortunately it emerges yet again that the better circles, especially the intellectuals, do not understand our Jewish policy and are placing themselves in part on the side of the Jews. As a consequence [news of] our action has been betrayed prematurely so that a whole crowd of Jews has slipped through our hands."

In the war diaries and reports of the *Rüstungskommandos* there were no more expressions of criticism or regret. The only factors thought worthy of mention related to the "disruption" caused and the "replacements" in the firms. In view of the army of millions of slave labourers and prisoners of war which had now been brought to Germany, the fate of Jewish forced labourers was no longer considered important.

In Berlin the *Rüstungskommandeur* ordered an entry to be made in the service diary:[68]

"On 27th February, suddenly and abruptly, there occurred the withdrawal of all Jews still involved in the labour process, 11,000 of whom were in the armaments sector. As in many cases the Jews were put to work in self-contained units, sometimes on important programmes, every attempt had to be made to find extensive replacements. This was only possible by calling up all the Western workers who arrived in the first half of March exclusively for this purpose, as well as other workers who became available, especially as a result of the compulsory registration action and as a result of closures. Thus the shutdown of specific manufactures could be prevented and there were merely certain interruptions caused by the initial training period of the new workers."

Such "interruptions" occurred in the *Elektro-Motorenwerk* of *Siemens Schuckert Werke*, where the disappearance of the Jews caused problems "in the deliveries for the U-boat programme, particularly of converters and control motors for fire-control facilities".[69] As was reported by *Rüstungskommando I*, the *Oberkommando der Marine* immediately applied for the assignment of "20 lathe operators, 10 fitters, 18 electrical mechanics and 20 women". *Rüstungskommando III* in Berlin reported that "the complete removal of the Jews ... in the Adolf Hitler tank programme" had caused a number of difficulties. To ensure the manufacture of tanks on schedule, the labour exchange promised "to provide a replacement supply of 100% in smaller and medium-sized firms, and of at least 50% in larger firms, within 48 hours".[70]

In the area covered by Berlin *Rüstungskommando V*, the "last Jews [were] removed without immediate supply of replacement". Disruption was recorded only in those firms with "a particularly high percentage of Jews working in them".[71] *Rüstungskommandos* in other German regions were hardly affected by the "factory actions". Jewish forced labourers had disappeared from many areas long before. The remainder were in individual armaments concerns or with firms making their contribution to the war effort by collecting and re-cycling rags and scrap. For example, a report came in from the *Rüstungsbereich* Düsseldorf:[72]

"On the basis of an order of the RSHA all Jewish workers had to be removed from the firms by 27th February 1943. There was no possibility of objecting. For the armaments concerns this measure was of little significance. It was somewhat greater for rag-sorting institutions, scrap dealers and similar firms."

The "factory action" pointed the way to the end of Jewish forced labour in Germany. Further *Gestapo* decrees ensured that all firms became "Jew free". Only a few forced labourers remained and these, in accordance with Himmler's programme for the Final Solution, were put to "self-contained work which is revocable at any time".[73] Still tolerated and exploited were the "non-Aryan" workers who were protected by having non-Jewish spouses or by classification as a *Mischling*.

After being dismissed without notice from their firms, the forced labourers and their families were given the *Gestapo*'s "place on the list" for "resettlement" in the East. Their interim and final destinations were the compulsory ghettos of Theresienstadt, Lodz and Warsaw, Riga and Kovno, Minsk and Izbica, and the extermination camps of Chelmno and Belzec, Treblinka and Auschwitz. In all these places of organised mass murder German Jews – who had already suffered all the preceding stages of defamation and victimisation – were confronted with a reality which was terrible beyond their imagination. In this de-humanised world of bar-

barisation and death, they shared their fate with other Jews. Their encounters with the *Ostjuden*, their "brothers and sisters" from Eastern Europe, have recently been impressively described by Avraham Barkai.[74] The slave labourers were "selected" on the loading platforms of the extermination camps. Usually it was young women and men, fit for work, who were recruited once again for forced labour on the building sites, in the camp factories and firms of the SS, the *Wehrmacht*, industry or trade. There they were exploited by a system which adopted the maxim of "destruction through labour".

In the occupied territories of the East, the military representatives of the war economy at first tried to retain the potential of Jewish labour until adequate replacements were guaranteed. This guideline permitted them to make interventions and protests, but prohibited mass resistance or refusal to obey. When the *Rüstungsinspektionen* and *Rüstungskommandos* found themselves unable to decide the timing of "withdrawals" or even to ensure the arrival of new workers, they – like other military offices – accepted the inevitable "losses"; the attitude they adopted was "to shrug their shoulders and look the other way".[75] This approach was demonstrated to perfection in a report written at the beginning of 1943 by the Baranowicze branch office and sent to the Minsk *Rüstungskommando*. The head of the branch – a *Rittmeister* – reported that the last "Jewish action" had taken place on 17th December 1942 and had ended with the "final removal of all Jews from the firms". He continued:[76] "The fact that all Jewish skilled workers have also disappeared in this way, making up about 50% of the workforce, is regrettable in the interests of production but cannot be helped."

The absolute priority accorded by Nazi racial fanatics to the extermination of the Jews ultimately clashed once again with the material interests of the system. As the military and economic situation deteriorated, there was increasing pressure to retain the economic potential of those Jewish slave labourers who were still "available" in the concentration camps. Moreover, demands were even made for them to be sent back to work in a Germany which was now almost completely "*judenfrei*". In April 1944 the *Eichmann-Referat* opposed any "so-called open deployment of labour in firms in the *Reich* ..., as it would ... contravene the *Entjudung* of the *Reich* which has been largely completed in the meantime".[77] But this veto was overridden. The reservoir of non-Jewish workers was virtually exhausted. Though almost 7.7 million foreign workers and prisoners-of-war had been harnessed to the German war effort, they were not enough. Jewish workers were now required to cover the shortfall. While the gassings and shootings continued and the last centre of European Jewry was destroyed with the deportation of the Hungarian Jews, both Jewish and non-Jewish concentration camp inmates were deported to the *Altreich* from early summer 1944. Once more the SS, businesses and factories hired out their slaves. Some of these weak, emaciated and half-starved women

77

and men, girls and boys, were crammed into accommodation provided by the firms, which often resembled conditions in the camps themselves; others were forced to march to work from the numerous satellite and permanent camps. Once again their routes and workplaces could be seen by the German people, though these – with few exceptions – took little notice of the survivors of the "Final Solution". Even today, the material "compensation" for the victims is a matter of dispute.

The vast majority of Jewish forced labourers in Germany, in the event, shared the fate of their co-religionists in countries occupied by the Nazis. Their harsh exploitation for the German war effort had been, at best, no more than a temporary reprieve. The extermination of Jews included the slave labourers in Germany as soon as – and often even before – replacements, in the shape of foreign workers and prisoners-of-war, could be found for them. Appeals for "exemptions" from deportation for skilled or essential workers had small hope of success in a system based on irrationality, racial hatred and mass murder, and geared to the enslavement of a whole continent. Forced labour in the Nazi war machine was only another step along the path of destruction for the Jews in Germany.

Notes

1 Nürnberger Dokument (Nbg.) Dok. PS-3663. Brief Reichsministerium für die besetzten Ostgebiete (RMfdbO) an Reichskommissar für das Ostland (RKO), 31st October 1941.
2 *Ibid.* Brief RKO an RMfdbO, 15th November 1941.
3 *Ibid.* Brief RMfdbO an RKO, 18th December 1941.
4 An excellent critical survey of the historical interpretations and controversies can be found in Ian Kershaw, *Der NS-Staat*, Reinbek 1988; see also Dan Diner (ed.) *1st der Nationalsozialismus Geschichte? Zu Historisierung und Historikerstreit*, Frankfurt a. Main 1987. See now Richard Breitman's seminal study, *Himmler, Architect of Genocide*, New York 1991. I am grateful to him for having provided me with two relevant documents for this article (see notes 57 and 76).
5 Susanne Heim and Götz Aly, "Sozialplanung und Völkermord", in *Konkret*, 10 (1989), p. 82. See also *idem*, "Die Ökonomie der 'Endlösung'. Menschenvernichtung und wirtschaftliche Neuordnung", in *Sozialpolitik und Judenvernichtung*, Berlin 1987.
6 Ulrich Herbert, "Rassismus und Rationalität", in *Konkret*, 12 (1989), pp. 56–60.
7 Christopher R. Browning, "Vernichtung und Arbeit", in *Konkret*, 12 (1989), pp. 64–69.
8 Dan Diner, "Die Wahl der Perspektive", in *Konkret*, 1 (1990), pp. 68–72.
9 Avraham Barkai, *Vom Boykott zur "Entjudung". Der wirtschaftliche Existenzkampf der Juden im Dritten Reich 1933–1943*, Frankfurt a. Main 1988, pp. 173–181; see also Konrad Kwiet, "Nach dem Pogrom. Stufen der Ausgrenzung", in *Die Juden in Deutschland 1933–1945. Leben unter nationalsozialistischer Herrschaft*, ed. by Wolfgang Benz, Munich 1988. Parts of this contribution have been adapted for this Year Book article.

10 Ulrich Herbert, *Fremdarbeiter. Politik und Praxis des "Ausländereinsaizes" in der Kriegswirtschaft des Dritten Reiches*, Berlin–Bonn 1985; and *idem*, "Arbeit und Vernichtung. Ökonomisches Interesse und Primat der 'Weltanschauung im Nationalsozialismus'", in *1st der Nationalsozialismus Geschichte?*, *op. cit.*, pp. 198–236.

11 See here Rolf-Dieter Müller, "Die Mobilisierung der deutschen Wirtschaft für Hitlers Kriegführung", in Bernard R. Kroener, Rolf-Dieter Müller and Hans Umbreit (eds.), *Das Deutsche Reich und der Zweite Weltkrieg*, vol. V/1, Stuttgart 1988, pp. 349–689; also "Die Mobilisierung der Wirtschaft für den Krieg – eine Aufgabe der Armee? Wehrmacht und Wirtschaft 1933–1942", in *Der Zweite Weltkrieg*, ed. by Wolfgang Michalka, Munich 1989, pp. 349–362; Georg Thomas, *Geschichte der deutschen Wehr- und Rüstungswirtschaft (1918–1943/1945)*, ed. by Wolfgang Birkenfeld, Freiburg–Boppard 1966.

12 Joseph Walk (ed.), *Das Sonderrecht für die Juden im NS-Staat, Eine Sammlung der gesetzlichen Massnahmen und Richtlinien – Inhalt und Bedeutung*, Heidelberg 1981.

13 Nbg. Dok. PS–1720. Arbeitseinsatz der Juden, 20th December 1938.

14 Bundesarchiv Militärarchiv (BA/MA) RW 20–3/9. Geschichte der Rüstungsinspektion (RüIn) III, Heft I, 1st September 1939–30th September 1940, p. 29; see also BA/MA RW 20–3/12. Lagebericht RüIn III, Heft 1, 21st September 1939–11th January 1940; see also the vital contribution by Bernhard R, Kroener, "Die personellen Ressourcen des Dritten Reiches im Spannungsfeld zwischen Wehrmacht, Bürokratie und Kriegswirtschaft", in *Das Deutsche Reich und der Zweite Weltkrieg*, vol. V/1, *op. cit.*, pp. 693–989.

15 BA/MA RW 20–3/10 Geschichte der RüIn III, Heft 2, 1st October 1940–31st December 1941, p. 15.

16 BA/MA RW 20–3/15. Lageberichte der RüIn III, Heft 4, Lagebericht von 15th October 1940, p. 1.

17 BA/MA RW 20–3/15. Lageberichte der RüIn III, Heft 4. Lagebericht von 15th January 1941, p. 6.

18 Walk, *op. cit.*, p. 174.

19 BA/MA RW 20–9/25. RüIn IX, Lagebericht, 15th January 1941–15th May 1941, p. 19. On the deliberations before the outbreak of the war as to how to utilise Jewish labour see Appendix.

20 BA/MA RW 20–3/15. Lageberichte, RüIn III, Heft 4, 15th July 1940–15th August 1941, p. 6.

21 Barkai, *Vom Boykott zur "Entjudung"*, *op. cit.*, p. 176.

22 BA Koblenz, NS 19 neu/1570.

23 *Reichsgesetzblatt*, 1941 I, p. 675.

24 Raul Hilberg, *Die Vernichtung der europäischen Juden*, Berlin 1982, p. 110.

25 Hans Rosenthal, *Zwei Leben in Deutschland*, Bergisch-Gladbach 1980, p. 45.

26 Wiener Library (WL) P IIIe, No. 1185.

27 Jochen Klepper, *Unter dem Schatten deiner Flügel*, Stuttgart 1956, pp. 922 and 1136.

28 WL P IIId, No. 1141.

29 Peter Hanke, *Zur Geschichte der Juden in München zwischen 1933 und 1945*, Munich 1967, p. 339.

30 BA/MA RW 20–3/15. Lagebericht der RüIn III, Heft 4, 15th July 1940–15th August 1941, p. 8.

31 Quoted from Konrad Kwiet and Helmut Eschwege, *Selbstbehauptung und Widerstand. Deutsche Juden im Kampf um Existenz und Menschenwürde 1933–1945*, 2nd edn., Hamburg 1986, p. 255.

32 Kwiet, "Nach dem Pogrom", *loc. cit.*, pp. 581–589; see also Monika Richarz (ed.), *Jüdisches Leben in Deutschland*, Bd. 3. *Selbstzeugnisse zur Sozialgeschichte*, Stuttgart 1982, Veröffentlichung des Leo Baeck Instituts.

33 WL P IIIb, No. 616.

34 WL P IIa, No. 90.

35 WL P IIId, No. 1097.

36 WL P IIId, No. 1141.

37 Robert A. Kann, *Erinnerungen von Valerie Wolffenstein aus den Jahren 1891–1945*, Vienna 1981, p. 37.

38 Michael Brenner, *Am Beispiel Weiden. Jüdischer Alltag im Nationalsozialismus*, Würzburg 1983, p. 99.

39 Inge Deutschkron, *"Ich trug den gelben Stern"*, Cologne 1978, p. 75.

40 Joel König (Esra Ben-Gershom), *David. Aufzeichnungen eines Überlebenden*, Frankfurt a. Main 1979; Anneliese Ora Borinski, *Erinnerungen 1940–1943*, Ms. in Institut für Zeitgeschichte (IfZ) ZS 43/2; see also Werner T. Angress, "Auswandererlehrgut Gross-Breesen", in *LBI Year Book X* (1965), pp. 168–187; and *idem, Generation zwischen Furcht und Hoffnung, Jüdische Jugend im Dritten Reich*, Hamburg 1985.

41 See Kwiet/Eschwege, *op. cit.*, pp. 114–139; Eric Brothers, "On the Anti-Fascist Resistance of German Jews", in *LBI Year Book XXXII* (1987), pp. 369–382. On the current state of research see Arnold Paucker, *Jüdischer Widerstand in Deutschland. Tatsachen und Problematik.* Beiträge zum Widerstand 1933–1945, Gedenkstätte Deutscher Widerstand, Heft 37, Berlin 1989. (A revised and enlarged English version, published by the *Gedenkstätte*, is now in print.)

42 WL P IIId, No. 1141.

43 WL P IIId, No. 26.

44 BA/MA RW 21–19/9 RüKdo Frankfurt/M *Kriegstagebuch* (KTB) No. 8, p. 10.

45 BA/MA RW 21–4/8 RüKdo Berlin III KTB 8, 23rd October 1941, p. 12.

46 *Ibid.*, 28th October 1941, p. 14.

47 Heydrich's guidelines on deportation of October 1941 have – to the best of the author's knowledge – not yet been located. References to them can be found in the "circulars" issued by regional state police headquarters and in a KTB entry of the Frankfurt *Rüstungskommando* on 22nd November 1941: BA/MA RW – 19/9. KTB No. 8, p. 13. Similarly, in the later, surviving deportation guidelines issued by the RSHA, "temporary exemption … of Jewish workers in work of importance to the war effort" is permitted. See H. G. Adler, *Der verwaltete Mensch, Studien zur Deportation der Juden aus Deutschland*, Tübingen 1974, p. 188.

48 BA/MA RW 21–19/9 RüKdo Frankfurt/M KTB No. 8, 2nd November 1941, p. 13.

49 BA/MA RW 21–4/8 RüKdo Berlin III, KTB No. 8, 29th November 1941, p. 32.

50 *Ibid.*, p. 33.

51 BA/MA RW 20–3/16, RüIn III, Heft 5, 15th September 1941–15th February 1942, p. 9.

52 BA/MA RW 20–3/10, RüIn III, Heft 2, 1st October 1940–31st December 1941, p. 15.

53 On the arguments with the SS see Albert Speer, *Der Sklavenstaat*, Stuttgart 1981 (an account with a pervasive tone of apologia); for criticism see Matthias Schmidt, *Albert Speer. The End of a Myth*, London 1985. Typical of Speer was his attempt to exert his influence to delay the withdrawals of Jews. An entry of the KTB, Chef WI Amt of 22nd September 1942 contains the following:

"Speer wants to speak to the *Führer* because of the withdrawals of Jews from the industrial economy. His proposal concerns creating self-contained *Juden-Betriebe* (firms made up of Jews) until further notice." BA/MA RW 19/186.

54 BA/MA RW 19/186. KTB Chef Wi Amt, 12th September 1942.
55 Quoted from Helge Grabitz and Wolfgang Scheffler, *Letzte Spuren*, Berlin 1988, pp. 310–312.
56 Grabitz/Scheffler, *op. cit.*, p. 312.
57 NA Washington T 175 roll 22–2527369.
58 Grabitz/Scheffler, *op. cit.*, p. 179.
59 On the establishment of "forced labour camps for Jews (*Zwangsarbeitslager*= ZAL(J) in the *Reichskommissariat* 'Ostland' " see Alfred Streim, "Konzentrationslager auf dem Gebiet der Sowjet-union", in *Dachauer Hefte*, 5 (1989), pp. 174–187.
60 Grabitz/Scheffler, *op. cit.*, p. 179.
61 Speer, *op. cit.*, pp. 349–350.
62 IfZ ED 83/2. Joseph Goebbels, *Tagebuch*, 30th September 1942.
63 BA/MA RW 21–4/12, RüKdo Berlin II, KTB No. 12, 1st October 1942–31st December 1942, p. 19.
64 *Ibid.*, p. 17.
65 BA/MA RW 21–3/2 RüKdo Berlin II, KTB, 1st October 1942–31st December 1942, p. 19.
66 BA/MA RW 21–4/13 RüKdo Berlin III, KTB No. 13, Sonderrundschreiben No. 2 of 20th January 1943.
67 IfZ München Fa 246/2. Goebbels, *Tagebuch*, 2nd March 1943.
68 BA/MA RW 21–2/3 RüKdo Berlin I, KTB, 1st January 1943–31st March 1943, p. 17.
69 BA/MA RW 21–2/3 RüKdo Berlin I, KTB, 1st January 1943–31st March 1943, p. 7.
70 BA/MA RW 21–4/13 RüKdo Berlin III, KTB No. 13, 27th February 1943, p. 29.
71 BA/MA RW 21–6/1 RüKdo Berlin V, KTB, 28th February 1943, p. 15.
72 BA/MA RW 21–16/12 RüKdo Düsseldorf, KTB, p. 20.
73 Walk, *op. cit.*, p. 481.
74 Avraham Barkai, "German-Speaking Jews in Eastern European Ghettos", in *LBI Year Book XXXIV* (1989), pp. 247–266; see also *idem*, "Between East and West. Jews from Germany in the Lodz Ghetto", in *Yad Vashem Studies, XVI* (1984), pp. 271–332.
75 Klaus-Jürgen Müller, *Das Heer und Hitler*, Stuttgart 1969, p. 45.
76 NA Washington T 77 R 1159 141. Aussenstelle Baranowicze, RüKdo Minsk, p. 9.
77 Quoted from Ulrich Herbert, "Von Auschwitz nach Essen", in *Dachauer Hefte*, 2 (1986), p. 18.

18

POVERTY AND PERSECUTION

The Reichsvereinigung, the Jewish
population, and anti-Jewish policy in the
Nazi state, 1939–1945[1]

Wolf Gruner

Source: *Yad Vashem Studies*, 27 (1999), 23–61. Translated from the German by William Templer.

This job can no longer provide any satisfaction. It now has very
little in common with what we used to understand as welfare work.
And when it's people that are involved, not property, liquidation is
particularly rough. Yet just because we're dealing with human
beings, you have those occasional moments when there seems to be
some real meaning in still being here.[2]

Hannah Karminski (1897–1942), July 1942

These lines, which bespeak a sense of both profound resignation and social
obligation, are from a letter by Hannah Karminski only a few months
before she was deported to her death. Karminksi, a former managing
director of the Jewish Women's League, was active from 1939 on as a
senior staff member in the welfare department of the National Association
of Jews in Germany (Reichsvereinigung der Juden in Deutschland, RV).
Her description brings into sharp relief the traumatic dependency of the
officials and personnel in Jewish welfare offices on their persecutors, as
well as their Sisyphean daily labors in trying to struggle with poverty on a
mass and previously unknown scale within the Jewish population in
Germany after years of persecution.

This article does not attempt to describe welfare work as a response by
Jewish institutions to poverty either as a temporally limited social phenomenon precipitated by crisis or war or as a permanent feature of a specific social stratum. Rather, it focuses on analyzing the ways in which
Jewish institutions sought to grapple with the consequences of a process of

structural pauperization as driven by deliberate policy. That process was initiated by the Nazi state in 1933, through a diverse array of persecutory measures, in order to expel German Jewry from the Reich. In the wake of the November 1938 pogrom, as prospects for the success of previous policy seemed to fade, the process was pushed forward with relentless rigor. The Jews' material bases for survival as a collectivity defined by National-Socialist racial policy were attacked, undermined, and destroyed. Even state welfare benefits for this population were later specifically revoked. A newly devised organization, the Reich Association of Jews in Germany, was ordered by the Nazi state to shoulder responsibility for social care and welfare.

Background conditions and the establishment of the RV

Already under the impact of the Great Depression, penury and want were on the rise in the Jewish population. But it was the policies of persecution introduced by the Nazi state, beginning in 1933, that set into motion a structural process of pauperization and immiseration. Rapidly, it resulted in a disproportionately large percentage of Jews among the jobless and destitute in the German Reich, in marked contrast with the general upward trend in the economy.[3] Despite mass emigration, the ranks of unemployed Jews swelled to over 60,000 by the summer of 1938, almost twice the number than when the Nazis had seized power.[4] Longer and longer lines of needy Jewish Germans were applying for public-welfare assistance.

Local welfare offices reacted to this surge in new applications by introducing ever-more stringent practices. As early as 1936, the Jewish poor in a number of towns were being singled out: in some, supplementary benefits were cancelled; in others, welfare payments were reduced; in still other localities, all welfare recipients were conscripted for compulsory labor in segregated work squads. In the German Council of Municipalities (Deutscher Gemeindetag), municipal officials and mayors were already busy batting about more extensive steps designed to oust Jews from the state network of social welfare. Finally, in the summer of 1938, the Interior Ministry drafted an expedient decree.[5]

The planned move to exclude all needy Jews in Germany from social welfare was to have grave consequences, and the autonomous incorporated Jewish Communities (Gemeinden) and institutions were confronted with grave problems that virtually defied solution. For one thing, Jewish social welfare—like welfare aid from other religious organizations—had previously operated on the basis of "charity," providing assistance supplementary to state welfare benefits. Moreover, from 1933 on, Jewish welfare offices found themselves up against ever-more pressing financial problems as municipal subsidies for care in Jewish institutional homes were cancelled, along with a rapid drop in the level of funds available for welfare as many former contributors had emigrated.[6] Between 1933 and 1938, Jewish organizations abroad had already recognized the need to lend a greater hand and boosted their financial assistance to Jewish institutions in Germany.[7]

At the same time, the massive pauperization had an early recoil effect on the central policies of state persecution pursued by the Nazi leadership. By 1936, in ministry-level discussions, officials were emphasizing that poverty constituted an obstacle to expulsion. In 1938, that conflict of interest came to a rapid head. The step-up in anti-Jewish measures was fueling increased poverty, yet the few potential countries of immigration were wary of welcoming the destitute.[8] Consequently, after the *Anschluss* of Austria, the Nazi leadership shifted gears, opting for a policy of force over the shorter term in order to coerce Jews into leaving. On the heels of a mass deportation of Polish Jews in late October 1938, therefore, came the infamous *Kristallnacht* pogrom.

Yet the pogrom failed to accelerate the exodus of the German Jews to the levels the Nazi leaders desired. As a result of all subsequent new measures, such as forced Aryanization, special taxes, and a ban on commercial activity, the German Jews were now doomed to unemployment, and the indigent among them to dependence on welfare.[9] Many no longer had sufficient funds to emigrate.[10]

For that reason, within the span of a few brief but fateful weeks, the Nazi top echelon began to revamp its approach, adopting a new two-pronged strategy: to impel Jews able to leave to emigrate, while forging ahead with the social separation of those remaining behind. Since it was now no longer "merely" a policy of social exclusion, but of erecting separate structures for the Jews in Germany, this new approach was more than a simple radicalization of previous practices. It spelled a fundamental new direction in persecution policy. This policy was pressed forward by the flurry of decrees from the end of 1938 on, ordering the segregation of Jews in education, culture and social welfare, housing and the labor market. The aim of the Nazi state was to systematically isolate some 300,000 individuals within the strictures of a Zwangsgemeinschaft, a compulsory community inside the state, an undertaking historically unprecedented in scope and intent.[11]

One building block in this new orientation was the creation of a compulsory inclusive organization. A recently discovered fact is that only days after the pogrom, on November 15, 1938, Heydrich invited officials to an inter-ministerial meeting to prepare the groundwork for setting up a "Reich Association for the Care of Jewish Emigrants and Needy Jews."[12] The idea had been cleared with Göring, who had given his approval. On December 1, representatives of the ministries and the Security Police decided that this "Reich Association" should also be given the task of setting up a separate school system.[13] By February 1939, the organization of the bureaucratic apparatus was apparently complete.[14] It was to make partial use of the personnel and infrastructure of the National Representation of Jews in Germany (Reichsvertretung der Juden in Deutschland), which had been created in the autumn of 1933 as an umbrella organization of the local Jewish Gemeinden and the Jewish state and regional associations.[15]

Yet contrary to what some historians contend, the utilization of an existing infrastructure is certainly no proof that the Reichsvereinigung was launched with no outside influence from the Nazi authorities.[16] Even if, since the spring of 1938, and under the impact of state persecution on Jewish institutions, representatives in the Reichsvertretung had themselves been bandying about the idea of forming a more strongly centralized body,[17] these ministerial discussions and other new documentation suggest a different picture. Thus, on February 5, 1939, the head of the Security Police informed all state police offices in the Reich about a scheme to consolidate the "means lying scattered in diverse Jewish organizations into a single body":

> the National Representation of Jews in Germany [has been] ordered to form a so-called National Association of Jews. At the same time, it must take steps to assure that all existing Jewish organizations disappear. Their entire facilities are to be placed at the disposal of the National Association.

The local Gestapo was to monitor but not disrupt this process, because the "necessary control and surveillance functions" would be handled centrally from Berlin.[18]

While the planned organizational structures were set up quickly, their "legal approval" was dragged out. Initially, the plan called for the Reich Association to be launched subsequent to a police decree. Yet in early March, the Nazi leadership suddenly switched to the idea of issuing a new "Decree on the Reich Citizenship Law."[19] However, the inter-ministerial agreement this required was held up. That was the main reason the Reich Association was not officially established until July 4, 1939.[20]

The Tenth Decree on the Reich Citizenship Law vested the new Reichsvereinigung der Juden in Deutschland with responsibility for a separate welfare and school system; its main purpose was to "promote emigration." According to the bylaws of July 7, 1939, given the stamp of approval by the Security Police (Heinrich Müller) for the Reich Ministry of Interior, the new compulsory organization also had "to fulfil all additional tasks ... assigned it by the Reich Interior Minister."[21] The RV bylaws could be altered only with the approval of the so-called control agency (or Aufsichts behörde, as the Gestapo was euphemistically called).[22]

The aims and structure of the organization were fundamentally differ-ent from those of the old Reich Representation, where the local Gemein-den, State Associations, and regional welfare societies had functioned as constituent members of the umbrella organization. Moreover, they also differed from internal Jewish plans, in the summer of 1938, for a proposed Reich Federation (Reichsverband).

The specified purpose of that Reich Federation was to encompass all Jews in the German Reich and to "promote their religious, cultural, social and other needs"—not emigration. All persons of the Jewish faith who belonged to a Jewish community were regarded as potential voluntary members. By contrast, all "Jews" so defined by the Nuremberg Laws and resident in the territory of the Reich were required to belong to the new compulsory Reich Association. Instead of a confederation of all communities or independent Jewish organizations represented on the council of the envisaged Reich Federation, the Reichsvereinigung con-sisted solely of branches dependent on directives handed down by the appointed executive board, the larger communities and a total of eighteen district offices that encompassed the smaller Gemeinden under their juris-diction. Only in one sphere, namely religious functions, did the Jewish communities still enjoy a modicum of autonomy.[23]

The altered situation in Jewish welfare in 1939

Although the RV bylaws specified that one of its three principal tasks was the creation of a separate welfare system, strangely enough—in contrast with educational matters, for example—no single individual on the execu-tive board was vested with responsibility for this area. Dr. Conrad Cohn was appointed director of the welfare department, Hannah Karminski was made head of the "General Welfare" section, and Dr. Walter Lustig took over as chief of medical welfare.[24] Just as in organizational structure, there was only a superficial similarity between the tasks of the Reich Associ-ation and its predecessor, the Reich Representation. Welfare now no longer consisted of Jewish self-help to supplement state benefits. Rather, it was an institution for social welfare for the entire Jewish population that had been imposed from above by force, separately organized and centrally controlled by the Gestapo.

For the Jewish side, the starting conditions were negative in the extreme. During the November pogrom, many community centers, cloth-ing distribution points and public kitchens had been demolished; goods, foodstuffs and money had been confiscated and personnel had been arrested.[25] From that point on, the fate of the Jewish communities was overseen and sometimes even governed by the local Gestapo.[26] This new constellation spawned unanticipated conflicts of interest with various authorities, since within the framework of the new concept of Zwangsgemeinschaft, the Security Police were now concerned to guarantee (and at times even augment) the ability of Jewish social institution to function. In most localities, it was evidently the Gestapo that supervised Jewish welfare. Only in Frankfurt am Main was there a special municipal officer appointed for this purpose,[27] and in some towns the local welfare authorities were charged with keeping tabs on Jewish welfare.[28]

Even if after a time confiscations were reversed or facilities repaired in a makeshift way, the capacity and financial means of the Jewish offices were often far too limited to provide the necessary relief for the rising tide of those in need. On November 19, 1938, a new decree excluded Jews from the public-welfare system, shifting the state obligation to provide welfare literally overnight to the shoulders of the Jewish communities.[29]

Neither in terms of structure nor budget were the hard-strapped Gemeinden prepared to provide basic social welfare for tens of thousands of impoverished Jews. Moreover, most municipalities and their welfare offices were eager to eliminate the Jewish poor from their public rolls, quickly and totally. In a number of localities that initiative failed, because the Gestapo intervened on the side of the Jewish institutions. In Berlin, for example, there was a special audit of the books of the Jüdische Gemeinde, and the conclusion was that the community lacked the requisite funds to provide for all the needy. Thus, the municipal welfare authority had to continue to give assistance to Jews in need. For such reasons, there were initially quite diverse schemes, based on local circumstances, when it came to compulsory involvement on the part of Jewish communities in the financing of public welfare.[30]

Even if public-welfare benefits continued to flow, these were only a minimum aid package, varying from locality to locality.[31] This increased the need for supplementary aid from the Jewish Winter Relief (*Jüdische Winterhilfe*). The scope of that program also points up just how dramatically the general social situation had deteriorated, because, in addition to Jews on welfare, the Winter Relief was also assisting pensioners, white-collar employees, and factory workers with small incomes. At the end of 1938, there were 70,682 recipients, i.e., one in every four Jews in Germany. The previous winter, the numbers had been one in every five.[32]

Along with the concrete destruction wrought by the pogrom, the general progressive erosion of Jewish institutional infrastructure since 1933 posed a formidable problem for the creation of a separate welfare system inside the Reichsvereinigung. Driven by persecution, pauperization, and emigration, the number of Gemeinden had shrunk from 1,610 in January 1933, to only 1,480 at the official birth of the Reich Association in early July 1939; of the original thirty-four state and regional associations, only eleven were still in existence.[33] Associations had been forcibly closed down by the police, or had disbanded due to difficulties in staffing or financing. In 1933, there had been nearly 3,700 Jewish institutions; only a third of these had survived. (In Berlin, the number of Jewish organizations had plummeted from 990 to 221.) Out of 586 welfare organizations, 302 were still operating; only eighty *chevrot kadishah* (burial societies) were left from an original 582. Of forty-three kindergartens, six remained, and not a single of the 113 lodges had survived.[34]

These still extant institutions were now either slated to be eliminated or incorporated into the RV,[35] like the Central Welfare Agency for German Jews (Zentralwohlfahrtsstelle der Juden in Deutschland).[36]

Due to the expansion of a separate welfare net, Jewish welfare institutions (hospitals, homes for children and the elderly, asylums for the insane and the blind) were initially exempted from compulsory "Aryanization."[37] For example, the Jewish Benevolent Society in Leipzig operated a canteen, a day-nursery, and a home for the elderly. The urgency of the social situation is evident in a letter from the society to the state police headquarters in Leipzig requesting more staff: "The extent of privation among the elderly and indigent Jews we must care for and accommodate has necessitated expanding the old people's home from 14 to approximately 30 persons."[38]

Thus, the creation of the Reichsvereinigung was no mere attempt to breathe new life into diverse Jewish institutions for self-help; rather, it involved the carefully monitored construction of a separate edifice of welfare in the framework of this new compulsory organization. The purpose of that system of welfare was to come to effective grips with the social problem of mass pauperization within the Jewish population as driven by the policy of discrimination. In the eyes of the rulers, the mass penury constituted a major hindrance to expulsion.

The new poverty and Jewish welfare, 1939–1940

The formal creation of the RV in July 1939 had accelerated the shifting of welfare burdens from state agencies to the Jewish institutions. More and more towns and villages now categorically rejected any support for needy Jews. The last such decision was in Hamburg, effective December 1, 1939.[39] Beginning in November 1939, the RV had to take over funding throughout Germany both for institutional care (so-called *Geschlossene Fürsorge*), i.e., the accommodation of the handicapped or mentally ill in nursing homes and mental institutions and, from 1940 on (except in Berlin), also for non-institutional care (*Offene Fürsorge*), i.e., regular ongoing assistance for the needy living on their own.[40]

At the end of 1939, almost one in every three Jewish residents was on the Jewish welfare rolls, a total of more than 52,000.[41] That led to staggering financial problems. Once established, the RV was authorized to collect dues officially from its compulsory membership. It used these revenues to finance its main programs and balance out the budgetary burden between the local communities. Help also arrived from abroad in the form of increasing contributions from organizations such as the American Jewish Joint Distribution Committee.[42] From the spring of 1939 on, income from the newly introduced "emigration tax" levied on every Jewish emigrant was also employed to finance various activities, including welfare.[43]

In Hamburg, the Gestapo had already jumped ahead of the rest of the Reich, imposing just such a "levy" in December 1938. According to the local ordinance, it applied to all Jewish emigrants regardless of whether or not they were community members. The local Gemeinde later commented in retrospect:

> With the introduction of the emigration tax, the Community was walking in the footsteps of our ancestors. In the 18th century, every Jewish Community member who moved out of Hamburg was required to pay a high tax assessed on the value of their assets.[44]

This is a striking example that points up the way in which the RV or Gemeinde representatives often sought to weave official orders from the authorities into the woof of their own history—probably in order to preserve some modicum of self-respect and forestall a serious loss of face in the eyes of the broader Jewish population.

Many articles in the *Jüdisches Nachrichtenblatt*, the official RV paper, specially invoked Jewish tradition as part of a reaction to the new situation in which the RV had been saddled with sole responsibility for welfare for the poor. At the same time, such references to tradition were intended as an appeal to galvanize internal solidarity within German Jewry in the face of mounting persecution. Yet precisely in this context of galloping privation, a problem arose: some Jewish communities were apparently paying out higher benefits to the needy than the levels permitted in public welfare for Jewish recipients. The RSHA decided to clamp down, taking steps at the end of 1939 to curb this practice. It ordered the Reichsvereinigung to introduce a system of "self-surveillance." On principle, it was necessary that the Jewish poor receive less than their Aryan counterparts; at the same time, the RV budget should not be overburdened "unnecessarily."[45]

Thus, only on rare occasions could the Jewish poor be given special ancillary aid over and above the regular welfare payments. In many towns Jewish institutions set up new welfare soup-kitchens and clothing-distribution shops.[46] Though the provision of shoes or clothing remained one of the traditional services of relief offices, that function went through two rapid fundamental transformations. First, when, in the aftermath of the November 1938 pogrom, the newly founded RV and its district offices were saddled with the task of welfare provision, they found themselves confronted with a daunting task: how to erect a social network on a new scale in order to provide for the needs of tens of thousands of impoverished Jews—a network it was only partially possible to build up on the foundations of existing institutions. Due to the sharp rise in the number of the needy, the RV thus found itself forced over the short term to rely completely on clothing donations from the Jewish population.[47]

Second, the problem was compounded once the war had broken out and the Nazi state had made another fateful decision: German Jews now had to maintain themselves by *Sonderversorgung*, a special segregated system for providing basic necessities. From the beginning of 1940, Jews had been prohibited from purchasing new clothing and shoes, so the circuit of clothing-distribution shops had to be expanded once again to cope with the new and urgent demands.[48]

In a parallel development, the JWH, on orders from the Reich Ministry of Interior, suddenly broke with its long-standing principle of distributing nothing but material goods to the needy: indigent Jews were now permitted to receive only financial aid. The reason behind this move was that the Nazi authorities wished to prevent any new articles from ending up in Jewish hands via donations channeled through the Winter Relief. Poverty-stricken Jews now had to depend on the meager "free market," itself further restricted by the regulations of *Sonderversorgung*, in order to purchase food, used clothing, or fuel.[49]

Along with the efforts by welfare services and the Jewish Winter Relief to stem the tide of structural poverty, the RV also provided care for the elderly, medical welfare, and aid for the war-disabled. In particular, care for the aged expanded into an ever-larger component of RV activity. The Reichsvereinigung now had to guarantee the provision of such care, replacing services previously furnished largely by private foundations or aid societies.

Large numbers of young people had opted for emigration, leaving many elderly or sick relatives behind alone, often without any family maintenance. These developments led to a drop in the number of private families taking in persons requiring special care. That decline was further compounded by the effects of the anti-Jewish Rent Law of April 1939, because "uncertainty over whether the occupants would not themselves soon lose their apartment" often discouraged people from taking in such boarders.[50] By the summer of 1939, in Berlin alone, there were already some 3,000 applications for places in homes for the elderly. Although it was difficult to find space for rent, purchase of property was forbidden, and no funds were available for new construction, RV officials managed to make do: by 1940, they had almost doubled the number of such homes.[51] Facilities were now located in former synagogues or schools, and even in apartments that had been combined to accommodate several Jewish families.[52]

The medical welfare program of the RV concentrated in particular on expectant mothers, medical services in schools and institutional homes, health cures at spas, rest cures and health care for emigrants. The principal obstacle here was the state licensing of physicians. For example, there were only two Jewish "medical practitioners" licensed to practice in the whole area of Pomerania, East Prussia, Schleswig-Holstein and Mecklenburg, and no specialists.[53] This welfare district had been particularly ravaged by the destruction wrought to its infrastructure. Of the ninety rest and recuperation homes in Germany in 1932, what remained in the wake of *Kristallnacht* were nothing but two homes for adults and one for children.[54]

In addition, the RV welfare department also had to become involved in the two other compulsory main task areas of the organization, namely emigration promotion and schooling. Both had been hard hit by the structural pauperization of the Jewish population. Thus, many indigent Jews were provided the cost of passage, clothing, or tools and equipment in order to assist them to flee from Germany, as long as flight was still possible.[55] Indirectly, they also helped potential emigrants by covering the costs of occupational retraining, since the skilled had better prospects abroad: in 1939, 80 percent of all agricultural trainees and 70 percent in the manual trades were being supported, a total of more than 2,000 persons.[56]

In addition, previously unknown categories of aid to the needy emerged in the aftermath of the pogrom. As part of new directions in anti-Jewish policy, the labor offices began, in early January 1939, to conscript jobless Jews for heavy manual labor in road construction or at garbage-disposal sites. They received the minimal wages for unskilled laborers. Many Jewish officials initially hoped that forced-labor deployment in segregated work brigades (so-called *Geschlossener Arbeitseinsatz*) would at least guarantee minimum maintenance levels for a group that had already swelled to some 20,000 Jewish workers and their families by the summer of 1939. Such expectations soon soured to bitter disappointment.[57] Commenting at the end of 1939, the RV noted:

> These individuals were recruited almost exclusively for unskilled manual labor. Many are housed together in labor camps and separated from their families. Since their earnings are often insufficient to provide for their dependents, the Jewish welfare services were frequently obliged to step in. On top of that, in many instances they also had to make funds available to cover the cost of work clothes for conscripted laborers.[58]

Huge social problems were also generated in many localities by the strictures of the anti-Jewish Rent Law. Since countless German Jews had lost their apartments by spontaneous eviction notices from individual landlords or by systematic "evictions" at the hands of the municipal authorities, the

Gemeinden had to move quickly to set up shelters for the homeless and to enlarge existing facilities for the elderly.[59] People were often forced to vacate their apartment at short notice several times over even a few short months. For the victims, this meant not just the loss of their accustomed surroundings and comforts; they also usually had to give up any right to privacy, because in the so-called *Judenhäuser* ("Jews" houses') set up in many cities, a family as a rule was allotted only a single room. As a result, people had to get rid of their furnishings and belongings, resulting in a further decline in their daily living standards, quite apart from whatever capital they might still possess.

The privation generated and driven by the policy of persecution now struck almost all groups in the Jewish population. Malnutrition plagued the aged, the sick, children, and forced laborers in the wake of the policy of *Sonderversorgung* imposed after the outbreak of war in 1939 and the concomitant reduction in rations.[60] Since there was little butter or kosher meat, rabbis were forced to be extremely flexible in how they interpreted traditional dietary laws when it came to margarine and meat so as to assure the basic provision of kosher food for Jewish canteens or institutional homes.[61] Alongside such latent problems, numerous emergency relief operations were undertaken, such as the swift response sparked by the first deportations from Pomerania in February 1940: on short notice, Jewish offices rushed to the aid of individual victims, providing them with money and food, and arranging shelter for those who later returned.[62]

Poverty and the budget of the Reichsvereinigung in 1940

At the beginning of 1940, the RV anticipated that another 45,000 Jews would soon join the ranks of the indigent, necessitating additional annual expenditures in excess of RM 20 million. Thus, they projected a total budget of RM 125 million required for the following three fiscal years. Of this, it was likely that not even half the cost could be met by contributions, liquidations of assets, or funds from Jewish organizations abroad, such as the Joint. In light of a potential deficit of RM 71 million, the newly erected compulsory edifice of the RV appeared to be tottering on the financial brink.[63]

Yet the budget for the first six months of 1940 had initially been drawn up without taking these projections into account. In any event, the largest single item in the total budget of over RM 22 million was the figure of RM 11.3 million for welfare,[64] made up at this point of the general welfare, support for institutional homes (for the aged, children, the handicapped and rest homes), medical care (clinics and hospitals), and welfare aid for war victims.[65]

Since late April and early May of 1940, RV representatives had been hoping they might economize on welfare expenditures,[66] because the

Labor Administration Authority had extended the nets of forced-labor deployment to all Jews fit and able to work. Previously, official policy was that "only" those being supported by state benefits were to be conscripted.[67] In order to potentially relieve the strain on the RV welfare budget by means of the wages (however paltry) paid to forced workers, the district offices were now also supposed to order the indigent on Jewish welfare to register with their local labor office.[68] However, Jewish officials believed there was a certain limit to this strategy, since the working conditions for conscripted laborers were becoming ever harsher.[69]

The actual RV expenditures for the first half of the year ran to RM 22.5 million; the outlay for welfare, RM 9.5 million, was somewhat less than projected. Membership dues provided only RM 5 million; and more than half of the total expenditures, RM 11.7 million, was covered by "assets." Of the latter, one million came from "genuine" assets, 10.6 million from emigration tax revenues.[70] For the second half of 1940, the RV had a projected budget of RM 10.4 million for welfare and had pared down the total budget to just under RM 20 million.[71]

Against the backdrop of new budget planning and in the afterglow of the *blitzkrieg* victory over France, the Security Police informed the RV on June 25, that "a fundamental solution" for the Jews from Europe was now envisaged following the anticipated victorious end of the war in the autumn, namely, the "readying of a colonial reservation." The structures and finances of the RV were to be mobilized logistically to this end, and its officials were thus instructed to "begin examining this problem carefully in advance so that potential plans can be put on the table when demanded."[72]

Although labor offices across the Reich inducted Jews in a second massive wave of conscription for industrial labor deployment in the autumn of 1940, contrary to what many had hoped, the social decline in the Jewish population had not been halted. By the eve of the new year, the number of male and female forced laborers had already soared to some 40,000.[73] Bearing in mind the effects of the deportations at the end of October from western Germany, the RV noted:

> Outlay will be reduced due to the discontinuance of welfare payments for the Jews in Baden and the Palatinate and, to a limited extent, because of labor deployment as well. On the other hand, effective January 1, 1941, previous expenditures will be augmented by assumption of total welfare costs for the Jews in Berlin.[74]

With this takeover of all welfare costs in Berlin, the forced transfer of state welfare to the RV inside the *Altreich* was largely complete. The upshot was that new economy measures notwithstanding, the RV had to increase its budget once more for the first half of 1941 to RM 22.5 million.

Half of the projected expenditures were reserved for welfare. Since anticip-ated income revenue was less than RM 13 million, due to pervasive poverty, the plan was to increase the 1941 membership dues assessed on the basis of declared wealth, and, in particular, to utilize the emigration tax and Gemeinde assets to help cover the deficit.[75] Consequently, plans were drafted in the community institutions to slash personnel and operating costs.[76]

In the midst of these deliberations on how to cut costs, Jewish officials received the next bit of bad news: effective January 1, 1941, a new special 15-percent surtax was to be introduced on all Jewish income, the so-called *Sozialausgleichsabgabe*. One consequence of this "social compensation tax" was that many forced laborers and employees in Jewish institutions were now at risk of joining the ranks of the needy.[77]

Attempts by the RV to exploit conflicts of interest

Although the RV representatives had no possibility whatsoever of altering the basic thrust of the persecution policy, the occasional contradictions, based on conflicts of interest, between the diverse agencies in the Third Reich involved in policy planning could sometimes be exploited for the benefit of the Jewish population as a whole or individuals directly affected. Occasionally, they were even successful.

Thus, in 1939–1941, the Reichsvereinigung was able to induce the RSHA to intervene and block a number of initiatives by other agencies that went beyond the RSHA's own general aims in the persecution policy. Those initi-atives included, for example, local hassles in the supply of food[78] or early plans by some municipalities for barracks camps.[79] As we have already described, regional welfare authorities and municipal welfare offices were interested in just how fast they could cut off the Jewish poor from social-welfare benefits. The RSHA restrained more radical demands for the RV to assume welfare costs for non-members as well, such as foreign Jews and those in "mixed marriages." Against the selfish concerns of the municipali-ties to reduce the number of poor on their welfare rolls, the RSHA was interested in making sure that the Gemeinden and the RV would not be weighed down by too heavy a financial burden over the medium term so as to guarantee continued functioning of the separate school and welfare systems.[80]

Diverse conflicts were also generated as a result of the autonomous labor deployment program organized in the Reich by the labor offices. The RV was able to exploit the interest of the SD and Security Police in expanding the schemes of vocational retraining as preparation for emigra-tion in order to shield Jews from the grasp of the labor offices and con-scripted labor. However, their venturous attempt in 1940, to have Jewish prisoners released from the concentration camps for work as forced labor-ers under the Labor Administration Authority ended in failure.

94

The RV also managed to avert a number of planned local operations against the Jewish population with a "helping hand" from the RSHA. In 1939–1940, the labor offices in Baden and Silesia refused to grant Jews unemployment benefits, arguing that Jewish welfare could also take them under its wing. In this instance, the RSHA, fearing that Jewish welfare offices might be swamped by requests for aid and unable to cope, backed Jewish officials in their petition to the Labor Ministry.

In another case, the RV defended its position by a contrary tactic, this time with backing from the Labor Administration Authority. When, in October 1940, the RSHA suddenly demanded that 10,000 male laborers be made available for work on autobahn construction, the Jewish authorities responded by pointing out that almost all workers were already busy on the job: they had long since been integrated into the forced-deployment scheme run by the labor offices. This special recruitment operation was subsequently abandoned.[81] However, such scope for maneuvering disappeared abruptly once it had been decided in 1941 to press ahead with deportations to the East.

The dismantling of the RV in the course of deportations

In mid-March 1941, some six months before the beginning of deportations from the *Altreich*, the RSHA commented to Jewish officials that "a projected emigration by all Jews capable of being resettled would necessitate substantial funds."[82] In preparation, drastic economy measures were ordered, involving a radical paring of the organizational structures just set up. The number of communities in the RV as yet not included within district offices had to be pruned from eighty-two to seventeen: these were only in the larger cities and were now termed Kultusgemeinden. District offices had to be reduced from eighteen to thirteen, and now encompassed more and more communities.[83] The number of members on the RV executive board was cut back; the number of departments was limited to those dealing with education and retraining, social services, finance/administration, and emigration.[84] The RV was ordered to slash expenditures for personnel and education.[85]

The RV and communities had to sack thousands of employees; to avoid new welfare burdens, they were registered in the labor offices for conscripted labor deployment.[86] The RV district offices received similar directives: all expenditures for welfare were to be reviewed in order to channel every fit and able individual on the welfare rolls into conscripted labor.[87]

With this "aid" from the RSHA, the labor offices managed once again to recruit more than 10,000 men and women by the summer of 1941. With between 51,000 and 53,000 deployed forced laborers, there were virtually no potential Jewish workers left in the *Altreich* to conscript.[88] Due to the strenuous, monotonous, and often poisonous working conditions in industry, the grind of shift work, the long distances to and from the job, inadequate diet, and a lack of rest and recreation, Jewish officials expected that the health of nearly all such conscripted laborers would suffer.[89] In Berlin, the city that still retained the most favorable social and economic conditions in the teeth of persecution, there were now some 30,000 persons living on forced labor and 11,000 on welfare, amounting to two-thirds of the Jewish population there.[90]

In connection with these economy measures, the RV had instructed its district offices in late February that, in future, cash welfare payments would have to be replaced by material aid; clothing distribution points and canteens would have to be expanded.[91] Under the press of persecution, the public kitchens in Jewish institutions had long since cast off their original character as canteens for the needy. They now resembled communal dining halls, their operation geared to the rhythms of forced labor. Welfare work for the young took on a similar thrust, now concentrated in the main on care for the children of forced laborers. The emergency welfare services operated four homes in cities for persons who had relocated from rural areas, transients, the homeless, and those who had been bombed out in air raids. Social welfare was also provided for prisoners.[92]

In numerous cities, the RV had to contend with the social consequences of forced resettlement into *Judenhäuser*. On top of this, in the summer of 1941, the Gestapo ordered the RV to finance the construction of at least thirty-eight labor and residential camps at closed mines, in evacuated monasteries, or in military barracks. Camp facilities such as Milbertshofen in Munich and Kapellenstrasse in Bonn were now set up in order to intern the Jewish population of entire towns or rural districts prior to deportation.[93]

Some 167,000 Jews still remained in the *Altreich*; almost 60 percent were female, and the percentage of the elderly was extremely high.[94] Mass privation was the product of an eight-year-long process of systematic persecution. Half of all RV expenditures, now some RM 3 million a month, went for welfare. In Berlin, the proportion spent on welfare was even greater, hovering at about 70 percent. Only a scant 5 percent of the budget in Berlin was allocated to education and culture, 15 percent was set aside for administrative costs, and 10 percent for other communal activities.[95]

Since the revamping carried out in the spring of 1941, there was a master budget for the whole organization, replacing the former system of independent, separate budgets for the individual communities. On orders from the RSHA, the only revenue sources that could be used to finance the RV budget were dues paid in by its compulsory members, monies from the JWH and from the new *Jüdische Pflicht* scheme, which had been initiated that same spring. It was now strictly forbidden to utilize any other funds, such as capital from property liquidations, etc., because remaining RV assets were earmarked to serve one exclusive and paramount purpose: the financing of the now-imminent deportations.[96]

In mid-September 1941, after the introduction of the compulsory yellow badge, the RV district office in Brandenburg, East Prussia, received a letter from Selma Ebert. Together with her three children, she had been left by her "Aryan" husband and had been resident since April 1939 in the Ladeburg poorhouse after having been evicted from her apartment. Frau Ebert wrote:

> Please send me two badges. One for myself and one for my son Gerhard ... I dread the winter, I don't have any coal or overcoat. If I could buy some coal, but I don't have the money. What's going to become of me? Nobody can stand any more of this suffering and pain. My dear Mrs. Löwenthal, couldn't you possibly see your way to granting me a few marks to buy some coal? Because there's no gas here and I'm totally dependent on coal. Maybe I could get some as an advance from the Winter Relief, cause when the two truckloads of coal that the dealer's got have run out, I won't get any till January. Since that's when he'll receive new supplies. My heartfelt thanks in advance, Selma Ebert.[97]

The situation of this isolated and totally impoverished woman is reflective of the plight of a large segment of the Jewish population in the autumn of 1941, on the eve of the deportations. In September, the Nazi leaders finally decided on a concrete date for the long-prepared deportations; at the end of the month, it informed Jewish officials of this fact and ordered them to take part in organizing the planned transports.[98] The Kultusgemeinden were required to establish camps for those to be deported and equip the transports, which were slated to begin in mid-October. In Hamburg alone, the costs for food, blankets, clothing, travel, etc., for the period October to December 1941, amounted to almost a quarter million marks.[99]

The initial transports precipitated new social problems, since among the deportees were thousands of forced laborers who had been supporting their relatives with their meager incomes. Overnight, the number of places in homes for the aged or in homes for children torn from their foster families had to be increased once again.[100] Although the burden on Jewish welfare offices was eased as a consequence of the drop in the number of needy community members, reduced spending for schools, etc., this was cancelled out by the new financial constraints. Confiscation by the Reich of the property and assets of deportees in accordance with the Eleventh Decree on the Reich Citizenship Law also put an abrupt end to maintenance payments from blocked accounts for needy relatives or friends.[101]

As the deportations got under way, the RV was told to reduce by 20 percent all welfare payments from Jewish institutions.[102] This meant, for example, that benefits for the Jewish needy in Berlin fell below the estimated minimum for survival.[103] Yet due to special taxes, the take-home pay of those still on forced labor was also insufficient. This proved especially disastrous in cases where relatives had to be fed and cared for. For that reason, many forced laborers were also compelled by circumstances to work illegally at another job, concealing their yellow badge, while others sold their last belongings in a bid to improve their desperate lot.[104] Large families were particularly pinched, with too little money even to buy the reduced food rations.[105]

Starvation had begun to spread. Of the approximately 130,000 Jews still in Germany in the winter of 1941–1942, some 18,880 were dependent on welfare from the JWH. In Breslau, almost one in three of the 6,467 Jews there had to be given supplementary welfare relief; that was in marked contrast with the picture in Berlin, where only 9 percent of the Jewish population of 58,000 were receiving extra aid. The labor situation in Berlin was characterized by a large number of Jews employed in Jewish institutions and especially conscripted to work in industry.[106]

Deportations, suspended toward the end of the winter, were resumed in late March 1942. On April 2, Heydrich issued a directive that the assets of the RV should in future be utilized "primarily for the final solution of the Jewish question in Europe." Consequently, these were to be regarded "as assets already earmarked for purposes of the German Reich."[107] Subsequent to a decision by Hitler, Eichmann informed RV representatives at the end of May that preparations were being made for the "entire evacuation of the Jews . . . to a place of permanent residence"; i.e., all those under the age of sixty-five were to be sent East and the elderly and disabled veterans were to be confined in Theresienstadt.[108]

Now the German state literally stole the last shirt off the backs of the German Jews. They were ordered to surrender all articles of clothing not essential for a "modest standard of living,"[109] along with necessary household appliances such as electric heaters, hotplates, and vacuum cleaners.[110] Education for Jews was totally banned.

From this point on, poverty or welfare dependence were regarded as sufficient grounds for early deportation. The Gestapo informed the Jewish Community in Berlin that anyone receiving any form of social assistance had, "for budgetary reasons, to be induced to go."[111] This applied to everyone receiving support from Jewish institutions, which, at that point in the Reich, meant a total of 2,718 Jews, including the elderly.[112] This was followed in September by the largest deportation wave for 1942—more than 12,000—about 10,000 of whom were sent to Theresienstadt.[113]

By the spring of 1943, most of the Jews still remaining in Germany had been shipped East to be murdered. In June, the RSHA dissolved the organizational structure of the RV, along with its district offices. After the Reich had confiscated its entire assets, a newly created "rump" organization was allocated a mere RM 5 million for all expenditures.[114] This "New Reichsvereinigung" was headed by Dr. Walter Lustig and consisted only of the central office, a medical department, and a welfare section. The latter was now directed by Dr. Königsberger.[115] The officials newly appointed to replace those who had been deported and the new staff workers, largely from "mixed marriages," had to take up their work in rooms at the Berlin Jewish Hospital on Iranische Strasse. The hospital served simultaneously as a sick ward, a prisoner camp, and a makeshift children's home. In place of the previous RV branches, i.e., the Gemeinden and district offices, there were now "agents" in forty-one cities whose task was to maintain contact with Berlin and organize welfare services locally.[116]

Down to the war's end, Jews in "mixed marriages" and Jewish "*Mischlinge*" (with one or two Jewish grandparents) were subjected to new conditions of persecution modeled on the compulsory community. Forced labor and residential concentration in *Judenhäuser* were once again characteristic features of such persecution.[117] Even in these dire circumstances, RV-officials attempted to make social conditions more tolerable for the victims, so as to enable them at least to survive.[118] Yet only with the Allied victory did genuine prospects emerge: not just for the small numbers of Jews who had survived the slaughter in the East, but also for the development of an independent, self-determining, pluralistic Jewish welfare system such as was soon to crystallize in the DP camps.

Conclusion

The anti-Jewish policy of the Nazi state, which, particularly in 1938, had aspired to demolish the very foundations of existence for German Jewry, deliberately and systematically, led to massive pauperization. From 1939 on, there was no longer any upper class within the Jewish population. Even when assets still existed, they lay deposited in blocked accounts. Conditions were compounded by a ban on commercial activity and forced labor, which closed the door on any ways to earn an independent living. The abrogation of state welfare in the wake of the *Kristallnacht* pogrom— at the same moment that vast numbers of Jews found themselves dependent for the first time on welfare support—created a completely new situation for Jewish welfare offices. Up until that juncture, they had provided only "charitable" aid intended to supplement public-welfare benefits. But the policies of the Nazi state brought an abrupt end to the voluntary community of solidarity and responsibility based on donations by the wealthy and care for the needy.

The traditional aid was supplanted by a Zwangsgemeinschaft, a compulsory community of the Jews in Germany. The new direction in "persecution policy" after the November 1938 pogrom was the driving force behind both the establishment of the new Reichsvereinigung under RSHA supervision and the creation of a separate "Jewish" welfare system. Even if some of the same personnel, all the way to members of the executive board, and part of the infrastructure of the old Reichsvertretung were utilized to set up the new compulsory organization, the RV, the differences in historical, political, and social conditions between the two organizations are striking, as is the discontinuity in previous goals and perspectives.

Under the press of constraints, assistance for individuals was no longer its main concern; rather, the work of Jewish welfare came to center on securing the subsistence of tens of thousands of persons condemned to a life of poverty and want. To effect this, it was necessary to build up a whole separate system of basic welfare care. In contrast with the previously dominant view among historians, there was thus no simple demolition or dismantling of Jewish welfare. Rather, the new situation was characterized by the historical paradox of an *expansion* of Jewish institutions in 1939 and 1940, under the stringent surveillance of the Security Police. This new centralized structure replaced the pluralistic infrastructure of earlier aid societies and welfare institutions.

Priority was given to those interests that served the persecution policy; there was also close surveillance over the organizational bureaucracy, finances and their use. In the spring of 1941, a radical disassembly of the system was initiated once again in light of the imminent deportation of the German-Jewish population. After the completion of the deportations, an organizational rump was allowed to carry on, perforce as a shadow of its former self and geared to providing for Jews in "mixed marriages" and so-called *Geltungsjuden*.[119]

The lack of any future perspective constituted the fateful fundamental constellation for the self-sacrificing and dedicated work of many officials, staff workers, and volunteers employed in the Jewish welfare offices. A long-term welfare policy was impossible. From 1939 on, to combat mass poverty in the Jewish population in the Third Reich meant creating halfway acceptable social conditions for a burgeoning number of the needy using a shrinking base of funds. After the war broke out, aid was oriented only to securing the basis for survival. Instead of positive promotion of the economy, the daily tasks centered initially on helping people to flee and, later on, easing the fate of forced laborers, prisoners and deportees.

Relief for structural poverty due to persecution resembled the labors of Sisyphus, because what one day had been laboriously constructed under the watchful eyes of the Gestapo was called into question the next by new harsh measures. The lives of officials and their staff workers were in constant danger. The "control agency" shipped off several members of the RV executive board to concentration camps for minor infractions. Among them was the head of the welfare department, Dr. Conrad Cohn, who perished in 1942 in Mauthausen.

The mass poverty generated by the persecution had a significant impact on fundamental political decisions by the Nazi leadership that affected the fate of the Jewish population as a whole, as well as their segregation and later deportation. For the individual victim of that policy, poverty and the welfare aid it necessitated consituted an enormous obstacle to successful emigration in the years 1938–39. In 1939 and 1940, both factors provided the labor offices with an argument for conscripting individuals for forced labor—and finally, in 1942, with a rationale for early deportation by the Gestapo.

Notes

1 This article is an expanded version of a paper presented at an international conference on "Jews and Poverty" organized by the Simon Dubnow Institute for Jewish History and Culture at the University of Leipzig in September 1997; the original German will be published in the conference proceedings, forthcoming.

2 Letter to Dr. Schäffer, July 24, 1942, reprinted in *Leo Baeck Institute Year Book* [LBIYB], 2 (1957), p. 312.

3 Cf. the more recent description of the fate of specific individuals up to 1933, and particularly in the subsequent period, by Stefanie Schüler-Springorum, "Elend und Furcht im Dritten Reich. Aus den Akten der Sammelvormundschaft der Jüdischen Gemeinde Berlin," *Zeitschrift für Geschichtswissenschaft*, 45 (1997), pp. 617–641, translated in this volume as "Fear and Misery in the Third Reich." On the general process of pauperization after 1933, see Shalom Adler-Rudel, *Jüdische Selbsthilfe unter dem Naziregime 1933–1939* (Tübingen: Verlag Mohr, 1974); Avraham Barkai, *From Boycott to Annihilation. The Economic Struggle of German Jews 1933–1943* (Hanover, NH: University Press of New England, 1989; German original, *Vom Boykott zur "Entjudung"* [Frankfurt am Main: Fischer, 1988]).

4 Avraham Barkai, "Der wirtschaftliche Existenzkampf der Juden im Dritten Reich 1933–1938," in Arnold Paucker, ed., *Die Juden im Nationalsozialistischen Deutschland. The Jews in Nazi Germany 1933–1943* (Tübingen: Verlag Mohr, 1986), p. 156. See Clemens Vollnhals, "Jüdische Selbsthilfe bis 1938," in Wolfgang Benz, ed., *Die Juden in Deutschland 1933–1945. Leben unter nationalsozialistischer Herrschaft* (Munich: C.H. Beck, 1988), pp. 314–412, here p. 374.

5 Wolf Gruner, "Die öffentliche Fürsorge und die deutschen Juden 1933–1942. Zur antijüdischen Politik der Städte, des Deutschen Gemeindetages und des Reichsministeriums," *Zeitschrift für Geschichtswissenschaft*, 45 (1997), pp. 599–606.

6 Wolf Gruner, *Judenverfolgung in Berlin 1933–1945. Eine Chronologie der Behördenmassnahmen in der Reichshauptstadt* (Berlin: Edition Hentrich, 1996), pp. 17–33. See Michael Wildt, ed., *Die Judenpolitik des SD 1935–1938. Eine Dokumentation* (Munich: Verlag R. Oldenbourg, 1995), pp. 82–84, doc. no. 6: "Lagebericht Sicherheitsdienst der SS (SD) D II 112 vom 25.6.1936"; Reichsvertretung der Juden in Deutschland, *Informationsblätter*, 6 (1938), no. 1/2, p. 4.

7 Funding from organizations such as the American Jewish Joint Distribution Committee or the Central Jewish Fund accounted for more than half of the

outlay for the Central Committee for Aid and Rehabilitation in the Reichsvertretung during the period 1933–1938; Vollnhals, "Jüdische Selbsthilfe," p. 317. For a thorough treatment of the Joint, see Yehuda Bauer, *My Brother's Keeper. A History of the American Joint Jewish Distribution Committee 1929–1939* (Philadelphia: Jewish Publication Society of America, 1974).

8   See Gruner, "Die öffentliche Fürsorge," p. 598.

9   The oft-cited figure of 16 percent of Jews still employed in the labor market, based on the May 1939 census, does not refer to the number remaining of those formerly in gainful employment, but indicates the extent of new, supervised job categories. Along with the small number of "medical practitioners" and "legal consultants" (so-called *Krankenbehandler* and *Konsulenten*, which were new Nazi terms for still-practicing physicians and lawyers), the figure included a few skilled manual workers, white-collar employees in Jewish institutions, and, in particular, conscripted laborers, whose ranks had swollen by then into the thousands; Wolf Gruner, *Der Geschlossene Arbeitseinsatz deutscher Juden. Zur Zwangsarbeit als Element der Verfolgung 1938 bis 1943* (Berlin: Metropol, 1997), p. 92.

10 If a person still had any assets, they were frozen in blocked accounts; "Arbeitsbericht der Reichsvertretung der Juden in Deutschland für das Jahr 1938" ["Arbeitsbericht Rvtr. 1938"], ms. (Berlin, 1939), Jerusalem, Leo Baeck Institute, pp. 15–16.

11 For a more extensive, initial exploration of this concept of persecution, see Gruner, *Der Geschlossene Arbeitseinsatz*, pp. 58–62, 334–335.

12 "Reichsvereinigung für die Betreuung jüdischer Auswanderer und fürsorgebedürftiger Juden"; see letter, "Werner Best (CdS) an Auswärtiges Amt," November 15, 1938, cited in Imtrud Wojak, *Exil in Chile. Die deutsch-jüdische Emigration während des Nationalsozialismus 1933–1945* (Berlin: Metropol, 1994), p. 46.

13 The holdings of the Federal Archives, formerly housed in different locations, have now been brought together and are mostly deposited in Berlin. "Vermerk über die Besprechung betr. Neuerteilung des Schulunterrichts an Juden am 1.12.1938" (n.d.), Federal Archives Berlin (Bundesarchiv; BA), 49.01 RMWiss, No. 11787, fols. 100–103; see also "Anwesenheitsliste und Niederschrift ü, die Besprechung betr. Neuerteilung des Schulunterrichts an Juden am 1.12." December 1, 1938, ibid., fols. 106–109RS.

14 On February 2, 1939, the welfare department of the newly created compulsory organization issued its first circular: "*Die Reichsvereinigung der Juden in Deutschland ist nunmehr als Gesamtorganisation aller Juden im Deutschen Reich—mit Ausnahme der Ostmark—geschaffen worden*"; Otto Dov Kulka, ed., *Deutsches Judentum unter dem Nationalsozialismus*. Vol. 1: *Dokumente zur Geschichte der Reichsvertretung der deutschen Juden 1933–1939* (Tübingen: Mohr-Siebeck, 1997), pp. 447–448. On February 17, 1939, the "Jewish public" was also informed of its establishment; *Jüdisches Nachrichtenblatt* (February 17, 1939), p. 1. See Kulka, *Deutsches Judentum*, pp. 448–449.

15 On the history of the Reichsvertretung, see Kulka, *Deutsches Judentum*.

16 Cf. for this opinion Esriel Hildesheimer, *Die Jüdische Selbstverwaltung unter dem NS-Regime. Der Existenzkampf der Reichsvertretung und Reichsvereinigung der Juden in Deutschland* (Tübingen: J.C.B. Mohr, 1994); Kulka, *Deutsches Judentum*, especially pp. 27–31, 441–446. See also Hans-Erich Fabian, "Zur Entstehung der 'Reichsvereinigung der Juden in Deutschland,'" in Herbert A. Strauss and Kurt R. Grossmann, eds., *Gegenwart und Rückblick. Festgabe für die Jüdische Gemeinde zu Berlin 25 Jahre nach dem Neubeginn* (Berlin: Lothar Stiem Verlag, 1970), pp. 165–179, and especially p. 170.

17 Cf, the relevant documents in Kulka, *Deutsches Judentuin*, pp. 410–430.

18 "Chef der Sipo und des SD (Müller)-Runderlass," February 5, 1939, Yad Vashem Archives (YVA), 051/OSOBI, no. 8 (500–2–87), fols. 1–2; see Kurt Pätzold, ed., *Verfolgung, Vertreibung, Vernichtung. Dokumente des faschistischen Antisemitismus 1933–1942* (Leipzig: Reclam, 1983), pp. 222–223, "Runderlass der Stapoleitstelle Düsseldorf," February 20, 1939, doc. no. 186.

19 "Schreiben Stuckarts (RMdI)," March 7, 1939, BA, R 18 RMdI, no. 5519, fol. 378. A draft of that same date was virtually identical with the later decree regarding the Reich Citizenship Law; see Kulka, *Deutsches Judentum*, p. 442, n. 5.

20 *Reichsgesetzblatt* (1939) I, p. 1097.

21 Publication of the decree and bylaws in *Jüdisches Nachrichtenblatt* (July 11, 1939), pp. 1–2.

22 "Bericht der Dt. Treuhand- und Revisionsanstalt (Stand vom 30.6.1940)," BA, 80 Re 1, no. 5019, fol. 7.' I am grateful to Thomas Jersch (Berlin) for calling this document to my attention.

23 "Satzungsentwurf des Reichsverbandes von 1938," in Kulka, *Deutsches Judentum*, pp. 418–424. "Satzung der Reichsvereinigung" in *Jüdisches Nachrichtenblatt* (July 11, 1939), pp. 1–2. Cf. in part similar arguments on discontinuity put forward earlier by Günter Plum, "Deutsche Juden oder Juden in Deutschland?," in Benz, ed., *Die Juden in Deutschland*, pp. 70–72.

24 *Jüdisches Nachrichtenblatt* (July 21, 1939). Only after Cohn had joined the executive board "via a by-election with approval by the control agency" subsequent to Heinrich Stahl's resignation in February 1940, was the area of welfare now represented *in persona*, even though Cohn was nominally in charge of the department that dealt with preparations for emigration; "Bericht der Dt. Treuhand- und Revisionsanstalt (Stand vom 30.6.1940)," BA, 80 Re 1, no. 5019, fols. 6–7; likewise, ibid., "Vermerk über RV-Vorstandsitzung," February 19, 1940, 75 C Re 1, no. 1, fol. 190.

25 On Württemberg, see Paul Sauer (comp.), *Dokumente über die Verfolgung der jüdischen Bürger in Baden-Württemberg durch das nationalsozialistische Regime 1933–1943*, II (Stuttgart: Kohlhammer, 1966), pp. 134–138, doc. nos. 375–377; on the Palatinate, see Kurt Düwell, *Die Rheingebiete in der Judenpolitik des Nationalsozialismus vor 1942* (Bonn: Ludwig Röhrscheid Verlag, 1968), p. 155; on Darmstadt, see "Jüdische Notstandsküche an IKG Darmstadt," May 15, 1939, Central Archives for the History of the Jewish People (CAHJP) Jerusalem, Darmstadt III, no. 145, no fol.; on Frankfurt am Main, see Kommission zur Erforschung der Geschichte der Frankfurter Juden, ed., *Dokumente zur Geschichte der Frankfurter Juden* (Frankfurt am Main: Verlag Waldemar Kramer, 1963), VI 43–VI 45, pp. 319–323; on Göttingen, see "Notizen," December 7, 1938, and February 16, 1939, Municipal Archives Göttingen, Sozialamt, Acc. No. 407/77, no. 47/1, no fol.

26 In Hamburg, the Gestapo dissolved the Council of Representatives, abrogated the community constitution and appointed Dr. Max Plaut as director of a newly created Jewish Religious Association (Jüdischer Religionsverband) and head of all Jewish organizations in Hamburg; see "Bericht über Arbeit der Religionsgemeinde Ende 1938 bis Ende 1940" (c. May 1941), State Archives Hamburg, 522–1 Jüdische Gemeinden, no. 991 a, fol. 33.

27 In 1939, he acted initially on instructions from the municipality, from 1940 on as ordered by the Gestapo; see Lutz Becht, "Der Beauftragte der Geheimen Staatspolizei bei der jüdischen Wohlfahrtspflege in Frankfurt am Main," in *Frankfurt am Main, Lindenstrasse. Gestapozentrale und Widerstand* (Frankfurt am Main: Campus-Verlag, 1996), pp. 87–99.

28 "Dr. Conrad Cohn (RV) an IKG München," August 26, 1940, BA, 75 C Re 1, no. 761, fol. 94.
29 *Reichsgesetzblatt* (1938) I, p. 1649.
30 Gruner, "Die öffentliche Fürsorge," pp. 606–610. Cf. "Arbeitsbericht Rvtr. 1938," p. 16.
31 Privileged groups, such as small pensioners, disabled veterans or war widows, and war orphans, no longer received any special benefits. Only severely disabled Jewish veterans were left in a somewhat better position; "Arbeitsbericht Rvtr. 1938," p. 17. On the whole, there were diverse welfare practices in different cities; Munich, for example, introduced a reduced "payment schedule for Jews" (*Judenrichtsatz*); Gruner, "Die öffentliche Fürsorge," p. 609.
32 Wolf Gruner, "Die Berichte über die Jüdische Winterhilfe von 1938/39 bis 1941/42. Dokumente jüdischer Sozialarbeit zwischen Selbstbehauptung und Fremdbestimmung nach dem Novemberpogrom," *Jahrbuch für Antisemitismusforschung* 1 (1992), pp. 307–341. Cf. Adler-Rudel, *Jüdische Selbsthilfe*, pp. 164–165. Jewish communities such as Hamburg also utilized funds from the Winter Relief to ease their budgetary burden in providing for institutions and institutional homes; "Bericht über Arbeit der Religionsgemeinde 1938 bis 1940" (c. May 1941), State Archives Hamburg, 522–1, no. 991 a, fol. 30.
33 "Bericht der Abwicklungsstelle für Organisationen bei der Reichsvereinigung über die Entwicklung des Vereinswesens 1933–1941," November 7, 1941, BA, 75 C Re 1, no. 31, fol. 235.
34 Ibid. In Frankfurt an der Oder, for example, there were forty-two associations in 1937; that number had plummeted to just eighteen by the end of 1938; "SDOA Ost Bericht," January 13, 1939, YVA, 051/OSOBI, no. 47, no fol.
35 Some of the central institutions were formally incorporated in October 1939 into the RV; among the social institutions were the Jewish Employment Aid Office (Jüdische Arbeitshilfe) and the National Committee of Jewish Youth Associations. This was also the case with the remaining professional associations and political organizations, most of which had been forced to shut down their operations in November 1938; "Bericht der Abwicklungsstelle für Organisationen bei der Reichsvereinigung," November 7, 1941, BA 75 C Ro 1, no. 31, fols. 235–237.
36 As a leading welfare organization, the Central Welfare Agency for German Jews had belonged, since 1924, to the German League of Independent Welfare Services. On its history until 1933, see Giora Lotan, "The Zentralwohlfahrtsstelle," *LBIYB* 4 (1959), pp. 185–207. After 1933 it lost its top-level status and had to withdraw from the League, which a short time later was restructured as the Reich Association of Independent Welfare Services (Reichsgemeinschaft der freien Wohlfahrtspflege); on this, see Christoph Sachsse and Florian Tennstedt, *Der Wohlfahrtsstaat im Nationalsozialismus. Geschichte der Armenfürsorge in Deutschland*, vol. 3 (Stuttgart: Kohlhammer, 1992), pp. 132–136.
37 "Anordnung des Stellvertreter des Führers Nr. 1/39," January 17, 1939, *Der Prozess gegen die Hauptkriegsverbrecher vor dem Internationalen Militärgerichtshof* [IMT], vol. XXV (Nuremberg, 1948), pp. 131–132. Cf. Sauer, *Dokumente über die Verfolgung*, II, no. 339, pp. 83–84. See also on the decree on the deployment of Jewish assets, *Jüdisches Nachrichtenblatt*, no. 16 (February 24, 1939).
38 "Israelitischer Wohltätigkeitsverein an Stapoleitstelle Leipzig," March 15, 1939, State Archives Leipzig, Polizeipräsidium Leipzig-V, no. 4442, fol. 6.

39 The social-welfare office in Hamburg had reserved for itself the right to oversee payments. Officials in the Jewish community anticipated that welfare expenditures would rise from RM 643,000 in 1938 to almost RM 1.5 million in 1940. This also meant that there was no longer a positive balance between outlay and revenue as in times past, and the budget was now overdrawn. An initial deficit of RM 500,000 for 1939 doubled the following year, due in the main precisely to the spurt in welfare costs; "Sitzung des Vorstandes am 23.10.1939," State Archives Hamburg, 522–1, no. 985 c, fol. 1; "Sitzung Ende November 1939," ibid., fol. 4; see also "Bericht über Arbeit der Religionsge-meinde Ende 1938 bis Ende 1940" (c. May 1941), ibid., no. 991 a, fols. 10–12.

40 From November 1, 1939, the RV had to take over all costs for institutional welfare; Gruner, "Die öffentliche Fürsorge," p. 610. For the RV this meant that instead of participating with a partial payment of RM 15 per individual, it had to assume the full expenses (RM 90 per person) for some 1,000 mentally ill in public nursing homes; see "Arbeitsbericht der Reichsvereinigung der Juden in Deutschland für das Jahr 1939" ["Arbeitsbericht RV 1939"], ms. (Berlin, 1940), p. 38.

41 "Arbeitsbericht RV 1939," p. 32.

42 Funding for Germany just from the Joint jumped from $686,000 in 1938 to $978,102 in 1939; see Bauer, *My Brother's Keeper*, p. 258.

43 The so-called *Auswandererabgabe*; "Arbeitsbericht RV 1939," p. 8.

44 Revenue from this "tax" was initially utilized to cover the budget deficit in Hamburg and, after March 1939, was passed on to the RV; "Bericht über Arbeit der Religionsgemeinde Ende 1938 bis Ende 1940" (c. May 1941), State Archives Hamburg, 522–1, no. 991 a, fols. 38–39.

45 The welfare department of the RV had to caution people to adhere to the guidelines; "Rundschreiben Nr. 1017," December 14, 1939, CAHJP Jerusalem, JCR/S no. 7, fol. 199; see also "Dr. Conrad Cohn (RV) an IKG München (Dr. Neumeyer)," August 26, 1940, BA, 75 C Re 1, no. 761, fol. 94.

46 "Arbeitsbericht RV 1939," p. 35.

47 See the call issued by the RV district office in Baden at the beginning of 1939 to hand in all "dispensable articles," such as shoes and underwear, for the clothing distribution shops. The synagogue councils were now organizing collections four times a year; see Josef Werner, *Hakenkreuz und Judenstern. Das Schicksal der Karlsruher Juden im Dritten Reich*, 2nd rev. ed. (Karlsruhe: Badenia, 1990), p. 296.

48 "Bericht über Arbeit der Religionsgemeinde 1938 bis 1940" (c. May 1941), State Archives Hamburg, 522–1, no. 991 a, fol. 35.

49 Gruner, "Die Berichte über die Jüdische Winterhilfe," p. 313.

50 "Notiz für Dr. Eppstein," July 7, 1939, BA, 75 C Re 1, no. 1, fol. 96.

51 At the end of 1938, there were sixty-seven homes; this had risen to ninety by the end of 1939, and to 122 with 7,000 places in 1940; Adler-Rudel, *Jüdische Selbsthilfe*, p. 170; "RV-Statistik über Zahl der Heime 1940," BA 75 C Re 1, no. 1, fol. 175.

52 Robert Prochnik, "Bericht über die organisatorischen und sonstigen Verhält-nisse der jüdischen Bevölkerung in Berlin und unter Berücksichtigung des gesamten Altreichs, Stand 31.7.1941," ms. (Vienna, 1941), pp. 23–27.

53 Adler-Rudel, *Jüdische Selbsthilfe*, p. 171.

54 "Arbeitsbericht RV 1939," p. 38.

55 Between January and September 1939, there was a huge wave of some 62,000 emigrants, many of whom received aid from Jewish relief agencies. Of the approximately 5,000 who emigrated from the outbreak of the war to the end

of 1939, some two-thirds received funds from the RV; see "Arbeitsbericht RV 1939," pp. 12–14.

56 Ibid., p. 29. These expenses had been divided between the communities and the RV. After the small communities were disbanded, the RV took on the total burden. In July 1939, there was a total of 3,425 training places (1,500 in the skilled manual trades; 1,555 in agriculture); see Adler-Rudel, *Jüdische Selbsthilfe*, p. 157 and appendix, p. 204.

57 On this entire complex, see Gruner, *Der Geschlossene Arbeitseinsatz*, pp. 55–119.

58 Cited in ibid., pp. 118–119; see Adler-Rudel, *Jüdische Selbsthilfe*, pp. 160–161.

59 See "Entwurf Eingabe RV (Dr. Arthur Lilienthal/Berthold Auerbach) an Reichsarbeitsministerium," July 17, 1939, BA, 75 C Re 1, no. 1, fols. 90–106. In Leipzig, a shelter for the homeless was set up in a former private synagogue, see *Leipziger Neueste Nachrichten* (October 31, 1939). On Munich, see IKG München an

60 On aid for forced laborers, see Gruner, *Der Geschlossene Arbeitseinsatz*, pp. 118, 132. In Bavaria, the RV welfare department, working together with the section for schools in the RV district office, saw to it that Jewish children also received vitamin tablet supplements, as was common practice in the public schools; "RV/Bezirksstelle Bayern an IKG Aschaffenburg," December 31, 1940, CAHJP Jerusalem, Inv. No. 346, no fol.

61 In order to make sure there was enough food, the standard generic brand of margarine was declared kosher parve, even though it contained animal fat. Since kosher meat was no longer available, other permitted types of meat were used in the canteens and prepared in strict accordance with religious dietary laws; "Sitzung des Vorstandes Ende November 1939," State Archives Hamburg, 522–1, no. 985 c, fol. 4; "Sitzung des Vorstandes November 1940," ibid., fol. 22.

62 For example, the RV provided aid for deportees from Schneidemühl, those who remained behind, and a certain number who later returned destitute from Poland to Germany; "RV-Schreiben an Hauptamt Sipo, Anlage," April 9, 1940, BA 75 C Re 1, no. 483, fols. 214–215; "Rücksprache im Gestapa am 1.4.1940," ibid., fols. 218–220.

63 "RV-Haushaltsplan für das 1. Halbjahr 1940," BA 75 C Re 1, no. 1, fols. 40–58.

64 The second-largest item in the budget was preparation for emigration, RM 4.2 million, though it also contained hidden welfare expenditures; third-largest was vocational training, amounting to RM 1.9 million, "Bericht der Dt. Treuhand- und Revisionsanstalt (Stand vom 30.6.1940)," BA, 80 Re 1, no. 5019, fols. 10–13; see also "RV-Haushaltsplan für das 1. Halbjahr 1940," BA, 75 C Re 1, no. 1, fols. 40–58; "RV-Voranschlag für das 2. Halbjahr 1940," BA, fol. 146.

65 "Anlage Organisation der RV (Stand vom 30.6.1940)," BA, 80 Re 1, no. 5019, fol. 30.

66 "RV-Voranschlag für das 2. Halbjahr 1940," BA, 75 C Re 1, no. 1, fol. 146.

67 Gruner, *Der Geschlossene Arbeitseinsatz*, pp. 133–150.

68 "Rundschreiben der RV-BSt. Baden vom 1.7.1940," CAHJP Jerusalem, JCR/S 7, no fol.

69 Thus, they tried concomitantly to integrate unemployed Jews into certain aid agencies or training programs; see Gruner, *Der Geschlossene Arbeitseinsatz*, p. 119.

70 "Bericht der Dt. Treuhand- und Revisionsanstalt (Stand vom 30.6.1940)," BA, 80 Re 1, no. 5019, fols. 10–13.

71 "RV-Voranschlag für das 2. Halbjahr 1940," BA, 75 C Re 1, no. 1, fols. 140–153.

72 "Vorladung ins Gestapa am 25.6.1940," BA, 75 C Re 1, no. 45, fol. 178.

73 Gruner, *Der Geschlossene Arbeitseinsatz*, pp. 161–178.

74 "Anhang zu Voranschlag für RV-Etat des 1. Halbjahres 1941," BA, 75 C Re 1, no. 64, fol. 9. More than 2,800 Jews who had been on the welfare rolls of the Berlin State Welfare Office until the end of 1940 lost their claim to benefits; Wolf Gruner, "Die Reichshauptstadt und die Verfolgung der Berliner Juden 1933–1945," in Reinhard Rürup, ed., *Jüdische Geschichte in Berlin. Essays und Studien* (Berlin: Hentrich, 1995), pp. 229–266, here p. 245.

75 "Vorstandssitzung des Jüd. Religionsverbandes," December 15, 1940, State Archives Hamburg, 522–1, no. 985 c, fol. 26.

76 "Voranschlag für RV-Etat des 1. Halbjahres 1941," BA, 75 C Re 1, no. 64, fol. 63. The maximum daily maintenance allowance for persons in institutional homes was reduced to only RM 0.90, and residents had to take care of all housework. Laundry had to be done in the homes themselves, and vegetable gardens had to be planted on institution grounds. In addition, they wished to set maximum levels for the salaries of community and RV staff; "RV/Abt. Fürsorge-Rundschreiben," January 5, 1941, BA, 75 C Re 1, no. 484, fols. 154–156; "Vorstandssitzung des Jüdischen Religionsverbandes," December 15, 1940, State Archives Hamburg, 522–1, no. 985 c, fol. 27.

77 "Protokoll der RV-Vorstandssitzung," December 20, 1940, BA, 75 C Re 1, no. 2, fol. 72; "Protokoll," January 6, 1941, ibid., fol. 69.

78 Jewish disabled veterans received benefits in accordance with existing legislation just like their "Aryan" counterparts. This was standard procedure for war victims in Hildesheim, Braunschweig, and Bielefeld; by contrast, in towns such as Minden and Wolfenbüttel, in actual practice full maintenance was not provided; "RV/Abt. Fürsorge-Kriegsopfer an RV Berlin," August 25, 1941, ibid., no. 752, fol. 177 + RS.

79 The RSHA thwarted attempts in Aachen, Brandenburg, and Munich to set up special camps for the Jewish inhabitants; "Aktennotiz 30/41 ü. Vorladung ins RSHA," March 21, 1941, BA, 75 C Re 1, no. 45, fol. 13; "Aktennotiz 19/41 ü. Vorladung ins RSHA," March 8, 1941, ibid., fol. 47.

80 Gruner, "Die öffentliche Fürsorge," pp. 610–613.

81 For all examples see Gruner, *Der Geschlossene Arbeitseinsatz*, pp. 121, 165–167.

82 "Notiz Nr. 27 über Vorladung," March 17, 1941, BA, 75 C Re 1, no. 45, fol. 26.

83 "RV-Organisationsplan (Stand vom 1.9.1941)," ibid., 75 C Re 1, no. 31, fol. 139. On the situation in 1940, see Bericht der Dt. Treuhand- und

84 Heavy cuts in numbers and personnel in the RV district offices were pushed through, which particularly affected emigration departments and their advisory positions; Prochnik, "Bericht," pp. 11–12.

85 For budgetary reasons, schools had to merge or downsize their teaching staffs; "RV-Vorstandssitzung," February 17, 1941, BA, 75 C Re 1, no. 2, fol. 64; "Sitzung RV-Vorstand," February 23, 1941, ibid., fol. 62.

86 Gruner, *Der Geschlossene Arbeitseinsatz*, p. 182.

87 "Aktennotiz 7/41 ü. Vorladung im RSHA," February 20, 1941, BA, 75 C Re 1, no. 45, fol. 77 + RS.

88 If one adds the small number in independent professions or training schemes and the more than 6,000 working in RV administration, welfare and district offices, the estimated 59,000 fit and able to work were all employed; Gruner, *Der Geschlossene Arbeitseinsatz*, p. 280.

89 *Der Aufbau* (August 1, 1941).
90 Prochnik, "Bericht," pp. 1–4.
91 "Rundschreiben," February 27, 1941, BA, 75 C Re 1, no. 4, fols. 14–15. The welfare department was forced to reduce the daily amount for maintenance in institutional homes, slashing it to RM 0.75 per person; "RV-Vorstandssitzung," February 17, 1941, BA, 75 Re 1, no. 2, fol. 64; "RV-Vorstandssitzung," February 23, 1941, ibid., fol. 62.
92 Prochnik, "Bericht," pp. 23–27.
93 Gruner, *Der Geschlossene Arbeitseinsatz*, pp. 249–262.
94 Prochnik, "Bericht," pp. 1–4.
95 Twenty percent went for non-institutional welfare (cash benefits, foster homes, non-institutional medical care). Forty-five percent was allocated for institutional welfare (benefits for wards/foster children, residents in RV-operated and other homes for the elderly, nursing homes for the infirm, youth homes, other types of residential institutions or hospitals) and 5 percent for meals for the needy; Prochnik, "Bericht," pp. 12–14.
96 Ibid., pp. 15–17.
97 "Brief von Selma Ebert an die RV-Bezirksstelle Brandenburg-Ostpreussen, eingeg. am 14.9.1941," BA, 75 C Re 1, no. 739, fol. 15. On her living conditions, see ibid., fols. 54, 130, 154; "Notizen," March 27 and February 14, 1939, June 14, 1940.
98 "Notiz über Vorsprache Löwenherz bei Brunner," October 2, 1941, cited in Hans Safrian, *Die Eichmann-Männer* (Vienna and Zurich 1993), p. 120. The Jewish Community in Berlin was informed on October 1 about the "partial evacuation"; "Bericht Hildegard Henschel," p. 3, YVA, 01/51, no fol.
99 Especially as a consequence of the transports, the clothing-distribution shops were under a heavy strain. In October, 840 persons had to be given clothing, as opposed to a previous monthly average of 300; "Bericht über Arbeit der Religionsgemeinde im Jahr 1941," State Archives Hamburg, 522–1, no. 991 a, fol. 48.
100 Ibid., fol. 42. See also Schüler-Springorum, "Fear and Misery," in this volume.
101 "Bericht über Arbeit der Religionsgemeinde im Jahr 1941," State Archives Hamburg, 522–1, no. 991 a, fols. 42–43.
102 *Reichsministerialblatt der Inneren Verwaltung* (1941), p. 1951; see "Vermerk der RV/Abt. Fürsorge vom 19.8.1942 als Anlage für das RSHA vom 20.8.1942," BA, 75 C Re 1, no. 759, fol. 1.
103 The Jewish Community in Berlin was permitted to provide the needy with only RM 24 a month per person instead of RM 30, which was the amount at the time deemed the necessary minimum for survival; "Tabelle mit Richtsätzen der RV-Bezirksstellen, Anlage zum Vermerk vom 19.8.1942," BA, 75 C Re 1, no. 759, fol. 2; Prochnik, "Bericht," p. 23.
104 Margarete S., a forced laborer at Siemens, was moonlighting at her old profession as a seamstress; see transcription of interview with Margarete S., Berlin, March 25, 1990, p. 9.
105 Schüler-Springorum, "Fear and Misery".
106 In Breslau, there were almost 2,000 persons, in Berlin 5,000. In 1940–1941, the total figure amounted to 37,000 of 170,000 Jews, slightly over 21 percent; "Bericht der RV/Abt. Fürsorge über die JWH 1941/42"; Gruner, "Die Berichte über die Jüdische Winterhilfe," p. 341, doc. no. 4.
107 "Runderlass RSHA (IV B 4)," April 2, 1942, Wiener Library, doc. no. 605, no fol. My thanks once again to Thomas Jersch for pointing out this reference.
108 "Notiz über Vorsprache im RSHA," May 29/30, 1942, cited in Hans Safrian, *Die Eichmann-Männer*, p. 175.

109 "Rundschreiben RV-Bezirksstelle Rheinland," June 17, 1942, CAHJP Jerusalem, HM-No. 4718, no fol.
110 *Jüdisches Nachrichtenblatt* (June 19, 1942).
111 "Notiz Henschel (RV) ü. Rücksprache bei Gestapo Berlin," September 28, 1942, BA, 75 C Re 1, film 52407–23, fol. 83. Cf. "Notiz Henschel über Vorsprache bei Gestapo Berlin," September 4, 1942, Leo Baeck Institute Archives New York, Max Kreuzberger Research Papers, Ar 7183, Box 2, Folder 2.
112 "Aufstellung der RV/Abt. Fürsorge vom 4.9.1942," BA, 75 C Re 1, no. 759, fol. 3.
113 "RV-September-Statistik," YVA, 08/no. 14, no fol.
114 "Vermerk Leo Schindler," August 12, 1943, BA, 75 C Re 1, no. 9, fol. 780.
115 "RV-Organisationsplan vom 1.7.1943," ibid., no. 10, fol. 7.
116 This refers to the so-called *Vertrauensmänner*. "Rundschreiben Nr. 1," July 9, 1943, BA, 75 C Re 1, no. 23, fol. 14. More generally, cf. Barkai, *From Boycott to Annihilation*, pp. 184–185; see also Wolfgang Benz, "Überleben im Untergrund," in Benz, ed., *Die Juden in Deutschland*, pp. 690–700.
117 Gruner, *Der Geschlossene Arbeitseinsatz*, pp. 322–330.
118 See "Notiz Kleemann," October 15, 1943, and "Bericht Neumann für Lustig," October 8, 1943, BA, 75 C Re 1, no. 61, fols. 45, 48.
119 In Nazi "racial biology," the category *Geltungsjude* comprised persons with two Jewish grandparents who were nonetheless "considered in legal terms" as full Jews (*Volljuden*)—and not as so-called first-degree *Mischlinge*—because at the time the Nuremberg Laws were promulgated they had belonged to the Jewish religious community or were married to a Jew; see Horst Seidler and Andreas Rett, *Das Reichssippenamt entscheidet. Rassenbiologie und Nationalsozialismus* (Vienna and Munich 1982), pp. 114–115.

19

IN THE SHADOW OF AUSCHWITZ

The murder of the Jews of East Upper
Silesia

Sybille Steinbacher

Source: Ulrich Herbert (ed.), *National Socialist Extermination Policies. Contemporary Perspectives and Controversies,* New York/Oxford: Berghahn, 2000, pp. 276–305.

At the largest of the National Socialist concentration and extermination camps, Jews from throughout Europe were gassed, shot, hanged, poisoned, and killed in medical experiments. At the outbreak of the Second World War, roughly 100,000 Jews were living within thirty kilometers of the future site of the gas chambers, in the province immediately surrounding Auschwitz. Their fate has never been the subject of historical research; nor has the concrete political history of the area around Auschwitz been examined.[1] And yet East Upper Silesia served as an advanced outpost for National Socialist policies of race and conquest. Not only was the region one of the principal sites of the murder of Jews in eastern Europe, as one of the four annexed eastern areas, it also played a significant role in policies of resettlement and Germanization. Along with the Ruhr, East Upper Silesia was also one of the most important centers of arms production in the German Reich. Unlike in the Warthegau, East Prussia, and Danzig-West Prussia, anti-Jewish policy was guided largely by economic principles. As the focus of conflicting economic interests and ideological dogmas, extermination policy in the province underwent a unique evolution. Given the immediate proximity of Auschwitz-Birkenau, certain questions all but clamor for answers: What became of the Jewish population? What were the consequences of the policies of race and conquest, resettlement and forced labor? Was the "Final Solution," in its organization and dynamics, attuned to the concentration and extermination camp?—or to put the matter another way: Were the Jews

110

of East Upper Silesia delivered especially swiftly and thoroughly into the machinery of destruction?

A wealth of newly released empirical material serves to focus our inquiries into "Jewish policy"[2] and the murder of the Jews of East Upper Silesia on several key connections within the context of a sophisticated study of the details of National Socialist extermination policy.[3] Against a background examination into the impetus toward increasingly radical measures arising in the occupied territories and affecting the decisions of the Berlin government, we shall investigate how resettlement policy and "Jewish policy" were functionally related, as well as how the anti-Jewish campaign was conceptually integrated into occupation policy. In addition, the role of agents operating at middle and lower administrative levels of persecution and extermination policy, their freedom of action, and their individual initiatives are of great interest in connection with an investigation of relevant bureaucratic processes of decision-making and implementation. Moreover, the issue of the influence exerted by individual circumstances on the long-range planning of anti-Jewish policy is of great importance, as is the issue of the role played by economic factors in the process of the "Final Solution." Not the least of our concerns is the role played by ideological factors in setting the murder of the Jews in motion.

I

Anti-Jewish policy was in no sense purposely steered toward mass murder in carefully prepared, increasingly radical phases. At least in the initial phase, a definitive program contrived to culminate in "eradication," destruction, and murder did not exist. On the contrary, interruptions and fluctuations were typical, with expulsion being the underlying aim of "Jewish policy" in East Upper Silesia in the early stages. That the occupying forces were ready to resort to open violence was clear from the beginning. Even the early days of September 1939 were marked by terror, when Einsatzgruppe z.b.V. under SS-Obergruppenführer Udo von Woyrsch began to advance from Kattowitz behind the rear guard of the 14th Army of Wehrmacht Army Group South. The force had been rapidly assembled from mixed units of security and regular police specifically for duty in Upper Silesia on Himmler's teletyped order of the evening of 3 September.[4] Due to the Silesian uprisings at the beginning of the 1920s, it was assumed that an especially large number of activists in the resistance would be operating in the region. Although the *SS-Einsatzgruppen* in the Polish campaign clearly had no orders to target Jews, Einsatzgruppe z.b.V., in contrast to other special units, unleashed a wave of systematic violence against the Jewish population, which included mass executions and attacks on Jewish institutions.[5] Presumably those acts were carried out on the personal initiative of SS-Obergruppenführer Udo von Woyrsch,[6]

111

who, as one of Himmler's favorites, clearly enjoyed broad freedom of action in "Jewish matters."[7] A genocidal mentality had already manifested itself in German units in the first days of the war. The brutality of their behavior is clear enough in those few but eloquent entries in the daily reports of Einsatzgruppe z.b.V. referring to "synagogues catching fire," "incidental shootings," "pacification actions," and "shooting insurgents."[8]

Even those East Upper Silesian Jews who initially managed to flee from the marauding troops were subjected to openly capricious violence. At least, 2,000 Jews, and possibly many more, were permanently forced into the Soviet sphere of influence when Eduard Wagner, General Quartermaster of the Army High Command, closed the border at the San.[9] Those who remained in the German sphere of influence suffered the full weight of racist policy. As early as 4 September, the Head of the Civilian Administration (CdZ) issued a decree concerning "the property of persons who have fled."[10] The exclusion of the Jewish population from the economic life of East Upper Silesia introduced by that decree was the first act of state-sponsored anti-Jewish policy. "Jewish policy" began so swiftly and with such vehemence that the Jews were already economically and socially marginalized before the administrative structure was fully in place. Within days the occupying forces had confiscated Jewish-owned landed property, houses and lots, businesses and shops, as well as closing and padlocking shops, freezing security bonds and bank accounts, and blocking access to safety deposit boxes. When German trustees, acting on orders from Georg Brandt, military commander for Upper Silesia, confiscated Jewish business enterprises, economic "aryanization" became systematic. Jews were dispossessed, deprived of legal rights, humiliated, and reduced to a state of panic from the very outset.

In September 1939, Jews comprised barely 5 percent of the entire population of the province. With its 7.46 million inhabitants, Silesia was the most populous of the four annexed territories in the East; covering roughly 48,000 square kilometers, it was also the largest. In a complicated administrative restructuring in October 1939, the two newly established administrative units in Oppeln and Kattowitz were added to the existing Silesian government districts of Breslau and Liegnitz, which had been part of the Old Reich.[11] Silesia was thus expanded to include not only the formerly Prussian industrial area around Kattowitz, Beuthen, Hindenburg, and Königshütte, along with the coal mines in the Dombrowa and Olsa region, but also territories lying far beyond the once disputed territory that had been awarded to Poland in accordance with the arbitration agreement reached in Geneva in May 1922. Thus, the Reich was expanded to include areas populated exclusively by Poles and Polish-speaking Jews. These were districts that, prior to the First World War, had been part of Russian-controlled Congress Poland and the Austro-Hungarian Kingdom of Galicia; they had never before belonged to the German—or Prussian—

sphere of influence.[12] These areas, bordering directly on the Government General, were added to the Kattowitz government district and officially annexed by the German Reich.

The administrative relationships in the new territories were of primary importance for the evolution of "Jewish policy," because plans for ethnic restructuring were strongly influenced by the location of the borders. The so-called police line, which was drawn at the end of November 1939, was of incomparably more importance for the Kattowitz district than its customs and administrative border with the Government General. It not only ran through the middle of the district but also created two legally distinct areas, each of which had its own political priorities.[13] Throughout the entire occupation, the Kattowitz district remained deeply divided both ethnically and administratively. To the west of the police line lay so-called East Upper Silesia—the main industrial "plebiscite" area. This area had been the bone of contention in the border dispute between the German Reich and Poland after the First World War. It contained about a million Poles, along with approximately 600,000 people of varying ethnicity—the mixed population typical of Silesia, which was bilingual and could not be definitively assigned to a single nation. In addition, there were about 300,000 Germans and people of German descent, as well as roughly 5,000 Jews. East of the police line, however, in the newly acquired, purely Polish areas, the population consisted almost exclusively of "people of alien ethnicity," totaling about 750,000 Poles and between 90,000 and 100,000 Jews. That area—which included Auschwitz, then a city with 7,000 to 8,000 Jews—was condescendingly referred to as the "East Strip." Auschwitz had second-class status for a short period following its annexation at the end of October 1939, but was, from May 1941 on, legally equivalent to cities in the Old Reich.[14] The Auschwitz of the "Final Solution"—and historical studies of the period have not registered this fact—did not lie in a geographically nebulous "East," but was a city on what was at that time German soil.

Because the Jewish portion of the Silesian population had been small to the point of being undetectable prior to the annexation of the East Strip,[15] the so-called Jewish question became an issue for the province only with its eastward expansion in the fall of 1939. The almost exclusively orthodox Jews in the East Strip had virtually nothing in common with the largely assimilated, German-speaking Jewish population living west of the police line. Bound by traditional rites and customs, with their ear locks and long beards, typically dressed in kaftans, they corresponded precisely to the stereotypes subscribed to by the German occupiers, who had been indoctrinated in antisemitism.

The occupation forces saw the large concentrations of Poles and Jews in the East Strip as posing serious risks to the Upper Silesian industrial area with its rich coal deposits, and its iron, zinc, copper, and steel works. In terms of economic and ethnic policy, the police line was intended to prevent ostensibly negative influences from coming in from the eastern districts. The line, which separated from the Old Reich all of Danzig-West Prussia and the Warthegau but only those parts of Silesia and East Prussia comprising the newly acquired regions, was not a national border. Nevertheless, as far as police matters and passport control were concerned, it effectively turned the annexed regions into foreign territories—or into Reich territories of second-class status.[16] In the Kattowitz district the police line was intended to secure the western part economically and promote its development as a self-contained, independent economic area. The line was supposed to protect the economy by reducing unwanted immigration from the East Strip, preventing smuggling and illicit trade, and safeguarding the western zones' labor force. The police line was an ethnic wall separating a western zone marked for Germanization from an area that was to be isolated and exploited in accord with ethnic policy. The line held the "ethnically alien" inhabitants within the East Strip, prevented free movement and flight, and thus had an important logistic function in the pursuit of the overarching political goal of "ethnic reordering."

In his new capacity as Reich Commissar for the strengthening of the German Nation (RKF), to which Hitler had appointed him on 7 October 1939, Reichsführer SS (RFSS) Heinrich Himmler was in charge of Germanization in the territories in western Poland.[17] Now responsible for the systematic expulsion of the "racially inferior" Poles and Jews, he succeeded in combining his existing authority in security matters with his new responsibilities so as to establish an enormous power base in the conquered East. The goal of the planned population transfers, for which Himmler created an independent SS apparatus, was to create through resettlement policy a durable core population of Germans cleansed of "racially alien elements" that would serve as a basis for the racial-biological restructuring of all of Europe under German hegemony. The ideological program was to pursue Germanization by radically denationalizing the occupied areas in the East, reconstituting them both economically and socially, and systematically repopulating them with "racially valuable" volksdeutsch and reichsdeutsch immigrants.[18]

That three-step master plan for implementing ethnic policy envisioned the liquidation of the intellectual and political elite along with property owners, the expulsion of all Jews and most Poles, and the strict segregation of the remaining Polish population from the settlers, who would be German or of German descent. That racist program, euphemistically called "resettlement," was organized in the annexed eastern territories through the so-called short-term plans (Nahpläne) and began to be implemented between October 1939 and March 1941. The violent methods employed in the name of "ethnic reordering" impacted the indigenous Jews and Poles in East Upper Silesia in equal measure. In this phase, anti-

Jewish policy and anti-Polish policy were based on exactly the same political premises, pursued the same goal, and were organized by the German bureaucracy as being essentially indistinguishable.[19]

II

During the tenure of Gauleiter and Oberpräsident Josef Wagner, relations between the civilian authorities on the one hand and the SS and police on the other were characterized by vigorous conflict over policies of ethnic restructuring. Wagner, a "veteran of the party's political struggle," hence a close confidant of Hitler, had governed in the province since 1935.[20] With the outbreak of the war, due to the constitutionally unique status of the annexed eastern territories,[21] his already far-reaching authority was expanded to embrace additional responsibilities. Together with Fritz Dietlof Graf von der Schulenburg, who served as deputy Oberpräsident in Breslau from 1939, Wagner developed ambitious measures for Germanizing the province. This area was an especially prestigious one because the *gauleiters* were carrying out a personal commission of the "Führer." Hitler proclaimed at the end of September 1939 that, "at the end of ten years," he demanded from them "just one announcement": "namely that their districts were German, and in fact pure German. He would not, however, ask what methods they had used in order to make their districts German, and he would not care if it was later demonstrated that the methods employed to secure control of the area had been neither nice nor exactly legal."[22]

In the area of Germanization policy, Himmler's desire to establish the SS in the conquered East as his own territorial regime independent of civilian authority stood in diametric opposition to the ambitions of Wagner and Schulenburg. In their struggle with the SS, however, the civilian authorities were never motivated by an inclination to object to the forcible expulsion of Poles and Jews on humanitarian grounds. Neither Schulenburg, who at a later stage was one of the leaders of the nationalist conservative opposition and one of the architects of the attempted coup of 20 July 1944, nor Wagner was likely to put up any opposition.[23] Both men were convinced that the "Aryan" race represented a superior level of civilization; they struggled with the SS solely over administrative control of ethnic matters while their interest in the racial and economic protection of the German people was quite in accord with the goals of the SS.

In the fall of 1939, full authority over resettlement policy lay with Gauleiter and Oberpräsident Josef Wagner. Wagner implemented the resettlement program ruthlessly until forced to surrender his authority to the SS once and for all after Himmler's intervention and, along with Schulenburg, officially to step aside for Himmler's favorite, Fritz Bracht.[24] Wagner was already a leading figure in the first deportation project—the so-called Nisko plan.[25] At the beginning of October 1939, as part of the projected establishment of the "Reichsghetto Lublin," Adolf Eichmann, who was at that time still directing the Central Office for Jewish Emigration in Vienna and Prague, prepared on his own initiative for the removal of 70,000 to 80,000 Jews from East Upper Silesia, along with additional Jews from Vienna and Mährisch-Ostrau. Wagner had already been considering expelling the Jewish population from his province's East Strip "beyond Cracow."[26] Once drawn by Eichmann into the Nisko plan, he played a prominent role in the planning but was unable to prevent the collapse of the entire project by the end of October 1939 due to organization and logistical difficulties.

From that point on, the shifting of populations in East Upper Silesia was the task of *Arbeitsgruppe Umsiedler* under the direction of Fritz-Dietlof Graf von der Schulenburg. Initial plans focused on the area west of the police line—the area that seemed to lend itself to immediate Germanization thanks to the large number of inhabitants who were either German or of German ancestry. The East Strip, on the other hand, was considered more of a problem area for ethnic policy due to the large number of "ethnically alien" inhabitants and was temporarily exempted from Germanization. This meant the roughly 100,000 Jews in the East Strip were temporarily spared deportation. Even so, Wagner's office regarded the area east of the police line as crucial to the Germanization program. The East Strip was quickly turned into an internal dumping ground for "racially undesirable" inhabitants of the area west of the police line.[27] That measure became necessary in early 1940, when the Government General reduced the numbers of Poles and Jews that it would accept from the annexed regions, and then later stopped such immigration altogether. Due to difficulties in implementing resettlement policy, the East Strip came to serve as an internal dumping area for "racially inferior" elements from within East Upper Silesia, much as the Government General did for the annexed areas in the East. Subsequently, there developed in that relatively small area a space problem that was to impact massively on the continued evolution of "Jewish policy." German authorities simply left the care and shelter of all the Jews of East Upper Silesia to the existing Jewish communities while herding all the Jews into the East Strip. The largest "deportation destinations" were three cities in the formerly Russian Congress Poland in which Jews had been living for a long time: Bendzin (Polish, Bedzin; Germanized after 1941 as Bendsburg), Sosnowitz (Polish, Sosnowice), and Dombrowa (Polish, Dabrowa). In Bendzin alone, 24,495 of 54,000 inhabitants were Jews; in Sosnowitz, 26,249 of 114,774; and in Dombrowa, 15,663 of 42,000.

III

When Fritz Bracht became the new Gauleiter and Oberpräsident of Upper Silesia, first on temporary, then on permanent appointment,[28] the change in administrative leadership brought a shift in the principles under-lying resettlement and Jewish policy. Very much the protégé of the Reich-führer SS, Bracht permitted Himmler to exercise the unfettered influence on the province's population policy that he had always craved. Jewish and resettlement policies, which civilian authorities had treated as one and the same, came under the permanent control of the SS in the fall of 1940. The two strands of ethnic policy were immediately separated and assigned to different departments: Fritz Arlt, a twenty-eight year old SS-Untersturmführer who held a doctorate in anthropology, took over as part of his job as Himmler's RKF representative the responsibility both for deporting the Polish population and for settling *volks-deutsch* and *reichs-deutsch* immigrants.[29] "Jewish policy," which was now elevated to the level of a separate department, became the province of SS-Oberführer Albrecht Schmelt, former chief of police in Breslau. Schmelt's office, which was established in October 1940 with headquarters in Sosnowitz, was a unique institution in conquered Poland. Created by Himmler himself, the office probably reported to him either directly or through the *Höherer SS- und Polizeiführer.*[30] Acting as special deputy of the Reichsführer SS, Schmelt created a new kind of system of forced labor "for exploiting and directing the ethnically alien work force in East Upper Silesia." He organized the system, quite in the spirit of the SS, so effectively that within a short period of time roughly 17,000 exclusively Jewish forced laborers, male and female, were being exploited in physically demanding labor a minimum of twelve hours per day. Deprived of social benefits as well as unemployment pay, pensions, health benefits, and birth and death benefits, the Jews were forced to contribute a large portion of their paltry wages to Schmelt's office.

In East Upper Silesia economic interests controlled anti-Jewish policy. Pragmatic labor policy and economic efficiency long took precedence over "racial" dogma. This was characteristic for the evolution and dynamic of the extermination policy, and it distinguished developments in the region from the processes at work in the other annexed regions in the East. Except for the Ruhr, East Upper Silesia had an all but unique status in the armament economy of the German Reich. Rich deposits of zinc, minerals, and lead, huge production sites for iron and steel, and one of the largest coal fields in Europe made the province "an armament factory for the Reich."[31] Himmler's specific interest in securing influence in the very center of the arms industry through the "Jewish investment" makes it clear that he was out to add to his control of security and resettlement policy unlimited economic power in the conquered eastern territories. "Jewish policy" was guided by the premise that the war economy was not to be enfeebled by population experiments, but rather productivity was to be enhanced through the recruitment of a Jewish work force that could be used as desired and exploited to the maximum. In the name of economic efficiency, the use of Jews as forced labor began in East Upper Silesia much earlier than anywhere else in the German occupied regions.[32] From the fall of 1940 on, anti-Jewish policy no longer aimed at expulsions but rather at the systematically organized use of forced labor. Jews were explicitly exempted from the rigorous deportations controlled by RKF Representative Fritz Arlt. Thus, the 17,993 victims of the Saybusch Action, the first resettlement of inhabitants of East Upper Silesia into the Government General, were exclusively Polish.[33] Between September 1940 and January 1941, 4,125 farmers from Galicia were moved into Polish houses, apartments, and farms.[34] Concerning the roughly 560 Jews in the Saybusch district, the order of the Gestapo in Kattowitz stated explicitly: "Jews must not be evacuated."[35]

Under the supervision of Schmelt's office, Jews worked in specially established camps at construction sites along the Silesian strip of the Reichsautobahn between Berlin and Cracow, in forced labor camps attached to various private businesses in open country or in the vicinity of large industrial sites, and in work areas of the Wehrmacht's factories, so-called "shops," which were established under German management in the Jewish cities in the East Strip.

The idea of employing Jews as forced labor in guarded camps was not new. It had been practiced in the Old Reich by the Reich's Institute for Employment and Unemployment Insurance since December 1938,[36] and even a few weeks longer in the Ostmark.[37] Since the outbreak of the war, forced labor had also been a core element of anti-Jewish policy in conquered Poland. Immediately following the invasion, Jews were forced as punishment and "for educational reasons" to clear away rubble, lay railroad tracks, dig anti-tank ditches, sweep streets, and perform ameliorative tasks. On the very day that the Government General was established, Hans Frank decreed forced labor to be obligatory for Jewish males from the age of fourteen, which was later extended to include women and children.

While in other areas the "Jewish investment" was primarily an instrument of social isolation and humiliation, in East Upper Silesia its purpose from the very outset was to achieve economic efficiency. Under Schmelt's monopoly, the use of forced labor was for the first time systematically organized as an instrument of anti-Jewish policy. In the late autumn of 1940, Himmler's special representative anticipated the practice of renting out prison labor; the IG Farben Works in Auschwitz was the first private business to adopt the practice in the spring of 1941.[38] It was ultimately introduced throughout the Reich with the founding of the SS Office of Economic Management (WVHA) in March 1942. Schmelt developed and personally controlled, independently of the Board of Concentration Camps, a blanketing network of more than 200 individual camps with exclusively Jewish inmates stretching from East Upper Silesia to Lower

Silesia. In essence, he was already practicing in his area what would be introduced throughout the Reich under the aegis of the Board of Concentration Camps in the middle of 1944 when around 500,000 concentration camp inmates in a dense system of camps were forced to perform forced labor in arms production.

Although Schmelt subjected the Jews of East Upper Silesia to a rigid system of control, repression, and exploitation, he had a calculated economic interest in maintaining their capacity to work. Pragmatic economic considerations had a retarding effect on dogmatic interpretation of "racial" principles. Consequently, anti-Jewish policy at first had less harsh consequences in the province than elsewhere in the occupied East. Of course, little is known about the productivity of the Jews in the forced labor system run out of Schmelt's office. Given the miserable living conditions, especially in the Schmelt camps located along the Reichsautobahn, the use of forced labor there may have been economical but can hardly have been profitable. One must assume that it proved about as nonsensical as the practice of recruiting concentration camp inmates for forced labor. The latters' productivity was less than 50 percent of that of a German worker, at times as low as 20 percent. But quite apart from the program's actual efficiency, Schmelt collected fees from firms for the loan of Jewish workers. The office realized such high profits that the forced labor program financed, among other things, a special fund established by Gauleiter and Oberpräsident Fritz Bracht to underwrite resettlement projects for *Volksdeutsche*[39] as well as supplementary aid for the families of fallen SS men.[40] Additionally, Schmelt's office was a main contributor to the state purchase of the *Gau*'s "model estate," Parzymiechy, which was to be used to "set up" *Volksdeutsche* as farmers.[41] Schmelt also made personal use of the monies derived from the "Jewish investment," building a private residence for himself in the idyllic Parzymiechy region, and depositing around 100,000 marks in his private bank account.[42]

Anti-Jewish policy in East Upper Silesia, while simultaneously embodying the principle of complete bureaucratic control and rigorously exploiting the work force, was tricked out in legal garb and legitimized with the aid of formal legislation. Its goal was isolation and "racial" segregation while simultaneously establishing legal practices in the area that would comport with the "Jewish policy" in the Old Reich. The first step was the introduction of the Nuremberg Laws, which went into effect on 11 June 1941.[43] In that same month, it was decreed that Jews must adopt the given names of Sara and Israel, which had been mandatory in the Old Reich since August 1938.[44] In September 1941, simultaneously with the Old Reich, East Upper Silesia introduced the requirement that Jews wear the yellow Jewish star; the armband that had been required before then was abolished.[45] Additional decrees introduced numerous minor harassments. Beginning in the spring of 1941, Jews might enter government offices only

119

with special permission[46]; in Sosnowitz a special post office for Jews had to be established.[47] Jews were not permitted to perform in or attend concerts.[48] Jews were forbidden to shop in grocery stores owned by non-Jews, and they might not engage in trade.[49] Jews were not permitted to use trains or busses.[50] Exceptions were made only for those who had to commute to and from work in the East Strip. For a time, a special streetcar for Jews, which displayed a blue Star of David and a sign reading "Only for Jews," ran between Sosnowitz and Bendzin.[51] As part of the "Pelzaktion" [fur drive] Jews were compelled to contribute their winter clothes and skiing equipment to German soldiers on the Eastern Front.[52] Ultimately, they were no longer permitted to keep cows or work animals.[53] Even their bicycles were taken away from them,[54] and—in an epitome of absurdity—they were permitted to walk only on the right side of the sidewalk moving in the direction of traffic.

IV

In the euphoria of victory, amid grandiose delusions of power polictics, as part of its campaign against the Soviet Union, the National Socialist regime also plotted its course for dealing with ideological enemy number one—the Jews. The ideological equation of Bolshevism and Jewry, which was typically mentioned in the same breath as plans for a "racial" war of extermination, was of decisive significance for the increasingly radical evolution of "Jewish policy."[55] Up until then deportation and resettlement strategists had been forced to endure inertia, obstructions, and impasses in their planning; now the dream of conquering a "gigantic empire in the East" opened a new dimension in the racial and political "reordering of Europe." Expulsion and extermination now became intermingled. Jewish deaths became a numerical value calculated into plans to "create space for Germans." From then on, the strategy underlying "Jewish policy" was to combine deportations with forced labor leading eventually to exhaustion and death. Those too old, too ill, or too young to work were to be driven into extinction centers near the Arctic Ocean, there to die.[56] When mass shootings of Jewish men began in the occupied areas of the Soviet Union at the end of June 1941, and when women and children were targeted for liquidation in many locations a month later, a "quantum leap"[57] in "Jewish policy" had been reached.

In all probability, systematic extermination resulted from a combination of more or less directed contingency plans that grew harsher in fits and starts. In the planning phase, decisions of the Berlin government were less decisive than the individual initiatives of lower-level officials in the regional civilian and police occupation authorities. Extermination policy was not centrally planned and organized according to the same rules in all areas; it was rather a normal component of each region's system of governance. Mass murder, although it cannot be explained in a way that is entirely free of contradictions, was in all probability the result of an exceedingly complex, long-term political process that for a long time was played out in public. Events were not controlled by a self-regulating, automatic process but rather by real people taking actions at all levels of the apparatuses of occupation in the individual territories.

A situation of enormous implications arose in the East Strip in March 1941, when, for logistical reasons, preparations for the Russian campaign led to the premature termination of resettlements into the Government General. The existing concentration of Jews now blocked the funneling in of other population groups. Thousands of Poles had to be assigned to mass housing, so-called Polish camps, east of the police line, while simultaneously people of German descent were streaming into the East Strip from the Romanian Buchenland. In the conflict over living space, the province's internal dumping ground became so crowded that the very existence of the Jews concentrated in that area became a source of conflict. Against this background, before Auschwitz-Birkenau became an extermination camp, an atmosphere of collapsing inhibitions and a latent readiness to commit murder was spreading throughout East Upper Silesia.

Among all the diverse causes leading to the murder of the East Upper Silesian Jews, obstacles to the implementation of resettlement policy played an essential role. Deporting and importing ethnic populations, though synchronized in theory, did not stay balanced in practice. Responsible officials in the RKF and the Reichssicherheits-hauptamt (RSHA) insisted on bringing masses of people into the province without arranging for housing and feeding. All these shifts of populations were going on simultaneously, and all of them were emptying into the same area. In the hierarchy of those to be provided for, the Jews were "racially" the least valuable. In the charged atmosphere of the war against the Soviet Union, the conflict over living space became a ready-made justification for local politicians, resettlement strategists, architects, and development planners to not even include Jews in their plans for the future. In the transition from a policy of deportation to mass murder, the logistical muddle in the East Strip provided an ostensibly rational pretext for causing the Jews simply to "vanish." When all activity relating to resettlement policy degenerated into a series of frantic attempts to control the chaos following the premature termination of resettlements in March 1941,[58] pushing the Jews out became about all the authorities could agree on.

Contrived justifications were part of the program of murder throughout the eastern occupied regions. Homicidal intentions were concealed beneath the weighing of practicalities, and rationalizations were put forward as excuses for increasingly radical actions. Thus, circumstances peculiar to a given situation, which civilian and police functionaries took to be insoluble dilemmas, provided an additional impetus for setting mass murder in motion. Utopian schemes for "sanitizing" society provided the driving force and the conceptual foundation of the program of murder. Those responsible justified their own actions as harsh but, given the goal of Germanization, unavoidable. Making cities and communities German, along with an expanding program for refurbishing the cities and modernizing the economy, provided the conceptual framework for setting mass murder in motion.[59]

Antisemitism, posturing as a master race, and the concept of *Lebensraum* coalesced in the hubris of planning for Germanization. But seeking the sole explanation of mass murder in that complex of supposedly rational justifications does not do justice to the complexity of the causal chain. The destruction of the Jews—and this must be stressed—was not a by-product of rationally devised plans for reordering Europe.[60] And yet the processes at work in East Upper Silesia demonstrate unambiguously that, against the conceptual background of Germanization, long-range plans for economic and social restructuring played a central role in setting the destruction of the Jews in motion—and that there existed a functional connection between Germanization and genocide. From the interplay of ideological motivations and the situational "necessity" of Germanizing the Polish and Jewish cities in the East Strip, there arose the dynamic of systematic mass killing.

Josef Wagner and Fritz Dietlof Graf von der Schulenburg had already created the logistical preconditions, when, in one of their last official acts, they permitted the East Strip, which had hitherto been exempted from the Germanization program, to be included in the area marked for ethnic reordering. The upgrading of the region's status was decreed on 10 October 1940 and, after details were clarified, approved by Himmler on 16 January 1941.[62]

At the same time, the number of Jewish inhabitants in Sosnowitz and Bendzin was constantly rising, because in the process of recruiting forced laborers, SS-Oberführer Albrecht Schmelt had caused small Jewish communities in the East Strip to be dissolved and their inhabitants moved to the large collection points.[63] The uninterrupted influx of Jews provoked massive criticism from Oberbürgermeister Franz-Josef Schönwälder in Sosnowitz and Bürgermeister Kowohl in Bendzin. Both municipal executives saw the Germanization program being seriously jeopardized, and both initiated measures to increase the pressure on the Jews. Schmelt's forced labor policy enjoyed the support of the municipal heads of government only when Jews were being moved to camps to work on the Reichsautobahn or in industries,[64] but not when they were being recruited as workers for the Wehrmacht "shops" in Sosnowitz and Bendzin. With the support of Police Chief Alexander von Woedtke, Kowohl and Schönwälder seriously impeded this usage of forced labor. Kowohl justified his position on the grounds that the German population should no longer have to "put up with" being thrown together with "Jewish parasites."[65]

In East Upper Silesia, anything that disrupted Germanization—from ramshackle houses to "racially" undesirable human beings—was ruthlessly swept aside. Rationalizations that stigmatized the Jews as harmful, disruptive, or superfluous and thus justified their disappearance did not, however, serve the purpose of overcoming any psychological inhibitions on the part of the officials. To assume as much would be to concede that they were aware of the injustice of their actions. Rapid Germanization was a political mandate, and the professional horizon of the local politicians was correspondingly narrow. Now that moral inhibitions had collapsed during the weeks of military rule, the responsible authorities lacked any awareness of the injustice of their actions. Their practice of justifying the disappearance of the Jews on ostensibly rational grounds reveals less a need for self-justification than a conscious conviction that what they were doing was right.

In the name of Germanization, mid- and lower-level officials set in motion a mechanism that was directly linked to the crimes of the SS in Auschwitz-Birkenau. Mass extermination—erroneously characterized after the war as a "regression to barbarism"—was motivated to a considerable degree by a desire to colonize and civilize. Simply put: The mass murder of the Jews was committed in order to bring "German culture" to the conquered eastern territories.

The labor policy of Schmelt's office, which gave priority to economic efficiency and strove to maintain the Jews' ability to work, conflicted with the eagerness of civilian administrative authorities to rid themselves of the Jews at once. The worse the military situation became following the German defeat before Moscow in December 1941, the more intensively the "Jewish investment" was exploited for the sake of arms production. A violent disagreement arose between Schmelt and the civilian authorities over the issue of the "working Jews." The conflict did not come about due to actions by the leadership of the regime, but rather developed locally—which indicates just how much freedom of action the local functionaries enjoyed. It appears most likely that Himmler laid down the basic tenets of "Jewish policy" relating to arms production, then granted his special representative Albrecht Schmelt the freedom to act on his own authority. Schmelt was supported by economic and Wehrmacht enterprises that were profiting from Jewish labor. The pressure to proceed more radically definitely came from the civilian authorities.

In connection with the Speer program, Schmelt stepped up his use of Jewish labor. Beginning in the spring of 1942, he had Jews trained for arms production, even as skilled laborers in concrete and construction.[66] Later, thanks to the serious labor shortage throughout the Reich, they became indispensable to the war effort. In the spring of 1942, 6,500 Jews were employed in forty armament factories crucial to arms production. In addition, numerous new Schmelt camps were established to support the production of submarines, airplanes, munitions, ceramics, freight cars, heavy machinery, tiles, light bulbs, and sugar—even highway construction and structural engineering. How successfully the SS strove to amass economic power is clear from an April 1942 communication from Higher SS- and Police Leader (HSSPF) Ernst Heinrich Schmauser to Himmler, in which Schmauser proclaimed himself especially pleased by the fact that Jews working in construction were being used in an area, "for which other workers are hardly available at all anymore."

The integration of Jews into arms production led to a slowing of the process of murder that was peculiar to the region. In contrast to what one might expect given the close proximity of Auschwitz-Birkenau, the Jews of East Upper Silesia were delivered into the machinery of murder neither remarkably rapidly nor especially thoroughly. On the contrary, most Jews were still alive after the Jewish populations of whole cities and regions in occupied Poland had already been exterminated. As late as November 1943, according to the figures of Richard Korherr, Chief Statistician for the Reichsführer SS, Schmelt still had at his disposal a total of 50,570 Jews. Thus, East Upper Silesia contained roughly a third of the Jews in the entire Reich who were still being employed as forced laborers.[68]

From the victims' perspective, working under the supervision of Schmelt's office offered protection and security against being transported to the extermination camps. For that reason, the province surrounding Auschwitz became a haven for Jews fleeing from other parts of occupied Poland. Several hundred Jews, especially from the Government General, tried to insinuate themselves into the East Upper Silesian forced labor camps in an effort to save their lives.[69]

In the final analysis, the labor program under Schmelt merely postponed murder; it did not prevent it. The first wave of systematic exterminations in East Upper Silesia began on 12 May 1942. From then until August, when mass murder temporarily reached a record pace, a total of roughly 38,000 Jews had been transported. More than half were judged unfit for work and transported directly to the Auschwitz-Birkenau camp; the rest went to the Schmelt camps.

Between October 1942 and March 1943, the Jewish quarters of Sosnowitz and Bendzin were sealed off as closed ghettos. Unlike the Jews in the Warthegau and the Government General, the Jews of East Upper Silesia had not previously been subjected to comprehensive ghettoization. Nor had starvation—an important tool of anti-Jewish policy in Warsaw and Lodz—been applied due to the economic interest in the Jews' productivity.

Presumably in response to the uprising of the Warsaw ghetto, Himmler ordered the destruction of all Jewish communities in the East Strip at the end of May 1943. The labor policy thus became obsolete; the extermination program could proceed unimpeded. A special supplement to an order of the Reichsführer SS of 21 May 1943 providing for all Jews to be deported from the Reich and from the protectorate of Bohemia and Moravia "to the east, or to Theresienstadt," made it clear that SS-Obersturmbannführer Adolf Eichmann, Chief of the Jewish Council in the RSHA, was to discuss with SS-Oberführer Schmelt "at once" "the issue of removing" the Jews of East Upper Silesia.[70] Four weeks later the death trains began running from Sosnowitz and Bendzin to the extermination camp at Auschwitz-Birkenau. By mid-August 1943 the ghettos had been liquidated, and more than 30,000 additional Jews had been taken away and killed. An order of the local SS command in Auschwitz read: "In recognition of work performed by all members of the SS in recent days, the commander has ordered that all service units shall have leave from 1300 hours on Saturday, 7 August 1943, through Sunday, 8 August 1943."[71] This directive related to the murder of East Upper Silesian Jews; it meant simply that the SS in the camp were being rewarded with a free weekend. The last transport from an East Upper Silesian forced labor camp, carrying a total of twelve Jews, pulled into Auschwitz-Birkenau on 23 July 1944.[72]

Roughly one of every ten inhabitants of the East Strip had been killed after the ghettos were dissolved; in Bendzin, more than half; in Sosnowitz, around a third of the city's population. The Executive Committee (Oberpräsidium) in Kattowitz under Fritz Bracht reported these figures to the chancellery of the NSDAP in September 1944. The "Jewish element," it was prosaically reported, had been "deported, which is to say, eliminated." That was demonstrated in two columns of figures showing former and current population counts under the terse headings: "formerly" and "now."[73]

In September 1943, Schmelt moved his offices to Annaberg in the region west of the police line, where he held civilian authority as Chairman of the Regional Council (Regierungspräsident) in the district of Oppeln.[74] On Himmler's instructions, between September 1943 and July 1944, the largest camps were removed from Schmelt's control and incorporated into the state system of concentration camps; the concentration camp at Groß-Rosen took over twenty-eight Schmelt camps, and Auschwitz-Birkenau absorbed at least fifteen;[75] Schmelt camps with fewer than 800 inmates were abolished at once.[76] Schmelt, however, retained both his title and, though considerably reduced in size, his system of forced labor, which he now operated with Polish workers. At the end of the war, however, Schmelt fell out of favor with Himmler when it was discovered that he was guilty of embezzlement. He was brought before an SS- and Police Court on charges of enriching himself through his office, but details of the proceeding are not known. Albrecht Schmelt committed suicide at the beginning of May 1945.

Although the use of forced labor ultimately proved to be but a stage in the process of murder that delayed, but did not prevent, extermination, subordinating "Jewish policy" to economic criteria was responsible for the fact that mass extermination in East Upper Silesia—despite the close proximity of Auschwitz-Birkenau—came relatively late. The majority of Jews stayed alive under comparatively "better" conditions for a relatively long period. The province's unique status in the Reich's economy and the consequent value placed on maintaining the Jews as a workforce were crucial in retarding the dynamic of the extermination policy within the province. That was the unique feature of the process of the "Final Solution" in the province. As the focus of conflict between, on the one hand, practical exigencies of the war economy, which required trouble-free operation and efficiency, and, on the other hand, ideological "racial" dogma, economic motivations could exert a retarding influence during a certain phase of the extermination policy—and this is shown clearly by conditions in East Upper Silesia. The lethal course of events relied on smooth cooperation between SS and civilian authorities. As far as extermination policy was concerned, the conflict between the apparatuses at the beginning of the war, which was already reduced with the appointment of a Gauleiter and Oberpräsident subservient to Himmler in the person of Fritz Bracht, faded fully into the background. In proceeding against the Jews, the SS and the civilian authorities acted in concert. The importance of regional initiatives in the overall context of mass murder, which originated in East Upper Silesia with functionaries at the bottom of the administrative hierarchy, cannot be overestimated.

The system of differentiated functions, division of labor, and isolation of areas of responsibility, which had already been established during the deportation program at the beginning of the war, became one of the most important organizational bases for systematic extermination after the shift to a policy of murder. The functional connection between resettlement policy and Jewish policy derived largely from experience in structure, organization, and personnel that had been gained during the period of short-term planning. The cooperation between the authorities had long proven effective by the middle of 1942, when murder replaced expulsion as the instrument of "Jewish policy." And yet psychological behavior models that interpret the radicalization of "Jewish policy" as the result of responsible officials in the RSHA having grown "disappointed" and "angry" at the difficulties of resettlement policy and then resorting to more and more brutal methods until mass murder was the sole instrument of anti-Jewish actions—such models are not very plausible.[77] Nor does it seem appropriate to speak of a "breakdown" of ethnic resettlement plans; rather it was a question of resettlement being set aside in favor of other priorities. Those plans were consistently pursued by the RSHA with great tenacity in the face of all obstacles until, in the atmosphere of war against the Soviet Union, they were transformed into projects that foresaw murder as a means of solving problems that plagued population policy.

Antisemitic convictions played an essential role in setting mass murder in motion. Ideology supplied the framework of justifications that permitted civil authorities and police to resort to drastic measures based on emergencies that had ostensibly arisen in the confusion of resettlement. In the name of Germanizing the East Upper Silesian cities, the systematic mass murder of Jews became part of a problem-solving strategy. The measure was justified as necessary to prevent German ethnicity (*Deutschtum*) from being compromised. The Jews of East Upper Silesia were certainly not shipped to the Auschwitz-Birkenau extermination camp in secret. On the contrary, violent expulsion was carried out so openly in the increasingly Germanized province that the regional press carried reports about it. The *Oberschlesische Zeitung*, for example, published in April 1944 under the headline "How Bendzin Became Bendsburg" an article accompanied by many photographs about the transformation of the ugly "nest of Jews" into an small, up-and-coming German city. It was reported with satisfaction that the once "almost completely Jewish" Bendzin, where "the most depraved discards of that race" had lived, was "now German and clean."[78]

Notes

1 This presentation is based on the results of my dissertation, " 'Musterstadt' Auschwitz. Germanisierungspolitik und Judenmord in Ostoberschlesien." The study will be published by K. G. Sauer Verlag (Munich) in 2000 as part of a research project on the social history of Auschwitz, which was directed by Norbert Frei at the *Institut für Zeitgeschichte, München* (Institute of Contemporary History, Munich). In the absence of recent research, the two early studies by Martin Broszat and Czeslaw Madajczyk continue to be basic texts as far as occupation policy is concerned, although East Upper Silesia receives little attention in either work; see Martin Broszat, *Nationalsozialistische Polenpolitik 1939–1945.* (*Schriftenreihe der Vierteljahrshefte für Zeitgeschichte Nr.* 2) (Stuttgart, 1961); Czeslaw Madajczyk, *Die Okkupationspolitik Nazideutschlands in Polen 1939–1945* (Berlin, 1987) (first published in Polish in Warsaw, 1970). Surprisingly, studies of specific geographic areas are not available—a circumstance that may be due to difficulty in accessing documentation, but which presumably also derives from the fact that the events in Silesia after the war, described as "flight and expulsion," obscured our view of National Socialist extermination policy. Inadequate in this regard: Norbert Conrad (ed.), *Deutsche Geschichte im Osten Europa, Vol 4: Schlesien* (Berlin, 1994). Frank Golczewski touches briefly on the situation in East Upper Silesia in his survey of the process of the "Final Solution" in occupied Poland; see Frank Golczewski, "Poland", in Wolfgang Benz (ed.), *Dimension des Völkermords. Die Zahl der jüdischen Opfer des Nationalsozialismus* (Munich, 1996) (first published as vol. 33 of *Quellen und Darstellungen zur Zeitgeschichte*, Munich, 1991), pp. 411–497, especially 412, 422, 450, 457, 460, and 468. Deborah Dwork and Robert-Jan van Pelt, *Auschwitz von 1270 bis heute* (Munich, 1998) (first published in English, New York, 1996), do not treat the structure and dynamic of extermination policy in East Upper Silesia in their study. The empirical

content of the research on Auschwitz in recent years has remained extremely paltry due to a lack of grounding in facts; hence, despite a wealth of publications, scientific studies based on source materials are, astonishingly, hardly in evidence.

2 Since this term cannot be reconciled with the classical concept of public policy, it will appear in quotation marks here.

3 For a survey of the most recent regional studies, see Ulrich Herbert (ed.), *Vernichtungspolitik 1933–1945. Neue Forschungen und Kontroversen* (Frankfurt a.M., 1998).

4 Himmler to Woyrsch, 3 September 1939, Institut für Zeitgeschichte (IfZ), *Nürnberger Dokumente* (Nürnb. Dok.) NOKW-1006.

5 More than 100 Jews died in Bendzin when the fire spread from the synagogue to the Jewish quarter. Another 30 Jews were shot in the middle of September for having allegedly set the fire themselves. ZStLu. V 206 AR-Z 394/67, 48–52. Notation of the Zentrale Stelle on the results of the investigation, 11 March 1968. In Trzebinia, Dulowa, and Krzeszovia, 43 Jews were killed, another 30 in Sosnowitz; ZStLu [Zentrale Stelle der Landesjustizverwaltungen, Ludwigsburg], 205 AR-Z. 1617/62. Proceeding against Fritz Stolz, unpaginated, Zentrale Stelle an Oberstaatsanwaltschaft am Landgericht Amberg, 6 December 1962. Between the beginning of September and the second half of October 1939, 40 synagogues were demolished and 45 completely destroyed by fire, BAK (Bundesarchiv Koblenz), Zeitgeschichtliche Sammlung 122/24; in addition: the Jewish cultural center in the Blachownia district to the office of trustees in Kattowitz, 19 November 1940, including a list of destroyed synagogues in the district, WAP Kat (Archivum Panstwowe w Katowicach), HTO 2876, Bl. 5. There are no exact figures of the total numbers of victims of Einsatzgruppe z.b.V. Estimates run between 1,400 and 1,500 (Madajczyk, *Okkupationspolitik*, 17) and 2,000 dead (Czeslaw Luczak (ed.), *Grabiez polskiego mienia na Ziemaiach Zachodnich Rzeczypospolitej "wcielonych" do Rzeszy 1939–1945*, (Poznan, 1969), p. 74).

6 See Broszat, *Polenpolitik*, p. 28; also: Helmut Krausnick and Hans-Heinrich Wilhelm (eds.), *Die Truppe des Weltanschauungskrieges. Die Einsatzgruppen der Sicherheitspolizei und des SD* (Stuttgart, 1981), pp. 13–278, specifically 54.

7 Woyrsch was in the vanguard of the struggle for National Socialist rule in Silesia. He played a leading role in building the party in 1925, then expanded the SS until it was the largest National Socialist formation in the eastern part of Germany, and also acted as a leader in the brutal suppression of the "Röhm Putsch" in the province. Woyrsch, who repeatedly entertained Himmler at his estate in Lower Silesia, enjoyed the privilege of addressing the Reichsführer SS with the familiar "*Du.*" For a brief biography: "Zeugenschrift Woyrsch," IfZ, ZS 1593; see Ruth Bettina Birn, *Die Höheren SS- und Polizeiführer. Himmlers Vertreter im Reich und in den besetzten Gebieten* (Düsseldorf, 1986,) p. 349.

8 The reports date from 6 to 22 September 1939; see Krausnick, *Einsatzgruppen*, p. 41, 52.

9 *Kriegstagebuch der Rüstungsinspektion VIII Breslau* (War Diary of Arms Inspection VIII Breslau), pp. 96–98, specifically 98, 12 September 1939, BA-MA (Bundesarchiv-Militärarchiv Freiburg), RW 20–8/1. The closing of the border was announced on 12 September 1939, *Sammelbericht* [Summary Report] Nr. 4 of CdZ Fitzner, 5 September 1939, BA-MA, RW 20–8/17, Bl. 69–95, specifically 73. The report refers to a "large number" of Jews who were turned back "again."

10 Order of the CdZ, 5 September 1939, GStAPK (Geheimes Staatsarchiv Preußischer Kulturbesitz Berlin) HA XVII, BA Ost Reg.Kat./3, Bl. 116.
11 The government district Oppeln covered 11,694 square kilometers and had 1.35 million inhabitants. The government district Kattowitz was somewhat smaller, covering 8,923 square kilometers, but was more densely populated, containing 2.43 million inhabitants. For developments in the territory, see Madajczyk, *Okkupationspolitik*, p. 35, which contains slightly different figures; also Dieter Rebentisch, *Führerstaat und Verwaltung im Zweiten Weltkrieg. Verfassungsentwicklung und Verwaltungspolitik 1939–1945*, Vol. 29 of *Frankfurter Historische Abhandlungen* (Stuttgart, 1989), pp. 196f.
12 Specifically the districts Saybusch (Zywiec), Wadowitz (Wadowice), Krenau (Chrzanow), Ilkenau (Olkusz), Warthenau (Zawiercie), Bendzin (after 1941 also Bendsburg, Polish, Bedzin), and Bielitz-Biala (Bielsko-Biala), from spring 1941 also Blachstädt (Blachownia); see Broszat, *Polenpolitik*, pp. 31ff., 36f.; see also Walther Hubatsch (ed.), *Grundriß der deutschen Verwaltungsgeschichte 1815–1945*. Reihe A: *Preußen*, Vol. 4: *Schlesien* (Marburg a.L., 1976), pp. 285–313.
13 Order of BdO Paul Riege for the exercise of police authority east of the existing toll border, order number 11, 16 November 1939, AGK (Archiwum Glownej Komsisji Badania Zbrodni przeciwko Narodowi Polskiemu Instytut Pamieci Narodowej, Warszawer), CA 850/6, Bl. 16–20, especially 20.
14 The term "Old Reich" refers to areas lying within the German borders of 1937.
15 In May 1939 a total of 17,257 Jews lived in the parts of Silesia belonging to the Old Reich, which amounted to 0.7 percent of the entire population; far and away the most Jews lived in Breslau (11,172 in all), which was at that time, the third largest Jewish community in the German Reich after Berlin and Frankfurt am Main. Since the Jewish population in the area of Silesia that belonged to the Old Reich fell under the Old Reich's laws, it is not the subject of this study.
16 See Broszat, *Polenpolitik*, p. 37; Rebentisch, *Führerstaat*, p. 172; Ludolf Herbst, *Das nationalsozialistische Deutschland 1933–1945. Die Entfesselung der Gewalt: Rassismus und Krieg* (Frankfurt a.M., 1996), pp. 281f.
17 Decree of the Führer and Reichschancellor for the Protection of German Ethnicity, 7 October 1939, BAB (Bundesarchiv Berlin), R 49/1, Bl. 1–2; also BAB, R 58/242, MF 6, Bl. 246–248; also IfZ, Nürnbg. Dok. Dok. NG-962 and NG 1467; reprinted in NMT, Vol. 13, p. 138.
18 Inhabitants of the German Reich were called "Reichsdeutsche." "Volksdeutsche" was the term for members of German minorities in foreign states.
19 Concerning the operation and personnel of "Jewish" and resettlement policy up to the radicalization of anti-Jewish measures, using especially the Warthegau as an example, see Götz Aly, *"Endlösung." Völkerverschiebung und der Mord an den europäischen Juden* (Frankfurt a.M., 1995); also Götz Aly, " 'Judenumsiedlung'—Überlegungen zur politischen Vorgeschichte des Holocaust," in Herbert (ed.), *Venichtungspolitik*, pp. 67–97. The connection between Jewish and resettlement policies was first established by Christopher Browning; see Christopher Browning, "Nazi Resettlement Policy and the Search for a Solution to the Jewish Question," in *German Studies Review* 9/3 (1986): 497–519; in German translation under the title "Die nationalsozialistische Umsiedlungspolitik und die Suche nach einer 'Lösung der Judenfrage' 1939–1941," in Christopher Browning, *Der Weg zur "Endlösung." Entscheidungen und Täter* (Bonn, 1998), pp. 13–36.
20 For a brief biography of Wagner, see Peter Hüttenberger, *Die Gauleiter. Studie*

zum Wandel des Machtgefüges in der NSDAP. (Schriftenreihe der Viertel-jahrshefte für Zeitgeschichte Nr. 19) (Stuttgart, 1969), p. 219; see in addition Karl Höffkes, *Hitlers politische Generale. Die Gauleiter* (Tübingen, 1986), pp. 367ff.

21 In the annexed eastern regions, a unique constitutional arrangement developed through the promulgation of special legislation that differed from the laws of the Old Reich. The Gauleiters governed nearly autonomously and largely independently of the Reich Ministry of the Interior; see Broszat, *Polen-politik*, p. 34. Broszat. *Der Staat Hitlers. Grundlegung und Entwicklung seiner inneren Verfassung* (Munich, 1981), pp. 162ff.; Rebentisch, *Führerstaat*, pp. 175ff.

22 Bormann to Lammers, 20 November 1940, where a statement made by Hitler on 25 September 1939 is quoted, BAB, R 43 II/1549, Bl. 47–50; also IfZ Fa 199/51, Bl. 47–50.

23 The postwar myth surrounding Schulenburg also contributed to a transfigura-tion of Wagner. In the scholarly literature, Wagner is presented surprisingly uncritically as "thoughtful statesman" and an especially "mild" politician on the resettlement issue. And yet his policy appears relatively "restrained" only in comparison to the racial policies of the zealot Arthur Greiser in the Warthe-gau. It would certainly be wrong to speak of opposition to the Germanization policy on humanitarian grounds on either his or Schulenburg's part. On Schu-lenburg, see the glorifying and strongly apologetic biography by Albert Krebs, *Fritz-Dietlof Graf von der Schulenburg. Zwischen Staatsraison und Hochverrat. (Hamburger Beiträge zur Zeitgeschichte Nr. 2)* (Hamburg, 1964); see also the more recent and more critical study by Ulrich Heinemann, *Ein konservativer Rebell. Fritz-Dietlof Graf von der Schulenburg und der 20 Juli* (Berlin, 1990).

24 The background of Wagner's dismissal cannot be precisely reconstructed. Himmler's machinations may have been decisive, but Hitler's territorial plans for Silesia may also have been the cause. Since Wagner was an avowed opponent of the recent subdivision of Silesia into *Gaus* for Upper and Lower Silesia, which Hitler had desired, Hitler's knowledge of that fact may have moved him to recall Wagner from Breslau. He did, however, leave Wagner as Gauleiter in South Westphalia with offices in Bochum for more than a year, and Wagner was also permitted to retain his authority as *Reich-spreiskommissar* for the entire Reich. Wagner's ultimate fall at a meeting of *Gau* leaders in Munich in November 1941, though its details are equally impossible to reconstruct, had nothing to do with his policy in Silesia. Perhaps Wagner's critical statements concerning Germany's chances of victory in the Russian campaign persuaded Hitler to strike at his former confidant with unaccustomed harshness.

25 Eichmann's note of 6 October 1939. A facsimile appears in *Nazi-Dokumente sprechen*, published by the Rat der jüdischen Gemeinden in den böhmischen Ländern (Council of Jewish Communities in the Bohemian Lands) (Prague) and by the Zentralverband der jüdischen Gemeinden in der Slowakei (Central Association of Jewish Communities in Slovakia) (Bratislava), Prague (no year of publication), no pagination; also reprinted in Hans-Günther Adler, *Der ver-waltete Mensch. Studien zur Deportation der Juden aus Deutschland* (Tübingen, 1974), p. 128; also in Miroslav Karny, "Nisko in der Geschichte der 'Endlö-sung'" in *Judaica Bohemiae* 3 (1987), no. 2; 69–84, especially 74. On the depor-tation plans, see Seeve Goshen, "Eichmann und die Nisko-Aktion im Oktober 1939. Eine Fallstudie zur NS-Judenpolitik in der letzten Epoche vor der 'Endlösung.'" in *Vierteljahrshefte für Zeitgeschichte* 29 (1981); 74–96, especially

79ff.; Seev Goschen, "Nisko—Ein Ausnahmefall unter den Judenlagern der SS," in *Vierteljahrshefte für Zeitgeschichte* 40 (1992); 95–106; see also Jonny Moser, "Nisko. The First Experiment in Deportation," in *Simon Wiesenthal Center Annual* 2 (1985): 1–30; Hans Safrian, *Die Eichmann-Männer* (Vienna, 1993); second edition with the title: *Eichmann und seine Gehilfen* (Frankfurt a.M., 1995), here pp. 68–85.

26 Notation on the conversation between Eichmann and Wagner, 11 October 1939; reprinted in *Nazi-Dokumente sprechen*, unpaginated.

27 Confidential memorandum of the Kattowitz Gestapo to the regional councils, mayors, district administrative heads, chiefs of police, Chief of Staff of the Security Police, and all Gestapo offices on foreign soil, 23 February 1940, containing information on the target area of the planned deportations, WAP Kat. RK 2833, Bl. 21–23, especially 21, also WAP Kat. HTO 62, Bl. 225.

28 Following the partition, the newly established *Gau* of Lower Silesia, with its capital in Breslau, was governed by Oberpräsident and Gauleiter Karl Hanke.

29 For Arlt's biography, see Götz Aly and Susanne Heim, *Vordenker der Vernichtung. Auschwitz und die deutschen Pläne für eine neue europäische Ordnung* (Frankfurt a.M., 1993) (first published in Hamburg, 1991), especially pp. 168–187, 207–222; see also Götz Aly and Karl Heinz Roth, *Die restlose Erfassung. Volkszählen, Identifizieren, Aussondern im Nationalsozialismus* (Berlin, 1984), pp. 71–74, 84f.

30 While the office's internal correspondence did not survive, important parallel documentation is available. Of central importance are the legal communications of public prosecutors of the Federal Republic after the war. Because of difficulties with documentation, Schmelt's office has not been systematically studied in scholarly research. For an important, albeit cursory, treatment, see Alfred Konieczny, "Die Zwangsarbeit der Juden in Schlesien im Rahmen der 'Organisation Schmelt,'" in *Beiträge zur nationalsozialistischen Gesundheit-sund Sozialpolitik* (1983), no. 3: *Sozialpolitik und Judenvernichtung. Gibt es eine Ökonomie der Endlösung?*, pp. 91–110; Schmelt's unit is also mentioned briefly in Wolf Gruner, *Der Geschlossene Arbeitseinsatz deutscher Juden. Zur Zwangsarbeit als Element der Verfolgung 1938–1943*, Vol. 20 of *Dokumente-Texte-Materialien des Zentrums für Antisemitismusforschung der Technischen Universität Berlin* (Berlin, 1997), p. 264 note 293 and passim.

31 Robert Ley, NSDAP-Reichsorganisationsleiter, wrote in his greeting on the occasion of the first anniversary of Upper Silesia's independence, which appeared under the title *"Ein Jahr Gau Oberschlesien* [Upper Silesia After One Year]" in the *Kattowitzer Zeitung* on 1 February 1942: "As one of our mightiest arms producers, the *Gau* of Upper Silesia has the task of contributing to the strengthening of the German armament industry and thus to the achievement of the final victories of our arms."

32 On forced labor as an instrument of "Jewish policy," see Gruner, *Arbeitseinsatz*.

33 Transport list of the *Umwandererzentralstelle (UWZ)* of Litzmannstadt, 23 September to 14 December 1940; reprinted in Biuletyn Głównej Komisji Badania Zbrodni Hitlerowskich w Polsce (BGKBH) (1960) 12. Document 106. Broszat calculates 17,413 deportees but does not include the last transport of 29 January 1941; see Broszat, *Polenpolitik*, p. 99.

34 Himmler's instructions of 1 August 1940. BAB, 17.02/428, unpaginated.

35 Guidelines for the Evacuations in the Saybusch Area, 14 September 1940; reprinted in *Documenta Occupationis Teutonicae*, Vol. 11, *Polzenie Ludnosci w Rejencji Katowickiej w latach 1939–1945*, Waclaw Dlugoborski (ed.) (Posnan, 1983), pp. 166–171.

36 See Dieter Maier, *Arbeitseinsatz und Deportation. Die Mitwirkung der Arbeitsverwaltung bei der nationalsozialistischen Judenverfolgung in den Jahren 1938–1945*, Vol. 4 of *Publikationen der Gedenkstätte Haus der Wannsee-Konferenz* (Berlin, 1994), pp. 18, 22ff., 29; also Gruner, *Arbeitseinsatz*; Ulrich Herbert, "Arbeit und Vernichtung. Ökonomisches Interesse und Primat der 'Weltanschauung' im Nationalsozialismus," in Dan Diner (ed.), *Ist der Nationalsozialismus Geschichte? Zu Historisierung und Historikerstreit* (Frankfurt a.M., 1987), pp. 198–236; also in Ulrich Herbert (ed.), *Europa und der "Reichseinsatz." Ausländische Zivilarbeiter, Kriegsgefangene und KZ-Häftlinge in Deutschland 1939–1945* (Essen, 1991), pp. 384–426, especially 392.

37 See Gruner, *Arbeitseinsatz*, pp. 48ff.

38 See for now the dissertation by Bernd Christian Wagner, *IG Auschwitz. Zwangsarbeit und Vernichtung von Häftlingen des Lagers Monowitz 1941–45.* This study is also part of the research project on the social history of Auschwitz directed by Norbert Frei at *Institut für Zeitgeschichte.*

39 Note by Rudolf Höß (unpublished parts), IfZ. F 13/1–8, Bl. 31f.; excerpts published in *Faschismus-Ghetto-Massenmord*, Document 173, Bl. 226. War diary of the office of armaments inspection of defense district VIII in Breslau, 1 January–31 March 1941. Notation on the employment of "Schmelt Jews" in the clothing industry, along with a reference to the special fund. BA-MA, RW 20/8–6, Bl. 87.

40 Correspondence between the *Hauptamt für Verwaltung und Wirtschaft* (Main Office for Administration and Economy) (later WVHA) and HSSPF Schmauser of the NSDAP-Reichsleitung and Himmler about Schmauser's request for funds ("schwarze Kasse [black fund]"), 17 November 1941–26 January 1944, IfZ, MA 303, 2589715–25898758.

41 IfZ, Nürnb. Dok. Nr. 3182. Greifelt to Brandt, personal staff of the RFSS; contains notes relating to a presentation at the headquarters of the Reichsführer SS on 28 May 1942, and notation of the use of "surplus funds deriving from the Jewish work program (Schmelt) in Upper Silesia."

42 Testimony of Schemlt's former secretary, Anneliese F. before the state office of criminal investigations in Hannover, 23 November 1971. Public Prosecutor's Office (StA) Dortmund, 45 Js 27/69, Vol. 18, pp. 213–216, Proceeding against Fritz Arlt.

43 RGBl (Reichsgesetzblatt) 1941, no. 50, 4 June 1941, Bl. 297, Decree for the Introduction of the Nuremberg Laws in the Annexed Territories, 31 May 1941. AZIH (Achiwum Zydowskiego Instytutu Historycznego, Warszawa). Jewish Council of Bendzin, 212/1, Bl. 14. Announcement by the representatives of the Jews of Bendzin of the introduction of the Nuremberg Laws, June 1941.

44 Official journal of the Regierungspräsident of Kattowitz, 26 April 1941; official journal of the Regierungspräsident of Kattowitz, 17 May 1941; police order of 9 May 1941, effective as of 1 June 1941, IfZ, Dd. 56.14. Announcement of the assumption of an additional given name, undated, probably in the middle of June 1941, AZIH, Jewish Council of Bendzin, 212/1, Bl. 5.

45 Announcement regarding the obligation to obtain and wear the Jewish star, 20 September 1941, AZIH, Jewish Council of Bendzin 212/1, Bl. 48. Announcement regarding how the Jewish star is to be displayed, 2 October 1941, AZIH, Jewish Council of Bendzin 212/1, Bl. 52. The badges had to be bought for ten pfennig at specially designated shops in the East Strip.

46 Decree of Woedtke, Chief of the Sosnowitz Police, to the Central Jewish Council in Sosnowitz, 17 April 1941, AGK CA 171/32, Bl. 14. Announcement of the representatives of the Jews of Bendzin regarding Woedtke's order of 28 May 1941 banning Jews in Bendzin, 30 May 1941, AZIH, Jewish Council of Bendzin, 212/1, Bl. 3.

47 See contemporary eye-witness account of Nathan Eliasz Szternfinkiel, *Zaglada Zydow Sosnowca* (Katowice, 1946), p. 20 (German translation: *Die Vernichtung der Juden von Sosnowitz* in the investigative documents of the public prosecutors office in Dortmund. StA Dortmund 45 Js 27/69, enclosures. Proceeding against Fritz Arlt.)

48 Chief of the Sosnowitz Police to the Gestapo in Kattowitz, 17 December 1941, WAP Kat. Sosnowitz Chief of Police 315, Bl. 1.

49 *Kattowitzer Zeitung*, 30 November 1940, police order regarding conducting business with Jews, promulgated 23 November 1940, effective as of 1 December 1940.

50 Order of the Sosnowitz Chief of Police excluding Jews from public transportation, 6 February 1941, amended 19 March 1941, AGK, CA 171/32, Bl. 5, 11. Announcement of the Police Command regarding the use of trains by Jews, 30 April 1941, AGK, CA 171/32, Bl. 15.

51 See Szternfinkiel, *Zaglada*, p. 20.

52 Circular from Moshe Merin, Chairman of the Central Jewish Council in Upper Silesia, to all local councils of elders, 20 December 1941, AZIH, Jewish Council of Bendzin 212/1, Bl. 58; see Szternfinkiel, *Zaglada*, p. 31.

53 Chief of Sosnowitz Police regarding the confiscation of cattle owned by Jews, 8 May 1941, AGK, CA 171/31.

54 Situation report of the NSDAP District Directory in Bendzin to the NSDAP Provincial Directory, October 1941, undated, WAP Op. NSDAP Gauleitung 207, Bl. 22. Report of the NSDAP District Directory in Bendzin to the NSDAP Provincial Directory, October 1941, undated, WAP Op. 2481/281, Bl. 22.

55 The close ideological connection is explicitly established in Andreas Hillgruber, "Die 'Endlösung' und das deutsche Ostimperium als Kernstück des rassenideologischen Programms des Nationalsozialismus," in *Vierteljahrshefte für Zeitgeschichte* 20 (1972): 133–153. While Hillgruber assumes that the murder of the Jewish population had already been planned by the beginning of the Russian campaign, in a more recent study Burrin expresses the view that the bleak course of the military campaign was decisive; see Philippe Burrin, *Hitler und die Juden. Die Entscheidung für den Volksmord* (Frankfurt, 1993) (first French edition, Paris, 1992).

56 For the basic details, see Aly, *Endlösung*, pp. 273ff., 392.

57 Christopher R. Browning, *The Final Solution and the German Foreign Office* (New York, 1978), p. 8.

58 Notation by Butschek, RKF Ansiedlungsstab [Resettlement Staff] in Kattowitz, regarding a discussion on 19 March 1941 in Berlin on how to solve settlement problems, 20 March 1941, BAB. Film 16786, Deutsches Auslandsinstitut, unpaginated.

59 The relationship between municipal development and the murder of the Jews has not hitherto been explicitly investigated. For general information on city planning under National Socialism, especially in the Warthegau, see Niels Gutschow and Barbara Klein, *Vernichtung und Utopie. Stadtplanung Warschau 1939–1945* (Hamburg, 1994), especially pp. 21–41; Werner Durth and Niels Gutschow, *Träume in Trümmern. Stadtplanung 1940–1950* (Munich, 1993), especially pp. 75–112.

60 See the controversial theses of Götz Aly and Susanne Heim concerning the relative importance of economic considerations of population policy in setting mass murder in motion; Aly and Heim, *Vordenker*; on the controversy, see Wolfgang Schneider (ed.), *"Vernichtungpolitik." Eine Debatte über den Zusammenhang*

von Sozialpolitik und Genozid im nationalsozialistischen Deutschland (Hamburg, 1991); on the importance of racism, see in the aforementioned volume, Ulrich Herbert, "Rassismus und rationales Kalkül. Zum Stellenwert utilitaristisch verbrämter Legitimationsstrategien in der nationalsozialistischen Weltanschauung," in Schneider (ed.), *"Vernichtungspolitik,"* pp. 25–35.

61 Schulenberg to Himmler via *Reichsstelle für Raumordnung*, 20 May 1940, BAB, R 49/902, unpaginated.

62 Note of the RKF-Planungshauptabteilung (Main Planning Office) on a conversation between Himmler, Bracht, and Bach-Zelewski, 11 September 1940, BAB, R 49/902, unpaginated; Arlt's list of suggestions to the RFK-Planungshauptabteilung, 5 October 1940; note of a discussion on 10 October 1940 at the invitation of the HSSPF in Kattowitz; participants included Bach-Zelewski, Ziegler, Springorum, and a representative of the RKF-Planungshauptabteilung, 14 October 1940; note on the same discussion, 26 October 1940, BAB, R 49/902, unpaginated; Himmler's general directive RKF No. 10/1 1, 16 January 1941, IfZ, MA 125/13, No. 38718. A similar recommendation had already been discussed on 30 July 1940 in the Oberpräsidium, minutes of the meeting, WAP Kat, OPK 1810, Bl. 3–4; on subdividing into zones, see also Greifelt's communication to Bracht, 23 November 1940, BAK, R 113/7, Bl. 117; also BAK, R 113/7, Bl. 147–148; *Kattowitzer Zeitung*, 10 November 1940, "Raumplanung in den Ostgebieten [Development Planning in the Eastern Territories]." Development, organization, and performance of the Office of the Gauleiter and Oberpräsident as representative of the Reichsführer SS, Reich Commissioner for the Protection of German Ethnicity in Upper East Silesia, September 1939 to January 1943, Bl. 55; includes a sketch of the zones of settlement I and Ia, BAB, 17.02/318; the sketch is also reproduced in Robert-Jan van Pelt, "A Site in Search of a Mission," in Yisrael Gutman and Michael Berenbaum (eds.), *Anatomy of the Auschwitz Death Camp* (Washington, 1994), pp. 93–155, especially 107.

63 File memorandum on a discussion at police headquarters in Sosnowitz, 12 November 1941, WAP Kat, RK 2780, Bl. 95–99, especially 97; Woedtke's note on resettling Jews as discussed on 19 November 1941, written on 25 November 1941, AGK, CA 171/32, Bl. 41; order of the Sosnowitz police, also WAP Kat, Chief of Sosnowitz Police, Bl. 316, 78.

64 Schönwälder to Springorum, situation report for November 1940, 30 November 1940, GStAPK, HA XVII, BA Ost. Reg. Bez./13, Bl. 112–121, especially 116. Schönwälder expresses satisfaction in the fact that the "idly lounging about, shadily dealing" Jews have "finally" disappeared.

65 Kowohl to the District Council of Bendzin, 24 June 1941, WAP Kat, RK 2785, Bl. 18.

66 Notes by Rudolf Höß (unpublished part), 1 November 1946, IfZ, F 13/1–8, pp. 31ff.; excerpts published in *Faschismus-Ghetto-Massenmord*, Dok. 173, p. 226. In contrast to Höß's assertions, there were no efforts to abolish the Schmelt camps in 1941. Quite to the contrary, the camps became more important than ever due to the Speer program. Also false, because based on Höß's memoirs: Israel Gutman editor-in-chief, Eberhard Jäckel, Peter Longreich, and Julius Schoep, editors of the German edition, *Enzyklopädie des Holocaust. Die Verfolgung und Ermordung der europäischen Juden* (Munich, 1995), p. 1071.

67 Schmauser to Himmler, 20 April 1942, IfZ, Nürnb. Dok. NO-1386, excerpts reprinted in Adler, *Mensch*, p. 230.

68 *Die Endlösung der europäischen Judenfrage. Statistischer Bericht des Inspekteurs für Statstik beim Reichsführer SS. Geheime Reichssache* (The Final Solu-

tion to the Jewish Question. Statistical Report of the Chief of Staff for Statistics for the Reichsführer SS. Secret Matter of State), 1 January 1943, BAB, NS 19/1570, Bl. 4–10, or 12–28, especially 8, 25; Korherr spoke of the "use of Schmelt camps," counting among the 50,570 East Upper Silesian Jews some 42,382 "stateless" Jews, by which he meant Jews who had always lived in the province. Of these 8,188 were treated in the subcategory of "foreign" Jews; these were Jews whom Schmelt caused to be removed from the transports on their way from Holland and France to Auschwitz-Birkenau. Additional extensive networks of forced labor camps existed from the summer of 1941 under the control of SSPF Friedrich Katzmann in east Galicia and also under the authority of SSPF Odilo Globocnik in the Lublin district of the Government General, including the camps along *Durchgangsstraße IV*, the axis connecting central Poland and the Crimea. There has been to date no systematic study of the major forced labor projects. See (for the present) Thomas Sandkühler, "*Endlösung*" in *Galizien. Der Judenmord in Ostpolen und die Rettungsinitiative von Berthold Beitz 1941–1944* (Bonn, 1996), pp. 46f.; Dieter Pohl, *Nationalsozialistische Judenverfolgung in Ostgalizien 1941–1944. Organisation und Durchführung eines staatlichen Massenverbrechens*, Vol. 50 of *Studien zur Zeitgeschichte* (Munich, 1996), pp. 132ff., 331–355; lacking in new contributions: Daniel Goldhagen, *Hitlers willige Vollstrecker. Ganz gewöhnliche Deutsche und der Holocaust* (Berlin, 1996) (first American edition, New York, 1996, pp. 335ff.).

69 Circular of the Kattowitz Gestapo, 26 February 1942; includes an announcement of "illegal Jews," APOSW (Archiwum Panstwowe Muzeum w Oswiecimiu), Bürgermeister Oswiecim, 1, Bl. 34; also the contemporary, eye-witness account by Szternfinkiel, *Zaglada*, pp. 46f.

70 Telex of the RSHA, 21 May 1943. ZstLu, 205 AR Z 308, Bl. 67. Proceeding against Baucke et al., volume of enclosures without pagination. No documents relating to the discussion between Eichmann and Schmelt have survived.

71 Headquarters and garrison orders of the Auschwitz concentration camp 1940–1945, edited manuscript, StB 31/43, 6 August 1943.

72 See Franciszek Piper, *Die Zahl der Opfer von Auschwitz. Aufgrund der Quellen und der Erträge der Forschung 1945 bis 1990* (Oswiecim, 1993), pp. 183–186, Table 15.

73 Director of the Gau office for municipal policy at the Kattowitz Oberpräsidium in Bracht's name to the NSDAP Party Chancellery, 6 September 1944, WAP Kat, RK 1654, Bl. 103–107, specifically 104; also *Akten der NSDAP Parteikanzlei*, Teil II, Bd. 3/4, Bl. 12118–12122, especially 12119, containing the statement: "The Jewish element, which accounts for most criminals, the anti-German Polish intelligentsia, and the criminal element, have been resettled, i.e., eliminated, so that extraordinary levels of criminal activity are no longer a prospect." In addition: Reich Ministry of the Interior (RMI) to the Headquarters of Police, 10 October 1944, IfZ, Nürnb. Dok., NG-2660; the statistics were used by the Ministry of the Interior in a communication to the Headquarters of Police. Following the murder of the Jews, the number of inhabitants in Sosnowitz dropped from 130,000 to 101,788; in Bendzin, from 54,739 to 25,595; in Dombrowa, from 41,491 to 29,018; in Czeladz, from 23,000 to 20,571; in Zagorze, from 16,400 to 12,556; in Nikwa, from 12,550 to 11,083; and in Schümenschütz, from 28,560 to 24,669.

74 Schmelt to Arlt, 13 September 1943, announcement of the office's new address and telephone number, AGK 865/7, 75.

75 Unpublished parts of the notes of Rudopf Höß, IfZ, F 13/1–8, Bl. 31f.; excerpts

printed in *Faschismus-Ghetto-Massenmord*, doc. 173. Höß again errs in dating the absorption of the Schmelt camps by the concentration-camp bureaucracy in the spring of 1943 and in saying that the process was "completely accomplished" by that time.

76 *Vierteljahresbericht der Rüstungsinspektion im Wehrkreis VIII* [quarterly report of the Armament Inspectorate in Military District VIII] October-December 1943, especially "Judeneinsatz," undated, presumably January 1944, BAMA, RW 20–8/32, Bl. 49.

77 This is Aly's interpretation, which was generally anticipated in Browning, *Nazi Resettlement Policy* (in German translation: Browning, *Umsiedlungspolitik*). The shortcoming of this interpretation is that it fails to explain why the "failure" of population plans led to mass murder only in the case of the Jews, but not in the case of the Polish population.

78 *Oberschlesische Zeitung*, 4 April 1944, "Wie aus Bendzin Bendsburg wurde. Ein Bildarchiv erzählt von der Wandlung einer Stadt" (How Bendzin Became Bendsburg. Pictures Show the Transformation of a City).

Part 2

THE NAZI ASSAULT ON THE JEWS OF POLAND

20

THE ECONOMICS OF THE FINAL SOLUTION

A case study from the General Government

Götz Aly and Susanne Heim

Source: *Simon Wiesenthal Centre Annual*, 5 (1988), 3–48. Translated by Norma von Ragenfeld-Feldman.

On 31 July 1941 Hermann Göring commissioned Reinhard Heydrich to make the organizational preparations for the murder of the European Jews. Göring did this in his capacity as Plenipotentiary for the Four Year Plan,[1] a position in which he had already successfully directed both Aryanization and forced emigration. He was also responsible for the economic rationalization and the increasingly more effective economic exploitation of the German Reich and the occupied territories. In this, he was advised by a committee of state secretaries and experts, who can be considered as the actual "crisis managers" of the Third Reich.

These experts did not primarily use an ideological approach, but one of pragmatic rationality. They constantly used such concepts as "solution" (*Lösung*) or "total solution" (*Gesamtlösung*). They did not revel in myths of blood and race, but thought in categories of large-scale economic spaces, structural renewal, and overpopulation with its attendant food problems; and they were resolved to effectuate more rational methods of production, standardize products, and improve social structures. They always thought and acted at the expense of minorities, whose stigmatization and discrimination were prescribed by Nazi ideology. In this way, they attempted to secure advantages for the majority of the population, or at least guarantee its social status, by subjecting the minorities to extreme social disabilities that ultimately ended in death.

The policy of destruction in the Third Reich, it seems to us, must be understood as a systematic constituent of the social policy practiced at that time. In the context of our work on the murders committed against psychiatric patients, we have come across the connection between modernization and destruction. Thus in the "euthanasia operation," therapeutic progress and the advances made in the organization of traditional institutional psychiatry were explicitly intermingled with the killing of incurable patients who failed to respond to therapeutic treatment.[2] We encountered the same relationship in our investigation of economic planning in occupied Poland. There the draft of an economic development program was linked to the increasingly outspoken demand that Jews be eliminated from the artificial creation known as the General Government.[3]

In line with our working hypothesis, we are not interested in the irrational and pathological personality traits of a few Nazi leaders, who seem to us far more intelligent and discerning than is generally assumed; rather, we are concerned with the many institutions of the regime involved with planning, the gathering of statistics, and statistical analysis.[4] After 1938 these institutions became increasingly influential and counted such men as Fritz Todt, Albert Speer, Herbert Backe, and Reinhard Heydrich among their political representatives. They based their decisions on the work done at such research institutions as the German Labor Front Institute for the Scientific Study of Labor, the National Working Association for Spatial Research, certain departments of the SS Security Service (SD), the National Board for Economy and Efficiency, the Institute for German Projects in the East (*Ostarbeit*), the German Foreign Institute (*Auslandsinstitut*), as well as many others.

It is our hypothesis that between September 1939 and the summer of 1941, various groupings of Germany's educated elite involved with planning devised the "final solution" for logical reasons and implemented it in conjunction with the war against Russia. The "final solution" evolved from studies and proposals of subordinate planning officials, gradually moving from the lower to the higher bureaucratic echelons. It should be carefully noted that these planners, who did not always appear to be of importance within the hierarchy, did not themselves make the decisions but suggested them to superiors.

"Polish conditions"

The invasion of Poland confronted the Nazi planners with social problems they had not previously encountered in their own territorial sphere of domination. Nevertheless, the confrontation was not unexpected. Already during the 1930s, German social scientists from all disciplines had been concerned with the poverty, overpopulation, and structural underdevelopment in Eastern and Southeastern Europe; and professors such as Theodor Oberländer and Peter-Heinz Seraphim, Oberländer's former student, had acquired an exact overview of the situation from their social scientific outpost at Königsberg.[5] In 1935 Oberländer already stated:

140

The extraordinarily high agrarian density, combined with the lack of capital, creates especially for the zone adjacent to Russia the danger of heading, just as in Russia, toward a social upheaval arising from internal tensions and overpopulation pressures.[6]

The Nazi space and economic planners—and not they alone—viewed Poland as being overpopulated. Her economy suffered from too little labor productivity, that is, from a deficient labor organization and lack of capital. It was not by accident that the mixture of inefficiency, disorder, and poverty in Polish factories and farms was in Germany commonly referred to as "Polish conditions" (*polnische Wirtschaft*); and even today, in the jargon of German automobile workers, a nonstandardized machine screw is called a "Polish screw."

In order "to tie the eastern agrarian states to the Central European space"[7] and subject them to the notion of the economy of large-scale spaces (*Großraumwirtschaft*) under German hegemony, it was particularly important to solve the social question and break through this self-satisfied underproductivity. Thus, if conditions in Poland, as measured by German notions of economic and political order, had already appeared untenable to the Germans long before their invasion, then the situation must have deteriorated considerably after the so-called incorporation of western Poland into the Reich. With the conquest of the western Polish provinces, Germany incorporated not only the most important industrial regions of Poland, but also those agricultural regions where the surplus that was produced provided the Polish population with food and kept the foreign trade balance on a somewhat even keel. By contrast, the "remainder of Poland" (*Restpolen*), organized as the General Government, was for the Germans "a creation with little economic prospect."

Originally Hitler had intended to leave the General Government to its own devices. In late autumn of 1939, the Germans regarded it as a "heap of rubble" and manpower reservoir. They began to dismantle its industrial plants and used this territory, reduced in size by the war and sandwiched between German and Soviet spheres of influence, as the region designated for dumping the unwanted and expropriated. The deportees were to vegetate there under the worst conditions and, if need be, die from tuberculosis, typhus, hunger, and deprivation. But when the German civilian government developed the ambition in March 1940 to create a "Germanic development program," every planning step amounted to an attempt to decrease the density of the population or, at least, prevent further population growth.[8]

The Germans could achieve this if they found a way to eliminate the sizeable Jewish minority from the total population. After all, they constituted a good 10 percent of the population, and often much more in the cities that were difficult to control and provision. The extreme poverty of most Polish Jews precluded from the outset the application of traditional Nazi anti-Jewish techniques and policies (*Judenpolitik*), consisting of threats and expropriations forcing Jews to purchase their emigration at high prices. The so-called Eastern Jews (*Ostjuden*) thus represented a social "mass problem" whose "solution" would simultaneously make a large part of visible Polish poverty disappear. In November 1939 the Hamburg *Wirtschaftsdienst* published an article by Peter-Heinz Seraphim on "The Economic Significance of Polish Jews." Seraphim focused programmatically on the relationship between Jewish poverty and the social question:

> In Poland, as in the entire East European area of habitation, the Jewish question definitely is a mass problem.... Particularly in Poland, we find a large group of destitute people, the so-called Jewish *Luftmenschen*, that is, a people who live off air, from hand to mouth, thoroughly proletarianized, for the most part a demoralized element that is mobile in location and occupation. Several factors have reenforced this process of impoverishment in the postwar period. If one is to make a rough estimate of the extent of the pauperization of the East European Jews of Poland and understands by the Jewish pauper a character who is unable to maintain himself on the basis of his own economic strength without charity and outside Jewish help or whose standard of living is considerably lower than that of small peasants and industrial workers, then one can regard approximately 35 percent of all Jews in Poland thus defined as pauperized.[9]

Moreover, the poverty of Polish Jews increased massively due to the war and the discrimination that immediately followed in its wake.

Even earlier, in December 1939, an official of the German Foreign Institute mentioned the connection between poverty and the desirability of destruction in a report about his trip through occupied Poland. This official, Dr. Eduard Könekamp, reported his observations on the first mass resettlements from the annexed western part of Poland to the eastern edge of the newly formed General Government:

> Many Germans probably see Jews in such masses for the first time.... [The ghettos] are among the filthiest things imaginable. Here the Jews vegetate in quarters that are sometimes as much as four flights underground. The prevailing hygienic and moral conditions here are ghastly.

The kinds of "criminal Jewish types" milling about, his report continued, far surpassed the ones depicted by the *Stürmer*. But now "they are most vigorously enlisted to do labor, [and] those who do not appear for work are shot." The latter assertion, however, corresponded to Könekamp's imagined desires rather than the reality at the time.

Könekamp, who after World War II was appointed Deputy Mayor of Stuttgart by the Allies,[10] described in his 1939 report what were no doubt common German reactions when confronted with the poverty, exacerbated by wartime, of the Polish-Jewish residential quarters:

> The destruction of this sub-humanity (*Untermenschentum*) would serve the interests of the entire world. But this destruction poses an extraordinarily difficult problem. Executions will not work. Also, one cannot allow women and children to be shot. Here and there one can also count on the losses incurred during evacuations, and 450 are said to have perished during a transport of 1,000 Jews from Lublin.... All the agencies concerned with the Jewish question recognize the inadequacy of these measures. But a solution to this complicated problem has not yet been found.[11]

It took two more years until such visionary schemes of destruction, conceived by mid-level bureaucrats, were implemented. During this time German administrative practices produced conditions that made genocide appear reasonable and useful.

Tabula rasa

The scientists and experts who worked in the General Government and built their careers there were on the average quite young. Generally speaking, Germany probably never had a younger, more mentally agile, and more active administrative elite than during the Nazi period. Until the end of 1941, the power and influence of these 25- to 35-year-old managers grew as Germany expanded, enabling them to pay progressively less attention to obstinate realities while developing their plans. As Helmut Meinhold, one of the experts, wrote:

> [In the General Government] the economic planner is confronted with a totally new situation. The issue is not the location of a new industrial plant or the most advantageous development of a transportation network under a given set of economic conditions. Rather, in the economic sphere one basically finds oneself close to a *tabula rasa*.[12]

It is self-evident that no such tabula rasa actually existed in the densely populated General Government. It first had to be created by the appropriate terrorist policies. And since the economic factors such as capital, energy, raw materials, or transport capacities could not be manipulated and were, quite simply, in ever shorter supply as the war progressed, the only remaining economic factor that planners of this ilk could actually modify was the number and composition of the population. In a study on the "Expansion of the General Government to the East," Meinhold, who was then 28 years old and after the war became one of the most important advisers on social policy in the government of the Federal Republic of Germany, focused exclusively on "migration" (*Siedlungsbewegungen*), which he regarded as an absolute prerequisite were every additional annexation "to be economically useful."[13] Although Meinhold never contemplated the construction of a single railroad line, he did consider "removing part or all of the Poles" to the East in order to solve "the problem of overpopulation."[14] The Jews, however, he wanted "resettled" in any case.

In the view of such planning officials, the General Government served as a colonial zone for experimentation with respect to racial ideology, *völkisch* politics, population policy, economics, or whatever else one wants to call it. Like every young and power-hungry elite, these men pressed forward when the opportunity arose; they were determined to implement their ideas. This opportunism also explains why after 1945 the same men (moved by both indignation and self-pity) with agility and little effort found their way into new positions after their "reeduction." Their basic rule for planning and implementing policies was to clear away everything considered to be a nuisance, including every unpopular minority and the Jews in any case. At this point, their planning concepts intersected with racial ideology. And from the amalgam of both elements, resulted the plans for and implementation of the destruction of millions of human beings.

Population as a variable

The German spatial planners and economists considered "overpopulation" the main problem of the economic order in the General Government. This troublesome condition, however, was not caused by too high a population density per square mile. Overpopulation was—and always is—defined relatively and is proportionate to insufficient productivity and underemployment, that is, to the inadequate utilization of the available labor force. Moreover, the additional factor of "mentality" explained why the labor force in the General Government was "less efficient than the German one" since it "generally lacked what was natural to the German worker, namely the motivation to organize his own work with the purpose of attaining the highest labor efficiency possible ... [and also lacked] the impulse to reach a higher standard of living by increased productivity."[15]

From this perspective, "every other person in Polish agriculture" represented "nothing more than dead ballast."[16] In economic terms, it was

144

the system of self-contained home industries that determined the unprof-
itable conditions in the Polish villages. Money hardly played a role at all in
the system. The rural population produced not only foodstuffs but practically all basic commodities; at most, they engaged in a kind of barter trade
with other home industries located in the village or surrounding region, so
that in the view of the economic planner Helmut Meinhold, who worked
at the Institute for German Projects in the East in Cracow, "there basically
existed no economy in the actual sense of the term."[17]

Concepts such as "marketing," "market control," or "development"
made the self-sufficient conditions of life in the Polish villages appear
absurd. The self-contained home industries were an economic factor that
could not be moved at will, but rather a barrier to the plans of economic
planners, population policy makers, and SS officers. Not only did the villages provide the social backing for the resistance—how else could both
hunted partisans and those who had evaded forced labor exist?—but they
also assured the survival of the rural population itself. Given the system
of subsistence economy, the occupation forces, determined to cart agricultural products off to Germany, could enforce the steadily increasing
delivery quotas only with difficulty, even after the hunger of the Polish
population had already been calculated as part of the quotas. It was
impossible to draw profits from this economy. Furthermore, it resisted
every kind of rationalization. On the one hand, unemployment did not for
the most part manifest itself openly; and on the other hand, a natural
economy made the accumulation of capital as a prerequisite for
investments for the purpose of raising the productivity level virtually
impossible.[18]

According to such analyses, the agrarian overpopulation not only
spelled disaster for agriculture itself, but gradually also affected an
increasing number of other economic sectors. A natural produce economy
and barter trade (that is, production for the local and, at best, regional
markets) resulted in only small surpluses in agriculture-related trade and
industry (partly also in home industries as, for example, blacksmithing and
cart making) and also in extremely low labor productivity. To rationalize
these not easily transparent relationships within the self-sufficient
economies of the Polish households, villages, and districts, Meinhold was
not satisfied with just describing the phenomena of overpopulation and the
"low labor return"; he also postulated the mathematical relationship of the
two factors to each other. He adopted from Oberländer the so-called
Mombertian Formula,[19] which reads as follows:

The space available for food (*Nahrungsraum*, or N) equals the
size of the population (*Volkszahl*, or V) times the cost of living
(*Lebenshaltung*, or L).
In abbreviated form: $N = V \times L$.

The actual function of this formula lies in it being abstracted from its substantive content and thereby suggests the possibility that individual factors can be manipulated with and written, for example, as:

$$V = N/L$$

(Population size equals the space available for food divided by the cost of living.) But if the space for food was limited and the cost of living had already been reduced to a subsistence level, then the thing to do would be to reduce the size of the population (V).

Thus expressed in manageable terms, population size became a magnitude that was, alongside others, variable at will. Mass murder, forced resettlements, invasions of other countries, or the deliberate policy of starvation were equated with "reduction of the size of the population," "expansion of nutritional space," or "reduction of living costs"; and thus metamorphosed into sanitized scientific terms, they became part of the repertory of economic planning.

A less aggressive possibility of expanding the space for food lay in increasing the yield per hectare of land, but Meinhold dismissed this as an alternative, since it did not provide new work opportunities to alleviate the agrarian overpopulation. As he concluded, "Thus the only possibilities left are the reduction of the size of the population or the extension of the space allotted to food production to non-agrarian sectors."[20]

Without intervention from the outside, however, the demographic conditions in the General Government would constantly deteriorate due to the excess of births over deaths by about 140,000 people per year and the deportations from the annexed western provinces of Poland: "Indeed, one can even foresee the time when the rural population will sink below the subsistence level, although by German standards it has been below the minimum of economic subsistence for several decades." This did not necessarily upset the German intellectuals in Cracow. What it did mean to them, however, was "that the region ... becomes a burden on the rest of the grand region (*Großraum*), and therewith practically on the Reich itself, at least as far as covering the costs of administration, transport, and economic organization are concerned."[21]

In his calculations, Meinhold also used the "greatest possible labor productivity in the grand region" as a yardstick to apply to the General Government. According to this criterion, he ascertained the "size of the labor force ... that would be needed if agricultural labor were organized correctly" and compared "this size ... to the size of the labor force actually available."[22]

Thus, a country was ultimately considered overpopulated to the degree its labor productivity lagged behind the greatest possible labor productivity within the "European grand region." Therefore, a subsistence economy

146

that hardly produced surpluses had automatically to be considered over-populated if measured against such thoroughly capitalized states as the German Reich, no matter how many people lived in it. Finally, Meinhold calculated the effect of two variants (the same organization of labor as in the Reich, or a somewhat less favorable one) and arrived at a surplus population amounting to 4.5 million or 5.83 million people, that is, roughly 30 percent of the total population of the General Government.[23]

Once a beginning had thus been made, the entire project assumed gigantic proportions, which did not remain limited to the General Government. In Southeastern Europe, "in the case of a radical solution of the agrarian labor problem," a decision to use migratory labor meant that "12 to 15 million workers ... [would be] set into motion." And that was not all, since these workers also had families so that "a rough total of 50 million people would have emerged out of their hitherto virtually self-contained home economies and, in accordance with this, market relations too would experience major changes. ... It is a task fit for the notion of the grand region and a basis for the ideological justification of the grand region as a concept."[24] The "ideological justification of the concept," however, had a material side to it. Since previously "the market in the whole overpopulated zone is not worth much despite the large number of over one hundred million inhabitants," favorable market conditions would first have to be created by a restructuring process. "It is therefore quite certain with respect to the eastern and southeastern territories that the reorganization, even if it occurs in conjunction with industrialization, can only expand the market for German industry."[25]

Meinhold's planning led to an obvious conflict of goals. The released labor force, amounting to millions of workers in the occupied European countries, would try to find both work and bread, while migrating from east to west. An even greater "population pressure" would result for the eastern districts of the Reich, and the Germanization projects would simply be undermined by economic mechanisms, threatening the social stability of the grand region. This would have to be counteracted "through the following measures ... implemented either singly or in concert":

(1) Labor in the Reich, especially migratory labor, will be regulated by law in such a way that it will represent no threat, in terms of its nature and extent, to the German national terrain.
(2) The number of available jobs in the General Government will be increased as much as possible.
(3) The population density in the General Government will be reduced.
(4) The extent and pace of the economic use of the organization of labor in the General Government will be adjusted as far as possible to the other three measures as they become effective.[26]

In conquered Poland, the number of industrial jobs had declined under German domination.[27] Meinhold knew this; he was well informed about current statistics. Thus his proposal "to reduce the density of the population in the General Government," which he thought appropriate in addition to labor deportations, gained in importance.

Finally, Meinhold concluded that "above all, the possibility [should be] mentioned ... that by settling the Jewish question a number of jobs will become available and, at the same time, a reduction—albeit not a sufficiently large one—of the size of the population will occur." Thus, "considerable relief for the strained labor market ... could temporarily alleviate the situation in the General Government."[28]

For this, however, speed was required, as Meinhold's assistant, Hans Kraft Nonnenmacher, noted:

> As overpopulation increases, the chances of eliminating overpopulation decreases, and the results will contribute to still more overpopulation. For with constantly diminishing labor productivity, the population is no longer capable of saving the capital necessary to heighten the efficiency of the factories. But this heightened efficiency, in turn, is the precondition for creating new employment opportunities, in agriculture as well as in industry which, if savings were accumulated at a higher rate, would gradually rebuild itself. Here we see ourselves confronted by a vicious circle, which steadily leads to the growing pauperization (*Verelendung*) of the population. The manifestations and further consequences resulting from this condition are manifold.[29]

This notion did not imply that the "excess" population would just be killed. After all, that did not happen. The destruction of part of the population through hunger and deportation was a means to break through the diagnosed vicious circle of underproductivity, that is, to force an opening into the self-contained economic system and thereby create the prerequisites for rationalizing the entire economy as well as the productive utilization of the rest of the population.

Evidently, these theories also achieved popularity in the planning staffs of German firms. In 1942, the economic department of IG Farben considered the massacres of several hundred thousands of Serbs by the Croatian Ustasha as a constructive contribution to the solution of the overpopulation problem in the Balkans.[30] In the camouflaged language of the times, a report about the economic structure of Croatia stated:

> Furthermore, in connection with the removal of numerous Serbian peasants, it is hoped that the problem of the large agrarian overpopulation of particular regions—for example, Zagoria,

148

Dalmatia, and the Lika—will be solved by a generous internal colonization. At the same time, the crop yield per hectare, still far
below the European average, is to be increased by a more intense
cultivation of the land.[31]

The transformation of racial science into sociology

To segregate the Jews according to plan, the General Government's ministry of interior, known as the Central Office (*Hauptabteilung*) for Internal
Administration, set up from the beginning a special office and assigned it a
name with many facets: Office for Population Policy and Welfare (*Abteilung
Bevölkerungswesen und Fürsorge*). The significance of this office for the
destruction of the Jews living in the General Government has hardly been
examined thus far; that is, its assessment in the literature is flawed.[32] The
office was first directed by Dr. Fritz Arlt, a member of the SS Security
Service. A student of Arnold Gehlen, Arlt was a theologian, sociologist, and
population specialist, who had gathered relevant experiences in Silesia and
Leipzig in connection with his bureaucratic activity of sorting out minorities,
in particular Jews.[33] In his first progress report of May 1940, he provided the
following summary: Among the most necessary instruments of a German
National Socialist administration over alien peoples (*fremdvölkische*) is an
official agency that is specifically concerned with the ethno-political (*volkspolitische*) structure of the region, because ethno-political knowledge of all
kinds—national, racial, statistical, historical, and so on—is basic for every
practical administrative task, ranging from the calculation of the expected
tax revenues to the distribution of the police force.[34]

Such a comprehensive task required experts who were qualified and
interested; Arlt as well as his successor Lothar Weirauch fulfilled such
requirements. Both were not only convinced race researchers, who as
members of the master race made no secret of their arrogance toward
Poles and Jews, but also clear-thinking social planners and demographers.
The most pressing task of the office was the racial assessment of people
and their division into different ethnic groups. The divisions not only were
expressed in statistical terms; they also determined the sum total of the
material conditions of life. Hence, alongside the desks for social welfare,
state welfare, resettlement, statistics, and the procurement of lineage certificates (*Sippenamt*), there were, respectively, special desks for Ukranians,
Jews, Poles, and ethnic Germans. As was stated, "each individual ethnic
group will be handled by a special desk (*Referat*)."[35] And the tie to welfare
was said to be necessary "in order to influence indirectly the ethnic policy
(*volkspolitische*) situation."[36]

This was thus a graduated system, sometimes positive and sometimes
negative, of social services and discriminations, ranging from food allocations

for resettled ethnic Germans to compulsory labor for Jews. Later on, the Office for Population Policy and Welfare coordinated and directed (*feder-führend*) ghettoization and the deportations, with the SS and police providing official assistance (*Amtshilfe*).[37]

Weirauch, who after the war described his work as having been purely charitable and received from former co-workers written confirmation that he had resisted the ethnic population policy of the SD by acting in favor of the Polish population,[38] characterized the office under his supervision at the beginning of 1943 as follows:

> Since my office is in charge of all ethnic policy issues—also including those dealing with resettlements—that concern the administration of the General Government, I have always been informed of the essential features of every evacuation and resettlement (*Aus- und Umsiedlung*). ... May I point out that in 1940 and 1941 my office managed the reception and accommodation of the evacuees from the incorporated eastern regions and, in addition, centrally managed and supervised all military defense settlements that had been created earlier or are now being set up. As the government's central agency for all ethnic policy questions, I am presently involved in two military defense planning projects.[39]

On 27 October 1942 Weirauch, at that time director of the Office for Population Policy and Welfare, participated as the General Government's representative in the third "Conference on the Final Solution."[40] A private letter of his deputy, Walther Föhl, documents the daily routine of the office:

> Every day we receive and take care of trains from all over Europe, each carrying over 1,000 Jews. We put them up more or less provisionally or, for the most part, push them off into the White Ruthenian swamps, in the direction of the Arctic Ocean where, if they have survived (which the Jews from the Kurfürstendamm or from Vienna and Bratislava certainly will not), they will all congregate toward the end of the war, but not before having built some highways. (But one should not talk about this!)[41]

Arlt and his men, among them the informant of the Foreign Institute in Stuttgart, Dr. Hans Hopf,[42] were faced in the General Government with a wealth of qualitative and quantitative problems. Thus Weirauch lamented the incapacity of the Polish workers and peasants to be civilized: "Just as each individual person is at a great loss to understand the most primitive requirements concerning his bodily cleanliness, so the workers and peasants as a whole demonstrate little love of order, organization, and little determination to achieve something."[43]

Arlt admitted that the racial hatred of the German occupation forces for the Polish "subhumans" and the Eastern Jews in the General Government was identical with the hatred of the propertied for the poor, thus reclassifying class differences as racial categories: "The social stratification of the population in the General Government is therefore simultaneously a racial stratification."[44] Racial policy was associated with a social regrouping process, and thus the Office of Population Policy and Welfare regarded it as the task of the German administration in the General Government to

> eliminate the influence exerted by the Polish upper classes that was damaging to the whole of the country but, at the same time, give them the opportunity to do useful work for the general reconstruction. In addition, it was necessary to pull the mass of Polish workers and peasants out of their dull inertia and encourage them to engage in productive activity.[45]

The factor disturbing the statisticians of the Office for Population Policy and Welfare in this task was the overpopulation in the General Government, "for the size of the population corresponds in no way to the possibility of satisfying the needs of the population."[46] As with Meinhold, the way to resolve the situation was through the "expansion of the space for food," which meant land improvement and increased crop yields per hectare in agriculture, or else the "reduction of the size of the population." In this respect, a beginning had already been made. As Arlt calculated, "thousands have dropped out of the population stock as victims of war." Moreover, "due to the consequences of war ... mortality [is] higher ... than it has been until now." Infants, old people, those who are too weak to live, the infirm, and the sick are "the groups most subject to the dying-off process."[47] Yet at the same time, the activity of Arlt himself intensified the problem of overpopulation. He reported in June 1940:

> We helped to implement the evacuations and resettlements from the *German eastern territory*, the *1st immediate plan* (40,000 Poles and Jews), *2nd current plan* (120,000 Poles and Jews), as well as a portion of the 35,000 *gypsies* who were announced to us. In cooperation with the district chiefs, the number of resettlements have thus been established district by district and the necessary provisioning as well as the transports have been taken in hand.

In addition, there was a plan for the "remigration of escaped and prisoner-of-war Poles from *Hungary and Rumania*."

> We are dealing here with approximately 40,000 men from each country. 450,000 Jews are to be deported to the region of the

151

General Government *from Greater Germany*. [Moreover, it is] planned to resolve the *gypsies* question by deporting approximately *35,000 gypsies* into these parts.[48]

The groups forcibly driven into the General Government burdened its economic structure all the more as all their possessions had been seized:

In view of the high degree of overpopulation, the problems of the General Government can no longer be solved without recourse to the public welfare system. There is the added factor that the number of those who cannot support themselves on their own, or must be supported in their daily lives by the public at large, is constantly rising.[49]

The solution Arlt had proposed was not only to cut down population growth by means of forced resettlements, but also to remove at once the original overpopulation. And like Meinhold, Arlt too wanted to combine the expulsion and destruction of human beings with the "rehabilitation" of both economy and population policy, as well as the modernization of the General Government. With the removal of the Jews, "the living space of the General Government would be relieved of about 1,500,000 Jews." Population density would thus be reduced from 126 to 110 people per square kilometer, a size which, "while the possibility of seasonal migration to the German labor market is maintained," promises to be a "successful, constructive solution." Thus,

At first, a great number of employment opportunities would be provided for the local, non-Jewish population; that is, that part of the Polish population that is unemployed or underemployed would experience essential relief ... By way of a sociological restructuring process, some of these Poles could then occupy the positions in industry, trade, and the crafts that the Jews had previously possessed. This would constitute an essential contribution to the social recovery of the Polish agricultural proletariat. At the same time, such relief for the majority of rural workers would provide further opportunities for dealing constructively with the problem of overpopulation.[50]

The sociological concept of "social regrouping"—"socially regrouped Jews" (*Umschichtungsjuden*)[51] were also mentioned—became a synonym for deportation. For Arlt and Weirauch, the destruction of the Jews was a matter of population policy; and they also knew how to assert that way of looking at things outside their office and impose it even upon the coterie of their opponents.

In December 1942, the public health officer (*Amtsarzt*) in Warsaw, Dr. Wilhelm Hagen, wrote a worried letter to Hitler. At a meeting on tuberculosis, he had learned from Weirauch that while resettling 200,000 Poles "so that German military peasants (*Wehrbauern*) could be settled," it was intended "to proceed against a third of the Poles—70,000 old people and children under ten years old—in the same manner as against the Jews, that is, to kill them." Hagen suspected that "the idea probably arose because at the moment there seems to be no space for the Poles that are to be resettled, insofar as they cannot be utilized directly for labor work in the armaments industry."[52]

Hagen's scruples, however, involved only the fact that it was intended to proceed against the Poles "in the same manner." He objected because, on the one hand, this would supply new grounds for agitation to the Reich's opponents in the General Government as well as in foreign countries and, on the other hand, in terms of the population policy, he thought such a procedure unreasonable:

> From the perspective of population policy, thorough considerations have convinced me that we have no interest in the reduction of the size of the Polish population or the impairment of the upward population trend. Of all foreign laborers, the Pole should be regarded, in the racial sense, as an element that is close to us and very much less of a danger than the races of the southeast, whose population pressures we will not be able to withstand permanently with just our own strength.[53]

If one follows Hagen's line of argument, then genocide based on population policy was indeed something worth discussing, something already practiced; and Hitler and Hagen obviously agreed that, insofar as the Jews were concerned, population policy required that they be killed.

The project concerning the Polish middle class

The idea of a far-reaching rearrangement at the cost of the Jews in Poland, as Arlt had developed from a sociological point of view, supplemented economic policy strategies. When Dr. Walter Emmerich of Hamburg, who had been appointed on 13 June 1940 as the new chief of the Central Office for Economy in the General Government, explained "the basic principles of the economic policy he intended to pursue" to Hans Frank, they resembled Arlt's population policy plans. According to Emmerich, "the prerequisite for a successful economic activity" consisted of "a fundamental change in the entire economic structure." Already in his first days in office, it was clear to Emmerich how this was to take place. As he explained to Frank, "first, a significant rationalization has to take place in the Jewish sector." Moreover, "in place of the many small businesses, viable medium-sized businesses must be established," of course by non-Jewish Poles: "Compression of the Jewish sector would create the possibility for advancement of the Polish sector ... Naturally, this commercial migration would have to be organized in such a way that it does not transpire without restraint."[54] Emmerich meant thereby the orderly despoilment through the use of laws, trustees, and the exertion of the state's monopoly of power.

The small Jewish retail trade (*Kleinhandel*) could not be controlled by German wholesalers, but this could be done through the newly created and artificial "medium-sized enterprises" (*Mittelexistenzen*). If locally limited Jewish trade had made the imperialist penetration of the newly conquered "spaces" difficult, the projected "commercial migration" would open up the markets of the East. For this purpose, Emmerich suggested the establishment of a German-Polish chamber of commerce with the proviso that the leadership of all its institutional functions rest in German hands: "Poles should only cooperate, but should not make decisions." Frank assured his new economics minister of his "unconditional support" for these plans.

The appointment of Emmerich turned out to be an economic policy coup for Hamburg. Severely cut off from its old trading partners by the war, the commercial firms of the Hanseatic city demanded compensation in the East.[55] The warehouses of the trading companies of Hamburg and Bremen were filled with goods, which since the outbreak of war could not be exported and would find no buyers in Germany either. The products, favored by the high, artificially maintained course of the zloty, would be dumped on the new General Government market. The Reich Economic Ministry initially gave these firms the right to import goods valued at ten million reichsmarks into the General Government.[56] After only three months, the markets had already been divided among the firms. The *Ostdeutscher Beobachter* reported that "a number of trustworthy German wholesale trading firms [have been] commissioned ... to set up a commercial enterprise in each of the 40 districts." As investment capital, they had already brought along supplies of goods that, due to the war, the Reich could no longer export. As their umbrella organization, the firms established "The German Merchants Trading Company, Inc." in order to "achieve a satisfactory position vis-à-vis production in the General Government as well as in transactions with the authorities."[57] Altogether, 22 of the most prestigious commercial firms from Hamburg and nine from Bremen established themselves in the General Government as "district wholesale traders" doing business without competition.[58] Ultimately, the Germans also planned to extend this practice, which they also pursued after the occupation in the Soviet Union in the General Commissariat *Ostland*, with the inclusion of Dutch, and even French, Belgian, and Swiss wholesale trading firms.

154

Emmerich did not arrive in Poland by himself. To head the desk that handled basic economic policies in his office, Emmerich appointed Max Biehl, who had formerly edited the *Wirtschaftsdienst* of Hamburg. To head the economics section in the German Institute for Projects in the East, Emmerich, who simultaneously (in *Personalunion*) headed this Institute, procured Helmut Meinhold, an economist who in 1935 had received his economics degree in Hamburg. Meinhold's two assistants, Hans Kraft Nonnenmacher and Erika Bochdam-Löptien, also came from Hamburg. Emmerich himself had studied economics in Hamburg between 1922 and 1930 and had then worked at the University of Hamburg until he transferred in 1934 to become a civil servant in the agency for economics of the government of Hamburg. In Cracow, he saw himself "as the man from Hamburg in an exposed and advanced position," as one of those persons "who have the courage to make himself available for work in the east" and took care that "the lines to Hamburg" would not be cut off.[59] Emmerich and his co-workers not only represented the economic interests of Hamburg; they also belonged to the Kiel-Hamburg school, especially famous through the Kiel Institute of World Economics, which combined economic theory and economic practice in such an excellent and farsighted manner.

Frank's appointment of the highly educated Emmerich as the economics minister of his government in Cracow, which was just being consolidated, was part of a comprehensive concept that placed expertise above party dogmas. Emmerich had joined the Nazi Party only in 1937 in order to promote his official career, and his attitude to it remained quite critical. He regarded it as his task to make clear to the uneducated minor officials of the party in Cracow that they knew nothing about economic policy and should leave the restructuring of this important sector to specialists and experts, such as himself.[60]

But there were substantial points of contact between the racial program, on the one hand, and the efficiency-oriented economic leadership, on the other. Insofar as racial policy fell into line with the tenets of social and economic policy, it also became, among other things, an auxiliary political instrument. In a series of articles published by the *Berliner Börsenzeitung*, Emmerich wrote:

> If the production apparatus of the General Government is at the disposal of the entire greater-German market, and if it is being granted all kinds of easements that are justifiable due to its close relationship to the Reich, then the most essential prerequisite will have been created in that this country, which is not favored by nature, will also find its economic equilibrium and can be lead, step by step, toward greater prosperity. The orientation of the economy toward such economic policy bases will go hand in hand

with the far reaching changes brought about by elimination of the Jews from the economy. Their dominant position in the economic life of the earlier Polish republic is known. Here we have an important starting point to counteract in a planned way the alien manifestations that were evident in trade as well as the crafts, and thus to give to this densely populated country an internal structure through the formation of a broad and non-alien middle class stratum.[61]

In the context of Aryanization, which had already progressed considerably by then, most small-sized Jewish businesses were closed, and the most profitable among them were consolidated. This tremendous push toward rationalization created larger economic units and reduced the number of middlemen, that is, the chain of retail dealers that was typical for Poland at the time, and thus, by reducing trade margins, would bring down prices. In this way, the purchasing power of the Polish population was to be raised without the producers having to suffer a loss of income. This measure was important for the middleman trade in both agrarian products and the so-called cottage industries, which Polish peasant families pursued as secondary sources of income and which allegedly were until then the special "objects of exploitation by Jewish contractors."

By consolidating businesses, however, only the middle level of trade, the retail trade, was reorganized, since on the level of the wholesale trade it was above all the Germans who were to profit from Aryanization and economic restructuring. "Aryan" Poles were trained to replace the many Jewish small retail merchants and small businessmen; these Poles were to take over the rationalized businesses and form the basis of a new Polish middle class. In the crafts industry the procedure was similar, though slower, in that "Polish-Aryan replacements" were trained and Polish craftsmen received Jewish enterprises. This project of social upward mobility served both as an outlet for the agrarian overpopulation and, in general, as an offer to appease the Polish population.

The Germans created for themselves in the General Government a comprehensive apparatus for managing the economy, which manifested itself in various institutions such as, for example, the Transfer Agency (*Transferstelle*) for the Warsaw ghetto; to manage rationalization in the various branches of the economy, they created, for example, the trusteeship administration, economic management agencies, the Central Chamber for the Economy, and the General Government Office of the Reich Board for Economy and Efficiency. All these institutions were to make possible not only the full use of economic capacities, but also a comprehensive rationalization: that is, the introduction of industrial standardization; compulsory bookkeeping for businesses beyond a specific size; the introduction of the Refa Time Measurement System; the training in rational plant management, Taylorization, piecework; and the establishment of qualifications for Polish craftsmen and skilled workers, who were also to be used in the Reich as needed. In sum, the principles of productivity, thinking in terms of efficiency, order, and work discipline, were to replace production hitherto geared toward meeting immediate needs and also supplant the "eastern-Slavic attitude of mind" in the "Polish economy," and thus make this "tributary land of the Reich" into a well-functioning segment of the European grand region (*Großraum*).

On 27 March 1941, at the first working conference of the Frankfurt Institute for the Investigation of the Jewish Question (*Institut zur Erforschung der Judenfrage*), the economist Peter-Heinz Seraphim presented these plans to an "expert public" (*Fachöffentlichkeit*) that considered the "Jewish question" ripe for decision. At the same time, Seraphim pointed beyond Poland: the proportion of Jews in Eastern Europe amounted to between six and twelve percent, in the rest of the European countries to about one percent. The "Jewish problem" was a problem particularly for those places where the occupation force was devising the administrative and economic structure for the new regions, namely the cities. Precisely because so many Jews did live there, "a sudden solution of the question" would pose technical and economic difficulties; nevertheless, it would have to be tackled systematically as well as judiciously, and replacements would have to be provided. Seraphim continued:

> Without doubt such a possibility does exist, since among the peasant population of the Romanians, Magyars, Ukrainians, Slovaks, and Poles there is a population "superpressure" (*Überdruck*) that opens the way for replacing the Jewish petty bourgeoisie with native elements of the population. For years, the Jewish elements in the cities prevented succeeding generations of peasants from nations long settled on the land to advance in the cities. The cities have been "blocked," so to speak, by the Jews. Now the moment seems to have arrived for breaking the monopoly.[62]

"Construction" (*Aufbauwerk*) in the General Government, about which the Germans still boasted even after the war, included the creation, at the expense of the Jewish population, of a Polish petty bourgeoisie that was prepared to collaborate. The following excerpts from contemporaneous newspapers provide evidence for this practice:

The Polish middle class

According to reports in the Polish papers, a measure has been introduced in the Warsaw district with the generous assistance of

157

the German authorities, which is of the greatest significance for the positive social-political development of the Polish population. By establishing numerous Polish trade schools (*Fachschulen*), it is intended to promote the formation of a healthy Polish middle class, which was almost entirely lacking in the Poland of earlier times. A number of such schools have already been opened in the Warsaw district, including agricultural and commercial schools, schools for metal workers and electrical engineers, as well as other schools.[63]

Basketmaking

In the basketmaking crafts of the Cracow district, which represented one of the biggest branches of the home industry there, and which before the war employed a total of 50,000 persons in the two main regions of Rudnik and Radscha, the Jewish distributors and dealers, who previously predominated up to 95 percent, have been completely eliminated.[64]

Development and extension

There can be no doubt, however, that in the distant future the question of reordering trade requires an irrevocable solution. The aim can only be the recovery of trade by limiting the number of commercial enterprises, the limitation and elimination of Jewish trade, insofar as this is feasible and economically justifiable, the development and extension of a Polish cooperative system in order to detach the peasant from the Jew, strict controls over trade, and the ruthless struggle against unfair business methods which, as far as trade in the General Government is concerned, have been the order of the day up to now.[65]

Competition

Radom, 30 January. The German administration wishes to offer an opportunity to the Polish crafts industry, which hitherto has had to fight the tough competition of the Jewish crafts industry, to broaden its skills and thus assist in its attainment of a sound working basis. The director of the Chamber of Crafts in Radom, Dr. Lichtenhäler, wants to introduce special training for the Polish tailors of Radom, which is to be handled by a specialist from Warsaw.[66]

Warsaw businesses

Warsaw, 13 March. In one of the lecture evenings at the German Center for Popular Education (*Volksbildungsstätte*), the chief of the Resettlement Office of the District Chief of Warsaw, *Reichsamtsleiter* Schön, dealt with the theme of ethnic order (*Volkstumsordnung*) in the Warsaw district. The speaker emphasized that the elimination of Jewry in the economic sphere would encourage the establishment of a sounder economic structure for the Polish population. A Polish middle class was until now always absent, since the sources of livelihood for this population group were in Jewish hands. If up to now, for example, it has been possible to distribute 4–5,000 stores and workshops to the Poles in Warsaw, then this already constitutes an important beginning for the formation of a Polish middle class.[67]

Cracow

The order about the formation of a Jewish quarter in Cracow, the capital city of the General Government, was issued already some time ago. The District Chief has now issued the implementation decree. It concerns the Jewish business and factory enterprises in Cracow and their possible transfer, the changeover of merchant and craft establishments, and the liquidation of enterprises in whose continued operation there is no public interest.[68]

In Aryan hands

The City Commissioner of Neu-Sandez, Dr. Friedrich Schmidt, works with all possible energy to give the city a German appearance. In place of the dirty and inhospitable Jewish shops there are to be bright and clean businesses. Thus about 70 shops in Neu-Sandez previously owned by Jews have been taken over by Aryans. The city took care that the shops not only changed hands, but also changed character. From two or sometimes even three filthy cubbyholes, which the Jew considered to be shops, there frequently arose beautiful, spacious stores, which also would be infused with light and air. For the Polish business world located near the throughways, it became a matter of course to have the signposts and street names in two languages. The many ugly advertising signs, formerly jutting out into the streets, have vanished.[69]

Economic surgery

When it became known two years ago that the German administration intended to eliminate the Jews rapidly and totally from Polish economic life, Polish economic circles were at first clearly fearful that this drastic intervention would result in a massive setback for the economy, which had already suffered a considerable breakdown due to the lost military adventure against the Reich. There was great surprise when, thanks to the carefully preplanned precautionary and transition measures, the massive surgery performed on the Polish economy proceeded almost without pain. This surprise changed into relief when for many a Pole, who had been able to salvage parts of his wealth from the debacle, the possibility opened up to move, in place of a Jew, into the partial ownership of an enterprise. Suddenly countless professional positions opened up for the young people in the crafts. Rapidly the German authorities had to organize the trade school system and the retraining of unused labor forces, so that the young people needed for the jobs would be available.[70]

Segregation and advancement

Due to the absolute predominance of the Jews, it has been impossible for employees to acquire experience by rising to managing positions in either technical or commercial fields, or to secure in this way for themselves the necessary connections to buyers, suppliers, and the authorities. In the meantime, the segregation of the Jews will create for the population of the General Government opportunities for upward mobility, with the precondition, however, that the applicants, aside from demonstrating the necessary open-mindedness, also acquire sufficient specialized skills.[71]

Beautiful successes

In the crafts concerned with textiles and leather wear, the elimination of Jewish craftsmen has necessitated a particularly vigorous supply of skilled labor. The efforts made in this respect have led to beautiful successes and they demonstrate that a restructuring of the crafts groups is possible within a relatively short period of time. It will thus also be possible to satisfy the special needs currently arising in metal crafts. The rural crafts can likewise be promoted in the interest of agriculture and can be strengthened numerically.[72]

Rationalization

Already in early summer 1940, the RKW established the "General Government Bureau." The RKW, an institution that dated back to the Weimar period, had an excellent reputation. At that time the abbreviation RKW stood for Reich Board for Economy and Efficiency (*Reichskuratorium für Wirtschaftlichkeit*). Today RKW stands for an institution with the same purpose, namely, modernization and efficiency, and is called Board for the Rationalization of the German Economy (*Rationalisierungskuratorium der deutschen Wirtschaft*). The director of the Cracow bureau, Dr. Rudolf Gater, had already known Emmerich in Vienna. In 1938–1940, Gater, then at RKW's Vienna branch, saw to it that Jewish properties were not simply despoiled and transferred, but that Aryanization was linked to modernization and concentration of the supposedly backward economy of the "*Ostmark*." Emmerich, then representative of Hamburg interests in Vienna and economic plenipotentiary on the staff of Josef Bürckel, the Reich Commissioner for Austria's Reunion with the German Reich, implemented the Aryanization of export firms with the least possible friction. In Cracow, too, Gater pursued his task with the energy he had exhibited in Vienna; he was clearsighted and shunned ideological insipidness. His bureau's reports were always stamped "strictly confidential" or "classified," and only a few numbered copies were distributed.

Gater and his co-workers characterized the productive capacities of the Polish workers as being "without exception smaller" than those of their German counterparts. This was partly so because "the Polish worker [could] not be described as diligent." Realistic as he was, however, Gater mainly attributed this low productivity, which was 40 percent lower by comparison, to an "anti-German attitude" and, above all, to hunger. The persistent demands made by Gater's bureau, and later also supported by Frank, always included improved nutrition for the Polish industrial workers and the distribution of food rations through the factories.

If the industry of the General Government was to become somewhat competitive, the high Polish protective tariffs would have to be reduced. Their step-by-step reduction, which over a long-term period could be entered into the calculations of the entrepreneurs, was similar to the comparability procedure used in the Common Market today and was described by Gater as the "transformation of protective tariffs into educational tariffs." Furthermore, Gater demanded a "stronger division of labor"; the "establishment of more rational production methods (mass production, assembly-line production)"; the introduction of "bookkeeping and cost calculation methods";[73] and by militarizing work to a certain degree, "a stricter work and factory discipline, which is adapted to the Polish worker." Gater emphatically demanded the rationalization of agriculture. The areas to be cultivated were to be enlarged through land reform and the reparcelling of the agricultural land of communities so that the mechanization of agriculture—which Gater intended to push through by introducing the compulsory buying of agricultural machinery—would pay off.

Only if Germanophobia, hunger, the lack of work discipline, a weak infrastructure, and the chaotic organization of enterprises in industry, in the skilled trades, and in agriculture were combatted simultaneously, could the low wage level of the General Government serve as a wage advantage. Only then would it be possible to construct a "supplemental economy in the grand region." In December 1940 Gater concluded a report about the "Economic Foundations of the General Government." He calculated that on the average there were 129 persons per square kilometer in the General Government, while in East Prussia, which as a predominantly agrarian area was particularly well suited for comparison with the General Government, the average was only 63 persons. For Gater, who measured all economies against those of the German Reich, the social structure in the General Government seemed comparatively miserable; and because of the excessively high birth rate, there was no improvement in sight:

> When reflecting on the exceedingly unfavorable social structure of the G[eneral] G[overnment], one must also consider the population increase, which in the years between 1931 and 1939 amounted to an average of 1.2 percent per year. If one assumes a future population growth of only 1 percent per year, there will be a population increase of about 120,000 persons per year. Since agriculture can no longer absorb anyone and, on the contrary, shows a large excess of an underemployed population, the steady population increase will produce a considerable intensification of the social problems in the G[eneral] G[overnment]. Even if the G[eneral] G[overnment] per se is industrialized to only a negligible extent, which means that an increase is indeed possible, it is still out of the question to transfer the high excess of people to industry ... Just to absorb the population increase, the yearly growth rate, after the level of 1938 has again been reached, would have to be ca. 11 percent.[74]

This calculation already included a reduction of the yearly excess of the population from 1.2 percent to 1 percent and thus allowed for 24,000 people per year to disappear from the statistics. But even in this manipulated version, it seemed impossible that newly created industrial jobs would absorb the yearly population increases; the real growth of 11 percent was illusory.

According to Gater, forced labor in the Reich would not suffice to make the huge population excesses of the General Government productive. Three hundred forty thousand Poles were already subjected to it, and Gater shrewdly predicted that the number of forced laborers could "perhaps be raised to two million persons old enough to work."[75] Furthermore, even voluntary emigration did not hold out the prospect of reducing the population of the General Government sufficiently.

Already in this study, Gater implicitly called for a "solution" to the so-called overpopulation problem, a solution that in a wider sense could be described as the policy of "evacuation" by force:

> Even if the big and particularly work-intensive public construction projects planned for the coming years (above all, the extension of the interior waterways, the water supply, and road construction) will be accompanied by a certain lessening of the population pressure, by and large the problem of overpopulation will still remain. To solve it exclusively within the space (*Raum*) formed by the G[eneral] G[overnment] will cause extraordinarily great difficulties.

The problem was further intensified by the approximately eight million Poles living in the newly incorporated German eastern territories. "Since above all West Prussia, southeast Prussia, and the Wartheland are to become a peasants' land (*Bauernland*) settled by Germans," about six million Poles, according to Gater's calculation, had to be "removed" from there in the course of time. Since the General Government was in no position whatever to take on these people, the rationalization expert Gater, who saw himself as an unpolitical scientific expert and did not belong to the Nazi Party, wrote as follows:

> Thus other means must be sought otherwise to accommodate these people *and* the excess overpopulation of the G[eneral] G[overnment], after deducting the Jews that are to be resettled (*auszusiedeln*) from this total number.[76]

While Gater in December 1940 thus regarded the statement "the Jews that are to be resettled" as a firmly established factor in his calculation concerning population and economic policy (and it should be noted that these were the Jews from the General Government), he made the removal of the Poles dependent on the victorious outcome of the war and the "new possibilities" that would then become available. Thus Gater, too, must have belonged to the German planners in Cracow who, regardless of how the war developed and without regard to voluntary or forced emigration, already considered in 1940 the possibility of eliminating the Polish Jews from the population of the General Government; and how could this be done except through physical destruction?

In the section entitled "The Jews in the Economy," Gater urged that a consistent, as well as graduated, procedure to remove the Polish Jews from commerce and the crafts of the General Government be adopted. As was the case with Emmerich and Arlt, Gater's concept combined the "creation of a viable Polish middle class" with the economic and social expropriation of the Jews:

> The *exclusion* (*Ausschaltung*) of Jewish traders and craftsmen will be ... expediently undertaken *in stages*, so that in the interim period the necessary replacements can be procured. The detachment of the Jews from trade and workshops takes place, on the one hand, by closing a certain number of enterprises so as to get rid simultaneously of considerable overstaffing and, on the other hand, by retraining the Poles who are to replace the Jews...
>
> The removal of the *Jewish entrepreneur and landlord* takes place through trustees taking over enterprises and real estate. The proceeds from such assets are used in part for retiring the debt and developing the enterprises. Only a very small portion goes to the support of the former owners. *The rest will go to the government of the G[eneral] G[overnment]*. The Jewish workers, due to the above mentioned measures now available, will be utilized, individually or in brigades, for work designated by the labor exchanges. Out of the 1.7 million Jews living in the G[eneral] G[overnment], 400,000 have been registered at present in the *Jewish Card File* (*Judenkartei*) as capable of work. Any further participation of Jews in the economy of the General Government will be limited by the decree concerning the acquisition of industrial enterprises, businesses, and shares.

> The *total task* for the immediate future can be stated somewhat more precisely in that, little by little, Jewry is to be totally eliminated from the industrial economy. By creating a viable *Polish middle class*, it will then be possible to achieve a considerably more harmonious population structure.[77]

In May 1941, the General Government Bureau of the Reich Board for Economy and Efficiency produced a confidential report about the crafts in the General Government. This study described the scope and economic significance of the crafts, differentiating between "Jews and non-Jews" and between individual districts. It concluded that before the war an average of 50 percent of all craftsmen in the General Government had been Jews; this percentage was in part much higher in the cities, but less by half in the country. Thus, it was precisely in the crafts that the expulsion (*Vertreibung*) of the Jews had to lead to substantial structural changes.

Nevertheless, the jobs and the workshops of the ghettoized Jews were not to be distributed to Polish craftsmen simply at will, but to those in particular who had been forcefully removed from the annexed western part of Poland. The study estimated their number at 50,000; further, the study concluded that, "by already having pushed back the Jewish crafts and by eliminating them completely later on," these Polish craftsmen "can be accommodated in full in the crafts industry of the G[eneral] G[overnment]."[78] The takeover of Jewish workshops by Poles was to be managed by the Trustee Office according to the pattern of Aryanization that had proved a success in Austria. The Polish craftsmen were to receive credit in order to buy new means of production; moreover, they were to be supported by receiving public contracts for the production of, for example, uniforms, ammunition pouches, ammunition cases, and other goods.

The economy of the ghetto

The controlling economic authority of the Warsaw ghetto, the Transfer Agency of Warsaw, was established at the time of the ghetto itself. Max Bischof, the director of a Viennese bank, was appointed to head the agency.[79] With respect to economic policy, the ghetto was treated as a "foreign country," for which the Germans sought an even balance of trade. The ghetto was a country, however, that, aside from its inhabitants' labor power, had almost no resources and had to buy all means of production as well as foodstuffs from the outside and pay for them with manufactured products or in cash. The Transfer Agency supervised the legally permitted imports and exports of the ghetto; managed its material assets; collected dues for services and utilities (rent, gas, water, electricity, etc.); and negotiated production contracts between German and Polish firms, on the one side, and Jewish enterprises in the ghetto, on the other. It thus had control over the crucial levers with which to regulate the living standard of the ghetto, a control that was nevertheless partially undermined by the so-called black market. Raul Hilberg describes the situation as follows: Bischof did not curb the black market and therefore could not harness the total production of the ghetto, as the *Gettoverwaltung* in Lodz had done, for the maximization of German gains; but like his colleagues in Lodz, he could always neglect to send enough food and fuel into the ghetto, thus constraining its cost.[80] This gave Bischof the opportunity to even out the balance of foreign trade, that is, to have the surplus from the ghetto flow into the Aryan sector. The ghettoization "was an act of total spoliation,"[81] which took place by way of the black market as well as the Transfer Agency.

In the short term, the creation of the ghetto had not only brought profits to the economy (through Aryanization and forced labor), but also saved the state money, since the Jews themselves had to provide police and administrative services for the Jewish sector of the population and had to assume as well all welfare costs. At the government meeting on 3 April 1941, the city commandant of Warsaw, Ludwig Leist, ascertained with satisfaction that the establishment of the ghettos signified

> great relief for the city, particularly with respect to personnel matters. All services hitherto performed by the city are now being shifted on the Jewish community.[82]

But by despoiling the Jews of all their material resources and incarcerating them in the ghetto, the Germans also deprived them of the possibility of earning their livelihood on a permanent basis. In this manner, the ghetto in Lodz, one of the first created in occupied Poland, became an operation that had to be subsidized by the occupation authorities. Although the Jews there were forced to work for the army or for private firms, the ghetto in Lodz required, according to the report of the Reich Budget Office (*Reichsrechnungshof*), a monthly subsidy of one million marks,[83] simply because there were an insufficient number of production facilities and the ghetto inhabitants manufactured far below the required technical standards. Of course, even the subsidies for the ghetto in Lodz ultimately came from Jewish assets, that is, from the budget of the Central Trustee Office East (*Haupttreuhandstelle Ost*), which managed Aryanized firms and confiscated Jewish capital.

The occupation authorities in the General Government utilized the experiences gained in Lodz when they created the Warsaw Ghetto. In General Governor Frank's opinion, however, there was no alternative to establishing a ghetto. "Even if this measure did create expenses," he still had the "reassuring feeling of having half a million Jews under control."[84] Moreover, it was assumed that ghettoization was necessary to combat the black market generated by the German occupation and that the economic order in the General Government could not be guaranteed without it.

At two government meetings in April 1941, the governors and economic experts of the General Government dealt intensively with the possibilities of building up an efficient ghetto economy and, in contrast to Lodz, of reaching a positive balance of trade for the ghetto. On this occasion, Emmerich handed Frank a report by the Reich Board for Economy and Efficiency concerning "The Economic Balance of the Jewish Quarter in Warsaw" and had also brought along the report's author, Dr. Gater. According to Gater, in contrast to the ghetto in Lodz, where at the start all supplies and means of production had been removed from the ghetto, which was then completely shut off from the outside world, the Warsaw ghetto, although it should be "an economic district in itself," nevertheless "must be connected with its surroundings." Gater had calculated that every ghetto resident must do an average of 93-Groschen worth of work per day in order to cover the value of imports into the ghetto from the outside, that is, to meet the demands made by the Germans, which added up to a sum total of approximately 500,000 zloty a day.

These conclusions, as Gater himself noted, were not based on a system that calculated the minimum living wage, "but on a system of calculation that only took into consideration the value of the external balance of payments." Therefore, it was all the same whether the goods imported into the ghetto sufficed to sustain its residents or not. If not enough was imported, either the ghetto residents attempted to secure for themselves supplies of food, coal, and so on in other ways—such as through the black market at excessive prices—or they had to starve to death. From the perspective of the economic expert, the only important factor was whether the Jews were in a position to pay for the imports to the ghetto.

As the allocation of food and raw materials lay in German hands, so too the possibility for ghetto residents to produce the necessary quantities in order to pay for the imports to the ghetto depended on German decisions. For an estimation of the profitability of the ghetto, it was of essential importance, of course, to know the level of wages of the Jews working in the labor camps outside the ghettos. Gater assumed that on the average "one could reckon with approximately 10 zloty per week." This led him to the following conclusion:

> In view of the fact that the individual Jew can only be used for seven to eight months per year in external labor (*Außendienst*), one can calculate that three Jews will have to be used for work outside in order to maintain the balance of payments value (*Außenbilanzwert*) of one Jew in the ghetto. If one were to use higher payments in the camps as the basis for these calculations, the ratio would perhaps be improved to two to one.

In terms of the ghetto's balance of payments, the forced labor organized by the state thus yielded next to nothing. The Jews had to provide a large part of their necessities of life through their own material and physical resources, while the occupation authorities or, alternatively, German and Polish private enterprises enriched themselves at their expense. Yet the profitability of the ghetto, and thereby ultimately also the right of its inhabitants to exist, depended on wages that were arbitrarily fixed. "Regarding the question of what the Jew could earn from his work in the Jewish quarters," Gater had "no real experiences as yet"; nevertheless, he started with the assumption of considerably more favorable orders of magnitude. First of all, he based his calculations on a daily productivity of five zloty per head and reached the conclusion that "as a result 60 to 65,000 Jews would have to be employed productively in order to [achieve] the necessary balance" for the whole ghetto. But the rationalization expert

Gater also noted the fact that without prior investment this balance could in no way be attained. He estimated that the credit needed to finance the necessary machines and raw materials would require a loan of 30 to 40 million zloty. To this, Emmerich added the proposal that for the purpose of carrying out their contracts German wholesale trading firms be moved to the ghetto, for which, of course, they would also have to be allowed a certain influence on the organization of Jewish labor so "as to insure that all requirements with respect to quality, delivery dates, etc. are met with satisfaction."[85]

The district governors and the heads of the central offices of the General Government agreed that the "whole ghetto issue be dealt with strictly according to the guidelines of the Central Office for the Economy (*Hauptabteilung Wirtschaft*)." This meant above all that in the ghetto, capitalist profit for private economic gain would not be permitted; rather, a system of strict management would be instituted, enabling the Central Office to determine the utilization of Jewish labor as well as the allocation of raw materials for the ghetto. The firms admitted to the ghetto were to be able to draw a maximum of added value from Jewish labor, while, at the same time, as high a proportion as possible of the costs for the support of the ghetto could be shifted to the Jewish community. In short, the goal to be achieved was "to manage the ghetto in such a way that it cost the state virtually nothing."[86]

The ghettos were regarded as a temporary arrangement. Nevertheless, in April 1941 Emmerich still thought that this was "not a matter that could already be liquidated in one year." Thus, until the prerequisite provisions for the "final solution of the Jewish question" were in place, one had to be economical with the means at hand. But very soon it was clear to the men around Emmerich

> that the ghetto was financially not viable. It could not live without subsidies if the aim was to maintain the ability of the Jews to survive. With this statement, nothing is said as yet about the justification for the ghetto. It is, after all, a temporary concentration camp until such time as the Jews can be deported.[87]

Actually, the export surplus rose steadily after July 1942.[88] But the economic success was based on the hunger of the ghetto residents and the terror of the first deportations to Treblinka. It was a success that impressed the president of the Central Office for Construction, Theodor Bauder, to such a degree that he "suggested an operation against the Poles also, an operation similar to the one carried out these days against the Jews. For it has been demonstrated that the Jewish operation has resulted in a great onrush of Jews to be employed."[89]

Rumors of the approaching "resettlements" circulated in the ghetto even before the deportations began. Since "unproductive" people—

children, the old, and the sick—were transported first, employment remained for the ghetto inhabitants the only hope for survival. But a positive trade balance for the ghetto, that is, achieving a surplus of required exports, did not delay the deportations from the ghetto by a single day; nor did it save the lives of the ghetto inhabitants. In the under-capitalized economy of the ghetto and, in particular, under conditions of the war economy, production was inefficient, even if the Jews did manage to produce a bit of a surplus; for it tied up scarce resources that could produce considerably greater values with a better organization of labor and a more favorable combination of work and capital.

At the meeting of April 1941 concerning the Reich Board's report on the ghetto, Emmerich himself had still raised the question "whether ghetto enterprises should be favored in allocating raw materials, even at the risk of thereby throwing workers in the non-Jewish Polish enterprises out of their jobs."[90] At that time the question remained open, but a decision became increasingly apparent in the months that followed. The more the food situation became decisive for the retention of German domination over occupied Poland and for the outcome of the war, the less the Germans could afford the capital drain of a backward ghetto economy. This was especially true if other capacities remained unused, or as long as the "Aryan" enterprises quite frequently failed to meet their quotas because workers became sick from malnutrition or were engaged in illicit trading, and finally as long as the enterprises produced considerable quantities for an illegal market. In October 1942, the Armaments Inspector of the General Government, Lieutenant General Schindler, still complained, "In general, 25 percent of the work force drop out because of absenteeism, in some individual plants even up to 70 percent during the summer months." According to Schindler, a plant would therefore have to employ 30 percent more workers than were actually necessary. His constant interventions were henceforth aimed at tying the workers to their work places by granting them and their families bigger food rations and by cheaply selling the vitally necessary objects and textiles within the plant.[91] Also, production based on cheap forced labor from the ghetto would undercut the capitalized enterprises in the Aryan sector and prevent their modernization by means of dumping prices.

At the first meeting of the armanents commission of the General Government on 24 October 1942, Lieutenant General Schindler (at whose suggestion, by the way, the Reich Board for Economy and Efficiency supposedly wrote its report on the efficiency of the Warsaw ghetto) declared the following with respect to the imminent loss of Jewish workers:

In addition, about 50,000 Jews are employed in plants working for the Wehrmacht, but at the beginning of next year the Jews are supposed to be removed from these plants; that is, they have to be

169

replaced by other workers. Therefore, some way must be found to procure new workers. This can only be done by shutting down plants that these days still manufacture products that are not important for armanents and, on top of it all, are not lucrative; moreover, they frequently produce solely for the black market, use black market materials in processing goods, and deprive the armaments industry of its first-rate skilled workers. It will be the task of the Central Office for the Economy to identify these plants, close them down, and draw up a plan for those remaining.[92]

Schindler asked Emmerich to arrange for these measures and, at the same time, concluded a consulting contract with Rudolf Gater. The argument of labor scarcity was thus to be used to release material and human resources and promote the further concentration of the entire war economy. This development would soon apply to the Reich as well. The *Speer-Chronik* thus reported about a meeting of office chiefs on 9 August 1943:

In order to digest the big bite taken with the "industrial war economy," three new offices have been established: raw materials, planning, and production of consumer goods. The latter even had to tolerate the name "Despoilment Office" (*Amt zur Ausplünderung*). It encompassed also those economic sectors that were to be engaged particularly strongly in transplanting workers to the armaments factories.[93]

The Despoilment Office, which explicitly gave rationalization and concentration of the war economy priority over the quantitative expansion of forced labor, was headed by Georg Seebauer, Gater's old director at the Reich Board for Economy and Efficiency.

In the first quarter of 1943, 834 plants in the industrial sector of the General Government were then actually shut down because they either lacked importance or did not produce sufficiently. Gater worked out rationalization proposals for individual enterprises such as, for example, the German Factory for Enamelled Goods in Cracow. By the third quarter of the year, 250 more plants were already shut down in favor of a "limited group of those operating most rationally," the so-called concentration plants. Parallel to this, "the operation of concentrating the crafts" involved 13,600 shutdowns. The Armaments Inspection judged the overall results as quite positive. In his fourth quarter report for 1943, Schindler noted under the key word *rationalization*:

Due to the elimination of the Jews, the destruction of Aryan enterprises by the Bolsheviks in Galicia, and the shutdowns, the number of enterprises have been reduced to 32 percent of those existing in 1939, that is, to 89,000 enterprises. At the same time, the number of persons employed in the crafts industry, which for 1939 can be estimated at approximately 600,000, declined by the end of 1943 to approximately 195,000 persons.[94]

Similar proportions applied to the commercial sector.

In our view, the Armaments Inspector was not concerned with preventing the deportation of the Jewish armaments workers. He merely wanted to make sure that their replacement by Polish workers and, above all, by more rational production methods, would be accomplished in an orderly fashion, gradually and without major production stoppages.

Postwar confessions

The theory of overpopulation described—and describes—relatively backward economic conditions. Underemployment prevails because more people are engaged in certain work processes than would be required by the general technological state of development. Relatively widespread general poverty arises from such conditions, which can also be depicted as the unfavorable combination of animate and inanimate production, that is, of human labor and capital. The situation itself prevents capital accumulation and thus remains stable. If rationalization is then introduced from the outside, labor forces will be "set free"; that is, they will become visibly unemployed and idle. In this process, the population will be almost inevitably divided into those who work more intensively and those who no longer work at all. A palpable overpopulation is in the making. The question of who should belong to the productive and who to the unproductive sector of the population can be managed by the state. By taking the optimal organization of labor, rather than the sustenance of human beings, as the yardstick for economic organization, the existing forces of production, and thus social conditions based on might, are accepted as fixed variables, while the number of human beings can be varied through administrative measures of the state.

Since the Nuremberg Laws, and especially after the experiences in Vienna, the Nazi economic and population policy planners vigorously promoted such procedures at the expense of the Jewish minority. This neutralized the political resistance of the broad majority, since it benefitted from the process. But those who had become unemployed due to the advances made by productivity and, in addition, were forced to contribute their assets to finance that progress became dependent on government or private welfare; or new jobs had to be created for them.

For occupied Poland this procedure was ruled out in the short run for three reasons. First, the people who were to be "set free" there by way of

171

structural changes, not through force, counted in the millions; they were said to comprise 30 percent of the total labor force. Second, the Germans were not prepared to surrender the necessary capital in the form of credits; it was supposed to be raised only through the labor of those who worked in the new, more productive ways. However, this could succeed only with an organization of labor that prevented the unemployed from eating up the newly created surpluses. Third, it makes sense to those who want either to develop or to compel an advance in productivity to keep the factor of labor as much as possible to a minimum until such time as the maximal level of technology has been reached. For it was only then that cheap labor, as in occupied Poland, for example, would become a wage advantage that reduced costs. Cheap labor forms the vortex for rationalization. This also applied to the war economy after its lightning successes had passed. It had a chance only when it managed, for example, to produce boots not as hand-made items by coerced Jewish shoemakers, but in the production line of big factories employing many machines and unskilled labor.

In this sense, the ghetto economy was anachronistic. It tied down resources such as raw materials, machines, transport facilities and, above all, clothes, foodstuffs, heating materials, and living accommodations, without even remotely attaining the desired modern level of production. The deportation and the killing of unemployed Jews meant a massive saving; and the murder of the last 50,000 "Armaments Jews" (*Rüstungsjuden*) in the General Government, which was announced half a year ahead of time, became a stimulus for further rationalization. The destruction of the Jews as the "unproductive overpopulation" saved foodstuffs that would, at least in theory, supply the Polish armaments workers with more food. If that succeeded, according to the realistic assumption of the generals commanding the German war economy, then work productivity would increase more than if two half-starved workers shared a work place between them.

Overpopulation theories and ruthless economic rationalization provided an immanently rational reason for the destruction of the Jews. This was true in the summer of 1941 when the Nazi regime pushed its utopian social redevelopment schemes at the height of its power; and this remained true even when its military successes took a turn for the worse.

A few months after the German defeat, Helmut Meinhold was commissioned by the British military government to write an expert review about the economic reconstruction of Hamburg.[95] In this report he also analyzed the opportunities that were offered through the immense destruction. The tabula rasa returned with him and with men of his ilk from occupied Poland to the society of the killers (*die Gesellschaft der Endlöser*). Thus Meinhold saw "Polish conditions" in Germany: high overpopulation due to the refugees, destroyed production facilities, and lack of capital. From this perspective, the loss of human beings through war had not kept step with the loss of capital, at least not for the Germans.

In this situation, Meinhold saw only two solutions: either "the granting of credits" or the delivery of machinery for production in return for agrarian products along with the simultaneous reduction of food imports. In Poland, the German economic administration had taken the latter path. "Hence," Meinhold wrote in the summer of 1945, "one part of the population would have to die of starvation or, at least, perish through diseases of malnutrition."[96] If there was no credit forthcoming in this situation of crises and shortages, either capital would be literally exhausted because it was being used up to cover the minimum needed for existence, or people would have to starve to death for the benefit of capital formation. "Even for the sake of creating work," Meinhold wrote, "Germany cannot afford to have the kind of work done that uses up materials and thereby engenders a reduction in vitally necessary substances."[97] This also meant that emergency public works projects "would have to be consistently left undone," even if they "hardly utilize any materials" as, for example, in clearing up the rubble of destroyed cities.

The analysis considers labor at a level below the given state of technology as tantamount to the destruction of capital, since invested capital can pay for itself only if the labor force is more effectively utilized. Such an amortization, however, could not be achieved in occupied Poland through emergency public works projects and simple gang labor, and thus Meinhold could consistently claim that "overpopulation [manifests itself] as the effective erosion of capital."[98] If one thinks of this notion the other way around, then the killing of human beings, for whom there are no meaningful work places available that correspond to the existing technological level, signifies a form of indirect capital amortization. Moreover, if little is being invested, as in wartime, then there will be less capital erosion.

In his Hamburg study, Meinhold explains this theory, which could conceivably be called mass murder as a factor of economic reconstruction:

Hitherto we have presumed the intention (and we will do so likewise in the future) that at present it must be the economic aim to preserve rather the whole population, even if only wretchedly so, than to supply one part of the population with more food and let the other part perish. On that basis it is thus more correct to employ only 50 workers out of 100, who will then carry (*durchschleppen*) the other 50 until the situation improves again, than to have 75 people work and 25 starve to death. The prerequisite for this, however, is the possibility of improvement later on . . .

It is also possible, of course, to take another point of departure, especially if the aforementioned possibility is in doubt. Therefore, one could say: in the struggle for existence, it is better if the 75, who have proven themselves capable, stay alive and the remainder die at once than if, in the last analysis, all 100 perish. Such a standpoint would be justified if in fact selection (*Auslese*) was at issue.[99]

In Poland, "one" had chosen this other "point of departure" and made the concomitant "selection."

The economic calculations of a Helmut Meinhold explain why the Germans did not have the Jews simply dig canals after the Germans had deprived them of their rights and their property, but instead used up transport, labor, and materials to kill them: The death of the Jews provided the simplest and most viable means of slowing down capital erosion and of keeping open the possibility for an economic upswing in occupied Poland. Helmut Meinhold, Walter Emmerich, Rudolf Gater, and with some probability also Otto Ohlendorf and Konrad Meyer, as well as many other German intellectuals, were engaged in what can be called the political economy of the "final solution." This was an activity that, precisely because it appeared so abstract and neat, tells us more about the causes for the destruction of the European Jews than do the actions performed by subordinate executors.

Through the activities of these men, an originally racist concept such as the "solution of the Jewish question" underwent a fateful change of values. The intellectual planners did not use the concept emotionally, as if they were filled with hatred, but scientifically as technical terminology. Hate and base motives were transformed into the necessities of population and structural policies. Only thus, rendered rational endogenously, could the "final solution" be implemented with the appearance of being a reasonable measure.

Notes

This article originated at the Institute for Social Research in Hamburg in conjunction with the project entitled "Biographies of the Perpetrators" (*Täterbiografien*). Together with Peter Chroust, Hans Dieter Heilman, and Christian Pross, our project group focuses on the careers of German intellectuals before, during, and after the Third Reich. Our investigations have directed us to the rational core of a regime that by virtue of its historically unique crimes is usually characterized as extremely irrational. Tracing the development of individual careers, how they intersected and converged at certain points, we have come across personalities that do not fit the image of the henchman at all, yet provided the reasons and the means for the mass murders committed by the Nazi state. For a different version of our thesis, see *Beiträge zur nationalsozialistischen Gesundheits- und Sozialpolitik*, Vol. 5 (Berlin, 1987), pp. 11ff.

1 *Trial of the Major War Criminals before the International Military Tribunal* [Blue Series], 42 vols. (Nuremberg, 1947–49), 26: 266ff.

2 See *Beiträge zur nationalsozialistischen Gesundheits- und Sozialpolitik*, Vols. 1 and 2 (Berlin, 1985).

3 Susanne Heim and Götz Aly, *Ein Berater der Macht: Helmut Meinhold oder der Zusammenhang zwischen Sozialpolitik und Judenvernichtung* (Hamburg and Berlin, 1986). Because Meinhold had since 1959 been one of the most important political advisers on domestic affairs for all West German governments, this essay was originally conceived as part of a political dispute surrounding the planned celebration in his honor.

4 Preliminary studies about this subject are to be found in Götz Aly and Karl Heinz Roth, *Die restlose Erfassung. Volkszählen, Identifizieren, Aussondern im Nationalsozialismus* (Berlin, 1984).

5 See Peter-Heinz Seraphim, *Das Judentum im Osteuropäischen Raum* (Essen, 1938); Theodor Oberländer, *Die agrarische Überbevölkerung Polens* (Berlin, 1935); F. Ross, *Der Bevölkerungsdruck im deutsch-polnischen Grenzgebiet*, ed. Theodor Oberländer (Ms. Königsberg, 1936); Peter-Heinz Seraphim, ed., *Polen und seine Wirtschaft* (Königsberg, 1937).

6 Oberländer, *Agrarische Überbevölkerung*, p. 116.

7 Peter-Heinz Seraphim, "Wirkung der Neustaatenbildung im Nachkriegseuropa auf Wirtschaftsstruktur und Weltniveau," *Weltwirtschaftliches Archiv* 41 (1936): 399.

8 For German economic policy in the General Government generally and its dangerous turn toward becoming a constructive policy, see Tadeusz Kudyba, "Die strukturelle Veränderung der polnischen Wirtschaft während der Besatzungszeit," rer. pol. diss., University of Bonn, 1950. Kudyba, who had grown up in the area of Zamosc and was later incarcerated in Mauthausen-Gusen, reached at that time a conclusion that is partly similar to ours, but which thereafter was not raised again in the literature. His conclusion stated that "in the context of the German body politic, the economic structure of the Polish region was not to be rationalized by improving on the factor at fault, that is, by increasing the number of places of work, but by reducing the factor that existed in excess, namely, the human beings, achieving this through a process of destruction." Ibid. p. 158. See also Ludwik Toronczyk, "Die deutsche Wirtschafts-, Kultur-, und Bevölkerungspolitik im Generalgouvernement und in den eingegliederten Ostgebieten in den Jahren 1939–1945," Ph.D. diss., University of Vienna, 1951; Gerhard Eisenblätter, "Grundlinien der Politik des Reiches gegenüber dem Generalgouvernement, 1939–1945," Ph.D. diss., University of Frankfurt, 1969; Berthold Puchert, "Fragen der Wirtschaftspolitik im okkupierten Polen 1939 bis 1945, mit besonderer Berücksichtigung der IG Farbenindustrie AG," Habilitation, University of Berlin [East], 1968.

9 Peter-Heinz Seraphim, "Die Wirtschaftsbedeutung des Judentums in Polen," *Wirtschaftsdienst*, No. 11 (1939): 362.

10 See Maria Zelzer, *Stuttgart unterm Hakenkreuz* (Stuttgart, 1983), pp. 253, 389; Karl Strölin, *Stuttgart im Endstadium des Krieges* (Stuttgart, 1950), p. 64. (This reference was kindly provided by Mr. Hans Heilman.)

11 Koblenz, Bundesarchiv [hereafter cited as BA], R 57 [Deutsches Auslands-Institut]/344, 345: Dr. Könekamp, Polenfahrt vom 29.11 bis 9.12.1939 (Umsiedlung der Juden ins östliche Generalgouvernement).

12 Helmut Meinhold, review of *Die räumliche Ordnung der Wirtschaft* (Jena, 1940) by August Lösch, in *Die Burg* 3, no. 3 (1942): 360.

13 BA, R 52 IV/144a: Helmut Meinhold, "Die Erweiterung des Generalgouvernements nach Osten. A. Allgemeines" (Manuskriptreihe des Instituts für Deutsche Ostarbeit, vertraulich), July 1941. Apparently, this is identical with the less aggressively cited report "Die östlichen Nachbargebiete des Generalgouvernements. A. Allgemeines," documented in *Die Burg* 3, no. 3 (1942): 357.

14 Ibid.: Meinhold, "Erweiterung des Generalgouvernements nach Osten," p. 1.
15 Helmut Meinhold, "Die Arbeiterreserven des Generalgouvernements," *Die Burg* 3, no. 3 (1942): 80 [hereafter cited as "Arbeiterreserven"].
16 Idem, "Die nichtlandwirtschaftliche Überbevölkerung im ehemaligen Polen," *Ostraumberichte*, Neue Folge 1 (1942): 128.
17 Ibid., p. 132. From January 1941 to August 1942, Meinhold served as an expert in the economics section of the Institute for German Projects in the East, and was in practice its head. At this institute the bases for the practical policies of the German occupation forces of the General Government were developed. In 1943 Meinhold was transferred by his superior and patron Walter Emmerich, the economics minister of the General Government, to the Central Office for Economics.
18 BA, R 52 IV/144d: Helmut Meinhold, *Die Industrialisierung des General-gouvernements* (Manusckriptreihe des Instituts für Deutsche Ostarbeit, Nur für den Dienstgebrauch), Dec. 1941, p. 52 [hereafter cited as *Industrialisierung*].
19 Ibid., p. 140. Mombert's study does not discuss the space available for food (*Nahrungsraum*), but the scope for getting food (*Nahrungsspielraum*). With this is meant, to the exclusion of all else, the capacity to supply food; that is, the combination of the productive factors of labor, land, and capital, but never space in the geographic sense of the word. By changing the formula, Meinhold brutalized the scientific concept at the same time. The expansion of the space available for food can thus always mean the military conquest of other countries. But even if he was cited incorrectly in a significant way, Mombert's way of looking at things was basically not dissimilar from that of Meinhold. Mombert, too, was not primarily concerned about how to secure a sufficient supply of food for human beings, but about the optimal yield that can be gained from labor; he also dealt with a variable population size. Nevertheless, the context in which he evolved his "population science" was diametrically opposed to Meinhold's. Mombert confronted above all the question of the declining birth rate in industrialized countries. Thus, the question never arose for him of how to remove excess population, but, on the contrary, how to assure a sufficiently large population. According to his ideal notion, the "optimum population" was to be found

> in the development population and economy in such a way that the population is sufficiently large to utilize all gifts of nature to the fullest extent so that the yield of labor, and therewith also the standard of life, can reach the highest level under the given economic conditions. Of course, it can be the case that ... this optimum of the population cannot be reached, indeed, that a nation, when its population is declining, might be thrown back from this optimal situation after it might have almost reached it at one time.

> Paul Mombert, "Bovölkerungslehre," *Grundrisse zum Studium der Nation-alökonomie* (Jena, 1929), Vol. 15.

20 *Industrialisierung*, p. 140.
21 Ibid., pp. 135f.
22 Ibid., pp. 41f.
23 See "Arbeiterreserven," pp. 282f.
24 *Industrialisierung*, pp. 167f.
25 Ibid., p. 186.
26 Ibid., p. 161.

27 See Waclaw Dlugoborski, "Die deutsche Besatzungspolitik und Veränderungen der sozialen Struktur Polens 1939–1945," in *Zweiter Weltkrieg und sozialer Wandel*, ed. Waclaw Dlugoborski (Göttingen, 1981), p. 350.

28 *Industrialisierung*, p. 165.

29 Hans-Kraft Nonnenmacher, "Die Wirtschaftsstruktur des galizischen Erdölgebietes," *Deutsche Forschungen im Osten* 1, no. 6 (1941): 15ff.

30 The Ustasha was the fascist movement of Croatia, whose leaders established a particularly bloody regime in 1941 as the puppet government of the Germans.

31 Zentrales Staatsarchiv der DDR: Volkswirtschaftliche Abteilung der I.G. Farbenindustrie AG, "Die Wirtschaftsstruktur Kroatiens (Vowi 4479), Bericht vom 23.3.1942, gez. Dr. Br." For this reference we wish to thank Dr. Martin Seckendorf of the Staatliche Archivverwaltung der DDR, who is an acknowledged authority on Nazi policies in Southeastern Europe.

32 Michael Weichert, *Jüdische Selbsthilfe 1939–1945* [Yiddish] (Tel Aviv, 1966) provides a totally erroneous interpretation of the Office for Population Policy and Welfare, which minimizes its role. Dr. Weichert was the director of the Jewish Social Self-Help (*Selbsthilfe*) and was involved in many negotiations with Arlt, Föhl, Türk, and Weirauch. He did not see through the German functionaries sitting across from him, and he arrived at a wrong assessment of the Office by viewing it only from the perspective of charity. See also Michael Weichert, *Der Krieg* [Yiddish] (Tel Aviv, 1963). The same mistake is made by a newer Polish work, which takes up on this longtime taboo theme. See Bogdan Kroll, *Rada Growna Opiekunncza* (Warsaw, 1985). By contrast, the Jewish historical commission in Poland correctly documented the Office quite early and correctly. See Josef Kermisz, ed., *Dokumenty i Materialy, Dziejow Okupacji Niemieckiej W Poloscz*, Vol. 2: "*Akcje i Wysiedlenia*" (Warsaw, Lodz, Cracow, 1946).

33 Prior to this, Arlt had been chief (*Gauamtsleiter*) of the Race Political Office (*Rassenpolitisches Amt*) in Silesia; he belonged to the SD and had organized courses in Jewish Studies for Eichmann's Office (*Referat*) IV b 4 of the Central Office for Reich Security (*Reichssicherheitshauptamt*). During his activities as director of the Office for Population Policy and Welfare in Cracow, he retained some of his functions in Kattowitz. For example, from 1940 to 1942, he worked as plenipotentiary of the Reich Commissar for the Consolidation of the German Race (*Reichskommissar zur Festigung des deutschen Volkstums*) in both Cracow and Kattowitz, and at the end of 1940 he shifted the main focus of his work to Kattowitz. After the war, he first found accommodation at the Red Cross; then he became a managing member of the Federal Association of the German Employers' Union (*Bundesvereinigung Deutscher Arbeitgeberverbände*) as well as its representative *inter alia* at the Youth Board of the West German Government and the Board of the German-French Youth-Work (*Deutsch-Französisches Jugendwerk*). He also maintained excellent relations with the trade unions. Although Fritz Arlt's file at the Berlin Document Center [BDC] contains a lot of information, the judicial proceedings against him (Staatsanwaltschaft Dortmund, Verfahren 45 Js 49/61) failed, due to the incompetence, or perhaps the unwillingness, of the authorities; and they were suspended in 1966. The records of the proceedings contain few relevant documents, and no attempts were made to shed light on the former activities of the Office for Population Policy and Welfare.

34 BA, R 52 II [Kanzlei des Generalgouverneurs]/247: Bericht über den Aufbau der Verwaltung im Generalgouvernement, p. 182.

35 Ibid.

36 Ibid.
37 See *Dokumenty i Materialy*, Vol. 2, passim.
38 BA, Ost Dok. 13, no. 248: Affidavit of Else v. Scheidt, 2 June 1947.
39 BA, NS 19/1210: Lothar Weirauch, Leiter der Abt. Bevölkerungswesen und Fürsorge, to HSSPF Wilhelm Krüger, 4 Dec. 1943.
40 See *The Wannsee Protocol*, Vol. 11 of *The Holocaust: Selected Documents*, ed. John Mendelsohn (New York, 1982), pp. 120ff. (from Nuremberg Document NG-2586). After the war, Weirauch became a *Ministerialdirigent* in Bonn and conducted an almost friendly, but from Weirauch's side thoroughly mendacious, correspondence with Weichert (located in BA, Ost Dok. 13, no. 246: Briefwechsel Weichert-Weirauch).
41 BDC dossier Walter Föhl: Föhl to "SS-Kameraden zuhause," 21 June 1942.
42 Another career can explain why so little was known about the Office for Population Policy and Welfare. Dr. Hans Hopf worked there as a "genealogist," which means that he directed the careful selection and recording of human beings according to their "ethnicity"; this was an important bureaucratic prerequisite for the Holocaust. After the war, Hopf became an archivist at the West German Federal Archives in Koblenz. There Hopf created the "Documentation East" (*Ostdokumentation*), a sizable, largely pseudo-documentary sanitizing operation for former members of the German occupation authorities. Nevertheless, this little used collection, which is not exactly being pushed on archive users, is an interesting source if used correctly.
43 Lothar Weirauch, "Die Volksgruppen im Generalgouvernement," *Europäische Revue* 18 (May 1942): 251 [hereafter cited as "Volksgruppen"].
44 Fritz Arlt, *Übersicht über die Bevölkerungsverhältnisse im Generalgouvernement* (Cracow, 1940), p. 41 [hereafter cited as *Übersicht*].
45 Weirauch, "Volksgruppen," p. 251.
46 Arlt, *Übersicht*, p. 19.
47 Ibid., p. 9.
48 BA, R 52 II/247: Bericht über den Aufbau der Verwaltung, p. 201.
49 Ibid., p. 196.
50 Arlt, *Übersicht*, p. 21.
51 See, for example, the important article by Miroslav Karny, "Die 'Judenfrage' in der nazistischen Okkupationspolitik," *Historica*, 21 (Prague, 1982): 178.
52 BA, NS 19/1210: Dr. Wilhelm Hagen, Stadtmedizinalrat von Warschau, to "Führer des Großdeutschen Reiches, Adolf Hitler," 7 Dec. 1942.
53 Ibid.
54 *Das Diensttagebuch des deutschen Generalgouverneurs in Polen*, ed. Werner Präg and Wolfgang Jacobmeyer (Stuttgart, 1975), pp. 244f. [hereafter cited as *Diensttagebuch*]. Sections of the diary not included in this abbreviated published edition will be cited by date from the complete diary located in BA, R 52 I.
55 On this, see also *Bremer Nachrichten*, 21 June 1940:

> The director of the Office for Economy, Privy Councillor Dr. Zetsche, was relieved of his responsibilities in accordance with his own wish. He is replaced by the Syndicus of the Senate and departmental adviser, Dr. Emmerich from Hamburg. In order to supply the General Government with goods, namely agrarian products, a number of German wholesale trading firms, which previously were engaged in export and are situated mainly in the Hanseatic cities, have been taken to the General Government. Firms from Danzig are said to follow.

56 *Diensttagebuch*, p. 226.
57 *Ostdeutscher Beobachter*, n.d. [ca. April 1940].
58 See BA, R 52 VI [Generalgouvernement, Hauptabteilung Wirtschaft]/20, for a list of the district wholesalers in the General Government (and their parent branches). They were as follows: Staudt & Co., Berlin; Breckwoldt & Co., Hamburg; C.F. Eckhardt, Fürth i.B.; H.A. Lerchen & Co., Berlin; Athen & Haupt, Hamburg; Schütte & Bünemann, Bremen; Jos. Hansen & Söhne, Hamburg; C. André & Co., Hamburg; Willi Fuhrhop, Hamburg; Fredk. Möller Söhne, Bremen; Deutsch-Westafrikanische Handelsgesellschaft, Hamburg; "Webbers" Gebr. Webendörfer, Hamburg; Walther C. Többens, Bremen; Jos. Hansen & Söhne, Hamburg; Hansing & Co., Hamburg; Bieling Gebrüder, Hamburg; Heinrich Kramer, Bremen; Dietrich Dirksen, Danzig; Georg Kadgiehn, Bromberg; "Edeka," Danzig; H. Hommel, Kom-Ges., Köln; Georg Fröde, Marienburg (Westpreußen); Gerhard Eggebrecht, Danzig; Gebr. Weyersberg, Solingen-Ohligs; C. Illies & Co., Berlin-Charlottenburg; Tetzlaff & Wenzel, Danzig; Hugo Claassen, Danzig; Fritz Bogut, Danzig-Schidlitz; C. Woermann, Hamburg; G.L. Gaiser, Hamburg; "Dekage" Handels-Aktiengesellschaft, Hamburg; Gollücke & Rothfos, Bremen; C.F. Corssen & Co., Bremen; Overbeck & Co., G.m.b.H., Bremen; Schmidt & Luhmann, Bremen; Wilhelm Eicke & Co., Bremen; Carlowitz & Co., Hamburg; Breckwoldt & Co., Bremen; Kunst & Albers, Hamburg; Gesellschaft für Außenhandel m.b.H., Wien; Adolf Gleue, Hamburg; Louis Delius & Co., Bremen; J. Winckler, Hamburg; Ulrich Thomas, Danzig; Deutsch-Ostafrikanische Gesellsch., Berlin; Oscar H. Jencquel, Hamburg; F.D. Warnholtz, Hamburg; G.L. Gaiser, Hamburg.
59 See BA, R 52 IV, pp. 69, 82, 89, for the personnel files of Meinhold, Bochdam-Löptien, and Nonnenmacher.
60 Based on oral communications from various persons who had either worked closely with Emmerich or known him well. After the war Emmerich was interned in Neuengamme for two years, but a request for his extradition by the Polish government failed because of the resistance of the British military government.
61 Walter Emmerich, "Aufbau im neuen Wirtschaftsraum," *Berliner Börsenzeitung*, 30 Nov. 1940.
62 Peter-Heinz Seraphim, "Bevölkerungs- und wirtschaftspolitische Probleme einer europäischen Gesamtlösung der Judenfrage," *Weltkampf: Die Judenfrage in Geschichte und Gegenwart* 1, no. 1–2 (1941): 44ff.
63 *Wochenspiegel*, 28 Feb. 1940.
64 *Ostdeutscher Beobachter*, 11 Dec. 1940.
65 *Danziger Wirtschaftsdienst*, 1 Jan. 1941.
66 *Krakauer Zeitung*, 30–31 Jan. 1941.
67 Ibid., 13 Mar. 1941.
68 *Rheinisch-Westfälische Zeitung*, 23 Apr. 1941.
69 *Krakauer Zeitung*, 28 June 1941.
70 *Die deutsche Stimme*, 10 Dec. 1941.
71 *Die wirtschaftliche Leistung* 1, no. 5, 15 Dec. 1942. This newspaper appeared in German and Polish.
72 Ibid. 2, no. 2 (1943).
73 Gater published a book on this subject in both Polish and German: Rudolf Gater, Rudolf Wittich, and Fritz Gerlach, *Der Einheitskostenplan für Industriebetriebe im Generalgouvernement: Leitfaden für die Einführung eines geordneten Rechnungsverkehrs* (Berlin, 1942).

74 Freiburg, Bundesarchiv-Militärarchiv [hereafter cited as BA-MA], RW 19 Anh. I/1349: RKW-Dienststelle Generalgouvernement, "Die wirtschaftlichen Grundlagen des Generalgouvernements" (Dec. 1940), pp. 6ff. For the RKW-report on the manufacture of agricultural machinery in the General Government, see BA-MA, RW 19 Anh. I/1350.

75 BA-MA, RW 19 Anh. I/1349: "Die wirtschaftlichen Grundlagen," p. 6.

76 Ibid., p. 7.

77 Ibid., pp. 30f.

78 BA R 52 VI/18, p. 25: RKW-Dienststelle Generalgouvernement, "Das Handwerk im Generalgouvernement" (May 1941).

79 For the successful activity of Max Bischof, see Warsaw, Archiv für neue Akten, Die Regierung des Generalgouvernements, Personalakte Max Bischof, 1324/1, Blatt 84: Distriktgouverneur Fischer to Bischof, 25 Apr. 1944. This letter is a kind of character reference supplied by Fischer in connection with a proceeding against Bischof because of the alleged Jewish origins of his wife.

80 Raul Hilberg, *The Destruction of the European Jews*, 2nd rev. ed., 3 vols. paginated throughout (New York and London, 1985), p. 257.

81 Ibid., p. 266.

82 *Diensttagebuch*, p. 346: minutes of the meeting of 3 Apr. 1941.

83 Ibid., p. 361: minutes of the meeting of 19 Apr. 1941.

84 Ibid.

85 Ibid., pp. 344f.: minutes of the meeting of 3 Apr. 1941.

86 BA, R 52 I: minutes of the meeting of 19 Apr. 1941: comments by District Governor Fischer and Under Secretary Kundt.

87 BA, R 52 I: minutes of the meetings of 3 Apr. and 16 Oct. 1941: comments by Emmerich.

88 See BA-MA, RW 23/3 for the letter of Governor Fischer to the director of the Transfer Agency in Warsaw, Bischof, of 25 Apr. 1944.

89 BA, R 52 I: minutes of the meeting of 13 July 1942.

90 BA, R 52 I: minutes of the meeting of 3 Apr. 1941.

91 See, for example, Ba-MA, RW 23/2, Bl. 41: fourth quarter-yearly report of the Rüstungsinspektion des Generalgouvernements.

92 BA-MA, RW 23/2.

93 Hans Kehrl, *Krisenmanager des Dritten Reiches* (Düsseldorf, 1973), pp. 313f.

94 BA-MA, RW 23/3.

95 Bibliothek des Instituts für Weltwirtschaft an der Universität Kiel: "Grundlinien des industriellen Wiederaufbaus von Groß-Hamburg," ed. Helmut Meinhold (Ms., Nov. 1945) [hereafter cited as "Grundlinien"].

96 Ibid., p. 12.

97 Ibid., p. 16.

98 *Industrialisierung*, p. 213.

99 "Grundlinien," pp. 16f.

21

THE ORIGINS OF "OPERATION REINHARD"[1]

The decision-making process for the mass
murder of the Jews in the
Generalgouvernement

Bogdan Musial

Source: *Yad Vashem Studies*, 28 (2000), 113–53. Translated from the German by William Templer.

The question of the decision-making process leading up to the mass murder of the European Jews during World War II remains a controversial topic in the historical research. Recent studies suggest that the decision was a complex, step-by-step process, and the most crucial decisions were made in the summer and fall of 1941.[2]

The contemporary debate generally posits two basic decisions, separate in time, that set the "Final Solution" in motion. The first, leading to the murder of Soviet Jewry, is assumed to have been reached in July or August 1941[3]; that is, only after the destruction of the Soviet Jews was underway was the decision made to annihilate all the Jews in Europe. The second decision is dated to September or October 1941.[4]

L.J. Hartog and Christian Gerlach have sought to modify this two-phase sequencing of the decision-making process for the "final solution." They argue that Hitler did not reach the decision to murder all European Jewry until the beginning of December 1941. Gerlach adds: "At least that is when he first made it public."[5] While this thesis offers a plausible explanation for several previously unanswered questions, at the same time it reintroduces questions that the previous thinking had appeared to clarify. One such question concerns the purpose behind the construction of the Belżec death camp, on which work commenced at the end of October 1941. Gerlach himself concedes: "It is still unclear what conceptions about future developments were associated with construction of the Belżec camp."[6]

181

It seems that both Hartog and Gerlach and those who argue for the commonly accepted chronology are correct. This apparent contradiction can be resolved by the addition of a third, very important, stage to the decision-making process, which enables us to answer various questions more plausibly. Moreover, adding a third phase significantly enhances the plausibility and persuasiveness of the thesis of a step-by-step decision-making process underlying the genesis of the "final solution."

This third stage was the separate decision to proceed with the murder of the Jews in the *Generalgouvernement* (GG). Significantly, this affected a particularly large population, numbering some 2.5 million Jews.

The chronology I suggest frames the following decisions:

1. The first—the destruction of the Soviet Jews—was taken in July or August 1941.
2. The second—to murder the Jews in the GG—was made at the end of September or beginning of October 1941. At about the same time, it was decided to murder the Jews in the *Warthegau.*
3. Only then did Hitler take the final decision, made known in December 1941, to annihilate *all* European Jews.
4. This absolute order for destruction was apparently modified in early 1942: all able-bodied Jews capable of employment in the war economy were, for the time being, to be spared. However, in the spring of 1942, a decision was made once again to push ahead with the more radical version of the "final solution."

This article concentrates on the question of precisely when the decision was taken to murder the entire Jewish population in the GG. It will attempt to show that the substantive order for this operation was given in the first half of October 1941. The author of this decision was Odilo Globocnik, the *SS- und Polizeiführer* (SS and Police Leader; SSPF) in the Lublin District, and his initiative was closely bound up with resettlement plans to "Germanize" the area—first the Lublin District, and then the entire GG. The final decision was then made by Hitler after Himmler had presented Globocnik's proposal to him. This argument is based on an array of sources, conclusions from the circumstantial evidence, and a critical examination of the documentation. When examined concurrently, this evidence can convincingly piece together the puzzle of the decision-making process that led to the liquidation of the Jews in the *Generalgouvernement.*

The discussion in Lublin, October 17, 1941

The discussion in Lublin on October 17, 1941, as recorded in Hans Frank's official diary, is one of the most important pieces of evidence for this discussion. Previous research has evidently overlooked the significance of this conference for the preparatory stage of Operation Reinhard. Participating were Governor-General Hans Frank; Dr. Ernst Boepple, undersecretary in the GG administration; Ernst Zörner, governor of the Lublin District; the senior administrative head (*Amtschef*) in the Lublin District, Wilhelm Engler; and Globocnik. Four items were on the agenda; the third concerned the "Jewish Question." The participants came to the following decision:

> All Jews, with the exception of indispensable craftsmen and the like, are to be *evacuated* from Lublin. Initially, 1,000 Jews will be transferred across the Bug River. Responsibility for this is placed in the hands of the SSPF. The *Stadthauptmann* will select the Jews to be evacuated.[7]

An analysis of this discourse reveals that the meaning of "evacuating of the Jews across the Bug" was clear to all the participants—it was synonymous with their murder.[8] Thus, this "evacuation" was planned as a prelude to the state-organized mass murder. The code "evacuation over the Bug" stemmed from the autumn and winter of 1939/1940, when Jews were indeed expelled from the GG "across the Bug" into Soviet-occupied eastern Poland.[9]

A glance at the location of Lublin in the autumn of 1941 shows that a literal interpretation of the notion "across the Bug" would have meant evacuating Jews from the Lublin District either to the northeastern corner of the Galicia District, or into the *Reichskommissariat* Ukraine. Yet a priori it was impossible to contemplate evacuating the Jews over the Bug into Galicia, thereby keeping them in the GG. Deportation into the *Reichskommissariat* Ukraine was also out of the question at this juncture. Three days earlier, on October 14, Frank had asked Rosenberg about the possibility of transferring the Jews in the GG into the occupied eastern territories. Rosenberg's reply was unambiguous: "At the moment he [Rosenberg] could see no possibility for implementing such resettlement plans."[10]

It is also noteworthy that Globocnik was the official charged with carrying out this "evacuation." Until then, the *civil administration* had ordered and implemented expulsions of Jews within the GG.[11] Yet if one assumes that, for the participants in this discussion, "evacuation" was synonymous with death, it seems only understandable that Globocnik was given the job of implementing this operation. As SSPF, he was the only one in the Lublin District with sufficient personnel at his disposal, namely the SS and the police, for organizing mass murder. In addition, according to the most recent findings, it seems that, during their meeting on October 13, 1941, Himmler ordered Globocnik to begin construction of the first extermination camp in Bełżec.[12]

Another piece of significant evidence is a casual remark made by Hans Frank in an address on October 17, 1941, while the government was in formal session in Lublin. In this speech, Frank noted inter alia: *"On the basis of a special assignment I've been given by the Führer,* I'll be coming here quite often in the near future and so will have the good fortune to visit Lublin fairly frequently."[13] It is quite plausible that Frank was referring here to the murder of the Jews and the subsequent re-populating of the Lublin District with ethnic Germans. There was no other "assignment" at this time that would have required Hitler's special approval or even his official order.

Frank's remark suggests that Hitler had decided on the destruction of the Jews and that Hans Frank regarded this decision as a direct order from the *Führer.* It also indicates that Frank proceeded from the premise that as governor-general, it was his duty to assist in the forcible "removal" of the Jewish population from the GG.

However, in order to reconstruct the path of the decision-making with regard to the murder of the Jews in the Lublin District, and throughout the GG, it is necessary to examine more closely the personality and activities of Odilo Globocnik. We may assume that Globocnik was, in fact, the man who initiated this mass murder. Previous research has viewed him as Himmler's close associate and subordinate and, most particularly, as the official in charge of Operation Reinhard. That approach tends to overlook the considerable impact of his enormous activism on behalf of *volk*-ethnic policy and his racial ideas on occupation policy and the decision to murder the Jews in the GG. Moreover, there is still no comprehensive biography of Globocnik.[14]

For Globocnik and his bureaucratic apparatus, as for other SSPFs in the *Generalgouvernement,* the "Jewish Question" had, since the summer of 1940, come to represent a major security and racial-political problem. This resulted once the civil administration had, for all practical purposes, assumed authority over the Jews in regard to areas of residence, food supply, and forced labor.[15] This constellation changed, from Globocnik's perspective, once he and his highest commander Himmler had decided to implement the ambitious plans for settling the Lublin District with ethnic Germans as part of the "General Plan for the East." Götz Aly has convincingly demonstrated the close link between settlement plans in general and the destruction of the Jews.[16] Contemporary documents indicate that it was Odilo Globocnik who displayed extraordinary initiative in drafting plans for the Germanization of the East. In the period of July 20–31, 1941, Himmler put him in charge of *"SS und Polizei Stützpunkte"* in all the occupied Eastern territories, i.e., the GG and the USSR.[17] This fact is also corroborated by later accounts by contemporaries, such as Jakob Sporrenberg, Globocnik's successor as Lublin SSPF,[18] Dr. Boepple,[19] and Globocnik's adjutant.[20] In his Krakow jail cell, Rudolf Höss, commandant of Auschwitz, wrote that Globocnik had drafted fantastic plans of bases stretching all the way to the Urals ... He didn't see any difficulties here and rejected all criticism with a superior sweep of the hand. Insofar as he did not need them for labor at "his" bases, he wanted to liquidate the Jews in these areas on the spot.[21]

The large number of such postwar statements pointing to Globocnik's unusual level of activism regarding questions of racial policy in the Lublin District is striking. Yet both directly and indirectly, the extant contemporary sources also confirm Globocnik's involvement in such activities in the Lublin District and throughout the GG.

Already in August 1940, Globocnik presented Himmler with a project to set up fortified rural farmsteads (so-called *Wehrbauernhöfe*) in the Lublin District. However, Himmler at that time wished to concentrate only on SS and police camps. In the fall of 1940, these were then actually constructed on six large estates; the following spring, they were manned by SS men. Their task, inter alia, was to "make a significant contribution to the creation of a new order of land and settlement throughout the GG. They will become vital German centers on the plains."[22]

In the spring of 1941, Globocnik had a SS-*Mannschaftshaus* in Lublin, where plans and projects for future settlements could be developed. As a result of his intense activism on these questions, he was far ahead of the relevant plans stemming from the SS Race and Settlement Office in Berlin, the authority actually responsible for this project.[23] Yet Globocnik did not limit himself to devising projects and setting up SS and police bases. In the spring of 1941, he began with the "Germanization" of the first settlements in the Lublin District. These comprised five villages near the city of Zamość, where German farmers had indeed settled in the eighteenth century, only to be Polonized in the course of the next.[24] In the spring of 1941, the so-called anthropological commissions set up by Globocnik began work in the Lublin District.[25] This was within the framework of the *volk*-political operation *"Fahndung nach deutschem Blut"* ("In Search of German Blood").[26]

Heinrich Himmler was very interested in Globocnik's projects and plans and put his trust in him to help fulfill Himmler's dream to resettle Germans in the East. Himmler paid numerous visits to the Lublin District, and, during such a visit on July 20, 1941, one month after the attack on the Soviet Union, Himmler reached several fateful decisions: (1) "The ancient German city center [in Lublin] should be included as part of the overall construction plan envisioned for the SS and police quarter." (2) "The operation 'In Search of German Blood' will be expanded to include the entire *Generalgouvernement*; a major settlement area will be created in the German colonies near Zamość."[27]

Yet from the perspective of those involved, an absolute prerequisite for realizing these plans was the "cleansing" of this area of the Jews and Poles living there. This was pointed out in a report by SS-*Hauptsturmführer* Helmut Müller, dated October 15, 1941:

> [Globocnik] considers the ... gradual cleansing of the entire *Generalgouvernement* of Jews and Poles necessary in order to secure the eastern territories, etc. ... He is full of excellent and far-reaching plans on this. The only thing that prevents him from realizing them is the limited power of his present position.... It is SS-*Brigadeführer* Globocnik's idea to push ahead with the German settlement of the entire district by concentrating first on a small section of it. Moreover, building on this (longer-term aim) and in conjunction with the Nordic or German-settled Baltic lands, Globocnik wishes to forge a link via Lublin District with the German-settled areas in Transylvania. He thus intends to "encircle" the remaining Poles in the western intervening area by a noose of new settlement, gradually throttling them both economically and biologically.[28]

The shift in Globocnik's planning perspective in the summer of 1941 is noteworthy. Until then he had evidently been concentrating mainly on preparations for Germanizing the Lublin District. In the summer of 1941, after the attack on the Soviet Union, Himmler had him expand his plans to encompass the entire GG and the USSR. This expanded portfolio is reflected in the fact that, in late summer of 1941, Globocnik set up the Plannungs-und Forschungsstelle im Generalgouvernement (Office for Planning and Research). This office was to provide him the "scientific-technical foundation for his plans and ideas and their preparation."[29] Up until that time, these matters had been dealt with by staff in the SS-*Mannschaftshaus* in Lublin.

In this connection, it should be noted that, already in March 1941, Hitler had reached a decision that the entire GG should be Germanized in the near future. In a GG government session on March 25, 1941, Governor-General Frank proclaimed:

> The *Generalgouvernement* as an expedient structure is now coming to an end.[30] ... The GG will now be given greater assistance and in particular will be emptied of its Jewish population. ... The Poles will also accompany the Jews in their exodus from this area. The *Führer* is determined to make this region, over the course of the next 15 to 20 years, into an area that is purely German.[31]

However, there were apparently still no concrete plans for this endeavor. In any event, it was evident to Hans Frank that such plans could

186

be realized only after the victorious end of the war. In the speech cited above, he stated in no uncertain terms: "Yet at the moment, it is inappropriate to embark upon longer-term experiments in *volk* policy. *Reichsmarschall* Göring commented recently: 'It is more important for us to win the war than to push ahead with racial policies.'"[32]

Still, even with the absence of operative plans in the summer of 1941, the above indicates that ideas about Germanizing the GG were nothing new. Globocnik was the man who wished to forge ahead immediately, translating these plans into action, at least in part. In Himmler he found a ready ear for his ideas—and probably, via Himmler, with the *Führer*.

Summer–fall 1941: plans for settlement in the Lublin district and the military situation

A review of the military situation and the prevailing mood of Hitler and his closest associates in the summer and fall of 1941 are important prerequisites to an understanding of Himmler's decision of July 20, 1941 (regarding the settlement of ethnic Germans in the Lublin District) and subsequent developments.

The assumption both in the GG and the Reich in the summer of 1941 was that the opportunity would soon be created for deporting the Jews to the East. On June 19, 1941, three days before launching Operation Barbarossa, Hitler promised Hans Frank that "the Jews would be removed from the *Generalgouvernement* in the near future."[33] In other words, there would soon be enormous areas available in the East for moving ahead with population transfers on a huge scale. In the Lublin District alone, hundreds of thousands, indeed millions, would have to be "displaced" in order to settle Germans in their stead.

In the first weeks of the eastern campaign, victory seemed to be in the offing. On July 9, 1941, Hitler said to Goebbels: "the war in the East has basically been won. We still have to fight a series of difficult battles, but Bolshevism will not be able to recover from the defeats it has suffered."[34] This suggests that Himmler's decision on July 20, 1941, to Germanize the Lublin District was taken in an atmosphere of premature euphoria over victory and a sense of omnipotence. Clearly Hitler was at least informed about such a historic resolution. On July 27, one week after Himmler's decision, Hitler reportedly was musing about future settlement plans and the settlement of armed German "militia farmers" as a defensive wall in the East.[35]

During the end of July and the beginning of August 1941, the mood in the *Führer*'s headquarters shifted regarding the military situation in the East. On August 1, 1941, a diary entry by Goebbels noted: "People are openly admitting they were a bit mistaken in their assessment of Soviet fighting power." Nine days later, on August 10, 1941, Goebbels wrote:

187

"We're going to have to face some very tough and bloody confrontations until we've smashed the Soviet Union."[36] During August, the initial euphoria over imminent victory finally evaporated. Hitler was suffering from an attack of prolonged diarrhea, terribly disconcerted, as Goebbels noted, by the military developments in the East. No longer did they anticipate a quick victory on the eastern front. In the meantime, Hitler was even hoping to come to some peace accord with Stalin, as long as he could retain the bulk of the conquered territory in the East, something that was "absolutely out of the question" one month earlier. On September 10, Goebbels wrote: "I believe that we gradually have to prepare the people to accept the notion of a prolonged war. . . . It's time to finish with all these illusions."[37]

In September 1941, Hitler gradually recovered from his initial shock and rallied to a new optimism. His hope was to win important battles before winter descended on the troops, and he was contemplating winter encampments for the Wehrmacht in the East.[38] At the beginning of October 1941, Hitler was once more completely certain of ultimate victory, though unable to say exactly when. In a discussion on October 4, Goebbels asked Hitler whether he thought "that Stalin at some point would capitulate. . . . The *Führer* thinks it possible, though improbable given the present state of affairs." Hitler went on: "It's impossible as yet to say what the coming winter may bring. We have to be prepared for any eventuality." Yet Hitler "came to the clear conclusion that victory would be ours."[39]

Expostulating at one of his table talks in the early hours of October 27, Hitler noted: "In order to exploit Europe's India, the Ukraine, all I need is peace on the western front, not in the East too. . . . As far as the East is concerned, I have no interest whatsoever in arranging some sort of negotiated end to the war."[40] Two weeks later, on November 10, Hitler told Goebbels: "No one can say how long the war against the Soviet Union will last. Whether we'll ever arrive at some sort of peace is uncertain. . . . It's conceivable the struggle there will drag on *for years to come*."[41]

Though the triumphant euphoria in the *Führer*'s headquarters was gone in September and October 1941, the shock of late July and August 1941 had meanwhile been overcome. There was a new optimism that the war could be won after all, even if it would be protracted.

In the meantime, Globocnik was busy at work finalizing preparations for the settlement of ethnic Germans in the Lublin District. In September 1941, the time appeared ripe to put the plans drafted by him and his staff into practice.[42] Initially, however, the area had to be "cleansed" both of Jews and Poles. The imminent "deportation" of Jews to the East anticipated in the early phase of the war against the Soviet Union had not materialized.

This military situation ruled out any option of deporting hundreds of thousands of Polish Jews to the territory behind the lines of the eastern front. It is virtually inconceivable that the military top echelon would have permitted the deportation of hundreds of thousands, indeed millions, of persons into these areas. They would then have been uprooted, homeless, destitute, and with no assured source of food for survival. Deportation to the East was possible only after "resolving the military questions," as Hitler expressly stated to Goebbels in September.[43] Yet even after months and years, no such "resolution" was on the horizon.

Hypothetically, there was another alternative; namely, to carry out a "resettlement" operation within the GG. However, that option was just as impracticable, since the *Generalgouvernement* was saddled with an acute housing shortage. The area was so overcrowded that, in the spring of 1941, for example, the civilian administration had tried unsuccessfully to ghettoize the Jews in the Lublin District.[44] This was also the reason behind the failure, in 1939–1941, of all the attempts to totally "cleanse" the eastern territories that had been incorporated into the Reich, especially the *Warthegau*, of "undesirable elements," such as Poles or Jews.[45] The cities and villages in the GG were overcrowded with displaced persons, refugees, and expellees (Poles and Jews). This precluded implementing a "resettlement" inside the GG.

This territorial bottleneck, blocking any "larger-scale" mass resettlement, is confirmed by the following exchange. Franz Rademacher from the Foreign Office asked Eichmann whether there was any option for shipping Serbian Jews to Poland or Russia. On September 13, 1941, he received an unambiguous reply, which he noted in a memorandum: "Residence in Russia and GG impossible. Not even the Jews of Germany can be lodged there. Eichmann proposes shooting."[46] It should be stressed here that the Jewish population within the Lublin District, a small area of about 24,000 sq. km, was twice the size of the Jewish population in all of Germany in its 1937 borders. In September 1941, there were some 160,000 Jews in Germany; the number in the Lublin District was some 320,000.[47]

Moreover, a "deportation" of the Jews to the East did not constitute a lasting, long-term solution, because these territories, as envisioned in *Generalplan Ost*, were to be dominated by Germans and gradually colonized and Germanized. Yet for fundamental ideological reasons, there was likewise no room for the Jews in the Greater German Reich. Hitler confirmed this in a remark during his table conversation on October 17, 1941, in connection with the future settlement of the East by German settlers. "The indigenous population? Well, we'll proceed to sift through them. We'll completely kick out the destructive Jew."[48] Thus, over the short term, continuing hostilities—and, over the longer term, the ideological considerations—ruled out the "deportation" of the Polish and other European Jews to the East.

It was now logical and consistent, from the perspective of Himmler, Globocnik and their ilk, to ponder the prospect of murdering the Polish

Jews instead of waiting until they could be deported to the East, since such a removal was, in any case, ideologically misconceived. One example of this view is Eichmann's September 13, 1941, suggestion to execute the Jews in Serbia on the spot since there was "no room for them" in the GG or Russia. In the late summer of 1941, thinking among the Nazi leadership began to look to a "solution of the Jewish Question" by means of mass murder.

If one considers Globocnik's untiring activism—his adjutant confirms he worked at a phenomenal pace[49]—it is quite possible that he arrived independently at the idea of killing Jews on the spot. The postwar statement by Rudolf Höss cited earlier also suggests this. Since the mass murder of the Soviet Jews was in high gear at this time, the idea to murder the Jews was not new. Moreover, Globocnik was notorious for his brutality and absolute hatred of Jews, which will be referred to below.

Yet in his capacity as Lublin District SSPF, Globocnik could not himself decide on a question of such historic magnitude. As Browning asserts, "there is not the slightest evidence that any major change in Nazi Jewish policy took place without the knowledge and approval of Adolf Hitler."[50] In his October 15, 1941, report, Helmut Müller likewise referred to Globocnik's dilemma in realizing his far-reaching plans to Germanize the Lublin District within the confines of his limited power.[51]

Yet it was possible for Globocnik to present such a proposal to Himmler, who, as *Reichsführer*-SS and Chief of German Police, was the responsible official. Globocnik's October 1 letter to Himmler should be interpreted as just such a proposal:[52]

Reichsführer! In line with implementation of your aims regarding the Germanizing of the district, I passed on the *detailed prepared documents* to *Obergruppenführer* Krüger yesterday. SS-*Obergruppenführer* Krüger wished to present them immediately to you. He regarded this as urgent in the light of the emergency in which the ethnic Germans in the *Generalgouvernement* now find themselves. This has taken on such serious proportions that one can easily claim their situation in Polish times was better ... Since preparations for concentrating them are now complete, implementation could commence immediately. ... In this connection, I would also like to point out that by bringing them together in concentrated settlements and by a radical and thorough *forced removal of alien ethnic elements* here in the Lublin District, we can achieve a substantial political pacification. Because both the political activism among the Poles and Ukrainians and the influence of the Jews, augmented by the influx of thousands of escaped POWs, have taken on a form that here, too, simply in regard to implications for security policy, necessitates a rapid response.... SS-*Obergruppenführer*

Krüger has ordered me to request you, *Reichsführer*, for the possibility of an audience with you in the near future.[53]

The following points are clear from the letter:

1. Preparations for "Germanizing" the Lublin District personally ordered by Himmler had been completed, except for the "forced removal." But the "forced removal of alien ethnic elements" was an absolute precondition for the "ingathering" (*Zusammensiedlung*) of ethnic Germans in the district.

2. Plans for "forced removal" and "ingathering" were drafted in Lublin.

3. Globocnik was pressing for a quick decision so as to be able to commence with the "forced removal" and "ingathering" operations. He asked Himmler for an appointment in order to discuss the matter personally. He was granted that appointment, and the questions were indeed discussed, since there is a handwritten note on the document: "disc. orally."

4. It is not absolutely clear from the document that there were plans to murder Jews. Yet it would be mistaken to expect this to be *explicitly* stated in such an official document that later was placed in Globocnik's personal file. Such matters were strictly confidential.

Himmler probably received Globocnik's letter shortly after October 1. Yet the decision was of such fundamental political importance that Himmler must have presented Globocnik's proposal—doubtless seconding it—to Hitler. From the perspective of the protagonists, this involved a decision of the greatest historical significance, one that could only be taken by the *Führer*. Moreover, the planned measures constituted such a serious encroachment on the ambit of Hans Frank's authority that Himmler had to seek a way either to gain Frank's agreement or to neutralize him.[54] There is no evidence that Himmler sought consensus with Frank on this question. Yet there are some indications to suggest that, by having Hitler take the decision, Himmler in effect neutralized Frank to some extent.

Other circumstantial evidence also points to a personal decision by Hitler. Hans Frank's comment on October 17, 1941, about a "special assignment" he had been given by Hitler in the Lublin District, probably entailed the murder of the Jews and repopulating the district with Germans. Likewise, it is probably not coincidental that, on that very same day, Hitler mused about the settlement of the East by German settlers, "sifting" the indigenous population, and "completely kicking out" the Jews. He then went on:

There is only one task: to carry out Germanization by bringing in German settlers and to regard the indigenous population as Indians ... My approach to this matter is cold and calculating. I feel I'm acting here only as the agent of a historical will. I'm only sad I'm not a lot younger. Todt, you've also got to expand your program! You'll get the workers.[55]

These remarks indicate that Hitler had been confronted with this question shortly before, and that decisions already had been reached. The phrase "completely kick out the Jews," just like "evacuation across the Bug," indicates the intent for their destruction—which, indeed, then did occur.

Minister Todt evidently took Hitler's instruction to expand his construction program seriously, as was to be expected. Globocnik's adjutant later remarked: "It is noteworthy that *Reichsleiter* Todt, Speer's predecessor, was in constant contact with Globocnik consulting with him about the situation in the East regarding construction schemes in the pipeline."[56] However, such contacts can only have taken place prior to the end of January 1942, because Todt was killed in an airplane accident on February 8, 1942.[57] This is an additional indication pointing to Globocnik's bellwether role in plans to Germanize the East.

It should also be stressed that, in Hitler's eyes, a primary war aim against the Soviet Union was to conquer new *Lebensraum* for the German people. As early as 1923, he had written:

> ... we National Socialists must hold unflinchingly to our aim in foreign policy, namely, *to secure for the German people the land and soil to which they are entitled on this earth.* And this action is the only one which, before God and our German posterity, would make any sacrifice of blood seem justified ...
>
> If we speak of soil in Europe today, we can primarily have in mind only *Russia* and her vassal borders states. Here Fate itself seems desirous of giving us a sign. By handing Russia to Bolshevism, it robbed the Russian nation of that intelligentsia which previously brought about and guaranteed its existence as a state.[58]

In a discussion on July 16, 1941, with his closest associates, Hitler stated that a final solution in the war against the Soviet Union was now in the works: "We have to create a Garden of Eden from the newly won eastern territories; they are absolutely vital for us."[59]

What role was set aside for "the destructive Jew" to play in this "Garden of Eden"?[60] On October 17, 1941, within his fanciful visions for the future in the East, Hitler commented "several times that he would like to be 10 or 15 years younger in order to watch this development unfold."[61] Thus, Globocnik's concrete plans for settlement in the Lublin District amounted to a first attempt to realize Hitler's vision of the future—at least in part.

It is my thesis that, after Hitler took what he believed was a historic decision, Himmler informed Globocnik. On October 13, 1941, there was indeed a two-hour conference in which Himmler, Krüger, and Globocnik participated.[62] We have no record of what was discussed, but we can assume that the resettlement of the Germans and the murder of the Jews were both broached and given some sort of approval. The Higher SS and Police Leader (HSSPF) Krüger took part in the consultation both because he was Globocnik's direct superior and because the nature of the measures discussed involved the entire GG, for which Krüger was responsible.

However, the fact that this discussion took place on October 13, also means that Hitler must have reached his decision several days after October 1, but before October 13. If we can believe Goebbels, who met with him on October 4, Hitler was in excellent spirits during this period: "He looks superb and his mood is exuberantly optimistic. He simply radiates optimism." At the same time though, Hitler did not want to pin himself down as to a date for the final victory over the Soviet Union.[63] He thus was in a mood that could certainly tempt him to decisions aimed at the practical realization of his visions for the future.

Hans Frank, who was in the Reich October 1–14, must also have learned during this time of the decision Hitler seems to have taken.[64] After all, he was Governor-General and thus personally responsible to the *Führer* for everything that occurred in the territory of the GG. This fits well with the discussion on October 17 in Lublin and Frank's casual mention that day of his "special assignment" from the *Führer*.

Yet the discussion between Frank and Rosenberg can be read as contradicting the above supposition. If Frank knew that the Jews were slated to be murdered on the spot, then why did he ask Rosenberg whether it might be possible to deport the Jews from the GG to the East? Perhaps Frank felt in a sense "uneasy" about the prospect of murdering "his" Jews directly on the spot, in the GG, leading him to attempt to have them "deported" to the East, and even contacting Rosenberg personally with this in mind. In his notorious speech on December 16, 1941, Frank alluded to Rosenberg's refusal: "We were told in Berlin: why all this trouble? We can't do anything with them in the *Ostland* or the *Reichs-kommissariat* either. So liquidate them yourselves!"[65] Under these circumstances, Frank evidently could see no other alternative except to bow to the *Führer*'s order. For example, in a speech on March 4, 1944, to his closest associates, he stated: "Just call to mind what a horribly difficult task we had to take upon ourselves in order to solve the Jewish problem."[66]

It appears that the principal motive for Hitler, Himmler, and Globocnik to "remove" the Jews from the Lublin District and the entire GG at that point in time was bound up with the visions for future settlement. In order to "Germanize" Lublin and other areas, these first had to be "cleansed" of Jews and then of Poles. What were decisive here were the race-political factor and the paranoid hatred of the Jews, which completely ruled out any option for the continued existence of the Jews in areas under German control.

Other factors also infused the October 1941 decision with added dynamism. The mass murder of the Soviet Jews was in high gear at this point, making a decision in favor of the mass liquidation of the Jews no novelty. The threshold to mass murder had already been crossed. A compounding factor was the resettlement of the Volga Germans and the imminent catastrophe with regard to the food supply, as the signs were now clearly visible.

At the beginning of September 1941, the Soviet leadership announced it was resettling approximately 400,000 Volga Germans to Siberia and Kazakhstan, "since the possibility cannot be excluded that there are fifth columnists in their ranks."[67] Hypocritically, Goebbels branded this measure "indeed one of the greatest national dramas history has ever witnessed."[68] However, in the paranoid worldview of the Nazis, the Bolsheviks, now busy deporting the Volga Germans to Siberia, were scum to be equated with the Jews. They thus accused the Jews of some complicity in this measure.

At the same time, there were ever-more evident signs, especially in the eastern territories under German control, of the threat of starvation. On October 9, 1941, Goebbels noted in his diary: "the food supply situation in the occupied territories is taking such a catastrophic turn that it increasingly threatens to overshadow all other considerations." On October 17, he wrote: "Over a large part of Europe, there looms for the coming winter the terrible cloud of famine."[69] At that day's GG government session in Lublin, Frank said that "provision of food" was the major problem in all districts of the *Generalgouvernement*.[70] Yet most of the approximately 2.5 million Jews in the GG were, from the German standpoint, "useless mouths to feed," since they were not deployed in the German war economy. In his December 16 speech, Frank even accused the Jews in the GG of being "noxious gluttons."[71]

The spiraling death rate among the hundreds of thousands of Soviet POWs who had been left to die a miserable death by starvation and its associated illnesses in the prisoner camps of the Wehrmacht was also a factor. On October 17, Goebbels wrote: "There are catastrophes of starvation there that simply defy description."[72] It is a short leap from there to the murder of hundreds of thousands of hated and despised Jewish women, children, and men who were "unfit for labor." After all, the Soviet soldiers who were basically able-bodied and fit to work had also been left to die of starvation. An unambiguous statement by Hitler on January 25, 1942, also points in this direction: "Why should I look at a Jew differently from the way I see a Russian POW? Many are dying in the prisoner camps because we've been forced into this situation by the Jews."[73]

Whereas, in September and October 1941, there was a coalescence of circumstances and events that, compounded with the paranoid hatred of the Jews, provided a justification from the viewpoint of Hitler and his minions for the murder of Polish Jews, initially it was necessary to "limit" operations to Polish Jews. The time was not yet ripe for murdering

German Jews, because there were apprehensions about possible resistance within certain strata of the German population, such as intellectual circles or the church.[74] In any case, it was imperative to avoid any unnecessary unrest. Goebbels, doubtless one of the best-informed men in the entire Reich in this regard, angrily wrote in his diary on October 28, 1941:

> Our intellectual and social strata have suddenly rediscovered their sentiments of humanity for the poor Jews.... The Jews just need to send a little old lady with the Star of David badge hobbling down the Kurfürstendamm and the plain honest German [der deutsche Michel] is already inclined to forget everything the Jews have inflicted on us over the past years and decades. But not us, we cannot forget! ... Before the year is over, we have to try to remove the last remaining Jews from Berlin.... Whether I'll succeed I don't yet know because the Jews can still find powerful protectors in the highest offices of the Reich. It is curious what a lack of good healthy instinct still exists in our social and intellectual circles when it comes to the Jewish Question.[75]

It was thus anticipated that opposition to the murder of German Jews would be far greater than opposition "just" against the law for the obligatory Star of David badge introduced in September 1941, or against an expulsion. It was precisely in August 1941 that the government had been constrained to call a halt to the Euthanasia Program (Operation T-4) in order to placate the outraged German population. Here was an evident gap between aims to liquidate the Jews and options for translating that into practical reality. Hitler and his intimates were aware that the murder of German Jews had to be carried out "unobtrusively." An example of that perspective is the indirectly attested remark by Himmler to Vicktor Brack regarding the murder of the Jews (probably on December 14, 1941): "For purposes of concealment alone, it ought to be done as quickly as possible."[76]

But in September 1941, it was still unclear in Berlin how that could be effected. By contrast, the East, with the GG included, was an area unencumbered by the rule of law. With its indigenous population paralyzed by permanent terror, there the Nazis could manage things as they saw fit.

Extermination camps with stationary gas chambers—a prerequisite for implementing the murder of the Jews in the GG

One of the primary prerequisites that initially facilitated the concrete decision regarding the mass murder of the Jews in the GG was a new and efficient technology for murder, the stationary gas chambers. Utilizing previously employed mass-murder methods—i.e., shooting—it would have proved difficult to implement the mass liquidation in the GG. After all, the task involved the murder of millions of persons, as inconspicuously as possible, with the use of limited personnel. The *technical* problem as to how to implement the mass murder was extremely significant.

In the occupied Soviet territories, Jews were slaughtered en masse under the pretext of combating partisans, and large numbers of personnel were necessary for the executions. Such numbers were not available in the GG, nor was there any war going on against partisans. When Stalin, on July 3, 1941, publicly called for a partisan war to be waged behind the German front lines, Hitler also could find some "positive" sides to that call to arms. Thus, on July 16, 1941, he remarked: "This war against partisans has some advantages too; it gives us a convenient possibility to liquidate those who are against us."[77] From the Nazi perspective, the Soviet Jews were enemies in a double sense—racially as Jews and ideologically as putative Bolsheviks.

Moreover, shootings were an exhausting, physical burden for the shooters. When Himmler witnessed an execution in Minsk in mid-August of 1941, he is reported to have said: "That's not how it's done." Then he is reported to have ordered Arthur Nebe, head of Einsatzgruppe B, to search for more "humane" methods of killing that would place less of a burden on the personnel pulling the trigger.[78]

Yet the use of gassing vans was no substantial relief as far as the perpetrators were concerned. Due to the relatively low killing capacity of such facilities, the procedure would have taken too long. This means that, in the late summer of 1941, none of the customary murder techniques previously used was practicable under the given circumstances as an effective means for disposing of approximately 2.5 million Jews in the GG. That "dilemma" was reflected in Frank's December 16, 1941, remark to a session of the GG government: "We cannot shoot these 3.5 million [sic] Jews, we cannot poison them. Yet we'll be able to take measures to destroy them that will somehow result in success."[79]

The idea of building stationary gas chambers, which, in sheer efficiency and capacity, exceeded by far anything previously available, thus emerged as "the" solution. Death camps with stationary gas chambers were the technical prerequisite for the "final solution." As Browning writes: "The extermination camps equipped with gassing facilities were not, after all, an obvious invention, immediately self-evident the moment Hitler decided to kill the Jews."[80]

In other words, the development of stationary gas chambers preceded the *concrete decision* for the mass murder of Polish and European Jewry—not vice versa. On the other hand, the *will* for mass murder was a precondition for the development of the gas chambers. This is no contradiction, as there is a clear distinction between intentions (or the resolve) and the practical possibilities for their realization. Situational and cognitive factors in the decision-making process leading up to the "final solution" were mutually contingent. Far too much importance is attached to the historiographical controversy between the "intentionalists" and "functionalists," and I am in basic agreement with Browning, who deals in detail with this question in his book *The Path to Genocide*.[81]

The idea of employing stationary gas chambers for the mass murder of the Jews must have arisen in September 1941, at the latest, because, by the end of October 1941, construction had begun on such installations at the Bełżec death camp. It is also possible that this idea was developed in Lublin. There is circumstantial evidence and other considerations to support that hypothesis.

Dieter Wisliceny, a close associate of Eichmann, commented in 1946: "According to Eichmann's own statements to me, Globocnik was the first to employ gas chambers for mass extermination."[82] Eichmann himself stated for the record in Jerusalem that Heydrich had informed him two to three months after the attack on the Soviet Union: "the *Führer* has ordered the physical destruction of the Jews." He also said that Heydrich had given him the following order: "Go to Globocnik. The *Reichsführer* SS has already given him appropriate instructions. See how far he's gotten with the project."[83]

I believe Eichmann was mistaken in dating the order for the murder of all Jews to the summer of 1941—an error explicable by the distance in time from the event. But it is improbable that he was wrong about the event's "core"; namely, that he should inspect the technology of murder by gas chamber being set up by Globocnik—which he did after Hitler had given the order for all Jews to be murdered.

Rudolf Höss also reports that annihilation camps were already in existence in the GG when Himmler ordered him to build extermination facilities in Auschwitz.[84] Work on the Auschwitz-Birkenau death camp was not started until May 1942.[85] At that juncture the death camps Bełżec and Sobibór were already operational.

It should be recalled in this connection that, at about the same time, though independently of each other, the decision was taken for the systematic murder of the Jews in the *Warthegau* and in the GG. The fact that different murder methods were developed in each place indicates that the idea for death camps with stationary gas chambers had been developed locally in Lublin. Of the five death camps with stationary gas chambers— Bełżec, Sobibór, Treblinka, Majdanek, and Auschwitz—four were under Globocnik's overall command.

In addition, it is difficult to imagine that when, on October 1, 1941, Globocnik requested permission for "forced removal" of the population, he had no concrete idea as to how he might carry it out. Deportation to the East at this juncture, as already described, was impracticable for military reasons and misconceived for ideological ones. Resettlement within the GG was likewise out of the question, since there was no expendable territory available there. Moreover, when Globocnik received the desired "authorization" to push ahead with "forced removal" on October 13, 1941, there were evidently already detailed draft plans in Lublin for construction of the extermination camp. Globocnik's October 1 letter to Himmler mentioned "*ausgearbeitete Unterlagen*"—detailed prepared documents. At the end of that month, construction commenced on the Bełżec facility.[86]

A postwar statement by Ferdinand Hahnzog, then commandant of the gendarmerie (rural police) in the Lublin District, supports the argument that the mass-murder method of using stationary gas chambers was developed in Lublin. He reported on "a primitive facility near Bełżec hidden deep in the forest bordering on Galicia ... consisting of a sealed shed into which the Security Police and the SD from Zamość pumped exhaust fumes from the vehicles used to bring the '*morituri*' there!" These experiments had been carried out already "in the spring of 1941, if not earlier, in the fall of 1940."[87] Experiments with new techniques of murder were certainly nothing unusual at the time. Similar "experiments" went on in Minsk or Mogilev in the summer of 1941.[88]

Thus, Globocnik's staff of experts from various fields at work on individual "projects" were already pondering this method of mass murder by the summer of 1941 at the latest. In addition, he himself had the requisite background. In the 1920s, he had graduated from the Higher State Institute for Mechanical Engineering and had worked as a site engineer and supervisor on various construction sites.[89] Since 1939, in his capacity as SSPF in Lublin, he had been occupied with systematic murder. This means that he brought both theoretical knowledge and practical experience to this new project. His adjutant Max R. was strongly impressed by Globocnik's abilities: "I was quite astonished about his knowledge in the most diverse fields, whether political, technical or geographical."[90]

Gerlach believes that the construction of Bełżec was an attempt "to experiment with methods for mass extermination of Jews by poison gas in stationary gas chambers then carry out the first efforts."[91] However, several considerations speak against the experimental character of the Bełżec facility. If it indeed had been experimental, then less time and energy would have been invested in it. Dr. Janusz Peter, a member of the Polish resistance movement from Tomaszów Lubelski, 7 kilometers from Bełżec, reported as an eyewitness regarding the origins of the death camp in Bełżec. Initially, so-called *Askaris*[92] arrived in Bełżec, along with Germans dressed in the uniform of regular police. Then

> the camp commandant's office hired local workers whose job was
> to cut down the trees in a wooded area at the end of a dead track,
> build a sidetrack and replace the rotted sleepers. After a square

had been cleared in the wooded area and fenced in with barbed wire, the hired carpenters and bricklayers went to work ... At the end of January 1942, all civilian workers were let go and the *Askaris* took over completion of the work.[93]

This description seems to contradict the argument that Belżec was experimental. The area fenced in during the autumn of 1941 was not expanded later on; only the gas chambers were dismantled and replaced by larger ones, as will be discussed below. A simple building would have been sufficient for an experimental facility, which could have been guarded and concealed with far less expenditure on manpower. If so much effort were invested, then they must have already had concrete conceptions that this method of killing was practicable and, in particular, efficient.

It is clear that Globocnik, who was a fierce antisemite, had no qualms about mass murder. In April 1941, his direct superior in the GG, HSSPF Krüger, gave the following assessment: Globocnik "grasped intellectually the magnitude and greatness of the tasks facing us" and possessed "the resolute mercilessness" necessary to *commence with* these tasks and *carry them out.*[94] SS-*Gruppenführer* von Herff had an analogous evaluation:

Little concerned about external appearance, *fanatically obsessed with the task* ... One of the best and most vigorous pioneers in the GG. Responsible, courageous, a man of action. His daredevil character often leads him to overstep the given limits and to forget the boundaries laid down within the [SS] Order, although not for reasons of personal ambition, but rather due to his *obsession* with the cause.[95]

Himmler also praised Globocnik for his "enormous energy and dynamism ... a man made like no other for the tasks of colonization in the East."[96]

There is no doubt that, by the fall of 1941, Globocnik and his henchmen had long since crossed the psychological threshold to mass murder. We might wonder whether he had any threshold of inhibition. An obsessed fanatic, ready to risk his own freedom and life for a delusive idea, he most likely had even fewer scruples when it came to sacrificing the freedom and lives of persons he despised and hated for the sake of his ideology.[97] From his perspective, these individuals were a hindrance blocking the path to the realization of his "visions."

The question arises: did the decision of early October 1941 to murder the Jews apply only to the Lublin District, or to the entire area of the GG? Gerlach assumes that the decision to construct the annihilation camp in Belżec cannot be equated with the decision to murder all the Jews in the GG, since the original "killing capacity" of this death camp was insufficient.

He agrees in this assessment with Dieter Pohl, who hypothesizes that Globocnik's task was increasingly expanded later on.[98]

In contrast, my argument is that there was an expectation already in October 1941 that the destruction of the Jews throughout the entire GG would soon commence. On October 21, 1941, the construction of new ghettos in the Galicia District was forbidden, "since there are hopes the Jews can be deported from the *Generalgouvernement* in the near future."[99] Yet an actual "deportation" of Jews to the East at this time was, for military considerations, out of the question.

In October 1941, Globocnik probably also assumed that the Jews were to be murdered throughout the GG and not just in the Lublin District. The earlier cited report by Helmut Müller on October 15, 1941, points in that direction. Müller reported that Globocnik "considered it necessary gradually to empty all of the GG of Jews and Poles in order to bolster the security of the eastern territories."[100] In Globocnik's view, the entire GG was to be best regarded as an "internal German area" that "consequently would soon be populated 100 percent by Germans ... Inside the GG, population policy is thus closed."[101] So Globocnik was at least contemplating the future prospect of "removing" all Jews from the GG in order to be able to Germanize the area.

The argument that the "killing capacity" of the Bełżec camp was insufficient for murdering all Jews from the GG over a brief span is not persuasive. According to figures arrived at by Janina Kiełboń, a total of nearly 58,000 Jews were gassed there between March 15 and 31, 1942.[102] Höfle, one of Globocnik's close associates, stated, on March 16, 1942, that he could "handle 4–5 transports a day of 1,000 Jews each for the final destination Bełżec."[103] At the opening of the extermination facilities at Bełżec, the perpetrators thus expected to be able to murder 4–5,000 Jews per day. This was quite adequate for the planned "gradual emptying of all of the GG of Jews."

Before Operation Reinhard was launched, the murderers could assume that, within the course of two years, the roughly 2.5 million Jews in the GG could be put to death at Bełżec. In mid-June 1942, the original gas chambers were torn down, and new, large ones were erected in their place.[104] This suggests that the perpetrators did not determine the actual, limited "killing capacity" of the Bełżec facility until it had become operational.

In addition, it cannot be ruled out that first preparations for constructing the death camp at Sobibór were made simultaneous with the building of the Bełżec extermination camp. Several historians, such as Jules Schelvis, now accept this view: "Roughly at the same time as the construction of Bełżec, the first activities in Sobibór that outsiders could note commenced in the fall of 1941."[105]

This is corroborated by Ferdinand Hahnzog, who reported that first there were "experiments" with gas chambers in Bełżec. Then, in October 1941, an unprecedented auditing of his office was undertaken by SS-*Standartenführer* Walther Griphan, the new commandant of the regular police in the Lublin District and a colonel in the municipal police (Schupo). After the audit, Griphan took Hahnzog aside

> to explain quite plainly that the moment had now arrived for settling accounts with all enemies of the Reich—Poles, Jews and even Germans! ... This first shock was soon followed by a second: probably in November 1941, once again completely unprecedented, I was ordered, just as suddenly and unexpectedly, to report to Globocnik himself. He introduced me to a young SS leader who had been given the job of setting up the Sobibór camp and wanted the support of the gendarmerie office in Wodawa for that purpose.[106]

Hahnzog's report is unambiguous—provided he is describing events that actually took place. The report seems credible, since all other data given by Hahnzog are reliable and correct insofar as can be ascertained based on a comparison with contemporary documentation and other witnesses' testimony. Another striking aspect of this report is its relatively exact reconstruction of the chronology of events, which Hahnzog was able to recall in connection with the associated incidents. Finally, in his capacity as commandant of the gendarmerie in the Lublin District, Hahnzog was doubtlessly well informed about the events transpiring there. After all, he was a member of SSPF Odilo Globocnik's staff.

If two annihilation camps were under simultaneous construction in the Lublin District in the fall of 1941, the intended aim was not only to liquidate Jews from the Lublin District. It can also be argued—although this may sound more macabre—that, if necessary, it would have been possible to carry out the murder of the Jews in the Lublin District by using the methods of killing that had been employed until then. This was done, for example, in the *Warthegau*, and the number of Jews in the *Warthegau* and in the Lublin District was roughly the same.[107] Moreover, the decisions to murder them were reached at about the same time. But for the millions of Jews living in the GG, it was necessary to come up with something "special."

In addition, if one assumes that the concrete decision to murder the Jews in the Lublin District directly triggered the settlement measures planned there, then the physical destruction of these Jews would not have constituted a definitive final solution. The Jews represented only one segment of those in the Lublin District who were now slated for "forcible removal." In addition to the 40,000 Jews in the city of Lublin, there were some 100,000 Poles who also had to disappear. In the entire district, there were more than 300,000 Jews; yet there were also some 1.8 million Poles and 300,000 Ukrainians.[108] Murdering only the Jews in the district would not have opened the necessary territorial space in order to be able to displace hundreds of thousands of persons in the Lublin District (or even throughout the entire GG) in a short time and thus effect a successful "forced removal" of the population. As in the case of the Jews, a quick deportation of Poles to the East on short notice was likewise out of the question. There can be no doubt that Globocnik and Himmler were well aware of these problems.

This dilemma became especially clear in connection with the trial run "forced removal" of the population of six villages in the vicinity of Zamość carried out in November 1941. The 2,089 expelled Polish farmers were initially brought to Zamość. From there they were transported to villages in Hrubieszów county (*Kreis*) along the Bug River. But the German military is reported to have voiced opposition to their deportation further east because it did not wish to have the hostile Poles in the rear of the eastern front. The expellees were then left to their fate and permitted to go where they chose. Of course, a return to their home villages was out of the question, since ethnic Germans had in the meantime been settled there.[109] If the relocation of a mere 2,000 expellees had spawned so many difficulties, then far greater ones could be expected in connection with the planned "removal" of hundreds of thousands, indeed millions.

This means that the imminent demographic displacements associated only with the settlement schemes in the Lublin District presupposed large areas of open territory that simply did not exist in the fall of 1941. By contrast, the murder of all Jews in the GG promised to open up such territory. The plan was to deport the able-bodied Poles to the Reich as forced laborers and to house those unfit to work in the evacuated ghettos.

The events of the autumn of 1942 prove that this was no mere speculation. At that time, operations got underway to "empty" the by-now "de-Judaized" city of Lublin of its Polish population as well. The Poles marked for removal from the city of Lublin were to be placed in the emptied ghettos in Pulawy county and in the northern parts of Lublin-Land county. In a memorandum dated October 15, 1942, it was noted: "In both these counties, it is not yet possible to bring in Poles immediately, since the resettlement of Jews is still underway."[110] At the beginning of October 1942, Brandt, *Kreishauptmann* in Pulawy, declared that "Opole along with Kudl could also be filled immediately if the 8,000 Jews still located there could be removed."[111] In the fall of 1942, however, relatively few Lublin Poles (approximately 3,000) were relocated, due to the associated economic difficulties that entailed. On November 23, 1942, Globocnik and Lublin *Stadthauptmann* Dr. Curt Engländer agreed that "in keeping with circumstances, the pace of resettlement can now be significantly reduced so as to avoid harming the Lublin economy."[112]

The difference in the treatment of Poles vs. Jews is principally attributable to ideology. Poles were urgently needed as "slave labor" back in the Reich, a role attributed to them by Nazi ideology. In contrast, a permanent presence of Jews within the territories controlled by the German Reich was, for ideological reasons, out of the question. Nevertheless, there are indications that there were already ideas being broached to liquidate the "useless" Poles (i.e., those unfit for labor) from the areas designated for repopulation by Germans. That intended aim prompted Dr. Hagen, a German doctor in Warsaw, to write directly to Hitler on December 7, 1942:

> In a government discussion on combating tuberculosis, the head of the Department of Population and Welfare, *Oberverwaltungsrat* Weihrauch, disclosed to us the secret state information that, in connection with the removal and resettlement of 200,000 Poles in the eastern part of the *Generalgouvernement* in order to make room for the settlement of armed farmers, there was a definite plan or the idea was being given consideration: namely to deal with about a third of the Poles, some 70,000 elderly people and children under the age of 10, as the Jews had been dealt with, i.e. to kill them. .... *The idea of such action against the Poles probably arose because there seems at the moment to be no room for the Poles slated for removal*—unless they can be deployed directly in the armaments industry.[113]

In October 1941, this same idea could well have played a similar role in connection with the envisaged murder of Jews in the Lublin District. In the fall of 1941, there was even less space for the Jews from Lublin or Zamość than for Poles. By the end of the autumn of 1942, ghettos in the GG either stood empty or had been partially evacuated. However, the plan to kill the "useless" Poles probably had to be scrapped for two reasons: first, the situation on the eastern front deteriorated dramatically at the end of 1942; second, there were fears of a general revolt, and there were already first inklings of this possibility in the resettlement areas. But the entire supply and reinforcement route for the eastern front ran directly through occupied Poland and would be endangered by a revolt.

The change in the absolute annihilation order for the murder of the European Jews, spring 1942

Let us summarize the findings briefly once again. The concrete decision to murder the Jews in the GG was taken at the beginning of October 1941. That decision presupposed the development of annihilation camps equipped with stationary gas chambers. On the other hand, the *will* for the mass murder was a precondition for the employment of gas chambers. The mass murder of 2.5 million Jews in the GG had to be carried out swiftly, inconspicuously, and with a limited number of personnel. The destruction of Soviet Jewry, in high gear at this time, was carried out under the pretext of the so-called war against the partisans and by employing a relatively large number of personnel, which was unavailable in the GG. The development of stationary gas chambers in the extermination camps was also the prerequisite for the later decision to murder all the Jews in Europe. As Gerlach convincingly argues, Hitler announced that decision on December 13, 1941.

If Hitler's decision to murder all the Jews in Europe was an absolute order for destruction, as Hartog and Gerlach contend, then that dictate was, I believe, altered in the spring of 1942. Initially, only Jews "unfit for labor" were to be liquidated. During the deportations to the annihilation camps in the Lublin District in the period from March to the summer of 1942, not all Jews were deported to the gas chambers. Rather, initially, there was a relatively costly selection process separating between the able-bodied and those unfit for labor, where the former as a rule were permitted to remain in their places of residence. Those "unfit for labor," by contrast, were sent to be gassed. This procedure was also in keeping with the interests of the civilian administration there, which was pressing for the "deportation" of Jews "unfit for labor." At the same time, the bureaucracy had repeatedly and unambiguously voiced the desire, most particularly within the labor administration, initially to retain those "fit to work." It should be expressly underscored once more that in the Lublin District and throughout the GG, the overwhelming majority of Jews were classified as "unfit for labor" according to the Nazi criteria prevalent at the time (in the Lublin District, some 80 percent).[114] If the intention at this time had been to murder all Jews without exception, then it is not clear why this elaborate and costly selection process was carried out, instead of just systematically evacuating all the ghettos one after the other.

This thesis is no mere speculation, jumping to questionable conclusions based on the limited perspective of a regional study. Postwar statements by Dieter Wisliceny and Rudolf Höss, who played a leading and super-regional role in the "final solution," also point in this direction. In 1946, Wisliceny testified:

> I am convinced that Hitler's decision ordering the biological destruction of the Jews must have fallen in the period after the beginning of the war with the United States.... Himmler, either on his own initiative or at a suggestion from [Oswald] Pohl, exempted able-bodied Jews from biological destruction; he wished to deploy them as slave laborers in the large factories in the concentration camps.[115]

Wisliceny stated that, in the summer of 1942, Eichmann showed him

Himmler's spring 1942 order regarding the "exemption of able-bodied Jews."[116] Rudolf Höss's statement, written in prison in Krakow, is in basic agreement:

> According to the order of the *Reichsführer*-SS of the summer of 1941, all Jews were to be annihilated.[117] The RSHA expressed great misgivings when the RFSS, at Pohl's suggestion, ordered that the able-bodied were to be sorted out from the rest. The RSHA was always in favor of the total elimination of all Jews, and viewed every labor camp, every thousand able-bodied workers, as a germ harboring the danger of liberation, of somehow staying alive. No office had a greater interest in seeing death statistics for Jews mount than the RSHA, the Office for Jewish Affairs. By contrast, Pohl had orders from the *Reichsführer*-SS to deploy as many prisoners as possible in the armaments industry.[118]

In July 1942, there was evidently a renewed intensification in Hitler's order, which had been modulated in the spring of 1942, for the biological destruction of the Jews in Europe. It appears that Globocnik, in turn, played an important role in this shift.[119] However, the investigation of that problem lies beyond the scope of this paper.

Notes

1 The plan for the murder of the Polish Jews in the *Generalgouvernement* was given the cover name "Operation Reinhard" after the assassination of Reinhard Heydrich in Prague in May 1942, in order to honor his memory. See Dieter Pohl, *Von der "Judenpolitik" zum Judenmord. Der Distrikt Lublin des Generalgouvernements 1939–1944* (Frankfurt am Main: Peter Lang, 1993), p. 129.
2 An overview of the most recent research can be found in Christopher R. Browning, *The Path to Genocide. Essays on Launching the Final Solution* (Cambridge: Cambridge University Press, 1992); idem, *Der Weg zur Endlösung. Entscheidungen und Täter* (Bonn: Dietz, 1998); expanded translation of English ed.); see also Christian Gerlach, "Die Wannsee-Konferenz, das Schicksal der deutschen Juden und Hitlers politische Grundsatzentscheidung, alle Juden Europas zu ermorden," *WerkstattGeschichte* 18 (1997), pp. 7–44; This also appeared in English, "The Wannsee Conference, the Fate of German Jews, and Hitler's Decision in Principle to Exterminate All European Jews," *The Journal of Modern History* 70 (December 1998), pp. 759–812.
3 Ralf Ogorreck, *Die Einsatzgruppen und die "Genesis der Endlösung"* (Berlin: Metropol, 1996), chap. 7–8, pp. 176–222, is persuasive. He argues that, in August 1941, a comprehensive order was handed down to liquidate all Soviet Jews, irrespective of age or gender. Similarly, see Philippe Burrin, *Hitler und*

die Juden. Die Entscheidung für den Völkermord (Frankfurt am Main: Fischer, 1993); Browning, *Path*, argues against the notion that this decision was made in July 1941.

4 Thus, for example, Burrin, *Hitler*, pp. 133 ff. (September) and Browning, *Path* (October).

5 L.J. Hartog, *Der Befehl zum Judenmord. Hitler, Amerika und die Juden* (Bodenheim: Syndikat, 1997), pp. 63–77; Gerlach, "Wannsee-Konferenz," p. 8.

6 Gerlach, ibid., p. 43.

7 Archiwum Głównej Komisji Badania Zbrodni przeciw Narodowi Polskiemu w Warszawie (Archive of the Main Commission on Investigating the Crimes Against the Polish People; AGK), *Das Diensttagebuch des deutschen General-gouverneurs in Polen 1939–1945*, Vol. XIII/1, pp. 951 f. (hereafter, *AGK Diensttagebuch*). The German *Stadthauptmann* was the principal official in the municipal administration.

8 This discussion is evaluated in a similar way by the historians who prepared the edition *Der Dienstkalender Heinrich Himmlers 1941/42*, edited and annotated by Peter Witte, et al. (Hamburg: Hans Christians, 1999), pp. 233 f., n. 35.

9 Bogdan Musial, *Deutsche Zivilverwaltung und Judenverfolgung im General-gouvernement. Eine Fallstudie zum Distrikt Lublin 1939–1944* (Wiesbaden: Harrasowitz Verlag, 1999), pp. 127 f.

10 Werner Präg und Wolfgang Jacobmeyer, eds., *Das Diensttagebuch des deutschen Generalgouverneurs in Polen 1939–1945* (Stuttgart: Deutsche Verlags-Anstalt, 1975), p. 413.

11 Musial, *Zivilverwaltung*, pp. 157–159.

12 *Dienstkalender Himmlers*, p. 233, fn. 35; Peter Witte, "Zwei Entscheidungen in der 'Endlösung der Judenfrage': Deportationen nach Lodz und Vernich-tung in Chelmno," *Theresienstädter Studien und Dokumente* (1995), p. 61, fn. 16; also Pohl, *Judenpolitik*, p. 101; Peter Longerich, *Politik der Vernichtung. Eine Gesamtdarstellung der nationalsozialistischen Judenverfolgung* (Munich: Piper, 1998), pp. 452–456.

13 *AGK Diensttagebuch*, vol. XVII/1, p. 30 (emphasis added).

14 In 1997, Siegfried Pucher published a short biography of Globocnik: "... *in der Bewegung führend tätig—Kämpfer für den 'Anschluss' und Vollstrecker des Holocaust*" (Klagenfurt: Drava, 1997). However, the book treats Globoc-nik's life in Lublin without evaluating the decisive West German trials against former associates and the archival materials stored in Poland. In contrast, the period before 1939 appears to be relatively well researched.

16 Götz Aly, *"Endlösung". Völkerverschiebung und der Mord un den europäis-chen Juden* (Frankfurt am Main: Fischer, 1995).

17 *Dienstkalender Himmlers*, pp. 185–186, 189, and notes.

18 Interrogation of Jakob Sporrenberg, December 16/17, 1949, AGK SAL 193/4, fol. 996. See also the December 15, 1960, interrogation of Konrad G., who directed Wehrmacht counterintelligence in Warsaw, Zentrale Stelle der Lan-desjustizverwaltungen in Ludwigsburg (ZStL) 208 AR-Z 74/60, fol. 447, and the 1960 statement of a former Wehrmacht intelligence officer, Hans W., October 21, 1960, Niedersächsisches Hauptstaatsarchiv Hannover (HStA), Nds, 721 Hild, Acc 39/91, no. 28/55, fols. 141 f.

19 Interrogation of Boepple, May 11, 1946, Zuffenhausen, AGK SAKr 1, fol. 18.

20 Interrogation of Max R., January 28, 1963, HStA, Nds, 721 Hild, Acc 39/91, No. 28/188 (no pagination).

21 Rudolf Höss on Globocnik, January 1947, Institut für Zeitgeschichte, Munich (IfZ) F 13/6.

22 Gerhard Eisenblätter, *Grundlinien der Politik des Reiches gegenüber dem Generalgouvernement 1939–1945* (diss.), Frankfurt am Main, 1969, pp. 202 f.; "Bericht über den Aufbau der SS- und Polizeistützpunkte" (n.d.), Bundesarchiv, Berlin (BA) BDC (Globocnik).

23 Helmut Müller, "Bericht über die Verhältnisse in Lublin," October 15, 1941, BA BDC (Globocnik); Józef Marszalek, *Majdanek, obóz koncentracyjny w Lublinie* (Warsaw: Interpress, 1981), pp. 17 f. The SS-*Mannschaftshaus* was a kind of think tank sponsored by the SS in major German universities in the 1930s. It attracted young academics, mostly doctoral candidates. Such institutions were also established in occupied countries during the war. See Michael G. Esch, "Die 'Forschungsstelle für Ostunterkünfte' in Lublin," *Zeitschrift für Sozialgeschichte des 20. und 21. Jahrhunderts*, vol. 11, no. 2 (1999), pp. 67–96.

24 "Lagebericht des Kreishauptmannes Weihenmaier," February 4, 1941, AGK NTN 280, fol. 185.

25 *Krakauer Zeitung*, July 15, 1941; Czeslaw Madajczyk, *Generalna Gubernia w planach hitlerowskich* (Warsaw: Ludowa Spóldzielnia Wydawnicza, 1961), p. 116.

26 Under the code name "*Fahndung nach deutschem Blut*," Globocnik began, in the fall of 1940, to seek out "submerged" German folk culture. The focus was on German settlers who had settled in the area of the later GG in the eighteenth and nineteenth centuries and had been Polonized over the course of time; they were to be "re-Germanized." Cf. Bruno Wasser, *Hitlers Raumplanung im Osten. Der Generalplan Ost in Polen 1940–1944* (Basel: Birkhäuser, 1993), p. 11; see also *Himmlers Kalender*, pp. 65 f.

27 Memorandum, Himmler, July 21, 1941, BA BDC (Globocnik); Czesaw Madajczyk, *Zamojszczyzna—Sonderlaboratorium SS* (Warsaw: Ludowa Spóldzielnia Wydawnicza, 1977), vol. 1, pp. 26 f.

28 Müller, "Bericht über die Verhältnisse in Lublin."

29 Ibid.

30 Originally the GG was meant to serve as a kind of reservation for Poles living there and for "undesirable elements" (Poles, Jews, Gypsies) from the Reich. For a more detailed account, see Eisenblätter, "Grundlinien," pp. 66–109.

31 Präg and Jacobmeyer, *Diensttagebuch*, p. 335.

32 Ibid., p. 336.

33 Ibid., p. 386.

34 Elke Fröhlich, ed., *Die Tagebücher von Joseph Goebbels. Teil II. Diktate 1941–1945* (Munich: Saur, 1995), vol. 1, p. 35.

35 Werner Jochmann, ed., *Adolf Hitler. Monologe im Führerhauptquartier 1941–1944. Die Aufzeichnungen Heinrich Heims* (Hamburg: Knaus, 1980), p. 48.

36 Goebbels, *Tagebücher*, vol. 1, pp. 160, 208.

37 Ibid., pp. 33, 257–265, 392.

38 Entry for September 24, 1941, ibid., vol. 1, pp. 480–483.

39 Entry for October 4, 1941, ibid., vol. 2, pp. 49–56.

40 Jochmann, *Monologe*, p. 110.

41 Entry for November 10, 1941, Goebbels, *Tagebücher* vol. 2, p. 263 (emphasis added).

42 In a letter to Himmler on October 1, 1941, Globocnik stated: "Since preparations have been completed for concentrating [the population], implementation could start immediately." BA BDC (Globocnik).

43 Entry for September 24, 1941, Goebbels, *Tagebücher*, vol. 1, p. 480.

44 Musial, *Zivilverwaltung*, pp. 141–145.

45 Eisenblätter, *Grundlinien*, pp. 178–194.

46 Memorandum, Rademacher, quoted in Browning, *Path*, p. 134.
47 Musial, *Zivilverwaltung*, p. 102; Ino Arndt and Heinz Boberach, "Deutsches Reich," in Wolfgang Benz, ed., *Dimension des Völkermordes. Die Zahl der jüdischen Opfer des Nationalsozialismus* (Munich: R. Oldenbourg, 1991), p. 36.
48 "Den destruktiven Juden setzen wir ganz hinaus," Jochmann, *Monologe*, p. 90.
49 Interrogation of Max R., May 29, 1968, ZStL 208 AR-Z 74/60, fol. 8685.
50 Browning, *Path*, p. 120.
51 Müller, "Bericht über die Verhältnisse in Lublin."
52 Similar in Witte, "Zwei Entscheidungen," p. 61, fn. 16; *Dienstkalender Himmlers*, p. 233, n. 35.
53 Globocnik to Himmler, October 1, 1941; BA BDC (Globocnik) (emphasis added).
54 On Hans Frank's position as Governor-General, see Musial, *Zivilverwaltung*, pp. 13–20.
55 Jochmann, *Monologe*, pp. 90 f. Fritz Todt was the munitions minister and head of the semi-military construction company Organisation Todt.
56 Interrogation of Max R., May 29, 1968; ZStL 208 AR-Z 74/60, fol. 8686.
57 *Dienstkalender Himmlers*, p. 341.
58 Adolf Hitler, *Mein Kampf*, trans. by Ralph Mannheim (London: Hutchinson & CO, 1969), pp. 596–598 (emphasis added).
59 "Aufzeichnungen Bormanns über die Besprechung Hitlers mit seinen Mitarbeitern über die Ziele im Krieg gegen die Sowjetunion, 16.Juli. 1941," in *Internationaler Militärgerichtshof. Der Prozess gegen die Hauptkriegsverbrecher* (*Trial of the Major War Criminals Before the International Military Tribunal: Official Text*), 42 vols. (Nuremberg, 1947–49) (hereafter, *IMT*), vol. XXXVIII, p. 88; Czeslaw Madajczyk, ed., *Vom Generalplan Ost zum Generalsiedlungsplan* (Munich: Saur, 1994), pp. 61–64.
60 Browning, *Path*, p. 105.
61 "Notiz des persönlichen Referenten von Alfred Rosenberg, Dr. Koeppen, über das Gespräch mit Hitler am 17. Oktober 1941," in Madajczyk, *Generalplan Ost*, pp. 22 f.
62 Entry for October 13, 1941, *Dienstkalender Himmlers*, p. 233.
63 Goebbels, *Tagebücher*, vol. 2, pp. 49, 52, 55 f.
64 Präg and Jacobmeyer, *Diensttagebuch*, pp. 410–413.
65 Ibid., p. 457.
66 Ibid., p. 810.
67 *Völkischer Beobachter*, September 11, 1941.
68 Entry for September 9, 1941, *Goebbels Tagebücher*, vol. 1, p. 384.
69 Ibid., vol. 2, pp. 82, 133.
70 *AGK Diensttagebuch*, vol. XVII/1, p. 29.
71 Präg and Jacobmeyer, *Diensttagebuch*, p. 458.
72 Goebbels, *Tagebücher*, vol. 2, p. 132.
73 Jochmann, *Monologe*, p. 229.
74 Hans Mommsen, "What Did the Germans Know about the Genocide of the Jews?," in Walter H. Pehle, ed., *November 1938. From "Kristallnacht" to Genocide* (New York: Berg, 1991), p. 205.
75 Goebbels, *Tagebücher*, vol. 2, pp. 194 f.
76 Brack to Himmler, June 23, 1942, BA BDC (Globocnik); see also Nuremberg doc. NO-205. On the dating of Himmler's statement, cf. *Dienstkalender Himmlers*, p. 290, fn. 48.
77 "Aufzeichnungen Bormanns über die Besprechung Hitlers mit seinen Mitar-

beitern über die Ziele des Krieges gegen die Sowjetunion, 16. Juli. 1941," in *IMT*, vol. XXXVIII, p. 88.

78 Quoted in Ogorreck, *Einsatzgruppen*, p. 182; Longerich, *Politik der Vernichtung*, p. 442; Breitmann, *Architect*, pp. 191–194; Eichmann described to Rudolf Höss the mass executions of Soviet Jews by Einsatzkommandos: "There were reported to have been horrific scenes; the wounded trying to run away, the killing of the wounded, especially women and children.... Most members of these mobile killing units took a bit of alcohol to help get over this gruesome work." Notes of Rudolf Höss: *"Meine Psyche. Werden, Leben und Erleben* (1946–1947)," AGK Archivum Jana Sehna 22, fol. 127.

79 Präg and Jacobmeyer, *Diensttagebuch*, p. 458.

80 Browning, *Path*, p. 117.

81 Ibid., pp. 86–121.

82 Dieter Wisliceny, "Bericht: Die Bearbeitung der jüdischen Probleme durch die Sicherheitspolizei und den SD bis 1939," November 18, 1946, IfZ Fa 164 (Wisliceny), p. 8.

83 Jochen von Lang, ed., *Das Eichmann-Protokoll. Tonbandaufzeichnungen der israelischen Verhöre* (Berlin: Severin und Siedler, 1982), pp. 82 f.

84 Jean-Claude Pressac, *Die Krematorien von Auschwitz. Die Technik des Massenmordes* (Munich: Piper, 1994), pp. 51–55, fn. 132; Karin Orth, "Rudolf Höss und die 'Endlösung der Judenfrage.' Drei Argumente gegen deren Datierung auf den Sommer 1941," *WerkstattGeschichte* 18 (1997), pp. 52 f.

85 Pressac, *Die Krematorien von Auschwitz*, pp. 48–50; the first murders by poison gas took place in December 1941; ibid., pp. 41 f.; idem, with Robert-Jan van Pelt, "The Machinery of Mass Murder at Auschwitz," in Yisrael Gutman and Michael Berenbaum, eds., *Anatomy of the Auschwitz Death Camp* (Bloomington: Indiana University Press, 1994), pp. 183–245.

86 Witte, "Zwei Entscheidungen," p. 61, fn. 16; Pohl, *Judenpolitik*, p. 100; Longerich, *Politik der Vernichtung*, p. 455.

87 "Zustände und Begebenheiten im Distrikt Lublin des Generalgouvernements von Januar 1940 bis April 1942 aufgrund persönlicher Erinnerungen von Ferdinand Hahnzog, Juli 1962," HStA, Nds, 721 Hild, Acc 39/91, no. 28/113, fol. 245. Hahnzog remained in Lublin from January 1940 to April 1942. Data in his other statements is generally reliable and correct.

88 Longerich, *Politik der Vernichtung*, pp. 442–445 (Minsk); Ogorreck, *Einsatzgruppen*, pp. 211–214 (Minsk and Mogilev); Breitmann, *Architect*, pp. 196 f.

89 Pucher, *In der Bewegung*, p. 22.

90 Interrogation of Max R., ZStL; 208 AR-Z 74/60, fol. 8686.

91 Gerlach, "Wannsee-Konferenz," p. 43.

92 These were former Soviet POWs that had been trained in the Trawniki camp near Lublin and had later been deployed for action in the framework of Operation Reinhard. That is why they are also termed Trawniki men.

93 Janusz Peter, *Tomaszowskie za okupacji* (Tomaszów Lubelski: Tomaszowskie Towarzystwo Regionalne, 1991), pp. 188 f.

94 Krüger to Himmler, April 2, 1941. BA BDC (Globocnik).

95 Note of assessment in connection with the official trip by SS-*Gruppenführer* von Herff through the *Generalgouvernement* in May 1943; ibid. (emphasis added).

96 Himmler to Wendler, August 4, 1943, ibid.

97 Before the incorporation of Austria (*Anschluss*) into the Reich, Globocnik served eleven months in jail for political activity in the NSDAP; see Pucher, *In der Bewegung*, pp. 22–30.

98 Gerlach, "Wannsee-Konferenz," p. 9; Pohl, *Judenpolitik*, p. 101.

99 Präg and Jacobmeyer, *Das Diensttagebuch*, p. 436; the ban on the construction of new ghettos in the GG was issued in July 1941; in September 1941, the Galicia District evidently was granted a special permit. Dieter Pohl, *Nationalsozialistische Judenverfolgung in Ostgalizien 1941–1944. Organisation und Durchführung eines staatlichen Massenverbrechens* (Munich: Oldenbourg, 1996), p. 141.
100 Helmut Müller, "Bericht über die Verhältnisse in Lublin," October 15, 1941.
101 "Globocniks Stellungnahme zur der Frage: 'Behandlung Fremdvölkischer,'" March 15, 1943; AGK NTN 255, fols. 210 f.
102 Janina Kielboń, *Migracje ludności w dystrykcie lubelskim w latach 1939–1944* (Lublin: Państwowe Muzeum na Majdanku, 1995), pp. 149, 170.
103 Memorandum, Reuter, March 17, 1942, Archiwum Państwowe w Lublinie (APL), GDL 270, fol. 34.
104 Yitzhak Arad, *Belzec, Sobibor, Treblinka. The Operation Reinhard Death Camps* (Bloomington: Indiana University Press, 1987), p. 73.
105 Jules Schelvis, *Vernichtungslager Sobibór* (Berlin: Metropol, 1998), pp. 37 f.; similar in Witte, "Zwei Entscheidungen," p. 61, fn. 16; Longerich, *Politik der Vernichtung*, p. 455.
106 Hahnzog, "Zustände und Begebenheiten," pp. 245 f.
107 According to estimates by Frank Golczewski, there were some 260,000 Jews in the *Warthegau* and 250,000 in the Lublin District; see Frank Golczewski, "Polen," in Benz, ed., *Dimension des Völkermordes*, p. 457. However, my estimate is that there were some 320,000 Jews living in the Lublin District. I was unable to check the figures given for the *Warthegau*; Musial, *Zivilverwaltung*, p. 102.
108 "Konfessionelle Gliederung der Bevölkerung des Distrikts Lublin nach dem Stande 9.12.1931 (Schätzung)"; APL, GDL 728, fol. 8.
109 Expert opinion by Dr. Zygmunt Klukowski, January 27, 1950; AGK SAL 193/3, fols. 614 f. Klukowski was a physician, historian and member of the Polish resistance movement from Szczebrzeszyn, near Zamość. On the difficulties with housing "expellees" in November 1941, cf. several contemporary documents published in Madajczyk, *Zamojszczyzna*, vol. 1, pp. 49–52.
110 Memorandum, October 15, 1942; AGK OKBZH Lublinie 257, fols. 1 f.
111 Memorandum, October 14, 1942; ibid., fol. 3. The *Kreishauptmann* was the principal official in the country administration.
112 Memorandum on the discussion of November 23, 1942; ibid., fols. 35 f.
113 Hagen to Hitler, December 7, 1942 (copy); AGK NTN 412, fol. 3 (emphasis added).
114 See Musial, *Zivilverwaltung*, pp. 242–248, 262–267, 273–276, 292–300.
115 Wisliceny, "Bericht: Die Bearbeitung der jüdischen Probleme durch die Sicherheitspolizei und den SD bis 1939," Bratislava, November 18, 1946; IfZ Fa 164, pp. 8 f.
116 Ibid.
117 This statement by Höss that the order for the extermination of the Jews was given in the summer of 1941 has recently been questioned by Karin Orth, *Rudolf Höss*. She argues convincingly that Höss was mistaken about the dating of this order.
118 Rudolf Höss, "*Meine Psyche. Werden, Leben und Erleben* (1946–1947)," AGK Archivum Jana Sehna 22, p. 140.
119 See *Dienstkalender Himmlers*, p. 483 (n. 35), p. 493 (n. 82); Brack to Himmler, June 23, 1942, BA BDC (Globocnik); Browning, *Der Weg*, pp. 151–159, who persuasively argues that this intensification occurred in July 1942.

22

JEWISH WORKERS IN POLAND

Self-maintenance, exploitation, destruction

Christopher Browning

Source: Christopher Browning, *Nazi Policy, Jewish Workers, German Killers*, Cambridge: Cambridge University Press, 2000, pp. 58–88.

Historians of the Holocaust have generally accepted that the Nazi regime gave a fundamental priority to racial ideology over economic utility in carrying out the Final Solution.[1] Perhaps the most succinct and emphatic statement in this regard was the cryptic message of December 18, 1941: "In principle, economic considerations are not to be taken into account in the settlement of the [Jewish] problem."[2] It is my purpose not to dispute but rather to qualify this axiom of Nazi Jewish policy through an examination of the German exploitation and destruction of Jewish labor in Poland.

I will argue for four points. First, Nazi policy toward the use of Jewish labor in Poland differed in both time and place. Conclusions drawn from a single camp or single phase of occupation are generalized only at the risk of considerable distortion.[3] The story is a complex one. Second, in the German use of Jewish labor in Poland, economic considerations were taken seriously by many Germans but only within and not as a challenge to the parameters set by political and ideological factors. Third, even within these ideological parameters there was no consensus among the Germans over the use of Jewish labor, and productive utilization of Jewish labor often faced opposition and sabotage from both local and higher authorities. In 1942–43, Himmler himself was the driving spirit behind the destruction *of* Jewish labor, apparently finding "destruction *through* labor" an unsatisfactory policy in most circumstances. Fourth, both early in the war when the ultimate goal was Jewish expulsion and later when the ultimate goal was Jewish extermination, there was an initial period of conflict and confusion followed by a period in which advocates for a productive use of Jewish labor were permitted brief and precarious opportunities to pursue their goals. In these brief periods, select Polish Jews were not to be starved or killed systematically. Rather they were to work productively (and intensively) for the moment, though always with the clear expectation that they would be expelled or killed sometime later. In these brief periods, the ultimate ideological goal was never superseded, just temporarily deferred, but this deferral was the difference between life and death for many survivors.

I would also suggest that an examination of Nazi policies toward Jewish labor in Poland is necessary in order to understand what in the experience of Polish Jews led them to put so much faith in the strategy of "survival through labor." Why could they not understand the Nazi priorities that seem so self-evident to historians today? There were indeed all too many occasions on which Jewish "work" was organized in an utterly irrational way from the point of view of economic utility and constituted in practice merely another cruel means to imposing additional humiliation and suffering before death. But that is not the whole story. Jewish leaders were not deluded in believing that many local German authorities had a strong interest in the productive exploitation of Jewish labor. They were mistaken, however, in their desperate hope that the fate of their communities lay in the hands of these local authorities and that the combination of their vested interests and the clear demonstration of Jewish productivity on behalf of the German war economy could ultimately save a remnant of the Jewish community. One reason, however, for this mistaken hope placed in the power of local authorities was that frequently the advocates of a productive use of Jewish labor did prevail temporarily over vociferous opposition. An examination of the Nazi exploitation of Jewish labor is also helpful in understanding how a minority of Jews from some labor camps but not others were, contrary to Nazi intentions and against all odds, able to survive.

In the first weeks of the occupation, local German authorities rounded up Polish Jews for forced labor on an ad hoc basis. These razzias frequently became occasions for German amusement and Jewish suffering. Initiatives to bring greater order to the use of Jewish labor came from both sides. In Warsaw, the paralyzing fear and disruption caused by such roundups induced the newly appointed head of the Jewish Council, Adam Czerniakow, to negotiate an agreement in late October 1939 with the Security Police, whereby the Jewish council would supply and pay for a labor battalion on a regular basis,[4] an example that was followed by other Jewish councils.[5] Also in late October, the newly appointed head of the General Government, Hans Frank, issued an edict imposing forced labor on all Jews and authorizing implementation through the HSSPF Friedrich Wilhelm Krüger.[6]

Krüger was quite aware that random local roundups constituted a relatively irrational and unproductive use of Jewish labor potential. Particularly in Poland there were many skilled Jewish craftsmen, he noted, and "it would be a pity, if this manpower were not profitably employed." Krüger

212

therefore ordered the Jewish councils to create card files for the systematic registration of all male Jews by profession.[7] Himmler and Heydrich also expressed interest in exploiting Jewish labor, but in a different way. In early 1940 both envisaged vast Jewish forced labor camps to work on border fortifications – a so-called *Ostwall* on the demarcation line – and other construction projects.[8]

For the Germans a number of questions had to be answered. Who would allocate or assign Jewish labor? Were the Jews to be concentrated in vast labor camps or employed selectively according to skill? And how would Jewish labor capacity be maintained over time? After considerable recrimination, especially between the civil administration and SS in the Lublin District and Frank's insistence on a solution,[9] guidelines were announced by the head of Frank's labor division, Max Frauendorfer, in the summer of 1940.[10] In principle, Jewish labor was conceded to be a police matter, but in practice, allocation of Jewish labor would now take place through the Labor Division and its local labor offices. The use of Jewish labor was "urgently necessary," he wrote, because many Polish workers had been sent to Germany, and in contrast to Reich Jews, many Polish Jews were "good skilled workers and craftsmen." Jews were to be employed in the normal labor market as the best way to utilize their skills. Moreover, as the resources of the Jewish councils were exhausted, and it was in German interest to maintain the strength of these workers, they would have to be paid at 80 percent of the Polish wage. "One could not forget that the Jews, so long as they were there, had to be provided for in some way," he noted. Only Jews who were not employed in the free economy were to be summoned to forced labor, many of them to work in camps along the frontier on large projects. But this was an "experiment" (*"Versuch"*); only the future would show how far one could go in this direction.

There was nothing inherently flawed or economically irrational about Frauendorfer's approach. Precisely such an approach of combining paid Jewish labor on the free market with selective conscription for the labor camps of *Organisation* Schmelt was successfully employed in East Upper Silesia.[11] One result was that Jewish mortality rates remained at the prewar level there for the first 2 years of the war. But there is nonetheless a surreal aspect to reading the documents on Frauendorfer's seemingly rational approach to the use of Jewish labor, for implementation of the plan in the General Government failed in every way.

First, those who had enjoyed the fruits of uncompensated Jewish forced labor were not prepared even to pay cut-rate wages. Frauendorfer continued to insist on the 80 percent wage rate, because "otherwise the maintenance of the strength of the working Jews would not be guaranteed."[12] Such exhortations had little effect. The *Kreishauptmann* of Czestochowa, for example, replied defiantly, "I assume that this regulation can be lost locally and have acted accordingly."[13] In any case, the issue of employing Jews in the free labor market at whatever wage was increasingly rendered moot by ghettoization, one major effect of which was to sever Jews from employment in the regular economy.

This is an issue to which we shall return. In the meantime, however, the initial experiment in work camps had also failed completely. Labor camps were planned in the Lublin district to house 50,000 Jews working on both military fortifications as well as road construction and water control projects. The Jews were to come from not only the district of Lublin but also those of Warsaw and Radom. Allocation of workers was to be the task of the labor offices, which issued certificates of exemption to Jews already employed in the regular economy.[14]

Reality was otherwise. The SS and police leader (SSPF) in the Lublin district, the notorious Odilo Globocnik, systematically ignored the labor offices and their certificates of exemption, as his men seized Jews at random to fill his own camps.[15] In the end only 13 kilometers of worthless antitank ditches were dug before the military turned its attention to preparing offensive staging areas instead of defensive fortifications.[16] But the human cost was staggering. When Globocnik finally shifted Jewish workers from his own camps to those of water control projects in October 1940, one inspector noted: "The Jews ... who have been delivered from the Jewish camp at Belzec unfortunately had to be released, because they had been driven to the utmost by those in charge there (SS) and were totally incapable of work."[17] The SS was not alone in this regard. Reports on the water control camps also detailed absolutely dreadful conditions.[18]

These labor camps for water control projects were also shut down over the winter months.[19] However, the Lublin water control projects were resumed in the spring of 1941 with Jewish camp labor, and a whole new network of such camps was opened in the Warsaw district as well. These camps became quickly known for terrible food shortages, poor sanitation and medical care, guard brutality,[20] and inadequate pay. Indeed, one camp employer shamelessly announced that, after deductions for food, shelter, salaries for guards, and medical care, his workers owed him money.[21] The camps produced suffering and death but little else. As one German official who inspected the camps calculated, the camps had cost 4.5 times as much to construct as the value of the labor performed there.[22] By late August 1941, when the Germans in Warsaw had finally given up on the water control camps, the head of the labor office for Jews there noted that the use of Jewish labor camps elsewhere in the General Government was also in decline. "The inclination to use Jewish labor in camps is, after many bitter experiences, no longer great. The cost stands in no profitable relationship to the labor output."[23] When the idea of reviving the Jewish labor camps for water control projects was broached once again in Warsaw in the spring of 1942, this same man successfully opposed the proposal. On the basis of past experience, he noted, he wanted "no camps of emaciated men, no impossible work demands that even German workers could not surmount."[24] As an experiment in the productive use of Jewish labor, the first generation of Jewish labor camps in the General Government had clearly failed.[25]

Everywhere in German-occupied Poland the Jews faced wholesale confiscation of their property, exclusion from many economic activities, and vast economic hardship. Nowhere did this hardship become so acute as in the two largest Jewish communities in Poland, namely Lodz in the Warthegau and Warsaw, where hermetically sealed ghettoization quickly led to mass starvation. Here a debate over the use of Jewish labor, between factions that I have elsewhere dubbed "productionists" and "attritionists," emerged in the most acute form.

Everywhere German occupation authorities faced two common factors that in retrospect favored ghettoization: first was the dashed expectation of a quick expulsion of Polish Jewry, and second was, in Warsaw ghetto commissioner Heinz Auerswald's words, "the desire to segregate the Jews from the aryan environment for general political and ideological reasons."[26] Nonetheless, there was no uniform policy of ghettoization in Poland, which proceeded in different ways at different times in different regions for different combinations of reasons.[27] Let us examine the Lodz and Warsaw cases more closely.

In the Warthegau in December 1939, Gauleiter Arthur Greiser determined that the Jews had "hoarded colossally" and thus they were to be sealed in ghettos "until what they have amassed is given back in exchange for food and then they will be expelled over the border."[28] In short, a hermetically sealed ghetto in Lodz was initially viewed as a "transition measure" ("*eine Übergangsmassnahme*")[29] for extracting through deliberate starvation the last remnants of Jewish wealth prior to their expulsion, not as a source of productive labor. Little attention was given, therefore, to the initial proposals of the head of the Jewish council, Chaim Rumkowski, to organize ghetto labor and production in order to purchase food for the poor Jews in the ghetto.[30] With the emphasis on extraction, not production, the Germans calculated that the resources of the ghetto would be totally exhausted by July 1940, but deportation of the Lodz Jews was still expected in August.

Two factors then forced the Germans to recalculate. First, the expected August expulsion of Lodz Jews into the General Government was postponed indefinitely,[31] and second, the death rate in the ghetto skyrocketed.[32] The Germans faced a decision. The head of the ghetto administration, Hans Biebow, now argued that every effort had to be made "to facilitate the self-maintenance of the Jews through finding them work."[33] Biebow's rabidly antisemitic deputy, Alexander Palfinger, emphatically opposed the idea of a self-sustaining ghetto. He argued that "especially in the Jewish question, the National-Socialist idea ... permits no compromise" and that "a rapid dying out of the Jews is for us a matter of total indifference, if not to say desirable ..."[34] (*"Völlig gleichgülitg, um nicht zu sagen, wünschenswert ist uns das rasche Absterben der Juden"*). The local decision went against Palfinger, when in mid-October 1940 "it was established ... that the ghetto in Lodz must continue to exist and everything must be done to make the ghetto self-sustaining."

A similar pattern of decisions, first to ghettoize and then to harness Jewish labor for self-maintenance, was repeated in Warsaw. The Warsaw Jews were hermetically ghettoized in the fall of 1940 after many false starts, including Frank's summer ban on further ghetto construction as "for all practical purposes illusory" in view of the Führer's Madagascar Plan.[35] The demise of this plan in September, combined with dire warnings of German public health doctors in the General Government about the threat of epidemic posed by Warsaw Jews, triggered Frank's decision for their ghettoization.[36]

As in Lodz, the creation of a sealed ghetto cut the Jews of Warsaw off from any employment and business on the outside. All economic relations with the outside world were now to take place through a so-called Transfer Agency (*Transferstelle*), presided over by none other than Alexander Palfinger. Having been bilked of his opportunity to engineer a deliberate mass starvation of the Jews of Lodz, he now controlled the economic lifeline to a Jewish community in Warsaw that swelled to a maximum of 445,000 in the spring of 1941.[37]

Reports reached Cracow in mid-January 1941 that food supplies to the Warsaw ghetto had been stopped entirely.[38] Two months later, in mid-March, Frank went through one his mercurial changes of mood. He cited Göring approvingly that "it is more important that we win the war than implement racial policy." Thus one had to be happy over every Pole or Jew working in a factory, whether he "suits us or not."[39] This burst of pragmatism provided a propitious moment for two of his economic advisers, Dr. Walter Emmerich and Dr. Rudolf Gater, to present an analysis of the economic viability of the Warsaw ghetto and propose an immediate, basic reorientation.[40] Fundamentally, they argued, the Warsaw ghetto was supposed to last five years, but cut off from the outside economy, it consumed far more than it produced. Once the existing wealth of the ghettoized Jews was exhausted, the Germans would face one of four choices: (1) subsidize the ghetto; (2) accept the consequences of inadequate provisioning; (3) harness the Jews to productive labor; or (4) loosen the seal around the ghetto to allow the resumption of direct economic ties with the surrounding population. Gater and Emmerich accepted the impossibility of the first and fourth options, which is to say that they did not challenge the wider ideological parameters. Thus the choice was simple; one could either view the ghetto "as a means to liquidate the Jews" (*"als ein Mittel ... das jüdis-*

che Volkstum zu liquidieren") or as a source of productive labor, and Emmerich and Gater clearly supported the later option.

Rather than openly arguing for a deliberate policy of mass starvation for its own sake, Governor Ludwig Fischer of the Warsaw district and his minions in reply consistently denied any impending hunger crisis. Emmerich brushed such claims aside as mere fantasy. As the ghetto had been created for the long haul, economic planning had to be done accordingly. "The starting point for all economic measures concerning the ghetto has to be the idea of maintaining the capacity of the Jews to live. The question is whether one can succeed in solving this problem in a productive manner...."[41]

Frank sided with the Cracow "productionists" over the Warsaw "attritionists." In May 1941, on the very eve of Germany's "war of destruction" against the Soviet Union, a change of personnel in the Warsaw ghetto administration ensued. Heinz Auerswald, a lawyer who at least on one occasion could not remember when he had joined the Nazi Party,[42] was made the new commissioner, and a Viennese banker, Max Bischof, whose wife was half Jewish,[43] took over the Transfer Agency in place of the odious Palfinger, with the explicit task of creating a self-sustaining ghetto economy.

One point should be clearly made. The ghettoized Jews of Lodz and Warsaw were not to be kept alive in order to work; rather they were to be put to work in order to be kept alive by their own efforts and at their own expense. The Germans did not yet perceive themselves facing a serious labor shortage, and Jewish labor was thus not viewed as essential to the war effort. But the local Germans who had improvised ghettoization without direction from Berlin were now left to improvise solutions to the dilemma posed by ghettoization once expulsion was indefinitely postponed and mass starvation loomed. They were neither philo-Semitic nor humanitarian, but they were concerned about public health and public aesthetics. Starving Jews threatened to spread epidemic, and even the "attritionist" governor of the Warsaw district, Ludwig Fischer, conceded "that the corpses lying in the street create a very bad impression."[44] The military commandant in Warsaw was more blunt: "The ghetto was developing into a cultural scandal, a center of disease...."[45] Local ghetto administrators assumed that in accordance with central policy, one day the Jews would disappear. Left to themselves in the meantime, they conceived of the creation of self-sufficient ghetto economies harnessing productive Jewish labor as being in Germany's interest and hence their patriotic and professional duty.

To create ghetto economies, the ghetto managers had to operate under many constraints. The ideological parameters had already made impossible either a loosening of the ghetto seal or feeding the Jews at German expense. The ghettos were temporary phenomena destined to be emptied at some point in the future and thus ranked low in any claim on priorities. Most importantly, the incarcerated Jews were at the bottom of the Nazi racial hierarchy with the least claim to scarce resources. Thus the ghetto managers were free to improvise ghetto economies only as long as they worked with marginal resources not claimed by others. What they could not do was to achieve a reallocation of scarce resources, especially food, to benefit Jews at the expense of anyone else.[46]

Operating under such constraints, the ghetto managers were only partially successful. Hunger and disease continued to haunt Warsaw and Lodz, and the skyrocketing death rates were only gradually and precariously stabilized. Yet, in the end, Jewish labor in both ghettos became productive, though along different organizational models.

In Lodz Hans Biebow was determined to keep all strings of the ghetto economy in his own hands. He set about collecting all of the unused machinery in the Warthegau and then machinery that had been confiscated from Jews in Germany. He also toured Germany in search of new contracts that would allow him to add new workshops and new products.[47] After the terrible winter of 1940, employment began a steady rise in the spring of 1941. By the summer of 1941, 40,000 Jews were working in the Lodz ghetto; by the following spring the figure was 53,000; by the spring of 1943, it stood at 80,000. Chief among the contractors was the Wehrmacht. Though initially "dubious" about the quality of goods that would be produced in the ghetto, it was soon ordering military supplies of all kinds.[48] Ghetto productivity was not increased only by procuring new machinery and contracts, however. Biebow ordered the work week extended from 54 to 60 and finally to 72 hours and imposed draconian factory discipline. The result – in Isaiah Trunk's words – was "the most industrialized ghetto in all of Eastern Europe."[49]

In contrast to the controlled economy in Lodz, a decentralized, laissez-faire economy gradually emerged in Warsaw, though it turned the corner toward economic viability quite belatedly, only in the spring of 1942. The initial attempts of Auerswald and Bischof in the summer of 1941 to increase employment within the ghetto failed miserably. The Jews were reluctant to register with the labor office, for fear that they would be sent to the notorious labor camps. And the Wehrmacht was reluctant to place orders.[50] More success was obtained when the Transfer Agency got out of the business of trying to run workshops and allowed private firms to create their own shops in the ghetto, procure their own contracts, import their own raw materials, and deliver their own products outside the control of the Transfer Agency.[51]

As late as mid-October 1941, a discouraged Bischof confessed that the ghetto economy was a "field of ruins"[52] ("*Ruinenfeld*"). However, in early 1942 a significant change in the ghetto economy began to occur. German employers in Poland began to appreciate the potential of Jewish labor as awareness of a major labor shortage spread through the war economy. As laborers were taken from Poland back to the Reich, the ghetto increasingly was seen as a reservoir of replacement labor essential to the local economy.[53]

In April, May, and June 1942, demands for Jewish labor rose dramatically, new firms opened operations in the ghetto and others expanded their operations there, and production figures skyrocketed. And in May 1942 the monthly death rate fell below 4,000 for the first time in 12 months.[54] The destruction of the Warsaw ghetto that commenced in late July 1942 did not occur because the Warsaw Jews had stubbornly survived a policy of deliberate starvation or because "impossible circumstances" deliberately engineered by cynical local authorities compelled a radical solution; rather, the local experiment in a self-sufficient ghetto economy in Warsaw was just beginning to bear fruit when basic changes in policy fashioned in Berlin rendered such local experiments obsolete.

As the idea of murdering all the Jews of Europe had crystallized within the Nazi leadership in the fall of 1941, Reinhard Heydrich had quickly perceived a major threat to the comprehensive nature of the emerging plan. In a discussion of the Jewish Question with officials of Alfred Rosenberg's Ostministerium (Konrad Meyer and Georg Leibbrandt) on October 4, 1941, he observed: "There is in any case the danger that above all, those in the economic sector will in numerous cases claim their Jewish workers as indispensable and no one will make the effort to replace them with other workers. But this would undo the plan for a total resettlement of the Jews from the territories occupied by us."[55] Heydrich's fears in this regard could only have been intensified during the month of October, as evidence of a severe labor shortage in the German war economy inexorably mounted, and on October 31, Hitler gave in to economic realism and ordered the large-scale labor exploitation of Soviet POWs on Reich territory.[56] Berlin stuck to the hard line concerning Jewish labor, however, even into December. When officials of the Ostland inquired whether all Jews should be liquidated regardless of age, sex, and economic interest, Berlin replied "economic interests are to be disregarded in principle" in solving the Jewish Question.[57]

Several factors brought about a change in this hard-line policy in winter of 1941. The mirage of solving Germany's current labor shortage through the exploitation of Soviet POWs evaporated when the staggering mortality and debilitation they had suffered became apparent.[58] And after the Soviet counteroffensive and Pearl Harbor in the first week of December, it was clear that the demands of the war economy for labor would only intensify. The Nazi regime accepted the necessity of importing vastly increased numbers of civilian forced laborers from the east, especially Russians, Poles, and Ukrainians.[59] At the same time, Himmler and Heydrich altered the SS position on the use of Jewish labor. More as the exception than the rule, Himmler had already approved two local systems of SS controlled Jewish labor camps: first those of *Organisation* Schmelt in East Upper Silesia in the fall of 1940, and second, the so-called D-4 camps to provide Jewish labor for road construction in Galicia in the fall of 1941.[60] When Heydrich voiced the intention to use Jewish labor on a large scale for the first time at the Wannsee Conference, he annunciated what has become known as the doctrine of "destruction through labor." This was already the policy in practice in the D-4 camps, if not in those of *Organisation* Schmelt, and indeed, Heydrich's specific reference at Wannsee to decimating the Jews through road construction might well have been a quite concrete reference to them.[61]

Five days later Himmler informed the head of the concentration camp inspectorate, Richard Glücks, "now that Russian prisoners of war cannot be expected in the near future," he could expect that 150,000 Jews would be sent to the camps for "large economic missions and tasks."[62] As Oswald Pohl informed his camp commanders, the camps were to be "as productive as possible" and prisoner employment was to be, "in the true meaning of the word, exhaustive."[63] The official SS vision for the use of Jewish labor was, therefore, quite clear. Jews capable of labor were to work productively and die in the process.

The totality and clarity of this murderous vision was not fully and immediately comprehended by Germans in Poland, nor did Himmler remain content with it for long. When the vastly increased numbers of civilian workers began to be sent from Poland to the Reich in the spring of 1942, local authorities responded with a policy of substitution, in which Jewish labor would fill the void. The first planned act of substitution of Jewish for Polish laborers seems to have taken place in the course of the expulsion of the Jews from Mielec to the Lublin district on March 9, 1942. Those Jews selected as capable of work were not expelled but sent instead to a nearby airplane factory. The military deemed the experiment a success.[64] Indeed, so much so that in early May 1942, the Armaments Inspectorate endorsed the employment of a further 100,000 skilled Jewish workers, thus freeing Polish and Ukrainian workers to be sent to the Reich.[65]

At the same time, just prior to the first deportations from Lublin to Belzec, the ghetto was divided into A and B sections for nonworkers and workers. Though not always honored in the chaos and brutality of the ensuing ghetto-clearing operation, certificates of exemption were given to essential workers who were to be resettled in a temporary "work ghetto" of Majdan Tatarski. And Globocnik's deputy, Hermann Höfle, informed the civil administration concerning incoming transports from Slovakia and the Third Reich that the trains would stop in Lublin for a selection of able-bodied Jews before the others were sent to Belzec to "never again return."[66] Höfle then proceeded to enlist the local officials of the Lublin district to take a census of working and nonworking Jews, one of whom replied emphatically: "In these deportations only old people, incapable of work, women and children may be seized, and such men who are not employed by German agencies. Craftsmen must under all circumstances remain here for the moment."[67] Frank himself remained in a pragmatic mood: "If I want to win the war, I must be an ice-cold technician. The question what will be done from an ideological-ethnic point of view I must postpone to a time after the war."[68]

In Poland, indeed, anti-Semitic ideology and economic pragmatism seemed quite compatible at this point. The initial argument of the ghetto managers had been that Jews had to be put to work so that they might live, not that they should be allowed to live so that they might work. But this gradually changed. In their attempt to justify greater food supplies for the malnourished and starving ghetto inhabitants, the ghetto managers increasingly reversed the terms of the argument. Because these Jewish workers were making a significant contribution to the war economy, they should be better fed to enhance their productivity. The corollary, of course, was that nonworking Jews were a burden not deserving of food. The ghettos had never been viewed as permanent; now that Berlin had decided finally to "evacuate" the ghettos, relief from the burden of non-working Jews was welcomed by all.[69] This widespread view was expressed by Frank's state secretary, Josef Bühler, at Wannsee, when he had urged that the Final Solution begin in the General Government, since most of the Jews there were already incapable of work.

The only critical concern voiced in the General Government, therefore, was not about the deportation of nonworking Jews but about whether labor of the working Jews left behind would be properly exploited. On May 5, 1942, Bühler told his division heads that:

> According to the latest information, there are plans to dissolve the Jewish ghettos, keep the Jews capable of work, and to deport the rest further east. The Jews capable of work are to be lodged in numerous large concentration camps that are now in the process of being constructed.

Bühler feared that using Jewish labor in large camps would destroy the existing organizational forms within which Jews were working and damage their "multifaceted use" ("*Mehrfaches des Nutzes*").[70] Labor Department head Max Frauendorfer, perhaps fearing a repeat of the 1940 camps, urged that the Jews "should be maintained capable of work for the duration of the war." He was convinced that with so many Polish workers in the Reich, the General Government was "for the time being absolutely dependent upon the use of Jewish labor," and he was also convinced that Himmler, Albert Speer, and Fritz Sauckel all increasingly valued the use of Jewish labor as well.[71]

Indeed, even into the summer of 1942 the dominant tone among Frank's officials was not fear over the possible loss of Jewish labor (whose continuing presence they took for granted) but impatience that they had not yet been fully relieved of the burden of their non-working Jews. HSSPF Krüger did nothing to disabuse them of their assumptions about working Jews in late June when he stated that not only would Jewish workers in the armaments industries be retained but their families would be also.[72] The situation then abruptly changed in late July, when Himmler issued a December deadline for clearing the General Government "of the entire Jewish population." This included all Jewish labor "except in internment camps." Massively accelerated deportations ensued, which threatened to leave behind only a fraction of the number of Jewish workers earlier envisaged.[73]

The German historian Christian Gerlach has now brilliantly analyzed a hitherto neglected dimension to our understanding of this concerted assault upon Jewish labor in the summer of 1942.[74] Perhaps owing to the all-too-frequent use of transparently formulaic rationalizations in German documents of the period, many historians – myself included, I must emphasize – have simply read past the many references to the Nazi perception of a looming food crisis in 1942 in connection with the Final Solution. But Gerlach convincingly demonstrates that these references were not formulaic but instead reflected an obsession gripping many leading Nazi officials at the time. In my opinion, Himmler's determination to liquidate the "work Jews" stood independent of the "food crisis." It began before and continued long after the crisis was at its most acute stage. But the widespread concern over food shortages – constantly associated with so-called Jewish blackmarketeering – contributed greatly to Himmler's leverage, as the near-total liquidation of the Jews could now be seen as offering immediate economic advantages to offset the economic disadvantages related to loss of scarce labor.

The reaction among the civil administration and military to this decimation of the "work Jews" differed, but in general complaints were minimal. In Warsaw, Bischof chronicled the total collapse of the ghetto economy.[75] But other officials in this stronghold of erstwhile "attritionists" expressed no doubt about either their priorities or the fate of the deported Jews. "These economic disadvantages must ... be put up with, because the extermination of the Jews is unconditionally necessary for political reasons."[76]

In the end only certain elements of the German military in the General Government openly broke with the consensus and tried to impede, however temporarily, Himmler's designs. On July 17, 2 days before Himmler issued his end-of-the-year deadline to clear the General Government of Jews, Krüger met with Generalleutnant Maximilian Schindler, head of the Armaments Inspectorate, and announced that all previous arrangements between Schindler and the SS concerning Jewish labor were now null and void. Krüger announced a new arrangement, whereby the SS would build conveniently located labor camps in which Jewish workers necessary for military production would be incarcerated. Moreover, Krüger assured Schindler, the Jewish ghettos would only be dissolved in agreement with the Armaments Inspectorate.[77]

Quickly, however, the military was literally flooded with reports that production at firms with which they had contracted for supplies had been disrupted owing to the seizure without notice of Jewish workers.[78] The military then sought the assurance of the SS that "Jewish actions" would take place only after the military had been informed and had approved because, "with the complete combing-out of Polish workers for the Reich, Jews are the sole available labor manpower."[79]

At a following meeting, Krüger's representative announced flatly that the plan of substituting Jewish for Polish workers – so in vogue just months earlier – had been given up. He then invoked Göring, often an advocate of economic pragmatism in the past:

> In the opinion of the Reich Marshal one must give up the notion that the Jew is indispensable. Neither the Armaments Inspectorate nor any other agencies in the General Government would retain Jews until the end of the war. The orders that had been issued were clear and hard. They were valid not only for the General Government but also for all occupied territory.[80]

The SS position was quickly supported by Wilhelm Keitel and the Armed Forces High Command (Oberkommando der Wehrmacht, or OKW), which on September 5 ordered that Jewish workers were now to be replaced with Poles.[81] Having planned in the spring of 1942 to replace Polish workers sent to the Reich with Jewish workers, Germans in the General Government were now being told that the Jewish workers were only temporary substitutes who were to be replaced yet again with Poles!

On September 18, 1942, Kurt Freiherr von Gienanth, the military commander in the General Government, composed and sent to the OKW the only unequivocal denunciation of the economic absurdity being perpetrated in the General Government, though not of course even mentioning the much greater moral outrage being committed in the death camps.[82] Twelve days later, the "war diary" of the senior quartermaster noted succinctly, "General of the Cavalry, Freiherr v. Gienanth, has been retired, effective immediately."[83] His successor was explicitly ordered to comply with SS labor policies,[84] and an incensed Himmler also threatened harsh consequences for anyone else who opposed him "with alleged armaments interests" but "in reality merely wanted to support the Jews and their business."[85]

Himmler's policy distinguished between "so-called" armaments workers who "merely" worked on such things as clothing and footwear on the one hand, and "actual" armaments workers who produced weapons and munitions on the other hand. Those in the former category were to be collected immediately in SS camps, where they would fulfill military orders. Those in the latter were to be held in closed barracks at their factories, which in effect would become "concentration-camp enterprises" ("*Konzentrationslager-Betriebe*"), which paid the SS per head for the use of these laborers.[86] Even these work Jews were eventually to be transferred to large SS camps in eastern Poland. Then they, too, Himmler insisted, "will also disappear some day in accordance with the wish of the Führer." The only concessions gained by the military were the temporary sparing of the "so-called" armaments workers producing uniforms alongside the "actual" armaments workers and the promise of sufficient time to sort out those truly essential workers who were to remain.[87]

If the Jewish workers most essential to military production were temporarily spared, their families usually were not. Nor were the Jews in other sectors of the economy even when vital to replacing Poles taken to Germany or working in ways at least indirectly important to the war economy. For example, in December 1942, Frank belatedly regretted the loss of Jewish workers that brought numerous railway construction projects to a halt:

> In our time-tested Jews we have had a not insignificant source of labor manpower taken from us. It is clear that the process of mobilizing labor is rendered more difficult when in the midst of this wartime labor program the order comes that all Jews are to be left to their destruction.[88]

Himmler's triumph in 1942 was nearly total. The civil administration in the first half of the year had expected to be rid of the nonworking Jews but still enjoy the widespread use of Jewish labor, especially to replace Polish workers sent to the Reich. This expectation had been totally dashed in July 1942. Of all the employers in the General Government, only the military had been granted a temporary reprieve for essential armaments workers, but only if they were turned over to the SS by their former employers, incarcerated in either SS or factory camps, and rented back at 5 Zloty per head per day. For Himmler this was a brief political concession to remove the chief pretext for military opposition, not a recognition of the indispensability of Jewish labor to the war economy. Well into 1943, Himmler would push for both ever greater control over the still-living Jewish armaments workers and their even more total destruction, regardless of economic considerations and the disastrous German defeats in the Russian and Mediterranean theaters. Owing to Himmler's relentless pursuit throughout 1943, far more Jews – classified as essential workers the previous year – would be murdered outright than would die through an exhaustive "destruction through labor." In his zeal to murder the remaining work Jews, Himmler far outstripped even the most murderous henchmen he had employed for the destruction of Polish Jewry – namely Odilo Globocnik and Friedrich Wilhelm Krüger.

In the last half of 1942, when the bulk of Polish Jewry had been deported to death camps, usually a remnant of some 10 percent to 20 percent of each community had been granted the treasured work exemption and left behind. Since large SS camps to hold such numbers did not exist, these remnants of work Jews were incarcerated either in factory camps or fenced-in areas of the Jewish quarters now renamed *Arbeitsghettos* or *Restghettos*. These "work ghettos" or "remnant ghettos" served not only as improvised forced labor camps (*Zwangsarbeitslager* or ZAL) but also as illusory sanctuaries to lure Jews out of hiding.

Himmler had no intention of allowing the situation to stabilize. In January 1943 he descended upon Warsaw and was furious to discover that no further progress had been made in shifting Jewish workers out of the ghetto to SS camps. He ordered that under Globocnik's supervision the work Jews were to be transferred to SS camps in Lublin, after which the ghetto was to be torn down completely. In a fit of pique, he also ordered that the factory proprietors who had allegedly arrived in Poland with nothing and made themselves wealthy on "cheap Jewish labor" be sent to the front.[89] While the liquidation of the Warsaw ghetto led to the great uprising in April 1943, the liquidation of the *Restghettos* elsewhere was driven forward. This process amounted to yet another mass selection, in which some Jews (now a remnant of a remnant) were sent to work camps and the others were either shot on the spot or deported to a death camp.

Unlike in Warsaw, SSPF Julian Scherner in Cracow had already ordered the transfer of his work Jews to Plaszow as soon as the construction of the enlarged camp was complete.[90] The liquidation of the Cracow ghetto followed on March 13–14, 1943, and 14,000 Jews were sent to Plaszow for labor, whereas 3,000 were deported to Auschwitz and nearly as many were shot on the spot.[91] In March, April, and May the *Restghettos* of the Lublin district (Piaski, Cholm, Wlodawa, Izbica, Leczna, Miedzyrzec, and Lukowa) were liquidated, with at least some of the Jews sent to Majdanek for labor but many others to their immediate deaths in Sobibor and Treblinka.[92] From April through June, SSPF Fritz Katzmann launched the final savage assault on the remaining ghettos in Galicia – by far the largest contingent of Jews still alive in the General Government.[93] On June 30, 1943, Katzmann proudly informed Himmler that over 434,000 Jews had been "deported" ("*ausgesiedelt*") from Galicia, and all ghettos there had now been dissolved. The remaining 21,000 Jews were in camps under the control of the SS and their numbers would be steadily reduced.[94] The Radom district was no exception. The *Restghettos* of Kielce and Tomaszowa-Mazowiecki were cleared in late May, with the surviving remnants of worker groups sent to nearby work camps.[95] In late June the so-called little ghetto of Czestochowa was also liquidated, with only a minority of the work Jews left alive.[96]

This ongoing drive to liquidate the "work ghettos" and vastly reduce the number of Jewish workers left alive traced clearly to Himmler, though with declining support from his key SS men in Poland. Indeed, a new factor now weighed on Himmler that made him even more determined. The Warsaw ghetto uprising that began in April 1943 clearly shook Himmler. In addition to his inveterate suspicion that virtually every claim about the indispensability of Jewish labor to the war economy was both a pretext for personal profit and manifest evidence of the insidious temptation to corruption that the Jews – if left alive – represented, his ideologically conditioned obsession with the Jews as a security risk and the cause of all unrest behind the lines was now also fully activated. On May 10, 1943, Himmler discussed police reinforcements to the General Government and particularly the use of SS units, "as for example in street fighting in the Warsaw ghetto." He then declared:

> I will not slow down the evacuations of the rest of the some 300,000 Jews in the General Government, but rather carry them out with the greatest urgency. However much the carrying out of Jewish evacuations causes unrest at the moment, to the same degree they are the main precondition for a basic pacification of the region after their conclusion.[97]

The repercussions were quickly felt in the General Government, where Krüger stated before Frank and Heydrich's successor Ernst Kaltenbrunner among others that he had "just recently again received the order to carry out the removal of the Jews in a very short time." They were to be taken out of armaments factories and other businesses producing for the military and placed in large concentration camps, from which they would be made available to the armaments industry. "But the Reichsführer wishes that even the employment of these Jews ceases." Krüger then voiced open disagreement. These work Jews were "Maccabeans, who work wonderfully" ("*Makkabäer, die ausgezeichnet arbeiten*"). He did not think that Himmler's wish could be fulfilled, because among the Jews were skilled workers who could not be replaced. He asked Kaltenbrunner to explain the situation to Himmler and "beseech him to refrain from taking away this Jewish manpower"[98] ("*ihn zu ersuchen, von der Wegnahme dieser jüdischen Arbeitskräfte Abstand zu nehmen*").

Himmler was clearly not swayed by economic arguments, however, and in this regard received full support from Hitler. As Himmler noted after a meeting on June 19, 1943, once again devoted to security concerns: "To my presentation on the Jewish question, the Führer spoke further, that the evacuation of the Jews was to be carried out radically and had to be seen through, despite the unrest that would thereby arise in the next 3–4 months"[99] (*"Der Führer sprach auf meinen Vortrag in der Judenfrage hinaus, dass die Evakuierung der Juden trotz der dadurch in den nächsten 3 bis 4 Monaten noch entstehenden Unruhen radikal durchzuführen sei und durchgestanden werden müsste"*).

The assault on the work Jews continued along two lines. Targeted were both Jews already in work camps who were not deemed essential to military production on the one hand and Jews in the few still-existing major "work ghettos" throughout eastern Europe on the other hand. Beginning in late June and culminating in two days of coordinated, multiple massacres on July 22–23, 1943, the Galician D-4 labor camps for road construction were systematically liquidated.[100] And four *Restghettos* that had been converted into labor camps in the eastern Cracow district (Przemysl, Tarnów, Bochnia, and Rzeszów) were closed down simultaneously in the first 3 days of September, with only a portion of their workers distributed to work elsewhere.[101]

The bigger targets for Himmler, however, were the remaining major "work ghettos" of Bialystok, East Upper Silesia, and Lodz as well as the remaining ghettos even further east, such as Minsk. For Bialystok and Lodz, as in Warsaw the previous spring, he enlisted the services of Odilo Globocnik, who hoped to pillage both manpower and machinery for his own growing empire in Lublin. At this point, at least, both Himmler and Globocnik viewed the SS camps of Lublin as the last repository of the remnant of a remnant of work Jews, who in turn would work in SS-controlled industries rather than private firms. The model for this was the transfer of the Többens and Schultz firms, along with their machinery and workers, from Warsaw to camps in Poniatowa and Trawniki.[102] Here they were slated to be taken over by a SS firm known as Osti (Ostindustrie) created specifically to utilize Jewish workers and property as well as the machinery of ghetto firms.[103]

The Lublin camp conglomerate thus included the concentration camp at Majdanek (under the Wirtschafts-und Verwaltungshauptamt [WVHA], the Economic and Administrative Main Office of the SS), the two Lublin work camps at Lipowa and the "old airport,"[104] a Heinkel factory at Budzyn, Globocnik's private workshop at Krasnik, and the new work camps at Poniatowa and Trawniki. Globocnik boasted of 45,000 Jewish workers, most of whom had recently come from Warsaw. Furthermore, he expected this number to increase "significantly more in the coming months" (*"in den nächsten Monaten noch bedeutend"*) because of a similar windfall of workers and machinery from Bialystok. He also proposed the same fate for Lodz.[105] And in August Himmler ordered additionally that Jews of Minsk were to be taken to Lublin as well.[106]

Globocnik's staff did indeed help carry out the liquidation of the Bialystok ghetto in mid-August 1943 and received the bulk of the workers not gassed at Treblinka.[107] However, the transfer of Jews from Minsk to Lublin never materialized, except for one small contingent of Jews from Minsk selected at Sobibor.[108] And the great prize of Lodz, moreover, eluded Globocnik entirely. Though Himmler approved the transfer in principle in September 1943,[109] the scheme came to naught as the entire Globocnik empire collapsed precipitously in the fall of 1943 with fatal consequences for the Jewish workers.

Globocnik had been useful to Himmler in carrying out the liquidation of the work ghettos while providing the cover, however implausible, that war production would not be impaired. But Himmler's obsessive suspicions about the seductive lure of wealth produced by Jews must have made him uneasy about Globocnik's growing ambitions for the Lublin labor camp empire. In any case, with the last work ghettos liquidated, Himmler transferred Globocnik to Trieste in September 1943. Then came the event that inflamed Himmler's other obsessive suspicion about the Jews as a dangerous security risk, when on October 14, the inmates of Sobibor staged a successful revolt and outbreak. This followed upon the Treblinka breakout and unsuccessful resistance at Bialystok.

The Germans had already shown a well-grounded fear that to begin a gradual elimination of work camps would give warning and invite resistance among desperate prisoners who had nothing to lose, once the last hope of survival through labor was dashed. Thus the elimination of entire labor camp systems – the D-4 camps in Galicia on July 22–23 and in eastern Cracow district on September 1–3 – had been coordinated, simultaneous operations. In the former case, at least, outside killing units were brought in and even German camp personnel were not warned ahead of time. Himmler now ordered that this same scenario be played out in Lublin on a much vaster scale. Police and SS units were brought in from all over Poland and even the Protectorate, and on the 2 days of November 3 and 4, some 42,000 Jews – virtually the entire Jewish labor force in Lublin – were massacred in what was cynically dubbed Operation *Erntefest*, or "harvest festival."[110]

The assault on the labor camps did not end there, however. One day after *Erntefest*, on November 5, the labor camp at Szebnia in the Cracow district was liquidated, when its nearly 4,000 workers were shipped to Auschwitz.[111] And on November 19, the 4,000 inmates of the last major Jewish labor camp in eastern Poland – the Janowska Road camp in Lwów where thousands of Jews had already perished under what was perhaps the most terrifying and murderous regime of all the Jewish labor camps – were also massacred.[112]

In the entire region of Galicia, Lublin, Bialystok, Warsaw, and Cracow, only the major labor camp at Plaszow and a few minor camps such as the Heinkel plane factory at Budzyn and the oil refinery at Drohobycz remained in existence.[113] In March 1943 before Himmler's assault on the work ghettos and labor camps, more than 300,000 Jews had been temporarily spared as "work Jews" in these regions.[114] At the end of November 1943, perhaps 25,000 were still alive.[115] The overwhelming majority of fatalities had not been caused by "destruction *through* labor." Instead, they had been victims of a Himmler-driven campaign for the "destruction *of* labor" through outright massacre.

November 1943 was a turning point, however. The work camps of Plaszow, the Radom district, and East Upper Silesia were not liquidated in turn. Himmler even permitted Lodz to continue as a work ghetto, rejecting Oswald Pohl's bid to turn it into a concentration camp.[116] And in the Radom district, in contrast to Plaszow and East Upper Silesia, the camps also remained "factory camps" distantly supervised by the SSPF but not incorporated into the concentration camp system (of the WVHA). These camps continued in operation until the approach of the Red Army forced closure, and even then the inmates were not killed on the spot but rather evacuated westward. Moreover, within at least some camps, the murderous regimen was significantly moderated over time.[117] The massive selections and gratuitous killings were curtailed, and death from exhaustion, malnutrition, and disease dropped significantly as well. Compared with the horrendous conditions within the Jewish labor camps and their near total liquidation further east by November 1943, a new period of precarious stability began. With the war clearly lost and the labor shortage clearly insurmountable, a weak glimmer of economic pragmatism was belatedly tolerated. At least in some camps neither a regimen of "destruction of labor" nor a regimen of "destruction through labor" characterized this period. Rather, it was "work now, destruction later" until the chaotic period of evacuations and death marches set in, and the fate of the surviving remnant of Polish "work Jews" was inextricably mixed with that of other slave laborers being driven westward in the closing months of the war.

In summary, German attitudes toward the exploitation of Jewish labor in Poland were mixed and changing, though always within the parameters of the Nazi regime's ideology and ultimate political priorities and goals. During the period when expulsion was envisaged as the ultimate goal and no overall labor shortage was perceived, the Nazi exploitation of Jewish labor was as wasteful and inefficient as it was cruel. When expulsion stalled and local authorities were left to deal with the large concentrations of impoverished Jews cut off from employment in the regular economy, at least in the two largest ghettos of Lodz and Warsaw advocates of a productive use of Jewish labor prevailed over advocates of attrition through starvation. Precarious ghetto economies were established for the purpose of maintaining the ghettoized Jews at their own expense. Though death rates soared and hunger and suffering remained immense, the Jews of Lodz, Warsaw, and the rest of Poland did not suffer the same fate as the

Soviet POWs who died by the millions in the first 9 months after Operation Barbarossa.

The situation in Poland was fundamentally altered by two decisions in Berlin in the fall of 1941, one calling for a massive increase in the use of foreign labor and the other substituting extermination for expulsion as the goal of Nazi Jewish policy. Local authorities assumed that they would reconcile these conflicting policies by exploiting Jewish labor to replace deported Polish labor while simultaneously ridding themselves of what they considered the unwanted burden of the nonworking Jews. This time, however, Berlin did not leave local authorities to themselves. Himmler intervened consistently and savagely from July 1942 through November 1943 to force the destruction of the working Jews in Poland, a goal that he achieved throughout the districts of Galicia, Bialystok, Warsaw, Lublin, and most of Cracow.

Local authorities of the SS, military, and civil administration all saw this as a clear conflict between political and economic goals. Despite their full awareness of the damage to the war economy, however, they almost without exception conceded priority to the regime's political goal of the Final Solution. For Himmler and Hitler, however, no such conflict existed. All claims of Jewish indispensability to the economy were dismissed as invalid. Indeed, such claims were seen as evidence that the Jewish spirit of profiteering was still threatening to infect the Germans, and hence inspired an even more fanatical determination to exterminate Jewish labor. Jewish workers clung desperately to the strategy of survival through labor, until Himmler's policy left no option but hopeless resistance. The Warsaw ghetto uprising in turn activated another Himmler obsession that the Jews stood behind all resistance to the Germans and their total removal was the prerequisite for pacification. To Himmler's ideologically driven delusion about Jews and the economy was now added a mechanism of self-fulfilling prophecy concerning Jews and resistance.

Then in November 1943 came the last turn. With the war lost and German labor shortage insurmountable, Himmler's obsessive campaign to destroy Jewish labor slackened. The surviving Jews of Radom, Lodz, and East Upper Silesia did not suffer the same fate as those further east, and local authorities were once again left to make their own decisions. As a result, they treated their Jewish captives once again as slave laborers to be exploited mercilessly and draconically but not as objects to be destroyed immediately and totally. Unlike further east, from these camps there would be a surviving remnant, and it is to their story and their testimony that we turn next.

230

Notes

1 There are a few historians who do not accept the primacy of ideological over
economic factors and who have argued in one way or another that the Final
Solution was a by-product of economically motivated decisions. For instance,
Götz Aly and Susanne Heim have argued at one time that the murder of the
European Jews was for the Nazis a "logical" means to solving a problem of
overpopulation that blocked the path to economic modernization. Most
important among the numerous publications of Aly and Heim in this regard
are: "Die Ökonomie der 'Endlösung': Menschenvernichtung und
wirtschaftliche Neuordnung," *Beiträge zur nationalsozialistischen Gesund-
heits-und Sozialpolitik*, vol. V, *Sozialpolitik und Judenvernichtung: Gibt es
eine Ökonomie der Endlösung?* (Berlin, 1987), pp. 7–90; "The Economics of
the Final Solution; A Case Study from the General Government," *The Simon
Wiesenthal Center Annual*, V (1988), pp. 3–48; "Sozialplannung und Völkermord: Thesen zur Herrschaftsrationalität der natsionalsozialistischen Vernichtungspolitik" and "Wider die Unterschätzung der nationalsozialistischen
Politik: Antwort an unsere Kritiker," *Vernichtungspolitik: Eine Debatte über
den Zusammenhang von Sozialpoliitk und Genozid im nationalsozialistischen
Deutschland*, ed. by Wolfgang Schneider (Hamburg, 1991), pp. 11–24 and
165–75; and *Vordenker der Vernichtung: Auschwitz und die deutsche Pläne für
eine neue europäische Ordnung* (Hamburg, 1991).
   For the most recent broad critique of this approach, see: Michael Burleigh,
"A 'political economy of the Final Solution'? Reflections on modernity,
historians, and the Holocaust," *Ethics and Extermination: Reflections on Nazi
Genocide* (Cambridge, 1997), pp. 169–82.
   Arno Mayer has argued that the murder of the European Jews (outside the
Soviet Union) is to be seen within the context of the economic imperatives of
total war and commensurate "hyerexploitation" of labor, in which the intensi-
fying persecution of the Jews was "calibrated in accordance with the produc-
tivity-utility precept." Arno Mayer, *Why Did the Heavens Not Darken? The
"Final Solution" in History* (New York, 1989).
2 Nuremberg Document PS-3666 (Otto Bräutigam to Hinrich Lohse, 18.12.41),
printed in: *Documents on the Holocaust*, ed. by Yitzhak Arad, Yisrael
Gutman, and Abraham Margoliot (Jerusalem, 1981), p. 395.
3 For instance, Daniel Goldhagen – narrowly focusing on two Lublin labor
camps during the height of the killing – has argued for a far-reaching consensus among Germans on the use of Jewish labor as a means for not only the
destruction of Jewish life but also German psychological gratification derived
from the economically wasteful opportunity to inflict punishment and suffering. At the same time he has depicted concerns for a productive use of Jewish
labor as an extremely marginal and insignificant phenomenon. See Daniel
Jonah Goldhagen, *Hitler's Willing Executioners: Ordinary Germans and the
Holocaust* (New York, 1996), esp. Part IV.
4 *The Warsaw Diary of Adam Czerniakow* (hereafter cited as WDAC), ed. by
Raul Hilberg, Stanislaw Staron, and Josef Kermisz (New York, 1969), p. 84
(entry of 20.10.39).
5 Isaiah Trunk, *Judenrat: The Jewish Councils in Eastern Europe under Nazi
Occupation* (New York, 1972), p. 72.
6 *Faschismus-Getto-Massenmord* (hereafter cited as FGM) (East Berlin, 1960),
p. 203 (decree of 26.10.39).
7 *Das Diensttagebuch des deutschen Generalgouverneurs in Polen 1939–1945*,

ed. by Werner Präg and Wolfgang Jacobmeyer (Stuttgart, 1975), p. 77 (Abteilungsleitersitzung, 8.12.39).

8 *Biuletyn Glownej Komisji Badania Zbrodni Hitlerowskich W Polsce* (hereafter cited as *Biuletyn*), XII, 66F–75F (NO-5322; Heydrich conference of 30.1.40); Halder, *Kriegstagebuch*, I, 184 (entry of 5.2.40); Rolf-Dieter Müller, *Hitlers Ostkrieg und die deutsche Siedlungspolitik* (Frankfurt/M., 1991), pp. 20–22. Experiments with Jewish forced labor camps had already been undertaken in Germany. Wolf Gruner, *Der Geschlossene Arbeitseinsatz deutscher Juden: Zur Zwangsarbeit als Element der Verfolgung 1938–1945* (Berlin, 1997); for non-German Jews in forced labor camps in, Germany, Wolf Gruner, "Juden bauen die 'Strassen des Führers': Zwangsarbeit und Zwangsarbeitslager für nichtdeutsche Juden im Altreich 1940 bis 1943/44," *Zeitschrift für Geschichtswissenschaft* 9 (1996), pp. 789–808.

9 *Trials of the War Criminals before the International Military Tribunal* (hereafter cited as IMT), vol. 29, pp. 448–56 (2233-PS: Polizeisitzung, 30.5.40).

10 Frank, *Diensttagebuch* pp. 230–2 (Wirtschaftstagung, 6–7.6.40); *Documenta Occupationis* (hereafter cited as DO), VI, 568–72 (Frauendorfer circular, 5.7.40).

11 For East Upper Silesia, see: Alfred Konieczny, "Die Zwangsarbeit der Juden im Schlesien im Rahmen der 'Organisation Schmelt'," *Beiträge zur nationalsozialistischen Gesundheits und Sozialpolitik*, V (1987), pp. 91–110; Avihu Ronen, "The Jews of Zaglembie During the Holocaust, 1939–1943," Ph.D. thesis, Tel Aviv University, 1989 (abstract in English); and Sybil Steinbacher, "Judenverfolgung im annektierten Osten Schlesiens 1939–1945," German Studies Conference, Washington, D.C., September 1997.

12 FGM, p. 215 (Labor Division meeting, Cracow, 6.8.40).

13 Yad Vashem Archives (hereafter cited as YVA), JM 814, Situation report of Czestochowa, 14.9.40.

14 YVA: JM 2700, Cracow conference on Jewish labor, 6.8.40; and O–53/79/102 (Ramm Vermerk to Jache and Hecht discussion with Globocnik, Wendt, and Hofbauer, 8.8.40).

15 YVA: O-53/79/197–98 (Hecht Vermerk, 23.7.40); pp. 116–17 (Zamosc labor office report on events of 13–14.8.40); pp. 118–19 (Ramm Vermerk, 15.8.40); pp. 141–42 (Ramm to Globocnik, 19.8.40); p. 137 (Ramm Vermerk to Jache and Hecht, 20.8.40); p. 130 (Labor Division to Globocnik, 20.8.40); p. 136 (Ramm Vermerk to Jache and Hecht, 20.8.40); p. 140 (Globocnik, to Labor Division, 23.8.40); and p. 138 (Labor Division to Globocnik, 24.8.40). YVA, JM 2700, Vermerken of 21.10. and 15.11.40.

16 Müller, *Hitlers Ostkrieg und die deutsche Siedlungspolitik*, p. 22.

17 YVA, JM 2700, undated note to Labor Division Cracow.

18 FGM, pp. 218–21 (excerpts from reports on the Lublin work camps). Army inspection of the camps produced two very conflicting reports. Major Braune-Krikau, the chief of staff of Oberfeldkommandantur 379 in Lublin, reported very critically on camp conditions, of which the Jews were the victims. In contrast, Lieutenant Börner of the Abwehr blamed the unsatisfactory conditions on the Jews, because "most of the working Jews went around in rags and also showed no interest whatever in cleanliness" (*"die meisten der arbeitenden Juden in Lumpen gehen und für Reinlichkeit auch wohl sowieso kein Interesse haben"*). His suggestion was to assign more guards to enforce camp regulations effectively. National Archives (hereafter cited as NA), T-501/212/634–6 (Anlage 290a: report of Braune-Krikau, Oberfeldkommandantur 379, Lublin, 23.9.40); and pp. 637–42 (Anlage 290: report of Lt. Börner, Abwehrnebenstelle Lublin, 24.9.40).

JEWISH WORKERS IN POLAND

19 At least a few Jewish labor camps for water control projects continued in exist-
    ence in the Lublin district until December 1942. Peter Witte, "Letzte
    Nachrichten aus Siedliszcze: Der Transport Ax aus Theresienstadt in den
    Distrikt Lublin," *Theresienstädter Studien und Dokumente*, III/1996, pp. 98–113.
20 One military report described the treatment of the Jews in the work camps as
    "bestial" (*"viehisch"*) but conveniently implied that this was due solely to the
    Polish guards. NA, T-501/212/456 (excerpt from the monthly report of Kom-
    mandantur Warschau, 16.4–15.5.41).
    For another vivid description of conditions in a Jewish work camp at this
    time, see Yitzhak Zuckerman, *A Surplus of Memory: Chronicle of the Wassaw
    Ghetto Uprising* (Berkeley, CA, 1990), pp. 135–145.
21 YVA, O-53/105/II/339–41 (Wielikowski report, 10.5.41).
22 YVA, O-53/105/II/336–7 (Meissner report, 30.6.41).
23 YVA, JM 3462, monthly report of October 1941 for Labor Division branch
    office of the Jewish district (Hoffmann).
24 YVA, JM 3462, conference on Jewish labor, 20.3.42.
25 For greater detail, see my: "Nazi Germany's Initial Attempt to Exploit Jewish
    Labor in the General Government: The Early Work Camps 1940–1941," *Die
    Normalität des Verbrechens: Bilanz und Perspektiven der Forschung zu den
    nationalsozialistischen Gewaltverbrechen*, ed. by Helge Grabitz, Klaus
    Bästlein, and Johannes Tüchel (Berlin, 1994), pp. 171–85.
26 YVA, JM 1112, Heinz Auerswald, "Two Year Report," 26.9.41.
27 Christopher R. Browning, "Nazi Ghettoization Policy in Poland, 1939–1941,"
    Central European History 19/4 (1986), pp. 343–68; Philip Friedman, "The
    Jewish Ghettos of the Nazi Era," *Roads to Extermination: Essays on the
    Holocaust* (New York and Philadelphia, 1980), pp. 59–87.
28 Berlin Document Center, Greiser Pers. Akten, Besuchs-Vermerk of the Staff
    of the Führer's Deputy, II.I.40. I am grateful to Dr. Hans Umbreit for a copy
    of this document.
29 FGM, p. 81 (Rundschreiben of Uebelhoer to party and police officials,
    10.12.39).
30 YVA: O-58/78/296–7 (Rumkowski to Marden, 6.4.40); JM 799/209 (Vermerk
    of conferences of 26 and 27.4.1940). DiM, pp. 74–5 (Oberbürgermeister to
    Rumkowski, 30.4.1940).
31 Frank, *Diensttagebuch*, pp. 261–3 (entry of 31.7.40).
32 In the brief period between June 16, 1940, and January 31, 1941, nearly 5
    percent of the ghetto population perished. *The Chronicle of the Lodz Ghetto
    1941–1944*, ed. by Lucjan Dobroszycki (New Haven, 1984), p. xxxix.
33 YVA, JM 798, Activity Report for September 1940.
34 YVA, O-53/78/76–82, Palfinger's "Critical Report," 7.11.40.
35 FGM, p. 110 (Schön report, 20.1.41).
36 Christopher R. Browning, "Genocide and Public Health: German Doctors and
    Polish Jews, 1939–1941," *Holocaust and Genocide Studies*, 3/1 (1988), pp.
    147–52.
37 Yisrael Gutman, *The Jews of Warsaw*, p. 63; YVA, JM 814, February Situ-
    ation Report of Warsaw District, 10.3.41.
38 Frank, *Diensttagebuch*, p. 328 (conference of 15.1.41).
39 Frank, *Diensttagebuch*, p. 337 (Regierungssitzung, 25.3.41).
40 YVA, JM 10016, "Die Wirtschaftsbilanz des jüdischen Wohnbezirks in
    Warschau." The entire document has now been published in: *Beiträge zur
    Nationalsozialistischen Gesundheits und Sozialpolitik*, vol. 9,
    Bevölkerungsstruktur und Massenmord: Neue Dokumente zur deutschen

Politik der Jahre 1938–1945 (Berlin, 1991), ed. by Susanne Heim and Götz Aly, pp. 74–138. For a very different interpretation of the Gater memorandum and the events surrounding it, see: Susanne Heim and Götz Aly, "Die Ökonomie der 'Endlösung': Menschenvernichtung und wirtschafliche Neuordnung," *Beiträge zur Nationalsozialistischen Gesundheits und Sozialpolitik*, vol. 5 (Berlin, 1987), pp. 7–90.

41 Frank, *Diensttagebuch*, pp. 337 and 343–6 (entries of 25.3.41 and 3.4.41).

42 YVA, O-53/49/103–4, personnel questionnaire of Auerswald's.

43 Götz Aly, *Vordenker der Vernichtung*, p. 324.

44 WDAC, p. 239 (entry of 21.5.41).

45 NA, T-501/roll 212/456 (Monthly report of the Warsaw commandant, 16.4–15.5.41).

46 In this regard, the reactions of Greiser in the Warthegau and Frank in the General Government to requests for an increased food supply to the Lodz and Warsaw ghettos were identical. DiM, III, p. 248 (Ventzki Aktenvermerk, no date); YVA, JM 112 (Frank Tagebuch, 15.11.41).

47 YVA: O-53/78/137–8 (Gettoverwaltung memorandum, 24.3.43); JM 798 (Activity report, February 1941); JM 800/148 (Aktennotiz, 10.3.41). DiM, III, 114–16 (Biebow to Treuhandstelle Posen, 26.3.42).

48 YVA, O-53/78/137–9 (Gettoverwaltung memorandum, 24.3.43); DiM, III, 177–9 (Marder to Uebelhoer, 4.7.41) and 243–5 (Biebow to Fuchs, 4.3.42).

49 Isaiah Trunk, *Judenrat*, pp. 84, 91.

50 YVA, JM 3462 (Hoffmann reports of October and November 1941).

51 WDAC, p. 401 (appended document: Auerswald to Medeazza, 24.11.41); Gutman, *The Jews of Warsaw*, p. 75; Trunk, *Judenrat*, p. 78–81.

52 Archivum Panstwowe m. St. Warszawy, Der Kommissar für den jüdischen Wohbezirk in Warschau, Nr. 132, speech of Max Bischof, 15.10.41.

53 Ulrich Herbert, *Fremdarbeiter: Politick und Praxis des "Ausländer-Einsatz" in der Kriegswirtschaft des Dritten Reiches* (Bonn, 1985), esp. pp. 137–49; YVA, JM 3462, Conference on labor, 20.3.42.

54 YVA: JM 3462 (Hoffmann reports of April and May 1942, and Czerniakow report, May 1942); O-53/101 (Hummel's monthly reports to Bühler, January through May, and bi-monthly report of June/July 1942).

55 Nuremberg Document NO-1020 (Meeting of Heydrich, Meyer, Schlatterer, Leibbrandt, and Ehlich, 4.10.41). Philippe Burrin, *Hitler and the Jews: The Genesis of the Holocaust* (London, 1994), p. 123.

56 Ulrich Herbert, *Fremdarbeiter*, pp. 137–43. In his article "Labour and Extermination: Economic Interests and the Primacy of Weltanschauung in National Socialism," *Past and Present*, No. 138 (February 1993), pp. 153 and 168, Herbert suggests that the decisions over the fate of the Jews and over the use of Soviet labor were made by the same people at the same time and were inherently interrelated – that is, the decision to use Soviet POW labor freed the Germans to exterminate potential Jewish labor. I am not convinced of the causal connection. First, I think the key concluding decision for the Final Solution was made by Hitler in early in October at the height of victory euphoria, and the change in attitude toward Soviet labor came in the following weeks as both the evidence of labor shortage and an unconcluded war mounted. Second, the notion of using Jewish labor does not seem to have been brought into the discussion until the following January.

57 Nuremberg Document 3663-PS (Ostministerium, Berlin, to RK Ostland, 18.12.41).

58 Christian Streit, *Keine Kameraden: Die Wehrmacht und die sowjetischen*

Kriegsgefangen (Stuttgart, 1978), pp. 9, 136. According to Herbert, *Fremdarbeiter*, p. 149, by March 1942 only 5 percent – some 167,000 – of the 3.35 million Soviet POWs captured in 1941 were capable of labor.

59 Herbert, *Fremdarbeiter*, pp. 144–5, 152–61.

60 Hermann Kaienburg, "Jüdische Arbeitslager an der 'Strasse der SS,' " *1999*, 1/96, pp. 19–20; Thomas Sandkühler, "Judenpolitik und Judemord im Distrikt Galician, 1941–1942," *Nationalsozialistischen Vernichtungspolitik*, p. 136.

61 Kaienburg, "Jüdische Arbeitslager an der 'Strasse der SS,' " *1999*, pp. 13–14.

62 Nuremberg Document NO-500 (Himmler to Glücks, 25.1.42).

63 IMT, vol. 38, pp. 365–6 (Nuremberg. Doc. R-129: Pohl circular, 30.4.42).

64 YVA: JM 3462, Warsaw labor conference, 20.3.42; O-53/130/601–2, quarterly report of Rü Kdo Krakau, 1.10.–21.12.42.

65 NA, T-501/219/347 (Kriegstagebuch, Oberquartiermeister, entry of 8.5.42). For a pioneering analysis of the pertinent military documents, see: Hanns von Krannhals, "Die Judenvernichtung in Polen und die 'Wehrmacht,' " *Wehrwissenschaftliche Rundschau*, 15 (1965), pp. 571–81.

66 DiM, II, pp. 32–3 (Türk note, 17.3.42).

67 DiM, II, p. 54 (Lenk to SSPF Lublin, 9.5.42).

68 Frank, *Diensttagebuch*, p. 489 (entry of 14.4.42).

69 For the emergence of the distinction between working and nonworking Jews, see also: Götz Aly, "*Endlösung*," pp. 263–8.

70 Frank, *Diensttagebuch*, p. 495 (entry of 5.5.42).

71 Frank, *Diensttagebuch*, p. 516 (Hauptabteilungsleitersitzung, 22.6.42).

72 Frank, *Diensttagebuch*, pp. 507–9 (Polizeisitzung, 18.6.42).

73 Nuremberg Document NO-626: Himmler to Berger, 28.7.42. Christopher R. Browning, "A Final Hitler Decision for the 'Final Solution'? The Riegner Telegram Reconsidered," *Holocaust and Genocide Studies* 10/1 (spring 1996), 3–10.

74 Christian Gerlach, "Die Bedeutung der deutschen Ernährungspolitik für die Beschleunigung des Mordes an den Juden 1942," *Krieg, Ernährung, Völkermord* (Hamburg, 1998), pp. 167–257.

75 YVA, O-53/105/II/220–30 (*Transferstelle* reports of 5.8, 5.9, and 8.10.42).

76 YVA, O-53/113/348–61 (Bimonthly report for August/September, 1942, from the district of Warsaw to the State Secretary, General Government, 15.10.42).

77 NA, T-501/216/927 (Krüger account of meeting with Schindler, 17.8.42). Excerpts from many of the documents pertaining to the military-SS negotiations have been printed in: Helge Grabitz and Wolfgang Scheffler, *Letzte Spuren* (Berlin, 1988), pp. 306–15.

78 NA, T-501/219 (Kriegstagebuch of Oberquartiermeister): pp. 380 (entry of 20.6.42), 412 (entry of 5.8.52), 414 (entry of 8.8.42), 422 (entry of 17.8.42), 434 (entry of 2.9.42), 442 (entry of 13.9.42). NA, T-501/216/966 (Oberquartiermeister to MiG, 5.8.42).

79 NA, T-501/216/927 (Forster to GenQu, 5.8.42).

80 NA, T-501/216/923–6 (meeting on Jewish labor, 14.8.42).

81 Grabitz/Scheffler, *Letzte Spuren*, p. 310.

82 NA, T-501/216/350–2 (Gienanth to OKW, 18.9.42). Printed in: FGM, pp. 444–6.

83 NA, T-501/219/452 (entry of 1.10.42).

84 YVA, O-53/130/575–6 (copy of telegram of OKW, circulated by Forster, 10.10.42).

85 FGM, pp. 446–7 (Nuremberg Document NO-1611: Himmler to Pohl, Krüger, Globocnik, Reichssicherheitshauptamt [Reich Security Main Office, or RSHA], and Wolff, 9.10.42).

86 The payment arrangement was first worked out in Warsaw by SSPF Sammer-Frankenberg. Anordnungen of 14.9.42, facsimile in: Grabitz/Scheffler, *Die Letzte Spuren*, pp. 172–3.

87 NA, T-501/216/776–7 (Forster to WiG, 20.10.42); YVA, O-53/130/573 (Forster memos, 14 and 15.10.42).

88 Frank, *Diensttagebuch*, p. 588 (Regierungssitzung, 9.12.42).

89 Nuremberg Document NO-1882 (Himmler to Krüger, 11.1.43); NO-2514 (Himmler to Pohl, 16.2.43); NO-2494 (Himmler to Krüger, 16.2.43). FGM, pp. 449–50 (Sammern-Frankenegg to Himmler, 2.2.43). For the transfer of the Schultz firm from Warsaw to Trawniki, see: Grabitz/Scheffler, *Letzte Spuren*, pp. 179–210, 318–27.

90 FGM, doc. nr. 357, p. 448 (Scherner circular to factory managers, 14.12.42).

91 Staatsanwaltschaft StA Hanover, 11/2 Js 481/69 (indictment of Körner, Heinemeyer, and Olde), p. 116 (Zentral Stelle der Landesjustizverwaltungen [hereafter cited as ZStL], II 206 AR 641/70, vol. 13).

92 Dieter Pohl, *Von der "Judenpolitik" zum Judenmord: Der Distrikt Lublin des Generalgouvernements 1939–1944* (Frankfurt/M., 1993), pp. 165–6. For the liquidation of Miedzyrzec and Lukow, see: Christopher R. Browning, *Ordinary Men: Reserve Police Battalion 101 and the Final Solution in Poland* (New York, 1992), pp. 133–4.

93 Dieter Pohl, *Nationalsozialistische Judenverfolgung in Ostgalizien 1941–1944* (Munich, 1996), pp. 246–65; Thomas Sandkühler, *"Endlösung" in Galizien: Der Judenmord in Ostpolen und die Rettungsinitiativen von Berthold Beitz 1941–1944* (Bonn, 1996), pp. 194–8.

94 IMT, vol. 37, p. 401 (Nuremberg Document 018-L (Katzmann report to Himmler, 30.6.43).

95 For Kielce: StA Darmstadt 2 Js 1721/64 (indictment of Wollschläger), pp. 88–89. For Tomaszow-Mazowiecki: Landgericht Darmstadt, 2 Ks 1/69 (judgment against Böttig, Fuchs, and Reichl), p. 49 (YVA, TR-10/861).

96 Landgericht Lüneburg 2 a Ks 2/65 (judgment against Degenhardt), pp. 31–35 (YVA, TR-10/585).

97 FGM, p. 355 (Himmler Aktennotiz, 10.5.43). Greifelt recorded Himmler's comments two days later: "It is an urgent task in the General Government to remove the 3–400,000 Jews still present there" (*"Eine vordringliche Aufgabe im Generalgouvernemnt sei es, die dort noch vorhandenen 3–400,000 Juden zu entfernen"*). FGM, p. 356 (Nuremberg Document NO-3173: Greifelt note on Himmler presentation of 12.5.43).

98 Frank, *Diensttagebuch*, p. 682 (Arbeitssitzung, 31.5.43).

99 YVA, O-53/130/438–9 (Himmler note on his meeting with Hitler at the Obersalzberg on 19.6.43).

100 Pohl, *Nationalsozialistische Judenverfolung in Ostgalizien*, pp. 348–55.

101 For Przemysl: StA Hamburg 147 Js 39/67 (indictment of Stegemann, Benesch, et al.), pp. 152–87 (YVA, TR-10/945). For Rzeszow: Landgericht Memmingen Ks 5 a-d/68 (judgment against Schusster, Dannenberg, Lehmann and Öster), pp. 22–3 (YVA, TR-10/687). For Tarnow: Landgericht Bochum 16 Ks 2/70 (judgment against Baach and Wunder), pp. 99–101 (YVA, TR-10/751). For Bochnia: Landgericht Kiel 2 Ks 4/66 (judgment against Müller), pp. 45–50, 63 (YVA, TR-10/725).

102 Grabitz/Scheffler, *Letzte Spuren*, pp. 179–210, 318–23.

103 Enno Georg, *Die wirtschaftlichen Unternehmungen der SS* (Stuttgart, 1963), pp. 90–9; *Trials of the War Criminals before the Nürnberg Military Tribunals* (hereafter cited as TWC), V, pp. 512–24 (NO-1271: Fischer report, 21.6.44).

104 Daniel Goldhagen, *Hitler's Willing Executioners*, pp. 283–316.
105 Nuremberg Document NO-485 (Globocnik to Brandt, 21.6.43, and Vermerk), printed in: Grabitz/Scheffler, *Letzte Spuren*, pp. 322–7.
106 TWC, XIII, p. 1206 (Nuremberg. Doc. NO-3304: Brandt to Berger, 20.8.43).
107 Landgericht Bielefeld 5 Ks I/65 (judgment against Altenloh et al.), pp. 297–310; StA Dortmund 45 Js I/61 (indictment of Zimmermann), pp. 121–4; StA Hamburg 147 Js 24/72 (indictment of Michalsen et al.), pp. 157–63.
108 Grabitz/Scheffler, *Letzte Spuren*, p. 266.
109 FGM, 369 (Nuremberg Document NO-519: Pohl to Himmler, 9.2.44).
110 On the *Erntefest* massacres, see: Grabitz/Scheffler, *Letzte Spuren*, pp. 262–72, 328–34; Jozef Marszalek, *Majdanek; The Concentration Camp in Lublin* (Warsaw, 1986), pp. 130–4; Browning, *Ordinary Men*, pp. 135–42; Pohl, *Von der "Judenpolitik" zum Judenmord*, pp. 170–4.
111 StA Munich 116 Js 15/67 (indictment of Unterhuber), p. 16 (YVA, TR-110/717).
112 Pohl, *Nationalsozialistische Judenverfolgung in Ostgalizien*, pp. 332–8, 359–60.
113 For the survival of a remnant of work Jews of Drohobycz, see in particular: Sandkühler, *"Endlösung" in Galician*, pp. 290–406.
114 Nuremberg Document NO-5193 (Korherr report, 19.4.43), printed in: *The Holocaust: Selected Documents in Eighteen Volumes*, ed. by John Mendelsohn (New York, 1982), vol. 12, pp. 212–19; Nuremberg Document NO-5194 (Korherr report, 23.3.43), excerpts printed in: *Documents on the Holocaust*, ed. by Yitzhak Arad, Yisrael Gutman, and Abraham Margoliot (Jerusalem, 1981), pp. 332–4.
115 For a similar estimate, see: Frank Golczewski, "Polen," *Dimension des Völkermords: Die Zahl der jüdischen Opfer des Nationalsozialismus*, ed. by Wolfgang Benz (Munich, 1991), pp. 479–81.
116 Nuremberg Document 519 (Pohl to Himmler, 9.2.44; and Greiser to Pohl, 14.2.44), printed in FGM, pp. 369–70.
117 Felicya Karay, *Death Comes in Yellow: Skarzyksko-Kamienna Slave Labor Camp* (Amsterdam, 1996), pp. 125–6.

Part 3

LOCAL INITIATIVES, 'ETHNIC CLEANSING', AND REGIONAL GENOCIDES

23

THE EXTERMINATION OF THE JEWS IN SERBIA

Walter Manoschek

Source: Ulrich Herbert (ed.), *National Socialist Extermination Policies. Contemporary Perspectives and Controversies*, New York/Oxford: Berghahn, 2000, pp. 163–85.

When German troops invaded Yugoslavia without a declaration of war on 6 April 1941, approximately 80,000 Jews lived in that country. About 55,000 to 60,000 Yugoslavian Jews and another 4,000 or so foreign Jewish refugees ended up falling victim to the Holocaust.[1] As a result, Jews in Yugoslavia suffered one of the proportionately highest death rates of all European Jewish populations.

After Yugoslavia's military capitulation in mid-April 1941, the Yugoslavian state was shattered and divided up among the Axis powers. The process of exterminating Yugoslavia's Jews varied along regional lines. Depending on whether they lived under Bulgarian, Hungarian, Italian, or German occupation, or in the territories of the Croatian Ustasha state, they fell into the clutches of the extermination apparatus at varying times and under differing circumstances. Thus, the majority of Jews living in Croatia were murdered in the numerous camps of the Croatian Ustasha (such as Jasenovac or Stara Gradiška, to give only two of the most notorious examples), and a relatively small minority were deported to Auschwitz since 1943 in the course of the "Final Solution." Whereas about 16,000 Jews living in the regions annexed by Hungary, such as the South Baranya and Bacska, managed to avoid mass extermination until German troops marched into Hungary in March 1944. In Serbia the head of the Security Police (Sicherheitspolizei or Sipo) and SD, Emanuel Schäfer, was already able to report in June 1942: "Serbia is free of Jews."[2] In little more than one year of military occupation, the Wehrmacht and Security Police murdered the entire population of 17,000 Jews living in Serbian territory.[3]

I

The attack on the Balkan states in April 1941 was not planned as an ideo-logically-motivated war of racial extermination. The destruction and parti-tion of the Yugoslavian state, coupled with the Axis occupation of Greece, was primarily intended to secure the Reich's southeastern flank, with the smallest possible number of troops, for the war against the Soviet Union, while the region's resources were to be plundered for the German war economy. After the rapid capitulation of the Yugoslavian and Greek armies, the Wehrmacht continued to occupy only Serbia in its pre-1912 borders and a relatively small part of Greece.

Following the withdrawal of German combat forces from the Yugosla-vian theater, four specially-created occupation divisions were dispatched to Serbia and Croatia. Two of these, the 717th and 718th Infantry Division (ID), were established in the Ostmark (Austria's provincial designation after the Anschluss in March 1938). The composition of the units bespoke their geographic origins: in both divisions, Austrians made up a majority of officers and enlisted men. The occupation divisions were supplemented by six Landesschützenbataillone (Home Guard Battalions), of which four also stemmed from the Ostmark. Thus, foot soldiers from the Ostmark constituted the core of the military occupation apparatus after the spring of 1941.[4] The disproportionately strong representation of Austrians was by no means a coincidence. In fact, where Serbia was concerned, Hitler had, according to Franz Neuhausen, the general plenipotentiary for the Serbian economy, "assumed the same standpoint that the Austrians had taken in 1914. As an Austrian, he never wavered from that standpoint, in accord-ance with which he ordered strict measures against the Serbs. Further-more, he believed that only the Austrians knew the Serbs and that they were the only ones competent to assess the political, economic, and other questions in Serbia."[5]

The traditional hostile image of Serbia from 1914—the Austrians held the Serbs responsible for the war which cost them their empire—formed a solid foundation upon which the racial-ideological objectives of National Socialism could be built in 1941. In early 1941, the Wehrmacht leadership had been committed to participating in a "crusade against Jewish Bolshe-vism" (according to the Chief of the Wehrmacht Supreme Command, Field Marshal Wilhelm Keitel) and the institutional cooperation between the army, on the one hand, and Himmler's "special political police units," (the Security Police, the SD, and the SS) on the other hand, had been for-malized.[6] In the Balkan lands, Himmler's "special units" were empowered to act not only against "emigrants, saboteurs, terrorists, etc.," but also against "Jews and Communists."[7]

The first steps in the process of exterminating the Jews immediately fol-lowed the establishment of the occupation regime. They occurred in the same sequence previously employed in other occupied countries: registration, marking, deprivation, social exclusion. Two days before the Yugoslavian army capitulated, the chief of the *Einsatzgruppen* (Action Squads) in Belgrade, Wilhelm Fuchs, had ordered all of the city's Jews to report for registration. "Jews who fail to obey this order will be shot dead,"[8] decreed posters pasted on the walls.

From the beginning, military agencies were also active in persecuting the Jews. Already in April 1941, for example, in the Banat city of Groß-betschkerek (Zrenjanin), the local commandant mandated that Jews wear the Star of David and arranged for the approximately 2,000-member Jewish community to be committed to a ghetto of the city.[9] In Belgrade, the field commander, Colonel von Kaisenberg, decreed limitations on Jews' freedom of movement and on the hours that they could shop.[10]

Wehrmacht organizations were also involved in robbing Jews of their property. The military police confiscated Jewish apartments and businesses, as well as their inventories. Moveable goods were deposited in warehouses, from which members of the occupation forces could purchase them at affordable prices, with appropriate certification issued by the field command's administrative organization.[11]

The effect of the material deprivation of the Jews on the consciousness of Wehrmacht members should not be underestimated. A staff officer stationed in the Banat described the practical advantages of persecuting the Jews in a field mail letter: "Just a few weeks ago the war still raged here. Now, there are no traces to be found, since the enemy only turned and ran, and our tanks followed him. But there are traces, however, insofar as the Jews have been chased out, shot, and incarcerated. Entire palaces, mansions in all their pomp stand empty. Our infantrymen, noncommissioned officers, etc., feel very much at home in them. They are living like kings in there."[12]

Wehrmacht propaganda, too, fostered the image of the "Jew as enemy." Thus, Jews were held responsible for the anti-German sentiment in Serbia. In their reports on the public mood, the propaganda department determined "that the negative attitude of the intellectual circles has in no way changed. Here, the Jews play an important role." In May 1941, the "start of a large-scale anti-Jewish propaganda effort was made." "Presentations on the Jewish question" were prepared for radio broadcasts, while "up-to-the-moment information to counter Communist propaganda, as well as on the activities of Jewry in the Balkans, was made available" for the Serbian press.[13]

If the first measures of Jewish persecution took place in an unsystematic and uncoordinated fashion, then the following stages of oppression were coordinated between the highest military authorities and the remaining occupation agencies. Six weeks after the occupation began, the Wehrmacht commander in Serbia, General Ludwig von Schröder, decreed the identification, registration, and marking of Jews and Gypsies with yellow armbands; their dismissal from all public offices and private operations; the "aryanization" of their property and assets; and the introduction of forced labor.[14] Thereby, the measures of racist persecution attained a level of uniformity, with a common denominator for the entire Serbian area of occupation.[15] In other words, the three first steps of the extermination process were set in motion in a single day. Concurrently, German authorities considered establishing a Jewish ghetto in the Serbian town of Majdanpek.[16] That plan, however, did not come to fruition. In response to the dynamics of unfolding events, the phase of ghettoization, as previously implemented in Poland, was "leapfrogged" in Serbia, where a locally-developed variant of the "solution to the Jewish question" emerged.

In coordination with the civilian and police agencies, the military commander enacted measures against Jews and Gypsies from the very beginning. As far as can be determined from the sources, cooperation on Jewish and Gypsy policies functioned without a hitch. In the first phase, until the invasion of the Soviet Union, the racist norms that already obtained in other occupied regions were adopted and adjusted to the conditions in Serbia. Wehrmacht agencies were tied into this process at every level of racist persecution and shared responsibility for it. Military pretexts or special justifications were not required. The process of registration, marking, deprivation, and social exclusion already constituted an integral component of National Socialist Jewish policies and the Wehrmacht, in addition to the police and security forces, shared responsibility for making it such.

With the attack on the Soviet Union in June 1941, the situation for the German occupiers of Serbia changed radically. As the German Ostheer (Army of the East) marched into the Soviet Union on 22 June 1941, with 136 divisions and over three million men, only four occupation divisions with a total of approximately 25,000 men, augmented by three police companies and their own Home Guard regiments, remained in Serbia. The average age of the soldiers was thirty years, considerably higher for the men of the Home Guard units. These men had no combat experience and their military education was limited to a training course lasting only a few weeks, which consisted of little more than repeated trips to the firing range. With the exception of a handful of noncommissioned officers, none of these men had any active service and even the officer corps consisted exclusively of reservists.[17] This was an occupation mechanism designed for "quiet times." But the quiet times in Serbia came to an abrupt end in the early summer of 1941, when the partisans under Tito's leadership took up their armed struggle. The occupying forces were now confronted with a well-organized guerrilla movement, for which they were prepared neither tactically nor by their training experience.

At first, the new military commander, General Heinrich Danckelmann, assigned the *Einsatzgruppe* of the Security Police and the Security Service

(SD), the Secret Military Police, a police battalion, and the regular military police to combat the partisans.[18] The so-called "police struggle against the partisans" meant, in plain language, shooting and hanging civilians "suspected of being partisans." As a precautionary measure, a "hostage reservoir" had already been accumulated by the time of the Soviet invasion. It consisted of those groups that had been identified as targets for extermination in the eastern campaign: Jews and Communists.[19] By the summer of 1941, the murder of hostages had already become an everyday occurrence in the occupation.

Lieutenant Peter G. reported on this "anti-partisan struggle" at regular intervals in his letters:

26 July 1941: Entire hordes of Communists are now shot and hanged almost daily. Otherwise, the situation is relatively calm.

29 July 1941: Do you receive Belgrade with your radio, which also gives German news evenings at 8 p.m. and 10 p.m.? Maybe you'll have the chance some time to listen? Don't get scared, though, if they happen to announce the totals of executed Communists and Jews, which they give at the end of the news broadcast. Today there was a record! This morning in Belgrade, we shot 122 Communists and Jews. You can even hear my town ... from time to time. It is often mentioned ... yesterday, over 30 people were shot.[20]

With complete openness, Lieutenant G. tells of attacks by the Communists and of the occupiers' reaction: the shooting of Communists *and* Jews. These actions were announced on public broadcasts and proudly described in letters destined for home. Within a few weeks, the fight against "Jewish Bolshevism" turned into an everyday norm in the microcosm of Serbia, as it did elsewhere. The crimes occurred with the knowledge, and in accordance with the orders of, the military commander and in front of the troops' own eyes. Against the backdrop of increasing partisan activity, the Wehrmacht leadership, but also the troop units, had quickly adjusted to the new norms and values of *Gegnerbekämpfung* (the fight against opponents) and internalized them, although the core of the troop units had not yet acquired first-hand experience of these brutal repression policies. Because of the small size of the German occupation administration in Serbia, and in the face of a threatening situation, there developed very rapidly, across all organizational boundaries, clear indications of a sense of community, characterized by a circle-the-wagons mentality and bound by a code of loyalty customary in such situations.

Despite a balance of over 1,000 shot or hanged Jews and Communists in July and August 1941, the activities of the partisans spread ever more rapidly. In August 1941, Hitler assigned the Wehrmacht the task of combating partisans in Serbia: "On account of the rise in disturbances and acts of sabotage, the Führer expects the army to take immediate action to restore law and order through swift and severe intervention."[21] With that, the members of the SD, police, and Wehrmacht closed ranks in a mutual struggle against their opponents. Each battalion established mobile pursuit teams (*Jagdkommandos*), consisting of soldiers, policemen, and SD members. These mixed pursuit teams represented a transition in the anti-partisan struggle from a policy of divided labor to direct cooperation between the army and the police apparatus. Through the subsequent commingling of personnel, the soldiers absorbed the combat methods and specialized forms of *Gegnerbekämpfung* favored by the police forces and SD.

Neither the methods of conducting this combat nor the definition of the enemy groups changed with the Wehrmacht's assumption of the anti-partisan struggle. Since fighting the partisans with available forces proved to be militarily hopeless, the policy of murdering hostages (*Geiselmordpolitik*) remained the centerpiece of the campaign. Jews and Communists were the primary victims.

The German failure to militarily subdue the partisans eventuated in uncoordinated acts of revenge against the Serbian civilian population. The murder of innocent civilians at the hands of soldiers did not result in a single prosecution by the military courts. To the contrary, commanders took an understanding approach to these breaches of military discipline, though they also acknowledged negative consequences: "It is understandable that soldiers who are ambushed by Communist bands should cry out for revenge. In the course of such operations, people who happen to be out in the fields are frequently arrested and executed. In most cases, however, one will not capture the guilty parties, who have long since disappeared, but instead innocent people, and thereby create a situation where the previously loyal population goes over to the partisans, out of fear or embitterment.... That German soldiers may under no circumstances execute women without judicial process, except when these attack the soldiers with weapon in hand, goes without saying" read one directive that was circulated to all companies.[22]

That directive makes clear how far the Wehrmacht had distanced itself from the legal norms of warfare. Partisans, or persons suspected of being partisans, with the exception of women, were allowed to be executed without any sort of judicial proceedings. For murdering innocent civilians, soldiers were not prosecuted by the military courts. Their murderous actions mainly met with the approval of their superiors and were rejected only for political or tactical reasons, not because they violated legal principles of war.

The army's murderous activities in the summer of 1941 had the characteristics of spontaneous acts of revenge, set off by frustration over the failures in the anti-partisan campaign. These acts of excess, did not result in military prosecutions but nevertheless proved to be counterproductive in the end. Not only were they impotent to check the spread of partisan activity, but they also endangered the internal discipline of the troop units. In place of such spontaneous excesses, therefore, a policy of systematic repression was introduced.

For that, the Wehrmacht leadership in Berlin sought a suitable candidate, a man who was prepared to execute Hitler's directive "to restore order with the severest means."[23] The task fell to Franz Böhme, a general of Austrian parentage. Recommended by his superior, General Field Marshal List, as a "first-rate expert on the Balkan situation,"[24] Böhme was appointed by Hitler in September 1941 as plenipotentiary commanding general in Serbia and all military and civilian agencies there were placed under his command. The former director of the Austrian military intelligence service had long enjoyed Hitler's trust. In February 1938, during a meeting with the Austrian Chancellor Schuschnigg at the Obersalzberg, the Führer had demanded that Böhme be appointed chief of the Austrian general staff. After the war in Poland and France, Böhme had participated in the invasion of Greece as commanding general of the XVIII Army Corps.

By the time General Böhme arrived in Belgrade in mid-September, Serbia, with the exception of only the largest cities, had fallen under the control of the partisans and the nationalist Chetnik bands. Böhme recognized that his forces were too weak to bring the country back under the control of the occupiers by military means, despite the recent arrival of reinforcements. Instead, he withdrew the fragmented units that had been scattered all across Serbia—and thus presented an ideal target for partisan attacks—to strategically important areas. Thereby, he hoped to reduce losses and reverse the trend toward demoralization among the troops. Concurrently, Böhme set the ideological, disciplinary, and organizational course for systematizing what had previously been uncoordinated measures of repression.

The conviction that Bolshevism and Judaism shared a structural identity—a conviction that extended far beyond the ranks of professed National Socialists—served to legitimize that summer's police and SD killings of Communists and Jews, which were labeled "measures of atonement." Whereas in the war against the Soviet Union, the racist mantra of "subhuman Slavs" helped destroy moral inhibitions over exterminating entire populations, in Serbia the Austrian Böhme resorted to an ancient Austrian image of the Serb as enemy. Fully aware that the overwhelming majority of his soldiers were Austrians, he invoked the historical dimension of their mission: "Your objective is to be achieved in a land where, in 1914, streams of German blood flowed because of the treachery of the Serbs, men and women. You are the avengers of those dead. A deterring

247

example must be established for all of Serbia, one that will have the heaviest impact on the entire population. Anyone who carries out his duty in a lenient manner will be called to account, regardless of rank or position, and tried by a military court."[25]

The war against the civilian population thereby acquired a new legitimacy. No longer did the killing of civilians at the hands of the Wehrmacht constitute an "understandable," if unsoldierly "violation," an officially unsanctioned breach of military discipline. Instead, it became a legalized and integral component of German military occupation policy. By invoking memories of the First World War, the army attempted to establish a historical justification as it accommodated its code of military justice to the National Socialist values system.

So that any potentially diverging subjective sense of moral right on the part of the soldiers would be brought in line with the National Socialist legal outlook, Böhme redefined the norms of appropriate behavior. "Leniency" toward the civilian population now counted as "a sin against the lives of comrades"; whoever was unwilling to accept these rules and act in accordance with them would be threatened with military legal proceedings, "regardless of rank or position." This directive of Böhme's, which was to be destroyed once disseminated, was intended to instill in the troops a sense of their ideological and historic mission, and to accustom them to the collective punishment of the Serbian civilian population. The disciplinary pressure from above, coupled with the opportunity for soldiers to take out on the civilian population their fears, frustrations, and aggressions that had accumulated in the course of the unsuccessful anti-partisan operations, created the psychological preconditions for the planned mass murder.

Böhme's order established new foundations for the occupation policy in Serbia, which Omer Bartov also identifies as the symptomatic characteristics of the military occupation in the East. The army, according to Bartov, "reverted to the most primitive moral rules of war, in accordance with which everything that secured one's own survival was permitted (and therefore considered moral) and everything that could threaten it in even the remotest sense (and was by definition immoral) must be destroyed."[26]

General Böhme had received the directive from Hitler "to restore order with the severest measures." This was one of Hitler's characteristically vague orders; it did not specify the measures to be taken to restore "law and order" in Serbia and left much room for individual decision-making. Execution depended upon the decoding abilities of each military commander ("What does the Führer expect?") and on their respective readiness to throw overboard the legal conventions of war and human rights, as well as to accommodate their views of military justice to the new values system.

A directive from OKW Chief Keitel, issued on the day that Böhme took up his post in Serbia, served as an indicator of the way the new commander would proceed. For the fight against "the movement of Communist uprisings in the occupied territories," Keitel established a guideline for all of German-occupied Europe: "As penance for the life of one German soldier, the death penalty for 50–100 Communists must be considered appropriate in these cases. The method of execution must serve to raise the deterrent effect."[27]

II

When General Böhme assumed his post in Serbia in mid-September 1941, the geographic concentration of Jews was already underway. In August, the Jews were deported from the Banat to Belgrade, and from the beginning of September the male Jews and Gypsies of the capital were also interned.[28]

Since the middle of August, the German envoy in Serbia, Felix Benzler, and the "Jewish expert" sent by the Foreign Office to assist him, Edmund Veesenmayer, had become active in shaping Jewish policy. In numerous telegrams to the Foreign Office in Berlin, they emphatically demanded the deportation of at least 8,000 male Jews from Serbia, since the "speedy and draconian solution to the Serbian Jewish question was the most urgent and expedient necessity."[29] They justified their demands with arguments couched in the language of security policy: Jews had emerged as culprits in numerous disturbances and cases of sabotage; concentrations of Jews detained and endangered the troops; Jews were demonstrably making decisive contributions to the unrest in the country; the initial deportation of male Jews was the necessary prerequisite for restoring orderly conditions—so read several of the justifications formulated by the German envoy.[30] After Adolf Eichmann, in response to a query from the Foreign Office, had declared the transfer of Jews from Serbia to occupied Poland or the Soviet Union to be impossible, State Secretary Martin Luther recommended to his envoy in Belgrad "a hard and inflexible proceeding" against the Jews, so as to "deprive them of their appetite for spreading unrest in the country. The Jews that have been collected in camps will just have to serve as hostages to guarantee the good conduct of their comrades-in-race (*Rassegenossen*)."[31]

This "security policy" argument for the ideology of racial extermination went hand in hand with General Böhme's military "pacification concept." At first, Böhme, together with Minister Benzler, pushed Reich Foreign Minister Ribbentrop to authorize the deportation of the Jews that were already interned in camps, so that enough space might be cleared for the planned incarceration of tens of thousands of Serbian civilians. Only a few days later, however, Böhme recognized the possibilities that the already-accomplished imprisonment of the male Jews presented: Jews and Gypsies stood available as "hostages on call" for executions.

After a fire-fight with partisans, which cost twenty-one Wehrmacht members their lives, General Böhme for the first time resorted to shooting Jews in retaliation. Böhme established the organizational blueprint for the course the mass executions would take and determined the selection of victims: "As reprisal and atonement, 100 Serbian prisoners will be shot immediately for every murdered German soldier. The chief of the military administration is requested to select 2,100 prisoners from the concentration camps Šabac and Belgrade (predominantly Jews and Communists) and to establish place, time, and burial sites. The execution details shall be formed by the 342nd Division (for the Šabac camp) and Corps Intelligence Detachment 449 (for the Belgrade camp)."[32]

With this order, General Böhme inaugurated a new phase in the persecution of the Jews. The existing practice of murdering Jews and Communists through *Einsatzgruppen* was now systematized, militarily decreed, and carried out by the soldiers themselves. If in the summer it had been the SD and the police who executed Jews and Communists, from now on the task would be carried out by the army. The Security Police would be called upon to assist only by delivering a specific number of execution victims upon demand.

Even as the first mass executions of Jews and Communists at the hands of the Wehrmacht were underway, General Böhme identified who the victims of future shootings would be: "All Communists, male residents suspected of being Communists, all Jews, a certain number of nationalist and democratically-minded residents"[33]—with the exception of collaborators, virtually the entire population was potentially affected.

Shifting "hostage shootings" from Himmler's special units to Wehrmacht soldiers presupposed that the soldiers' sense of moral right was already so distorted that they would be prepared to carry out these murderous actions. The troop commanders—General Böhme in the lead—now attempted to prepare the soldiers psychologically and mentally for their role in the bloody program of suppression. That occurred in a wide range of ways. Above all, the troops were inculcated with reminders of their "historic mission." "The streams of German blood that in 1914 flowed because of the treachery of Serbs, men and women," according to General Böhme, were to be avenged in 1941. The soldiers' senses of honor and comradeship were instrumentalized: General Böhme ordered that, "whenever possible," the "troop unit that suffered the loss be tasked with the execution." The pressure of disciplinary measures was increased; in the event of "cowardice in the face of the enemy," soldiers were threatened with military legal proceedings. Male fears were stirred up; although the commanders possessed evidence to the contrary, the chain of command pointedly spread the rumor that soldiers would suffer genital mutilation in the event of capture by the partisans.

This agglomeration of historical animosities, propaganda scare stories, perverted conceptions of discipline and comradeship, and the associated summons to officially-sanctioned mass murder would prove to be an effective, goal-oriented method by which the Germans' wounded sense of superiority and racist animosities could be channeled, militarily legitimized, and converted into mass murder. The orders from above, and the growing readiness below to carry out those orders, unleashed a dynamic of mass murder in the fall of 1941.

In the process, the logic of racist extermination was closely bound to the practical rationale of occupation rule: the overwhelming portion of approximately 8,000 adult male Jews, the unsettled Gypsies, and "suspicious Communists" were already interned in camps and stood "on call" at all times for executions. Now, the victims were selected in accordance with the National Socialist racial hierarchy: first, all Jews and Gypsies; then, those persons suspected of being Communists; and finally, the remaining populace, whereby assignment to either of the latter two groups was in practice rather arbitrary. Accordingly, the Jews and Gypsies were the first to be murdered. After suffering losses in the anti-partisan struggle, units requested from the appropriate staff agency that a contingent of hostages (in the ratio of 1:100 for each killed soldier, 1:50 for each wounded soldier, respectively) be made available to them. The administration chief, Dr. Harald Turner, conducted the selection of hostages and determined the time and place of the executions. A volunteer firing squad from the unit in question drove a truck to the camp, picked up the victims, and transported them to the execution site. The site would be cordoned off at a considerable distance and the victims dug their own graves before they were shot. The executions were filmed by the propaganda company and photographed. After the completion of the operation, the presiding officer prepared a detailed report on the "shooting of Jews and Gypsies," which was forwarded to higher military headquarters in Serbia, as well as to the 12th Superior Army Command in Salonika, Greece, the highest Wehrmacht headquarters in the Balkan region. Larger shootings lasted from early morning until evening, and often required several days to complete.

In one execution report from 1 November 1941, the officer in charge discussed advantages and disadvantages of this process:

> In coordination with the SS office, I picked up the selected Jews and Gypsies from the Belgrade prison camp. The trucks of Field Command 599 that were made available to me for this purpose proved to be unsuitable for two reasons:
>
> (1). They are driven by civilians. Maintaining secrecy can therefore not be guaranteed.
>
> (2). They were all without a cover or a canvas, so that city's residents saw who we had on the vehicles and to where we then drove. In front of the camp, the Jews' women had gathered, screaming and crying as we drove away.

The place where the execution was carried out is very propitious. It lies north of Pančevo, directly on the road from Pančevo to Jabuka, which is bordered by an embankment that is so high, a man could climb up it only with difficulty. Across from this embankment is swampy terrain, behind that a river. During flood conditions (as on 29 October), the water reaches almost to the embankment. Any escape attempt by prisoners can therefore be prevented with a handful of men. Also advantageous is the sandy soil there, which makes digging the pits easier and therefore also shortens the work time.

After arriving approximately 1.5 to 2 km before the selected site, the prisoners disembarked, marched to the spot on foot, while the trucks with their civilian drivers were immediately sent back, in order to provide as few clues as possible for them to develop any suspicions. Then I had the road blocked off for reasons of safety and secrecy.

The execution site was secured by 3 1. M.G. [light machine guns—W.M.] and 12 riflemen:

(1). Against escape attempts by the prisoners

(2). For self defense against eventual attacks by Serbian bands.

Digging the pits takes up the largest portion of the time, while the shooting itself goes very quickly (100 men, 40 minutes).

Baggage and valuables were collected beforehand and transported in my truck, to turn them over to the National Socialist People's Welfare Organization (*Nationalsozialistischen Volkswohlfahrt* or NSV).

Shooting the Jews is easier than shooting the Gypsies. One has to admit that the Jews go to their deaths in a very composed manner—they remain very calm—while the Gypsies sob, scream, and continue to move around, even when they are already standing on the spot of their execution. Several even jumped into the pit before the firing volley and pretended to be dead.

Initially, my soldiers were not affected. On the second day, though, one noticed that this one or that one doesn't have the nerves required to carry out an execution over a longer period of time. My personal impression is that one doesn't experience any mental reservations during the execution itself. However, these begin to set in when after a few days one thinks about the events in the quiet of the evening.[34]

A first lieutenant reported with regret that the detail under his command had to be relieved during an execution: "All in all, 449 men were shot dead on 9 and 11 October 1941 by the mentioned units. Unfortunately, because of operational reasons (*Einsatzgründen*), a further execution by the mentioned units had to be discontinued and responsibility for the assignment transferred to Major Pongruber's unit."[35]

While some carried out their duties with enthusiasm, in other executions "human weakness" and "mental reservations" came to light. It is important to hold on to the fact that soldiers were not forced to take part in the shootings. Whoever proved to have nerves that were "too weak" or was unable to overcome possible moral inhibitions could get out of such assignments. Nevertheless, the mass executions performed by the Wehrmacht came off smoothly. In their execution, no notable delays or impediments occurred. Alone in the two shooting actions described above, a total of 4,400 Jews and Gypsies were murdered. There are no indications of any negative effects on the internal discipline of the troops.

Where Jews and Gypsies did not exist in sufficient numbers for mass executions, other Serbian civilians filled out the pool of victims, for example in the cities of Kraljevo and Kragujevac, where among others, units of the 717th Infantry Division shot over 4,000 residents in the span of a few days. The manner in which these massacres were carried out characterizes the army's coordination system. In Kraljevo, 300 "Communists, nationalists, democrats, and Jews" were first murdered, before 1,400 randomly accumulated men fell victim to the execution squads on the following day.[36]

In Kragujevac, a similar "selection process" occurred. First, Jews, Communists, and prisoners from the local jail were shot; the troops liquidated the rest of the civilians only the next day—a total of 2,300 people.[37]

By the fall of 1941, massacres of Jews, Gypsies, and other Serbian civilians belonged to the established everyday routine of the Wehrmacht occupation. During these unrestrained mass murders, oversight over the victims was lost—even collaborators were caught up in the liquidation machinery. The head of the military administration, Turner, called upon the district and field commanders to be more selective in choosing their hostage victims, although he was fully aware of the Germans' self-made problem: at a ratio of 1:100, adequate numbers of victims "can no longer be produced, if at least a minimal degree of guilt, even based solely on the general attitude of those to be arrested, is still to be taken into account."[38]

In the case of Jews and Gypsies, however, such diluted selection criteria did not need to be taken into consideration: Turner emphasized that "in all cases, all Jewish men and all male Gypsies (would continue to) be held available for the troops."[39]

In relation to the high demand for shooting victims, the number of available Jews and Gypsies was relatively low. Although this "hostage reservoir" had been enlarged by the 400 or so male, mostly Austrian captured Jewish refugees from the "Kladovo transport,"[40] it was nonetheless exhausted after only a few weeks. Already in early November 1941, Legation Counsel Rademacher, the Foreign Office official entrusted with the "solution to the Jewish problem," reported: "The male Jews will all be shot by the end of this week, thereby the problem addressed in the mission report will be resolved."[41]

In their correspondence, the occupation agencies attempted to legitimize the extermination of the Jews and Gypsies through military euphemisms and pseudo-argumentation. Thus, the head of the military administration, Turner, justified the extermination policies to military agencies by observing "that the Jewish element is considerably involved in leading the bands [of partisans] and especially Gypsies are responsible for exceptional atrocities and intelligence gathering."[42]

Among friends, Turner did not need to fall back on such justification techniques. In a private letter to SS-Gruppenführer Richard Hildebrandt, Turner quite openly laid out the actual motivations for the killings: "In the last 8 days, I have had 2,000 Jews and 200 Gypsies shot dead, following the quota of 1:100 for brutally murdered German soldiers, and a further 2,200, also nearly all Jews, will be shot in the next 8 days. That is not pleasant work! But it must be done, in order to make it clear to people what it means just to attack a German soldier, while at the same time, the Jewish question solves itself most quickly in this way. Actually, it is wrong, if taken literally, that for murdered Germans, for whom the ratio of 1:100 should come at the expense of the Serbs, 100 Jews will now be shot, but they are the ones we happened to have in the camp—besides, they are also Serbian citizens and they, too, have to disappear."[43]

The soldiers who participated in the executions were also fully aware that the logic of the Jewish executions was skewed. In an interview, a soldier who took part in shootings of Jews admitted it was obvious to all involved "that the shooting of Jews bore no relation to partisan attacks, which were used only as an alibi for the extermination of the Jews.... Most of the members of the firing squad never fired a shot in anger, neither before nor after (the executions)."[44]

Pushing the war beyond the boundaries of all existing norms of warfare was the shared undertaking of all occupation authorities. The genocide of the Jews and of portions of the Gypsy population was a collective endeavor of all occupation agencies, as were the massive repressions against the remaining civilian population of Serbia. In the process, the Wehrmacht, as the reigning authority on the scene, had seized the initiative to issue the orders during the decisive phase in the fall of 1941. The soldiers, in turn, translated these orders into deeds.

The balance that General Böhme left behind in December 1941, after only two months as plenipotentiary commander in Serbia: 160 killed and 278 wounded Wehrmacht members were offset by an official total of 3,562 partisans killed in action,[45] and between 20,000 and 30,000 executed civilians—including all adult male Jews and Gypsies.[46]

III

Even as the murder of male Jews was underway in the fall of 1941, the military administration chief, SS-Gruppenführer Harald Turner, enacted the first measures for interning Jewish women and children in the Sajmište concentration camp near Belgrade: "Preliminary work for Jewish ghetto in Belgrade completed. Following the liquidation of the remaining male Jews, already ordered by the commander in Serbia, the ghetto will contain approximately 10,000 Jewish women and children."[47]

With that, the initiative in the extermination of the Jews passed back again from the Wehrmacht to the police and SS organizations, enabling the Wehrmacht to legitimize the incarceration even of women and children with absurd military pretexts. To justify the abduction of women and children to the Sajmište concentration camp—a former fairgrounds near Belgrade—the counter-intelligence unit Ic/AO in Salonika (to which Kurt Waldheim would belong a few months later) insisted: "All of the Jews and Gypsies are being transferred to a concentration camp in Semlin (Sajmište). ... They were proven to be pillars of the intelligence service of the insurgents."[48]

Around the turn of the year 1941–1942, approximately 7,000 Jewish women, children, and old men, as well as 500 Jewish men—they had been spared from earlier executions in order to serve on the camp security force (*Ordnungsdienst*)—and 292 Romany women and children were committed to the Sajmište concentration camp.

At the time of their incarceration—in other words, prior to the Wannsee Conference in January 1942—their fate was already determined. Late in 1941, the military administration chief, Turner, with the assistance of the SD office in Belgrade, requested from Berlin the latest technological innovation for exterminating Jews: a gas van.[49]

The Sajmište concentration camp was situated within view of Belgrade on the other side of the Sava River. With binoculars, it was possible to recognize the camp's inmates from the Belgrade fortress, the Taš Majdan. The former fairground structures had been only inadequately converted to housing for 7,000 people. Women and children were quartered in makeshift barracks that could barely be heated. As a consequence, the mortality rate, especially among children, was very high during the ice-cold winter of 1941–1942.[50]

The concentration camp's administration was relatively simple. The approximately 500 Jewish men who had been exempted from that fall's shootings administered the camp in so-called "self-administration." They were responsible for distributing food, dividing up labor, and organizing a Jewish guard force, which patrolled along the camp's barbed wire fence.[51] The camp's exterior was guarded on a rotation basis by 25 members of Reserve Police Battalion 64.[52]

The camp commandant since January 1942 was the native Austrian SS-Untersturmführer Herbert Andorfer. At the beginning of March 1942, Andorfer received the word from the BdS office (Befehlshaber der Sicher-heitspolizei-SD/Commander of the Security Police-SD) in Belgrade that a special van had been sent from Berlin, which would make it possible to gas the Jewish camp inmates. Immediately thereafter, the Romany women and children were released from the camp.

In order to ensure that the gassings would proceed smoothly, Andorfer put out announcements to delude the prisoners into believing they would soon be transferred to another, better-equipped facility. Andorfer even posted fictitious camp regulations and announced that prisoners would be allowed to take their baggage with them.

Prisoners registered in droves for the alleged transfer, hoping to escape the gruesome conditions of the Sajmište camp. In the time between early March and early May 1942, trucks drove every morning, with the exception of Sundays, from Belgrade to the Sajmište camp. Once there, 50 to 80 women and children stowed their baggage and boarded another, grey-painted Saurer truck, where they took their places on ten benches that had been set up in the interior. Then, both vehicles drove off in the direction of Belgrade. After crossing the bridge over the Sava that led to Belgrade, the baggage truck branched off and delivered the victims' belongings to the Belgrade depot of the National Socialist Volksfürsorge (Peoples Welfare).

The gas van stopped briefly. One of the two drivers, Wilhelm Götz or Erwin Meyer, got out and turned a lever on the van's exterior, causing the exhaust fumes to be channeled into the van's interior. During the sub-sequent drive straight through Belgrade toward the destination, Avala (about 15 km southeast of the capital), the Jews in the back of the van were gassed. Once arrived at the Avala shooting range, a detail of prison-ers from the Belgrade prison unloaded the dead, supervised by members of Reserve Police Battalion 64, and buried them in previously dug pits.

Until the beginning of May 1942, during a span of only two months, the approximately 7,500 Jewish camp inmates were murdered in this fashion. After the completion of this murderous mission, the gas van was returned to Berlin. There, it received a technical upgrade and was sent on to Belorussia, where it was used to gas Jews in Minsk.

The gassing sequence transpired in an efficient manner, according to the logic of the perpetrators. The transport of the victims from the concen-tration camp in the gas van ran very smoothly. The killing required only limited personnel: both gas van drivers; seven prisoners for unloading the dead, and digging and filling in the graves—after the last gas transport, they, too, were shot—and four police officers to guard the prisoners.

Despite the small numbers of people involved in the killings, word quickly spread of the mass murders. Within the SD it was, according to the camp commandant's adjutant, Edgar Enge, an "open secret that the Jews were gassed with this van."[53] In Reserve Police Battalion 64, too, one knew what was going on. Accordingly, a policeman involved in the gassing operations said in an official statement that their activities, "in spite of all security measures, were gradually leaking through to the company, particularly since a guard detachment from our company was also posted at the gas van's parking site and had numerous opportunities to see the gas van."[54] In a postwar witness statement, a department head in Turner's administration once again remembered hearing "from ethnic German circles in early 1942 that the Jewish prisoners of the camp were gassed to death."[55]

The staff of the military commander also was informed about the gradual decimation of the Sajmište camp's inmates. The staff section's ten-day reports duly recorded the systematic decline in the number of the camp's prisoners.

The Wehrmacht's soldiers also had at least a partial view into the proceedings. The victims' bodies were buried at the Avala shooting range, where German soldiers regularly held firing exercises. A truck driver of the Belgrade field command recalled how he discovered pits containing the bodies of gassed Jews while setting up firing targets for his unit's marksmanship training at the end of the range. To the left and right of the road, he noticed the contours of numerous four-sided mounds, which emitted the sweetish smell of decomposing flesh. He saw that women's clothing stuck out from crevices in the mounds and deduced that they must contain the mass graves of women.[56]

In the early part of 1942, the murderers were not so particular in their efforts at secrecy. Only later, as the German defeat began to seem like a distinct possibility, did they frantically attempt to wipe away the traces of their mass murders. In November 1943, the "special commando 1005" of *Einsatzgruppe* leader Paul Blobel arrived in Belgrade. For four months, the corpses of those who had been shot in the fall of 1941 and gassed in early 1942 were dug up, stacked on massive pyres, and incinerated.[57]

When General Löhr returned to the Balkans as Wehrmacht Commander Southeast in August 1942, the head of the military administration in Serbia, Harald Turner, proudly reported: "Jewish question, just like Gypsy question, completely liquidated: Serbia the only country in which the Jewish question and Gypsy question solved."[58] After Estonia, Serbia became the second land in the National Socialist empire that was made "free of Jews."

IV

The process of extermination in Serbia occurred in four uninterrupted sequential phases: (1) the identification of the victims, their loss of legal rights, their social exclusion, and confiscation of their possessions in the first half of 1941 was followed, with the beginning of the partisan struggle that summer, by (2) the murder of some male Jews by police and members of the SD. When the Wehrmacht assumed responsibility for the anti-partisan fight, and with the arrival of General Böhme, the army (3) extended the extermination program to all male Jews. While the men were still being murdered, (4) the women and children were interned in the Sajmište concentration camp and gassed in early 1942.

The extermination of the Gypsies occurred only partly parallel to the extermination of the Jews. The anti-Jewish directives of early 1941 counted only briefly for all Gypsies. After a few weeks, the occupiers differentiated between Gypsies with and without domicile: Serbian citizens of Gypsy descent who held respectable jobs, led an orderly lifestyle, and whose ancestors could be proven to have been settled since at least 1850, were exempted from anti-Jewish directives after July 1941. It is not possible to determine exactly how many Gypsies fell victim to the Wehrmacht's mass shootings in the fall of 1941. If one examines the ratio of Jewish and Gypsy women and children interned in the Sajmište camp (7,000 to barely 300), then their total may have been relatively low. The Romany women and children were released from the Sajmište camp shortly before the start of the gassings of Jews.

The first phase of the extermination program depended on neither the existence of a comprehensive order for Jewish extermination nor on Hitler's approval of the systematic murder of the Jews. In Serbia, the German occupation authorities determined independently to begin the "Final Solution of the Jewish question" in their sphere of responsibility.

The institutional chaos that typified the National Socialist system also existed in Serbia. The coexistence of individual agencies whose competencies overlapped, and were never clearly spelled out, consistently produced often bitter power struggles and turf battles between various occupation authorities.[59] All the more noticeable, then, the seamless way in which the various occupation elements augmented one another, and their smooth cooperation, in the area of Jewish policy.

The Holocaust in Serbia, then, was a collective deed of all the occupation agencies in which immediate responsibility shifted from one agency to another. Whoever took the momentary lead in the various phases of the persecution—the Wehrmacht or the *Einsatzgruppen*, the military administration or the embassy—depended on the situation at hand. To the extent that general guidelines from central headquarters in Berlin were even necessary, they were immediately adapted to the situation on the ground. In the process, the political police and the civil and military occupation authorities succeeded or supplemented one another as needed in taking the lead on Jewish policy. From the beginning, all occupation agencies were in complete agreement over the common goal to make the Jews "disappear." And they were able to come to quick agreement over precisely what means should be used to accomplish that goal as the situation demanded.

Notes

1 Holm Sundhaussen, "Jugoslawien," in *Dimension des Völkermords: Die Zabl der jüdischen Opfer des Nationalsozialismus*, ed. Wolfgang Benz (Munich, 1991), p. 329.

2 Walter Manoschek, " '*Serbien ist judenfrei': Militärische Besatzungspoltitik und Judenvernichtung in Serbien 1941/42*," in *Schriftenreihe des Militärgeschichtlichen Forschungsamtes* (Munich, 1995, 2nd edition), Vol. 38.

3 The exact number of Jewish victims cannot be established. Of the approximately 12,500 Serbian Jews, 4,200 Jews from the Banat, and approximately 1,000 foreign Jewish refugees, only a tiny number managed to survive, either by fleeing in time or going into hiding as "U-boats."

4 Bundesarchiv-Militärarchiv Freiburg (from hereon BA-MA), RH 26-718/3 and RH 20-12/121; Georg Tessin, *Verbände und Truppen der deutschen Wehrmacht und der Waffen-SS im Zweiten Weltkrieg 1939–1945* (Osnabrück, 1976), Vol. 13, pp. 127–132.

5 Interrogation statement of the former general plenipotentiary for the economy in Serbia, Franz Neuhausen, while in the Yugoslavian military prison in Belgrade, 20 September 1947; cit. from Venceslav Glisič, "*Der Terror und die Verbrechen des faschistischen Deutschland in Serbien von 1941 bis 1944*" (Ph.D. Thesis, Berlin, 1968), p. 31.

6 Directive of the Supreme Commander of the Army on the Regulation of the Engagement of the Security Police and the SD in Association with the Army during the Invasion of the Soviet Union, 28 April 1941, citation from *Deutsche Besatzungspolitik in der UdSSR*, ed. Norbert Müller (Cologne, 1988), pp. 42–44.

7 OKH, GenStdH/GenQu., Abt. Kriegsverwaltung (Army Supreme Command, General Staff of the Army/General Quartermaster, Department War Administration), Nr. 11/0308/41 g.K. Chefs. bis zum "Operationsbeginn," from 2 April 1941, cit. from Helmut Krausnick and Hans-Heinrich Wilhelm, *Die Truppe des Weltanschauungskrieges: Die Einsatzgruppen der Sicherheitspolizei und des SD 1938–1942* (Stuttgart, 1981), p. 137.

8 Military Historical Archive in Belgrade, German Archive, 50–4–4.

9 VO from 23 April 1941, Nbg. Dok. NOKW 1100.

10 Military Historical Archive in Belgrade, German Archive, 12–1–66.

11 Central Office of the Landesjustizverwaltungen Ludwigsburg (from hereon ZStL), 503 AR 12/62, Beiakte Bd. 6, Witness statements of Willi J. and Anton W.

12 Field mail letter of Lieutenant Peter G., 24 May 1941, Bibliothek für Zeitgeschichte, Stuttgart, Sammlung Sterz (Library for Recent History, Stuttgart, Sterz Collection).

13 Situation and Activity Report of the "*Propagandaabteilung S(erbien)*" (Propaganda Department S[erbia]), May-August 1941, BA-MA, RW 4/v.231.

14 Directive concerning the Jews and Gypsies, 30 May 1941, Jewish Historical Museum, Belgrade, 21–1–1/20.

15 Henceforth, the fate of the Gypsies in Serbia unfolded only partly parallel to that of the Jews. Thus, in July 1941, those Gypsies whose ancestors had been

settled since 1850 were excepted from these measures; the women and children were released from the camp before the gassing operation. The decisive reason why the Gypsies were only partially exterminated lay in the impossibility of categorizing them in accordance with their religious affiliation. The Gypsies who in the fall of 1941 were interned in the "hostage camps" in Belgrade and Šabac were executed as well as the Jews. For the extermination of the Gypsies in Yugoslavia, see Donald Kenrick and Grattan Puxton, *The Destiny of Europe's Gypsies* (London, 1972), reference is to German edition, *Sinti und Roma: Die Vernichtung eines Volkes im NS-Staat* (Göttingen, 1981); Karola Fings, Cordula Lissner, and Frank Sparing, "... *einziges Land, in dem Judenfrage und Zigeunerfrage gelöst": Die Verfolgung der Roma im faschistisch besetzten Jugoslawien 1941–1945* (Cologne, n.d.); and most recently Michael Zimmermann, *Rassenutopie und Genozid: Die Nationalsozialistische Lösung der "Zigeunerfrage"* (Hamburg, 1996), pp. 248ff.

16 Politisches Archiv, Auswärtiges Amt Bonn (from hereon PA-AA), *Botschaft Belgrad, Judenangelegenheiten Bd 62/6, Aufzeichnung über Besprechung über Judenfragen beim Militärbefehlshaber in Serbien am 14.5.1941* (Embassy in Belgrade, Jewish Matters Vol. 62/6, Memorandum on discussion of Jewish questions in the office of the military commander in Serbia, 14 May 1941).

17 Supporting documents in BA-MA, RH 26-718/3 and RH 20-12/121.

18 Directive concerning the engagement of the Security Police and the SD, 17 July 1941, BA-MA, RW 40/79. For concurrent developments in France (where many of the same conditions prevailed), compare the contribution by Ulrich Herbert, "The German Military Command in Paris and the Deportation of the French Jews" in this volume.

19 On 22 June 1941, the head of the military administrative staff, Privy Counsel (*Staatsrat*) Harald Turner, ordered the arrest of all leading Communists and veterans of the Spanish Civil War. Concurrently, the Jewish community in Belgrade had to provide forty men on a daily basis, who would be shot as hostages in the event of partisan attacks; Bundesarchiv Koblenz (BA-K), 70 Jugoslawien/33, *Anklageschrift gegen den Befehlshaber der Sipo-SD (BdS) Belgrad*, Dr. Emanuel Schäfer (70 Yugoslavia/33, Indictment against the Commander of the Security Police and SD in Belgrade, Dr. Emanuel Schäfer), p. 19.

20 Field mail letters of Lieutenant Peter G., 9th Company/Infantry Regiment 721, 714th Infantry Division, 27 July 1941, 29 July 1941, and 3 August 1941, Bibliothek für Zeitgeschichte Stuttgart, Sammlung Sterz.

21 Chief of the Wehrmacht Supreme Command (OKW) to military commanders in Serbia, 9 August 1941, BA-MA, RW 40/5.

22 Chief of the Higher Command LXV, General Bader, to all companies, 23 August 1941, BA-MA, RW 40/5.

23 Führerweisung Nr. 31a., 16 September 1941, cit. from *Hitlers Weisungen für die Kriegsführung 1939–1945: Dokumente des Oberkommandos der Wehrmacht*, ed. Walter Hubatsch (Munich, 1965), pp. 149f.

24 Teletype message from General Field Marshal List to Wehrmacht Supreme Command (OKW) and Army Supreme Command (OKH), 12 September 1941, NOKW-Dokument 1898.

25 Böhme to all units of the 342nd ID, 25 September 1941, BA-MA, RH 26–342/8.

26 Omer Bartov, *Hitler's Army: Soldiers, Nazis and War in the Third Reich* (New York, 1991), reference is to German edition, *Hitlers Wehrmacht: Soldaten, Fanatismus und die Brutalisierung des Krieges* (Reinbek, 1995) p. 109.

27 Keitel's order of 16 September 1941, BA-MA, RH 26–104/14.

28 Situation report by Turner, NOKW-Dokument 892, 21 September 1941.

29 Telegram from Veesenmayer and Benzler to the Foreign Office, 8 September 1941, PA-AA, Inland IIg.
30 See correspondence between Benzler, Veesenmayer, and the Foreign Office in Berlin (PA-AA, Inland IIg).
31 Luther to Benzler, 16 September 1941, NG-Dokument 3354.
32 Böhme's telephonic order to Quartermaster Section, 4 October 1941, BA-MA, RH 24–18/213.
33 Böhme's order, 10 October 1941, BA-MA, RH 26–104/14.
34 Activity report from the 704th ID, 1 November 1941, BA-MA, RH 26–104/15.
35 Report on the shooting of Jews on 9 and 11 October 1941, BA-MA, RH 24–18/213.
36 Walter Manoschek, "Serbien ist judenfrei": Militärische Besatzungspolitik und Judenvernichtung in Serbien 1941/42 (Munich, 1995, 2nd edition), pp. 155–158.
37 Ibid., pp. 158–168.
38 Turner's order to all district and field commands, 26 October 1941, NOKW-Dokument 802.
39 Ibid.
40 Compare Gabriele Anderl, Walter Manoschek, Gescheiterte Flucht: Der jüdische "Kladovo-Transport" auf dem Weg nach Palästina 1939–42 (Vienna, 1993).
41 Rademacher's notes on the results of his official visit to Belgrade, 7 November 1941, PA-AA, Inland IIg.
42 Turner's order to all district and field commands, 26 October 1941, NOKW-Dokument 802.
43 Turner's letter to Hildebrandt, 17 October 1941, NO-Dokument 5810.
44 Author's interview with A.A. on 22 February 1990 (tape recording excerpt).
45 Aktennotiz Sühnemaßnahmen bis 5.12.1941 (file note "atonement measures" until 5 December 1941), BA-MA, RW 40/23.
46 For estimates of the number of victims, compare Manoschek, "Serbien ist judenfrei," p. 166, note 60.
47 Memorandum from Turner, 20 October 1941, NO-Dokument 3404.
48 Comments on the occasion of the visit of the Deputy Supreme Commander to Belgrade, 5 December 1941, NOKW-Dokument 1150.
49 Partial copy of Turner's letter to Wolff, 11 April 1942, ZStL, 503, AR-Z 372/59.
50 Menachem Shelach, "Sajmište: An extermination camp in Serbia," Holocaust and Genocide Studies 2 (1987): 243–260.
51 Christopher Browning, Fateful Months: Essays on the Emergence of the Final Solution (New York; London, 1985), p. 71.
52 Unless otherwise noted, the reconstruction of the gassing operations is based on proceedings against the BdS Serbia, Emanuel Schäfer (ZStL, AR 1256/61), and against Herbert Andorfer (Landesgericht Wien, 27e, Vr 2260/67), and the judgement against Herbert Andorfer (ZStL, 503 AR 2656/67); in addition, see Manoschek, "Serbien ist judenfrei," pp. 169–184.
53 Witness statement of Edgar Enge, 2 May 1966, Landesgericht Wien, 27e, Vr 2260/67.
54 Witness statement of Karl W., 24 November 1964, ZStL, AR 1256/61.
55 Witness statement of Dr. Walter U., 5 April 1952, ZStL, AR 1256/61.
56 Witness statement of Anton W., 9 August 1962, ZStL, AR 12/62.
57 Investigation of members of "Sonderkommando 1005," ZStL, AR-Z 115/77.
58 29 August 1942, NOKW-Dokument 1486.
59 Compare Christopher Browning, "Harald Turner und die Militärverwaltung in Serbien 1941–1942," in Verwaltung contra Menschenführung im Staat Hitlers, ed. Dieter Rebentisch und Karl Teppe (Göttingen, 1986).

24

THE WAR AND THE KILLING OF
THE LITHUANIAN JEWS

Christoph Dieckmann

Source: Ulrich Herbert (ed.), *National Socialist Extermination Policies. Contemporary Perspectives and Controversies*, New York/Oxford: Berghahn, 2000, pp. 240–75.

On 24 June 1941, only two days after the war with the Soviet Union began, in the small Lithuanian town of Gargždai, the first killings of Jews in the German-occupied Soviet Union took place. That afternoon, a commando from the German Security Police and the security service (the SD) from Tilsit and a division of the Security Police from Memel shot 201 people.[1] After this massacre of civilians, a series of further shootings followed along the Lithuanian border. In this way, by 18 July 1941, more than 3,300 people had been killed.

The killings on June 24 in Gargždai have been described by the Stuttgart historian Eberhard Jäckel, according to whom the head of Einsatzgruppe A, Dr. Walter Stahlecker, did not stop at the killing of adult men but allowed "also Jewish women and children" to be shot. This led Jäckel to the conclusion that Stahlecker received verbal instructions on 17 June 1941, during a conversation with his commanding officer Reinhard Heydrich, the head of the Reichssicher-heitshauptamt (RSHA, the headquarters of the security service of the Reich), "that he had to, or had permission to, kill all Jews."[2]

This view, which has great significance for the analysis and interpretation of the development of the genocide of the Jews as a whole, rests on the opinion given by the Munich historian Helmut Krausnick as an expert witness in the Federal German court proceedings in Ulm in 1958 with reference to statements from those charged with the killings in the Lithuanian border regions. According to Krausnick, on 23 June 1941, Stahlecker had instructed the local police leaders in Tilsit to "implement the special treatment of all Jews, including women and children, as well as of Lithuanians suspected of Communism."[3]

This assumption appears questionable, both in the light of more recent sources and from the evidence given in the records of the Ulm *Einsatzgruppen* trial itself. The approximately 10,000–12,000 (predominantly Jewish) victims of the first wave of killings in German-occupied Lithuania were in the first place Jewish men and Communists. Jewish women and children were as a rule excluded from these shootings. The first half of this chapter reappraises this discussion of the context and the issuance of orders for the first killings in Lithuania.

In August 1941, a new phase was launched. The German civil authorities, already established at the end of July 1941, switched over to a policy of massacring very nearly the entire Jewish population—men, women, children—in the rural areas. From August 1941 on, the Jewish population in the larger towns of Lithuania were subjected to mass selections to which tens of thousands of Jews fell victim. Within a few months at least 120,000 Jews were shot and killed by German and Lithuanian police, who carried out their task with an inconceivable brutality. The Lithuanian police were established by the German occupation authorities in the very first days of the war, and came under German control. Approximately 45,000–50,000 Jews survived these selections. They were confined to ghettos in order to be put to work for a short period for the German war industry.[4]

The second part of this chapter focuses on the background to this transition from the first to the second phase of the murderous German policy in Lithuania in August 1941. If, as I am trying to show, no order had been given for the total annihilation of the Lithuanian Jews by the beginning of the war in June 1941, how did it come to be that only six weeks later the German leadership then decided to kill not only Jewish men as previously envisaged, but also women and children, in hundreds of mass shootings? In comparison to other regions in occupied Soviet territory, what happened in Lithuania came especially early and amounted to a policy of almost total annihilation—but why? In order to investigate questions about the motives and the timing of the radicalization of the anti-Jewish policy in Lithuania, a reconstruction of the German decision-makers' views of the events is needed. How did the regional German authorities perceive the situation, and how did it appear to the leadership of the Reich?

The war with the Soviet Union, launched with high expectations, took center-stage in the thinking of the National Socialist regime. It is common to argue that there was a close ideological connection between German war aims, the conduct of the war, and the killing of the Jews. By early 1941, the German leadership, as Andreas Hillgruber argued as long ago as 1972, was depicting this war against the Soviet Union as a *"Weltanschauungskrieg"* to exterminate "Jewish Bolshevism" and to procure *"Lebensraum"* for the German people.[5] In this light, the killing of Eastern Jewry during the course of the war would appear at the very least to have already been decided at the outset of the war. Other authors have laid more emphasis on the unexpectedly poor progress of the war, which led the National Socialists to switch their focus, influenced by their antisemitic *Weltanschauung*, to killing the Jews at once, as a "sacrifice and an act of vengeance" for the difficulties encountered in the pursuit of the war and for the prospect of the defeat of the Third Reich: an act of vindictiveness, one might say.[6]

The doubt as to whether these arguments give a satisfactory analysis of the concrete relation between war, antisemitism, and the killing of the Jews in occupied Soviet territory marks the starting point for the following considerations about the structures and motives of the German murder campaign in Lithuania in the summer and fall of 1941.

The initial phase: the first shootings and pogroms of June-July 1941

The 176th Infantry Regiment under Major General Robert Sattler, part of the 61st Infantry Division, was given the task, as part of Army Group North, of conquering the town of Gargždai on the first day of the attack on the Soviet Union. Through Gargždai ran the only road in the entire region covered by the corps. The bridge there over the Minija was of important strategic significance and could be quickly secured by skirting around Gargždai. However, the Second Battalion's intention "to take the place by surprise" was thwarted because Russian frontier troops defended the area obstinately.[7] In the battle, which lasted until the afternoon of 22 June, probably about 100 Germans lost their lives. Of the approximately 3,000 inhabitants of the small town, there were 1,000 Jews, living particularly in the area to the west of the town, which was most heavily fought over, where the Soviet frontier troops had their emplacements.[8] German troops reported that "civilians had also" taken part in the battles.[9] On 23 June, many of the towns people, who had tried for the most part to take shelter in cellars, were driven onto the marketplace. There the Jewish population and alleged Communists were probably separated from the rest of the population by frontier police from Memel and the helping hands of Lithuanians from Gargždai. Some 600–700 Jews had to remain overnight in the town gardens. The frontier police officials took those Jewish men above fifteen years of age away to a meadow to the west of the town, where they were guarded by German customs officials.[10] Following the directive to impose collective punishments against the civilian population in places which resisted,[11] a German company leader, with the agreement of the division leadership, informed the nearby frontier police position of the situation in Gargždai. The case was handed over to the frontier police, since the company had to make haste in order to catch up with the regiment, which had already moved on. The mobile units of the Wehrmacht were not themselves to carry out "special search and cleansing actions," since their priorities were to engage in "battle and [forward] movement."[12] The frontier police commissariat at Memel informed their superiors at the state police station in Tilsit, which then made a request to the RSHA in a special priority telex for directions as to what was to be done in view of the fact that the numbers of people arrested by the Wehrmacht had grown appreciably.[13]

On 24 June, the leader of the state police station, Hans-Joachim Böhme, and the head of the SD, Werner Hersmann, met with Stahlecker. Whereas Böhme and Hersmann, as they put it when charged in 1958, said that they had received the order to kill the Jews of Gargždai from Stahlecker, their report to the RSHA of 1 July 1941, read quite otherwise. There it was stated that they had discussed the situation with Stahlecker on 24 June, who "in principle" gave his "agreement to the cleansing actions in the area around the German borders."[14] In this document there is no question of an order, but rather of Stahlecker's "agreement," which therefore suggests that Stahlecker was reacting to the recommendations of Böhme and Hersmann. Seventeen years later, the State Court of Ulm mistakenly took these statements to mean that the accused had been given an "imperative order" (*Befehlsnotstand*).

In fact, however, the state police station at Tilsit instructed Gestapo Chief Dr. Erich Frohwann and SD-Chief Edwin Sakuth from the frontier police commissariat at Memel to prepare for the shooting of 200 able-bodied men. On 24 June, 200 men—Communists and predominantly Jews—were shot under the direction of the state police station in Tilsit and of the frontier police commissariat in Memel, their valuables having been taken before the shootings. A woman who had married a Russian commissar was also killed. The remaining Jewish women and children were locked up in barns guarded by Lithuanian police at the other end of the town and the women were put to work. Almost three months later, on 14 and 16 September, these approximately 300 women and children were then shot by German and Lithuanian police in two "actions" in a forest six to seven kilometers north-east of Gargždai.[15]

The state police station in Tilsit received Stahlecker's agreement not only to shoot Communists and Jews in Gargždai but also to further killings in the Lithuanian border region. Already on the following day, 25 June, the same Kommando shot 214 men and a woman in Kretinga, and 111 men two days later in Palanga. In Kretinga on 25 June, Jewish women and children were explicitly excluded from the killings, according to the state police report.[16] In Palanga, the local commander, also commander of the airbase there, placed at the Kommando's disposal a firing squad of sixteen to twenty men from the 6th Air Training Company of a fighter squadron from the airfield nearby.[17] Luftwaffe soldiers from Airfleet 1 had already driven the Jewish men into the synagogue, where they guarded them while the women were isolated in the Pryšmančiai Farmyard. As in Gargždai, the Jewish women and children from Palanga and Kretinga were shot by Lithuanian and German units two months later, at the end of August and the beginning of September 1941.

In the process of the first killing actions, a further Einsatzkommando was formed, grouping Wehrmacht units with the frontier police commissariat at Memel and the state police station in Tilsit, under their ambitious leader Hans-Joachim Böhme.[18] This Kommando had received extensive authorization for "cleansing actions" in the Lithuanian border area for which Sonderkommando 1b under Erich Ehrlinger and Einsatzkommando 3 under Karl Jäger had already been assigned. On 4 July, Heydrich's authorization was transmitted to the other *Einsatzkommandos*. According to Heydrich, in order to secure and ensure the freedom of movement of the *Einsatzgruppen* and *Einsatzkommandos* he had given state police stations the "authorization to carry out cleansing actions in newly-occupied territories across the border from their sectors."[19]

The defense strategies of the accused in the trials in Ulm of 1958 gave rise to the myth that Stahlecker and Heydrich had issued an order for the killing of Jewish men, women, and children to the state police station at Tilsit at the beginning of the war. As in the Nuremberg Einsatzgruppen trials, here it was a question not of historical fact, but of the "defense line" with which the accused sought to exonerate themselves.[20] Stahlecker's "agreement," Heydrich's "authorization," and the fact that it was above all Jewish men of an age for military service and Communists who were murdered contradict the supposition that at the beginning of the war precise instructions were given for the murder of the whole Jewish population in occupied Soviet territory. When on 30 June 1941, the Lithuanian police chief of Alytus, a town in the south of Lithuania, offered to kill all of the Jews in the whole region with a squad of 1,050 Lithuanian police and partisans in a few days, it was rejected by the German side.[21]

There are some rather clearer hints in another set of instructions given to the *Einsatzkommandos* in Lithuania at the beginning of the war. Hans-Joachim Böhme, the head of the Tilsit state police station, who used the situation in the first days of the war to become the head of one of the *Einsatzkommandos*, was apparently instructed by Stahlecker and Heydrich "to shoot Jewish men aged sixteen or over as well as dangerous Communists." Böhme himself named one such order in defending himself in court, when he sought to deflect the charge that he was responsible for the murder of Jewish women and children.[22] A similar instruction is documented for the region bordering Kaunas. On 15 August, SS-Hauptsturmführer Joachim Hamann of Einsatzkommando 3 in Kaunas instructed the head of the Lithuanian constabulary to seize and isolate all Jewish men older than fifteen in the provincial commissariat of Kaunas, as well as all Jewish women who had been active Communists.[23] The testimony of

Böhme was of course given in connection with the question of his responsibility for the shooting of women and children, and the instruction from Hamann to the Lithuanian police was issued at a later time, but the presumption that there was an instruction for the killing of Jewish men over fifteen years old as well as all persons suspected of being Communists is confirmed by the practice of the killings in these first weeks of the war.

Only those Jewish men who were seen as absolutely necessary for the continued operation of industries central to the war effort were explicitly excepted from these killings, in particular Jews who were skilled workers. They were allowed to live after the intervention of the German industrial detachments for whom they worked in ghettos under German control. The general instruction in this regard was sent from the Economic Directorate of the East (Wirtschaftsstab Ost, WiStab Ost) to the regional industrial units on 15 July 1941. These received an order "to leave Jewish skilled laborers in service [where working on] production important for the war effort [and] where no substitute is available and the maintenance of production depends on it."[24]

The systematic action of the Tilsit state police station *Einsatzkommando* in the Lithuanian border region—involving the targeted arrest and murder of specific groups of Communists and of Jewish men and the isolation of the Jewish population, gathering them for the most part into places on the outskirts of the areas in which they lived—was typical of the campaign of the German and Lithuanian police against the Jews before mid-August across the whole of Lithuania. Einsatzkommando 3 in Kaunas and the part of Einsatzkommando 2 active in northern Lithuania up to the beginning of October also focused on these groups.

SS-Unterführer Krumbach from the state police station in Tilsit, under interrogation for his role in the shooting of Jewish men in Kretinga, described the situation in June 1941 with greater clarity than his superiors did when defending their action in court on the ground that they were only following "imperative orders." To the question "How and why was the shooting of all of the Jews to take place, as it was explained to you? Were women and children also discussed?" Krumbach answered "Böhme and Hersmann explained to me then that according to an order from the Führer, the whole of Eastern Jewry had to be exterminated so that there would no longer be Jewish blood available there to maintain a world Jewry, thus bringing about the decisive destruction of world Jewry. This affirmation was by itself not new at that time and was rooted in the ideology of the Party. The *Einsatzkommandos* of the Sipo [Security Police] and of the SD were instituted for this task by the Führer. ... To my question what should happen to the Jewish women and children who remained and to the families of the Soviet officers, who after all had to be taken care of and supported, I received the reply that these would in all probability be accommodated in specially constructed camps. Full particulars of these were however still not known, and the time was also not yet ripe for a decision to be made."[25]

In an analysis which appeared in 1991, Peter Longerich argued that the "commanders of the extermination units" had received a "kind of general authorization to kill the Jewish population in the conquered territories, without numerical restriction, which was leveled to begin with essentially against men."[26] Even if Longerich's thesis "of a technique of instruction based on interaction" were to hold true,[27] the assumption that the heads of the *Einsatzgruppen* were given a "general authorization" is too vague. One should rather speak of a specific conception of terror and murder on the part of the Security Police as a systematic means of waging war, which determined the activities of the German death squads formed in the first months of the war. Many statements made before and after 22 June 1941, point to the fact that to the German political, military, and Security Police leadership this was a matter above all else of quickly eliminating the "Jewish-Bolshevik leadership strata," which from the National Socialist point of view constituted the core of the Soviet state. The concept rested on the line laid down by Hitler: "The Jewish-Bolshevik intelligence must be removed since up until now they have been 'oppressors' of the people."[28] The German leadership believed that the murder of these most important *"Weltanschauungsträger"* [carriers or vehicles of an ideological world-view] would greatly accelerate the collapse of the Soviet state.

The model for this concept was provided by the murderous progress of the Security Police in Poland after September 1939 against the Polish leadership stratum.[29] In spring 1940, it was used by the General Government as a means to secure the "complete control of the Polish people in this area" as a permanent feature of the German occupation regime, when Hitler gave the following instruction to General Governor Frank: "What we have now identified as the leadership level in Poland, that is to be liquidated; [if a new leadership were to] grow again, it is to be apprehended and done away with in an appropriate period of time."[30] In a more extreme and expanded form this concept was to be executed during the war against the Soviet Union and now took in those Jewish men "fit for military service."

The discussion of the plans for killing campaigns in the spring of 1941, i.e., before the war, shows that the "commissar instructions" and the "legal decree" dealt with not only the political commissars in the Red Army but also the entire group defined by the National Socialists as the "leadership strata" of the Soviet state, whose murder was eventually undertaken both by the army and by the *Einsatzgruppen*. On 25 April 1941, Alfred Rosenberg turned—in view of the lack of personnel—against the option "of a *general* elimination of all state, communal, and local functionaries. . . . A *general* extermination, as both one of the first acts of battle and also later through the use of civil authorities, would be a measure which, politically and socially, would later inevitably be revenged terribly."[31] There was however no dissent with respect to the "senior and the highest commissars." It was self-evident, according to Rosenberg, "that naturally tens of thousands of oppressors of the peoples of the East would have to be wiped out."[32] The Wehrmacht leadership by contrast turned against the restriction that "only high and very high functionaries should be executed," since it appeared to be difficult to have to separate "the different levels of officials," and it would also be a waste of time.[33]

In the last draft of these "Directions for the treatment of political commissars" of 6 June 1941, there was, then, no further mention of the "treatment of political functionaries"; the Wehrmacht was now only concerned about the political commissars, but only in a broad sense.[34] The rest of the "carrier stratum" in the occupied regions of the Soviet Union was to be turned over to the security divisions and *Einsatzgruppen*, who would thus have more time for "sorting" and investigating those with political responsibilities. General Quartermaster Eduard Wagner had negotiated this division of responsibilities with Heydrich, with the result that the security divisions were to concentrate on the big transportation roads while "the forces of the Reichsführer SS in the hinterlands would mainly take charge of the areas between the runways."[35] The German forces' short- and long-term goals no longer appeared to be in conflict with each other, since the killing of Communists and Jewish men would create "the basis for the final removal of Bolshevism," and at the same time would "secure the areas lying between the supply routes."[36]

The well-known statements made by Heydrich in his letter to the leadership of the SS and the police of 2 July 1941, accordingly envisaged "hitting the Jewish-Bolshevik leadership strata as effectively as possible."[37] Heydrich's instructions took account of Rosenberg's objections of April 1941 to the murder of persons "still useful for industry, union work, and trade." Of the lower levels of officials, "solely" the "radicals" were to be done away with, while all middle-ranking and senior political functionaries were to be killed immediately.

Heydrich's orders to the Security Police and the criminal instructions of the Wehrmacht should be seen as an expression of a process of the division of labor in a "war of *Weltanschauungen*" to which both were committed. Both series of instructions were linked by a concept which emerged from within the Security Police: to kill off the leadership of the Soviet state so as to be able to subjugate the whole country quickly. In the RSHA and Security Police leadership group around Heydrich, but also far beyond that group as well, Jewishness was seen as the "racial" basis of Bolshevism. The murder of the Jewish men was seen as a way of executing the order to "liquidate" the Soviet leadership stratum.[38]

During these initial phases, the male members of the "Jewish intelligence strata" were to be wiped out, not only in the border areas of Lithuania but in the whole of Lithuania.[39] The systematic progress of the German and Lithuanian police in the towns and villages of Lithuania, registering, arresting, and finally killing the upper class of the Jewish community of the day, came out of this concept of radical preventive terror. In addition, the numerous "pogroms" which took place in many parts of Lithuania in the first weeks after the outbreak of war were as a rule of a systematic character: frequently Lithuanian, but also German, police made targeted arrests. In some areas, and above all in Kaunas, the head of Einsatzgruppe A, Stahlecker, instigated deadly pogroms in which the entire Jewish quarter of a town was attacked. In two nights in Kaunas alone, over 2,000 Jews were barbarically murdered. Although Einsatzkommando 7A notified the RSHA from Vilnius (Vilna) that the "self-cleansing efforts" had been intensified there, they did not succeed in organizing a manhunt as murderous as the one in Kaunas.[40] One objective of the pogroms was nevertheless achieved: a "campaign of arrests" was immediately introduced and Communists and Jewish men were taken into custody.[41]

Heydrich's calculation, however, had still further ramifications. The leaders of the *Einsatzgruppen* had to give these pogroms the appearance that Lithuanians had "spontaneously" begun them, taking revenge on "the Jews" in brutal massacres and wild mass shootings for their supposed Bolshevik activity,[42] so that in this way they might prevent the responsibility of the German Security Police for these killings from becoming known "outside."[43] In the wake of these "wild" pogroms, the Security Police could even appear to be a guarantee of order—and here there are clear parallels with the utilization of the pogroms in Germany of 9 November 1938, by the Security Police and SD.[44] Heydrich wanted to set up a basis for legitimizing—in the eyes of "German circles"—the implementation of anti-Jewish policy by force. The Jews had to disappear from the occupied territories on the grounds of peace, order, and coexistence with the indigenous population in these areas, ruled by relatively few German personnel. The Security Police wanted to secure its position as an institutional check on the "wild wrath of the people" and claimed sole responsibility for anti-Jewish policy in the occupied Soviet Union, against the claims of other German bodies, and above all that of the civil administration. Nevertheless, the Security Police only received an all-encompassing authority for this area in 1943.

Before the beginning of the war, the German leadership had planned on a quick Wehrmacht victory over the Soviet Union, a matter of a few months. After this victory, the Jews were to be deported "to the East," as it was generally said; in June and July 1941, this referred more concretely to the northern regions of the Soviet Union around the Arctic circle, where a large proportion of the Soviet Gulag were. Beyond such vague hints, there were thus far, however, no written plans or material on this project; all deliberations on it thus stand on an insecure foundation.[45]

From March 1941 on, all previous planning undertaken by the RSHA and the Reich Commissar for the "resettlement" of the Jewish population could not be implemented to the expected extent. The war for "loot, *Lebensraum*, and annihilation" had also to make it possible for National Socialist population policy planners to overcome the difficulties they were facing in making the "ethnic cleansing of the land" a reality.[46]

As absurd as such a plan for the deportation of European Jewry "to the East" may seem today, in June 1941 the National Socialist leadership clearly took it to be a real possibility. The living conditions there, whether it be in the Pripyat marshes or in the camps of the Gulag Archipelago, were so abject and cruel that in this scheme the prospect of a genocide was visible.

It can thus be asserted that with respect to the first seven weeks of the war in the areas under German occupation, there was in June 1941 still no order envisaging the total elimination of the Jewish population during the war. In expectation of a speedy military defeat of the Soviet Union, vague but exceedingly brutal plans were laid to deport the Jews living in the area under German control to more easterly areas of the occupied Soviet Union after victory. For those people seen by the National Socialists as the most dangerous potential opponents of German rule—the "carrier class" of the Soviet state, Jewish men of fighting age, and especially "the intelligentsia"—an immediate killing campaign was discussed and adopted. This killing program followed from a racist preventive-policing concept and was tuned to the interests of the military. The defeat of the other side in the war was thus to be accelerated and the risk of potential resistance minimized. To this end, a division of labor was discussed and set out between the Wehrmacht, Security Police, and the leaders of the future civil authorities of the occupied Soviet Union. The first instructions given to the Einsatzgruppen were to arrest and kill all Communists and Jewish men over fifteen years of age. The first killings also then took place in those areas from which there had been reports of actual resistance.

The second phase: August to November 1941

In mid-August 1941, in contrast with the earlier period covered above, the killings suddenly developed on a greater scale. In the north and northeast of Lithuania, German and Lithuanian units began to kill Jewish women and children. Within three months, by the end of November 1941, at least 120,000 Jews were shot.

A review of the literature on the German occupation regime in Lithuania makes clear that the background for the extension of the killing program to include Jewish women and children has rarely been investigated.[47] Aside from the later works of H.-H. Wilhelm,[48] there has been no more intensive reflection on the question because studies have proceeded from the assumption that a decision to kill *all* of the Jews in the Soviet Union had been taken before the war against the Soviets began. To be sure, Yitzhak Arad did describe the different phases of the anti-Jewish policy but merely conjectured that this was a product of a "technical" problem: the capability of the *Einsatzkommandos* to undertake a planned and graduated process.[49]

In order to trace the question of the radicalization of the anti-Jewish policy at this time in Lithuania, the developments of summer 1941 will now be examined in more detail, and above all from the perspective of the German decision-makers. What had changed for German decision-makers in the region and for those in Berlin? In pursuing this line of inquiry, it is necessary to contrast German expectations of the war with the Soviet Union and the actual progress on the ground. As a result of the unexpected turn in the war, two core areas of German occupation policy were now of the utmost importance: military security and the issue of supplies.

The overall objective of the German war plans was to encircle the main troop divisions of the Red Army in the first weeks of combat, in order that, according to the constantly-repeated formulation of Hitler, the "vital force of the enemy be annihilated."[50] The Commander-in-Chief of the Army, von Brauchitsch, envisaged the initial phase thus: "Presumably heavy battles at the borders, lasting up to four weeks. Subsequently there would only be a small amount of resistance left to be dealt with."[51] The Red Army would already be defeated before the German army reached the Dvina and Dniepr rivers, in the Baltic this meant a decisive conflict while still in Lithuania and west of Latvia.[52] Without considering any alternative whatsoever, every plan proceeded from the assumption "that they would in fact succeed in preventing the Red Army from escaping to the interior of the Soviet Union."[53] Army Group North, comprising twenty-eight divisions, was given the task of "preventing Russian forces capable of fighting from retreating from the Baltic to the east and creating conditions for further speedy advances in the direction of Leningrad."[54]

In the event, however, the military campaign did not develop as expected. Despite the speedy progress of Panzergruppe 4 and parts of the 18th and 16th Armies—Lithuania was fully under German occupation within five days—the main forces of the 8th and 11th Soviet Armies succeeded in pulling back behind the Dvina, partly in an unplanned retreat, partly on the order of their commanding officers. Although the 11th Soviet Army failed to establish lasting defensive positions either at the Dvina or in the area of Pskow and Ostrow, many of its divisions remained battleworthy, and in the Luga sector there was enough time for the Soviet troops to erect defensive lines.

This overturned the assumption underpinning German strategy that, after fierce battles at the beginning of the war behind the old borders of Russia, the path to Leningrad would essentially be free. Following similar developments in the area covered by the Germans' 16th and 18th Armies, the easy possession of the land which had been expected failed to materialize across the entire area covered by Army Group North. From mid-July 1941, it proved particularly difficult for Panzergruppe 4 and the 16th Army to stabilize their sectors at the front in the face of counterattacks from the Red Army.[55] On 26 July, the Chief of the General Staff, Halder, already foresaw the position over the entire frontline "ending in stable [entrenched] warfare," and two weeks later he declared, "What we are undertaking now are the last desperate attempts to prevent stable warfare setting in."[56] The "Blitzkrieg" had failed, since the main fighting forces of the Red Army in the north of the Soviet Union had not been defeated in the first weeks of the campaign.[57] The Germans' underestimation of the "Russian Colossus" became clear in the second half of July, the German attack having already failed to achieve its objective.[58]

However, the Soviet retreat and the German strategists' underestimation of the fighting power as well as the equipment of the Red Army were only one aspect of the impending collapse of the German military's tactical plans. Personnel and material requirements had not been calculated generously and supply and provisioning problems proved to be of major significance for the military situation of the German troops.

Starvation policy as a tool of war

Before the war against the Soviet Union a starvation policy of incredible proportions was planned against the Soviet population.[59] A central goal of the war against the Soviet Union was to tackle the economic constraints faced by Germany, in particular with respect to grain and oil, through the exploitation of Soviet resources. In order to attain this objective, it was decided with "approval from the highest level," that "many tens of millions" would have to be allowed to starve to death.[60] At the same time, the starvation policy was conceived of as a weapon of war. Within the shortest time, two-thirds of the entire German army was no longer to rely on the Reich for provisions, but—as it was put in the instructions of 23 May 1941, which laid the basis for the policy—they "had to be provisioned entirely from the East."[61]

In concrete terms, for the supply of Army Group North, in particular in relation to fuel and provisions, a supply base was to be constructed on the Lithuanian-Latvian border in Dvinsk (Daugavpils in Latvian), to replace delivery from the Reich with goods to be found in the occupied Baltic as quickly as possible. It was clear from the outset that east of the Dvina the supply operation would become more difficult.[62] In the event, however, Panzergruppe 4, racing ahead of the 16th and 18th Armies, faced far greater supply problems than expected. The distance which had grown between the Panzergruppe and the infantry armies behind it was enormous, the roads in an exceptionally poor condition and, on top of that, they were constantly overused. In this situation, the intervening areas were "not exploited economically"—as the Head of WiStab Ost, General Wilhelm Schubert, reported, "the population robbed energetically" and the Panzergruppe demanded "motorized economic guard troops," which could not be deployed.[63] From the outset, supply questions were seen as a problem of control and security and not only as a question of requisitioning, procuring, and transporting goods.[64] Already on 1 July, General Quartermaster Wagner noted that "The pacification of the hinterland is causing considerable trouble. The singularity of our military strategy has resulted in far-reaching insecurity in the hinterland, where there are isolated enemy detachments."[65] Moreover, both the infantry units of the 16th Army—which were to be supplied from Lithuania and parts of Latvia—and the units of the 18th Army in Estonia took to the field under conditions in which, as industrial detachments reported, the basic supply process was out of control. The orderly securing of goods to which the army had aspired was thus aggravated. The attempt to bypass the supply problems encountered on land by using supply ships in the Baltic also collapsed, since the German battle fleet had failed to capture the Baltic islands, which, still occupied by the Soviets, lay in the way.[66]

The supply and provisioning situation came further to the fore in mid-July together with the worsening military position on the front. On 17 and 18 July, the head of Panzergruppe 4, General Erich Hoepner, forcefully reproached those responsible for army supplies.[67] Hoepner's units often received only one train per day from the supply base at Dvinsk, instead of the planned ten trains. The whole of Army Group North, instead of receiving the thirty-four trains it claimed to need each day, only exceptionally received as much as eighteen trains per day. For the attack planned in the second half of July by Panzergruppe 4 on Leningrad the whole supply capacity of Army Group North would have had to be placed at their disposal, which would have brought the 16th and 18th armies to a complete standstill.[68] In the following weeks, the attack on Leningrad had to be postponed seven times solely because of supply problems.[69] At the same time the military position of the 16th and 18th armies was in a critical state.[70] On 23 July, Hitler had stressed that what interested him above all else was the attack on Leningrad, to which end "everything possible" should be dedicated.[71] However, General Quartermaster Wagner could not make the necessary supplies available to Panzergruppe 4.[72] For this reason in July 1941 it was already decided not to try to capture and destroy Leningrad and Moscow immediately, but instead to seal off and starve both cities.[73] Supply was not only increasingly endangered by transport conditions; in addition, the procurement of essential goods was already proving to be far more difficult than had been expected. The whole German war effort seemed to be threatened by this. At the end of July, a staff officer in the Economic Armaments Office (Wirtschafts-Rüstungs-Amt, WiRüAmt) summarized his view of the position in the areas covered by Economic Inspection Groups North and Center and outlined the limitations on troop movements caused by supply problems: "We have to be able to count on not finding any supplies in place. If the advance only goes this slowly, and with the ever-greater supply problems it will hardly be possible to go any faster, Russia will systematically burn everything down (viz. Minsk), as it has so masterfully accomplished in every campaign for hundreds of years."[74]

Supply difficulties in the area covered by Army Group North

The German organizations responsible for the supply of the Wehrmacht knew beforehand that the military's objectives rested essentially on whether they succeeded in securing the necessary supplies quickly enough. In the first days of the war, reports came from Lithuania that rich sources of basic provisions had been found. The picture changed very quickly however. The liaison officer with the General Quartermaster reported to the WiRüAmt: "On 27 June incoming reports corrected the previous picture. In Lithuania army stocks almost totally destroyed. Planned destruction of the remaining stocks prepared. Realization prevented by Lithuanian self-defense. For that reason, such large stocks as that in Kovno can generally not be counted on."[75] The various bodies dealing with procurement and transport were increasingly finding it difficult to procure the amounts of goods demanded of them and to transport them to the front.

The 16th Army, for instance, then constantly engaged in fighting with the Soviets, depended for its supplies on the Dvinsk supply center. As early as 17 July the Chief Quartermaster of Army Group North, Major Alfred Toppe, had arranged for this supply base to be established, "as far as possible using booty and supplies from the land," and to procure and secure resources in the area southwest of Dvinsk.[76] At the same time the first reports came in from the liaison officer of Wirtschaftsstab Ost at Army High Command 16 which appeared to affirm the supposition that east of Latvia and Lithuania a "famine, with all its consequences," had set in. The Russian officials had fled, German troops requisitioned supplies without being subject to any control, and the harvest was endangered. "The civilian population was threatened by the specter of starvation!"[77] The geographical spread of the famine was of course from the outset a calculated development. It was intended to facilitate the German war effort and not—as now in practice proved to be the case—to endanger it. German soldiers were often badly supplied, as a letter from the field of 23 July from the area near Dvinsk illustrates: "This war requires iron nerves and composure. That we are often short of provisions is only to be blamed on the bad rail and street connections. Often we are very tight with our provisions, but despite this we must endure. We must at this time last the whole day with half a loaf of bread. . . . How often I have longed for a proper meal, but unfortunately . . ."[78]

Hitler was informed by Halder of the great difficulties faced by the 16th Army.[79] Yet on 27 July, the whole of Panzergruppe 3 from Army Group Centre further south was also ordered to go to the supply base at Dünaburg for provisions, albeit not yet to support Army Group North militarily.[80] The Army Group leaders were clear that they were thus faced by "barely solvable problems" of supply.[81]

In mid-August the branch office responsible for the provisioning of Army Group North under General Quartermaster Wagner, Supply Region North (Versorgungsbezirk Nord), established that in the whole area covered by the 16th Army there was no more livestock left to be taken.[82] Reports came in that the farmers were already totally impoverished and lacked all provisions, even lacking nourishment for themselves.[83] From October all reports spoke of a catastrophic food situation northeast of the Baltic states.

In the wake of food shortages in the rural areas east of the Baltic frontiers, the food shortage came to a head particularly quickly in the Baltic cities. At the beginning of July, Kaunas had supplies of flour and meat for six weeks, and from Vilnius it was reported that remaining foodstuffs would last two weeks.[84] On 9 July, Wirtschaftsstab Ost reported to Wirtschaftsinspektion Nord in Kaunas that in order to secure the hinterland it would be necessary to feed the most needy of the native population. In pursuit of this aim, the "residues" of foodstuffs from the newly-established indigenous authorities were to be released.[85] Finally in Kaunas and Vilnius ration cards were given out, with the proviso that "the amount given out would not be fixed at the outset . . . but determined after each daily restocking."[86] Any right the inhabitants of the towns then held to specific quantities of provisions was to be disregarded. The stores that had been taken were low. Only 5,000 to 6,000 tons of grain were left in the depots from which the towns of Kaunas and Vilnius also had to be supplied.[87] In August and September, however, 6,500 tons were delivered to the Wehrmacht,[88] and the towns officially ran out.

Since the German troops, as predicted, were provisioned "off the land," the food situation in the Lithuanian towns next to the rural areas northeast of the borders was "extraordinarily difficult" at all times.[89]

Supply Region North made great efforts—in vain—to be informed of the extent of the "direct provisions taken for troops from the land," in order to be able to determine the magnitude of the provisions still needed.[90] In July 1941, the repeated strongly-worded instructions of Keitel and Wagner to the effect that the economic service centers should at least be kept informed of the involvement of German soldiers in obtaining provisions and livestock holdings, remained unheeded.[91] The quantity of consumers, on the other hand, was easier to record. In mid-July 1941, the Lithuanian administration responsible for the food industry in Kaunas arranged that by 1 September all mayors and regional directors count those of their inhabitants who did not grow their own food, meaning those "living in the villages and towns and not possessing a plot of land." This would help to determine "how many inhabitants needed to be provided with food centrally."[92] The German authorities eventually made their food provision budget on the basis of 803,000 inhabitants.[93]

At the end of July, the leadership of the Reich turned its attention to the economic problems faced in the war, since the "assumption that operations would be very quick could no longer be made."[94] The previous plans for the starvation policy and the economic exploitation of the occupied regions had to be modified.[95] On 22 July, Herbert Backe, State Secretary in the Reich Supply Ministry, gave a "Report on Provisions" to the main figure responsible for the war economy, Hermann Göring.[96] Göring then, on 27/28 July, summarily ordered that "agricultural products in the occupied regions of the East be centrally registered and be taken to the troops according to the advice given by German supply bases." Only those people "performing important tasks for Germany" were to receive provisions.[97]

From now on, in consequence, labor capability and potential decided who received provisions and who did not. The previous geographical division of the occupied lands into "contributory zones," condemned "to die off," and "surplus zones," which would become "production areas," was modified.[98] Those people from whom no more work in the service of German war industry could be expected were exposed to a merciless starvation policy.

Likewise on 28 July 1941, Wagner and the chief quartermasters of the three army groups decided to refill the holdings of the supply bases by 15 August. After 15 August, they were even to begin stockpiling.[99] Eventually on 12 August, two weeks later, Wagner laid down the requisitioning targets, the delivery quantities for each quarter of the year, to be made available from 1 September 1941, to 31 August 1942 under the jurisdiction of Supply Region North.[100] These targets were very high and amounted to 250,000 tonnes annually in grain for bread alone.[101] From that, at least 120,000 tonnes were to be supplied from Lithuania.[102] This amount was the equivalent of some 15 percent of the expected Lithuanian harvest of 800,000 tonnes of wheat and rye.[103] The economic departments of the German occupation authorities made the Lithuanian administration responsible for compliance with the delivery demands and for allocating individual districts with specific requisitioning demands. Nevertheless, these orders, too, proved far too difficult to fulfill.[104]

The German civil occupation administration was clear that this would aggravate the food problem for the population in the Baltic. The food and agriculture department of the Reichskommissariat pointed out that Göring "decided ... that the Wehrmacht takes absolute precedence as a consumer ... over the indigenous civilian population. The deficit in meeting the procurement needs of the Wehrmacht, which you know full well, will thus be fulfilled under all circumstances, in an emergency at the expense of the native civilian population."[105] On 31 July, a meeting was recorded in the records of the body with overall responsibility for economic policy in the occupied Soviet Union, Wirtschaftsführungsstab Ost: "Backe asked about the possibility of sending a letter from the Reich Marshal [Göring] to the places concerned. Körner informed the meeting that the clear instructions of the Reich Marshal were that the interests of the food industry of Greater Germany clearly were to take priority in all supply questions in the newly-occupied area."[106] In the same conversation, Backe and Hans Joachim Riecke, leader of Chefgruppe Landwirtschaft (agricultural economics) in WiStab Ost and at the same time the division leader for food and agriculture in the Ministry for the East, stressed that the civil administration also had "from now on to begin to supply the population with [only] the smallest rations." The delivery of food supplies was thereby directly connected to basic questions of not only a medium-term production increase, but also a fear of growing resistance in the territories which had been plundered.

The supply of provisions for Jews

The German occupation authorities in Lithuania sought from the outset to set up a racist hierarchy for the supply of food, which at the end of July 1941 was again intensified on the instructions of the leadership of the Reich. This hit the Jews on the one hand, where they did not appear useful to the Germans as skilled workers, and on the other the Soviet prisoners-of-war. Over 200,000 prisoners-of-war died in Lithuanian camps under the supervision of the Wehrmacht during the first six months of German occupation.

In the first half of July the military administration had already arranged food rationing for the whole of Lithuania. This established a distinction between Jews and non-Jews. The non-Jewish population was supposed to get the parsimonious amount of 1750 grams of bread, 200 grams of flour, 150 grams of grits, 400 grams of meat, 125 grams of lard and 125 grams of sugar per week. The Jewish population by contrast received practically nothing. For them, the allotted amounts each week totaled only 875 grams of bread, 100 grams of flour and 75 grams of grits.[107] Jewish quarters were cut off from the stocks of the town administration and from the kitchens of large factories.[108] When quotas were fixed for the stocks and coupons introduced on 12 July, Jews could only buy at specific times and from special shops, "in order to shorten queues."[109] In the registration of the population for their nutritional allowance, "persons of Jewish origin ... were to be registered separately."[110] On 5 August, the *Deutsche Zeitung im Ostland* (the German Newspaper in the East) summed up the most important orders of the civilian authorities under the heading "The new norms in this industrial area": "Goods must only be handed out to Jews if adequate stocks exist to meet the needs of other inhabitants."

In contrast to the starvation rations in the more easily-controlled prisoner-of-war camps, the draconian food rationing for the Jewish population could not be enforced in this way: insufficient personnel meant they could not control the procedure. The instructions nevertheless document the intention of the German regional occupation authorities to reduce the problems of supplying provisions at the cost of the Jewish population and rapidly to force this population into profound misery. The connection between National Socialist provisions policy and anti-Jewish measures did not only affect Lithuania. On 28 July, Göring instructed that the policy be applied by the entire German occupation administration in the Soviet Union. Moreover, in reply to a query from WiStab Ost he added "that the Jews in the areas administered by Germany had no business to be there any longer. Where they have to be put to work, this must take place in the form of work units. ... Provisions must be particularly regulated and overseen."[111] With these words the overall guidelines of the anti-Jewish policy of the Reich leadership at this time were formulated.

The civil administration established in Lithuania at the end of July was given the task of translating this policy into action, together with the SS and police authorities. The Reichskommissar for the East (*Reichskommissar für das Ostland*, RKO), Hinrich Lohse, spoke briefly afterwards, noting that "the decision of the Führer ... [was that the] Germanization of Reichskommissariat Ost should be the ultimate goal" and that the Jews should be "completely removed from this area."[112] However, what was really meant by the guidelines given by Hitler and Göring—that the Jews be "completely removed from this area," and that the Jews had "no more business to remain in areas occupied by Germany"—was still unclear. In the course of the discussion between the Security Police and the civilian administration in the next week-and-a-half over the "Provisional Guidelines on the Jewish Question in Reichskommissariat Ostland" issued on 13 August, a number of contradictory interventions were made on the subject. What is clear however is that a revision of the previous plans was under discussion. On 6 August, the head of Einsatzgruppe A, Stahlecker, observed in the margin of a letter giving his view of the draft guidelines for the civilian administration: "The draft foresees resettlement from the open country into the towns. If, now, resettlement is to be tackled, this must take place in a fundamental sense, as follows."[113] Stahlecker then outlined, evidently on the basis of previous plans, his conception of "areas reserved for Jews" into which the Jews could be "pumped" so that they could be "profitably used for work" there. Stahlecker's formulation with the emphatic "now" made clear that the Security Police were also having to change their plans with respect to the Jewish population as a whole. The "resettlement" had clearly been planned for later, probably after a speedy victory. This victory was retreating, however, farther and farther into the distance.

What were the results of the discussion between the civilian administration and Einsatzgruppe A? It is possible to reconstruct the decision-making process, in part from eyewitness statements from the postwar trials (which were sometimes very detailed), and partly from examining the policy as it actually developed at the time.

After the end of July 1941, the position of the Jews of Lithuania became more and more difficult. Those Jews who lived on the land were mostly isolated outside populated areas, in synagogues, barracks, barns and abandoned farms. Many thousands of men had already been arrested or murdered. Since women, children, and older men were basically forbidden to leave these improvised camps, they suffered from hunger and disease spread easily. A number of the women were put to work. The Lithuanian police and administration were responsible for guarding them and supplying provisions.

On both the local level and the level of regional commissariats, the worsening supply situation was now discussed *ad infinitum*. At this stage, as many witnesses recalled, it was already clear that with respect to the nutritional wants of Jewish women and children no further allocations were to be made. They were rather to be killed.[114] Thus a Gestapo official from Memel explained in the course of these discussions that Jewish women and children in any case did not work and, as useless consumers of food, had therefore to be done away with.[115] In response, the Lithuanian administration had refused to give food coupons to Jews. In July 1941, the mayor of Kretinga complained to the SD that he did not know how the Jews should be fed.[116] The Lithuanian mayor installed by the Germans in Gargždai pressed for foodstuffs to be provided for the Jewish women and children in Kretinga, the county seat. The German administration explained, however, that the Jews were "useless eaters" and instructions were for them to be killed.[117] The Regional Commissar of Šiauliai, Hans Gewecke, instructed the Lithuanian district president and mayors that they should have the Jewish women and children shot by Lithuanian police, overseen by Germans.[118]

All in all, the witness statements are largely in agreement; by contrast, the surviving records from the civilian administration only give a few signs of this, and these moreover require careful scrutiny. On 13 August, the order was issued for the ghettoization of all Jews in the Šiauliai regional commissariat within the next fourteen days: the rural Jews were to be concentrated in county towns and were to be supplied with provisions from the Lithuanian town administrations.[119] Because of the state of the sources, this must leave open the question of whether or not the statements of the leader of the Tilsit state police station, Böhme, made in connection with a massacre of over 500 Jewish women and children in Batakiai, are true. At the trial, he maintained that SS-Hauptsturm-führer Hans Merten, the town commissar charged with overseeing provisions for Taurage (Tauroggen), had said of these killings that a "definitive solution" of this kind followed from the civilian administration's guidelines of 13 August on the "Jewish Question," according to which the Jews "were to be ghettoized and at the same time subjected to a limitation of their food provisions."[120]

On 3 September 1941, the first clear reference found in the sources thus far was made to the effect that the German Security Police in an area in Lithuania had now been instructed "to liquidate all Jews."[121] Since the discussion between the civilian administration and the Security Police turned solely on the question of Jewish workers and their families, an agreement must have already taken place in the course of August that the remaining Jewish population be killed. The provisional guidelines "for the handling of the Jews in the area of Reich Commissariat East" of 13 August give some information about this arrangement: "The open country is to be cleared of Jews."[122] This took place in the next three months. The inclusion of Jewish women and children in the killings was not a subject of controversy between the civilian authorities and the SS, in contrast to the question of Jewish workers, as the events of the following weeks and months showed.

The killing of the Jewish women and children of Lithuania began on 15 August in the rural regions of northeast and north Lithuania and was then pursued in and around Kaunas. Of the over 90,000 Jews killed up to the middle of October 1941, over 40,000 had lived in the northern Siauliai regional commissariat and over 30,000 in the region of Kaunas.[123] On the basis of the witness statements above, largely in agreement on this point, it is clear that provisions problems in Lithuania and in the region of Army Group North in general constituted an important, and possibly a decisive, factor in the decision to kill, instead of feeding, "useless" Jewish women and children.

Results

This examination of anti-Jewish policy in the Baltic has shown that first the military and six weeks later the civilian occupation apparatus in this region came under massive and increasing pressure to act. The unexpectedly difficult position for the armies in the regions at the front, east of the borders of the Baltic, impacted in particular in two respects on the area which was now the *"hinterland* of the front." On the one hand, more and more goods from the occupied countries had to be requisitioned solely for supply and in the face of logistical transport difficulties be quickly placed at the disposition of the German troops. On the other hand, as the decision-makers saw it, supply and transport problems were inescapably tied to questions of security. The order from Wirtschaftsstab Ost of the beginning of July noted above, to feed only the most needy of the indigenous population, was motivated by the need to "secure the hinterland." In addition to this, the transports were not to be exposed to attacks, a risk which appeared to be a potent one because of the relatively thin security forces of the German occupation regime. Both of these problem areas—the procurement of foodstuffs and the securing of the "hinterland of the front"—appeared to the National Socialists to be resolvable through a more radical policy with respect to the Jewish population. In January 1942, Einsatzkommando 3 correspondingly recounted the murderous deeds of the so-called Hamann Kommando, responsible for the killing of some 60,000 Jews: "In the course of the work of this commando, which covered the whole of Lithuania, it was seen that it would not be possible to stabilize the sectors lying to the rear of the front through the liquidation of a few Jews."[124]

The killing of the Jews could be rationalized according to supposedly real constraints. A higher amount of foodstuffs was left for the remaining population and, most important of all, for German soldiers. At the same time it was said that this would improve the security position. The prospect envisaged before the war that the whole Jewish population would be deported "to the East" presupposed a victory over the Soviet Union and appeared for the time being to be unrealizable.

Facing a war which was claiming many victims, the National Socialist occupation authorities now confronted the question of whether foodstuffs should be placed at the disposition of the Jewish population isolated at the rural margins or go rather to the soldiers fighting at the front. The Lithuanian administration was made formally responsible for the provision of food to Jews in the country and in the ghettos, but the Lithuanian administration depended on the apportioning of foodstuffs under German control. The German administration was, however, unable to make deliveries to the soldiers of its armies and tank divisions without falling back on the Reich for supplies. Its instructions nevertheless read otherwise, and within weeks they became more and more urgent: the administration had to substitute increasing quantities of supplies from the Reich with supplies from the occupied territories. In addition, they faced the instructions issued by Wagner that from 15 August they were to begin to increase the stocks in the supply bases and shortly thereafter achieve very high quarter-yearly deliveries of bread, grain, meat, etc., to the armies. In this context, Göring's order to feed only those working for the German war industry clearly implied that the Jewish section of the population was to be denied the right to live. It was left to the regional occupation administration to determine how exactly the decrees of Hitler and Göring were translated into action.

In reconstructing the perspective of the German decision-makers in Lithuania during this period, it becomes evident that after mid-July 1941 their position appeared to come to a head in unexpected and—in terms of their objectives—threatening ways. The administration was soon placed under increasing time pressure and faced with increasing demands for greater supplies. In this situation the immediate killing of the Jews of Lithuania increasingly appeared from their antisemitic viewpoint to be a real option. The personnel for carrying out such a killing campaign was available thanks to the radical representatives of the German Security Police in the Baltic and Lithuanian policemen who were prepared to collaborate. This was even more true after the SS had widened its network of support bases and personnel in Lithuania at the beginning of August. Himmler had visited Kaunas on 29 July, and on 2 August ordered the SS posts to expand.[125] The Lithuanian police units were assimilated into the constabulary under the SS and police station chiefs,[126] who for their part were placed under the SS leaders, the heads of the police force, and the General Commissar for "police security."[127]

The regional occupation authorities, however, needed the authorization of the Reich leadership for the systematic murder of the Lithuanian Jews. This was a question of systematic mass murder on a scale which ultimately only Hitler could have authorized. Like the German authorities in Lithuania, the Reich leadership also saw that their objectives were increasingly sliding into the distance and that the time available for the campaign was running short. Before the war against the Soviet Union began, Hitler had stressed that it was essential that there be no delays.[128] In July 1941, Hitler therefore asked for an up-to-date timetable: "How much time do I still have before I have to be finished with Russia, and how much time do I still need?"[129] Canaris wrote of the situation in Hitler's headquarters "that the atmosphere there was very nervous, since the Russian campaign—as is increasingly the case—is not drawing to a close 'according to the rules of the game.' The signs are increasingly clear that the war has not led to the internal collapse we expected, but rather to a strenghthening of Bolshevism."[130]

The delays caused by the unexpectedly poor military progress of the war effort not only raised a question mark over the implementation of previous strategic planning: it also affected "Hitler's entire program."[131] The "serious crisis"[132] evident from mid-July to mid-August 1941 endangered the cornerstone of National Socialist war diplomacy, the hope of dragging England onto the German side through control of the European continent, and above all else the aspiration to stop the United States from entering the war. Indeed, exactly the opposite began to appear likely. Instead of a "lightning victory" over the Soviet Union, a long drawn-out war of attrition was emerging,[133] which would moreover in all likelihood have to be conducted against an alliance of states which would gradually cooperate more closely and which also had a greater military potential.

The exact date of the eventual conversation between the Reich leadership and the regional occupation authorities in the Baltic about the killing of the Jews in this part of the occupied Soviet Union has thus far not been pinned down. The leaders of the bodies responsible for the civil administration, the economy, the Security Police, and the Wehrmacht had many opportunities to make arrangements orally at the end of July or in early August.[134] The result of these conversations has already been shown above: Lohse spoke on August 1 of the "decision of the Führer" that the Jews be "completely removed from this area."[135] Two weeks later it finally became clear that there was no longer a question of deporting the Lithuanian Jews "to the East," but rather that they were to be exterminated by the German occupation authorities with Lithuanian assistance. On 15/16 August 1941, German and Lithuanian units killed 3,200 Jewish men, women and children in Rokiškis near Dvinsk, which fell within the regional commissariat of Šiauliai under Hans Gewecke, a close friend of Hinrich Lohse.[136] With respect to the date, it is probable that the note by Goebbels on a meeting with Hitler on 19 August also related to the killing campaign against the Lithuanian Jews which had now been embarked upon on a large scale: "We also spoke about the Jewish problem. The Führer is of the conviction that his earlier prophecy in the Reichstag—that if the Jews succeeded in provoking a world war once again, it would end with the extermination of the Jews—was coming true. In these weeks and months it has proven accurate with an almost uncanny certainty. In the East the Jews have to pay the price; in Germany they had in part already paid and they would in the future have to pay still more."[137]

This examination of the situation in the north of the occupied Soviet Union in summer 1941 lays bare a multitude of factors in the political process which contributed to the speed with which the Lithuanian Jews were killed. Already before the war the National Socialist leadership had planned that all of the Jews would, as soon as possible, be completely "transferred" out of the Reich Commissariat of the Eastern Territories. The plans also implied the very rapid and thorough pauperization of the Jewish population: the supposed "Jewish-Bolshevik intelligence" had to be destroyed immediately. National Socialist security policy was the most important element in this calculation. Nevertheless, it was not foreseen at this early date that the decision to kill all of the Jews would be taken during the war.

The fundamental historical context in which the racist and economic-ally-motivated plans to exploit and expel the Jews developed into the sudden murder of the majority of the Jewish population was primarily the unexpectedly unfavorable course taken by the war. There can be no doubt that the Germans' anti-Jewish policy had already escalated before the war against the Soviet Union to such an extent that the killing of the Jews had moved into the realm of the possible. The intent to exterminate the Jews was clear from the plans for deportations. The analysis of the policy as it actually developed makes it seem possible that further factors were also necessary. The modification of the racist starvation policy targeted at large parts of the Soviet population in Lithuania meant first and foremost the pauperization of the Jewish population, which was to be denied the right to live. The mass killings were in this connection legitimized on the grounds of National Socialist security policy, which saw in the Jewish population per se a threat to the "stabilization of the rearwards sections of the front." Food and security policy appear thereby to have been the two crucial aspects which led to a radicalization of anti-Jewish policy and made the decisive changes and transitions possible.[138]

With regard specifically to Lithuania, the sudden murder of a large part of Lithuanian Jewry while the war was still underway appeared to the National Socialist decision-makers in the occupation administration to be a means of reducing a threatening and unexpectedly difficult situation, first and foremost with respect to the German war industry, and at the same time as a way of minimizing security and policing concerns. With respect to the increasing time pressures and the rapidly-intensifying pressures to take action it was decided that "the Jews have to pay the price." In the antisemitic perception of National Socialist decision-makers this could even be portrayed as a legitimate "emergency defense" against the Jews, alleged to be the "mortal enemies" of the German people.[139]

It seems to me for these reasons to be questionable to claim that the basic frame of mind in which these decisions arose was chiefly a product of the intoxication with victory of the National Socialist leadership, rather than of more pragmatic considerations.[140] Perhaps it would be better to say that the successful radicalization of the policy was a product of the situation in which decision-makers were allegedly facing extremely threatening shortages and constantly increasing time pressures. These problems were then to be overcome by virtue of National Socialist "pragmatism," meaning with politically-motivated violence, the terror of a "racial deterrence policy," and targeted killing campaigns motivated by the argument that some must die so that others can live or fight better.

285

Notes

1 Incident reports, USSR (Ereignismeldungen UdSSR, abbreviated EM below) No. 26, 18 July 1941, Bundesarchiv (BA) R 58/214.

2 Eberhard Jäckel, "Die Entschlußbildung als historisches Problem," in Eberhard Jäckel and Jürgen Rohwer (eds.), *Der Mord an den Juden im Zweiten Weltkrieg: Entschlußbildung und Verwirklichung* (Frankfurt a.M., 1987), pp. 9–17, here pp. 16f.

3 Helmut Krausnick, "Hitler und die Befehle an die Einsatzgruppen," in Jäckel and Rohwer, *Mord*, pp. 88–106, here p. 99.

4 An overview of the killing of the Lithuanian Jews is given by Yitzhak Arad, "The 'Final Solution' in Lithuania in the Light of German Documentation," in *Yad Vashem Studies* 11 (1976): 234–272. The figures given for Jewish victims and survivors are both minimum numbers. Exact statistics are not likely to be found. The figure given by Dina Porat of 175,000 Lithuanian Jews killed by the end of 1941 is probably somewhat too high. Dina Porat, "The Holocaust in Lithuania. Some unique aspects," in David Cesarani (ed.), *The Final Solution: Origins and implementation* (London/New York, 1994), pp. 159–174, here p. 161.

5 Andreas Hillgruber, "Die 'Endlösung' und das deutsche Ostimperium als Kernstück des rassenideologischen Programms des Nationalsozialismus," in *VfZ* 20 (1972): 133–153. Compare Gerd R. Ueberschär, "Der Mord an den Juden und der Ostkrieg. Zum Forschungsstand über den Holocaust," in Heiner Lichtenstein and Otto R. Romberg (eds.), *Täter—Opfer—Folgen: Der Holocaust in Geschichte und Gegenwart* (Bonn, 1995), pp. 49–81.

6 See Philippe Burrin, *Hitler und die Juden: Die Entscheidung für den Völkermord* (Frankfurt a.M., 1993), p. 172, and Arno J. Mayer, *Krieg als Kreuzzug: Das Deutsche Reich, Hitlers Wehrmacht und die "Endlösung"* (Reinbek, 1989), p. 660.

7 Proceedings of the State Court of Ulm against Bernhard Fischer-Schweder and others, Staatsarchiv Ludwigsburg EL 322, Vol. 8, p. 1955. Testimony given on 30 January 1957, by the company commander of the 3rd/I.R. 176.

8 Statement of one inhabitant from Gargždai, Feliksas S. Ibid., Vol. 8, pp. 2095–2097.

9 Walther Hubatsch, *Die 61. Infantrie-Division 1939–1945. Ein Bericht in Wort und Bild* (Friedberg, 1983), p. 18.

10 Bill of indictment against Fischer-Schweder and others, ibid., Vol. 13, p. 3374. Rabbi Meir Levin and a Jewish doctor, Dr. Uksmann, who had been the district doctor under the Soviets, were cruelly mistreated and murdered. See Dov Levin (ed.), *Pinkas HaKehillot, Lita* (Book of the Communities) (Jerusalem, 1996), p. 190.

11 Decree of Hitler of 13 May 1941 about the exercise of martial law in the "Barbarossa" region and giving particular measures taken by the troops. Printed in *Anatomie des SS-Staates*, Vol. 2 (Munich, 1989), pp. 182f.

12 Covering letter of 24 May 1941 from Brauchitsch for the martial law decree of 13 May 1941. Printed in ibid., Vol. 2, pp. 185f.

13 See EM No. 2, 23 June 1941. BA R 58/214.

14 Registered letter from the Tilsit state police station of 1 July 1941 to the Reichssicherheitshauptamt (RSHA) IV A 1. Re: Cleansing campaigns on the other side of the former Soviet-Lithuanian border. Zentrale Stelle der Landesjustizverwaltungen zur Aufklärung von NS-Verbrechen in Ludwigsburg (ZStL), Sammlung UdSSR, File 245 Ag No. 254–257, pp. 2–5.

15 Only Rachel Jamai survived this massacre. See Pinkas HaKehillot, p. 190.

16 "A decision was taken not to renew the action since only Jewish women and children remained in Krottingen." Registered letter from the Tilsit state police station to the RSHA of 1 July 1941, see n. 14.

17 ZStL 207 AR-Z 72/60, Proceedings against H.-H. St. In these proceedings there are explicit descriptions of the murders, committed by Luftwaffe members. The degree of the participation of Wehrmacht units in the shootings at Kretinga is still not easy to clarify.

18 See also Jürgen Matthäus, "Jenseits der Grenze. Die ersten Massenerschießungen von Juden in Litauen (June–August 1941)," in *ZfG* 44 (1996): 101–117. Matthäus has not considered the role of the Wehrmacht correctly, since he had not seen the trial records in the Ludwigsburg State Archive and the appropriate evidence did not appear in the bill of indictment or in the text of the judgement.

19 Einsatzbefehl No. 6 from Heydrich to the heads of the *Einsatzgruppen*, 4 July 1941. Sonderarchiv Moskau 500–5–3, p. 48.

20 See Alfred Streim, "Zur Eröffnung des allgemeinen Judenvernichtungsbefehls," in Jäckel and Rohwer, *Mord*, pp. 107–119, here p. 111.

21 Letter from the "Self-Defense Leader" of the Alytus region, the chair of the executive committee of the regional authorities, and the regional police chief, to the German commanders of the town in Alytus, 30 June 1941, Lietuvos Centrinis Valstybes Archyvas (LCVA) (Central State Archive of Lithuania) R 1436–1–29, Bl. 12f.

22 Judgment of 28 August 1958, against Fischer-Schweder and others. Printed in C.R. Rüter and Adelheid L. Rüter-Ehlermann (eds.), *Justiz und NS-Verbrechen, Sammlung deutscher Strafurteile wegen nationalsozialistischer Tötungsverbrechen 1945–1966* (Amsterdam, 1976), Vol. 15, p. 201.

23 Circular letter from Hamann to Reivytis, 15 August 1941. LCVA R 693–2–2, Bl. 2.

24 Telegram from WiStab Ost to Verteiler B of 15 July 1941, Re: Employment of Jewish skilled workers, Latvijas Valsts Arhivs (Staatsarchiv Lettlands) (LVA) P 70–2–52, Bl. 202.

25 ZStL 207 AR-Z 51/58. Proceedings against A. Krumbach and others. Interrogation of A. Krumbach on 7 October 1958, Vol. 1, pp. 86–87.

26 Peter Longerich, "Vom Massenmord zur 'Endlösung'. Die Erschießungen von jüdischen Zivilisten in den ersten Monaten des Ostfeldzuges im Kontext des nationalsozialistischen Judenmords," in Bernd Wegner (ed.), *Zwei Wege nach Moskau: Vom Hitler-Stalin-Pakt zum "Unternehmen Barbarossa"* (Munich, 1991), pp. 251–274, here p. 267.

27 Ibid., p. 269.

28 Entry for 3 March 1941, Percy E. Schramm (ed.), *Kriegstagebuch des Oberkommandos der Wehrmacht (KTB OKW)* (Munich, 1982), Vol. 1, p. 341.

29 See Uwe Adam, *Judenpolitik im Dritten Reich* (Düsseldorf, 1972), p. 305.

30 Werner Präg and Wolfgang Jacobmeyer (eds.), *Das Diensttagebuch des deutschen Generalgouverneurs in Polen 1939–1945* (Stuttgart, 1975), pp. 211f.

31 Nuremberg document PS 1020. Memorandum No. 3. Re: UdSSR, p. 7f. Italics in original.

32 Ibid., pp. 6f.

33 Discussion notes made by Tippelskirch OKW/WFSt/Abt. L (IV/Qu) of 12 May 1941. Published in *Anatomie des SS-Staates*, Vol. 2, pp. 179f.

34 Directions for the treatment of political commissars from the OKW, 6 June 1941. Printed in *Anatomie des SS-Staates*, Vol. 2, pp. 188–191.

35 Thus Wagner on 15/16 May 1941, in a speech to Security Division 285, which

was later active in the Baltic. Cited by Ralf Ogorreck, *Die Einsatzgruppen und die "Genesis der Endlösung"* (Berlin, 1996), p. 42.

36 Statements on 6 June 1941, by Nockemann, the leader of RHSA Amt II, made in a conversation with General Quartermaster Wagner, representives from the Security Police, army officers and the counter-espionage department of the OKW. Cited by Ralf Ogorreck, "Die Einsatzgruppen der Sicherheitspolizei und des SD im Rahmen der 'Genesis der Endlösung'. Ein Beitrag zur Entschlußbildung der 'Endlösung der Judenfrage' im Jahre 1941," unpublished Ph.D. dissertation (FU Berlin, 1992), p. 42. The published version of Ogorreck's dissertation mentioned in n. 35 unfortunately omits 51 pages of the dissertation (pp. 36–87), which describe and analyze in the most thorough way to date the history of the genesis of the instructions which were later considered to have been criminal acts.

37 This is the formulation in EM No. 43 of 5 August 1941. BA R 58/214. Heydrich's letter of 2 July 1941, is published in Peter Longerich (ed.), *Die Ermordung der europäischen Juden* (Munich, 1989), pp. 116–118.

38 See Ulrich Herbert, *Best: Biographische Studien über Radikalismus, Weltanschauung und Vernunft, 1909–1989* (Bonn, 1996), pp. 163–180 and pp. 237–245.

39 See EM No. 32 of 24 July 1941. BA R 58/214.

40 EM No. 9 of 1 July 1941. BA R 58/214.

41 EM No. 10 of 2 July 1941. BA R 58/214.

42 Heydrich discussed this (orally) on 17 June, recalling it once again on 29 June and drawing up instructions for it in writing on 2 July 1941. Longerich, *Ermordung*, pp. 116–119.

43 See the full report of Einsatzgruppe A of 15 October 1941. There it appears as: "It was however not undesirable that they, [the German Security Police] at least initially, did not give the appearance of using the clearly unusually harsh measures, which would certainly elicit a stir in German circles. It must be shown to the outside world that the native population itself took the first measures, of its own accord, in a natural reaction against centuries of oppression by the Jews and the terror of the Communists in former times." Sonderarchiv Moskau, 500–4–93.

44 See Ulrich Herbert, "Von der 'Reichskristallnacht' zum 'Holocaust'. Der 9. November und das Ende des 'Radauantisemitismus'," in idem., *Arbeit, Volkstum, Weltanschauung: Über Fremde und Deutsché im 20. Jahrhundert* (Frankfurt a.M., 1995), pp. 59–79.

45 See Götz Aly, *"Endlösung": Völkerverschiebung und der Mord an den europäischen Juden* (Frankfurt a.M., 1995), pp. 268–279; Burrin, *Hitler und die Juden*, pp. 114–116; Hans Safrian, *Die Eichmann-Männer* (Vienna/Zurich, 1993), p. 169.

46 Aly, *"Endlösung,"* p. 319. Already at the end of March 1941, a plan put forward by Heydrich to Göring for the "Solution of the Jewish Question" faced jurisdictional questions from the future Ostministerium (Ministry for the East); memorandum of 26 March 1941, from Heydrich after meeting with Göring. Sonderarchiv Moskau, 500–3–795, Bl. 145. Until the end of September, Adolf Eichmann thought of the "occupied Soviet Russian territories" as a "territory for the establishment of clearance contingents"; see Aly, *"Endlösung,"* pp. 268–279. In October 1941, General Governor Hans Frank finally asked Alfred Rosenberg whether the Polish Jews could not now be deported to the occupied Soviet Union, since Hitler had already authorized Frank to make a general deportation of the Polish Jews in the second half of March

and once more on 19 June 1941; memorandum of 14 October 1941, on the visit of Rosenberg to Frank of 13 October 1941. Diensttagebuch, p. 412; see Aly, *"Endlösung,"* pp. 334–336, 338, and 351f.

47 Seppo Myllyniemi, *Die Neuordnung der Baltischen Länder, 1941–1944: Zum nationalsozialistischen Inhalt der deutschen Besatzungspolitik* (Helsinki, 1973); Roswitha Czollek, *Faschismus und Okkupation: Wirtschaftspolitische Zielsetzung und Praxis des faschistischen deutschen Besatzungsregimes in den baltischen Sowjetrepubliken* (Berlin, 1974); Hans-Heinrich Wilhelm, *Die Einsatzgruppe A der Sicherheitspolizei und des SD 1941/42* (Frankfurt, 1996); Knut Stang, *Kollaboration und Massenmord: Die litauische Hilfspolizei, das Rollkommando Hamann und die Ermordung der litauischen Juden* (Frankfurt et al., 1996); Juozas Bulavas, *Vokiškuju Fasistu Okupacinis Lietuvos Valdymas 1941–1944* (German Fascist Occupation Rule in Lithuania) (Vilnius, 1969); Kazys Rukšenas, *Hitlerininku Politika Lietuvoje 1941–1944 Metais* (Hitlerite policy in Lithuania in the years 1941–1944) (Vilnius, 1970); Yitzhak Arad, *Ghetto in Flames: The Struggle and Destruction of the Jews in Vilna in the Holocaust* (Jerusalem, 1980); Dov Levin (ed.), *Pinkas HaKehillot: Lita* (Jerusalem, 1996).

48 Hans-Heinrich Wilhelm, "Offene Fragen der Holocaust-Forschung: Das Beispiel des Baltikums," in Uwe Backes et al. (eds.), *Die Schatten der Vergangenheit: Impulse zur Historisierung des Nationalsozialismus* (Frankfurt a.M., 1992), pp. 403–425.

49 "The rate of extermination [was] dictated by the physical capability of the murder squads." Arad, *Final Solution*, p. 239.

50 As Hitler for instance put it on 23 July 1941, KTB OKW, Vol. 1, p. 1030; on 18 August 1941, KTB OKW, Vol. 1, p. 1054; on 22 August 1941, KTB OKW, Vol. 1, p. 1063ff. Hitler's formulation should be understood in military terms and refers to the destruction of the military potential of the Soviet Union with respect to human and material resources.

51 Note by von Brauchitsch of 1 May 1941, in conversation with Chef L on 30 April 1941, PS 873. International Military Court, Nuremberg, *Der Nürnberger Prozeß gegen die Hauptkriegsverbrecher vom 14. November 1945–1. Oktober 1946: Urkunden und anderes Beweismaterial*, Vol. 26, pp. 399–401; Andreas Hillgruber, *Hitlers Strategie: "Politik und Kriegführung 1940–1941"* (Bonn, 1993), p. 508.

52 Rolf-Dieter Müller, "Das Scheitern der wirtschaftlichen 'Blitzkriegsstrategie'," in Horst Boog et al. (eds.), *Der Angriff auf die Sowjetunion, Aktualisierte Ausgabe von Das Deutsche Reich und der Zweite Weltkrieg*, Vol. 4 (Frankfurt, 1991), pp. 1116–1227, here p. 1138.

53 Klaus Reinhardt, *Die Wende vor Moskau: Das Scheitern der Strategie Hitlers im Winter 1941/42* (Stuttgart, 1972), p. 35.

54 Deployment instructions of the OKH for "Barbarossa," 31 January 1941, Colonel-General Halder; *Kriegstagebuch: Tägliche Aufzeichnungen des Chefs des Generalstabes des Heeres 1939–1942*, Vols. 2 and 3, Stuttgart 1963/1964 (KTB Halder). Here Vol. 2, Appendix 2, p. 464.

55 See KTB Halder, Vol. 3, 17 July 1941, p. 88; KTB OKW, Vol. 1, p. 1029, and Hitler's "Ergänzungen zur Weisung Nr. 33" of 23 July 1941, in Walther Hubatsch (ed.), *Hitlers Weisungen für die Kriegführung* (Munich, 1965), pp. 166–168.

56 Entries for 26 July 1941 and 8 August 1941. KTB Halder, Vol. 3, pp. 121 and 170.

57 Moreover, Army Group South did not succeed either, and the initial

successes of Army Group Center were put in question in the battle around Smolensk which dragged on from mid-July 1941. See Reinhardt, *Wende*, pp. 28–35.

58 Müller, *Scheitern*, p. 1167; Gerhard L. Weinberg, *A World at Arms: a global history of World War Two* (Cambridge, 1994), p. 269. Weinberg was referring to the first weeks of August, by which time this failure was clear.

59 Götz Aly and Susanne Heim, *Vordenker der Vernichtung: Auschwitz und die deutschen Pläne für eine neue europäische Ordnung* (Hamburg, 1991). See esp. the chapter "Der Krieg gegen die Sowjetunion und die Vernichtung von 'zig Millionen' Menschen," pp. 365–393. See the contribution by Christian Gerlach in this volume.

60 Industrial policy guidelines of 23 May 1941, for Wirtschaftsorganisation Ost, Gruppe Landwirtschaft. *IMG*, Vol. 36, pp. 135–157, citing pp. 140 and 145.

61 Ibid., p. 148.

62 See Walter Chales de Beaulieu, *Der Vorstoß der Panzergruppe 4 auf Leningrad 1941* (Neckargemünd, 1961), pp. 21f.

63 Weekly report WiStab Ost 6–12 July 1941. Bundesarchiv-Militärarchiv Freiburg (BA-MA) RW 31/11.

64 The basic text on logistical questions relating to supplies is Klaus A. Schüler, *Logistik im Rußlandfeldzug: Die Rolle der Eisenbahn bei Planung, Vorbereitung und Durchführung des deutschen Angriffes auf die Sowjetunion bis zur Krise vor Moskau im Winter 1941/1942* (Frankfurt, a.M., 1987).

65 KTB Halder, Vol. 3, p. 32.

66 The command to capture the Baltic islands was issued on 11 July 1941. Werner Haupt, *Heeresgruppe Nord 1941–1945* (Bad Nauheim, 1966), p. 46.

67 Hoepner complained "most strongly" to all of the commanders on the Eastern Front about the inadequate supply of provisions. Müller, *Scheitern*, p. 1170. In his original plan Hoepner wanted to be in Leningrad by 13 July. Heinrich Bücheler, *Hoepner: Ein deutsches Soldatenschicksal des XX. Jahrhunderts* (Herford, 1980), p. 136.

68 Müller, *Scheitern*, p. 1146.

69 Ibid., p. 1147.

70 See Hitler's Directive No. 33 of 19 July 1941, in Hubatsch, *Hitlers Weisungen*, p. 163.

71 Notes by Halder on lecture by Hitler, 23 July 1941. KTB Halder, Vol. 3, p. 108.

72 Müller, *Scheitern*, p. 1147.

73 The Army High Command made the shift on 25 July 1941. KTB OKW, Vol. 1, p. 1036. Hitler had already told Halder on 8 July that he aimed to use the Luftwaffe on Leningrad and Moscow "to raze them to the ground in order to prevent men remaining there who we would have to nourish in winter." KTB Halder, Vol. 3, p. 52.

74 Report of 28 July 1941, by Gusovius for General Thomas on his journey in the area covered by industrial inspection teams (Wirtschaftsinspektionen, Wi In) Center and North of 23–27 July 1941. BA-MA, WiID 86.

75 Daily report to the WiRüAmt from the Liaison Officer (Verbindungsoffizier, VO) with the General Quartermaster (GenQu). Thomas saw this on 1 July 1941. BA-MA RW 31/90a.

76 Letter from branch office GenQu Nord Dept. II B to distributors on 17 July 1941, re. Registration of captured property and rural resources for the sustenance of operations. LVA P 70–1–3, Bl. 1.

77 Enclosure 52 (23 July 1941), war diary of the VO of OKW/WiRüAmt (IV

Wi) at the Army High Command (Armeeoberkommando, AOK) 16. 22 June-14 February 1942. BA-MA RW 46/261.

78 Letter from the field of 23 July 1941 from Private First Class M.F. of the 256th Inf. Div., which as part of the 9th Army (Army Group Center) had conquered the south of Lithuania. Extracts published in Hans Manoschek (ed.), "*Es gibt nur eines für das Judentum: Vernichtung*": *Das Judenbild in deutschen Soldatenbriefen 1939–1944* (Hamburg, 1995), p. 37.

79 Notes by Halder of 23 July 1941, for a report to Hitler. KTB Halder, Vol. 3, p. 127.

80 General Wagner to Halder on 23 July 1941. KTB Halder, Vol. 3, pp. 103 and 106. On 15 August 1941, Hitler decided to assign Army Group North three divisions from Panzergruppe 3 for military purposes too. KTB Halder, Vol. 3, p. 179.

81 Discussion between all three Army Group heads on 25 July 1941. KTB Halder, Vol. 3, p. 120.

82 Enclosure 96, KTB IV Wi AOK 16. BA-MA RW 46/261.

83 Enclosure 80, ibid.

84 EM No. 12, 4 July 1941, and No. 14, 6 July 1941. BA R 58/214. Report from Marrenbach on July 6 about journey of 1–4 July 1941, to Vilnius and Kaunas. BA-MA, RW 31/90b.

85 Telegram from WiStab Ost to Wi In Nord of 9 July 1941. LVA P 70–1–2, Bl. 2. On 11 July 1941, this instruction, in exactly the same wording, was sent as "Special Instruction No. 7" to all economic offices. LVA P 70–2–52, Bl. 190.

86 Report of 31 July 1941, from Captain Reiner and Kriegsverwaltungsrat Ihde of WiStab Ost about a reconnaissance trip to Riga, Dvinsk, and Kaunas. Sonderarchiv Moskau, 1458–40–221, Bl. 68–72.

87 Statement of account of IV Wi AOK 18 relative to stocks on 20 July 1941. LVA P 70–2–40, Bl. 2.

88 Statement of account re. Requirements of Army Group North (16th and 18th armies, Panzergruppe 4) for meat, lard, and flour in August and September 1941. LVA P 70–1–16, Bl. 39.

89 Full report of Einsatzgruppe A of 15 October 1941. Sonderarchiv Moskau 500–4–93, p. 68.

90 Branch Office Gen.Qu. Nord II B to AOK 18 on 4 July 1941, re. Guidelines for the management of the economy in the newly-occupied regions. LVA P 70–2–1, Bl. 14–15.

91 Entry of General Thomas on 18 July 1941, "Ergebnis der Vorträge beim Reichsmarschall und bei Keitel am 17.7.1941." BA-MA RW 19/512, Bl. 37–39. GenQu Wagner re. Land use in the hinterland. Copy to WiRüAmt, Stab 1a, on 1 August 1941. LVA P 70–1–2, Bl. 16.

92 The Kaunas food industry administration to the mayors of all towns and villages and community directors. 16 July 1941. LCVA R 1444–1–13, Bl. 162.

93 Note by the head of the agricultural economics directorate (Chefgruppe Landwirtschaft, Chefgr. La) of WiStab Ost re. Report on working trip around Riga, Kaunas, and Minsk in the period 24 October to 2 November 1941. LVA P 70–2–38, Bl. 83–88.

94 "Richtlinien für die Führung und den Einsatz der Wirtschaftsdienststellen in den neu besetzten Ostgebieten" of 11 August 1941. Published in Rolf-Dieter Müller (ed.), *Die deutsche Wirtschaftspolitik in den besetzten sowjetischen Gebieten 1941–1943* (Boppard, 1991), pp. 418–420.

95 Meeting of Wirtschaftsführungsstab Ost on 31 July 1941. BA-MA RW 31/11, Bl. 99–109. Brief by KTB WiRüAmt of 31 July 1941, entitled "Organisationsfragen Russland." BA-MA Wi-ID/1222.

96 Entry for 22 July 1941, in Göring's desk diary. IfZ Ed 180/5.
97 Order of Göring on 27 July 1941, "Schwerpunkte und Methoden der wirtschaftlichen Ausbeutung der Sowjetunion." BA-MA RW 31/188, Bl. 74–76. Report of 29 July 1941, from General Nagel giving the replies of Göring to questions put by WiStab Ost. BA-MA RW 31/97.
98 Economic policy guidelines of 23 May 1941 (n. 62), p. 156f.
99 KTB Halder, Vol. 3, pp. 125 and 129.
100 This is made clear in a letter from Supply Region North of 11 September 1941, to the Chief Intendant with the Wehrmacht Commander-in-Chief in the East, re. Supply requirements for rations for Army Group North, 15 September to 15 December 1941. LVA P 70–1–4, Bl. 54.
101 Owing to the poor harvest, the distribution of bread grain was lowered by 55,000 tonnes in the autumn. 195,000 tonnes of supply needs remained to be delivered. Statement of account for Food and Agriculture Department in the RKO of 31 January 1942: provision conditions and delivery to the Wehrmacht. LVA P 70–1–16, Bl. 119.
102 Memorandum of a member of Chefgr. La. of WiStab Ost re. Report on working trip to Riga, Kaunas, and Minsk in the period 24 October to 2 November 1941. LVA P 70–2–38, Bl. 83–88.
103 Note by Krauss (RKO): conversation with the General Commissar in Kaunas, Food and Agriculture Department, 16–18 October 1941. Latvijas Valsts Vestures Arhivs [Latvian Historical State Archive) (LVVA) P 1018–1–155, Bl. 24.
104 Supply Region North, 1 October 1941, to Wi In Nord, re. Release of rationed food and luxury goods from the country to the food rationing offices. LVA P 70–1–7, Bl. 26.
105 Letter from Martin Matthiessen, leader of the economics department in the RKO, 5 November 1941, to division leaders in Kaunas, Riga, and Minsk, re. Utilizing the land for the Wehrmacht. LVVA P 69–1a–10, Bl. 537.
106 In the record for the head of WiStab Ost, this passage has been emphasized. RW 31/11, Bl. 99–109. The State Secretary responsible for the four-year plan, Paul Körner, was charged by Göring with the direction of Wirtschafts-führungsstab Ost.
107 Order of the garrison in Alytus to the civil authorities, 14 July 1941. LCVA R 1436–1–38. On 16 July the Lithuanian police were ordered to keep an eye on this food rationing. LCVA R 1436–1–29, Bl. 19–20. In the town garrison in Vilnius, at the beginning of July it had already been decided to leave only half as much rations for the Jews as for the rest of the population. Report from Marrenbach of 6 July on a trip to Vilnius and Kaunas, 1–4 July 1941. BA-MA, RW 31/90b.
108 EM No. 33, 25 July 1941. BA R 58/214.
109 EM No. 17, 9 July 1941. BA R 58/214.
110 Kaunas food industry administration to the mayors of all towns and villages and community superintendents. 16 July 1941. LCVA R 1444–1–13, Bl. 162.
111 Report of 29 July 1941, from General Nagel over the replies from Göring to the questions which WiStab Ost had submitted. BA-MA RW 31/97.
112 Record of 5 August 1941, of the "Discussion of the political and economic situation in the East in the meeting with Reichsminister Rosenberg on 1 August 1941." BA R 6/300, Bl. 1–5, here p. 2.
113 LVVA P 1026–1–3, Bl. 237–239. Noted by Stahlecker on the left side of Bl. 238. In the published version of this document this was wrongly transcribed as "If resettlement is now to be tackled 'here'." In Hans Mommsen and Susanne

Willems (eds.), *Herrschaftsalltag im Dritten Reich: Studien und Texte* (Düsseldorf, 1988), pp. 467–471, here p. 469, fn. 17.

114 Rüter, *Urteil*, Vol. 15, pp. 194–203. Proceedings against Fischer-Schweder et al., Bills of Indictment, Vol. 13, pp. 3466–3484.

115 Rüter, *Urteil*, Vol. 15, p. 200ff. Proceedings against Fischer-Schweder et al., Supplementary documents, Böhme memorandum, p. 48.

116 Proceedings against Fischer-Schweder et al., Bills of Indictment, Vol. 13, pp. 3468 and 3484.

117 Proceedings against Fischer-Schweder et al., Vol. 8, Statement by F.-S., p. 2100.

118 See in particular the statements of the Lithuanian Security Police Chief of Kretinga, Pranas Lukys. Proceedings against Fischer-Schweder et al., Vol. 10.

119 Šiauliai Regional Commissariat to the district heads and mayors of the municipalities on 14 August 1941 re. Directions and Guidelines from the Regional Commissar of 13 August 1941. LCVA R 1099–1–1, Bl. 153–155.

120 Proceedings against Fischer-Schweder et al., Supplementary documents, Böhme memorandum, p. 52.

121 Note by Gewecke on 3 September 1941, re. Jewish concerns in Schaulen [Šiauliai]. ZStL 207 AR-Z 774/61, Vol. 3, Bl. 529–530.

122 Provisional guidelines for the handling of Jews in the area under Reich Commissariat East. Printed in IMG, Vol. 27, pp. 19–25, here p. 24.

123 Full report of EG A up to 15 October 1941. Sonderarchiv Moskau 500–4–93.

124 Preliminary instalment of the second Stahlecker report, probably composed in January 1942. BA R 90/146.

125 Letter from Himmler of 2 August 1941, to HSSPF 101–103 and HSSPF East in Krakau, re. SS and police station leaders in the army regions [*Heeresgebieten*] as representatives of the HSSPF. LVVA P 1026–1–17, Bl. 279.

126 The corresponding order of 2 August 1941, for the Lithuanian units in Vilnius can be found in LCVA R 689–1–223, Bl. 16.

127 Himmler announced this on August 9, 1941. "Betr.: SS- und Polizeiorganisation in den besetzten Ostgebieten." Sonderarchiv Moskau 1323–1–50.

128 "We must have successes from the outset. There must be no setbacks." KTB Halder, Vol. 2, pp. 318f. On 4 June 1941, the commanders of the Army Groups were again addressed collectively by Halder: "Important: Speedy Accomplishment of Operation Barbarossa." KTB Halder, Vol. 2, p. 438.

129 Hitler's concern was reported by Keitel when he visited the leadership of Army Group Center in Borrisow at the end of July 1941. Cited by Reinhardt, *Wende*, p. 35. I am grateful to Christian Gerlach for this reference.

130 Diary of Erwin Lahousen, entry for 20 July 1941. IfZ Fd 47.

131 Reinhardt, *Wende*, p. 13.

132 Elke Fröhlich (ed.), *Die Tagebücher von Joseph Goebbels*, Part II Diktate, Vol. 1 (Munich et al. 1996), entry for 19 August 1941, pp. 257 and 261ff. On 29 July 1941, Goebbels noted for the first time that there was a "crisis." On 2 August 1941, he concluded from this that the German people must be prepared for a "hard and eventually a long war." Ibid., p. 139, 164. On 8 August 1941, he believed it was "highly unlikely" that the war against the Soviet Union could still end in 1941. Ibid., pp. 194f.

133 The ever more drastic orders on the security position in the occupied territories were all directed against the Jews, although this early on there was still hardly any resistance on the part of the Jews. On 16 July 1941, Hitler had stated that everyone was to be shot who only looked out of line. On 23 July 1941, Keitel declared: "The troops available for the security of occupied

eastern regions will only be sufficient in terms of the breadth of the area ... if the occupying power spreads such a terror which would be itself be sufficient to wipe out all desire on the part of the population to resist." Note for the record by Bormann about conversation between Hitler, Rosenberg, Lammers, Keitel, Göring, Bormann. IMG Vol. 38, 221–L, pp. 86–92; IMG, Vol. 34, pp. 258–9, 052–C.

134 On 24 July 1941, Lohse, the Reich Commissar for the Eastern Territories, before beginning his activities in the Baltic, was informed by General Quartermaster Wagner about the situation there; on 25 July he saw the Wehrmacht's Commander-in-Chief for the Eastern Territories, Walter Braemer; and he spoke on 26 July with Hitler. Shortly thereafter Lobse met with Himmler, the senior SS and police leader Adolf Prützmann and the head of the constabulary Karl Daluege, during Himmler's three-day journey in the Baltic between 29 and 31 July. Stahlecker had likewise "made contact" with the Reich Commissar "immediately after his installation." See the war diary of the diplomat Otto Bräutigam, in *Biedermann und Schreibtischtäter. Materialien zur deutschen Täter-Biographie: Beiträge zur nationalsozialistischen Gesundheits- und Sozialpolitik*, Vol. 4 (Berlin, 1987), p. 138ff. EM No. 35 (27 July 1941), BA R 58/214. Richard Breitman, *The architect of genocide: Himmler and the Final Solution* (Hanover/New England, 1991), p. 190. Landesarchiv Schleswig-Holstein, Lohse papers, Section 399.65, No. 10. Full report of EG A on 15 October 1941. Sonderarchiv Moskau 500–4–93, Bl. 3ff.

135 See above, n. 112.

136 "Gesamtaufstellung der im Bereiche des EK 3 bis jetzt durchgeführten Exekutionen" of 10 September 1941. BA R 70 SU/15, Bl. 78.

137 Goebbels, *Diktate*, entry for 19 August 1941, Vol. 1, Bl. 269.

138 See Ludolf Herbst, *Das nationalsozialistische Deutschland 1933–1945* (Frankfurt a.M., 1996), esp. chapters 12 and 13, here p. 378.

139 First fortnightly report WiStab Ost, 22 June-5 July 1941. BA-MA RW 31/90b.

140 See, for e.g., Christopher R. Browning, "The Euphoria of Victory and the Final Solution: Summer-Fall 1941," in *German Studies Review* 17 (1994): 473–481; Weinberg, *Eine Welt in Waffen*, p. 334.

25

GERMAN ECONOMIC INTERESTS, OCCUPATION POLICY, AND THE MURDER OF THE JEWS IN BELORUSSIA, 1941/43

Christian Gerlach

Source: Ulrich Herbert (ed.), *National Socialist Extermination Policies. Contemporary Perspectives and Controversies*, New York/Oxford: Berghahn, 2000, pp. 83–103.

No country in Europe was so severely affected by the Second World War as Belorussia. When liberated by the Soviet army in the summer of 1944, far fewer than 7 million of the original 9.2 million inhabitants remained in the country, and of these 3 million were homeless. Many villages and towns no longer existed. The enormous loss of state, community, and private property can scarcely be calculated. In Belorussia the Germans murdered about 700,000 Soviet prisoners of war, 500,000 to 550,000 Jews, 340,000 peasants and refugees as victims of the so-called "partisan struggle" and about 100,000 members of other population groups. In addition, more than 380,000 people were transported to the Reich as forced laborers.[1]

Three years earlier, in the summer of 1941, the German Army Group Center conquered Belorussia within a few weeks. Despite this rapid defeat, the Soviet authorities succeeded in evacuating 1.5 million people by train to the East, mostly out of eastern Belorussia, in an ad hoc evacuation campaign.[2] The evacuees included, above all, urban dwellers, particularly factory workers, civil authorities and functionaries, and perhaps 150,000 to 180,000 Belorussian Jews.[3] In the summer of 1941 the entire area of Belorussia fell under German military administration, which was replaced in the western half by various civil authorities between 1 August and 20 October 1941.[4] Though planned, the further expansion of the civil administration into the rest of Belorussia never occurred, and the eastern half of the country remained under military control for the duration of the occupation period.

Belorussia, never an independent state until 1991, for centuries occupied a difficult position in the field of political tension created by the politics of its large neighbors Poland and Russia. After 1920 it became a Soviet republic, with the exception of today's western Belorussia, which was part of Poland until the Soviet Union occupied and annexed east Poland in 1939.[5] A large Polish minority lived in the western districts, particularly in the cities. After this "reunification under socialist conditions" and at the time of the German invasion, Belorussia was in several ways a divided country: the Soviets persecuted the middle classes and the Poles—there were repeated waves of imprisonment and deportation from 1939 to 1941—while the Poles had repressed the Belorussians. Belorussia was even more divided economically and socially: in the west, industry was less developed, and by far the largest part of the agricultural economy was still in private hands. In the east, collectivized agriculture was the norm.

The German occupying powers divided Belorussia into no fewer than seven different large territories. The border between the areas under military and civil authority, although not identical with the prewar border between the USSR and Poland, ran directly through the country in a north-south direction. Almost all borders were changed or entirely redrawn and were more or less invented.

The so-called Generalkommissariat White Ruthenia, the sole administrative district under the Germans comprised solely of Belorussian territory, included the capital city Minsk and was part of the Reichskommissariat Ostland, with the capital city Riga. Larger parts of Belorussia, chiefly Polesje (the Pripyat Marshes), were divided between the Reichskommissariat Ukraine, the Generalkommissariat for Vohlhyn and Podolia, and the Generalkommissariat Shitomir. A further district, the Bezirk Bialystok, was annexed by the Reich and affiliated with East Prussia. The Bezirk Bialystok was not administered by the Ostministerium but by the East Prussian Gauleiter and Oberpräsident Erich Koch, who was also Reichskommissar for the Ukraine.

The eastern half of Belorussia was governed for the most part by the rear area of Army Group Center. Eastern Belorussia was divided into administrative districts controlled by the security divisions, field commanders, and district commanders. The General Quartermaster of the Army commanded administrative functions in the rear area of Army Group Center, while Army Group Center was responsible for military functions. In a military administrative district, economic organization required a special administrative body; in the area of Army Group Center, this task was fulfilled by the Economic Inspection Center, responsible to the Wirtschaftsstab Ost in Berlin.

In addition, there were Belorussian authorities at the city, Rayon (county district), community, and village levels, who were dependent on the German military and civil administrations. They were recruited in part from opponents to the Soviet system loyal to the Germans, in part from supposedly neutral persons; not a few secretly supported the Soviet powers and the political underground, and many maneuvered back and forth. But all-in-all the Belorussian support authorities "functioned," particularly in regard to anti-Jewish policies.

I begin the following essay with an analysis of the German plans, dating from 1941, to let millions of people in the Soviet Union starve to death, and the implications for Belorussia, particularly for Belorussian Jews. The second section examines how German units began to murder Belorussian Jews in 1941, and the step-by-step move towards total annihilation in the eastern part of the country. In the third section, I describe the liquidation campaigns in the different territories, which claimed as victims almost all Jews in western Belorussia in 1942. My analysis first concentrates on the course and to a certain degree on the structure of the mass murder of the Jews, and on its goals; second, I want to illuminate the connection between the overall concept of German occupation policies, which above all focused on economic interests, and the destruction of the Jews; and third, I examine the role played by the various occupation authorities in these events.

I

Toward the end of 1940, the Reich Ministry of Food and Agriculture prepared the annual report on the state of food for Hitler. State Secretary of the Reich Food Ministry Herbert Backe, who had already gained more power than his superior, Minister Darré, sent the report back two times, because its conclusions did not appear dramatic enough. Over the Christmas holidays of 1940, Backe simply sat down and wrote it himself.[6] His subsequent presentations to Göring and Hitler in January 1941 were the starting-point of the plan to use criminal occupation policies to obtain needed food stuffs from the Soviet Union. Göring immediately ordered a reduction in German meat rations for the summer, and in his meeting with Hitler, Backe for the first time argued that the Ukraine could be used as a "surplus area" for German food supplies, if deliveries to the remaining Soviet Union were stopped.[7] Shortly before this, on 18 December 1940, Hitler had signed the orders for the invasion of the Soviet Union.

After the failure of the attack on Great Britain in summer 1940, the strategic situation of Germany resembled that of the First World War, when the Reich was defeated because of its inferiority in capital, production capacity, raw materials, and food stuffs. Starvation had played a key role in the emergence of the revolutionary movement in 1918. In 1940, however, there was still no two-front war, larger territories had been occupied in comparison to the First World War, and Blitzkrieg campaigns had saved resources and war materials. But no Blitzkrieg existed for the economics of food and nourishment. By the end of 1939, almost entirely cut off from overseas transportation by the ocean blockade, Germany could no longer guarantee its own supplies of grain and oil-seeds. Victory in western Europe did not improve the balance of food stuffs—quite the contrary. Starvation was common in southeastern European countries, in part because they had already delivered so much food to the Reich. There was still no starvation in Germany. Supplies sufficed, but during 1940/41 grain stockpiles melted away. Because the end of the war was unforeseeable, this was a serious situation. During the summer of 1941, only a massive campaign brought in the new harvest without supply bottlenecks.[8] The campaign included measures for slaughtering fowl, because they required too much feed. This action took place under the official slogan "Eliminate the Bad Chickens!" (*Merzt die schlechten Hühner aus!*) Chickens were considered "bad" if they laid fewer than 100 to 120 eggs per year.[9]

Even with these domestic measures, the German government had difficulty supplying the population with food, and imports from the Soviet Union were also unreliable. Before the German invasion in 1941, the Soviet government had repeatedly declared that to avoid a drop in domestic consumption they did not want to raise appreciably grain exports to Germany. In any case, the Soviets demanded a high price, in highly valued industrial and military goods. The German government was moving towards a dependency that should not be underestimated,[10] and in response, the Reichs Food Ministry now drafted plans to let "*x* millions of people starve" after the invasion of Russia. This was the most extensive plan for murder yet known to history. It was aimed at two specific population groups: first, at the inhabitants of the agricultural "subsidy areas" of the "forest zones" in central and northern Russia, and with minor exceptions in Belorussia, where a "withering away (*Absterben*) of industry as well as a large part of the population" would need to be organized; and second, at the Soviet urban population as a whole. The occupation plans called for the re-establishment of large Russian agricultural exports as in the period before the First World War, and this required a return to the population conditions of that time. Although population levels in the USSR had remained static since 1918, the urban population had grown by some 30 million. To simply reduce rations for all inhabitants would have little effect, because of the uncontrollable black market. Nor could agricultural production be raised temporarily in the occupied Soviet territories, because planners realistically calculated that war-related destruction would result in considerable declines in production capacity.[11]

Besides these economic-agricultural motives, planners invoked a second tactical reason for instituting a policy of starvation against the Soviet population related to military strategy. The entire German operations plan had to deal with the difficulties caused by the enormity of the planned campaign.[12] For the army, this meant that the majority of the Red Army had to be destroyed in rapid maneuvers west of the Dniepr, to avoid its retreat into the inner reaches of the country and to prevent the establishment of a new, strong line of defense. The destruction of the remnants of Soviet resistance would require a deep attack into central Russia and the Caucasus before the onset of winter, and, as was foreseen, the range of German operations would be dependent on the provision of munitions, gasoline, and reserves. Maintaining supply lines in operations extending up to 2000 km was extremely difficult. This was well over the distances of about 400 km within which supplies could be easily transported by road, as in the war against France, and in the Soviet Union a large part of carrying capacity would be needed for the gasoline used by the trucks themselves. In addition, advances would require heavy rail support, but there were few extended east-west rail lines.[13] At the same time, a successful attack would require a rapid advance.[14] For these reasons, resupply transports would have to be relieved of everything that was not absolutely necessary.[15] The solution, in so far as there seemed to be one, was if possible to carry no food. The entire army on the Eastern Front, some three million men with extremely high ration requirements, would have to "live off the land," as it was called. In this way, the policy of starvation—in the logic of the German aggressor—became an unconditional military necessity. The plans implied that the greatest share of the extorted provisions would in practice be delivered to soldiers in the Wehrmacht rather than to citizens in the Reich, and this is in fact what happened. Reducing the supply of food stuffs to the Soviet population was thus entirely in the interest of the German army.

In response, the General Quartermaster of the Army, General Eduard Wagner, whose responsibility for both the organization of the military administration and lines of supply gave him a key position, had by February 1941 already devised guidelines for the future of the armed forces. The guidelines foresaw the relief of supply problems through the brutal enforcement of German interests and the "exploitation the countryside ... according to a well-thought-out plan." As if following the Backe plan, Wagner's order specifically states that "the individual countries are to be treated *differently*" and that Belorussia was to be handled particularly "ruthlessly."[16] After February 1941, the head of the Army Economics and Armaments Office of the High Command of the Armed Forces (OKW), General Georg Thomas, was one of the most passionate defenders and initiators of the starvation plan. By January, his office had already given up on plans to preserve the Soviet armaments industry by taking it into German possession.[17] From the beginning of March 1941, information folders for officers of the General Staff of the Army in the districts of the western Soviet Union illustrated the "disregard for the value of human life" in the region which seemed to allow brutal measures. The folders listed the number of Jewish inhabitants in urban areas, as well as other data on the "density of population" and the "density of the population in the countryside," which was irrelevant for military purposes. Such figures must have been included with the intent to change them.[18]

The starvation plan was approved by Hitler, co-initiated by Göring and the leaders of the Wehrmacht, and adopted by the responsible German State Secretaries on 2 May 1941. Experts at the German Reichsbank reviewed the economic considerations.[19] In June 1941 the economic guidelines in the "Green Folder," issued by Göring and signed by Chief of the OKW Keitel, became the basis for German occupation policies in the Soviet Union.[20] SS and police units were among others left responsible for realizing the guidelines, as demonstrated by surviving comments from Himmler and from Franz Six, Chief of the Vorkommando Moscow of Einsatzgruppe B. In July 1941, in the High Command of Army Group Center, Six declared that 30 million people would starve in "fire strips" (*Brandstreifen*) surrounding Moscow.[21] Himmler told a meeting of SS Group Leaders in the middle of June (the date is no longer a matter of doubt) that the Soviet population would be decimated by about 30 million people.[22] By chance or not: two days before that meeting occurred, Himmler spoke with Backe about agriculture in the Soviet territories planned for occupation.[23] It is noteworthy that Erich Koch, one of the most brutal of all National Socialist politicians, refused the post of Reichskommissar in Moscow because it was "an entirely negative task."[24]

We can thank the former Higher SS and Police Leader of "Russia Center" Erich von dem Bach-Zelewski for his confession in the Nuremberg trial about the Himmler statement cited above. Bach-Zelewski neglected to mention, however, that the plans called for the death of 20 million people in his region alone.[25] Bach-Zelewski's area of responsibility was initially Belorussia and later included central Russia. In the Wirtschaftstab Ost, one of the agricultural experts, most probably geographer Waldemar von Poletika, wrote "shall die" (*sollen sterben*) in the margins of a planning paper on Belorussia, alongside statements that 1,000,000 young, well-motivated, surplus workers could be transported from the region to Germany. Further marginal notes by von Poletika noted that the entire urban and half the rural population was supposed to die—a total of about 6.3 million people.[26]

Current scholarship makes isolated references to a *general* connection between the starvation plan and the suspected prewar plans for the destruction of the Soviet Jews, though we have virtually no sources to support this conclusion.[27] But the connection was quite concrete and direct: in Belorussia, for example, more that 90 percent of the Jews lived in towns and cities; they comprised a good 30 percent of the urban population.[28] This meant that the death of the mass of Belorussian Jews was planned beforehand. In addition, before 22 June 1941, besides the starvation plan, the most important elements of the German leadership had the *determined intention* to kill the vast majority of all Soviet Jews, who lived in the towns and cities of the western USSR—above all with starvation, supported by brutal occupation policies. But how and in what time period this mass murder could be actually carried out was still unclear. This is confirmed by postwar statements about the orders of the *Einsatzgruppen* Mitte in June 1941, which announced the general destruction of the Jews without comprehensive, concrete directives for the operation.[29] In addition, National Socialist ideology portrayed the Soviet Jews as potential enemies who should be fought with preventative measures, because they were the representatives and "wire-pullers" of the socialist system.[30] Supposedly Jews would offer particularly strong resistance to the destruction of socialism and the Soviet state apparatus, as well as to German plans for repression and exploitation.

To a great extent, plans for starvation and murder would quickly prove untenable. Nonetheless, the gain of agricultural surpluses at the cost of the population combined with de-urbanization and de-industrialization remained the main goal of German occupation policy in the Soviet Union until 1944.

II

In the first weeks after the German invasion, the SS and police units that entered Belorussia (*Einsatzgruppe* B and four police battalions) were not ordered to kill all Jews they encountered.[31] Nonetheless, they began to practice mass murder immediately; about 90 percent of their victims at this time were Jews. But as a report of *Einsatzgruppe* B stated,[32] the target group of these actions was "at first" limited: they killed men between about fifteen and sixty years of age, and not all of them, but rather those who could be labeled in Nazi jargon "Jewish intelligentsia"—teachers, lawyers, civil authorities, and state and party functionaries.[33] Broadly understood, these murders conformed to Heydrich's initial instructions to kill "Jews in state and party positions." There were practically no pogroms in Belorussia. In these first weeks, German liquidation operations were concentrated in the larger cities, above all Bialystok, Minsk, and Brest. The first Wehrmacht troops to enter Minsk interned all 40,000 men between fifteen and fifty living there—Jews and non-Jews—in a civilian prison camp. It was probably Generalfeldmarschall Günther von Kluge, the Commander in Chief of the (at that time) 4th Panzer Army, who authorized *Einsatzgruppe* B and the Army Secret Police to carry out the selection.[34] In the course of several weeks, they shot approximately 10,000 camp inmates, most of them Jewish. On the night of 7 July in Brest, Feldkommandantur 184 ordered police battalion 307 and part of the 162nd Infantry Division to undertake a mass internment. On the following day, the Police Battalion, a unit of the Security Police and SD from Lublin shot 4,000 Jewish men and 400 non-Jewish men. In Bialystok there were three mass shootings.[35] In smaller cities in July, SS and police "only" (meant relatively of course) carried out smaller massacres ranging from several dozen to several hundred Jewish men.

The military administration also ordered the first anti-Jewish regulations during these first weeks. These included forcing the Jews to wear a yellow badge or armlet, the establishment of Jewish Councils (which had to register Jewish inhabitants), the institution of various prohibitions (e.g., against buying food on the open market), and the establishment of ghettos. General orders for these actions came from regional authorities, the Army High Command, and the advancing commanders of the Army districts in the rear. The timing and course of implementation, however, was dependent on local military authorities. Ghettos were established because of local decisions, at first in particularly heavily damaged cities such as Minsk, Vitebsk, Bialystok, and Schklow, where there was an immense quartering and housing problem and where non-Jewish inhabitants were supposed to be helped at the expense of the Jews. The last ghettos in Belorussia were only established in May 1942 and some places never had one. General von Schenckendorff, the commander of the rear area of Army Group Center, issued the basic orders on 7 and 13 July 1941; at first the General Quartermaster of the Army, under whose jurisdiction this fell, gave no central orders to establish ghettos.[36]

The ghettos also served to limit the economic activity of the Jews as well as their consumption. After August 1941, their food ration was in most places set at 100 to 200 grams of bread per day, even smaller than that of the non-Jews.[37] This was not enough to live on, but the Jewish population survived, ensuring their supply of necessities through the black market, ersatz materials, and gardening. The numbers of dead from starvation remained *relatively* limited, although the Germans murdered many Jews for smuggling food. By August 1941, plans to let the Belorussian urban population starve to death had already been abandoned, in large part because the limited numbers of security troops could not prevent people from foraging in the countryside or buying food in the black market. And in this case, because the military could tolerate neither unrest related to hunger nor epidemics in the cities, the military administration worked in opposition to the agricultural authorities. In addition, the Wehrmacht required a working city infrastructure.

From the start, the use of Jewish labor was uncertain. In the beginning of July, the Wirtschaftsstab Ost frantically debated whether Jews would be allowed to work at all in the occupied Soviet territories in the future. If the Jews were denied work, their fate appeared grim indeed. After an initial inspection tour in Lithuania, leading economic functionaries declared that Jewish specialists were for the time being indispensable—as if before this, the assumption had been quite different.[38] On 15 July the Wirtschaftsstab Ost issued this order: "The local economic offices are to promote the maintenance of Jewish skilled workers in their posts in factories with production important to the war effort, when there is no available replacement and when production levels must be maintained." These orders were confirmed by Göring on 28 July and by the *Wirtschaftsführungsstab Ost* on 18 December 1941. By no means were all Jewish workers intended to be "retained"; instead there were numerous restrictions.[39] These orders also determined practice in Belorussia. In local negotiations, SS and police decided the life and death of Jewish people capable of work.

In actual fact, from the German point of view, the need for labor in the cities of Belorussia was very limited. German air attacks had destroyed many large cities and their factories. In eastern Belorussia, the Soviets had dismantled and transferred 109 factories and made others unusable. Many industrial areas lacked raw materials and energy. In addition, the German economic authorities shut down or cut back production in intact plants, when their products were meant "only" for the use of the civil population, as for example in the textile industry.[40] There was practically no real armaments industry. In many cities in 1941 and also into 1942, poor living conditions (a result of deliberate policy) forced non-Jewish inhabitants to move or flee, though the population had already dropped to about half of prewar levels because of evacuation, destruction, and flight.[41] Food, housing, and work shortages prevailed. Belorussian city administrators and the first German employment offices were hardly allowed to create new jobs. In the summer months of 1941 they saw only *one* practical means to lower high unemployment rates among non-Jews: to replace Jewish workers by the thousands.[42] The need for skilled labor was particularly low in Belorussia. Employment office statistics from 1941 and 1942 show that the share of labor in the general Jewish population was very low and that the quota of skilled laborers among all Jewish laborers was for the most part under 50 percent.[43] The reports of Jewish survivors show that they were rarely placed in the jobs they were trained for and often had to change positions. The authorities typically used Jews as short-term workers in periods when labor needs were particularly pressing.[44] For the criminal German authorities in Belorussia, most Jewish workers were by no means difficult to replace, despite historiographical assumptions to the contrary.

III

The question of why the mass murder of the Jews in the occupied Soviet territories was expanded in 1941 has been the focus of much discussion in the last decades. This expansion took place not in one step, as often assumed, but in two discernible phases. First, the killing units began to murder Jewish women and children, as well as men, in large numbers. The various killing units took this step at different times. *Einsatzkommando* 9, the first unit in *Einsatzgruppe* B, began this phase around July/August; the majority of *Einsatzkommando* 8, on the other hand, began to a great extent only in the beginning of September, likewise Police Battalion 322.[45] Because of the extensive source material, the SS Cavalry Brigade is a particularly good example. In mid-July 1941 Bach-Zelewski had asked Himmler if they could carry out a liquidation operation in Polesje. After a visit to Baranovitchi on 31 July, Himmler issued this radio message on the morning of 1 August: "Express orders for the RF-SS. All Jews must be shot. Drive Jewish women into the swamps."[46] By mid-August, the brigade had murdered at least 15,000 people between Baranovitchi and Pinsk—95 percent of them Jewish. In the most severely hit areas the "Jewish intelligentsia," broadly considered, were again particular targets for murder. The 1st SS Cavalry Regiment had killed all Jews in several small market towns, though they were spared in some other places. The 2nd Regiment shot 4,000 to 8,000 Jewish men in Pinsk on 5 August; two or three days later, in a separate operation, they killed 2,000 women, children, and elderly. In other places, this Regiment killed only Jewish men.[47] These actions marked the period of transition, but there was no clear break.

On 15 August 1941, Himmler visited Minsk, where Bach-Zelewski, Nebe (the head of *Einsatzgruppe* B), and *Einsatzkommando* 8 demonstrated a mass shooting action to their superior. It has recently been claimed, on the basis of statements made by accomplices, that Himmler gave the order for the "undifferentiated killing of all Jews encountered" at this meeting in Minsk,[48] but this is apparently wrong. In fact, Himmler had actually given orders for the expansion of the liquidation campaign to the 1st SS Infantry Brigade three days before, in a personal meeting with the HSSPF Rußland-Süd, Jeckeln. These orders were probably intended for broader implementation.[49] But the slightly decreasing number of murders committed by Einsatzgruppe B up to mid-September, and the remarks in several subsequent reports by Nebe on the "limited importance of the Jewish question," suggest that Himmler never gave the reputed order in Minsk.[50] Nor did his visit in any way mark the "birth of the gas chamber" or the mobile gas vans. Plans for these had already begun before this.[51]

The second step from mass murder to total destruction, scarcely noted in current research, was the start of the liquidation of entire Jewish communities. This step also took place in different regions at different times. After the end of August 1941, Section Troop Borisov of *Einsatzkommando* 8 first liquidated the Jewish communities between Borisov and Minsk.[52] Around the middle of September, *Einsatzkommando* 8 together with the Gendarmerie began a similar operation in the area of Mogilev, while *Einsatzkommando* 9 worked in the area around Vitebsk.[53] In September, the Security Police and the SD undertook a series of shootings of several hundred currently "unemployed Jews" in larger cities like Orscha, Bobruisk, Borisov, and Gomel.[54] An order of Keitel's forbidding the use of Jewish labor except in all-Jewish forced labor troops was now carried out.[55] On 2 October, the liquidation of the large ghettos in the rear areas of Army Group Center began with the shooting of 2,273 Jewish men, women, and children in Mogilev.[56] Within two months all of the ghettos had been liquidated: the Germans murdered 6,500 Jews in Mogilev, 4,000 in Vitebsk, 7,000 in Borisov, 2,000 in Orscha, 2,500 in Gomel, 7,000 in Polozk, and 7,500 in Bobruisk, where 7,000 had already been murdered by the SS Cavalry Brigade. During the same period, smaller ghettos were liquidated.[57] Only in a very few cities were several hundred Jewish workers allowed to stay alive. In the beginning of February 1942, only some 22,000 Jews remained alive, mostly in remote areas that the murder commandos had not yet been to.[58] These Jews were subsequently shot in early 1942. The liquidation was thus total very early on.

In any case, for organizational reasons the SS and police could not immediately begin the liquidation of the ghettos. The *Einsatzkommandos* in particular had first to complete several other tasks; inspecting local conditions, searching for political enemies and files, transmitting initial reports to Berlin, and collaborating with the rebuilding of the Belorussian supporting administration and police, whose existence as a functioning body was a necessary prerequisite for the larger liquidation operations. In addition, the commandos had to be stationed permanently in a fixed territory. Section Troop Borisov (noted above), under Werner Schönemann, was the first unit to achieve this in Belorussia at the end of July 1941.[59] In the entire occupied Soviet territories, *Einsatzkommando* 3 in Lithuania was the first to stay in a specific area and also the first to begin the liquidation of Jewish communities.[60] These different starting dates suggest not a single order for the expansion of murder, but rather a series of local, tactical orders.

The initial signal was given on 2 October by Higher SS and Police Leader Bach-Zelewski, on the same day—as he knew in advance—that Army Group Center began its offensive against Moscow.[61] Unlike the *Sonderkommandos*, most of the *Einsatzkommandos* were not moved forward in the military campaign, but were held back, obviously because they now had orders to kill all Jews in the rear area within a short period of time. At this point, the origin of this order is impossible to document. But the course of events shows that the resolution of the economic problems of the occupation authorities was the final, decisive impulse for the complete liquidation of the Jews in Army Group Center. For this reason, operations began in the large cities and ended in the outlying ghettos—in contrast to the situation in Lithuania. Local conditions likewise reveal the connections between economics and elimination: in Mogilev, at the time of both massacres, *non-Jewish* skilled workers escaped starvation and housing shortages by fleeing into the countryside, and *Einsatzgruppe* B reported that it had immediately afterwards returned the ghetto to the city administration.[62] Bobruisk experienced massive unemployment, and in Borisov food shortages were such that soon even local farmers were starving. Vitebsk suffered from a dire lack of provisions, and Jews there had received no food, with the result that most of them were actually starving by this time. Countless bodies lay in the ghetto, and *Einsatzkommando* 9 shot Jews who still lived because of the "danger of an epidemic."[63]

At the same time, large massacres of Jews in Generalkommissariat White Ruthenia took place. But in contradiction to many interpretations, these operations were not the product of blind rage, nor did they result in the total annihilation of the Jews in this region.[64] Despite ideological exhortation, these calculated acts of murder controlled by the regional Wehrmacht authorities actually had three limited, clearly defined goals. First, the 707th Wehrmacht Infantry Division was to murder all Jews in the countryside, or force them to emigrate from larger areas. Second, Reserve Police Battalion 11, with Lithuanian assistants, had the task of killing all Jews in the Soviet part of the Generalkommissariat, with the exception of Minsk. Third, the Jewish population was to be reduced in the small cities close to the major east-west roads and in the larger cities in formerly Polish areas, in order to relieve food and housing shortages. Indispensable Jewish labor, however, was to be spared; both operations were undertaken in the interests of the Wehrmacht troops quartered in the area. The 707th Infantry Division carried out these plans in towns; the Security Police and the SD from Minsk had responsibility for larger cities.[65] In Minsk, 12,000 Jews were shot to make room for in-coming transports of Jews from Germany. In Slonim, 9,000 "useless gobblers" (*unnütze Fresser*), in the words of the district commissar, were murdered. In both cases, the German authorities had determined an exact number of victims in advance. In Minsk, a second operation was planned and carried out, because the initial quota was not fulfilled.[66]

One element in particular stands out about the crimes in the Generalkommissariat White Ruthenia: in this area the Wehrmacht shot up to 19,000 Jews, clearly without a general from the OKW order to kill Jews,[67] but on the decision of a division commander. In this case, few other killing units were available. There was no Order Police Battalion, and only a weak commando of Security Police and SD in Minsk. On 4 October, at the request of the Wehrmachtbefehlshaber Ostland, Reserve Police Battalion 11 was transferred from Lithuania to Minsk by the commander of the Order Police.[68] The time parallels with events in the rear area under army control is remarkable, even more so when one notes the contemporaneous start of the mass shootings in east Galicia, in the Warthegau, and in Volhyn-Podolia.[69] The still limited character of the mass murder in the Generalkommissariat in 1941 (though 60,000 Jews were shot), in contrast to the rear area under army control, is explicable first because in eastern Belorussia, cities and factories were more heavily destroyed and practically no Jewish labor was needed. In addition, the pressures of starvation and housing shortages were greater in the cities because they had experienced direct assaults by the Wehrmacht. The larger picture showed similar tendencies: in September, because of the unforeseen conditions of war, Backe set up a new plan for wartime food supply that was sanctioned by Hitler and Göring. Backe, who demanded "extremely radical measures," exercised enormous pressure on the Wirtschaftsstab Ost, on the General Quartermaster of the Army, and on the OKW, and they unscrupulously passed it on.[70] A number of connected events occurred in the autumn of 1941: the transportation catastrophe of Army Group Center during the Battle for Moscow; the premeditated murder of prisoners of war incapable of work, which meant the starvation of the majority, especially in the rear areas of Army Group Center; the reduction of rations for non-Jewish city dwellers; and the intensification of the bloody struggle against "outsiders" (*Ortsfremde*)—starving refugees and scattered members of the Red Army.[71] Events in autumn 1941 marked the *transition from utopian plans for genocide to an implementable program of mass murder*. The initial criminal plans could still be realized, if only in part. In addition, to those responsible, it appeared more pressing to murder the Jews—seen as particularly "dangerous" political enemies—in the former Soviet territories than in the former Poland. This also explains the slaughter of the entire Jewish population in the small districts in the north of the Generalkommissariat of Shitomir (in the territory of the civil administration) between September 1941 and January 1942.[72]

In 1941 about 200,000 Belorussian Jews were murdered, practically all of those living in the eastern half of the territory. In the west, 300,000 were still alive. The military authorities above all shared political responsibility for these murders, because the intensification of the killing was directly connected to the implementation of plans to supply provisions to the Wehrmacht. In contrast to the liquidation of the prisoners of war, for which they were directly responsible, army agents themselves murdered Jews only in exceptional cases. Shootings of Jews by frontline troops during advances, which occurred in a number of cases, had the character of antisemitic attacks or brutal acts of retaliation. Killings by frontline troops, however, did not affect most cities; nor did they reach the massive dimensions of the massacres later carried out by the SS, police, and security troops.[73] After the advance, army participation was apparently limited: it is only possible to document the murder of so-called "country Jews" by several security divisions, the participation in massacres by Security Police with their own shooting commandos on the local level, and voluntary participation in shootings by numerous individual soldiers and officers.[74] The operations of the 707th Infantry Division are in fact an exception. It is of course clear that the army cooperated in and gave massive support to SS and police operations, for example in Bobruisk, Orscha, Borisov, Slonim, and Novogrodek,[75] and that they carried out ongoing transfers of captured Jews to the Security Police. In addition, army units made use of the police in mass murder operations or gave orders to carry them out, as in Brest or in the case of Reserve Police Battalion 11. But they rarely got their own hands dirty.

IV

The year 1942 was characterized by the implementation of campaign-style murder programs against the Jewish population of western Belorussia, above all in the Generalkommissariat White Ruthenia. On 2 and 3 March, for example, Security Police in Minsk, Baranovitchi, and Vilejka shot over 6,500 Jews, for the most part children, women, and unemployed. A crisis session of the Stadtkommissar in Minsk had earlier resulted in orders that despite the famine, the inhabitants could be "given no aid of any kind."[76] In a hearing after the war, Minsk Gestapo Chief Heuser remembered that "the main thing that was done in that severe winter crisis was saving lives 'worth living' [lebenswertes Leben], that is, White Ruthenians, at the expense of 'unworthy or sick' lives (Jews, Gypsies, the mentally ill, and prison inmates)."[77]

But these massacres did not seem to be sufficient for the authorities responsible for the murder campaigns. On 26 March, at a meeting in Riga (Kube was apparently present), the Generalkommissars of Reichskommissariat Ostland stated that "even though they may create a political inconvenience for us, it is seen as regrettable that the procedures pursued up to now [i.e., the mass shootings] have for the time being once again been abandoned. The current situation, in which the Jews receive no food whatsoever, is no solution." By November 1941, the Reichskommissariat had already de facto forbidden the murder of Jews through starvation because of the high risk involved, in so far as the Reichskommissariat was responsible for the prevention of epidemics spreading from the ghettos.[78] Negotiations now began between Kube, Zenner (SS and Police Leader of White Ruthenia), and Strauch (commander of the Security Police and SD), resulting in the selections of Jews, district by district, in all areas. Jews who, according to the Gebietskommissare (whose officials selected the Jews), could not be used as laborers were shot or murdered in gas vans. Kube ordered the district commissars to "select out all [Jews] not absolutely necessary to the national economy [Volkswirtschaft]."[79] The Reichskommissariat in Riga agreed; the local "Jewish expert" noted on a similar order, "corresponds to previous arrangements."[80] The selections first occurred in the region around Lida. In seventeen towns, between 8 and 12 May, the Security Police shot 16,000 Jews and let 7,000 live.[81]

Because of partisan attacks, mass flight of refugees and Jewish uprisings, and a lack of police manpower, the operations in the other districts took place in a somewhat less tightly organized manner. Skilled workers in the remaining ghettos were only killed in the last quarter of 1942. Nonetheless, the overwhelming majority of the estimated 112,000 Jews murdered in Generalkommissariat White Ruthenia in 1942 were victims of the campaigns between May and August. On 31 July Kube wrote a report, apparently on the request of Lohse, his Reichskommissar. Lohse immediately presented the results to Göring in Berlin, at a large conference on the food question in occupied Europe. Lohse answered a question from Göring with the remark that "now only a small part of the Jews remain alive; umpteen thousands are gone."[82]

In May 1942, in the Generalkommissariat Volhyn-Podolia, 326,000 Jews remained alive, including over 80,000 in the Belorussian area. On the basis of postwar statements, Gerald Fleming has already established that Hitler, not Himmler, gave the order for their elimination to Erich Koch in July 1942. Various sources show that the operation, with the internal slogan "A Jew-Free Ukraine!" (*Ukraine judenfrei!*), was actually controlled by Koch and the civil authorities, and that Koch had received dramatic demands for food deliveries to the Reich.[83] The role played by these demands is also demonstrated by the acceleration of the murders in August and by the course of events, which moved from the south, where the richest agricultural areas lay, to the north. On 9 July, Himmler took over the operation to "secure the harvest" in the Reichskommissariat Ukraine.[84] In September and October 1942, units of the Order and Security Police shot all the Jews in southwestern Belorussia, including 16,000 to 18,000 in Brest and up to 26,000 in Pinsk, the largest remaining Belorussian ghetto. The liquidation of the Pinsk ghetto has been seen as a perfect example of actions taken under a short-term order from Himmler based on ideological grounds—even though Koch had personally given the order several weeks before, and the civil authorities had already determined the course of events.[85]

The operation in Pinsk ended on 1 November; on the following day, almost 100,000 Jews in the Bialystok district were forced into internment centers, so they could be quickly deported to the Treblinka and Auschwitz extermination camps. The smooth cooperation between Security Police and SD and the civil authorities, here also responsible to Koch, was again evident. Technical obstructions in rail transport were the sole source of disruption.[86] By February 1943, in the area belonging to today's Belorussia, all 60,000 to 70,000 Jews were victims of this operation.

Approximately 20,000 Belorussian Jews remained in Minsk, Lida, and Glebokie. They were shot or deported at the latest in the summer and autumn of 1943. The head of the finance branch in the Reichskommissariat Ostland, Vialon, had obtained a promise from the SS that skilled

Jewish workers could remain employed, but the authorities in Generalkommissariat White Ruthenia did not allow this, because they could replace the Jews with Belorussians, with evacuees forced away from the front, and with new machinery.[87] In the end only several hundred Belorussian Jews were able to survive as forced laborers in the camps in Poland. In addition, about 30,000 to 50,000 Jews escaped from the Belorussian ghettos. However, fewer than half of them survived the so-called "Jew hunts" by Germans until liberation.[88]

In conclusion I would like to emphasize five main points:

1   The majority of Belorussian Jews were killed in regional murder campaigns. People were shot close to where they lived; relatively few were suffocated in gas vans. Thus the start, duration, and size of these programs was not determined by the distribution of rail transport or by the liquidation capacity of the death camps under the leadership of the Reichssicherheitshauptamt or the "Aktion Reinhard."

2   *Economic interests and crises* were far more important influences on the tempo of the liquidation of the Jews, *especially in the phases of acceleration.* The various liquidation programs in Belorussia, particularly those against non-Jewish population groups, were in large part responses to pressures related to food economics. This was the main interest of the occupying powers; on the central or regional levels, demanding food-delivery goals and local emergencies in the meager deliveries to non-Jewish urban populations produced decisions to murder either unemployed Jews, or all of them. Antisemitism and anti-Bolshevism were necessary preconditions for these murders, helping to establish the possibility of such ideas in the first place—but only economic pressure led to the massive killing campaigns, to the horrible dynamics of mass murder.

3   Thus the liquidation of the Jews was directly connected with the progress of the war. This was a concrete, palpable connection that cannot be explained by overly simple conceptual models of euphoria versus defeatism. Though the National Socialists were prepared in advance to commit crimes, at the beginning of 1941, the starvation program was a bitter necessity of war, for both the collective strategic situation of Germany and for the unavoidable supply problems related to the new military campaign. In the fall of 1941, both problems were greatly intensified: by developments at the front, in the transportation sector; through the newly developed war food plan necessary for supplying the Reich; and in the race for time in the battle for Moscow. Simplistic conceptions of the starvation policy now collapsed. In order to keep the situation in control, the burdens that emerged from the general intensification of the war were passed on more sharply to the

inhabitants of the occupied territories, above all to specific, delimited, stigmatized population groups. The undisguised mass murder of Jews and Soviet prisoners of war was the result. In spring and summer 1942, the new deliveries demanded by the Reich Food Ministry from the occupied areas to improve food supplies in the Reich were at the very least decisive for the acceleration of new murder programs against the Belorussian Jews.

4   The participating institutions—the military and civil authorities—did not act with restraint, nor did they simply give their consent. They were one of the driving forces behind the destruction of the Jews. The murder of the Jews and other population groups in Belorussia was hardly an exception in German occupation policies, but rather its means, and an essential part of its organization. As the liquidation of the Jews increasingly became a key part of the general strategy of occupation policies, the role of the SS and police declined in importance; they rarely determined the course of these policies. They did repeatedly seize the initiative in the mass murder of the Jews, their killing was unbelievably gruesome and hateful (which cannot be described here), and they at times exceeded the measures asked for by the authorities. But the massive liquidation campaigns took place only when they accorded with the combined interests of the administrative authorities. For example, in autumn 1941 Einsatzgruppe C did not succeed in carrying out their original goal of immediately killing all Jews in Volhyn-Podolia for political reasons, because the civil authorities still wanted to keep reserves of Jewish skilled laborers.[89] The well-known conflicts between Kube and the SS dealt only with how to proceed with the murders and was in any case limited to a personal level.[90]

5   In the search for explanations, above all for the events of 1941, the orders giving the commands for mass murder have up to now been represented somewhat too simply and directly, almost theatrically in the case of Minsk in August 1941. The expansion of the murders was a result of tactics, a response to regional possibilities for killing and so-called "killing requirements". The mass murder was carried out in a cold and calculated fashion, as the great majority of statements by perpetrators show, although few witnesses could clearly comprehend all the economic calculations that lay behind these actions. One *single* general order to kill all Jews was not enough to set the liquidation everywhere in motion. Mass murder always required supplementary local or regional planning, and it required interest, consensus, and initiative to ensure that the far-reaching destruction became a reality.

The analysis of events set out above is not intended to disregard and certainly not to disdain the victims of German murder campaigns in

Belorussia. It is vital to uncover the accurate reasons for why they were killed, whether because of racial insanity or murderous economic rationality. In occupied Belorussia both racist attitudes and brutal, goal-oriented calculation smoothed the way for ideas of liquidation; these motives rarely contradicted each other, and then only in limited ways. Following economic or partly national economic motives does not exonerate or excuse those who planned, initiated, or gave orders—rather the opposite, because this provides irrefutable proof of their intentions. Claims that they, at least, acted out of some sort of madness or insanity are indefensible.

Notes

1 The figures are based on the postwar territories of Belorussia and are from my dissertation "Die deutsche Wirtschafts- und Vernichtungspolitik in Weißrußland 1941–44" (Technical University of Berlin, 1997). The population figures before the German invasion agree with those those from Belorussia, see Jerzy Turonek, *Bialorus pod okupacja niemiecka* (Warsaw, 1993), p. 236. The figures I use for the number of "Ostarbeiter" transported to the Reich agrees almost exactly with the official data (376,362): *Collected Data on the Victims of German-Fascist Crimes in White Russia* (July 1945, in Russian), ZStA Minsk 845–1–58, Bl. 10. The number of homeless is from M. P. Baranowa and N. G. Pawlowna, *Kurze Geschichte der Belorussischen Sozialistischen Sowjetrepublik* (Jena, 1985), p. 124; Norbert Müller, *Wehrmacht und Okkupation* (East Berlin, 1971), p. 262.

2 See Klaus Segbers, *Die Sowjetunion im Zweiten Weltkrieg* (Munich, 1987), p. 183; Lothar Kölm, "Zur Standortverlagerung von Produktivkräften zu Beginn des Großen Vaterländischen Krieges der Sowjetunion (1941–1942)," in *Jahrbuch für die Geschichte der sozialistischen Länder Europas* 26, no. 2 (1983), p. 128; Turonek, *Bialorus*, p. 54.

3 My own figures, and see Mordechai Altshuler, "Escape and Evacuation of Soviet Jews at the Time of the Nazi Invasion," in *The Holocaust in the Soviet Union*, ed. Lucjan Dobroszycki and Jeffrey S. Gurock (Armonk and London, 1993), pp. 77–104, esp. 97.

4 The Bialystok district was established on 1 August 1941, the Generalkommissariat (GK) White Ruthenia as well as Volhynia and Podolia on 1 September 1941, the GK Shitomir on 20 October 1941.

5 Including the district around Bialystok, which was returned to Poland after 1945 and is not discussed here.

6 Backe to Darré, 9 February 1941, BA R 14/371, Bl. 19.

7 Backe's presentation to Göring was on 13 January, to Hitler before 29 January 1941; see Backe to Darré, 9 February 1941; see also the Reichsmarschall des Großdeutschen Reiches, Beauftragter für den Vierjahresplan V.P. 510/3g, 13 January 1941, BA R 14/371, Bl. 10/R and 16–20; for the meeting with Hitler, *KTB WiRüAmt/Stab*, 30 January 1941, BA-MA RW 19/164, Bl. 126. General Thomas (WiRüAmt) was informed during a high-level meeting with Göring and others including Backe, *Terminkalender Göring*, 29 January 1941, Institut für Zeitgeschichte (IfZ) ED 180/5.

8 See Akte BA R 14/128, especially *Vermerk* 24 May on a meeting on 20 May 1941 in RMEuL (Abschrift), Bl. 44–47.

9 NSDAP-Partei-Kanzlei, *Anordnung 32/41r*, 12 July 1941, with RMEuL, II B 4,

Betr.: Ausmerzung der schlechten Hühner, BA NS 6/821; RMEuL, II B 4, an die Landesbauernführer, 9 September 1941, BA R 43 II/613, Bl. 260/R.

10 See Rolf-Dieter Müller, "Von der Wirtschaftsallianz zum kolonialen Ausbeutungskrieg," in *Der Angriff auf die Sowjetunion*, ed. Horst Boog et al. (Frankfurt a.M., 1991), pp. 141–245, esp. 144–156; Ludolf Herbst, *Das nationalsozialistische Deutschland 1933–1945* (Frankfurt a.M., 1996), pp. 339–42; Andreas Hillgruber, *Hitlers Strategie: Politik und Kriegführung 1940–1941* (Frankfurt a.M., 1965), pp. 242 ff., esp. 256, on a new German-Soviet accord dated 10 January 1941 requiring increased deliveries to Germany of 2.5 million tons within fifteen months. See Herbst, *Deutschland*, p. 350. His conclusion that this "was enough to mask the [German] need for imports until 1943" is incomprehensible. See also Heinrich Schwendemann, *Die wirtschaftliche Zusammenarbeit zwischen dem Deutschen Reich und der Sowjetunion von 1939 bis 1941* (Berlin, 1993). The German leadership did not see this as an alternative to the emerging starvation plan. On the uncertainty of Soviet deliveries, see Generaloberst Halder, *Kriegstagebuch, Bd. II*, ed. by Hans-Adolf Jacobsen (Stuttgart, 1963), pp. 207, 311 (3 December 1940 and 13 March 1941).

11 Wirtschaftsstab Ost, Gruppe La, "Wirtschaftspolitische Richtlinien für Wirtschaftsorganisation Ost, Gruppe Landwirtschaft, 23 May 1941," in *IMT* (German edition), Vol. 36, pp. 135–157; "Aktionnotiz [of General Thomas] über Ergebnis der heutigen Besprechung mit den Staatssekretären über Barbarossa," 2 May 1941, in IMT, Vol. 31, p. 84. On the German starvation plan in general, see Müller, *Von der Wirtschaftsallianz*, pp. 184ff.; Götz Aly and Susanne Heim, *Vordenker der Vernichtung* (Hamburg, 1991), pp. 365–393.

12 See the analysis of Albert Beer, *Der Fall Barbarossa: Untersuchung zur Geschichte der Vorbereitungen des deutschen Feldzuges gegen die Union der Sozialistischen Sowjetrepubliken im Jahre 1941* (Ph.D. Thesis, Münster, 1978), esp. pp. 27–82.

13 Fundamental in this regard is Klaus A. Friedrich Schüler, *Logistik im Rußlandfeldzug: Die Rolle der Eisenbahnen bei Planung, Vorbereitung und Durchführung des deutschen Angriffs auf die Sowjetunion bis zur Krise vor Moskau im Winter 1941/42* (Frankfurt a.M., 1987), here pp. 106ff.

14 See Beer, *Barbarossa*, p. 194; Klaus Reinhardt, *Die Wende vor Moskau* (Stuttgart, 1972), p. 35; and Alfred Philippi, *Das Pripjetproblem* (Frankfurt a.M., 1956), esp. p. 10.

15 See Ihno Krumpelt, *Das Material und die Kriegführung* (Frankfurt a.M., 1968), pp. 140ff.

16 OKH, GenStdH, GenQu, Qu I/II Nr. I/050/41g.KdoS. Chefsache, February 1941, *Anlage 15: Anordnungen über militärische Hoheitsrechte, Sicherung und Verwaltung im rückwärtigen Gebiet und Kriegsgefangenenwesen*, BA-MA RH 3/132, here Bl. 78f. (author's emphasis).

17 Müller, *Von der Wirtschaftsallianz*, pp. 165f.; on the role of Thomas see idem, "Das Unternehmen 'Barbarossa' als wirtschaftlicher Raubkrieg," in *Der deutsche Überfall auf die Sowjetunion*, ed. Gerd R. Ueberschär and Wolfram Wette (Frankfurt a.M., 1991), pp. 125–157, esp. 137.

18 Military-geographical data on European Russia, Mappe A: General Survey (GenStdH, Abt. IV [Mil-Geo.], Berlin, 2nd, corr. printing/closed on 1 March 1941), Textheft, p. 36, and Anlage/Große Kartenskizzen zum Textheft, Enclosure 8, with printed note on the slip cover: "Enclosure 8—recorded at the last moment." In addition see Mappe E: Weißrußland. Closed on 27 March 1941.

19 On Hitler, see WiStab Ost, Gruppe La, "Wirtschaftspolitische Richtlinien für

Wirtschaftsorganisation Ost, Gruppe Landwirtschaft, 23 May 1941," in *IMT*, Vol. 36, p. 140. On Göring and the Wehrmacht, see the following passages and Müller, *Von der Wirtschaftsallianz*, 172ff. and 184ff. On the State Secretaries, see "Aktennotiz über die Besprechung am 2.5.1941," in *IMT*, Vol. 31, p. 84. On the German Reichsbank, see Referat A 4, Dr. Stamm, *Zur Möglichkeit, den großdeutschen Fehlbedarf an Getreide in Höhe von jährlich 3 Millionen t aus Sowjetrußland sicherzustellen*, 13 June 1941 (copy), BA 25.01, Nr. 7007, Bl. 233–256.

20 Der Reichsmarschall des Großdeutschen Reiches, *Richtlinien für die Führung der Wirtschaft in den neubesetzten Ostgebieten (Grüne Mappe), Teil 1* (2nd printing, July 1941), "Aufgaben und Organisation der Wirtschaft," Nbg. Dok. NG-1409, with a cover letter from the Chief of the OKW, WFSt/WiRüAmt, 16 June 1941; various summaries of the permanent, in-use "Grüne Mappe" in BA-MA RW 31/128D and /130–133.

21 Rudolf-Christoph Freiherr von Gersdorff, *Soldat im Widerstand* (Frankfurt a.M., 1977), p. 93; Wilfried Strik-Strikfeldt, *Gegen Hitler und Stalin: General Wlassow und die russische Freiheitsbewegung* (Mainz, 1970), p. 32. According to the reference label, the visitor was the leader of a "Vorauskommando Moskau" (v. Gersdorff), although both authors tried to leave uncertainties about his identity. Six was the leader of the "Vorkommando Moskau" of *Einsatzgruppe* B.

22 Examination of Erich von dem Bach-Zelewski, 7 January 1946, in *IMT*, Vol. 4, pp. 535f.; *Terminkalender Himmler* for 12–15 June 1941, OSOBYI Archives, Moscow 1372–5–23, Bl. 445; *Terminkalender* of Himmler's personal Referenten Rudolf Brandt for 12–15 June 1941, BA NS 19/3957, Bl. 87R–89R (inc. names of participants). Also see [Karl Hüser] *Wewelsburg 1933 bis 1945: Kultund Terrorstätte der SS* (Paderborn, 1982), pp. 3, 323. Peter Whitte et al. (eds.) *Der Dienstkalender Heinrich Himmlers 1941/42* (Hamburg, 1999), pp. 172–74.

23 Himmler to Greifelt, 11 June 1941, BA NS 19/3874, Bl. 9.

24 According to the account in Rosenberg to Lammers, 5 July 1941, BA R 6/21, Bl. 101.

25 Examination of Friedrich Jeckeln, 2 January 1946, BA Zwischenarchiv Dahlwitz-Hoppegarten (hereafter BA D-H) ZM 1683, A.1, Bl. 105. Six had mentioned similar things including Bach-Zelewski's responsibility; see v. Gersdorff, *Soldat*, p. 93.

26 Eugen v. Engelhardt, "Die Ernährungs- und Landwirtschaft der Weißrussischen Sozialistischen Sowjetrepublik," BA F 10772, Bl. 5895–6051, also BA-MA RW 31/299 and /300, here RW 31/299, Bl. 11 and 72. Bernhard Chiari has already discussed the marginal comments without making their full meaning clear in "Deutsche Zivilverwaltung in Weißrußland 1941–1944," in *Militärgeschichtliche Mitteilungen* 52, no. 1 (1993): 67–89, 78f., note 72. For the identity of the author of the marginal comments, see the accompanying text, Dr. Buchholz, "Kriegsverwaltungsrat beim WiStab Ost, zur Rückübersendung an Waldemar v. Poletika," 7 October 1941, BA-MA RW 31/299; *Kürschners Deutscher Gelehrten-Kalender, 8.–14. Ausgabe* (Berlin-W., 1954–83). Poletika (b. 1888) was a professor in Petrograd from 1919–23, emigrated in 1923 to Germany, was professor at the Berliner University from 1934/45, and for a number years the director of the Agrarwissenschaftlichen Forschungsstelle für die Oststaaten in Bonn after 1950.

27 See above all Ulrich Herbert, "Arbeit und Vernichtung: Ökonòmisches Interesse und Primat der 'Weltanschauung' im Nationalsozialismus," in *Ist der*

Nationalsozialismus Geschichte? ed. Dan Diner (Frankfurt a.M., 1993), pp. 203f. But, in view of the sequence of events—to the extent they can be reconstructed—one cannot share the view that "intentional destruction" (*Vernichtungsabsicht*) was "rationalized" by the agricultural experts only after the events. In any case, this was a selective program for murder. The same goes for assumptions based on the "primacy of the 'Weltanschauung.'"

28 See Mordechai Altschuler (ed.), *Distribution of the Jewish Population of the USSR 1939* (Jerusalem, 1993), pp. 38–41, 69–73 (I thank Dieter Pohl for calling my attention to this publication); *Bevölkerungsstatistik Weißrutheniens*, edited by the Publikationsstelle Berlin-Dahlem (Berlin, 1942).

29 See the examination of Alfred Filbert, 9 June 1959, Staatsanwaltschaft [hereafter StA] Munich I 22 Ks 1/61, Bl. 966–67R; and also 11 and 14 May 1959, StA Berlin 3 Pks 1/62, Vol. 1, Bl. 171 and 200f.; examination of Walter Blume, 2 July 1958, StA Munich I 22 Ks 1/61, Bl. 254, and also 20 May, 1960, StA Berlin 3 PKs 1/62, Vol. 6, Bl. 264R; examination of Ernst Ehlers, 17 April 1959, StA Munich I 22 Ks 1/61, p. 843/R. See Alfred Streim, *Die Behandlung sowjetischer Kriegsgefangener im "Fall Barbarossa"* (Heidelberg and Karlsruhe, 1981), pp. 88f.; for a different view see Ralf Ogorreck, *Die Einsatzgruppe und die "Genesis der Endlösung"* (Berlin, 1996), pp. 68–76.

30 The racist thinker who developed the supposed connections between Jews and their particularly active involvement in revolutionary politics is described by Fritz Nova, *Alfred Rosenberg: Nazi Theorist of the Holocaust* (New York, 1986), 103–24.

31 Ogorreck, *Einsatzgruppen*, pp. 110–27; Andrej Angrick and Martina Voigt, et al., "'Da hätte man schon ein Tagebuch führen müssen.' Das Polizeibataillon 322 und die Judenmorde am Bereich der Heeresgruppe Mitte während des Sommers und Herbstes 1941," in *Die Normalität des Verbrechens: Festschrift für Wolfgang Scheffler*, ed. Helge Grabitz, et al. (Berlin, 1994), pp. 325–385.

32 *Ereignismeldung* [hereafter EM] *43 des Chefs Sipo/SD*, 5 August 1941, BA-MA SF-01/28930, Bl. 1787.

33 Heydrich to the HSSPF im Osten, 2 July 1941, BA R 70 SU/32. Here Heydrich informed the HSSPF about the orders that he had already given the *Einsatzgruppen* before 22 June 1941.

34 See Paul Kohl, *"Ich wundere mich, daß ich noch lebe": Sowjetische Augenzeugen berichten* (Gütersloh 1990), p. 77, 84f., and 261f.; "Bericht Ministerialrat Dorsch (Zentrale der Organization Todt) 10 July 1941," in *IMT*, Vol. 25, pp. 81–83 (according to the report Kluge reserved the right to allow dismissals for himself); EM 20, EM 21, and EM 23, 12, 13 and 15 July 1941, BA-MA SF-01/28929, Bl. 1479ff., 1493, 1513 (Meeting btw Nebe and Kluge); GFP-Gruppe 570, Einsatzplan for 6–12 July, 1941, BA-MA WF-03/30429, Bl. 347–349.

35 For Brest, see EM 32, 24 July 1941, BA-MA SF-01/28930, Bl. 1637; Letter exchange 221st Sich. Div.-HSSPF Rußland-Mitte 7 and 8 July 1941, BA-MA RH 26–221/12a, Bl. 307 and 315; *Vermerk LKA* Baden-Württemberg/ZStL 23 February 1962, ZStL 202 AR-Z 52/59, pp. 3646–3676. For Bialystok, see Heiner Lichtenstein, *Himmlers grüne Helfer: Die Schutz- und Ordnungspolizei im Dritten Reich* (Cologne, 1990), pp. 69–93; Angrick and Voigt et al., *Tagebuch führen*, pp. 331–336.

36 Befehlshaber rückwärtiges Heeresgebiet Mitte, Abt. VII/Mil.-Verw., *Verwatungs-Anordnungen Nr. 1 und 2, 7, und 13.7.1941*, ZStA Minsk 409–1–1, pp. 71–73/R; RK Ostland, *Vorläufige Richtlinien für Behandlung der Juden im Gebiet des Reichskommissariats Ostland*, 18 August 1941, Ifz Fb 104/2; *Bekanntmachungen "Der Oberbefehlshaber der deutschen Armee,"* BA-MA WF-03/25645, Bl. 806 (Panzergruppe 3), WF-03/14270, Bl. 242 (4th Army) also

printed in Kohl, *Ich wundere mich*, p. 197 (9th Army). For the order of the GenQu 19 August 1941, see Befehlshaber rückwärtiges Heeresgebiet Mitte, Abt. VII/Kr.-Verw., in *Verwaltungsanordnungen Nr. 6, 12.9.1941*, BA F 40540, Bl. 795.

37 403rd Sich.Div., Abt. Ib, *Besondere Anordnungen für die Versorgung Nr. 23, 13.7.1941* (copy), ZStA Minsk 409–1–1, Bl. 14; Stadtkommissar Brest, *Lagebericht*, 21 November 1941, BA F 13752, Bl. 9; WiStab Ost, *Besondere Anordnungen Nr. 44*, 4 November 1941, BA-MA (BArchP) F 72745, Bl. 478–480.

38 Compare various reports in BA-MA RW 31/90b; *KTB WiStab Ost*, 3, 4, and 8 July 1941, BA-MA (BArchP) F 43384, Bl. 15, 17, 25; Chef WiStab Ost, Reports of 10 and 12 July 1941, BA-MA (BArchP) F 43390, Bl. 832, 836.

39 WiStab Ost, Fü/la, *Betr.: Beschäftigung jüdischer Facharbeiter*, 15 July 1941, BA-MA (BArchP) F 72745; Verbindungsstelle OKW/WiRüAmt bei Göring to Thomas, 29 July 1941, BA-MA (BArchP) F 44544, Bl. 103; *Niederschrift über die Sitzung des Wirtschaftsführungsstabes Ost* on 18 of 21 December, 1941, BA-MA (BArchP) F 623.

40 E.g., WiStab Ost, 2. *Vierzehntagesbericht (20.7–28.8)*, 9 August 1941, BA-MA (BArchP) F 43390, Bl. 870; WiIn Mitte, Chefgruppe Wirtschaft, *Besondere Anordnungen Nr. 1*, 12 July and also *Nachtrag* 13 July and *Anlage 1*, 19 July, 1941, BA-MA (BArchP) F 42747, Bl. 677, 685.

41 See e.g., *KTB Verbindungsoffizier IV* Wi OKW/WiRüAmt of the 4th Army, 5 and 6 July 1941, BA-MA (BArchP) F 42872, Bl. 9f; EM 21 and EM 145, 13 July and 12 December 1941, BA-MA SF-01/28929, Bl. 1489, 1491; and/28934, Bl. 3391.

42 WiIn Mitte, *KTB-Tätigkeitsbericht* for 20–27 July 1941, BA-MA (BArchP) F 42858, p. 668; Ortskommandantur Minsk, *Befehl Nr. 8*, 21 August, 1941, ZStA Minsk 379–2–4, p. 109; Gebietskommissar Slonim, *Lagebericht*, 25 January 1942, StA Hamburg 147 Js 29/67, Sonderband D.

43 See *Anzahl der Arbeitskräfte, die in mit Wehrmachtaufträgen belegten Betrieben beschäftigt sind, Stand: 10.10.1942*, BA-MA (BArchP) F 42898, Bl. 966f.; Kreiskommissar Grodno, "Kreiswirtschaftsamt, Bericht 9.12.1942," in Serge Klarsfeld (ed.), *Documents Concerning the Destruction of the Jews of Grodno*, Vol. 6 (Paris, 1992), p. 241.

44 For regulations against this, see e.g. the "Verordnung über Arbeitseinsatz, Verpflegung und Entlohnung der Juden des Stadtkommissars Minsk vom 25.8.1942" in *Minsker Zeitung*, 2 September 1942.

45 Urteil LG Berlin 3 PKs 1/62, 22 June 1962, in *Justiz und NS-Verbrechen*, Vol. 18 (Amsterdam, 1977), p. 616; see on the transitional phase e.g. B. *KTB Pol.Btl.322*, 31 August and 1 September 1941, BA F 56753, and *Bericht der Untersuchungskommission des Rayons Dribin*, 5 November 1944, Der Bundesbeauftragte für die Unterlagen des Staatssicherheitsdienstes der ehemaligen DDR [BStU] ZUV 9, Vol. 20, p. 17.

46 *Reitende Abteilung, SS-KavRgt. 2*, 1 August, 1941, 10:00 a.m., BA F 6296, Bl. 936; *Terminkalender Brandt*, 31 July 1941, BA NS 19/3957.

47 See the court proceedings ZStL 204 AR-Z 393/59 and LG Braunschweig 2 ks 1/63, in Staatsarchiv Wolfenbüttel, 62 Nds Fb. 2, No. 1264ff. See in general Yehoshua Büchler, "Kommandostab Reichsführer-SS: Himmler's Personal Murder Brigades in 1941," in *Holocaust and Genocide Studies* 1, no. 1 (1986): 11–25; Ruth Bettina Birn, "Zweierlei Wirklichkeit? Fallbeispiele zur Partisanenbekämpfung im Osten," in *Zwei Wege nach Moskau*; ed. Bernd Wegner (Zurich, 1991), pp. 275–290.

48 Ogorreck, *Einsatzgruppen*, pp. 179–183, 211 and 220 (for the citation).

49 Himmler was "very annoyed" and demanded daily case reports and increased brigade activity. On this, see the radio message from Grothmann (adjutant to Himmler) to Hermann (commander of the 1st SS-Inf. Brigade), 11 August (for the citation); and Knoblauch (Chef Kommandostab Reichsführer-SS) to Jeckeln and SS-Obersturmbannführer Wander to Knoblauch, both 12 August 1941, BA, NS 33/312, Bl. 18 and 26 and also NS 33/292 Bl. 23. See also the court procedure ZStL 202 AR-Z 1212/60 (1st SS-Inf. Brigade) and Ogorreck, *Einsatzgruppen*, pp. 190ff.

50 In July 1941, *Einsatzgruppe* B murdered on average 346 people per day, between 1 and 20 August 295 people per day, between 21 August and 13 September 285 people per day, between 14 and 28 September 419 people per day. Totals based on *Einsatzgruppe* B's own data in Em 31, EM 43, EM 73, EM 92, and EM 108, 23 July, 5 August, 4 September, 23 September, and 9 October 1941, BA-MA SF-01/28929–33, Bl. 1627, 1792, 2201, 2558, and 2863. Citation in *Einsatzgruppe* B, *Polizeilicher Tätigkeitsbericht für 17–23.8.1941*, BStU, ZUV 9, Vol. 31, Bl. 35.

51 See Christian Gerlach, "Failure of Plans for an SS Extermination Camp in Mogilev, Belorussia," in *Holocaust and Genocide Studies* 11, no. 1 (1997): 60–78, here 65.

52 See Res. Pol.Btl. 11, *Lagebericht*, 21 October 1941, ZStA Minsk 651–1–1, Bl. 4; judgement of LG Köln 24 Ks 1/63, 12 May 1964, in *Justiz und NS-Verbrechen*, Vol. 20 (Amsterdam, 1979), pp. 173ff.

53 See EM 92 and EM 124, 23 September and 25 October 1941, BA-MA SF-01/28932–33, Bl. 2552–54 and 3042; various court records of witnesses and perpetrators in ZStL 202 AR-Z 179/67, Dok.Bd. 1, Bl. 156ff., 199ff., 236ff., and Bd. 2, Bl. 27ff. and 170ff.; examination of L.A.M. 12 March and S. G.Z. 13 March 1949 as well as *Bericht der Untersuchungskommission des Rayons Dribin*, 5 November 1944, BStU ZUV 9, Vol. 20, Bl. 17, 111, 126.

54 EM 90, 21 September, EM 92, 23 September, EM 108, 9 October, EM 124, 25 October 1941, BA-MA SF-01/28932, Bl. 2479, 2552, /28933, Bl. 2859 and 3042f.

55 OKW/WFSt/Abt.L (IV/Qu), "Betr: Juden in den neu besetzten Ostgebieten" 12 September 1941, in *Deutsche Besatzungspolitik in der UdSSR*, ed. Norbert Müller (Cologne, 1982), p. 72; WiIn Mitte, *Lagebericht Nr. 8–10*, 6 November, 22 November, and 22 December 1941, BA-MA (BArchP) F 42862, Bl. 966, 1003, 1034.

56 For the course of events see Angrick et al., *Tagebuch führten*, pp. 346–350.

57 For an overview with at times different figures see Wila Orbach, "The Destruction of the Jews in the Nazi-Occupied Territories of the USSR," in *Soviet Jewish Affairs* 6, no. 2 (1976): 14–51.

58 Beauftragter des RMO beim Befehlshaber rückwärtiges Heeresgebiet Mitte, *Bericht Nr. 6*, 10 February 1942, BA-MA FPF-01/8212, Bl. 595.

59 Judgement of LG Köln 24 Ks 1/63, 12 May 1964 in *Justiz und NS-Verbrechen*, Vol. 20, pp. 173f.; Statements of Schönemann and of his translator R.L. (1962), StL 202 AR-Z 81/59, Vol. 3, pp. 598, 605f., 628, 695, 702, 773.

60 See the contribution by Christoph Dieckmann in this volume.

61 See AOK 9, Ic/A.O., to Panzergruppe 3, AOK 9/Ia, and Sonderkommando 7a, 28 September 1941, BDC, SL 47 F, p. 236. See also Helmut Krausnick, "Die Einsatzgruppen vom Anschluß Österreichs bis zum Feldzug gegen die Sowjerunion," in *Die Truppe des Weltanschauungskrieges*, ed. Krausnick and Hans-Heinrich Wilhelm (Stuttgart, 1981), pp. 179ff.

62 EM 133, 14 November 1941, BA-MA SF-01/28934, Bl. 3178 and 3188–90; Tätigkeits- und Lagebericht der Einsatzgruppen Nr. 7 for 1–30 November 1941, ZStL UdSSR Bd. 401.

63 See *KTB Wirtschaftskommando Bobruisk* for 1–15 October and 15–31 October 1941, BA-MA (BArchP) F 42901, Bl. 24; *KTB Gruppe IV Wi zb V Nr. 38* (Borisov) for 20–27 October and 3 December 1941, BA-MA (BArchP) F 43063, Bl. 955 and 958; *Rayonverwaltung Borisov* 23 December 1941, 23 January, 23 February, and 18 March 1942, Gebietsarchiv Minsk 624–1–1, Bl. 17, 20f., and 25; on Vitebsk e.g. examination of W.I.B., 29 August 1944, ZStL USSR Vol. 423, contents data to p. 65f.; *Berichte der Untersuchungskommission Vitebsk*, ZStA Minsk 861–1–5, Bl. 15, 23; Leni Yahil, *The Holocaust* (New York and London, 1990), p. 271.

64 See for another view Hannes Heer, " 'Killing Fields': Die Wehrmacht und der Holocaust," in *Mittelweg* 36, no. 3 (1994): 7–29, here 23–26.

65 On goals and the order of command, see Kommandant in Weissruthenien des Wehrmachtbefehlshabers Ostland, Abt. Ia, *Monatsbericht* 11 October-10 November, 1941, BA-MA RH 26–707/2, Bl. 1 (although here reports that the "total eradication of these alien [volksfremden] elements was carried out" are included alongside descriptions of local limitations on the operations and the evacuation of "country Jews" [Landjuden]); for the Res. Pol.Btl. 11 see Fschr. HSSPF Rußland-Nord to Himmler et. al., 6 and 10 October 1941, BA D-H ZB 6735, O.II, Bl. 111 and 115; and Akte ZStA Minsk 651–1–1.

66 See Gebietskommissar Slonim, *Lagebericht 25.1.1942*, StA Hamburg 147 Js 29–67, Sonderband D; a Jewish survivor received information on the motive and the planned number of victims from the deputy *Ortskommandant*, see court proceedings of A.O., 26 October 1960, ibid., Sonderband C1, Bl. 19, 22; also see the remarks of a perpetrator on the above mentioned appeal in the examination of X.H., 1 February 1974, ibid., Vol. 54, Bl. 10326f.; on the sudden halt of the operation when the "quota" had been reached see the statement by J.M. (1946), ibid., Vol. 1, Bl. 140, 142; and Nachum Albert, *The Destruction of Slonim Jewry* (New York, 1990), p. 87. On Minsk, see EM 124, 1 December 1941, BA-MA SF-01/28934; judgement of LG Koblenz 9 Ks 1/61, 12 June 1961 in *Justiz und NS-Verbrechen*, Vol. 17, pp. 510–14; Wassili Grossman and Ilja Ehrenburg (ed.), *Das Schwarzbuch*, pp. 242–45; Anna Krasnoperka, *Briefe meiner Erinnerung: Mein Überleben im jüdischen Ghetto von Minsk 1941/42* (Haus Villigst, 1991), pp. 22–27.

67 In this regard, see Herbert Jäger, *Verbrechen unter totalitärer Herrschaft* (Frankfurt a.M., 1982), p. 343.

68 BdO Ostland to Lohse, 17 October 1941, ZStA Minsk 651–1–1. Bl. 28.

69 See Dieter Pohl, *Nationalsozialistische Judenverfolgung in Ostgalizien 1941–1944* (Munich, 1996), pp. 139ff., and the contribution by Thomas Sandkühler in this volume; Götz Aly, *"Endlösung": Völkerverschiebung und der Mord an der europäischen Juden* (Frankfurt a.M., 1995), p. 355; Shmuel Spector, *The Holocaust of Volhynian Jews 1941–1944* (Jerusalem, 1990).

70 [WiRüAmt] Chef des Stabes, *Aktennotiz: Besprechung bei Staatssekretär Körner am 4.9.1941, 12:00*, BA-MA RW 19/177, Bl. 117–19; letter from GenQu Wagner to his wife, 9 September 1941, BA-MA N 510/48; Verbindungsstab des OKW/WiRüAmts bei Göring to Thomas 16 September 1941, in *IMT*, Vol. 36, pp. 107f.; *KTB WiStabOst* 23 September 1941, BA-MA (BArchP) F 43384, Bl. 146. Citation in Elke Fröhlich (ed.), *Die Tagebücher von Joseph Goebbels, Teil II., Bd. II* (Munich, 1996), 132 (17 October 1941). I am grateful to Peter Witte, Hemer, for pointing me to that source. See also ibid. on 23 October 1941 (p. 161).

71 See my dissertation (as in note 1).

72 For this, see the court proceedings ZStL 204 AR-Z 117/67, 119/67, 121/67, and

122/67; the reports of the investigation commission of the Polesje district, 20 June 1945, of the Kreis Kalinkowitschi, 15 December 1944, and Mosyr 12 January 1945, ZStA Minsk 845–1–12, Bl. 1–4, and 861–1–12, Bl. 25–30 and 71–76.

73 Frontline units murdered 20 Jewish people in Lida, 73 in Baranovitchi, 16 in Pinsk, several in Grodno and Lenin, at one time 10 and then 20 in Slonim, and 100–300 in Stolbzy. For details see my dissertation (note 1); for a different interpretation, see Heer, *Killing Fields*, pp. 7ff.

74 In February 1942 alone, Wehrmacht units killed 2,200 Jews in the area of Army Group Center, see Abwehrkommando III (B), *Tätigkeitsbericht Feber, 12.3.1942*, BA D-H FW 490, A, 28, Bl. 10; also see Hannes Heer, "Die Logik des Vernichtungskrieges, Wehrmacht und Partisanenkampf," in *Vernichtungskrieg: Verbrechen der Wehrmacht 1941–1944*, ed. H. Heer and Klaus Naumann (Hamburg, 1995), pp. 104–38, here 117. The statements in Heer, "Killing Fields", on a general "Wehrmacht liquidation program" beyond the actions of the 707th Inf. Div. should be relativized: the 354th Inf. Rgt. took part in large massacres "only" in operations of the section troop Borisov of Einsatzkommando 8 and did not carry them out alone (see Zentralstelle Dortmund 45 Js 9/64, e.g. Vol. 1, pp. 165f.; Vol. 2, pp. 3ff., 11f., 43f.; Vol. 3, pp. 102ff.; Vol. 6, pp. 131f.; Vol. 7, pp. 54f.; Vol. 9, pp. 106f.; Vol. 10, pp. 132; see ZStL 202 AR-Z 81/59, esp. Vol. 3). The at least 3,500 victims of the "fight against the partisans"—Operation "Bamberg" in early 1942—were not "mostly Jews" but rather for the most part non-Jewish farmers; only about 200 were Jews (see *Tagesmeldung der Einheiten der 707th Inf. Div.*, BA-MA RH 26–707/5 and BA-MA WF-03/7364, Bl. 471–94; and eyewitness accounts in Ales Admovitch, Yanka Bryl, and Wladimir Kolesnik, *Out of the Fire* (Moscow, 1980), pp. 31–56). In the Glebokie district (Glubokoje), in May and June 1942, 13,000 Jews were murdered not by the Wehrmacht but by the section troop Lepel of Einsatzkommando 9 under Heinz Tangermann with the assistance of the local German Gendarmes (Gebietskommissar Glebokie to GK Weißruthenien, 1 July 1942, ZStA Minsk 370–1–483, Bl. 15; in this regard see also Jürgen Matthäus, " 'Reibungslos und planmäßig': Die zweite Welle der Judenverfolgung im Generalkommissariat Weißruthenien (1942–1944)," in *Jahrbuch für Antisemitismusforschung* 4 (1995): 258f.; Heinz Tangermann, SS-Untersturmführer, *Bericht, Betr.: Bandenkampfabzeichen*, 30 March 1944, BA D-H ZM 635, A.1, Bl. 73–76 [fragment]).

75 See ZStL 202 AR-Z 64/60 against employees of the Bobruisk field airport; for Orscha, see Heer, *Vernichtungskrieg*, p. 122; for Borisov see Hans-Heinrich Wilhelm, "Die Einsatzgruppe A der Sicherheitspolizei und des SD 1941/42," in Krausnick and Wilhelm, pp. 576–81; on Slonim and Nowogrodek see Heer, *Killing Fields*, p. 25.

76 EM 178, 9 March 1942, BA-MA SF-01/28936, Bl. 3966; *Schwarzbuch*, pp. 249f.; on Baranovitchi, see also *Vermerk* ZStL 2 July 1969, StA Munich 1 113 Ks 1/65a-b, Vol. 7, Bl. 1203. On the meeting of 12 February, see Em 169, 16 February 1942, BA-MA SF-01/28935, Bl. 3846.

77 Examination of Georg Heuser, 1 March 1966, StA Hamburg 147 Js 31/67, Bl. 4291.

78 For this citation, see "Bericht des ständigen Vertreters des Ostministeriums beim RK Ostland 12. 5. über eine Besprechung bei Lohse" on 26 March 1942, IfZ Fb 104/2. There were massive murder "actions" in the following months in GK White Ruthenia alone, see RMO, 20 September 1941 (Durchschlag), BA R 6/387, Bl. 1; RKO, Abt.IIa4, *Betr.: Einsatz jüdischer Ärtze (gez.*

Trampedach) 3 November 1941, ZStA Minsk 370–1–141a, Bl. 183. It is especially noteworthy that this report was written not by the Health Department *(Gesundheitsabteilung)* but by the specialist for Jewish questions or "Jewish expert" *(Judenreferenten)* in the Political Department *(Abteilung Politik)* of the RKO.

79 GK White Ruthenia to the Gebietskommissare, 10 July 1942, IfZ Fb 104/2.

80 GK White Ruthenia, Abt, IIa, *Betr: Auftreten von Juden bei den Banditen*, 8 September 1942 (with Trampedach's marginal note), OSOBYI Archives, Moscow 504–1–7.

81 See court proceedings StA Mainz 3 Ks 1/67.

82 For the citation, see *Stenographisches Protokoll der Besprechung Görings mit den Reichskommissaren und den Militärbefehlshabern der besetzten Gebiete, 6.8.1942*, in *IMT*, Vol. 39, p. 402. See Kube to Lohse, "Betr.: Partisanenbekämpfung und Judenaktion im Generalbezirk Weißruthenien," 31 July 1942, printed in Ernst Klee, Willi Dreßen, and Volker Riess, *"Schöne Zeiten": Judenmord aus der Sicht der Täter und Gaffer* (Frankfurt a.M., 1988), pp. 169–71. On the different districts, see e.g. the court proceedings StA Hamburg 147 Js 29/67 (Slonim); StA Munich 1 113 Ks 1/65a-b (KdS-Außenstelle Baranovitchi). The figure of 112,000 Jews murdered in 1942 in GK White Ruthenia is based on data in my dissertation (see note 1).

83 See the figures in note 82; StA Frankfurt a.M., Anklageschrift 4 Js 901/62, 28 March 1968, ZStL 204 AR-Z 393/59, Vol. 17, Bl. 4629; Koch's remarks on the note about the meeting in Rowno on 26–28 August 1942 in *IMT*, Vol. 25, p. 318. See Gerald Fleming, *Hitler und die Endlösing: "Es ist des Führers Wunsch . . ."* (Wiesbaden and Munich, 1982), pp. 141–148. For figures on the Jewish population, see *Meldungen aus den besetzten Ostgebieten des Chefs Sipo/SD, Nr. 5, 29.5.1942*, BA-MA SF-01/28937, Bl. 430.

84 Himmler to Keitel 9 July and OKW (Warlimont) to Backe, 13 July 1942, BA-MA (BArchP) F 43386, Bl. 507, 510; and Spector, *The Holocaust of Volhynian Jews*, pp. 172ff.

85 See Himmler to HSSPF Ukraine 27 October 1942, in Helmut Heiber (ed.), *"Reichsführer . . .!" Briefe von und an Heinrich Himmler* (Stuttgart, 1968), p. 165; see also e.g. Raul Hilberg, *Die Vernichtung der europäischen Juden* (Frankfurt a.M., 1991), p. 400; in contrast see WFSt/Qu, *Betr.: Besprechung beim WBfh. Ukraine am 12.9.42*, notation of 14 September 1942, BA-MA RW 31/59b, Bl. 365 ("the Reichskommissar ordered the liquidation of these Jews"); GK Wolhynien-Podolien (KdS Rowno?) to various KdS-Außenstellen, 31 July 1942 (copy), Archiv der Polnischen Hauptkommission Warsaw, *Sammlung von Aktensplittern von SS- und Polizeieinheiten*, Vol. 77. I am grateful to Dieter Pohl for copies from these files.

86 See court proceedings LG Bielefeld 5 Ks 1/65, Nordrhein-Westfälisches Staatsarchiv Detmold D 21 A, Nr. 6134–6360. For an overview of the German "actions" see Yitzhak Arad, *Belzec, Sobibor, Treblinka: The Operation Reinhard Death Camps* (Bloomington and Indianapolis, 1987), pp. 131–135.

87 Reuben Ainstein, *Jüdischer Widerstand im deutschbesetzten Osteuropa während des Zweiten Weltkrieges* (Oldenburg, 1993), p. 89 and 233f.; court proceedings StA Mainz 3 Ks 1/67 (Lida); RK Ostland, II Fin, *Betr: Zusammenfassung der Juden in Konzentrationslagern*, 31 July 1943, BA D-H ZR 945, A.2, Bl. 22f.; on the "seamless replacement" *[reibungslose Ersetzung]* see WiIn Mitte, *Aktenvermerk über Besprechung mit GK Weißruthenien, 20.9.1943*, BA-MA (BArchP) F 42860, Bl. 1044; for a retrospective view see Gebietskommissar Glebokie, *Räumungsbericht 9.8.1944*, BA R 93/14.

88 This evaluation in Moshe Kaganowitsch, *Der Anteil der Juden an der Partisanenbewegung Sowjetrußlands* (contents summary), StA Hamburg 147 Js 29/67, Vol. 3, Bl. 594/R; Hauptkommissar Baranowitsche, *Bericht 27.8.1942*, Nbg.Dok. NG-1315; Shmuel Spector, "Jewish Resistance in Small Towns of Eastern Poland," in *Jews in Eastern Poland and in the USSR, 1939–1946*, ed. Norman Davies and Antony Polonsky (London, 1991), pp. 138–144, here 143f.; Kohl, *Ich wundere mich*, p. 75.
89 EM 133, 14 November 1941, BA-MA SF-01/28934, Bl. 3196.
90 See Helmut Heiber (ed.), "Aus den Akten des Gauleiters Kube," in *VfZ* 4 (1956): 67–92.

26

IMPROVISED GENOCIDE?

The Emergence of the 'Final Solution' in the 'Warthegau'[1]

Ian Kershaw

Source: *Transactions of the Royal Historical Society, 6th Series*, vol. 2, (1992), 51–78.

THE 'Warthegau'—officially the 'Reichsgau Wartheland', with its capital in Posen (Poznan)—was the largest of three areas of western Poland[2] annexed to the German Reich after the defeat of Poland in 1939. In the genesis of the 'Final Solution' it plays a pivotal role. Some of the first major deportations of Jews took place from the Warthegau. The first big ghetto was established on the territory of the Warthegau, at Lodz (which the Nazis renamed Litzmannstadt). In autumn 1941, the first German Jews to be deported at the spearhead of the combing-out process of European Jewry were dispatched to the Warthegau. The possibility of liquidating ghettoised Jews had by then already been explicitly raised for the first time, in the summer of 1941, significantly by Nazi leaders in the Warthegau. The first mobile gassing units to be deployed against the Jews operated in the Warthegau in the closing months of 1941. And the systematic murder of the Jews began in early December 1941 in the first extermination camp—actually a 'gas van station'[3]—established at Chelmno on the Ner, in the Warthegau.

Despite the centrality of the Warthegau to the unfolding of what the Nazis called 'the Final Solution of the Jewish Question'—the systematic attempt to exterminate the whole of European Jewry—the precise course of development of Nazi anti-Jewish policy in the Warthegau, though mentioned in every account of the origins of the 'Final Solution', has not been exhaustively explored.[4]

To focus upon the Warthegau in the genesis of the 'Final Solution' can, however, help to contribute towards answering the central questions which have come to dominate scholarly debate on the emergence of systematic genocide: how and when the decision to wipe out the Jews of

Europe came about, whether at the moment of German triumph in mid-summer 1941, or later in the year when the growing probability of pro-longed war in the east ruled out an envisaged 'territorial solution'; Hitler's own role in the shift to a policy of outright genocide; and whether the 'Final Solution' followed a single order or set of directives issued from Berlin as the culmination of a long-held 'programme' of the Nazi leader-ship, or unfolded in haphazard and piecemeal fashion, instigated by 'local initiatives' of regional Nazi bosses, improvised as a largely ad hoc response to the logistical difficulties of a 'Jewish problem' they had created for themselves, and only gradually congealing into a full-scale 'programme' for genocide.[5]

The deficiencies and ambiguities of the evidence, enhanced by the lan-guage of euphemism and camouflage used by the Nazis even among them-selves when dealing with the extermination of the Jews, mean that absolute certainty in answering these complex questions can not be achieved. Close assessment of the Warthegau evidence, it is the contention of this essay, nevertheless sheds light on developments and contributes towards an interpretation which rests on the balance of probabilities.

When the rapidly improvised boundaries of the newly created Reichs-gau Posen (from 29 January 1940 Reichsgau Wartheland or, for short, the Warthegau—taking its name from the Warthe, the central river of the province) were eventually settled, they included an extensive area centring upon the large industrial town of Lodz, which had formerly been in Con-gress Poland and had never been part of Prussian Poland.[6] The borders of the Reich were thereby extended some 150–200 kilometres eastwards of the boundaries existing before 1918. For Nazi aims at 'solving the Jewish Question', the significance of this extension was that it brought within the territory of the Warthegau—which was to be ruthlessly germanised—an area containing over 350,000 Jews (some 8% of the total population of the region). The most important figures in the Warthegau scene after 1939 were Arthur Greiser, Reich Governor and at the same time Gauleiter of the Nazi Party, and Wilhelm Koppe, the SS and police chief of the region. Greiser, born in the Posen province in 1897, was utterly ruthless and single-minded in his determination to make his region the 'model Gau' of Nazi rule.[7] He called upon a 'special commission', given to him by Hitler personally, whenever he encountered difficulties or obstructions.[8] He also stood high in Himmler's favour, and was given on 30 January 1942 the honorary rank of Obergruppenführer in the SS.[9] Koppe, born in Hildesheim in 1896, nominally subordinate to Greiser but in practice pos-sessing a high degree of independence as the leading SS functionary in the region, had effective control over deportation policy in the Warthegau.[10] He was well up in Himmler's good books and had the ready ear of the Reichsführer-SS. At the same date as Greiser's promotion within the SS, 30 January 1942 and precisely at the point when the killing of the Warthegau

Jews had begun, Koppe was promoted by Himmler to the rank of SS-Obergruppenführer and General der Polizei.' Like Greiser, he was notorious for his cold ruthlessness.

The tone for the administration of Poland was provided by Hitler himself. Admiral Canaris pointed out to General Keitel on 12 September 1939 that he had knowledge that extensive executions (Füsilierungen) were planned for Poland 'and that the nobility and clergy especially were to be exterminated (ausgerottet)'. Keitel replied that this had already been decided by the Führer. The Wehrmacht had to accept the 'racial extermination' and 'political cleansing' by the SS and the Gestapo, even if it did not itself want anything to do with it. That was why, alongside the military commanders, civilian commanders were being appointed, to whom the 'racial extermination' (Volkstums-Ausrottung) would fall.[12] On 17 October, Hitler spoke to a small group of those leaders most directly concerned of a 'hard racial struggle' which did not allow any 'legal constraints' or comply with principles otherwise upheld. The new Reich territories would have to be purged 'of Jews, Polacks, and rabble', and the remainder of the former Poland (the Generalgouvernement) would serve as the dumping ground for such groups of the population.[13] Hitler was involved at an early stage in schemes for a 'solution' to the 'Jewish Question' in Poland, though the ideas themselves emanated from Himmler (presumably in close collaboration with chief of the Security Police Reinhard Heydrich). At a meeting on 14 September 1939, Heydrich explained his own views on the 'Jewish problem' in Poland to the assembled Security Police leaders, adding that suggestions from the Reichsführer were being placed before Hitler, 'which only the Führer could decide'.[14] These were presumably the suggestions which became incorporated in Heydrich's directions to leaders of the Einsatzgruppen on 21 September 1939 for the concentration of Jews in the larger towns as a preparatory measure for a subsequent 'final goal' (to be kept 'strictly secret').[15] The 'final goal' was at this time evidently the eventual deportation of the Jews from Reich territory and from Poland to the intended reservation east of the Vistula, as Hitler himself indicated on 29 September to Alfred Rosenberg.[16] Hitler's views accorded precisely with guidelines which Heydrich drew up on that same day. The intention was to create a type of 'Reich Ghetto' to the east of Warsaw and around Lublin 'in which all the political and Jewish elements, who are to be moved out of the future German Gaue, will be accommodated'.[17] The plans for Poland, as they were gradually congealing in September and early October 1939, amounted, therefore, to a three-fold division: of those parts to be incorporated into the Reich and eventually wholly Germanised, and sealed off by an eastern fortification; of a German-run 'foreign-speaking Gau' under Hans Frank outside a proposed 'East Wall', centring on Cracow and coming to be called the 'General Government', as a type of buffer zone; and of a Jewish settlement to the east of this area, into which all Jews from Poland and Germany would be dumped.[18] The initial expectations, both of a Jewish reservation in the Lublin area and of the mass deportation of German Jews to the General Government rapidly, however, proved illusory. The organisational and administrative difficulties involved had been hopelessly underestimated. Eichmann's immediate attempt, in October 1939, to deport Vienna's Jews to the Lublin area was rapidly stopped.[19] And in the event, apart from small-scale deportations from Stettin and Schneidemühl in Pomerania to the Lublin area in February and March 1940—an SS 'intiative' which Frank's administration could not cope with, prompting a protest from the General Governor and a temporary ban announced by Göring on 24 March 1940 on deportation of Jews into Frank's domain[20]—Jews from the Altreich (Germany of the pre-1938 boundaries) were not deported to the east until autumn 1941.[21] From the measures for occupied Poland decided by the central Nazi leadership in September 1939, it can be seen that Hitler set the tone, and provided the ultimate authority for the brutality of racial policy; and that he had far-reaching but imprecise notions of future developments, drawing at least in part on policy initiatives suggested by Himmler, which rapidly proved unfeasible and impracticable. Precisely because Hitler's barbarous imperatives offered no more than broad but loosely formulated aims and sanction for action of the most brutal kind, they opened the door to the wildest initiatives from agencies of Party and State, and above all, of course, from the SS. The authorities on the spot in the Warthegau did not, in fact, reckon that they would have too much difficulty in tackling the 'Jewish Question', and consequently grossly underestimated the self-created logistical problems. The view prevailed that the real problem was Polish, not Jewish.[22] At the outset of the occupation, the Jews were seen by the Warthegau leadership as a sideshow.[23] The main issue in the Warthegau was thought to be less the 'Jewish' than the 'Polish question'.

Initially, it seemed that things were running more or less according to expectation. In his new capacity as Reich Commissar for the Strengthening of German Nationhood, under powers bestowed on him by Hitler on 7 October, Himmler on 30 October ordered all Jews to be cleared out of the incorporated territories in the months November 1939 to February 1940.[24] On the basis of the discussions on 8 November 1939 in Cracow, at which he was present, about 'the evacuation of Jews and Congress Poles from the Old Reich and from the Reich Gaue of Danzig, Posen' and other areas,[25] Koppe issued instructions on 12 November 1939 for the deportation from the Warthegau between 15 November 1939 and 28 February 1940 of, initially, 200,000 Poles and 100,000 Jews.[26] This appears to have been subjected to slight delay and an amendment of the numbers involved. For on 28 November, Heydrich ordered an initial 'short-term plan' (Nahplan) to deport 80,000 Jews and Poles from the Warthegau to the

General Government between the 1st and the 16th of December 1939 at a rate of 5,000 per day, to make way for 40,000 Baltic Germans.[27] These expulsions were immediately put into effect. Discussions with Eichmann in Berlin on 4 January 1940 then indicated the goal for the Warthegau as the deportations of 200,000 Jews and 80,000 Poles.[28] But at a meeting in Berlin on 30 January 1940, the first murmurings of complaint from the General Government about the number of expellees being deported from the Warthegau over the border could be registered.[29] By the time Koppe was forced to reply, in spring 1940, to the ever louder complaints, the total number of Jews and Poles deported had reached 128,011.[30]

By February 1940, deep divisions on deportation policy were apparent. While Himmler pressed for speedy deportation of Poles and Jews to make room for the planned influx of ethnic Germans into the annexed territories, Göring opposed the loss of manpower useful to the war effort and was backed by Frank, anxious to block the expanding numbers of expellees being forced into his domain.[31] In April, Greiser's request to deport the Warthegau Jews was deferred until the coming August.[32] But by the summer of that year it was plain that the intended deportations from the Warthegau into the General Government could not be carried out. An important meeting on the issue took place in Cracow on 31 July 1940.[33] Greiser emphasised at the meeting the growing difficulties in the Warthegau. He spoke of the 'massing' of Jews as the construction of a ghetto in Litzmannstadt (Lodz) had concentrated around 250,000 Jews there. This was, he declared, merely a provisional solution.[34] All these Jews had to leave the Warthegau, and it had been envisaged that they would be deported to the General Government. He had imagined that the modalities would be discussed at the meeting. But now a new decision—that is, to deport the Jews overseas, to Madagascar—had emerged. Clarification was crucial. The difficulties of feeding the Jews forced into the ghetto as well as the mounting problems of disease meant, he claimed, that they could not be kept there over the coming winter. A temporary solution had at all costs to be found which would allow for the deportation of these Jews into another territory. The Governor General, Hans Frank, reminded Greiser that Himmler had given him the assurance, on Hitler's command, that no more Jews were to be sent into the General Government. Koppe brought the discussion back to the looming crisis in the Warthegau. The position regarding the Jews was deteriorating daily, he claimed, repeating that the ghetto in Litzmannstadt had only been set up on the presumption that the deportation of the Jews concentrated there would commence in mid 1940. Frank replied that the germanisation of Litzmannstadt could not take place overnight and might well last fifteen years. The situation in the General Government, he stated, was in any case worse than that in the Warthegau. Greiser correctly drew the conclusion from the discussion that there was no prospect, even as an interim solution, of the General Government receiving the Warthegau's quarter of a million Jews. It was again stressed, however, by his entourage that there could be no question of the Jews remaining in Litzmannstadt and that 'the Jewish question must, therefore, be solved in some way or other'.[35] On 6 November 1940, Frank informed Greiser by telegram that further deportations of Poles and Jews from the Warthegau into the General Government were impossible before the end of the war. He had informed Himmler of this position, and given instructions to turn back any transports.[36]

Meanwhile, conditions for the Jews in the improvised ghettos and camps of the Warthegau were unspeakable. Outbreaks of epidemic disease were inevitable. At Kutno, where 6,500 Jews were confined in a former sugar factory, spotted fever (Fleckfieber) broke out on 30 October 1940. Breaking up the camp or dispersal of the inmates into buildings in adjoining streets was ruled out for fear of infecting Germans. Even fresh straw for bedding and hot water for delousing could not be provided. It was reported to Greiser that as things stood any possibility of combating the spotted fever in the camp could be ruled out. Worries were expressed about the situation in the coming winter. The epidemic was predictably unstoppable. By the summer of 1941 there had been 1145 cases, 280 of them fatal. The camp was finally closed in March 1942, by which time there had been 1369 cases, 313 leading to deaths.[37] A fate worse than spotted fever, of course, awaited the survivors. In the huge Lodz ghetto, whose Jewish population when hermetically sealed off from the rest of the city on 1 May 1940 numbered 163,177 persons, starvation went hand in hand with disease.[38] The problems of administration and control, of food provision and epidemic containment—that is the difficulties of coping with the internment of the Warthegau Jews which the Nazi leadership both in Berlin and in Posen had been in such a rush to bring about—were only too apparent to Greiser, Koppe, and other heads of the Warthegau administration, not least the Gestapo and the local government leaders in Lodz itself. The pressure which Greiser and Koppe had sought to put on Frank mirrored the pressure they were under from their own subordinates to do something about the mounting and apparently insoluble 'Jewish problem' in the province. But by mid 1941, there was no solution in sight.

It was at this juncture, however, in the summer of 1941, that talk began of new possibilities which might be contemplated. And the first evidence of such possibilities being envisaged can be witnessed in remarks issuing from the top echelon of the Warthegau administration. On 16 July 1941, the head of the Security Service (SD) in Posen, SS-Sturmbannführer Rolf-Heinz Höppner—a man close to both Greiser and Koppe—sent to Adolf Eichmann in the Reich Security Head Office in Berlin a summary, headed 'Solution of the Jewish Problem', of discussions, involving a variety of agencies, in the Reich Governor's headquarters. A possible solution to the

'Jewish Question' in the Reichsgau Wartheland had been broached. This amounted to the concentration of all Warthegau Jews in a huge camp for 300,000 persons close to the centre of coal production, where those Jews capable of working could be exploited in a number of ways with relatively easy policing (as the Police Chief in Lodz, SS-Brigadeführer Albert vouchsafed) and without epidemic danger to the non-Jewish population. The next item addressed the issue of what to do about those Jews incapable of working. A new, ominous, note was struck, offering a cynical rationalisation for genocide. 'There is the danger this winter', ran the minute, 'that the Jews can no longer all be fed. It is to be seriously considered whether the most humane solution might not be to finish off those Jews not capable of working by some sort of fast-working preparation. This would be in any event more pleasant than letting them starve'. Additionally, it was recommended that all Jewesses still capable of bearing children be sterilised, so that 'the Jewish problem' would be completely solved within the current generation. Reich Governor Greiser, it was added, had not yet commented on the matter. Government President Uebelhoer in Litzmannstadt had, however, given the impression that he did not want the ghetto there to disappear because it was so lucrative. Just how much could be made from the Jews had been explained to Höppner by pointing out that the Reich Labour Ministry was prepared to pay six marks a day from a special fund for each Jewish worker, whereas the actual cost amounted to only eighty pfennige a day. Höppner's covering note asked for Eichmann's opinion. 'The things sound in part fantastic', Höppner concluded, 'but would in my view be quite capable of implementation'.[39]

The Höppner memorandum demonstrates that there were still in July 1941 divergent views—even among the Lodz authorities themselves—about the treatment of the ghettoised Jews, now the ghettos appeared to be a long-term prospect rather than a transient solution.[40] But above all, the memorandum highlights the idea of genocide at an embryonic stage.

By July 1941, events elsewhere were already pushing German policy towards the Jews strongly in the direction of genocide. The preparations for the 'war of annihilation'[41] with the Soviet Union marked, it has been noted, a 'quantum jump' into genocide.[42] Certainly, a genocidal climate was now present as never before. But orders for a general killing of Jews were, recent research indicates, not, as is often presumed, transmitted orally by Heydrich to the leaders of the Einsatzgruppen before the invasion of the Soviet Union. The Einsatzgruppen did not initially behave in a unified fashion, and there was a gradual escalation of killing during the first weeks of the campaign. Only after clarification of the tasks of the Einsatzgruppen had apparently been sought and provided by Himmler in August 1941, was there a drastic extensification of the slaughter to all Jews, irrespective of age or sex.[43] Outside the Soviet Union, too, the obvious impasses in anti-Jewish policy were, from a number of differing directions, now developing a rapid, and accelerating, momentum towards outright and total genocide.

On 31 July 1941, Göring, who had been nominally in charge of coordinating the forced emigration of German Jews since the aftermath of the great pogrom of November 1938, commissioned Heydrich with undertaking the preparations for the 'complete solution of the Jewish question within the German sphere of influence in Europe'.[44] All Göring did, in fact, was to sign a document drawn up in Heydrich's office, almost certainly drafted by Eichmann.[45] The initiative came, in other words, from the Reich Security Head Office. The Göring mandate has frequently been interpreted as the direct reflection of a Hitler order to kill the Jews of Europe. Such an interpretation is open to doubt.[46] It seems more probable that the mandate still looked to a territorial solution, envisaging the removal of German and other European Jews to a massive reservation in the east—somewhere beyond the Urals. The war, it was thought, would soon be over. The opportunity of such a territorial solution would then present itself. The result, needless to say, would itself have amounted to a different form of genocide in the long run. But it was not the actual 'final solution' which historically emerged in the closing months of 1941 and the beginning of 1942. The territorial solution which was still being pressed for in the summer of 1941 was predicated upon a swift German victory. By September, this prospect was already dwindling. Before this time, Hitler, holding to his notion that the Jews could serve as 'hostages', had resisted pressure, especially from Heydrich and Goebbels, to deport the German Jews to the east.[47] In mid September, a Foreign Office enquiry about deporting Serbian Jews to the east was turned down by Eichmann on the grounds that not even German Jews could be moved to Russia or the General Government. Eichmann recommended shooting.[48] But around the same time, in mid September 1941, Hitler was persuaded to change his mind about deporting the German Jews.[49] In the next months, the crucial steps which culminated in the 'Final Solution' proper were taken. In October and November 1941 the threads of the extermination net were rapidly pulled together.

In this development, events in the Warthegau played a crucial role. Notification of the Führer's wish that the Old Reich and the Protectorate (Bohemia and Moravia) should be cleared of Jews, as a first stage to Poland and then in the following spring further to the east, was sent by Himmler to Greiser on 18 September 1941, four days after Rosenberg's apparently successful intervention in persuading Hitler to deport the German Jews. Evidently because of the immediate implications for the Warthegau of the deportation order, the letter was sent directly to Greiser as head of the province's government and administration. Himmler reported the intention to deport 60,000 Jews to Litzmannstadt for the duration of the winter. Further details, added Himmler, would be provided by Heydrich, either directly or via Koppe.[50] Whether the figure of 60,000 Jews was an error, or was rapidly revised, is unclear. But within a week the number concerned was referred to as 20,000 Jews and now 5,000 Gypsies.[51] Possibly, they were intended as the first 'instalment'. But even this number was far too great for the authorities in Litzmannstadt. The ghetto administration vehemently protested at the intended influx, and the protest—on the grounds of existing massive overcrowding, provisioning problems, economic dislocation, and danger of epidemics—was conveyed by the Government President of Litzmannstadt, Uebelhoer, in the strongest terms to Berlin.[52] But it was to no avail. Heydrich stated— though his telegram to Uebelhoer was overtaken by events and never sent—that the deportation was 'absolutely necessary and no longer to be delayed', and that Greiser had given his permission to receive the Jews in Litzmannstadt.[53] Himmler demanded the same understanding from Uebelhoer that he had received from Greiser. He sharply upbraided Uebelhoer, for whom Greiser intervened, for his objectionable tone.[54]

From this exchange, it is clear that the pressures for deportation were coming from Berlin, that Greiser was willing to comply despite the already mounting impossibility of 'solving' the Warthegau's own 'Jewish question', and that opposition from Litzmannstadt itself was simply ruled out by Reich Security Head Office. The stated aim, the further expulsion of the Jews the coming spring to the east, does not appear at this point to have been concealing an actual intention to exterminate the Jews in death camps in Poland. Clearly, Uebelhoer knew nothing of any such intention.[55] Hitler himself spoke at the end of the first week in October of transporting Czech Jews directly 'to the east' and not first into the General Government,[56] and both Heydrich and Himmler referred in early October to German Jews being sent to camps in the Baltic.[57] Here, of course, their fate, in view of the murderous onslaught of the Einsatzgruppen in the Soviet Union, would have been all too predictable. The decision to deport Jews into areas where they had already been killed in their tens of thousands was plainly in itself genocidal.[58] By this time, in late September or early October 1941, it would appear that the decision for physical extermination—at least of Jews incapable of working—had in effect been taken, though Russia rather than Poland was still foreseen as the area of implementation. The option of deporting the Jews 'farther east' to the Soviet Union rapidly vanished, however, in the next weeks with first transport difficulties, then the stalling of the German advance and the deteriorating military position in Russia. Far from a quick blitzkrieg victory, the end of the war in the east was nowhere in sight. And towards the end of October Eichmann was making it clear that the mooted further deportation to the east of Jews deported from Germany to Litzmannstadt referred only to Jews 'fit to work'.[59] Since Jews in the east incapable of working were already being earmarked for extermination, the implication was obvious.

New approaches to 'solving the Jewish Question' were meanwhile beginning to emerge. In circles closely connected with the 'Jewish Question', there was now ominous talk of 'special measures' for extermination.[60] Viktor Brack, of the Führer Chancellory and formerly the inspiration of the 'euthanasia action' (whose personnel, after the halting of the 'programme' in the Reich in late August, were now available for redeployment and carried with them 'expertise' derived from the gassing of the incurably sick), offered advice on the potential of poison gas as a means for tackling the 'Jewish problem', again at precisely this juncture.[61] In October, too, the SS commandeered Polish labourers at Belzec in eastern Poland to undertake the construction of the extermination camp there— one of the three camps (the others were Sobibor and Treblinka) which developed into 'Operation Reinhard', directed by the Lublin police chief Globocnik.[62] The former euthanasia personnel dispatched to liaise with Globocnik arrived in Lublin around the same time.[63] The first experimental gassings at Auschwitz (of Soviet prisoners-of-war) took place in late summer and autumn 1941, and construction of the extermination camp at Auschwitz-Birkenau was underway by the end of the year.[64] On 16 December 1941, Hans Frank spoke openly in a meeting of leaders of the General Government about the need to 'exterminate the Jews wherever we find them', pointing out that the Gauleiter of the eastern territories were saying they too did not want the Jews. They were asking why there was not a resort to 'self-help' to liquidate the Jews, rather than sending them to the east. Frank commented that he did not know how the extermination of the 3.5 million Jews in the General Government could come about, since they could not be shot or poisoned.[65] A comprehensive plan for the extermination of the Jews had evidently not yet been established. Physical extermination was, however, now unmistakably the intention.[66] The Jewish transports from Berlin, Prague, Vienna, and elsewhere had meanwhile been rolling into Lodz. The first German Jews arrived on 16 October 1941. By 4 November 1941, there had already been twenty transports, and the deportation target was reached.[67] With the number of Jews sharply increasing and the prospects of reductions through further deportations eastwards even more rapidly diminishing, killing the Jews of the Warthegau now emerged as a practical option.

The option was rapidly seized upon. Already in autumn 1941, and weeks before the transports from the Lodz ghetto to systematic extermination at Chelmno began, there were mass killings of Jews at locations in the southern part of the Warthegau. Polish underground sources smuggled out information, published in the United States in 1942, of the slaughter in October 1941 of the entire Jewish population—reputedly some 3,000 persons—of the Konin district, who had been gathered together in Zagarov (a village the Germans renamed 'Hinterberg') and then driven in truckloads into the Kaszimir woods where all trace of them ended.[68]

Postwar German investigations corroborated the essence of the report. They concluded that in an indeterminate period, probably between autumn 1940 and late summer or autumn 1941, and in various 'actions', a large number of Jewish men, women and children were driven into the woods between Kazimierz Biskupi and Kleczew and either shot or killed in a gas van. Most of the victims, it was noted, were from Zagorow (Hinterberg), where beforehand a large number of Jewish families from the Konin district had been concentrated. Witnesses said the killings were carried out by police and Gestapo.[69] Further postwar trial investigations in Germany established that, beginning on 26 November 1941 and lasting several days, an SS extermination squad had killed perhaps some 700 Jews—mainly elderly, ill, or feeble Jews and children—interned in a camp at Kozminek (Bornhagen in German) near Kalisch, by means of a gas van.[70]

Probably such killings were envisaged by the security police and liquidation squads as experiments in the extermination techniques which would soon need to be deployed for the far larger numbers in the Lodz ghetto. The major operation was not long delayed. At the beginning of December 1941,[71] regular and systematic extermination began at the site which had been selected specifically for the purpose, Chelmno, by a special 'task squad' which had already accumulated much expertise in gas van extermination.

In the framework of the 'euthanasia programme', which ran in the Reich between autumn 1939 and summer 1941, a 'special unit' under Herbert Lange had operated in the annexed areas of the east from a base in Posen. The most extensive of its mass killings had been the murder, between 21 May and 6 June 1940, of 1,558 mental patients from asylums in and around Soldau in East Prussia.[72] The technique used by Lange's Sonderkommando was the gassing of victims by carbon monoxide poisoning in a large van.[73] Lange's chauffeur, Walter Burmeister, recorded in postwar testimony that he had driven Lange around the Warthegau in autumn 1941, accompanied by other members of the Stapo-Leitstelle of Posen and a guard drawn from the Schutzpolizei looking for a suitable location to carry out killings of Jews. He then, presumably once an appropriate spot had been found, drove Lange to security police headquarters in Berlin and back. In November 1941, shortly after returning from Berlin, Lange's unit—now increased in size—moved from Posen to Chelmno, and at the beginning of December 1941 began the use of two gas vans (a third gas van arrived during the course of the month) sent from Berlin.[74] Thus began the killing process in the first of the extermination establishments to begin its operations.[75]

Did the initiative to begin the killing come from Berlin, or from within the Warthegau? In one postwar trial, it was accepted that orders for the 'resettlement' (that is, killing) of Jews from the Lodz ghetto to the extermination camp at Chelmno, went directly from the Reich Security Head Office in Berlin to the Gestapo office in Lodz.[76] Even if correct, this could be taken as consonant with a request emanating from within the Warthegau, then sanctioned in Berlin. However, neither a request from Lodz nor a general order coming from Berlin for 'resettlement' of the Lodz Jews could have by-passed the heads of the civil and police administration in the Warthegau, Greiser and Koppe. Moreover, the 'resettlement' of the Lodz Jews began only on 16 January 1942, more than a month after the killings in Chelmno had started.[77] If orders were transmitted direct from Berlin to Lodz, they must have been subsidiary to an initial decision to initiate the genocide in the Warthegau by exterminating the Jews incapable of work. And the balance of probabilities points towards seeing the initial impulses coming from within the Warthegau itself, and not directly from Berlin. The emergence of a genocidal 'solution' in the Warthegau corresponds exactly with the weeks in which the authorities there were having to cope with the reception of 20,000 Jews, accepted only under protest by the local authorities in Litzmannstadt. With the collapse of hopes of deporting the province's own Jews, then the forced reception of Jews from Germany, and finally the cutting off of an exit route for any of the Jews, Warthegau anti-Jewish policy had run ever further into a cul-de-sac.

Killing offered a way out. And, it will be remembered, it had already been talked of seriously among the Warthegau ruling elite as early as July 1941. The means, with the redeployment of Lange's special unit, were by autumn 1941 now to hand to implement what in July had been referred to in the Höppner memorandum as 'fantastic notions'. The mention in that memorandum of the names of the Lodz police chief Albert and the Government President Uebelhoer (who came, it will be recalled, in September to protest in the strongest terms about the orders for a new influx of Jews to the Lodz ghetto) indicates the centrality of the Lodz authorities to the internal Warthegau debate on the fate of the region's Jews. It is possible, as has been suggested (though there is no direct evidence to prove it), that when the position, from the point of view of the Nazi bosses in Lodz, became critical following the order to take in the tens of thousands of new deportees from the Reich in the autumn, the suggestion to liquidate them came initially from the Gestapo at Lodz.[78] On the other hand, the Sonderkommando Lange drew mainly for its personnel on the security police headquarters at Posen, where it was based before moving to Chelmno, and continued to liaise directly with the Posen office, not with Lodz.[79] Whatever part was played by the security police authorities in Lodz and Posen, the key role was almost certainly that of the overall head of the security services in the Warthegau, Higher SS and Police Chief Wilhelm Koppe.[80]

Koppe's own version of his involvement in the emergence of a genocidal 'solution' was given in connection with his trial in Bonn in 1960.[81] He portrays himself as the conscience-stricken recipient of orders from Berlin. Quite apart from the apologetics, the account has to be treated with caution. Koppe claimed he heard, either in 1940 or in 1941, that a Commissar (whose name he later learned was Lange) and a special SS unit were to be sent to him from Berlin to carry out the physical extermination of the Jews in the Wartheland. His understanding at the time, he said, was that this would apply only to Jews incapable of work—the impression, he added, also of Greiser. Koppe's view was that the Sonderkommando would carry out 'experiments', trying out gassing methods already devised by Brack of the Führer Chancellory. Koppe was adamant that he had heard of the deployment of the Lange unit from Ernst Damzog, Inspector of the Security Police and SD in the Wartheland, based in Posen, and learnt further from a telephone conversation with Dr. Rudolf Brandt from Himmler's personal office that an 'action' against the Jews was being prepared, and that Brack's gassing experiments, reaching completion in Berlin, were now to be deployed by Sonderkommando Lange, under Brack's direction, in the Wartheland. In a crisis of conscience, alleged Koppe, he consulted Greiser who, it was immediately obvious, was fully in the picture and stated that it was a matter of a 'Führer order' which could not be 'sabotaged' (since Koppe purportedly opposed such 'experiments' as inhumane).

In this account, it seems plain, Koppe is conflating the beginnings of the 'euthanasia action' in the Warthegau with the decision to kill the province's Jews. He could not possibly have heard of a decision to exterminate the Jews of the Warthegau in 1940. But nor did he encounter the name of Herbert Lange and existence of his Sonderkommando for the first time in 1941, and in connection with an 'action' against the Jews. For Lange and his men had by then already been stationed in Posen and at Koppe's behest for over a year, employed in the gassings of mental patients in the annexed areas of Poland. And whether in connection with the 'euthanasia action' or the extermination of the Jews, it seems unlikely that Koppe learnt of the deployment of the Sonderkommando Lange from Damzog, a subordinate. Finally, assuming that the telephone conversation with Brandt took place in autumn 1941 and along the lines Koppe described, it might be still be doubted whether it should be seen as relaying an order from Berlin as opposed to complying with a request from within the Warthegau to deploy the 'Brack methods' to exterminate the Jews. Without minimising the indispensability of empowering orders from Berlin, and accepting that by October 1941 a decision had been taken or sanctioned by Hitler to exterminate European Jewry—certainly those Jews incapable of working—it seems, nevertheless, probable, as we shall see, that Koppe was far more active in initiating the 'action' against the Jews in the Warthegau than his postwar account suggests.

At any rate, for well over a year before the killing of the Jews began, Koppe was in overall command of Lange's unit. Later, when it was renamed Sonderkommando Kulmhof (the German name for Chelmno) and placed under a new leader, Hans Bothman, Koppe had general control of the unit's personnel and economic matters,[82] delegating the practical running of the unit to Damzog's office.[83] In the summer of 1941 Koppe was among the circle of recipients—including by no means all the Higher SS and Police Leaders—of the 'Reports on Events' (Ereignis-meldungen), explicitly detailing the killings of Jews in the Soviet Union.[84] He knew, therefore, of the ravages of the Einsatzgruppen in Russia, and, of course, at first hand of the gassings of mental patients in the annexed Polish territories (since he had 'lent out' Sonderkommando Lange for that purpose). He was, as his own testimony shows, aware of Brack's experiments with techniques of mass killing by use of poisonous gas. There can be no doubt that he was involved in the deliberations which led to the Höppner memorandum in July 1941. He was in every way, then, well attuned to the progressively radical thinking on the possible 'solution to the Jewish Question' in the top echelons of the SS and at Reich Security Headquarters in Berlin.

The central role played by the regional command of the security police in the emergence and implementation of a policy of genocide in the Warthegau is obvious. But where did the overlord of the Warthegau, Reich Governor and Gauleiter Arthur Greiser, fit in to the decisions to move to outright genocide? Despite Koppe's assertion that Greiser was supinely carrying out a 'Führer Order' imposed on the Warthegau from Berlin, the evidence suggests, in fact, that the request to begin killing the Jews came directly from Greiser himself. As the letter from Himmler to Greiser of 18 September 1941, informing him of the decision to deport 60,000 Jews to the Lodz ghetto, shows, communication on such matters between the head of the SS and the leader of the Warthegau did not need to pass through the hands of Koppe.[85] Greiser himself had excellent relations with Himmler. But, as Koppe's testimony indicated, the Reich Governor and the regional police chief were of one mind on the 'Jewish Question', while the rounding up of Jews from the smaller ghettos of the Warthegau needed evident close cooperation between the security police and the administrative organs under Greiser's control.[86] It is clear that Greiser contacted Himmler directly in a number of instances relating to Chelmno and the Sonderkommando operating there.[87] And when, after a temporary end to the killing, the work of the Sonderkommando was recommenced in early 1944, it was on the basis of an agreement between Himmler and Greiser in which, it seems plain, the initiative was taken by the latter.[88] Something of Greiser's role can be gathered, too, from references to the killing of the Jews in mid 1942. A report of the Lodz Gestapo from 9 June 1942 noted that 'all Jews not capable of work' were to be 'evacuated'—a euphemism for liquidated—'according to the directions of the Gauleiter'.[89] This is probably to be linked with the killing of 100,000

Jews which Greiser himself had requested and referred to in a letter to Himmler dated 1 May 1942.[90] Greiser spoke in this letter of the completion, within the next two to three months, of 'the action, approved by you in agreement with the Head of the Reich Security Head Office, SS-Obergruppenführer Heydrich, for the special treatment [another camouflage term for killing] of around 100,000 Jews in the area of my Gau'. Although Greiser spoke of the 'action' being completed within two to three months, according to a memorandum from the Reich Security Head Office dated 5 June 1942, a total of 97,000 Jews had in fact already been killed in Chelmno since December 1941.[91] Greiser's request for permission to carry out the 'special treatment' must, therefore, have been made considerably earlier. Indeed, it conceivably marked the actual request to begin the killing before the commencement of operations in Chelmno at the beginning of December 1941.[92] Greiser went on in his letter of 1 May 1942 to request Himmler's approval of a further 'initiative' on his part: the use of the Sonderkommando, directly following on the 'Jewish action', to liquidate 35,000 Poles in the Gau suffering from incurable tuberculosis.[93] The tuberculosis episode is revealing in a number of respects for the light it casts on the likely decision-making process in the killing of the Jews. Greiser's letter to Himmler was immediately followed by a letter to the latter's personal adjutant SS-Sturmbannführer Rudolf Brandt from Koppe, recommending that the case be verbally explained to the Reichsführer and offering his own approval of the 'solution striven for by the Gauleiter'.[94] Brandt's reply to Koppe stated that he had passed on Greiser's suggestion for an opinion from Heydrich, but that 'the last decision in this matter must be taken by the Führer'.[95] Soundings were, in fact, taken a week later, on 21 May, from Heydrich, who replied on 9 June, stating that he had no objections, subject to thorough discussion of the necessary measures with the security police.[96] Himmler then wrote to Greiser, using Heydrich's wording as the basis of his own letter, towards the end of June.[97]

There matters appear to have rested until the autumn. Preparations for the 'action' presumably took some time.[98] In November 1942, however, before the 'action' had commenced, Greiser received a letter from Dr. Kurt Blome, deputy head of the Nazi Party's health office (Hauptamt für Volksgesundheit) in Berlin, raising objections on the grounds that it would be impossible to maintain the necessary secrecy, thereby arousing unrest and providing enemy propaganda with a gift. He specifically referred to the lessons to be learnt from the mistakes of such a kind made in the 'euthanasia action' in Germany. Consequently, he thought it necessary to consult Hitler, to ask whether, in the light of the 'euthanasia action' which Hitler had stopped (if only partially) for such reasons, the 'tuberculosis action' should go ahead.[99] Greiser wrote again to Himmler on 21 November in the light of Blome's objections. His comment is enlightening. He wrote: 'I myself do not believe that the Führer needs to be asked again in this matter, especially since at our last discussion with regard to the Jews he told me that I could proceed with these according to my own judgement'.[100] Himmler nevertheless regarded Blome's objections as serious enough to advise against the implementation of Greiser's suggestion.[101]

From this exchange, a number of points seem clear. The initiative for killing 100,000 Jews, and the later suggestion for the liquidation of 35,000 tuberculosis victims came directly from Greiser.[102] Approval in both cases was sought from Himmler, who in the latter case, certainly, then consulted Reich Security Head Office. The Warthegau head of security, Koppe, paved the way for the approval of the 'tuberculosis action' and probably did the same with regard to the 'initiative' on the Jews. It cannot be proved, but seems distinctly possible, that the initial suggestion came from him. In the case of the tuberculose Poles, it was pointed out that a decision could only come from Hitler, whose authorisation was essential, at which point doubts arose leading to Himmler's blocking of an initiative he had earlier approved. It seems inconceivable that the killing of the Jews could have been decided upon without some equivalent blanket authorisation by Hitler.[103] But it also appears plain that, as in the tuberculosis matter, all that would have been required of Hitler was authorisation for the implementation of initiatives coming from others. And, as Greiser pointed out, Hitler's response to his own request for authorisation on 'solving the Jewish Question' in the Warthegau had been to grant him permission to act according to his own discretion. Hitler's role here, as elsewhere, was to set the tone and then to provide the broad sanction for actions prompted and set in motion by others.

In the implementation of genocide in the Warthegau, it can be concluded that responsibility for the personnel and economic matters connected with the Sonderkommando at Chelmno rested with the Higher SS and Police Chief, Koppe, and was delegated by him to the Inspector of the Security Police and SD, Damzog, while general responsibility lay in the hands of Reich Governor and Gauleiter Greiser, operating with the permission of Reichsführer SS Himmler, and head of Reich Security Heydrich, and with the blanket authorisation to act as he saw fit provided by Hitler himself.[104]

This examination of the emergence of genocide in the Warthegau—admittedly tentative in places, and necessarily resting at times on the balance of probabilities—has suggested that improvisation by the German authorities on the spot played a decisive role in the autumn of 1941. It was only in the immediate aftermath of Himmler's order to receive tens of thousands of new Jews into the Warthegau and there into the overcrowded Lodz ghetto—following Hitler's authorisation to deport German and Czech Jews—that earlier 'fantasy' talk of liquidating Jews became transformed into a realisable prospect of extermination. The rapid conversion of the Sonderkommando Lange, conveniently to hand but before that date having no special link with a proposed 'solution' to the 'Jewish Question', into a unit deployed specifically in the systematic extermination of Jews, the prompt search for a suitable killing ground, the initial—seemingly experimental—slaughter of Jews at Zagorow and Bornhagen, and the establishment of Chelmno itself, all smack of improvisation. In this, the initiatives by the Warthegau rulers were highly important. Permission to kill a hundred-thousand Jews was actively sought by Reich Governor Greiser; no order to that effect was forced upon him by Himmler or Heydrich. Such a mandate had been requested by spring 1942 at the latest, but almost certainly well before this time and in all probability before the end of 1941. It is Greiser, too, who discusses the Warthegau Jews with Hitler himself at an unspecified date—at the latest by autumn 1942, but probably earlier—and is told to deal with them as he thinks fit. And, as we have seen, the Gestapo at Lodz recorded the fact that they were acting on Greiser's direct instructions in the liquidation of Jews incapable of work. Greiser was subsequently evidently well informed about what took place at Chelmno, and took a keen interest in the developments and in the work of Sonderkommando Kulmhof.[105] And, finally, it was Greiser, who on 7 March 1944 sent a telegram to Hitler, proudly reporting that in the Warthegau 'Jewry [had] shrunk to a tiny remnant'.[106]

Nevertheless, it seems more likely that Koppe, rather than Greiser, took the lead in initiating the move to outright genocide in the Warthegau.[107] Most probably it was Koppe, au fait with the thinking of Heydrich and Himmler, already having cooperated in Brack's gassing experiments through the use of the gas van by Lange's men to kill 'euthanasia' victims, and well aware of the antagonism in Litzmannstadt caused by the order to take in the new influx of Jews—possibly even prompted by the Gestapo there—who suggested to Berlin that a way out of the self-imposed problem would be to deploy the Lange unit to liquidate at least the Jews of the smaller ghettos where the problems in Nazi eyes were even greater than those of Lodz and where the possibility of moving them to Lodz was ruled out. It will be recalled that at the time that Höppner had sent his memorandum, in July, Greiser had not voiced an opinion on the solutions suggested. Evidently they had come from within the Security Police rather than from Greiser himself. And it seems likely that, several months later in the autumn, when the 'fantastic' notions mentioned by Höppner were being turned into reality, it was not Greiser, but Koppe, who was the actual initiator, with the Reich Governor approached when approval at the Gau level was needed.

It would be mistaken to conclude from this that 'local initiatives' acted in independence of central policy in Berlin; and even more so to imagine that central policy merely 'grew out of' practical improvisations at local or regional level.[108] An abundance of evidence has now been assembled, demonstrating beyond reasonable doubt that by the late summer and early autumn 1941 the decision physically to exterminate the Jews of Europe must have been taken by the Nazi leadership.[109] But the contrast between central planning and local initiative can easily be too sharply drawn. Whatever the nature of any central decision already reached, the fateful developments of autumn 1941 do have, within the overall goal of extermination of the Jews of Europe, an unmistakable air about them of improvisation, experimentation, and rapid adaptation to new policy objectives and opportunities. The 'Final Solution', as it came to emerge, formed a unity out of a number of organisationally separate 'programmes', one of which, arising from conditions specific to the Warthegau and remaining throughout under the direction of the province's own leadership rather than the central control of the Reich Security Head Office, was the extermination programme at Chelmno.[110]

At the time of Hitler's decision in mid September—against his earlier reluctance—to deport the German Jews to the east, knowledge of any already determined central extermination policy was clearly still confined to an extremely small circle of initiates. Plainly, Uebelhoer and the Litzmannstadt authorities were unaware in late September 1941 that the aim of anti-Jewish policy was systematic genocide. Otherwise, the vehemence of the objection to the influx of more Jews to the Lodz ghetto would be hard to comprehend.[111] But Koppe would have known, if anyone in the Warthegau did. His role as the police chief 'on the ground' aware of thinking at the centre was pivotal.

Hitler's own role in the emergence of a policy of systematic genocide was mainly to voice the need for a radical 'solution' to the 'Jewish Question', and to sanction and approve initiatives presented to him by those—above all Heydrich and Himmler—keen to translate the Führer's wishes into practical policy objectives. The evidence from the Warthegau—not least the authorisation to Greiser to act as he saw fit in the 'Jewish Question'—fits the picture of a Dictator whose moral responsibility is not in question but who was content to provide carte blanche for others to turn ideological imperatives into concrete directives for action.

By the date of the Wannsee Conference on 20 January 1942 the killing in the Warthegau had been in operation for over six weeks. By March 1942 the 'Final Solution' as it is known to history was in full swing.[112]

The killings at Chelmno began with the Jews from the neighbouring small ghettos and camps.[113] Transports from the Lodz ghetto began on 16 January 1942. Some 55,000 Jews from the Lodz ghetto itself had been killed by the end of May 1942.[114] By the end of 1942, the number of transports had declined, and at the end of March 1943 operations at Chelmno were ended and the camp dissolved. Greiser appeared in Chelmno, thanked the men of the Sonderkommando 'in the name of the Führer' for their work, invited them to a festive meal in a hotel in Warthbrücken, and attained through intercession with Himmler their further deployment, according to their wishes, as a unit attached to the SS volunteer division 'Prinz Eugen' in Yugoslavia.[115] The killings were restarted in April 1944, when Bothmann and the Sonderkommando were brought back to Chelmno for a second stint which ended on 17–18 January 1945.[116]

Of the leading provincial perpetrators of Nazi genocide in the Warthegau, Inspector of the Security Police and SD Ernst Damzog was killed in action in 1945. Head of the Posen SD Rolf-Heinz Höppner was sentenced in March 1949 in Poznań (Posen) to life imprisonment and released under an amnesty in April 1956. The Government President of Lodz, Dr. Friedrich Uebelhoer, disappeared after American internment under a false name. The Police President of Lodz, Dr. Wilhelm Albert, died in 1960. The Gestapo head in Lodz from April 1942 and, at the same time, Lord Mayor of the city of Lodz, Dr. Otto Bradfisch, responsible also for Einsatzgruppen shootings in Russia, was sentenced in Munich in 1951 to ten years in a penitentiary, and in Hanover in 1963 to thirteen years, less the time spent from his Munich imprisonment, for complicity in the murder of 15,000 and 5,000 persons. The head of the Jewish desk in Lodz, Günter Fuchs, was sentenced in Hanover in 1963 to life imprisonment for nine cases of murder and complicity in the murder of at least 15,000 persons. The head of German administration of the Lodz ghetto, Hans Biebow, was hanged in Lodz in 1947. Herbert Lange was killed in action near Berlin in 1945. His successor as head of the Sonderkommando Kulmhof, Hans Bothmann, hanged himself in British custody in 1946. Of the 160 men suspected of participating in the Chelmno murders, 105 could not be found; 22 were established as dead or missing in action, and two had been hanged in Poland. A total of 33 were located and interrogated, of whom 12 eventually stood trial in Bonn in 1962. The result of the trial and appeal was, finally, that on 23 July 1965, eight were found guilty of involvement in murder and sentenced to periods of between thirteen months two weeks in prison and thirteen years in a state penitentiary. In another three cases, the involvement was regarded as so slight that no punishment was fitting. The last case was stopped because the accused was unfit to stand trial.[117]

Arthur Greiser was condemned to death by a Polish court and hanged in Poznan in 1946—after a last-minute plea for intercession by the Papacy had failed.[118] Wilhelm Koppe escaped after the war and lived under a pseudonym for over fifteen years as a successful businessman, becoming director of a chocolate factory in Bonn before being captured in 1960 and finally, in 1964, being arraigned for his involvement in mass murder in Poland. He was deemed unfit to stand trial.[119] He died peacefully in his bed on 2 July 1975.[120]

The nearest estimates are that a minimum of 150,000 Jews and about

5,000 gypsies were murdered in Chelmno between 1941 and 1945.[121] Four Jews survived.[122]

Notes

1 I would like to express my warmest thanks and appreciation to the following for their most helpful contributions to the research for this article: Christopher Browning, Phillippe Burrin, Lucjan Dobroszycki, Gerald Fleming, Czesław Madajczyk, Stanisław Nawrocki, Karol Marian Pospieszalski, and the staffs of the Archiwum Państwowe Poznań, the Berlin Document Center, the Główna Komissa Badni Zbrodni Hitlerowskich w Polsce Archiwum Warsaw, the Instytut Zachondi in Poznań, and the Zentrale Stelle der Landesjustizverwaltungen, Ludwigsburg. I owe grateful thanks, too, to the British Academy and the Polish Academy of Sciences for their generous joint support of the research I undertook in Poznań and Warsaw in September 1989.

2 The others were West Prussia and part of Upper Silesia. In addition, in the north of Poland substantial tracts of territory were added to the existing German province of East Prussia. In each of the incorporated territories (least in Gau Danzig-Westpreußen, most by far in the Warthegau), the new boundaries included areas which had never hitherto belonged to Prussia/Germany. See Martin Broszat, *Nationalsozialistische Polenpolitik 1939–1945* (Frankfurt am Main, 1965), 36–41; Czesław Madajczyk, *Die Okkupationspolitik Nazideutschlands in Polen 1939–1945* (Berlin, 1987), 30–6.

3 *Der Mord an den Juden in Zweiten Weltkrieg*, eds. Eberhard Jäckel and Jürgen Rohwer (Stuttgart, 1985), 145.

4 Two essays appeared in Polish in the 1970s, but before much recent scholarly literature on the genesis of the 'Final Solution': Julian Leszczyński, 'Ż dziejów zagłady 'Żydów w Kraju Warty: Szkice do genezy ludóbojstwa hitlerowskiego', *Biuletyn Zydowskiego Instytutu Historycznego* 82 (1972), 57–72; and Artur Eisenbach, 'O należyte zrozumienie genezy zagłady Zydów', *ibid.* 104 (1977), 55–69.

5 For summaries and evaluations of the debate, see: Saul Friedländer, 'From Anti-Semitism to Extermination', *Yad Vashem Studies* 16 (1984), 1–50. Michael Marrus, *The Holocaust in History* (1988), chap. 2, and Ian Kershaw, *The Nazi Dictatorship. Problems and Perspectives of Interpretation* (3rd edn., 1993), chap. 5.

6 Broszat, *Polenpolitik*, 37–8.

7 I have contributed a brief character sketch of Greiser to the forthcoming second volume of Ronald Smelser, Enrico Syring, and Rainer Zitelmann (eds.), *Die braune Elite und ihre Helfer*. A character description by the prosecution counsel at Greiser's trial can be found in Zentrale Stelle der Landesjustizverwaltungen, Ludwigsburg (= ZSL), Anklageschrift aus dem Prozeß gegen Arthur Greiser, German translation (= Prozeß Greiser), Bl. 74–82. (A copy of the Polish text is in Polen-365h, Bl. 677–828).

8 See, for example, Główna Komisa Badania Zbrodni Hitlerowskich w Polsce (= GK), (Archive of the Central Commission for the Investigation of Hitlerite Crimes in Poland, Ministry of Justice, Warsaw), Process Artura Greisera (= PAG), vol. II, Bl. 52; and see also the comment by Carl J. Burckhardt, *Meine Danziger Mission* (Munich, 1962), 79.

9 Berlin Document Center (= BDC), Personalakte (= PA) Arthur Greiser, unfoliated, Führer decree awarding the promotion, 30 Jan. 1942. Greiser's

telegram to Himmler of the same date, thanking the Reichsführer-SS for his nomination to Hitler, stated that 'I am at your disposal at all times and without reservation in all my areas of work'.

10 Directly on Koppe, there is Szymon Datner, *Wilhelm Koppe—nie ukarany zbrodniarz hitlerowski* (Warsaw, 1963). Koppe figures prominently in Ruth Bettina Birn, *Die Höheren SS- und Polizeiführer. Himmlers Vertreter im Reich und in den besetzien Gebieten* (Düsseldorf, 1986). There is much valuable information on him in his personal file in the BDC. His trial indictment, ZSL, Landgericht Bonn 8 Js 52/60, Anklageschrift gegen Wilhelm Koppe wegen Beihilfe zum Mord (= Prozeß Koppe), Bl, 49–55, summarises his career and personality. He was said to have been unbureaucratic and unconventional in his workstyle—'ruling through the telephone', as one witness put it—and to have combined a propensity for unfolding new, sometimes fantastic, schemes, with pedantic attention to detail. *Ibid.*, Bl. 54.

11 BDC, PA Koppe, unfoliated, effusive handwritten letter of thanks to Himmler for the latter's good wishes on his promotion, 5 Feb. 1942. The headed notepaper already bore Koppe's new grade, which had been bestowed on him only a week earlier.

12 Broszat, *Polenpolitik*, p. 20.

13 *Ibid.*, 25.

14 ZSL, Verschiedenes, 301 Ar., Bl. 32.

15 ZSL, Polen 365n, Bl. 635–9. Printed in Broszat, *Polenpolitik*, 21.

16 Hans-Günther Seraphim, *Das politische Tagebuch Alfred Rosenbergs 1934/35 und 1939/40* (Munich, 1964), 99.

17 ZSL, Verschiedenes, 301 Ar., Bl. 39–40.

18 *Verfolgung, Vertreibung, Vernichtung. Dokumente des faschistischen Antisemitismus 1933 bis 1942* ed. Kurt Pätzold (Leipzig, 1983), 239–40.

19 See Seev Goschen, 'Eichmann und die Nisko-Aktion im Oktober 1939', *Vierteljahrshefte für Zeitgeschichte* 29 (1981), 74–96; and Jonny Moser, 'Nisko, the First Experiment in Deportation', *Simon Wiesenthal Center Annual 2* (1985), 1–30.

20 Pätzold, 262.

21 Some Jews were sent westwards in 1940. On 22–3 Oct. 1940, with Hitler's approval, 6,504 Jews from Baden and the Saarpfalz were deported into Vichy France. Hitler also authorised, at the prompting of von Schirach in October 1940, the deportation of Viennese Jews to Poland. These began in January 1941 but were stopped again in March. See Christopher Browning, 'Nazi Resettlement Policy and the Search for a Solution to the Jewish Question, 1939–1941', *German Studies Review*, IX (1986), 513.

22 A memorandum from the Reichsleitung of the Rassepolitisches Amt of 25 November 1939, for example, establishing guidelines for the treatment of the conquered population 'from a racial-political viewpoint', commented that the Jews in the rump of Poland (Restpolen) posed a less dangerous problem than the Poles themselves. 'The Jews here could certainly be given a freer hand than the Poles,' the memorandum ran, 'since the Jews have no real political force such as the Poles have with their Greater Polish ideology'. ZSL, Polen 365p, Bl. 449, 453.

23 Already in November 1939, on a visit to Lodz, Greiser spoke of meeting 'figures who can scarcely be credited with the name "person" ', but assured his audience that the 'Jewish Question' was no longer a problem and would be solved in the immediate future. GK, PAG, vol. 27, Bl. 167.

24 Instytut Zachodni (= IZ), Poznań, I-441, Bl. 144.

25 Institut für Zeitgeschichte, Munich (= IfZ), Eichmann 1458; and see Werner Präg and Wolfgang Jacobmeyer (eds.), *Das Diensttagebuch des deutschen Generalgouverneurs in Polen 1939–1945* (Stuttgart, 1975), (= DTB Frank), 6off. The Lodz Jews, however, the greatest number in what became the Warthegau, were not included in the first wave of deportees since it was at this stage not clear whether Lodz would belong to the Warthegau or *Generalgouvernment.*—Christopher Browning, 'Nazi Ghettoization Policy in Poland', *Central European History*, xix (1986), 346 and n.9.

26 IZ, I-441, Bl. 145–9.

27 IfZ, Eichmann 1460.

28 ZSL, Prozeß Koppe, Bl. 156. For deportation policy in general, see Robert Koehl, *RKFDV. German Resettlement and Population Policy 1939–1945* (Cambridge Mass., 1957). For the most reliable guide to the numbers of Poles expelled from the Warthegau under Nazi rule, see Madjczyk, *Okkupationspolitik*, appendix, Table 15.

29 ZSL, Prozeß Koppe, Bl. 158.

30 ZSL, Polen 179, Bl. 653–4. Koppe to Greiser (17 May 1940), enclosing a 'Stellungnahme' to the complaints, dated 20 April 1940, compiled by the Umwandererzentralstelle Posen. The expulsion figures (which do not differentiate between Jews and Poles) comprised 87,883 persons deported between 1 and 16 December 1939, and 40,128 from the 10 Feb. to 15 March 1940.

31 Browning, 'Resettlement', 506.

32 Browning, 'Ghettoisation.', 347.

33 All following from DTB Frank, 261–4, entry for 31.7.40.

34 DTB Frank, 261. Greiser had ordered the Lodz Jews to be ghettoised in December 1939 as an interim measure prior to their expulsion—he mentioned a figure of 'some 250,000'—'over the border'. The empty ghetto would then, he added, to be burnt to the ground. BDC, PA Greiser, Besuchs-Vermerk/Akten-Vermerk, Stabsleiter of the Reichsschatzmeister, 11 Jan. 1940, Bl. 3. At the establishment of the ghetto, the Government President of Lodz, Dr. Friedrich Uebelhoer, proposed in a communication to party and police authorities dated to December 1939 a 'temporary' solution to the problem of Lodz's Jews (which he numbered at about 320,000). He emphasised that 'the establishment of the ghetto is, it goes without saying, only a transitional measure'. Jüdisches Historisches. Institut, Warsaw, *Faschismus—Getto—Massenmord* (Frankfurt am Main, n.d. [1961]), 81.

35 DTB Frank, 264.

36 GK, PAG, vol. 36, Bl. 559–60.

37 Details in this paragraph based on reports in Archiwum Państwowe Poznań (= APP), Reichsstatthalter 2111.

38 *The Chronicle of the Lodz Ghetto, 1941–1944*, ed. Lucjan Dobroszycki (New Haven/London, 1984), xxxix, l-li. APP, Reichsstatthalter 1855 contains statistics of disease in the ghetto in 1941. And, for evidence of rocketing deathrates from summer 1940, see also Browning, 'Ghettoisation', 349.

39 GK, PAG, vol. 36, Bl. 567–8v.

40 See Browning, 'Ghettoisation', 349–51, for disputes between 'productionists' and 'attritionists' in Lodz. Dr. Karl Marder, the mayor of Lodz, signified in a letter to Uebelhoer of 4 July 1941—less than a fortnight before the Höppner memorandum—that the character of the ghetto in Lodz had changed, and that it should remain as an 'essential element of the total economy'. *Ibid.*, 350.

41 Hitler's description, prior to the invasion of the USSR, as noted by his Chief of Staff, Franz Halder, *Kriegstagebuch*, 3 vols., (Stuttgart, 1962–4), II, 336–7.

42 Christopher Browning, *The Final Solution and the German Foreign Office* (New York/London, 1978), 8.

43 These comments follow the analyses of Alfred Streim, *Die Behandlung sowjetischer Kriegsgefangener in 'Fall Barbarossa'* (Heidelberg/Karlsruhe, 1981) 74–93; and Philippe Burrin, *Hitler et les Juifs. Genèse d'un génocide* (Paris, 1989) 112–28. The counter-argument, that a general order to exterminate all Soviet Jews was orally given to the Einsatzgruppen leaders before the invasion of the Soviet Union, is most vehemently expressed by Helmut Krausnick, in Helmut Krausnick and Hans-Heinrich Wilhelm, *Die Truppe des Weltanschauungskrieges* (Stuttgart, 1981), 158–66, and in Jäckel and Rohwer, 120–1.

44 *International Military Tribunal: Trial of the Major War Criminals*, 42 vols., (Nuremberg, 1949), XXVI, 266–7, Doc. 710–PS.

45 That the document emanated from the *Reichssicherheitshauptamt* is certain, that Eichmann drafted it, very probable: see Raul Hilberg, *Die Vernichtung der europäischen Juden* (Frankfurt am Main, 1990), 1064 n.7; Jäckel and Rohwer, 15; Christopher Browning, *Fateful Months. Essays on the Emergence of the Final Solution* (New York/London, 1985), 21–2; Hans Mommsen, 'Die Realisierung des Utopischen: Die 'Endlösung der Judenfrage' im 'Dritten Reich', in Hans Mommsen, *Der Nationalsozialismus und die deutsche Gesellschaft* (Reinbek bei Hamburg, 1991) 207; and Richard Breitman, *The Architect of Genocide, Himmler and the Final Solution* (1991), 192.

46 See Burrin, 129–34; Mommsen, *Der Nationalsozialismus*, 207; and Arno Mayer, *Why did the Heavens not Darken? The 'Final Solution' in History* (New York, 1988), 290–2. See also Uwe Dietrich Adam, *Judenpolitik im Dritten Reich* (Düsseldorf, 1972), 308–9, though Adam presumes a Hitler directive behind the mandate, for which there is no evidence. Gerald Fleming, *Hitler und die Endlösung. 'Es ist des Führers Wunsch ...'* (Wiesbaden/Munich, 1982), 78, Browning, *Fateful Months*, 21–2, Breitman, 193, Krausnick in Jäckel and Rohwer, 201, with differing emphasis, hold to the view that the mandate inaugurated the 'Final Solution', Hilberg in Jäckel and Rohwer, 137–8, rather agnostically suggests a decision might have been taken around the date of the mandate, but that the evidence is inconclusive.

47 Burrin, 136–9; Christopher Browning, 'Zur Genesis der "Endlösung"', *Vierteljahrshefte für Zeitgeschichte* XXIX (1981), 103; Martin Broszat, 'Hitler und die Genesis der "Endlosung"', in *ibid.* XXV (1977), 750.

48 Browning, *Fateful Months*, 26.

49 Though impossible to be certain, it is probable that Rosenberg's influence was decisive in pressing Hitler to approve the immediate deportation of German Jews in retaliation for the Soviet deportation of Volga Germans to Siberia. See Burrin, 138–9; Browning, 'Zur Genesis', 103.

50 ZSL, USA 2, Bl. 310. Both Heydrich and Koppe were in receipt of copies of Himmler's letter to Greiser, which is, in fact, the only direct record of Hitler's deportation order.

51 *Ibid.*, Bl. 286, Gettoverwaltung to Regierungspräsident Uebelhoer, 24 Sept. 1941, signed by Werner Ventzki, the Oberbürgermeister of Lodz.

52 *Ibid.*, Bl. 286–309, Gettoverwaltung to Uebelhoer, 24 Sept. 1941; Bl. 277–9, Uebelhoer to Himmler, 4 Oct. 1941.

53 *Ibid.*, Bl. 280–2, Heydrich telegram to Himmler, 8 Oct. 1941; Brandt reply to Heydrich, same date.

54 Entire correspondence in the Uebelhoer case in *ibid.*, Bl. 257–85.

55 Broszat, 'Genesis', 751; Browning's reply, 'Zur Genesis', 103–4, seems weak on this point.

56 Cited Broszat, 751, n. 24.

57 Jäckel and Rohwer, 126.

58 Burrin argues (139–41), correctly in my view, that the deportation decision was tantamount to the decision to kill the European Jews.

59 Fleming, 83, letter from Dr. Wetzel, from the Ministry of the Occupied Eastern Territories, to Hinrich Lohse, Reich Commissar for the Baltic (Ostland), 25 Oct. 1941. The letter states categorically that there are no objections to the gassing of Jews unfit for work.

60 Browning, *Fateful Months*, 27.

61 Fleming, 81–3 (see note 59).

62 Jäckel and Rohwer, 127–8; Browning, *Fateful Months*, 30–1.

63 Browning, *Fateful Months*, 31.

64 Jäckel/Rohwer, 172–6; Browning, 'Zur Genesis', 107.

65 DTB Frank, 457 (entry for 16 Dec. 1941). 'Self-help' was, in fact already being resorted to in the Baltic, where—among many mass shootings—the first German Jews had been shot in Lithuania and Latvia in late November 1941. See Fleming, 14, 77–104.

66 Further confirmation is the reply from the Eastern Ministry in Berlin, on 18 December, to a request for clarification made the previous month by Gauleiter Lohse, the Reich Commissar in the Baltic, that economic considerations were deemed to be irrelevant to the settling of the 'Jewish problem'. Browning, *Fateful Months*, 33.

67 *NS-Vernichtungslager im Spiegel deutscher Strafprozesse*, ed. Adalbert Rückerl Munich, 1977, S. 257 n. 39 (henceforth cited as *NS-Vernichtungslager*). APP, Reichsstatthalter 1214, Bl. 7–9 has a statistical breakdown of the 17th and 20th transports on 1st and 4th Nov. 1941. For details of point of origin, date of arrival, and numbers involved, see Dobroszycki, *Chronicle*, lvii.

68 *The Ghetto Speaks*, 5 Aug. 1942 (Bund Archives of the Jewish Labor Movement, New York), 1. I am grateful to Prof. Lucjan Dobroszycki for a copy of this document. And see Dobroszycki, *Chronicle*, liv (where it is stated they were shot, though this is not stipulated in the report in *The Ghetto Speaks*).

69 ZSL, Verfahren 206 AR-Z 228/73. I am grateful to Dr. Wacker of the ZSL for providing me with this information.

70 *Justiz und NS-Verbrechen*, VII, Amsterdam, 1971, no. 231 b-2, 217–18, 230–1.

71 The date of 5 December 1941 was accepted at the Chelmno trial in Bonn (*Justiz und NS-Verbrechen*, XXI, Amsterdam 1979, 280), and at Koppe's trial (ZSL, Prozeß Koppe, Bl. 218) as the date of the first arrival of transports in Chelmno. Browning, *Fateful Months*, 30, dates the first gassing to 8 December 1941, as does Madajczyk, *Okkupationspolitik*, 380 (apparently, though not explicitly stated, based on early post-war Polish testimony). In a letter he sent me, dated 25 June 1991, Christopher Browning writes: 'I have seen no evidence given for either date, nor have I seen the discrepancy addressed'.

72 *NS-Vernichtungslager*, 258–9.

73 The killing was carried out by bottled carbon monoxide gas being released into the van. Lange's unit was to introduce at Chelmno a refined version of gassing, using the vehicle's exhaust. See Browning, *Fateful Months*, 59, 101 n. 8.

74 Eugen Kogon et al. (eds.), *Nationalsozialistische Massentötungen durch Giftgas* (Frankfurt am Main, 1986), 113–14, 310 n. 10; *Justiz und NS-Verbrechen*, XXI, 246. According to the evidence assembled for Koppe's trial (ZSL, Prozeß Koppe, Bl. 194), the initial drivers of the vehicles were SS men

from the unit who were subsequently replaced by two drivers coming from the RSHA in Berlin. Walter Burmeister, Lange's chauffeur, stated, however, that the drivers came together with the gas vans. Kogon, 114.

75 For the extermination at Chelmno, see above all *NS-Vernichtungslager*, Part 2. An important independent source is the account, compiled in 1945, of the Forest Inspector of the area, Heinz May. Part Three, 'Der große Judenmord', is printed (in German and Polish) in Karol Marian Pospieszalski, 'Niemiecki Nadleśniczy to Zagładzie Żydów w Chelmnie and Nerem', *Przeglad Zachodni Poznań* 18 (1962), 85–105. I am greatly indebted to Prof. Pospieszalski for providing me with a copy of this article, and with a translation into German of his introduction. An extract in English can be found in Dobroszycki, *Chronicle*, lv–vi.

76 *NS-Vernichtungslager*, 252.

77 *Justiz und NS-Verbrechen*, XXI, 280.

78 As claimed, though he cites no direct evidence, by Madajczyk, *Okkupationspolitik*, 380. Prof. Madajczyk acknowledges in a letter to me, dated 27 August 1991, that the assertion rested on inference. Christopher Browning (letter to me of 25 June 1991) points to the greater role of the Posen Security Police than the Lodz Gestapo in the build-up to the exterminations in Chelmno.

79 ZSL, Prozeß Koppe, Bl. 194–7; *NS-Vernichtungslager*, 262–4.

80 The centrality of Koppe's role is taken for granted in Birn, 181.

81 Printed in Kogon, 111–12. See also, for Koppe's dubious testimony, note 107 below.

82 *NS-Vernichtungslager*, 251, 258. See also ZSL, Prozeß Koppe, Bl. 212, 216–17.

83 According to one postwar witness, formerly a civil servant in Damzog's office, both Lange and Bothmann visited Damzog on a number of occasions, there was a special file on Chelmno in the office, and reports on the numbers killed were sent there. *NS-Vernichtungslager*, 252 & n. 22. Written reports of the Sonderkommando on the liquidation of the Jews were sent to Koppe, and Damzog and Bothmann were from time to time summoned by him to present verbal reports. ZSL, Prozeß Koppe, Bl. 197, 211, 216.

84 ZSL, Prozeß Koppe, Bl. 172.

85 *NS-Vernichtungslager*, 252 n. 25.

86 *NS-Vernichtungslager*, 252.

87 *NS-Vernichtungslager*, 252–3. See, for example, ZSL, USA-1, Bl. 91–4, the exchange of letters Greiser-Himmler. 19–27 March 1943, relating to the end of the operations of the 85 men of Sonderkommando Lange in Kulmhof.

88 *NS-Vernichtungslager*, 252–3; BDC, PA Greiser, for correspondence involving Pohl, Greiser, and Himmler, 9–17 Feb. 1944.

89 *Faschismus-Getto-Massenmord*, 285; *NS-Vernichtungslager*, 252, 290.

90 BDC, PA Greiser, Greiser to Himmler, 1 May 1942; printed in *Faschismus-Getto-Massenmord*, 278.

91 *NS-Vernichtungslager*, 290–1. Possibly, Greiser's request—though not specified as such—related to Jews from the Lodz ghetto, whereas the RSHA figure was a general one for the Warthegau. Around 55,000 Jews from the Lodz ghetto had been killed by 9 June 1942. Attention was turned in the summer to 'clearing' the surrounding rural districts, from where at least 15,000 Jews were transported to their death in Chelmno. A further 15,700, mainly weak and sick, Jews were taken from the Lodz ghetto in September 1942, bringing the total to around 70,000 Lodz Jews killed in Chelmno by the beginning of October 1942. *Ibid.*, 288–90.

92 This is presumed by Raul Hilberg, *The Destruction of the European Jews* (New York, 1973), 561, and—slightly more cautiously expressed—in the revised German edition (see above, note 44), 508.

93 BDC, PA Greiser, Greiser to Himmler, 5 May 1942. The number of Poles with tuberculosis was said to be around 230,000, those with the disease in an 'open' condition around 35,000.

94 BDC, PA Greiser, Koppe to Brandt, 3 May 1942.

95 *Ibid.*, Brandt to Koppe, 14 May 1942.

96 *Ibid.*, RFSS Persönlicher Stab-Untersturmführer Rutzen, 21 May 1942, with request from Brandt to Heydrich; Heydrich-Himmler, 9 June 1942.

97 *Ibid.*, Himmler-Greiser, 27 June 1942.

98 *Ibid.*, Greiser-Himmler, 21 Nov. 1942.

99 *Ibid.*, Blome-Greiser, 18 Nov. 1942.

100 *Ibid.*, Greiser-Himmler, 21 Nov. 1942. The date of this discussion between Hitler and Greiser cannot be precisely determined. Gerald Fleming, *Hitler und die Endlösung*, 35, states (though gives no supporting evidence) that Greiser had last seen Hitler on 1 Oct. and 8 Nov. 1942 (the English version of Fleming's book, *Hitler and the Final Solution* (Oxford, 1986), 22, has 11 Nov. 1942, but this seems a translation error). Fleming is followed in this by Friedländer, 'From Anti-Semitism to Extermination', 41, and by Czeslaw Madajczyk, 'Hitler's Direct Influence on Decisions Affecting Jews during World War II', *Yad Vashem Studies* XX (1990), 63–4. Both the dates mentioned by Fleming were large gatherings—a meeting of Gauleiter and Reichsleiter addressed by Hitler on 1 October, and the annual assembly of the Party faithful to commemorate the 1923 Putsch on 8 November (see Milan Hauner, *Hitler. A Chronology of his Life and Time* (1983), 179). Whether Greiser, presuming he attended both, had the opportunity for a private discussion with Hitler might be doubted. Since Greiser had requested, and been given, Himmler's permission to exterminate 100,000 Jews well before 1 May 1942, and these killings had already taken place before October–November 1942, the purpose of seeking a mandate from Hitler at such a date is not immediately obvious. The only explanations seem to be: a) that Greiser, for reasons which are unclear but were possibly directly to do with the proposed 'tuberculosis action', was trying at a late stage to obtain Hitler's retrospective dispensation for a free hand in liquidating the Jews; b) that he was asking Hitler for permission to extend the initial figure of 100,000, though it is scarcely imaginable that he would have needed to go beyond Himmler for such permission, nor that any permission at all would have been needed to widen the killing within the scope of what had by spring 1942 emerged as the fully-fledged 'Final Solution' programme; or, c) and perhaps most likely, that his discussion with Hitler relating to the Jews, took place at a significantly earlier date, and was simply being evoked by Greiser in autumn 1942 as a weapon in the tuberculosis matter.

101 BDC, PA Greiser, Himmler-Greiser, 3 Dec. 1942.

102 In other policy areas, such as the persecution of the Church, the instigation of draconian measures also came from Greiser and his subordinates rather than from central directives from Berlin. ZSL, Prozeß Greiser, 96.

103 As was necessary—finally even in written form—in the 'euthanasia action' (see Ernst Klee, *'Euthanasie' im NS-Staat. Die 'Vernichtung lebensunwerten Lebens'* (Frankfurt am Main, 1983), 100–1) as well as being called for in the case of the tuberculosis victims. The point is made by Burrin, 172.

104 *NS-Vernichtungslager*, 253.

105 ZSL, Prozeß Greiser, 99–102; USA-1, Bl. 91–4, exchange of letters Greiser-Himmler about Sonderkommando Lange; UdSSR-411, Bl. 13–15, testimony of Hermann Gielow from 15 May 1945 about Greiser's involvement in the work of Sonderkommando Bothmann at Chelmno between March 1944 and January 1945; Prozeß Koppe, 210, 216.

106 BDC, PA Greiser, (also in IfZ, MA-303) telegram to Himmler, 7 March 1944, thanking him for his generous support and giving the text of the 'proud report' he had sent the same day to the Führer. See also Fleming, *Endlösung*, 34.

107 Koppe's claims at his trial were both contradictory and incredulous. Having claimed (see above note 81) that he heard in 1940 or 1941 from Rudolf Brandt in Himmler's office of the forthcoming 'action' against the Warthegau Jews, he then alleged that—apart from rumours—he first heard of the 'Final Solution' and of the existence of the extermination camp at Chelmno from Greiser (following a telephone call to the latter from Philip Bouhler at the Führer Chancellor). He went on to claim that he had even successfully persuaded Himmler to end the 'Final Solution', but that Göring and Keitel had opposed it being halted.—ZSL, Prozeß Koppe, Bl. 290–1, 294.

108 See Broszat, 'Genesis', 753 n. 26.

109 See Browning, *Fateful Months*, chap. 1, esp. 32; Burrin, chap. 5; Jäckel and Rohwer, 125–98; Breitman, chap. 6–9.

110 ZSL, Prozeß Koppe, Bl. 297, emphasised the regional control of the Sonderkommando Lange/Bothmann. The Lodz ghetto was a 'Gaughetto' (*Faschismus-Getto-Massenmord*, 285)—a status Greiser was able to retain in February 1944 when Oswald Pohl, from the SS-Verwaltungshauptamt, was aiming to turn it into a concentration camp (BDC, PA Greiser, Greiser to Pohl, 14 Feb. 1944).

111 See Broszat, 'Genesis', 751.

112 Browning, *Fateful Months*, 30–4; chronology in Kogon, 328.

113 *NS-Vernichtungslager*, 268.

114 *Ibid.*, 276–7, and n. 69.

115 *Ibid.*, 280–2.

116 *Ibid.*, 282–6. Some 7000 Jews were killed at Chelmno in this second spell, though all between 23 June and 14 July 1944. *Ibid.*, 292–3. There were still at that time over 68,000 Jews in the Lodz ghetto, almost all of whom were, by 28 August 1944, sent to Auschwitz-Birkenau, Dobroszycki, *Chronicle*, lxiii–v.

117 *NS-Vernichtungslager*, 246–50, 257 n. 38; letter of ZSL, dated 20 June 1989 to Prof. Dr. Stanislaw Nawrocki (State Archives Poznań). I am most grateful to Prof. Nawrocki for a copy of this letter with details of the fate of some of the chief perpetrators.

118 GK Warsaw, Process Artura Greisera (36 files); ZSL, Prozeß Greiser (transl. of Anklageschrift); Polen-365h, Bl. 677–828, Anklageschrift; Polen-3650, Bl. 88–136, Greiser's final plea. The appeal for papal intercession was reported in *L'Osservatore Romano*, 22–3 July 1946. (I owe this information to the kindness of Dr. Gerald Fleming.) According to Dr. Marian Olszewski of the Instytut Zachodni in Poznań, currently working on a life of Greiser (letter to me from Prof. Nawrocki, Poznań, dated 15 May 1991), Greiser's defence lawyer, Heymowski, wrote intercession letters not only to the Pope, but also to President Truman. No response from either has come to light.

119 *NS-Vernichtungslager*, 251; ZSL, Prozeß Koppe. On Koppe's arrest, trial, and release on grounds of being unfit to stand: *Quick*, 15 July 1960; *Neue Zürcher Zeitung*, 21 Jan. 1965; *Frankfurter Allgemeine Zeitung*, 29 May 1965; *Allge-*

meine: Unabhängige jüdische Wochenzeitung, 17 Feb. 1967 (copies in IfZ, Munich).

120 Date of Koppe's death according to information from ZSL (see n. 117 above).

121 *NS-Vernichtungslager*, 288–93. While these figures provide a minimum estimate, they are far more accurate than the figure of 300,000 given at Greiser's trial (ZSL, Prozeß Greiser, Bl. 58).

122 *NS-Vernichtungslager*, 293 n. 96.

POLAND

■ Death Camp

—— Poland boundary before Sept. 1, 1939

•••••• Russian-German line, 1939

Annexed Land

General government

Generalkommissariats

27

FROM "ETHNIC CLEANSING" TO GENOCIDE TO THE "FINAL SOLUTION"

The evolution of Nazi Jewish policy, 1939–1941

Christopher Browning

Source: Christopher Browning, *Nazi Policy, Jewish Workers, German Killers,* Cambridge: Cambridge University Press, 2000, pp. 1–25.

Why the emphasis on decision and policy making, it might be asked. Is this not an exhausted topic whose time has come and gone with the intentionalist/ functionalist controversy of the late 1970s and early 1980s, characterized by unduly polarized alternative interpretations? The intentionalists emphasized the centrality of Adolf Hitler's ideology, predetermined plans, and opportunistic decision making, whereas the functionalists emphasized the dysfunction and unplanned destructive implosion of an unguided bureaucratic structure and tension-filled political movement that had driven themselves into a dead end. One approach perceived the Final Solution as being more like the Manhattan Project, a massive and well-planned program that produced the destruction intended, whereas the other perceived it as a kind of Chernobyl, the unintended but all too predictable by-product of a dysfunctional system.

If the intentionalist/functionalist controversy in this highly polarized form is no longer at the center of Holocaust research, nonetheless a much more nuanced debate over Hitler and the origins of the Final Solution, based on a much vaster documentary collection, has found new life in the 1990s. In this debate, virtually all the participants agree on the centrality of the year 1941 and an incremental decision-making process in which Hitler played a key role. What is being debated are the relative weighting of the different decisions taken in 1941 and the different historical contexts invoked to explain the importance and timing of those decisions. What is at stake is our differing understandings of how Hitler and the Nazi system functioned and how historically the fateful line was crossed between population decimation and genocide on the one hand and the Final Solution and Holocaust on the other.

The most recent controversy in this ongoing debate over the decisions for the Final Solution is the topic of my second lecture. But part of my argument is that the pattern of decision making that was practiced and the frustrations and failures that the Nazis experienced in racial empire building in Poland in the years 1939–41 are important for understanding the "fateful months" in which the Final Solution emerged. One crucial historical context for understanding the origins of the Final Solution, until recently overshadowed by the history of European and German anti-Semitism, the development of the eugenics movement, and the functioning of the Nazi system of government, is the visions of demographic engineering and plans for population resettlement that both inspired and frustrated Nazi racial imperialism in Poland between 1939 and 1941. I will argue that the theory and practice of what we now call ethnic cleansing was an important prelude to the decisions for the Final Solution that followed.

More specifically, I will argue that between September 1939 and July 1941, Nazi Jewish policy, as one component of a broader racial imperialism in the east, evolved through three distinct plans for ethnic cleansing to a transitional phase of implicit genocide in connection with preparations for the war of destruction against the Soviet Union. Hitler was both the key ideological legitimizer and decision maker in this evolutionary process, which also depended crucially upon the initiatives and responses elicited from below. For Hitler the historical contexts for his key decisions were the euphoria of victory in Poland and France and the galvanizing anticipation of a territorial conquest of *Lebensraum* and an ideological and racial crusade against "Judeo-Bolshevism" in the Soviet Union. Additionally, for the middle and lower echelon, regional and local authorities, key factors were not only their identification with Hitler's goals and personal ambition to make a career but also frustration over the impasse created by the ideological imperatives of the regime and their failure to implement the previous policies of ethnic cleansing.

In the months before the invasion of Poland, Hitler made clear on several occasions that the outbreak of war would set a new level of expectation on his part. For instance, in his Reichstag speech of January 1939, he prophesied that a world war would mean the destruction of the Jews in Europe. And to his generals on August 22, he called for a "brutal attitude," "the destruction of Poland," and the "elimination of living forces."[1] When Quartermaster General Eduard Wagner asked Reinhard Heydrich about the tasks of the Einsatzgruppen, he was bluntly informed: "Fundamental cleansing: Jews, intelligentsia, clergy, nobles" *(Flurbereinigung:*

Judentum, Intelligenz, Geistlichkeit, Adel).[2] But what did *Flurbereinigung* mean? How were Hitler's prophesies and exhortations transformed by his eager subordinates, especially Heinrich Himmler and Heydrich, into specific and concrete policies?

The arrest and decimation of Poland's leadership classes seem to have been decided even before the invasion.[3] But plans for a more sweeping demographic reorganization of Poland, including a solution to the Jewish question, emerged only during the month of September. On September 7 Heydrich told his division heads that Poland would be partitioned and Germany's boundary would be moved eastward. Poles and Jews in the border region annexed to the Third Reich would be deported to whatever remained of Poland.[4] A week later Heydrich discussed the Jewish question before the same audience and noted: "Proposals are being submitted to the Führer by the Reichsführer, that only the Führer can decide, because they will be of considerable significance for foreign policy as well."[5] The nature of these proposals was revealed the following week, when Heydrich met not only with his division heads but also the Einsatzgruppen leaders and his expert on Jewish emigration, Adolf Eichmann. Concerning Poles, the top leaders were to be sent to concentration camps, the middle echelon were to be arrested and deported to rump Poland, and "primitive" Poles were to be used temporarily as migrant labor and then gradually resettled, as the border territories became pure German provinces. According to Heydrich, "The deportation of Jews into the non-German region, expulsion over the demarcation line is approved by the Führer." This "long-term goal," or *Endziel*, would be achieved over the next year. However, "in order to have a better possibility of control and later of deportation," the immediate concentration of Jews into ghettos in the cities was an urgent "short-term goal," or *Nahziel*. The area east of Cracow and north of the Slovak border was explicitly exempted from these concentration measures, for it was to this region that the Jews as well as "all Gypsies and other undesirables" were eventually to be deported.[6]

This plan was slightly altered the following week when Germany surrendered Lithuania to the Soviet sphere and received in return Polish territory around the city of Lublin between the Vistula and Bug Rivers. On September 29, Hitler told Alfred Rosenberg that all Jews, including those from the Reich, would be settled in this newly acquired territory between the Vistula and the Bug. Central Poland west of the Vistula would be an area of Polish settlement. Hitler then broached yet a third resettlement scheme. Ethnic Germans repatriated from the Soviet sphere would be settled in western Polish territories incorporated into the Third Reich. Whether "after decades" the German settlement belt would be moved eastward, only time would tell.[7]

In short, by the end of September 1939 Himmler had proposed and Hitler had approved a grandiose program of demographic engineering based on racial principles that would involve the uprooting of millions of people. These policies were fully consonant with Hitler's underlying ideological assumptions: a need for *Lebensraum* in the east justified by a Social-Darwinist racism, a contempt for the Slavic populations of eastern Europe, and a determination to rid the expanding German Reich of Jews. These policies were also very much in tune with widely held views and hopes in much of German society concerning the construction of a German empire in eastern Europe. There was no shortage of those who now eagerly sought to contribute to this historic opportunity for a triumph of German racial imperialism. And the degree to which the widely held hopes and visions of these eager helpers would subsequently founder on stubborn reality, the greater their willingness to resort to ever more violent solutions. The broad support for German racial imperialism in the east was one foundation upon which the future consensus for the mass murder of the Jews would be built.[8]

Heydrich's plans for the immediate concentration of Jews in urban ghettos had to be postponed owing to army concerns over undue disruption.[9] But that did not deter one young and ambitious Schutzstaffel (SS) officer from taking the initiative to jump from the short-term to the long-term goal and implement the immediate expulsion of the Jews. On October 6, 1939, Eichmann met with the head of the Gestapo, Heinrich Müller, who ordered him to contact Gauleiter Wagner in Kattowitz concerning the deportation of 70,000 to 80,000 Jews from East Upper Silesia. Eichmann noted the wider goal of this expulsion: "This activity shall serve first of all to collect experiences, in order ... to be able to carry out evacuations in much greater numbers."[10]

Within days Eichmann had expanded this program to include deportations from both Mährisch Ostrau in the Protectorate and Vienna. He had also located a transit camp at Nisko on the San River on the western border of the Lublin district, from which the deportees were to be expelled eastward. By October 11, German officials in Vienna were informed that Hitler had ordered the resettlement of 300,000 Reich Jews, and Vienna would be completely cleared of Jews in 9 months.[11] And on October 16, Eichmann confidently informed Artur Nebe, head of the Criminal Police, that Jewish transports from the Old Reich would begin in 3 to 4 weeks, to which train cars of "Gypsies" could also be attached.[12]

In short, between mid-September and mid-October 1939, Nazi plans for the ethnic cleansing of the Third Reich of Jews and "Gypsies" from both its old and new territories had taken shape in the form of a vast deportation and expulsion program to the farthest extremity of Germany's new eastern empire – the Lublin district on the German–Soviet demarcation line.

Barely was implementation of the Nisko Plan underway, however, when it was abruptly aborted. On October 19, as the second and third transports were being prepared for departure, Gestapo Müller from Berlin ordered "that the resettlement and deportation of Poles and Jews in the territory of the future Polish state requires central coordination. Therefore permission from the offices here must on principle be in hand." This was quickly followed by the clarification that "every evacuation of Jews had to be stopped."[13]

The stop order in fact came personally from Himmler, which he justified to the irate Gauleiter of Vienna on the basis of so-called technical difficulties.[14] But what difficulties had caused Himmler to abort the Nisko Plan just days after it had been set in motion? Expelling Jews and "Gypsies," it turned out, was not the most urgent item on Himmler's agenda for the demographic reorganization of eastern Europe. Himmler had just gained jurisdiction over the repatriation and resettlement of ethnic Germans, and the first Baltic Germans had arrived in Danzig on October 15.[15] The problem of finding space for the incoming ethnic Germans now took priority over deporting Jews from East Upper Silesia, the Protectorate, and Vienna. The geographic center of Nazi resettlement actions suddenly shifted northward to West Prussia and the Warthegau as policy priorities shifted from expelling Jews to finding lodging and livelihood for ethnic Germans.

But despite the sudden demise of the Nisko Plan, the goal of ethnic cleansing remained, though it was now to be implemented in more gradual stages. On October 18 Hitler reiterated that "Jews, Polacks and riff-raff" ("*Juden, Polacken u. Gesindel*") were to be expelled from Reich territory – both old and new – into what remained of Poland, where "devils" work' ("*Teufelswerk*") remained to be done.[16] On October 30, Himmler issued overall guidelines for the *Flurbereinigung* of the incorporated territories that Hitler had once again sanctioned. Within 4 months, *all* Jews (estimated at 550,000) were to be expelled from the incorporated territories to a Lublin reservation between the Vistula and Bug Rivers. Also to be expelled were post-1919 Polish immigrants (so-called Congress Poles) and a sufficient number of anti-German Poles to bring the total to 1 million.[17] Jews in the recently established General Government were to be moved from west to east of the Vistula the following year.[18]

No one misunderstood the implications of this plan for a Jewish reservation in Lublin. Arthur Seyss-Inquart reported that the "extreme marshy nature" of the Lublin region "could induce a severe decimation of the Jews."[19] And the newly appointed general governor, Hans Frank, exulted: "What a pleasure, finally to be able to tackle the Jewish race physically. The more that die, the better."[20]

Clearly there were many Germans who were intoxicated by Hitler and Himmler's vision of vast and brutal population transfers within 4 months and who welcomed the loss of life, particularly Jewish life, that this would entail. But turning this vision into reality would prove difficult for the Germans actally entrusted with the task of implementation. The first flood of ethnic Germans arrived in Danzig–West Prussia, where space was found by both brutally clearing half the population of Gdynia (Gotenhafen)[21] and murdering the patients of mental hospitals.[22] But Gauleiter Albert Forster proved increasingly uncooperative about resettling further ethnic Germans.[23] By late November the higher SS and police leader for Danzig and West Prussia, Richard Hildebrandt, announced that "in the Danzig district itself the Baltic Germans will no longer remain but rather be sent on."[24]

On November 28, Heydrich intervened from Berlin, drastically scaling down the immediate task facing the Germans to a "short-range plan" (*Nahplan*) that differed from Himmler's guidelines of October 30 in significant ways. First, immediate expulsions were to take place only from the Warthegau rather than throughout the incorporated territories. Second, the quota was sharply cut from 1 million to 80,000 "Poles and Jews," whose removal would make room for 40,000 "incoming Baltic Germans." And finally, the racial and political criteria emphasized by Himmler gave way to more practical concerns. Housing and livelihoods had to be procured for incoming ethnic Germans, and "urgently needed" manual laborers were to be exempted.[25]

As a consequence, the emphasis on deporting Jews was diminished. Although by far the largest concentration of Jews in the Warthegau, those in the city of Lodz were not to be included, because it was not yet clear whether that city would ultimately be part of the General Government or end up within the boundaries of the Third Reich. Other Warthegau Jews were to constitute a deportation reservoir and be expelled only when needed to fill gaps and prevent delays, if the other priority-target groups were not available in sufficient numbers to fill the deportation quotas.[26]

The Germans in the Warthegau exceeded the quota and reported triumphantly that they had succeeded in deporting over 87,000 "Poles and Jews" by December 17, 1941. The primary thrust of the "first short-range plan" (*I. Nahplan*) was not to solve the Jewish question but rather to remove Poles who posed "an immediate danger" and find space for the Baltic Germans.[27] The reason why the precise number or percentage of Jews among the expellees was not reported becomes clear from local documents. In Lodz local authorities had been too incompetent or inefficient to identify "politically suspicious and intellectual Poles" in sufficient numbers to fill their quotas. Thus they had "had to fall back on Jews."[28] The indiscriminate seizure of Jews was obviously administratively easier than the selective seizure of Poles. In the end, about 10,000 Jews were deported, mostly from Lodz after all, owing to the insufficient number of deportable Poles identified and listed by the local authorities. This figure of 10,000 Jewish deportees from Lodz was not included in the self-congratulatory final reports on the "first short-range plan," because it was evidence not of a success in deporting Jews but rather of a failure to identify and seize Polish political activists and intelligentsia.

356

Immediately following the conclusion of the "first short-range plan," Heydrich's Jewish experts in Berlin once again posed the question "whether a Jewish reservation shall be created in Poland. ..."[29] Heydrich's response was threefold: he appointed Eichmann as his "special adviser" (*Sonderreferent*),[30] for the moment postponed any Jewish deportations from the Old Reich,[31] and ordered a "second short-range plan" for "the complete seizure of all Jews without regard to age or gender" in the incorporated territories and, "their deportation into the General Government."[32] On January 4, 1940, Eichmann reaffirmed that "On the order of the Reichsführer-SS the evacuation of all Jews from the former Polish occupied territories is to be carried out as a priority."[33]

However, despite the German recommitment to the immediate expulsion of all Jews from the incorporated territories, the problems that stood in the way of realization of expelling both Jews and Poles only multiplied in the new year. The arrival of 40,000 Baltic Germans was to be quickly followed by a further deluge of 120,000 Volhynian Germans. Hans Frank, so enthusiastic the previous fall, was now considerably sobered. He complained bitterly about the impact of the chaotic deportations of the "first short-range plan" and emphasized the limited absorptive capacity of the General Government.[34] The latter had been a matter of no concern in the fall of 1939 but increasingly became so as Hermann Göring insisted upon harnessing the productive capacities of the conquered territories to the war effort.[35] There were other problems as well. No trains were available until mid-February.[36] And Himmler, worried about a sufficient stock of German blood to repopulate the incorporated territories, insisted that cases of contested ethnic German status and Poles capable of Germanization not be deported without screening; hence only Jews and recent Polish emigrants but not longtime Polish residents were to be deported.[37] But that often meant exempting the political and economic leadership classes whose property was needed for accommodating incoming ethnic Germans while deporting the propertyless Polish workers most needed for economic production. The labor issue was intensified further when the Warthegau was targeted to provide 800,000 agricultural workers for the Reich. German occupation authorities immediately demanded that further deportations to the General Government had to be stopped if local labor needs were to be covered.[38]

Thus within the overall scheme for a demographic reorganization of eastern Europe that Himmler had proposed and Hitler approved in the fall of 1939, the Nazis had set for themselves three tasks: the ethnic cleansing of Jews from the Third Reich, of Poles from the Third Reich, and the repatriation of ethnic Germans from abroad. The plan for expelling the Jews had not been generated by the need to make space for the ethnic Germans but rather preceded it. But then the immediate urgency of resettling the Baltic Germans led to the temporary curtailment of Jewish expulsion, for the latter did not provide the necessary housing and jobs for the former. This conflict within German racial and resettlement policy was soon complicated by additional economic factors: the concern for labor and production, the shortage of trains, and the limited absorptive capacity of the General Government. The Nazi empire builders and demographic engineers had tied themselves in knots.

The Nazi leadership attempted to solve this welter of self-imposed contradictions with very limited success. On January 30, 1940, Heydrich chaired a meeting of leading officials from the occupied east, his own Reich Security Main Office, and Göring's representative, at which the hoped-for expulsion of all Jews was postponed once again. The deportation of 40,000 Jews and Poles for the purpose of "making room" (*Platzschaffung*) for the remaining Baltic Germans – the so-called intermediate plane (*Zwischenplan*) – was now to be followed by "another improvised clearing" of 120,000 Poles to provide space for the Volhynian Germans – a "second short-range plan." Unlike the urban Baltic Germans, the Volhynian Germans were a rural population, for whom the removal of Jews was even less relevant. Thus the evacuation of all Jews from the incorporated territories would take place only "as the last mass movement."[39]

The discussion was continued at a higher level yet, when Göring hosted Himmler, Frank, and the eastern Gauleiter at his Karinhall estate on February 12, 1940. Göring insisted that the first priority was to strengthen the war potential of the Reich, and in this regard the incorporated territories were to be the granary of Germany. Thus, "all evacuation measures are to be directed in such a way that useful manpower does not disappear." Jewish transports were to be sent only in an orderly manner, with prior notification and approval. Frank immediately adhered to Göring's position.

Himmler took for granted that the Baltic and Volhynian resettlements would continue in what were now designated the "intermediate" and "second short-range" plans. But Himmler agreed to postpone the resettlement of a further 40,000 Lithuanian Germans, 80,000 to 100,000 Bukovinian Germans, and 100,000 to 130,000 Bessarabian Germans, as well as the ethnic Germans west of the Vistula. However, the 30,000 ethnic Germans in the Lublin district east of the Vistula would have to be resettled, he insisted, because their present homeland was destined to become the *Judenreservat*. Finally, Himmler assured Frank that they "would reach agreement upon the procedures of future evacuations."[40]

Back in the General Government in early March, Frank explained what he thought had been agreed upon. The General Government would receive 400,000 to 600,000 Jews, who would be placed along the eastern border. "It is indescribable, what views have formed in the Reich, that the region of the General Government east of the Vistula is increasingly considered as some kind of Jewish reservation," he noted. The final goal was to make the German Reich free of Jews; but "that that shall not occur in a year and especially not under the circumstances of war, Berlin also recognizes." Moreover, no resettlement actions would take place without prior approval from the General Government. And most important, "the great resettlement ideas have indeed been given up. The idea that one could gradually transport 7.5 million Poles to the General Government has been fully abandoned."[41]

When Himmler attempted to exceed the Karinhall agreement and add Jewish deportations from Stettin to the "intermediate" and "second short-range plans," Göring and Frank exercised their power to block unauthorized transports. Himmler had to concede once again that the expulsion of Jews would commence only in August after the completion of the Volhynian Aktion or "second short-range plan."[42]

Himmler had seen his grandiose design for the sweeping racial reorganization of eastern Europe steadily whittled away. In the fall of 1939, he had envisaged the deportation of 1 million people (including *all* Jews) from the incorporated territories by March 1940, and eventually the removal of all Poles as well. By the spring of 1940, however, the deportation of Jews had been postponed to August, and Frank was boasting that the expulsion of 7.5 million Poles from the incorporated territories had been "fully abandoned." Moreover, Hitler himself seemed to have lost interest in the Lublin reservation as a solution to the Jewish question as well, indicating even to foreign visitors in mid-March 1940 that he had no space available for Jews there.[43]

Then suddenly Germany's stunning victory in France emboldened Himmler once again to try to override the pragmatic considerations of Göring and Frank. Himmler seized the propitious opportunity to revitalize his plans for the total expulsion of Poles from the incorporated territories and to suggest an even more radical expulsion plan for the Jews.

Sometimes in May 1940 Himmler drafted a memorandum entitled "Some Thoughts on the Treatment of Alien Populations in the East." The 15 million people of the General Government and 8 million of the incorporated territories – "ethnic mush" (*Völkerbrei*) in Himmler's view – were to be splintered into as many ethnic groups as possible for "screening and sifting" (*Sichtung und Siebung*). Himmler wanted "to fish out of this mush the racially valuable" to be assimilated in Germany, with the rest to be dumped into the General Government, where they would serve as a reservoir of migrant labor and eventually lose their national identity.

Along with the denationalization, in effect cultural genocide, of the various ethnic groups of eastern Europe, the Jews were to disappear in a different way. "I hope completely to erase the concept of Jews through the possibility of a great emigration of all Jews to a colony in Africa or elsewhere," he proposed. Concerning this systematic eradication of the ethnic composition of eastern Europe, Himmler concluded: "However cruel and tragic each individual case may be, this method is still the mildest and best, if one rejects the Bolshevik method of physical extermination of a people out of inner conviction as un-German and impossible" (*"So grausam und tragisch jeder einzelne Fall sein mag, so ist diese Methode, wenn man die bolschewistische Methode der physischen Ausrottung eines Volkes aus innerer Überzeugung als ungermansich und unmöglich ablehnt, doch die mildeste und beste"*).

With impeccable timing, Himmler submitted his memorandum to Hitler on May 25, a week after the German army had reached the English Channel. "The Führer read the six pages through and found them very good and correct" (*sehr gut und richtig*), Himmler noted. Moreover, "The Führer desires that I invite Governor Frank back to Berlin, in order to show him the memorandum and to say to him that the Führer considers it correct." Not content with this triumph, Himmler obtained Hitler's authorization also to distribute the memorandum to the eastern Gauleiter and Göring as well, with the message that the Führer had "recognized and confirmed" (*anerkannt und bestätigt*) the guidelines.[44]

This episode is of singular importance in that it is the only firsthand account by a high-ranking participant – Himmler – of just how a Hitler decision was reached and a "Führer order" disseminated in the shaping of Nazi racial policy during this period. Hitler indicated a change in expectations, in this case his abandonment of the Lublin reservation. At the opportune moment, Himmler responded with a new initiative in the form of a general statement of intent and policy objectives known to be in line with Hitler's general ideological outlook. Hitler indicated not only his enthusiastic agreement but also with whom this information could be shared. He gave no specific orders to the likes of Göring, Frank, and the eastern Gauleiter but simply allowed it to be known what he wanted or approved. The stage was then set for a new round of planning in the search for a solution to the Jewish question through expulsion or ethnic cleansing.

Heydrich rather than Himmler in fact met with Hans Frank on June 12. However, "in view of the dire situation" in the General Government it was agreed for the moment not to go beyond the Karinhall accord – that is, the Volhynian action then in progress followed by the general expulsion of Jews scheduled for August.[45] For Frank, even these expulsions loomed as catastrophic, given the food shortages in the General Government.[46] For the beleaguered Frank, a surprising order from Himmler suddenly stopping the impending expulsion of the Jews into the General Government came as a veritable deliverance.[47] Himmler had found his colony in Africa for the Jews!

For decades the island of Madagascar had exercised a fantastical attraction for European anti-Semites as a place for Europe's expelled Jews.[48] It had been frequently mentioned by leading Nazis since 1938, most recently by Frank in January 1940.[49] With the lightning defeat of France, it was a freakish idea whose time had suddenly come. In another example of timely initiative from below that dovetailed with changes in circumstances and policy at the top, the newly appointed Jewish expert of the German Foreign Office, Franz Rademacher, proposed that in planning for the peace treaty with France, Germany consider removing the newly acquired west European Jews to the French colony of Madagascar.[50] The proposal not only moved up the hierarchy with incredible speed but also was quickly expanded to include all European Jews. On June 18, both Hitler and Joachim von Ribbentrop mentioned the plan to use Madagascar for a Jewish reservation to Benito Mussolini and Galeazzo Ciano respectively in their talks in Munich over the fate of the French empire.[51] By June 24, 1940, Heydrich had gotten wind of the project and asserted his long-standing jurisdiction over Jewish emigration. He insisted that he be included in any discussions Ribbentrop was planning on a "territorial solution" to the Jewish question.[52] Ribbentrop immediately conceded, and henceforth planning on the Madagascar Plan was a mixture of cooperation and competition between the Foreign Office and SS.[53]

The demise of the Lublin reservation and the emergence of the new Madagascar Plan was, in Frank's words, a "colossal relief" (*"kolossale Entlastung"*) for German officials in the General Government.[54] Two fundamental changes in policy immediately resulted. First, "an order from Cracow [Frank's capital] was issued to stop all work on ghetto construction in view of the fact that, according to the plan of the Führer, the Jews of Europe were to be sent to Madagascar at the end of the war and thus ghetto building was for all practical purposes illusory."[55] Second, when Frank met with Gauleiter Arthur Greiser of the Warthegau in late July, the latter conceded that according to Himmler the Jews were now to be sent overseas. Nevertheless, as an interim measure he was still desperate to resettle Jews from the starving Lodz ghetto into the General Government in August as previously planned. Frank flatly refused and advised Greiser instead to see that the Lodz Jews were considered first in line for Madagascar if their situation were so impossible.[56]

Planning for Madagascar continued fervently until the end of August and then stopped abruptly. The defeat of France and seemingly imminent victory over Great Britain had promised both the colonial territory and the merchant fleet necessary for the plan's realization. But failure to defeat Great Britain was fully apparent in September, and the frenetic urgency behind its preparation in the summer months suddenly dissipated. Like Eichmann's Nisko Plan, Rademacher's Magadascar Plan was a timely low-level initiative that offered a way to implement policy decisions just made at the top. And like Nisko, real work on Madagascar was abruptly halted when circumstances changed. Just as the idea of the Lublin reservation continued as the official goal, even though it was consistently postponed in favor of more limited but temporarily more urgent Polish expulsions tied to ethnic German repatriation, Madagascar lingered as the official policy until an alternative was proclaimed. Not a "phantom solution" at first, it became one. Like Nisko/Lublin, Madagascar implied a murderous decimation of the Jewish population. If actually implemented, Hitler's Reichstag prophecy would have been proclaimed as completely fulfilled. And like the failure of Nisko/Lublin, the failure of Madagascar left the frustrated German demographic planners receptive to ever more radical solutions.

In the summer and fall of 1940, German ethnic cleansing continued to encounter difficulties. The Germans expelled over 70,000 people from Alsace-Lorraine and blocked the return of an additional 70,000 refugees who had fled.[57] Gauleiter Robert Wagner took the opportunity to propose expelling the Jews of Baden and Pfalz at the same time, and Hitler "impulsively" agreed.[58] Some 6,500 German Jews were expelled over the demarcation line into southern France, but the ensuing diplomatic complications with the Vichy government ensured that this measure was not repeatable.

In the east, the "second short-range plan" was somewhat expanded and considerably delayed. As part of the expanded plan, the so-called Cholmer Aktion for the repatriation of ethnic Germans from the eastern border of the Lublin district was particularly significant because it also involved the reciprocal exchange of Poles and ethnic Germans between the Lublin district and the incorporated territories.[59] These ethnic Germans came from within the German sphere and were thus in no imminent danger. In short, repatriating ethnic Germans to the incorporated territories was not just a reactive measure to rescue ethnic Germans from the Soviet sphere but a program carried out for its own sake. The vision of Germanizing the new borderlands fired Himmler's imagination as a historic mission of great consequence. This was the construction of German *Lebensraum* as understood at the time. Two years later, the Germans would try to reverse the Cholmer Aktion with the Zamosc Aktion, resettling Germans in areas from which they had in fact been recently removed. With ethnic German resettlement as with the Lublin and Madagascar plans, the hindsight perspectives of Generalplan Ost and Auschwitz are not the proper yardstick by which to measure Himmler's ideological horizon in the summer of 1940.

By the time the "second short-range plan" was concluded six months behind schedule in December 1941, the Germans had expelled some 460,000 people, of whom at least 36,000 or approximately 8 percent were Jews.[60] (Vastly greater numbers of Jews, of course, had fled on their own as refugees from the incorporated territories to the General Government and from the General Government over the demarcation line into the Soviet sphere). The Nazis, therefore, had achieved only a pathetic fraction of the overall goals and expectations of ethnic cleansing that they had set in the fall of 1939. Progress toward solving their self-imposed Jewish problem in particular was even more scant. In the repatriation of ethnic Germans, at least from the Soviet zone, they had come closer to meeting expectations, but the difficulties and delays in moving them from transit camps to permanent resettlement was yet another source of frustration.

Not surprisingly, therefore, the Nazis attempted to reinvigorate their lagging schemes for ethnic cleansing at the end of 1940. On three occasions – in the successive months of October, November, and December 1940 – Hitler made clear to Frank his "urgent wish" that more Poles be taken into the General Government, along with the Jews of Vienna.[61] With Hitler's support to override Frank, who now had no choice but to accept the expulsions as "one of the great tasks that the Führer has set for the General Government," Heydrich produced his "third short-range plan" (*3. Nahplan*) for 1941. Ethnic Germans were to be repatriated from the Balkans (Bessarabia, Bukovina, and Dobrudja) as well as a remnant from Lithuania. To make room in the incorporated territories, over 1 million Poles (200,000 of them at the behest of the army to clear land for a vast military training ground) were to be expelled into the General Government in one year, dwarfing the expulsions of 1939–40.[62]

As the pioneering research of Götz Aly has now shown, the "third short-range plan" for the intensified expulsion of Poles was paralleled by yet another plan for the expulsion of the Jews beyond those of Lublin and Madagascar. On December 4, Eichmann submitted to Himmler a brief summary on the status of the Jewish question, noting that 5.8 million European Jews had to be taken into consideration for resettlement to a destination mysteriously characterized as "a territory yet to be determined" (*"ein noch zu bestimmendes Territorium"*). Clearly the General Government was not this mysterious destination, for its Jews formed the bulk of the 5.8 million to be expelled, and as Himmler wrote concerning the General Government, in notes for a speech delivered 1 week later: "Jewish emigration and thus yet more space for Poles" (*"Judenauswanderung und damit noch mehr Platz für Polen"*).[63] Himmler's speech was given on the eve of the finalization of two important policies in December 1941, namely the "third short-range plan" for sending more than 1 million Poles from the incorporated territories into the General Government and the decision to invade the Soviet Union. The latter, because it obviously could not be talked about openly, had to be referred to in code language as a "territory yet to be determined" and was to provide the destination for Jewish expulsion. This in turn would break the demographic impasse in the General Government and create space for the realization of the ambitious "third short-range plan."

Planning for Operation Barbarossa remained secretive, and hence use of code language about "a territory yet to be determined" continued. The most detailed reference to this planning is contained in a memorandum written by Eichmann's close associate, Theodore Dannecker, on January 21, 1941:

In conformity with the will of the Führer, at the end of the war there should be brought about a final solution of the Jewish question within the European territories ruled or controlled by Germany.

The Chief of the Security Police and the Security Service [Heydrich] has already received orders from the Führer, through the Reichsführer-SS, to submit a project for a final solution.... The project in all its essentials has been completed. It is now with the Führer and the Reichsmarschall [Göring].

It is certain that its execution will involve a tremendous amount of work whose success can only be guaranteed through the most painstaking preparations. This will extend to the work preceding the wholesale deportation of Jews as well as to the planning to the last detail of a settlement action *in the territory yet to be determined* [italics mine].[64]

That Heydrich had indeed prepared and submitted a plan to Göring is confirmed in a meeting of the two on March 26, 1941. Heydrich's memorandum of the meeting, another archival find by Götz Aly, noted as point 10:

Concerning the solution to the Jewish question, I reported briefly to the Reichsmarschall and submitted my draft to him, which he approved with one amendment concerning the jurisdiction of Rosenberg and ordered to be resubmitted.

As Aly has pointed out, the reference to Rosenberg's jurisdiction – he was soon to be designated the future minister of the occupied Soviet territories – indicates once again that the proverbial territory yet to be determined was the Soviet Union.[65]

If Heydrich was busy drafting and submitting plans in the early months of 1941, what did Himmler think about it? There is an indication that at least in one regard he was somewhat troubled. In early 1941 he approached Viktor Brack of the Führer Chancellery and expressed concern that "through the mixing of blood in the Polish Jews with that of the Jews of Western Europe a much greater danger for Germany was arising than even before the war...." It is important to emphasize that such a concern made sense in the bizarre mental world of Heinrich Himmler only if a massive concentration of east and west European Jews were actually being envisaged in some area of resettlement, where this mix of Jews would produce offspring reaching adulthood in some 20 years! Clearly in Himmler's mind, this expulsion plan was not merely a cover for an already decided upon policy of systematic and total extermination. Himmler asked Brack, who worked with the "many scientists and doctors" assembled for the euthanasia program, to investigate the possibility of mass sterilization through X-rays. Brack submitted a preliminary report on March 28, 1941, which Himmler acknowledged positively on May 12.[66] Thereafter, however, Himmler showed no further interest.

The documentation for this last plan for expelling Jews into the Soviet Union is quite fragmentary and elusive in comparison to the Lublin and Madagascar Plans. This was due in part to the need to preserve secrecy concerning the identity of "the territory yet to be determined." And perhaps it was also because the Nazi leadership was caught up in the immediate preparations for Operation Barbarossa. But perhaps it was also because their hearts were no longer in it – that in the minds of Hitler, Himmler, and Heydrich the notion was beginning to take shape of another possibility *in the future*, if all went well with the imminent military campaign. Indeed, it was precisely in March 1941 that Hitler's exhortations for a war of destruction against the Soviet Union – like his earlier exhortations in 1939 preceding the invasion of Poland – were setting radically new parameters and expectations for Nazi racial policies.

Hitler's declarations that the war against the Soviet Union would not be a conventional war but rather a conflict of ideologies and races and that one avowed war aim was the "removal" of "Judeo-Bolshevik intelligentsia"[67] evoked responses from both the SS and the Wehrmacht. Himmler and Heydrich created the Einsatzgruppen and procured military agreement for their operation up to the front lines. The German military itself stripped the civilian population of protection of law by restricting military court martial jurisdiction and mandating collective reprisal. And it prepared to make its own contribution to the elimination of Judeo-Bolshevism through dissemination of the infamous "commissar order" and the equally infamous guidelines for troop behavior that equated Jews with Bolshevik agitators, guerrillas, and saboteurs.[68]

German preparations for the economic exploitation and demographic transformation of Soviet territory implied even greater destruction of life. The Economic Staff East (Wirschaftsstab Ost) of General Georg Thomas made plans for both feeding the entire German occupation army from local food supplies and exporting vast amounts of food to Germany.[69] The staff had no doubt that the "inevitable" result would be "a great famine," and that "tens of millions" of "superfluous" people would either "die or have to emigrate to Siberia."[70] The state secretaries fully concurred: "Umpteen million people will doubtless starve to death when we extract what is necessary for us..."[71]

Himmler was not to be outdone by the military and ministerial plans for the starvation death of "umpteen million" Soviet citizens and the forced migration to Siberia of millions more. Meeting on June 12–15, 1941, in his renovated Saxon castle at Wewelsburg with his top SS associates and the designated higher SS and police leaders (HSSPF) for Soviet territory,

Himmler sketched out his own vision of the coming conflict. "It is a question of existence, thus it will be a racial struggle of pitiless severity, in the course of which 20 to 30 million Slavs and Jews will perish through military actions and crises of food supply."[72] And on June 24, 1941, Himmler entrusted one of his demographic planners, Professor Konrad Meyer, with drawing up Generalplan Ost, which in one version would call for the expulsion of 31 million Slavs into Siberia.[73] In short, within the SS, ministerial bureaucracy, and military, there was a broad consensus on what the German scholar Christian Gerlach has aptly dubbed the "hunger plan" as well as ever vaster schemes of "ethnic cleansing."[74]

None of the Barbarossa planning documents or criminal orders of this period contain explicit plans concerning the fate of the Jews on Soviet territory. Certainly verbal orders were given to the Einsatzgruppen just prior to the invasion, the "most important" of which Heydrich relayed to the HSSPF "in compressed form" on July 2, 1941. Along with the general exhortation to carry out pacification measures "with ruthless severity," Heydrich's explicit orders for those to be executed included Communist functionaries, anyone engaged in any form of resistance, and "Jews in state and party positions."[75] Some historians, such as Helmut Krausnick, have interpreted this Heydrich execution order "in compressed form" as code language for the explicit and comprehensive verbal order given to the Einsatzgruppen prior to the invasion to murder all Soviet Jewry.[76] In contrast, I now share the view first advanced by Alfred Streim[77] and Christian Streit[78] and gradually endorsed by many other scholars[79] that the ultimate decision was made and orders were given for the Final Solution on Soviet territory beginning some 4 weeks after the invasion.

In my opinion, the last months before and the first weeks after the invasion of the Soviet Union can best be seen as an important transition period in the evolution of Nazi Jewish policy. The first two resettlement plans had failed and the third languished as the feverish and murderous preparations for Operation Barbarossa rendered it increasingly obsolete. Clearly, plans for the war of destruction entailed the death of millions of people in the Soviet Union, and in such an environment of mass death, Soviet Jewry was in grave peril. Indeed, Nazi plans for the war of destruction, when seen in the light of the past Nazi record in Poland, *implied* nothing less than the *genocide* of Soviet Jewry. In Poland, when large numbers of people had been shot, Jews had been shot in disproportionate numbers. When massive expulsions had taken place, it was never intended that any Jews would be left behind. And when food had been scarce, Jews had always been the first to starve. Now mass executions, mass expulsions, and mass starvation were being planned for the Soviet Union on a scale that would dwarf what had happened in Poland. No one fully aware of the scope of these intended policies could doubt the massive decimation and eventual disappearance of all Jews in German-occupied Soviet territories. Within the framework of a war of destruction, through some unspecified combination of execution, starvation, and expulsion to an inhospitable Siberia, Soviet Jewry, along with millions of other Slavs, would eventually be destroyed.

But the *implied genocide* in the future of Jews on Soviet territory was not yet the Final Solution for all Soviet Jewry, much less the other Jews of Europe. The old resettlement plans were dead, replaced by a vague genocidal vision that was unspecific about timetable and means and still comingled the fates of Jewish and non-Jewish victims. However, this vagueness and lack of specificity would soon come to an end. In the "fateful months" following Operation Barbarossa, a series of decisions would be made. Out of these decisions would emerge what the Nazis called "the Final Solution to the Jewish Question," a program of systematic and total mass murder, to begin and be completed as soon as feasibly possible, and for the first time with clear priority for the implementation of Jewish policy over the various other Nazi demographic schemes affecting ethnic Germans and Slavs.

Notes

1 *Nazi Conspiracy and Aggression* (hereafter cited as NCA), III, p. 665 (1014-PS); Franz Halder, *Kriegstagebuch* (Stuttgart, 1962), I, p. 25; Winfried Baumgart, "Zur Ansprache Hitlers vor den Führern der Wehrmacht am 22. August 1939," *Vierteljahresheft für Zeitgeschichte* (hereafter cited as VfZ), 1968, pp. 120–149.
2 Halder, *Kriegstagebuch*, I, p. 79.
3 Heydrich and Quartermaster General Eduard Wagner reached agreement in August that the Einsatzgruppen would arrest all potential enemies – that is, all "who oppose the measures of the German authorities, or obviously want and are able to stir up unrest due to their position and stature" (*die sich dem Massnahmen der deutschen Amtsstellen widersetzen oder offensichtlich gewillt und auf Grund ihrer Stellung und ihres Ansehens in der Lage sind, Unruhe zu stiften*). According to Wagner, the Einsatzgruppen had lists of 30,000 people to be sent to concentration camps. Edward Wagner, *Der Generalquartiermeister: Briefe und Tagebuch Eduard Wagners*, ed. by Elisabeth Wagner (Munich, 1963), pp. 103–4. In early September, Wilhelm Canaris pointed out to Wilhelm Keitel that he "knew that extensive executions were planned in Poland and that particularly the nobility and the clergy were to be exterminated." Keitel confirmed that "the Führer had already decided on this matter." NCA, V, p. 769 (3047-PS).
4 National Archives (hereafter cited as NA), T175/239/2728499–502 (conference of Heydrich's division heads, 7.9.39).
5 NA, T175/239/2728513–5 (conference of Heydrich's division heads, 14.9.39).
6 NA, T175/239/2728524–8 (conference of Heydrich's division heads, 21.9.39); NCA, VI, pp. 97–101 (3363-PS); Helmuth Groscurth, *Tagebücher eines Abwehroffiziers 1938–40*, ed. by Helmuth Krausnick and Harold Deutsch (Stuttgart, 1970), p. 362 (document nr. 14, Groscurth memorandum over verbal orientation by Major Radke, 22.9.39).

7 Das politische Tagebuch Alfred Rosenbergs, ed. by Hans-Günther Seraphim (Göttingen, 1956), p. 81. NA, T175/239/2728531–2 (conference of Heydrich's division heads, 29.9.39). According to Götz Aly, "Endlösung": Völkerverschiebung und der Mord an den europäischen Juden (Frankfurt/M., 1995), p. 39, the decision to repatriate all Baltic Germans from the Soviet sphere was reached between Hitler and Himmler only on September 27.

8 Aly, "Endlösung," esp. pp. 13–17; Aly and Susanne Heim, Vordenker der Vernichtung. Auschwitz und die Pläne für eine neue europäische Ordnung (Hamburg, 1991); Michael Burleigh, Germany Turns Eastward. A Study of Ostforschung in the Third Reich (Cambridge, 1988); Hans Mommsen, "Umvolkungspläne des Nationalsozialismus und der Holocaust," Die Normalität des Verbrechens: Bilanz und Perspektiven der Forschung zu nationalsozialistischen Gewaltverbrechen (Berlin, 1994), pp. 68–84. Deborah Dwork and Robert Jan van Pelt, Auschwitz: 1270 to the Present (New York, 1996), pp. 66–159.

9 Klaus-Jürgen Müller, Das Heer und Hitler. Armee und nationalsozialistische Regime 1933–40 (Stuttgart, 1969), pp. 671–2 (document nr. 47: Heydrich to Einsatzgruppen leaders, 30.9.39).

10 Yad Vashem Archives (hereafter cited as YVA), 0–53/93/283, Eichmann Vermerk, 6.10.39. For general studies of the Nisko Plan, see: Seev Goshen, "Eichmann und die Nisko-Aktion im Oktober 1939," VfZ 19/1 (January 1981), pp. 74–96; Jonny Moser, "Nisko: The First Experiment in Deportation," The Simon Wiesenthal Center Annual, II (1985), pp. 1–30; H. G. Adler, Der Verwaltete Mensch (Tübingen, 1974), pp. 126–140.

11 Gerhard Botz, Wohnungspolitik und Judendeportation in Wien 1938 bis 1945: Zur Funktion des Antisemitismus als Ersatz nationalsozialistischer Sozialpolitik (Vienna, 1975), pp. 164–86 (document VII: Becker memorandum, 11.10.39).

12 YVA, 0–53/93/299–300 (Eichmann to Nebe, 16.10.39) and 227–9 (Günther-Braune FS-Fernspräch, 18.10.39.

13 YVA, O-53/93/235–8 (R. Günther Tagesbericht, 19.10.39), 220 (undated R. Günther telegram), and 244 (R. Günther Vermerk, 21.10.39).

14 Botz, Wohungspolitik und Judendeportationen, p. 196 (document X, Himmler to Bürckel, 9.11.39).

15 Hans Umbreit, Deutsche Militärverwaltungen 1938/39 (Stuttgart, 1977), p. 218.

16 Trials of the War Criminals before the International Military Tribunal (hereafter cited as IMT), vol. 26, pp. 378–9, 381–3 (864-PS).

17 Faschismus, Getto, Massenmord (hereafter cited as FGM) [Berlin (East), 1960], pp. 42–3 (NO-4059); YVA, JM 21/1, Frank Tagebuch: Streckenbach report of 31.10.39; Biuletyn Glownej Komisji Badania Zbrodni Hitlerowskich W Polsce (hereafter cited as Biuletyn), XI, pp. 11F–14F, and Hans Frank, Diensttagebuch des deutschen Generalgouverneurs in Polen 1939–1945, ed. by Werner Präg and Wolfgang Jacobmeyer (Stuttgart, 1975), pp. 60–1 (conference of 8.11.39).

18 United States Holocaust Memorial Museum (hereafter cited as USHMM), RG 15.005m, 2/104/15 (Müller, RSHA, to EG VI in Posen, 8.11.39).

19 IMT, vol. 30, p. 95 (2278-PS).

20 FGM, p. 46 (Frank speech in Radom, 25.11.39).

21 Umbreit, Militärverwaltung, pp. 216–21.

22 Aly, "Endlösung," pp. 114–26.

23 Herbert Levine, "Local Authority and the SS State: The Conflict over Population Policy in Danzig-West Prussia," Central European History, II/4 (1969), pp. 331–55.

24 YVA; O-53/69/639–41 (Polizeisitzung in Danzig, 15.11.39) and 642–3 (conference of 20.11.39); JM 3582 (Hildebrandt speech, 26.11.39).
25 *Biuletyn*, XII, pp. 15F–18F (Heydrich to HSSPF Cracow, Breslau, Posen, Danzig, 28.11.39; and Heydrich to Krüger, Streckenbach, Koppe, and Damzog, 28.11.39).
26 USHMM, RG 15.015m, 1/5/4–7 (Rapp draft, 10.11.39) and 2/99/1–5 (Koppe circular, 12.11.39).
27 *Biuletyn*, XII, pp. 22F–31F, and USHMM, RG 11.001m, 1/88/185–202 (Rapp report, 18.12.39); YVA, JM 3582, and USHMM, RG 15.015m, 3/208/1–12 (Rapp report, 26.1.40).
28 USHMM, RG 15.015m, 3/218/13–14 (undated Richter report) and 27–35 (Richter report, 16.12.39).
29 YVA, JM 3581 (RSHA II/112 an den Leiter II im Hause, 19.12.39).
30 YVA, JM 3581 (Heydrich to Sipo-SD in Cracow, Breslau, Posen, Danzig, and Königsberg, 21.12.39).
31 YVA, JM 3581 (Müller to all Staatspolizeistellen, 21.12.39).
32 USHMM, RG 15.015m, 2.97/1–7 (2. Nahplan, 21.12.39).
33 *Biuletyn*, XII, pp. 37F–39F (Abromeit Vermerk of 8.1.40 on conference of 4.1.40).
34 *Biuletyn*, XII, pp. 37F–39F (Abromeit Vermerk of 8.1.40 on conference of 4.1.40; FGM, pp. 48 and 53 (reports of Gschliesser and Wächter); *Documenta Occupationis* (hereafter cited as DO), vol. 8, pp. 37–8 (report of Mattern); IMT, vol. 26, pp. 210–12. (661–PS); Frank, *Diensttagebuch*, pp. 93–7 (Abteilungsleitersitzung, 19.1.40).
35 Aly, "*Endlösung*," pp. 113–14.
36 USHMM, RG 15.015m, 1/96/12–13 (Krumey report, 30.1.40, on Leipzig Fahrplanbesprechung of 26–27.1.40).
37 Nuremberg Document NO-5411 (Creutz to Koppe, 18.1.40); *Biuletyn*, XII, pp. 44F–45F (Vermerk of Eichmann Seidl conversation, 22–23.1.40).
38 USHMM, RG 15.015m, 2/146/9–15 (meeting of 11.1.40).
39 *Biuletyn*, XII, pp. 66F–75F (NO-5322: conference of 30.1.40); USHMM, RG 15.015m, 12/109/1–3 (Rapp Vermerk, 1.2.40).
40 IMT, vol. 36, pp. 300–306 (EC-305).
41 Frank, *Diensttagebuch*, pp. 131 and 146–7 (Sitzung des Reichsverteidigungsausschuss, Warsaw, 2.3.40, and Dienstversammalung der Kreis und Stadthauptmänner des Distrikts Lublin, 4.3.40).
42 Frank, *Diensttagebuch*, pp. 158 (entry of 5.4.40) and 204 (entry of 19.5.40); *Dokumently i Materialy Do Dziejow Okupacji Niemieckiej W Polsce*, III, *Getto Lodzkie* (Warsaw, 1946), pp. 168–9 (Riegierungspräsident to officials of Bezirk Lodz and Kalish, 8.5.40).
43 *Documents on German Foreign Policy*, D, VIII, p. 912–13.
44 Helmut Krausnick, ed., "Einige Gedanke über die Behandlung der fremdvölkischen im Osten," VfZ, V/2 (1957), pp. 194–98.
45 *Biuletyn*, XII, pp. 94F–95F (R. Günther to Höppner, 1.7.40).
46 Frank, *Diensttagebuch*, pp. 210, 216 (Polizeisitzung, 30.5.40); Nuremberg Document NG-1627 (Frank to Lammers, 25.6.40).
47 *Biuletyn*, XII, pp. 96F–97F (Vermerk on Höppner-IV D 4 discussion, 9.7.40).
48 For the most recent scholarship on the European anti-Semitic tradition and the Madagascar Plan, see: Magnus Brechtken, "*Madagaskar für die Juden*": *Antisemitische Idee und politische Praxis 1995–1945* (Munich, 1997), and Hans Jansen, *Der Madagaskar-Plan: Die beabsichtigte Deportation der europäischen Juden nach Madagaskar* (Munich, 1997).

49 IMT, vol. 26, pp. 210–22 (661-PS).
50 Politisches Archiv des Auswärtigen Amtes (hereafter PA), Inland II A/B 347/3, Rademacher memorandum "Gedanken über die Arbeit und Aufgaben des Ref. D III, 3.6.40." A synopsis of this memorandum is Nuremberg Document NG-5764.
51 Paul Schmidt, *Hitler's Interpreter* (New York, 1951), p. 178; Galeazzo Ciano, *The Ciano Diaries 1939–43* (Garden City, NY, 1947), pp. 265–6. Two days later, on June 20, Hitler repeated his intention to resettle the European Jews on Madagascar to Admiral Raeder. Klaus Hildebrand, *Vom Reich zum Weltreich: Hitler, NSDAP, und koloniale Frage 1919–1945* (Munich, 1969), pp. 651–2.
52 PA, Inland IIg 177, Heydrich to Ribbentrop, 24.6.40.
53 For the details of this planning, see: Christopher R. Browning, *The Final Solution and the German Foreign Office* (New York, 1978), pp. 35–43.
54 Frank, *Diensttagebuch*, p. 248 (entry of 10.7.40) for HSSPF Friedrich Wilhelm Krüger's announcement of the news), and pp. 252 and 258 (Abteilungsleitersitzung, 12.7.40, and entry of 25.7.40) for Frank's boisterous reception.
55 FGM, p. 110 (Schön report, 20.1.40).
56 Frank, *Diensttagebuch*, pp. 261–3 (entry of 31.7.40).
57 IMT, vol. 31, pp. 283–94 (2916-PS); Akten der Partei-Kanzlei der NSDAP, 101 23821 (Chef der Zivilverwaltung in Elsass, 22.4.41, to Martin Bormann).
58 Bundesarchiv Koblenz, All. Proz. 6/Eichmann Interrogation, I, pp. 141–5; Jacob Toury, "Die Entstehungsgeschichte des Austreibungsbefehls gegen die Juden der Saarpfalz und Baden (22/23. Oktober 1940) – Camp de Gurs," *Jahrbuch des Instituts für Deutsche Geschichte*, Beihefte X (1986), pp. 435–64.
59 USHMM, RG 15.015m: 2/115/38 (conference of Ansiedlugnstab, Posen, 12.7.40), 40–41 (Höppner to Eichmann and Ehlich, 12.7.40), and 50 (Krumey Aktenvermerk, 21.8.40); 3/228/3 (Aufstellung der Cholmer Aktion).
60 The sources for these statistics are too lengthy to include here but are based on my manuscript, "The Origins of the Final Solution: The Evolution of Nazi Jewish Policy, September 1939–March 1942," to be published as part of Yad Vashem's multivolume history of the Holocaust.
61 At the October 2, 1940, meeting of Hitler and the eastern Gauleiter: IMT, vol. 39, pp. 426–9 (USSR-172). At the November 2, 1940, meeting of Hitler with Frank and Greiser: Frank, *Diensttagebuch*, p. 302 (entry of 6.11.40). For December: Ibid., p. 327 (entry of 15.1.41). For the Vienna Jews: NCA, IV, p. 592 (1950-PS).
62 Frank, *Diensttagebuch*, p. 327 (conference of 15.1.41); USHMM, RG 15.105m, 3/199/4–6 (Vermerk on conference of 8.1.41) and 8–9 (Höppner Aktenvermerk on Fahrplankonferenz in Posen on 16.1.41); *Biuletyn*, XII, p. 127F (Krumey to Eichmann, 6.1.41); YVA, JM 3582 (Abschlussbericht 1941).
63 Susanne Heim und Götz Aly, eds., *Beiträge zur nationalsozialistischen Gesundheits und Sozialpolitik*, vol. 9: *Bevölkerungsstrukture und Massenmord: Neue Dokumente zur deutschen Politik der Jahre 1938–1945* (Berlin, 1991), pp. 24–7 (Eichmann summary "submitted to the RFSS," 4.12.40; Aly, *"Endlösung,"* pp. 195–200.
64 Cited in: Serge Klarsfeld, *Vichy-Auschwitz: Die Zusammenarbeit der deutschen und französischen Behörden bei der `Endlösung der Judenfrage: in Frankreich* (Nördlingen, 1989), pp. 361–3. In February 1941 Heydrich also dropped reference to the Madagascar Plan and wrote Undersecretary Martin Luther in the Foreign Office about a "later total solution to the Jewish question" (*"späteren Gesamtlösung des Judenproblmes"*) to be achieved through "sending them off to the country that will be chosen later" (*"nach dem zukünftigen Bestimmungs-*

lande abzutransportieren") PA, Inland II A/B 809–41 Sdh. III, Bd. 1, Heydrich to Luther, 5.2.41.

65 Cited in: Aly, *"Endlösung,"* p. 270, with Aly's analysis, pp. 271–2. The document is from the Moscow Special Archives, 500/3/795.

66 *Trials of the War Criminals before the American Military Tribunal*, I, p. 732 (testimony of Viktor Brack, May 1947); Nuremberg Documents NO-203 (Brack to Himmler, 28.3.41) and NO-204 (Tiefenbacher to Brack, 12.5.41).

67 *Kriegstagebuch des Oberkommandos der Wehrmacht 1940–1941*, I, pp. 341–2 (entry for 3.3.41).

68 For the growing body of literature on Germany's preparation for a war of destruction in the Soviet Union, see: Hans-Adolf Jacobsen, "Kommissarbefehl und Massenexekutionen sowjetischer Kreigsgefangener," *Anatomie des SS-Staates* (Freiburg, 1965), II, pp. 161–278; Andreas Hillgruber, "Die 'Endlösung' und das deutsche Ostimperium als Kernstück des rassenideologischen Programmes des nationalsozialismus," VfZ, 20 (1972), pp. 133–53; Christian Streit, *Keine Kameraden: Die Wehrmacht und die sowjetischen Kreigsgefangenen, 1941–1945* (Stuttgart, 1978); Helmut Krausnick and Hans-Heinrich Wilhelm, *Die Truppe des Weltanschauungskrieges: Die Einsatzgruppen des Sicherheitspolizei und des SD, 1938–1942* (Stuttgart, 1981); Helmut Krausnick, "Kommissarbefehl und 'Gerichtsbarkeiterlass Barbarossa' in neuer Sicht," VfZ, 25 (1977), pp. 682–738; and especially the contributions of Jürgen Förster in *Das Deutsche Reich und der Zweite Weltkrieg*, IV, *Der Angriff auf die Sowjetunion* (Stuttgart, 1983), pp. 3–37, 413–47, 1030–88.

69 For military plans for economic exploitation: Rolf-Dieter Müller, "Von Wirtchaftsallianz zum kolonial Ausbeutungskrieg," *Das Deutsche Reich und der Zweite Weltkrieg*, IV, *Der Angriff auf dem Sowjetunion*, esp. pp. 125–29 and 146–52.

70 IMT, vol. 36, pp. 141–45 (126-EC: report of Wirtschaftsstab Ost, 23.5.41).

71 IMT, vol. 31, p. 84 (2718-PS: state secretaries' meeting, 2.5.41).

72 The Wewelsburg meeting has now been dated to June 12–15, 1941, according to Himmler's Terminkalendar found in the Moscow Secret Archives (Osobyi 1372-5–23. The accession number for the copy in the US Holocaust Memorial Museum is: 1997.A.0328). I am grateful to Dr. Jürgen Matthäus for providing me with a copy of this document. Testifying at the trial of Karl Wolff in Munich, Bach-Zelewski erroneously dated the meeting to March 1941. JNSV, XX (Nr. 580, LG München II 1 Ks 1/64), p. 413. At his even earlier Nürnberg testimony, Bach-Zelewski said that it had taken place early in 1941. IMT, vol. 4, pp. 482–88.

73 Dietrich Eichholz, "Der 'Generalplan Ost.' Über eine Ausgeburt imperialistischer Denkart und Politik," *Jahrbuch für Geschichte*, 26 (1982), p. 256 (Doc. Nr. 2: Meyer to Himmler, 15.7.41). Richard Breitman, *The Architect of Genocide: Himmler and the Final Solution* (New York, 1991), p. 168. Helmut Heiber, "Der Generalplan Ost," *Vierteljahrshefte für Zeitgeschichte*, 3 (1958), 300–313 (Doc.Nr. 2: Stellungnahme und Gedanken zum Generalplan Ost des Reichsführer SS, by Wetzel, 27.4.42).

74 Christian Gerlach, *Krieg, Ernährung, Völkermord: Forschungen zur deutschen Vernichtungspolitik im Zweiten Weltkrieg* (Berlin, 1998) pp. 13–30.

75 Heydrich to HSSPFs Jeckeln, v.d. Bach, Prützmann, and Korsemann, 2.7.41, printed in: Peter Klein, ed., *Die Einsatzgruppen in der besetzten Sowjetunion 1941/42: Die Tätigkeits und Lageberichte des Chefs der Sicherheitspolizei und des SD* (Berlin, 1997), pp. 324–5.

76 Helmut Krausnick and Hans-Heinrich Wilhelm, *Die Truppe des Weltanschau-*

ungskrieges: Die Einsatzgruppen der Sicherheitspolizei und des SD 1938–1942 (Stuttgart, 1981), pp. 150–65; *Der Mord an den Juden im Zweiten Welktrieg,* ed. by Eberhard Jäckel and Jürgen Rohwer (Stuttgart, 1985), pp. 88–106.

77 Alfred Streim, *Die Behandlung sowjetsicher Kriegsgefangenen im "Fall Barbarossa"* (Heidelberg and Karlsruhe, 1981), pp. 74–93.

78 Christian Streit, *Keine Kameraden: Die Wehrmacht und die sowjetischen Kriegsgefangenen 1941–1945* (Stuttgart, 1978), pp. 127 and 356.

79 In particular, see: Peter Longerich, "Vom Massenmord zur 'Endlösung.' Die Erschiessungen von jüdischen Zivilisten in den ersten Monaten des Ostfeldzuges im Kontext des nationalsozialistischen Judenmords," *Zwei Wege Nach Moskau: Vom Hitler-Stalin-Pakt zum "Unternehmen Barbarossa,"* ed. by Bernd Wegner (Munich, 1991), pp. 251–74; and Ralf Ogorreck, *Die Einsatzgruppen und die "Genesis der Endlösung"* (Berlin, 1996).